Guitar Player
Repair Guide 3rd Edition

Guitar Player
Repair Guide 3rd Edition

How to set up, maintain and repair electrics and acoustics

basic	d.i.y.	deep
What every guitar owner must know	Fix, finish, or modify any guitar	If you're ready to roll up your sleeves …

by Dan Erlewine

Backbeat Books

An Imprint of Hal Leonard Corporation
New York

Published in 2007 by Backbeat Books
An Imprint of Hal Leonard Corporation
19 West 21st Street, New York, NY 10010

Designed and edited by Tom Erlewine
Cover photos by Suzanne Burkey

We would like to thank Brian Blauser of Athens, Ohio, for his photos
from road trips with Dan to check out the guitars of the stars.
Thanks to Al Blixt of Ann Arbor, Michigan, for his photos of Buddy Guy.
Thanks also to Erick Coleman for his research on guitar electronics.

Printed in the United States of America

Library of Congress Cataloging-in-Publication Data is available upon request.

ISBN 10: 0-87930-921-0
ISBN 13: 978-0-87930-921-3

www.backbeatbooks.com

To my wife, Joan, and daughters, Meredith and Kate.
They didn't see a lot of me this summer.

And on behalf of my brother Tom, my partner in
creating this book, it's dedicated to Sue.

1 Cleaning and care — 1

basic
Supplies — 1
Cleaning the finish — 2
Cleaning the fingerboard — 4
Avoiding cracks, dealing with humidity — 6

2 Installing strings — 9

basic
Installing strings on electrics — 9
Installing strings on acoustics — 12
Installing strings on classicals — 13

3 Neck evaluation and truss rod adjustment — 15

basic
Neck evalution — 15

d.i.y.
Truss rod adjustment — 16
Understanding relief — 17
Pro-quality straightedges — 18
Typical neck adjustment scenario — 19

deep
Rescuing a broken truss rod — 21

4 Setup and action — 23

basic
What is a setup? — 23

d.i.y.
The basics of setup — 24
Setting up an electric guitar — 27
Setting up a guitar with tremolo — 29
Setting up an electric bass — 31
Setting up a flattop acoustic — 32
Setting up an archtop — 35
Setting up a classical — 36

deep
Low action and the blues — 40
Setups for pro players:
  Stevie Ray Vaughan and Jeff Beck — 44
  John Mooney's slide — 47
  Albert Collins — 50
  Buddy Guy — 52
  B.B. King — 57

5 Intonation and compensation — 63

basic
Understanding compensation — 63

d.i.y.
Setting intonation — 65
Adjustable bridges (electrics) — 65
Non-adjustable bridges (acoustics) — 65

deep
Buzz Feiten Tuning System — 66

6 Tuning machines — 69

basic
Tuner basics — 69

d.i.y.
Installing tuners — 71
Steinberger tuners — 72
Tuner repairs, broken mounting screws — 74
Damage from over-oiled tuners — 75

deep
Rotted plastic knobs — 77
Making new tuners look old — 78
Reconstructing rotted knobs — 80

7 Electric guitar bridges: non-tremolo — 83

basic
The many Tune-O-Matics — 83
TonePros and Pigtails — 85
Steve Rowen on T-O-M hardware — 87

d.i.y.
Slotting Gibson bridge saddles — 91
Adjusting an ABR-1 bridge radius — 92
Bridge posts and tailpiece studs — 93
De-rusting metal bridge saddles — 94

8 Electric guitar bridges: tremolos — 97

basic
Setting up your tremolo system — 97

d.i.y.
Floyd Rose installation and setup — 97
Kahler installation and setup — 103
Fine-tuning a Strat tremolo — 107
The Trem-Setter — 111
Roller nuts — 114

deep
String benders — 117

9 Acoustic guitar bridges — 121

basic
Fitting flattop bridge pins — 121
Evaluating acoustic action — 123

d.i.y.
Replacing a bridge saddle — 124
Archtop bridges — 127
Fitting an archtop bridge — 128

10 Acoustic body repairs — 131

d.i.y.
Clamps and glues — 132
Closing and gluing cracks — 135
Gluing loose braces — 143

deep
Reattaching loose bridges — 144
Bridge pad problems — 148
Neck resets — 152

11 Necks **157**

basic

Fender guitar neck shapes 158

Fender bass neck shapes 159

d.i.y.

Installing bolt-on necks 161

Fret buzz in the high registers 166

deep

Broken pegheads 166

12 Fretwork **169**

basic

What to expect from a fret job 169

d.i.y.

Loose frets 170

Fret files 171

Compound radius fingerboards 174

Fret dressing 177

Refretting: 184

Choosing your fretwire 190

Hammer-in method 194

Compression fretting 196

Martin bar-style fretting 199

The glue-in method 201

Bound fingerboards 207

Vintage Fender fretting 209

Fret slots and tang size 213

deep

The neck jig 214

The Plek machine 216

13 Nut replacement **219**

basic

About nut replacement 219

d.i.y.

12 steps for replacing a nut 220

Tools 220

Removing the old nut 221

Roughing in the blank 222

Cutting slots, finishing up 222

String spacing 223

14 Bindings and pickguards **225**

d.i.y.

Loose bindings 225

Shrinking Strat pickguards 227

Regluing an acoustic pickguard 229

15 Guitar electronics **231**

d.i.y.

Tools and supplies for electronics 231

Soldering technique 234

Using a multimeter 235

Caps and pots 235

Switches 237

Shielding 238

Acoustic guitar amplification 240

Semi-hollowbody wiring 250

Pickup replacement 251

Pickup repair 256

Rewiring, modifications 260

Wiring diagrams 262

deep

Wind your own pickups 264

16 Finishing and finish repairs **279**

d.i.y.

A basic finishing schedule 279

Spraying necks and bodies 287

Finish repairs 292

Supplies for finish repairs 294

Fixing chips 295

Fixing dents and scratches 301

Touching up color 302

deep

Faking an aged finish 304

17 Shipping a guitar or amp **305**

basic

How to pack a guitar 305

How to pack an amp 307

18 Tools **309**

basic tool list 309

d.i.y. tool list 310

deep tool list 310

Sharpening chisels and scrapers 312

19 Resources and schools **313**

deep

Training for a career in lutherie 313

Lists: schools, suppliers, organizations 315

Index **317**

Foreword

In my boundless optimism, I expected clues to sonic miracles. I was talking to Bob Ezrin, who produced Alice Cooper, Lou Reed, Pink Floyd, Kiss, Peter Gabriel and many others, and, in the process, conjured some of the hippest guitar sounds ever blasted across the airwaves. Surely, there must have been some voodoo in his microphone selection, his mic placement and his choice and manipulation of preamps, compressors and other arcane signal processors. But Ezrin made it clear that everything started with the guitar itself.

"An excellent setup is at the center of every good, complex guitar recording," he said. "The pickups must be in good shape, the electronics must be as clean as possible, and the fretboard must be buzz-free."

At a time when the quality of inexpensive, off-the-rack guitars can be downright awesome, we tend to forget how a beautifully set up instrument—more specifically, one tailored to a player's every ergonomic desire and technical idiosyncrasy—can enhance a guitarist's tone and performance. Perhaps we also forget that some guitars have souls that influence our playing in mysterious ways. (Just ask Clapton about Blackie, or B.B. King about Lucille, or Brian May about his Red Special.) The lesson here is just because you can easily replace an instrument that's broken, cranky or sickly, it doesn't mean that you should. In some cases, a few simple repairs can bring a guitar back to life—or even make it better than ever. And don't forget the whole concept of hot-rodding. With a little guidance and tech savvy, you can swap pickups, futz with wiring and enlist some other tricks to make a cheap guitar rage like a cornered panther, or turbocharge a fine guitar until it's something truly magical.

As Ezrin revealed, it all comes down to the guitar and what you do with it. And that's where Dan Erlewine becomes your guru, mentor, coach, visionary, taskmaster, guide and, most likely, savior. Dan knows more about guitars and guitarcraft than pretty much anyone left standing on this planet, and decades of his wisdom, tips, and techniques are encapsulated in this must-have book—which should now and forever be your guitar-repair bible.

Dan has been a vital and much-respected member of the *Guitar Player* family for many years, writing the seminal "Repairs & Modifications" column, as well as the "Repairs" column and the innovative "Mod Squad" feature (which profiled Dan's youthful shop crew pimping out various guitars) during my tenure as editor. Dan has also produced several how-to DVDs, and is currently developing a series of video repair guides for Guitar Player's Web television station, GPTV.

To quote a cliché, "Dan is the Man." But that's the whole truth. And after this book inspires you to transform your guitars into the easiest-playing, best-sounding machines you've ever plugged into an amp, you'll probably build a little shrine to Dan Erlewine in your music room, rehearsal space or home studio. Yeah, you'll be that thrilled with your instruments, and the man deserves it. Now, read on and start making your guitars play better and sound great!

Michael Molenda
Editor in Chief
Guitar Player

Introduction

You and I both want our guitars to stay in tune, play easily, sound great, and look good. Maybe that describes your guitar on the day you bought it, but is it still that way today? Things go wrong over time, but those things can be avoided, or can be fixed—that's what this book is for. More comprehensive than ever before, the *Repair Guide* now includes helpful information for all levels of experience:

basic You don't need to be good with tools to take good care of your guitar. Whenever possible, these chapters start with **basic** information—essentials for every guitar owner, things every player needs to know.

d.i.y. **Do-it-yourself** information is the soul of this book. If you're ready to tackle some of your own adjustments and repairs, let's get your guitars playing the way they were meant to.

deep In several chapters, I just can't resist taking you **deeper** into it. For example, after adding lots of new electronics help for do-it-yourselfers, we continue on to show how to make your own pickups!

Ready? Let's get started!

Dan

Dan Erlewine

Chapter 1

Cleaning and care

basic

Supplies	1
Cleaning the finish	2
Cleaning the fingerboard	4
Avoiding cracks, dealing with humidity	6

d.i.y.

deep

basic

Cleaning and polishing a guitar is the most basic maintenance task of all, and every player should know how to go about it. Maintaining a new instrument's clean good looks is simple if you keep it up from the beginning. But it's the lucky player who discovers a vintage piece who needs this chapter most: often that perfect guitar has a finish that's been dulled by years of sweat, dirt, and exposure to barroom smoke and the elements.

Guitar finishes become dirty and hazy because dirt particles come to rest on the finish, which always has a thin film of oil on it no matter how often you clean it. Some of these oils come from your body, while others become suspended in the air from cooking, manufacturing, pollution, etc. The oil and dirt create a "build" on the finish, which hardens in time and is quite tough to remove. That dirt itself has abrasive qualities, so when you remove it, you could be removing the finish too! That's why using the right cleaning technique is important.

The supplies needed for cleaning and polishing new or used guitars are few, inexpensive, and easy to use:

Clean, soft rags With several rags and plenty of time, you can clean the dirtiest guitar without polishes or cleaners, although polishes and cleaners help you do a faster, better job. The three best cleaning rags are: used, well-cleaned baby diapers, cotton T-shirts, and 100% cotton flannel. The soft rags that many manufacturers imprint with their company logo and include with a new instrument are made from flannel. You can also buy a yard of flannel at any fabric store for very little cost. Most other rags and fabrics are too coarse for delicate guitar finishes.

Naphtha (lighter fluid) is a great, all-around guitar cleaner. It's a degreaser for finishes, pickguards, fingerboards, bridges, tailpieces, and metal parts of all kinds. Used lightly on a rag (more dry than wet) it won't harm a delicate lacquer finish, and certainly won't hurt polyurethane or polyester finishes. Naphtha leaves a flat, dry haze on a finish, but it's generally used first in the cleaning process, and then guitar polish or a dry rag brings the sheen right back.

Guitar polish The creamy stuff in the little plastic squirt jars works as a cleaner because it's a liquid with an extremely fine abrasive. The liquid washes, and the abrasive lifts dirt. It's also a polish because it contains wax that protects and shines. The right polish won't scratch a finish. Martin makes a good polish/cleaner, and you can trust them to recommend something safe for high-quality guitar finishes, especially lacquer.

Swirl-mark remover is similar to liquid polish, but without the wax. It's a cleaner with an extremely mild abrasive, used in the auto industry for the final polish of newly sprayed finishes. A good swirl mark remover is Colortone #4 — a delicate, excellent cleaner that even without wax leaves a nice shine.

Liquid cleaners are light-duty buffing compounds with a mild abrasive but no wax. These are best for dirtier finishes, since the absence of wax allows unlimited cleaning time without the wax drying (along with the dirt) at every polish-stroke. The abrasive is coarser than swirl-mark remover or guitar polish, so it does a good job of removing heavy dirt buildup. Cleaners won't leave scratches, but as soon as the dirt lifts, switch to a milder polish or swirl-mark remover—you don't want to rub away more finish than needed! My choice for a liquid cleaner is Preservation Polish.

Warm water, used sparingly (your cleaning rag should be slightly damp—not sopping wet!), works wonders. Don't force water into checked, dry, or weathered finishes. Saliva (seriously) is an excellent cleaner too —but only if you're working on your own guitar!

Lemon oil is not for guitar finishes, although it's highly touted by some people. I occasionally use it on ebony or rosewood fingerboards, but I don't use it elsewhere because it feels as though I'm wiping kerosene onto the finish. I believe that lemon oil works its way into and under the finish, especially on older vintage instruments that have a lovely checked patina. This could cause the finish to lift and the wood to become saturated with oil—possibly dampening tone. Lemon Pledge should not be used on guitars!

Silicone is definitely not on the list, but it's added to some polishes and cleaners. These should be avoided! Armor All, which has silicone, is used by many music stores to keep guitar cases looking spiffy, but they should avoid it. Lacquer, glue, stain, and all sorts of guitar repair items just don't get along with the slippery residue of silicone, and subsequent repairs to an instrument exposed to silicone will be a hassle.

Elbow grease needs no introduction, so let's get on with the work.

Cleaning the finish

Cleaning and polishing are two different things. Polishing is what you do to a guitar that isn't really dirty, and this process doesn't have to involve polish at all. A clean, dry rag may be all you need to keep a new guitar's finish in shape by wiping off sweat and oil before they get a chance to build up and oxidize. Occasionally use the liquid guitar polish for its protective wax coating—but only on newer finishes that aren't weather-checked. Before polishing or cleaning, be sure to wipe, vacuum, or blow any gritty particles from your finish; otherwise you'll drag them around on the surface, causing scratches that you'll never get out!

Polishing an extremely dirty guitar doesn't make sense. You don't polish dirty instruments; you clean them first and then polish. Since guitar polish is also a cleaner, it takes care of both jobs at once if the finish isn't too bad. But cream polish also puts a nice shiny film on top of the dirt if you're not careful. And with polish or cleaners, it's easy to just move the dirt around without transferring it to your rag. Remember, getting dirt off the surface of the finish and onto your rag is the object! There's a knack to getting dirt to transfer, especially on old guitars where it's heavily oxidized. Here's how you do it:

Take a 4" x 6" section of a clean, dry rag, fold the corners into the center, and grab the rag like a "knuckleball." Bunch the corners and loose parts into your palm, so that the fingers and thumb are pinching the rag into a ball shape. In the finishing world this ball of cloth is known as a "tampon," "frenching-pad," or simply "pad." This kind of pad is used for French polishing, which is the art of applying a shellac finish by hand rubbing. It's also a good tool for cleaning and polishing your finish. Use

it with polish, naphtha, water, or cleaner, or use it clean and dry. A true French-polishing pad has a ball of cotton in the center to hold finish, and to help the pad hold its shape. The best pads are made from lint-free cloth (old linen bed sheets are great if you can find them).

There's no single best way to clean, but here's the low-tech method I generally start with: get very close and blow your warm, moist breath on the area until it fogs up, and then quickly polish off the dirt; it'll transfer to your rag. If this treatment doesn't remove all the dirt or haze, follow with a pad dipped lightly in naphtha, since it breaks down grease and sticky residues. Then follow with a pad dipped in water (it's a toss-up which to start with, naphtha or water). What naphtha or water won't remove, a polish or cleaner will. Give the whole instrument (or any area to be cleaned) a light wiping with naphtha before switching to a polish or cleaner.

Safety note Naphtha is a petroleum product, and you don't want it on your skin or in your eyes. Wear plastic gloves and safety glasses, and work in a well-ventilated area and away from sparks, heaters, or flame.

After the naphtha wash, use polish or cleaner (depending on the situation) and work small (4" to 6") areas at a time. As the dirt starts to loosen or "move," pick it up onto the face of your pad with a quick upward twist of the wrist. When one side of the rag gets loaded, switch to a clean part; otherwise you'll put the dirt right back onto the finish. The finish, rag, and dirt all become warm from the friction of rubbing, and the dirt that lifts away needs to be removed so it won't return to the finish. A good cleaning trick is to move the dirt off to an edge, where you can pick it up more easily.

Typical cleaning job Let's say the top edge of your Les Paul is sticky and showing some dirt where you rest your arm or picking hand. This type of hazy buildup can usually be removed without polish, using only a clean dry rag, so always try the dry rag first. Rub lightly in either a straight or circular pattern (circular motions blend in best). If you're not getting the dirt onto your dry rag, pour a dab of polish onto the rag's face or directly onto the finish, and continue rubbing, following the directions on the bottle (some polishes are wiped on and left to dry, some are rubbed off immediately).

Vintage guitars need special consideration
Often the moist-breath method is the best technique for extremely thin finishes that are riddled with checks (tiny cracks), since you don't want to work polish or cleaner down into these crevices. A light naphtha wiping is okay—"light" meaning that you tamp off the wetness onto another rag and wait until the naphtha starts to evaporate before wiping.

Warm water has its place in cleaning vintage instruments. If I use water, it's only to dampen the rag, which is wrapped tightly in one thin layer around my index finger. Sometimes a barely damp rag can be a big help in removing dirt or haze from a vintage piece where you're afraid of working any petroleum-based chemicals into a checked finish. You must be cautious of working water into a crazed finish, so it's a judgment call. Use the same light French-polishing motions that you used with the tampon, just barely hitting the surface to pick up the dirt. When nothing else works, saliva often dissolves the specks adhering to a finish. (Again, don't go spitting on somebody else's guitar!)

Beware of soft finishes! This rare phenomenon occurs with lacquer, varnish, or the shellac-based French polish, which was used on most instruments made before the 1930s. It's still used today on many of the world's finest classical guitars. Have you ever felt your skin stick to a wooden-armed chair with a gummy finish? When you know that if you dragged your fingernails along the finish they'd load up with sticky grime, that's a soft finish.

Finishes get this way because there are natural plasticizers (triglycerides) in your body that transfer through the skin—especially your hands. Lacquer "breathes," allowing moisture and certain chemicals such as polishes, cleaners, and plasticizers to migrate through it. The plasticizers go right through the finish and make the wood their home. Once a finish is softened this way, there's no cure except letting it totally air dry, and even then it may never be truly hard. The most common area of a guitar to suffer from this is the part of the body where you rest your arm when playing, although you may also see it on the neck or other areas. It's most common on dirty guitars that weren't cared for, since the oxidized dirt acts as a lid, holding the plasticizers down in the finish. If your axe suffers from these symptoms, I'm sorry, but don't try to rub, clean, or polish it away—that'll just make it worse.

How often should you clean and polish? When should you use a liquid cleaner or polish rather than just the dry rag? I haven't seen your guitar, so I can't tell you, but I can offer some ideas:

Polyurethane or polyester These catalyzed finishes seem impervious to anything; I suppose you can clean and polish them until the cows come home. New guitars with lacquer finishes (ask your dealer what type of finish is on your guitar) can stand up to cleaning or polishing quite well, since the finish surface is smooth and unchecked. Remember that lacquer "breathes," so when you rub polish onto your finish, you're rubbing it *into* the finish as well. Regular polishing helps keep the finish new-looking, and makes it less prone to checking because of the chemical nutrients in the polish.

When I buy a used guitar, I always clean it first thing. I haven't found a clean one yet, and I don't like someone else's dirt on my guitar. When possible I clean with naphtha and a dry rag, but often a liquid cleaner is necessary. I don't use commercial guitar polish on thin vintage finishes, because I'm afraid of the wax penetrating into the wood. After the initial cleaning, I may not use polish or cleaner on a used guitar for up to three years—sometimes longer. But I will use a dry rag every few months, or whenever the finish gets sticky. I really can't get too excited about rubbing any sort of liquid onto (into) a thin vintage finish. Polishes are for new guitars. They're formulated to penetrate and add essential ingredients that keep a finish softer, shinier, and more flexible. They can help keep your finish from becoming overly brittle, but I happen to like a dried-out finish on a 1930s Martin. And I

like the dried-out finish on my 1939 Gibson J-35!

I believe that dryness and brittleness are part of the reason old guitars have killer tone, so if you clean and polish a new guitar regularly, after 30 years the finish is less likely to be dry and brittle. It will look better, but may not sound as good as a guitar that was dry-polished (or given the moist-breath treatment) somewhat regularly but liquid-polished or cleaned only occasionally.

Cleaning the fingerboard

The condition of a guitar's fingerboard is essential to the quality of music that the instrument can produce. A clean fingerboard produces clean-sounding music because dirt is sticky and hampers smooth slides and fast playing. Dirt can also slowly rot the fingerboard, eventually causing the frets to work loose. Whenever I change strings, I always give the fingerboard at least a quick cleaning. There is a fine balance between a dirty fingerboard and one that has absorbed just the right amount of natural oil from your skin (a too-clean fingerboard wouldn't please many players).

Keep your strings clean When grime and dirt build  up along the edges of the fingerboard, and between the frets, and in the wood itself, it's time for a thorough cleaning. But if you always wipe your strings clean after playing, you won't give this dirt the chance build up. Years ago I was playing six nights a week alongside a pedal steeler, and I noticed that he would clean each string at the night's end, using a special cloth called a Blitz cloth, which was used by the Army to polish brass. I started using one, too, and found it to be the greatest string cleaner I'd ever seen. Back then, an army surplus store was the only place to find them. I guess the Blitz folks noticed how guitarists loved this thing, becasue today it's widely available as String Care by Blitz. Nowadays it's a two-cloth set: they include a dry polishing flannel with the Blitz cloth.

When cleaning strings after playing, be sure to lift each one out of the nut slot and off the bridge saddle, wiping that part of the string with your Blitz cloth, too. You may have to tune down slightly to do this. Once the strings are wiped and still a little slack, get in between them with the dry cloth (not the Blitz) and wipe down as much of the fingerboard as you can reach to get rid of the sweat. Occasionally use your thumbnail to press the rag into the crevice along the fret/fingerboard joint. This is where the wood can rot, since the fret slot (the groove that a fret is set into) has exposed end grain and will soak up any sweat and dirt that work their way under the fret. If you clean your strings faithfully—especially after a night's playing in a club or a long practice session—your fingerboard should only require an occasional polish with a soft, dry rag.

A filthy fingerboard is a different story. If the grime has accumulated for a long time, it may have hardened, and steel wool alone won't remove it. In this case, you'll have to scrape it off carefully. Be sure to use a scraper that won't cut into the wood and leave marks. In some cases you may wish to soften the dirt before trying to scrape it away. Use a cotton swab dipped in naphtha to wet the dirt and help loosen it. Then follow with your scraping tool—I prefer to use a radius gauge of the type used for measuring fretboard arc (page 24). Held at an angle, the radius touches all the board at once and removes the dirt like a snow plow removes snow. Also, its sharp tip is perfect for getting into that tight fret/fingerboard corner where most of the dirt cakes up.

Maple fingerboard caution: If your a guitar has a maple neck with a clear finish, don't use steel wool or a scraper on it! Use only a soft rag. For hardened dirt, dip the rag in a little lighter fluid if necessary; mostly, you will need a lot of elbow grease. Tape off the lacquered wood with masking tape while cleaning the fret/fingerboard edge

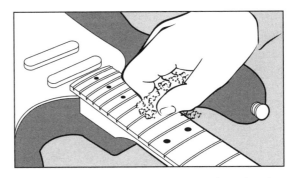

or polishing the fret tops. You may use steel wool on the finish, but it will remove the gloss and leave a dull, satiny finish. Some customers ask me to degloss their fingerboards in this manner, since they feel it leaves the surface more comfortable to play.

Pinch a ball of 0000 steel wool the size of a golf ball between your thumb and index finger, and push down with your thumbnail against the fret/fingerboard joint. This will clean right into that corner and smooth and polish the fret edges. 0000 steel wool is quite gentle— but still, try to avoid making excessive crosswise marks in the wood fingerboard. I prefer to protect the fingerboard with drafting tape. This is like masking tape, but less sticky. Remove any tape from the fingerboard slowly and carefully so you don't pull up any bits of finish or grain!

As you steel-wool the fret/fingerboard joint, you'll be polishing the sides of the fret. To finish the job, press your index finger on the steel wool again and rub back and forth on top of the fret to bring it to a good shine. This fret polishing is done along the fret's length (crosswise to the fingerboard). Finally, to remove any slight crosswise marks left by the fret polishing, use a fresh ball of wool to rub the entire fingerboard—wood and frets—in the direction of the wood grain along the entire fingerboard's length. This will give the fingerboard have a smooth, satiny look. Use only 0000 steel wool; nothing else is fine enough.

Conditioning the fingerboard with oil After cleaning, I occasionally apply a dab of lemon oil to the fingerboard, using a soft rag. Don't use oil every time you change strings; use it only when the fingerboard is dry and in need of it—perhaps several times a year for the average player. If the wood seems exceptionally dry after cleaning, it needs the lemon oil. Likewise, don't use steel wool each time you clean. Don't overdo it. I change strings every week when I'm playing on the weekends, but since I always clean my strings after the last set, I need to steel-wool the board only once a year or so.

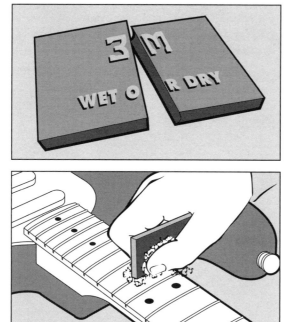

Tip for tool lovers Take a rubber squeegee (a 3M product used to remove water when wet-sanding cars, available at auto supply stores), and cut out a piece 1-1/2" by 2-1/2". With a small round file, make a slight groove on the long edge. Wrap the steel wool pad around your new homemade fret polisher, and use it as you would your finger. This tool saves a lot of wear on your fingertips and thumbnail when working the steel wool.

Avoiding cracks

If you heat your home with wood, keep a large kettle of water on or near the stove at all times to maintain some moisture in the air. Electric home humidifiers that are faithfully filled with water do a good job. There are also several in-case humidifiers available. You can make your own in-case humidifier by cutting a piece of kitchen sponge to fit a plastic soap box (the type used for storing soap when traveling) through which several small holes have been punched with an awl or icepick. Soak the sponge in water, squeeze out the excess until damp, and shut it in the plastic box. Kept in the accessory compart-

ment of your case, this helps protect your guitar from cracks due to the excess dryness in winter.

Dealing with humidity

Acoustic owners need to care for their delicate wooden instruments during the cold, dry months. Paying attention to humidity won't hurt electric owners either, so here's the skinny on chapped lips and cracked guitars.

In the humid summertime, guitars may suffer from becoming too wet, getting such symptoms as higher action (due to a more swollen top, which occasionally causes a bridge to loosen, as well) and a flat, "tubby" sound. Solve the high-action problem by having a lower "summer saddle" made for your guitar. The tubby sound goes away by itself in the fall, or whenever you have three or four nice, dry summer days in a row. Summer conditions aren't as dangerous as winter, however, since the wood seldom cracks due to over-humidification.

Low humidity occurs in the winter in most areas, and all year long in some desert and high mountain states. Heating your home, especially with forced air, adds to the dryness problem. When a solid-wood guitar dries out, the wood shrinks across the grain. The fingerboard shrinks, and the fret ends poke out from the sides. Tops flatten out or cave in, lowering the bridge and allowing the strings to buzz on the frets. The back may also flatten, and glue joints anywhere can come apart. If the wood dries too rapidly, the finish may check. In extreme cases, braces can come loose and the back, sides, and especially the top can crack. Most of these troubles can be avoid-

ed by adding moisture to the guitar's environment.

Use a hygrometer to measure your home's relative humidity; combination thermometer/hygrometers aren't expensive. If you're fortunate enough to have a furnace with a whole-house humidifier, use it; if you don't, consider having one installed. Check out the portable room humidifiers available through Sears and other companies. A natural approach is to leave bowls of water to evaporate on wood stoves and heater grates. Any of these measures will help, but they may not be sufficient protection against the dreaded crack monster.

Dampit

Humidipak

Lifeguard

Planet Waves

Soundhole humidifiers have gained popularity with many players and manufacturers. Two companies, Dampit and Kyser, manufacture soundhole humidifiers that sell for about $12.00. Simply put, these devices are dipped in water and then mounted in the soundhole when the guitar's not in use, and they slowly distribute moisture inside the guitar body. These humidifiers have soundhole covers that must be used to work properly. With the proper use of these humidifiers in the dry season and possibly a lower saddle in the wet season, your guitar should play consistently all year round.

I asked acoustic guitar experts **Dick Boak** from C.F. Martin, **Bruce Ross** at Santa Cruz Guitar Co. and **Bob Taylor** from Taylor Guitars for their thoughts on humidity and soundhole humidifiers:

Bruce: "Humidity control is most crucial to newer guitars. Once a guitar makes it through its first four seasons, it comes to terms with itself. Use the soundhole humidifier with care. I've seen them harm guitars, too, from over-wetting, which lets water drip inside."

Bob: "Lack of humidity control is the single source for over 90% of guitar problems. How you wax, clean, play, tote, strum, strap, oil, or loan a guitar is your business. These things don't matter a whole lot—the guitar will stand up to them. But when it comes to humidity, a little attention each time you play your guitar will make it last forever."

Dick: "Guitars sound terrible when they're full of moisture. But sometimes humidifiers are necessary—more so with newer guitars—and we sell both the Kyser and Dampit here at Martin. New guitars need special treatment for the first few years. Mostly watch the heat when it first comes on in the fall—don't 'force dry' your guitar. If all the drying happens in one day, you're in trouble. Keeping it in the case when you're not playing is a big help—with or without a humidifier."

Bob: "Try to keep a new guitar from any real shock (whether dry or wet) for three or four years. Lots of unnecessary and wasteful repair work is avoided by using a soundhole humidifier during the dry months. At Taylor, we include a Dampit with each guitar because it works. The Dampit is almost useless without the soundhole cover, but magic with the cover. We know of repair shops that use Dampits to fix guitars!"

Don't oversoak the humidifier; be sure to squeeze it out enough. Check the guitar's progress daily. Let your guitar tell you when it needs moisture. If the action's low and buzzy, and the top shows little or no arch, then you probably need to use your humidifier. If you're using a Dampit or Kyser for the first time on a guitar that's already dried out, expect to refill it after the first day—your guitar's thirsty. Keep your axe in the case during weather extremes, and learn to "read" your guitar—it's a great humidity gauge. When needed, use a humidifier from fall through spring. Soundhole humidifiers are inconvenient, but they're better than facing major repairs.

No system is perfect, especially when dealing with delicate wooden instruments that exist in a variety of climates. What's good for my guitar may not be good for yours, but many guitars will benefit from the use of a soundhole humidifier.

basic

Chapter 2

Installing strings

basic

Install strings correctly, and they'll stay in tune

Proper string installation has a lot to do with whether or not you'll stay in tune. Learning to tune a guitar or electric bass isn't easy—especially when you're just starting out. It's hard enough, in fact, that you'll want to know for sure that your guitar isn't working against you and causing tuning hassles that could be avoided. Outside of your ear, training, and playing experience, several factors determine whether your guitar can get in tune and stay there: the shape of the nut and bridge saddle(s), the quality and condition of the tuning keys, and how the strings are installed. Here are several tips that could help you out.

First off, the nut's string slots must not be too deep, and they shouldn't pinch the strings. This could cause a string to return flat after a string bend or tremolo dive, and may produce a catchy, "chinking" sound as you tune. If there are notches or grooves in your electric guitar's bridge saddles, be sure they're well-defined (but not too deep), smoothly rounded, and gradually tapered to the saddle's peak. In other words, each end of the string's "speaking length" must have a clean, neat contact point. Adding a tiny drop of lubricant such as Tef-lube, Vaseline, or powdered graphite at each of these points makes good sense, too.

I'm a firm believer in keeping vintage guitars stock, but I also know that replacing the tuning machines may be necessary. Your local music store can help you find exact tuner replacements (some retrofits have the same hole spacings, but better gears and a finer gear ratio). Be sure to save the original parts in case you decide to sell the guitar someday!

If "vintage" isn't an issue with you, installation of replacement tuners with locking string-posts will eliminate a great deal of tuning hassles. Some stock tuners' mounting holes will show after installing replacements—however, a good repairman can make these almost invisible. In fact, if you're not particularly skilled in

basic
Installing strings on electrics	9
Installing strings on acoustics	12
Installing strings on classicals	13

d.i.y.

deep

basic

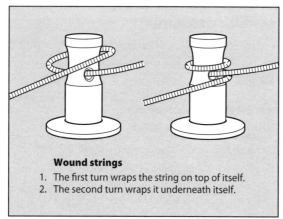

Wound strings
1. The first turn wraps the string on top of itself.
2. The second turn wraps it underneath itself.

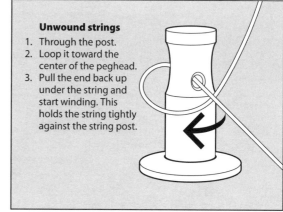

Unwound strings
1. Through the post.
2. Loop it toward the center of the peghead.
3. Pull the end back up under the string and start winding. This holds the string tightly against the string post.

guitar work, you'd be wise to have most tuners installed by a pro, unless the tuners are exact retrofits. Locking tuners are available from Schaller, Sperzel, and Gotoh.

Gibson-style electrics If your guitar has an angled peghead, like a Gibson, you'll benefit from jumping ahead to the acoustic stringing instructions on page 12. Your guitar shares some of the same stringing considerations as Martins and other steel string acoustics.

Fender-style electrics If your guitar has a bolt-on "slab" neck, Fender style, start here: With standard non-locking tuners, the way you install the strings may be the key to tuning troubles. With unwound strings (and sometimes a light, wound G), I run the string through the string post, pull it toward headstock center, loop it back underneath the string, and then pull it up against the post, so it wraps against itself as seen at left, above. This "locking tie" is more difficult with the thicker wound strings. Some people do it, although it can cause kinks, slipping, and string breakage in the heavier wound strings. Try it and see.

For many wound strings, especially the lighter D, A, and some low E gauges, make the first wrap over the string as it comes through the post, and the other wraps under as shown. With heavier gauge A and low E strings—especially on acoustic sets—just run the string through the post and make all the winds downward. Always wind it tight and neat.

If you have locking tuners, run the string through the post hole in a natural, straight line. Hold it taut, not tight, while you tighten the string-clamp. Then, in less than a turn, you'll be at pitch. Locking tuners make sense, and I

won't be surprised to find them as standard equipment on many guitars before too long.

How much string should you wind on? For Fender-style guitars, depending on string gauge, wind enough string to keep the angle from the tuner post to the nut somewhere between 5 and 12 degrees. This angle is less critical for non-tremolo guitars, but too great an angle will cause a string to bind in the nut slot when a tremolo's in use. Too shallow an angle will cause a string to pop out of the nut slot on Fender slab-style necks, or other necks with a shallow peghead angle. String trees, the hold-downs commonly used for the E, B, G and D strings, create the right string /nut angle for you.

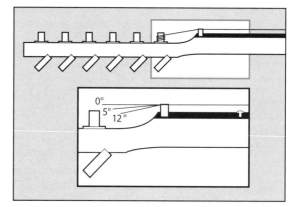

The simplest way of determining how much string to wind on a Fender guitar is to pull the length of string 2-1/2 string posts beyond the post you intend to use (that's about 2-3/4" of extra string length), and clip it to length. Then, one method of installing the string is to shove the end of the string down the hole of the slotted Safeti-Post vintage-stlye tuners, and make your string windings downward.

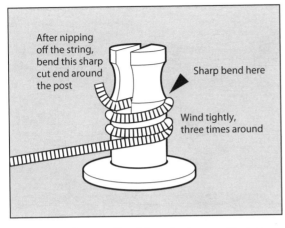

Here's another method for stringing up a Strat or Tele with Safeti-Post tuners:

1 Line the post slot parallel with to line of the string.

2 Pull the string tightly around the tuning post and, keeping constant pressure, wrap around three times —going from the bottom up.

3 After three full wraps, hold the string against the post with your finger, and with the other hand pull the string tightly through the slot. Finish this with a sharp bend in the opposite direction—making a "D" with a tail at the bottom. Then right at the bend, press the "tail" against the tuning shaft with the flat side of your wire cutters to make it hug the post, and clip it close. Tune to pitch.

For traditional tuners (with a hole in the post): Measure the string two tuning posts longer than the post for which you are stringing. Make a hard 90 degree bend in the string with your fingers. Thread the string through the post hole. Hold the bend of the string tight against the post, and with the other hand pull the short end of the string tightly forward, making another 90 degree bend in the opposite direction from the first. Still holding the string tightly at the first bend, begin winding (making the windings go down the post). The key here

is to keep the string tight and all bends at sharp right angles. This lets the edges of the tuning key hole grab the string to keep it from slipping.

Rules are made to be broken When I interviewed B.B. King, I learned that he installs the *entire* string— winding up all the slack onto each post. It seems like a lot of work, and I would never have thought of it, but Mr. King seldom goes out of tune—and as far as I'm concerned he *invented* string-bending!

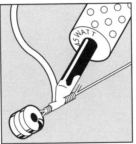

Soldering trick This is a bit of work if you change strings often (and a labor of love if your repairman does it for you). Using a hot soldering iron with 60/40 resin-core solder, tin each string's wrapping at the ball end. This keeps it from slipping or tightening like a hangman's noose at the tailpiece. "Tinning" is the process of lightly pre-coating an electrical lead with solder and letting it cool before making the final solder joint. Well-tinned string wraps should shine like silver, and never be gloppy or heavy with solder. The use of a 40–45-watt iron will enable you to get on and off the string in a flash, without overheating it. The low-wattage (15–25-watt) hardware store soldering irons will not work as well.

Don't do any soldering on, over, or near your guitar! Molten solder drips, splatters, and spits—and can make a beautiful finish look horrible. It's not good for your eyes, either, so wear safety glasses!

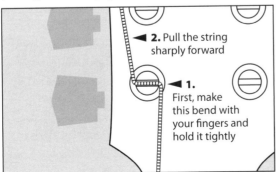

◀ **2.** Pull the string sharply forward

◀ **1.** First, make this bend with your fingers and hold it tightly

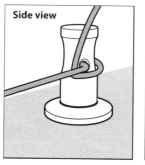

Side view   Top view

Martin's recommended string installation
This is the first step, which locks the string over itself.
Next give it two or three winds, and it will hold securely.

Installing strings on acoustics

Acoustic guitars with traditional angled pegheads (Martin, Gibson, etc.), and also electrics with angled pegheads, require a different number of string winds than bolt-on slab necks. You'll fine-tune what's right for you after going through a few sets of strings, but to give you a head start, here are the Martin factory specifications for string installation:

"Bass side strings passed through the string hole with string wound half way around post under longer portion of string, bent backwards over string and wound counter-clockwise two to three wraps around post toward the headplate. Follow this same specification for the treble strings with three to four wraps clockwise around the post."

The picture above shows the idea.

With most flattop guitars, something far more important is what's happening at the other end of the string: at the bridge pins.

Avoid bridge plate damage caused by sloppy string installation. If the ball ends are not correctly positioned, they'll wear away the wood inside—gnawing at the bridge pin holes every time you change strings.

I use an inspection mirror to check each ball end as I install every string, looking so see that the ball end is snug against the bridge plate in front of the pin, rather than off to the side (which happens if you're not watching). A telescoping inspection mirror is the easiest to find, although I prefer a 3"x8" rectangular mirror that I can lay inside the guitar.

Assuming that the bridge pins are well fit, and the bridge pin holes are clean and neat inside at the bridge plate, here's how to string up.

Pre-bend the strings
Pre-bend the ball end wraps using a needle-nosed pliers or a string bending stick—a dowel with a bent finishing nail at one end. The nail hooks the ball end as you wrap the string around the stick, bending it to fit the bridge. This makes it easy to install the strings with the ball ends forward toward the neck, up against the bridge pad in front of the pins. I prefer fluted (slotted) bridge pins. The flute faces the neck, aligning on the string to push the ball end snugly up against the bridge pad. Properly installed, the ball end will sit on the diagonal, with one corner nested in the bridge pin flute (small photo above).

On the other end of the bending stick is a nail for use with Bigsby vibrato tailpieces. This nail isn't bent—it's a straight pin to hold the ball end in the right position for pre-bending to fit a Bigsby. Make it a habit to pre-bend your strings. Even on a thin-bridged acoustic guitar, properly installed ball ends keep the string wrap from

pulling up out of the hole and onto the saddle (above). You don't want that!

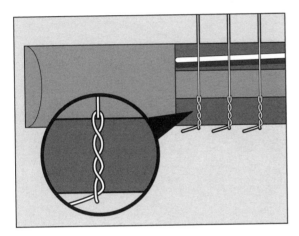

Installing strings on classicals

Nylon or gut strings (especially the wound bass strings) are more delicate than steel and must be handled more carefully to avoid kinks, nicks, breaks, and unwinding. To prolong the life of nylon strings, take special care while installing, detuning, or removing them. The nut slots and saddle crown must be perfectly shaped to avoid cutting the strings, and the ties used to install them at the bridge and tuners are important, too.

Most wound classical strings have a limp end and a stiff end, while the unwound treble strings often have a plain end and a colored one. The limp end of a wound string is simply a result of the manufacturing process; it is not meant to be tied onto the bridge, although many guitarists mistakenly do this because it's easier to wrap. The limp, loose, wrapped ends break sooner, and will not only mar the tie-block inlay, but scar the saddle as well, causing buzzing and intonation problems. Often the treble string ends are color-coded to identify the string tension (red=high; yellow=super high). Don't tie the col-

ored end to the bridge! As Jeff Elliott points out, "The color can transfer permanently to the finish of the top or the bridge, so I either clip it off or use the uncolored end. Whichever end you use for tying, heat it with a match or lighter to create a small ball end that helps it lock. To avoid burning it, remove the string from the flame the instant it begins to contract. If the nylon looks brown or burnt in any way, it will be too brittle, and will break off. In this case, cut it off and try again." Ball-end nylon strings, such as La Bella's Folk Singers, are available through your dealer, but they aren't generally used on fine classical guitars. They're used to simplify string installation on folk guitars or lesser-grade classicals.

For the standard wrap at the bridge, work about a 3" length of string through the tie block and out the back side of the bridge. Then bring the string end up and over the tie block, run it under the string, and loop or twist it toward the back edge of the tie block (shown above). Because the sixth, fifth, third and second strings have a similar large diameter, two twists are usually enough; the fourth and first strings should have three twists since their diameters are smaller. Regardless of the number of twists, the final twist should be at the back edge of the tie block, where you'll often find a strip of inlay material. The loose end must be tucked in under the string as it exits the string hole in the bridge. This isn't the only tie used on classical bridges, but it's the most common. The sharply trimmed string ends have a tendency to poke into the top after you've completed the wrap, so be sure to snip the string ends to avoid putting dings in the top.

Tying the strings correctly at the tuning key shaft is important, too. For the simplest tie, poke the string through the tuner barrel (roller) twice so that it can't slip, and then wind. This is not the approved method in classical guitar circles, though. Here's the traditional method for obtaining a tie that's good-looking and self-locking:

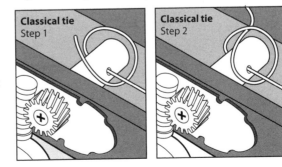

Classical tie
Step 1

Classical tie
Step 2

basic

Run the string through the hole, and then back over the barrel and under itself. Then hold the loose end while tightening the string, locking it against itself. Another similar self-locking tie runs back under itself and then threads up through the loop created by bringing the string back over the barrel (second drawing).

All makers don't necessarily wrap in the same direction or in the same way. **William Cumpiano**, for instance, believes: "You must have more than one wrap, and it's usually from three to five wraps by the time you get to pitch. Make the wraps around the barrel in the direction that creates the straightest string line to the individual string notches in the nut. Usually the D and G strings wind toward the center of the headstock, the outer two E strings wind toward the outer edges, and the A and B fall in between." **Jeffrey Elliott**, on the other hand, says, "Go through the barrel, keeping an inch or two of slack string, and come back up over the top and under the string as shown, but then wrap the string around itself twice. Then tighten the tuners, making the wraps around the barrel going toward the gears, unless the direction of the string won't get a clean shot from the barrel to the nut. Wrapping away from the gear causes the barrel to act as a lever, putting excess pressure and wear on the gear mechanism and shortening the gear's lifespan by years (especially if the gears are mounted poorly or have any loose components). But different guitars string up differently. The important thing is that a string doesn't touch another string, the channel, or the face veneer while on its way to the nut."

Richard Schneider advises: "Turn the tuning keys until the holes run almost up and down at right angles to the headstock face—maybe with the barrel holes leaning 5 or 10 degrees toward the nut. Run the string down through the hole, up the side of the barrel away from the nut, and back over and under the string. Wrap around the string twice, and then tighten the key while holding the loose end. I don't worry about undue pressure on the barrel or gears, because the tuners I use have a bearing on the shaft end in the headstock center." All of these methods will work. You'll have to experiment to get the correct number of wraps in the right direction so that the strings look neat and miss each other as they go to their respective slots in the nut.

basic

Neck evalution   15

d.i.y.

Truss rod adjustment   16
Understanding relief   17
Pro-quality straightedges   18
Typical neck adjustment scenario   19

deep

Rescuing a broken truss rod   21

Chapter 3

Neck evaluation and truss rod adjustment

basic

Neck evalution

Adjusting your guitar's truss rod is simple, and after reading this chapter you won't be afraid to do it. That adjusting nut is there for every guitar owner, not just repair shops. The key thing is to know when the neck is correctly adjusted, and that's explained here. Understanding truss rod adjustment is the first step to getting your instrument to play its best, and it's the first step for the do-it-yourselfer who's ready to move into setup and action adjustments.

When customers arrive at my shop wanting a guitar neck adjustment, it's usually because the strings are buzzing on the frets, or the action is too high (strings are up too far from the fingerboard). Fret buzz is especially common on the high frets overlapping the body (called the fingerboard "tongue"). Sometimes the guitar has intonation problems despite having a perfectly calibrated bridge. All of these are symptoms of a neck that needs adjustment.

To evaluate, or "read" your neck, you'll use a straightedge; do-it-yourselfers will use a variety of straightedges, but two will get you by. Always use your favorite gauge of strings, tuned to pitch, for these adjustments.

Sight the neck Place your nose close to the headstock and look along the fingerboard edge from the nut toward the body. You're looking for straightness, humps, up-bow (often called forward-bow), back-bow, and

d.i.y.

high frets. Up-bow pushes the surface of the fretboard away from the strings, while back-bow pulls the fretboard toward the strings. Check both the bass and treble sides, since they may look different. I wear safety glasses in case a string breaks. Neck sighting should be done in the actual "playing position," with the guitar on its side. Also in the playing position, double-check what your eye tells you with a good straightedge. The best entry level, inexpensive straightedges are a 12" combination square (the handle slides off, leaving only the blade), and a rafter square, which has two edges—16" and 24". These three lengths are adequate for most neck evaluations on guitar or bass.

d.i.y.

Truss rod adjustment

The typical truss rod isn't there to add metal and make the neck stiffer, it's there to pull the neck into the position you prefer. The truss rod has a threaded end with an adjusting nut at the peghead or the end of the fingerboard. Some acoustic guitars have adjusting nuts accessible through the soundhole. Find the nut and and the proper tool for turning it: usually an Allen wrench, nut driver socket, or a screwdriver.

Tightening (turning clockwise) pulls the neck back, straightening an up-bowed neck, and bringing the strings closer to the fingerboard. Loosening (counterclockwise) relaxes the neck, freeing it to lift into an upward bow which we call "relief" (the strings move up farther from the fingerboard). The old rule that sounds silly but works is: "righty-tighty, lefty-loosey."

On a workbench or tabletop, set the guitar (strung to pitch) on its side in the playing position with the neck unsupported. You'll need backlighting for the straightedge test, and I use white shelf paper on the benchtop—it makes an excellent visual background. Set the straightedge on the fingerboard between the third and fourth strings. It should run from the 1st fret to the 17th, covering most of the fingerboard. Hold the straightedge with one hand and, while adjusting the truss rod with the other, watch the light under the straightedge.

Don't despair if your straightedge isn't long enough. Any string makes an excellent straightedge when depressed between two frets (in this case the 1st and 17th).

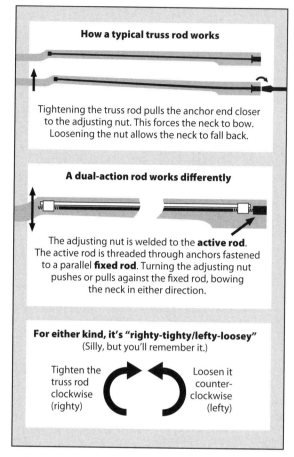

How a typical truss rod works

Tightening the truss rod pulls the anchor end closer to the adjusting nut. This forces the neck to bow. Loosening the nut allows the neck to fall back.

A dual-action rod works differently

The adjusting nut is welded to the **active rod**. The active rod is threaded through anchors fastened to a parallel **fixed rod**. Turning the adjusting nut pushes or pulls against the fixed rod, bowing the neck in either direction.

For either kind, it's "righty-tighty/lefty-loosey"
(Silly, but you'll remember it.)

Tighten the truss rod clockwise (righty)   Loosen it counterclockwise (lefty)

In fact, at Fender they always install a capo at the first fret for adjusting neck straightness and relief, or for setting the string height. The capo eliminates the nut height as a factor, and frees up one hand for measuring relief and adjusting the truss rod.

If the straightedge rocks on the fingerboard due to back-bowing, loosen the nut counterclockwise, watching for the fingerboard to come into level contact with the rule. If the strings are pulling the neck up in a slight curve, slowly tighten the nut clockwise until the rule rests flat on (hopefully) all the frets. If you loosen it now, the curve or bow will return to the fingerboard. This slight, controlled bow is called "relief." Remember how relief looks. When tightening a nut, it's best to first loosen it completely, then slowly tighten until it begins to grab and feel snug without exerting any real pressure. From this point, a quarter- to a half-turn usually straightens a neck against string pull. It would be rare to take a full turn. A squeak is a telltale sign that you are at the limit—stop there! Over-tightening can strip the nut, truss rod

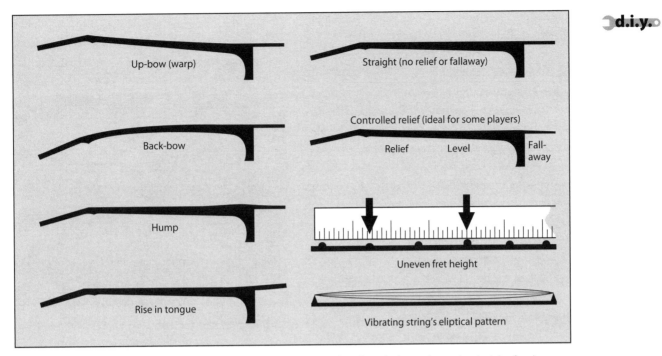

Up-bow (warp)

Straight (no relief or fallaway)

Controlled relief (ideal for some players)

Relief   Level   Fall-away

Back-bow

Hump

Uneven fret height

Rise in tongue

Vibrating string's eliptical pattern

d.i.y.

threads, or both. As you'll see shortly, it's always a good idea to clean and lubricate the threads of the truss rod and nut.

Caution: Some necks adjust more easily than others. With enough experience, you'll feel immediately whether the truss rod nut is turning properly or if it's seized up. Applying muscle to a seized truss rod could cause it to break inside the neck. This is rare, but it does happen. I'm not there to feel the wrench turning on your guitar, so I can only give you this caution: If you have doubts about whether it's working properly, call in someone with experience. Ask if you can look on and learn so you can do this yourself from now on.

Understanding relief Relief refers to a bit of controlled neck bow. I often find it's necessary in order to give a customer the playing action he wants — especially when he's a hard-strumming player who wants low action. In this section I'm going to describe relief in detail, but before I do I'd like to emphasize that my neck adjustment preference is a straight neck — with frets that have been dressed in the neck jig (page 214). I believe that loosening the truss rod to create relief sacrifices a whole bunch of tone. I've observed this hundreds of times, although many players are unaware of the potential loss of tone due to a bent, and therefore springy, neck.

Relief is often the key to low string height, few buzzes, and comfortable action. If you pluck a string, especially a wound one, the greatest movement occurs toward the center of the string length. The string moves in a long, elliptical pattern. By loosening the truss rod the fingerboard curves up, gaining relief and allowing a greater clearance for the vibrating portion of the string between the fretted note and the bridge. Relief can also eliminate buzzing on open strings near the nut and the first few frets, where the strings are lowest. Different amounts of relief are necessary depending upon a player's style and preferred string gauge, differing scale-lengths, and the height of the action. Experiment with adjusting relief in and out of the neck. Be sure to play the guitar at each stage to see the effect.

You may have to raise or lower the bridge saddle height after a neck adjustment. In fact, a pro will adjust the neck and string height simultaneously—tighten or loosen the rod, raise or lower the bridge—back and forth until the action is set. We set the string height separately in the next section of this chapter (later you'll use all the techniques together in a smooth, flowing operation with experience as your guide).

Not all guitars need relief. In fact, I always try to get an instrument to play with a perfectly straight neck first, and only add relief to eliminate unmanageable buzz-

d.i.y.

ing. Straight necks have lower, faster action—necks with relief play a little stiffer and mushier toward the center of the neck. Necks with too much relief and low action may buzz in the upper register.

Relief is measured by inserting a feeler gauge in the maximum gap between the top of the frets and the bottom of a straightedge sitting on the frets. Measure at the approximate midpoint between the nut and where the neck joins the body (normally between the 6th and 9th frets). Factory specifications for relief are listed elsewhere in this book, but as a rule relief will measure as follows: guitars from .004"–.012"; basses from .008"–.018".

For guitar, it's best to check relief with an 18" straightedge—one that will reach at least to the 15th or 17th fret. For bass you need a 24" straightedge. Study the illustration to understand how a "perfect" neck looks in both the straight and the relieved configurations. Relief should gradually disappear as the straightedge is slid further up the neck. You can see an exaggerated case of relief by clamping one end of a board to your workbench. Put a straightedge on the board, and lift the unclamped end. You'll see the most pronounced curve near the end you're lifting, and it will gradually straighten out to a flat portion at the other end. That's what your neck is doing when it's in relief. If there were a hump or rise at the clamped end (equivalent to your highest frets), you'd get fret buzz. In fact, a little "fallaway" is good up there to prevent buzz.

This slight fallaway in the last few frets would guarantee no buzzing in the upper register, but it's not a must—either dead flatness, or else fallaway, is correct. Whenever the upper register of the fretboard (called the tongue, or fretboard extension) rises instead of being flat or falling away, you have a symptom called "rising tongue" (drawing, page 17).

So relief really needs to be measured first with the long straightedge to see the whole board, and then double-checked with a shorter edge to view the flatter area of the board from around the 8th fret up. If that area shows a gap where it should read flat, then you really can't measure the whole board's true relief because of this "secondary relief," caused by the rise or hump. Many necks have this problem, and the only solutions are:

✔ Playing with some buzz on upper frets.

✔ Raising the string height.

✔ Filing the rise out of the frets.

✔ Removing the frets, flattening the wood properly, and replacing at least the last six frets.

Notched straightedge When you have symptoms such as humps and rises, it's far easier to isolate them using a notched straightedge. Several of my favorite straightedges are notched to fit over the frets, allowing me to read the fretboard instead of the frets (which may be worn in one area and not another, or poorly seated, and won't give a true picture of fingerboard flatness). I've named this technique the "MacRostie Method" after my good friend Don MacRostie, who invented the notched straightedge, and presented me with my first set.

After adjusting a bit of relief into your guitar's neck, rest a plain straightedge on the board and slide it one fret at a time toward the body. The edge should drop from fret to fret as it moves, indicating that each fret is slightly higher than the one following it. As you slide the rule, it should quit dropping and level out between the 7th and 10th frets, and remain flat the rest of the way. As we said earlier, it's OK when the frets from the 15th on up fall slightly away from the rule. This fall-away ensures clean notes in the upper register.

If you try to view the flat area with a too-long straightedge, you may find that it runs into the pickups and/or bridge before you can slide it onto the area you're after. This is why over the years my toolboxes have collected straightedges of all different lengths.

Pro-quality straightedges Inexpensive hardware-store straightedges can only give you a ballpark reading of a neck. Professional repair shops invest hundreds

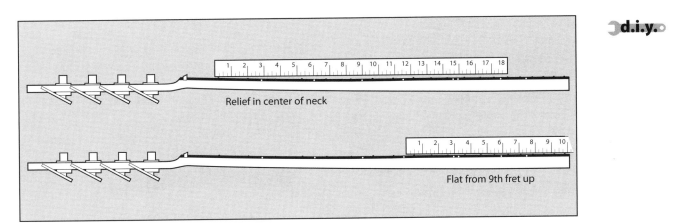

Relief in center of neck

Flat from 9th fret up

d.i.y.

of dollars in precision-ground straightedges of different lengths. At the entry level, you can get by with the straightedge and rafter square mentioned previously for both guitar and bass, but when you really want to know what's happening, check into professional straightedges. When I can find them, I prefer straightedges with a beveled edge since they give more accurate readings. High quality precision-ground straightedges have a thickness proportional to their length—the longer, the thicker—to keep them from curving due to flimsiness. An edge this thick, however, won't give a reading to suit me—so all of my longer straightedges must be beveled. I use the following lengths:

2", 3" These are "fret rocker" lengths for laying across any three frets (guitar or bass), looking for high frets. When there's a high fret, the straightedge will teeter on it. These straightedges are 1-1/2" wide. When set on end, they act as rockers for close frets.

8" For reading a guitar from 9th fret to fingerboard end

12" For reading general flatness, guitar or bass (also good from 9th fret to fingerboard end on bass).

15" Similar to above.

18" To look for relief/check flatness on guitar or bass.

24" To check relief and flatness on bass.

Notched, and beveled on one edge:

18" Notched short scale (24-3/4"/24.9").

18" Notched long scale (25-1/2"/25.4").

24" Notched standard scale bass (34").

I also took an extra of each of these three notched straightedges and cut it at the 9th fret. With these half-length notched edges I can read either the upper or lower portion of the fretboard independently.

Typical neck adjustment scenario

Neck adjustment problems are common to all acoustic or electric guitars and basses, and are most pronounced on the electric bass because of its long, slim neck. So the bass makes an excellent teaching example for neck adjustments. These techniques apply to all guitars, and to every scale length—basses just tend to need a little more help than guitars.

The straighter the neck, the lower the strings can be—but you must play with a light touch to avoid buzzes or fret rattle. If like low action and your style is to dig in hard, your neck will need some relief to avoid buzzes.

Vibrating string's elliptical pattern is accommodated by the neck relief

Under string tension, a perfect neck for many players is one that adjusts straight for low action and easy fret dressing, and eases from straightness into controlled relief. A properly relieved neck has a gradual up-bow between the nut and around the 9th fret, and then remains straight from the 9th to the last fret. The overall curve in the fret tops between the 1st fret and the body joint mimics the string's long elliptical pattern as it vibrates when plucked. This eliminates a lot of fret buzz.

Sighting a neck is the simplest way to see if it's straight, back-bowed, up-bowed or in controlled relief. This is how you determine what adjustments, if any, are needed. Hold your guitar on its side in the playing position to get a true reading from the neck. Support the body on a table, so its weight isn't tugging on the neck. Sight from the nut toward the body. If you have trouble

d.i.y.

looking along the fret tops, sight along the glue joint between the fingerboard and the wood of the neck—use that glueline as a straightedge. You can also check by holding down a string at the 1st fret and at the body joint, since a tight string is a good straightedge. To get an accurate reading, use a precision-ground straightedge.

Most necks adjust by tightening or loosening a truss rod nut. These adjusting nuts are located at the peghead or recessed into the body at the end of the fingerboard. Some acoustic guitars have an adjusting nut accessible through the soundhole. Find it and select the proper tool for turning it; most likely an Allen wrench, socket wrench, or screwdriver.

Tightening (turning clockwise) pulls the neck back, straightening an up-bow and removing relief.

Loosening (counterclockwise) allows a back-bowed neck to return to straight, or allows it to have relief.

Things to keep in mind:

✔ The adjustment nut on many bolt-on necks is at the body end. In that case, it's usually accessible only after loosening the strings and removing the neck.

✔ The first thing to do, always, is loosen the truss rod nut. It may already be as tight as it goes, and you'd hate to break it before even getting started. In fact, remove the nut completely and brush or blow any dirt from the threads of both the rod and the nut. Add a tiny dab of heavy-bodied lubricant on the threads inside the truss rod nut (GHS GraphitALL, Vaseline or StewMac Guitar Grease). Be careful not to get lubricant on the bare wood. Lubricating the threads makes for a smoother adjustment, especially on older instruments.

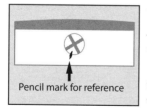

Pencil mark for reference

✔ Reinstall the nut until it's just snug (don't put tension on it). Then make a small pencil mark that crosses from the nut onto the neck. When this mark lines back up with itself, that's your snug starting point—a nice reference when making adjustments.

✔ One half-turn on a truss rod nut is a lot. Once a nut reaches snugness, tighten it one-eighth to one-quarter turn and then check your progress. If adjusting the nut requires neck removal, expect to remove and install the

neck several times during this process.

✔ The effect of a rod adjustment can take days or weeks to be complete. You may adjust a neck perfectly, only to find a day later that the neck has kept moving from the rod's tension—becoming too straight or even back-bowed. Don't panic if this happens; simply readjust it.

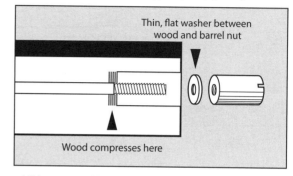

Thin, flat washer between wood and barrel nut

Wood compresses here

✔ If the truss rod barrel nut is extremely tight on the rod or recessed far into the hole, watch out! It was probably over-tightened by a previous owner or amateur "repairman." Some ill-informed people really crank those truss rods, which is a great way to break them, causing your neck to become permanently non-adjustable. Over-tightening can also cause the wood to compress, without straightening the up-bow. In this case, follow the removal, cleaning, and lubrication steps above, and then add one or two thin washers before threading the nut back on. Often this gives the nut a new grip and allows the rod to adjust further.

✔ With a stubborn neck, often it's best to loosen the rod completely, clamp the neck into straightness (or even a back-bow), and then tighten the truss rod nut. This method generally works when all else fails. Place a sturdy metal bar on two blocks of wood over the the finger-

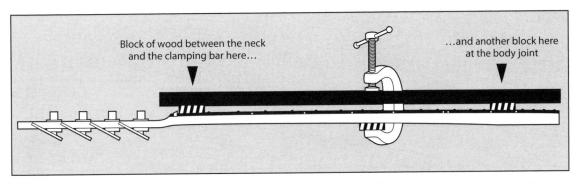

Block of wood between the neck and the clamping bar here...

...and another block here at the body joint

board. Using a caul to protect the neck surface, a clamp applies pressure that bends the neck into the position you want. The truss rod can be adjusted to hold this position that the clamping achieved.

 deep

Rescuing a broken truss rod

Many, many guitar necks have been thrown out because of adjusting nuts that no longer adjust. When something went wrong with the working parts (nut and threaded rod) buried in the wood of the neck, it's been next to impossible to repair. In some cases, the fingerboard could be removed and a new truss rod installed, but many guitars aren't valuable enough for this sort of costly surgery. The solution has often been to replace the neck entirely.

A while back, I had a conversation with my pal and fellow repairman Frank Ford, of *FRETS.com*. We imagined that if only there were a thread-cutting tool compact enough, it would be possible to get in there and fix a truss rod while it's still in the neck. Frank's an excellent machinist, and a few months later he'd managed it! He sent me a cutting die that was very close to what we needed. Its small size meant it was too delicate for lots of jobs, but I treasured it. I showed it to Don MacRostie and Al Rorick of Stewart-MacDonald's product development team, and they experimented and came up with the full-fledged neck-saving tool that Frank and I had dreamed of. It's now a bona fide lutherie tool for professional shops, and we named it the Truss

Rod Rescue Kit. This may be something you need to know about if you've got a truss rod that's called it quits.

Here's how to repair your standard 10/32" truss rod using this tool.

First, clean the threads Turn the truss rod's adjusting nut counterclockwise to remove it from the threaded rod. Sometimes, all you need is to clean up those threads that the nut turns on. Use the tool's thread-cutting die for this, turning it carefully onto the existing threads. By threading the die on and off once, you'll know the rod is cleaned and ready for its adjusting nut. If you feel resistance when turning the die, stop. This resistance means the tool has met with marred or dirty threads, or is starting to cut new threads in the metal rod. This requires a slow and careful approach, as detailed in step 3 in the instructions that follow.

The nut may be frozen to the rod, or it may even have broken off, taking the end of the truss rod with it. To repair a truss rod in this situation means removing wood from around the rod to make room before cutting new threads into the remaining rod (steps 1 through 5).

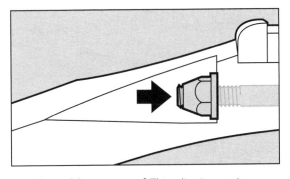

Good, working truss rod This adjusting nut is accessible, turns without too much force, and is flush against a metal washer that serves as a bearing surface.

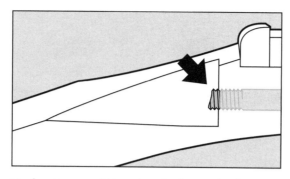

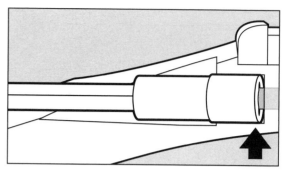

Broken truss rod Here, the adjusting nut has frozen to the truss rod and then broken off — taking part of the rod away with it. The remaining truss rod doesn't have enough thread exposed for an adjusting nut.

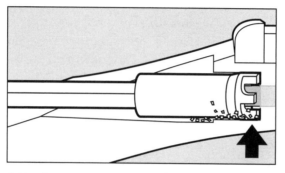

1 Use the cutter to remove wood until you have 5/8" of the truss rod exposed. Use only moderate pressure, and let the tool do the cutting. Stop frequently to remove wood chips from the cavity.

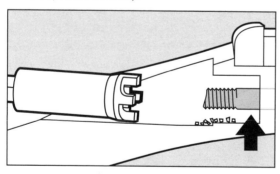

2 With the wood removed you now have access to more of the truss rod, but there may not be enough thread for the adjusting nut.

3 Switch to the die, using it carefully so you can feel it catch onto the threads. Turn the die slowly, and stop when it hits resistance. Note the position of the wrench at this point, then continue 1/4 turn — you've now started cutting threads. After 1/4 turn, back the die out and clean its threads. Also clean any shavings from the truss rod cavity. Continue thread-cutting 1/4 turn at a time, stopping to clean between each cut until you reach the bottom of the cavity. Cutting too quickly allows shavings to build up and places stress on the truss rod. A bit of lubricant in the die, such as petroleum jelly, Guitar Grease, paraffin, or beeswax will ease the job and produce cleaner threads. Don't use oil, or any other thin lubricant that might leech into the wood.

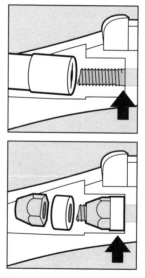

4 Now there is enough thread for the adjusting nut, but the die leaves a little bit of unthreaded rod at the deepest point in the cavity.

5 Use a spacer to cover that last bit of unthreaded rod and to provide a metal bearing surface.

Fender rods The tool has an adapter for use on Fenders (not pictured): a cylindrical "pilot" that fits into the end of the cutter bit, centering on the smaller (7/16" dia.) recess used on Fender truss rods. The pilot keeps the cutter aligned until it's started into the maple neck, then it's removed and the work proceeds, leaving a little extra space around the repaired truss rod nut.

Chapter 4

Setup and action

basic

basic

What is a setup?   23

---

d.i.y.

The basics of setup   24
Setting up an electric guitar   27
Setting up a guitar with tremolo   29
Setting up an electric bass   31
Setting up a flattop acoustic   32
Setting up an archtop   35
Setting up a classical   36

---

deep

Low action and the blues   40
Setups for pro players:
    Stevie Ray Vaughan and Jeff Beck   44
    John Mooney's slide   47
    Albert Collins   50
    Buddy Guy   52
    B.B. King   57

What is a setup?

A setup is the process of fine-tuning the guitar's overall action by making adjustments at the neck, bridge, and nut. If you've worked your way through preceding chapters, your guitar is clean, lubricated, strung to pitch, and you understand neck adjustment. You're ready to give it a setup.

On most electric guitars, the action height is adjusted by simply raising or lowering the bridge or its saddles. If you're working on an acoustic guitar, it probably has a non-adjustable bone saddle; to raise or lower it, you'll need to reshape or replace the saddle (page 124). If you encounter any of the following problems at this point, you'll need to address them before you're ready for setup:

Open strings are buzzing The nut needs to be raised, shimmed, or replaced (page 219).

Buzzing frets need to be dressed (page 177).

Inoperable bridge saddles on acoustics (page 123) or electrics (page 83).

Acoustic bridge needs to be reglued (page 144).

A repair shop technician does a setup by thinking of neck, bridge, fret, and nut adjustments together. Experience dictates which jobs need to be done, and in what order. For example, a professional wouldn't make a neck adjustment, re-string, fine-tune the nut, set the action and intonation, and then go back to dress the frets. If a professional is in the middle of a setup and discovers a bad nut, he or she will stop, make the nut, and then catch up to the leaving-off point. Some of these side trips involve repair work, such as shimming or replacing the nut, replacing an acoustic saddle, and replacing or dressing frets. These setup instructions assume your guitar's healthy, and you've already covered the following:

✔ The guitar is clean and strung to pitch.

✔ The frets are level and don't need dressing, etc.

✔ The neck is adjusted to what you think is right (the following setups may change that slightly).

⊃d.i.y.⊃

✔ The nut doesn't need replacement (lowering the nut may be part of a setup, but replacing it isn't).

✔ All bridge parts are functional.

⊃d.i.y.⊃

The basics of setup

You may need to adjust the action while you adjust the neck, and it's pointless to set the intonation until the action is where you want it. If the strings are either too high or too low, any fine-tuning of the intonation goes right out the window if you have to readjust the string height afterward. So be patient as you learn to set up your guitar, and understand that each adjustment might trigger other adjustments.

For years, this is how I set my action:

1 Lower the bridge until the strings buzz.

2 Raise it back up until the buzz stops, or is at a point you can live with.

It gets you in the ballpark, but these days I've moved on a more fine-tuned approach. I pay close attention to setup specs, and tweak my setups much more carefully.

Factory specs The place to start is with the setup specs used by Gibson, Fender, and Martin. These are good, middle-of-the-road specifications that satisfy most players. They ensure that a guitar leaves the factory in a playable state, but by the time it's purchased in arid Arizona or muggy Florida, the setup could feel quite different. Add player preferences into the mix and you can see that setup is something you want to tailor to each situation. Think of these factory specs as your starting point. If the guitar has a tremolo with a locking nut, you'll also want to refer to chapter 8.

Fretboard and saddle radius A certain amount of buzzing should be expected; metal strings on metal frets buzz a little. Proper neck adjustment and fret leveling will remove 90% of the buzzes, but the remaining 10% should be accepted as normal, and will play themselves out over time. Of course, any buzz can be eliminated by raising the action high enough, but this won't satisfy most players.

One cause of string buzz that's often overlooked is a mismatch between the radius curve of the fingerboard

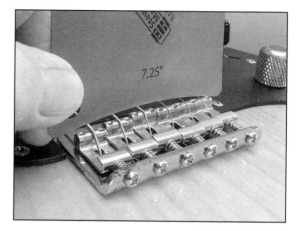

and the curved setting of the bridge saddle. Most steel-string guitars have curved radiused fingerboards, with the amount of radius differing between manufacturers (Martin and Gretsch seem to have the flattest fingerboards). If the bridge saddle curve is significantly flatter than the fingerboard's radius, the middle strings will be closer to the frets than the outer ones, causing buzzes. Correcting this poor saddle adjustment will often eliminate buzz immediately, also removing the need for fret leveling. You'll also find that a proper bridge setup makes for a more comfortable axe, especially when you play chords. Here's how to make and use a simple tool: a radius gauge for setting your bridge saddles.

Making a radius gauge It's not much trouble to make a radius gauge, so if you're unsure about which size you need, make them all and see which fits. The most popular fingerboard radii are: 7-1/4" (vintage Fender); 9-1/2" (some current Fenders); 10" (Kramer and many replacement necks); 12" (Gibson); and the 16"–20" range (Jackson, Martin, Gretsch, and others with a flatter fingerboard). I made my original radius gauges from Plexiglas, so that they'd be long-lasting. Stewart-MacDonald has

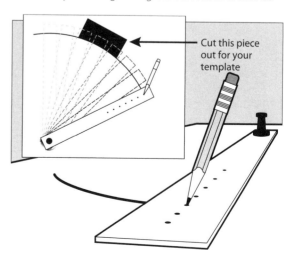

Cut this piece out for your template

reproduced these gauges in stainless steel, and that's what I use now. If you make cardboard or thin wood versions, they'll work fine if you're only occasionally setting up your own guitar.

Start with a piece of stiff cardboard or thin wood about 24" long and 1" wide. Draw a centerline on this piece and make a mark 1" in from one end—this is your axis. From this mark, measure the correct distance for the radii you want (7-1/4", 9-1/2", 12", etc.), and make marks accordingly. Lay this marked-out strip on a piece of smooth-faced cardboard and press a sharp pin through the center, pinning the strip to the poster board below. Now if you poke a second pin through any of the measured "radius" marks, you have a compass that can scribe the different radii onto the posterboard.

Cut out the gauges with a sharp blade, making them 4" wide (wide enough to span a guitar saddle). Thin wood or cardboard is hard to sand or shape, so make your first cut accurate. If you do need to custom-fit your gauge to the fingerboard, reinforce the cardboard by saturating it with water-thin super glue. Once it's dried, you'll find that you can carve, file, or sand the thin material much more effectively. Wear safety glasses when working with super glue, especially the thin stuff.

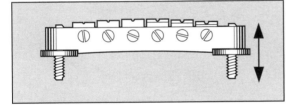

Use the gauge first to measure the fingerboard radius with the strings removed, and then sight across your guitar's bridge saddles, from E to E. On most electrics or acoustics, you'll see a gentle rise through the A and D strings, going back down through the G and B to the E. This curve should approximate the fingerboard's curve. Some guitars have a curve built into the bridge rather than using up/down adjustable saddles (Gibson Tune-O-Matics, etc.). With this type of bridge, the saddle radius can be controlled by the depth of the saddle slot filed into each bridge saddle insert, while overall string height is set by raising or lowering the thumbwheels on either end. Most Fenders have saddles that easily move up or down, making it easy to set your strings exactly to the fingerboard.

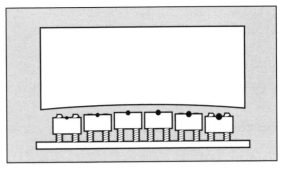

Fender bridge radius On Fender-style guitars, adjust the outside E strings to the action height that you like by measuring the gap between the bottom of the strings and the top of the 17th fret (refer to the factory specs chart). Now place your radius gauge on the two outer E strings just in front of the bridge saddles, and raise or lower the four middle strings until they, too, just touch the gauge—it's that simple. Your bridge saddle curve now matches the fingerboard.

With Fender's individually-adjustable saddles, you can match the fingerboard arch simply by measuring the clearance of each string at the 17th fret. But using the radius gauge is much easier.

When you sight across the bridge by eye, the curve may look right even when it's not. Often the middle strings are on too flat a curve and too close to the fingerboard, causing buzzes. Also, when the saddle curve matches that of the fingerboard, you'll like the feel of the action, especially for chords. Best of all, you'll usually find that you've eliminated that final 10% of annoying string buzz. If matching the radius doesn't feel exactly the way you like it, it's still the correct starting point from which to start personalizing your action—and it's much more accurate than eyeballing it.

Acoustic players use the radius gauge as a guide for tracing the proper shape onto a poorly shaped saddle, and then filing or sanding the saddle to match. This takes more care than working on electric saddles, since it's easy to screw up your saddle permanently and need to replace it. Also, removing and replacing an acoustic

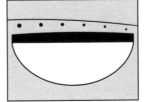

saddle is something to be done with care. See page 123 for help with this.

On both acoustics and electrics, saddles are shaped so that the strings

d.i.y.

gradually rise higher on the bass side. This compensates for the extra thickness of the wound strings and their wider, floppier vibration when struck. For this reason, when you perfectly match your fingerboard radius it's just a starting point. Expect to slightly raise the three lowest strings to get perfect results.

Customized radius gauges A fingerboard radius gauge set is perfect for most radius-checking, but they don't fit every possible bridge, so I've customized mine:

I cut the corners off of my radius gauge to fit between

the walls of a Tele bridge, to keep from hitting the bridge base on Gibsons, and to set pickup polepiece height.

The best way to set any bridge saddle radius is to check

the radius from underneath the strings—since measuring from the top doesn't take the height of the strings into account. Here I'm using a stainless understring radius gauge. You make your own by using the pencil compass method—or trace a radius gauge you made before onto a piece of cardboard and out the shape.

A notched radius gauge is useful because it fits over the

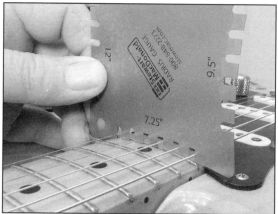

strings, so you can check the radius with the strings on!

Setup specs include:
✔ Maximum relief, or up-bow
✔ String height over the fretboard (controlled by adjusting the bridge saddle height)
✔ String height at the nut
✔ Bridge, tailpiece and tremolo adjustments
✔ Pickup height adjustment

All string height measurements are made by measuring the clearance between the bottom of a string and the top of a fret (or a pickup pole piece). Make your measurements with the guitar on its side, in the playing position. If the guitar's laying on its back, you'll get inaccurate measurements. You'll need a small ruler that reads in 1/64" increments, and a set of feeler gauges (which will read in thousandths).

I use a neck jig I created for fretting and setup work (page 214). It holds the guitar in the playing position, and allows me to take the strings off yet maintain the precise position of the neck as if it were under string tension.

Along with the factory specs, I've included measurements of my own from extremely well-playing guitars. These are always lower-than-factory-action, and in my opinion represent the best you can reasonably expect from a given type of guitar.

Setting up an electric guitar

Gibson factory specs For long (25-1/2") or short (24-3/4") scale guitars. Sample instruments used were a factory-fresh 1993 Les Paul, and my 1961 ES-345.

String height at the nut height is adjustable by filing the string slots for each string individually (page 222). Gibson measures clearance in 64ths; I've given the distances in thousandths as well, since I use feeler gauges to take these measurements.

Gibson factory specs vs. my specs		
Neck relief at 7th fret	Factory	Mine
On all strings:	.012"	.004"
String height at 12th fret	Factory	Mine
On the bass E string:	5/64"	3/64"
On the treble E string:	3/64"	3/64"
String height at the nut	Factory	Mine
On the bass E string:	2/64" (.030")	(.015")
On the A string:	2/64" (.030")	(.014")
On the D String:	1-1/128" (.022")	(.013")
On the G string:	1-1/128" (.022")	(.012")
On the B string:	1/64" (.015")	(.010")
On treble E string:	1/64" (.015")	(.009")

Gibson bridge and tailpiece adjustments At the factory, Gibson uses a mini-crowbar to lift the bridge while the thumb-wheels are spun up or down to raise or lower the bridge body. This "bridge jack" is made from steel that is heated and bent to a crowbar shape, and then padded with thick felt on the bend to keep from harming the top as the bridge body is pried up. If you lack this tool, you may have to detune the strings in order to get some thumbwheels to move (especially when raising the bridge).

The bridge saddle radius should match, or be slightly flatter than, the fretboard radius. This can be checked with a radius gauge. Most Gibson electric fretboards range between a 10" and 12" radius, and factory bridges have a radius of 12". By cutting the string notches slightly deeper on the middle strings, a flatter radius is achieved. The same files and techniques used for lowering the nut can be used for bridge saddles.

Stop tailpieces adjust by screwing the two studs in or out until the strings just clear the back of the bridge body. Many players go beyond this point and tighten the stop-bar snug against the body to increase sustain, but it's not proven that this works (try it). It does seem that every model, and even each individual guitar within the same model, has a perfect tailpiece height where the strings and action feel best and have the best tone. Raise your tailpiece up and down to find this sweet spot. I like to see the strings clear the body of the bridge. In the photo above, all the strings clear the back edge of the bridge; these saddles have been shaped and "deluxed" by me, the way I like 'em. You'll often lose this clearance when the stop-bar is screwed too far down. (Surely some harmonic qualities must be lost when the strings "ground out" on the bridge body?) Trapeze tailpieces are not, for all practical purposes, adjustable.

Gibson pickup height Height adjustments for pickups are best made with  both volumes wide open. Switch back and forth between pickups while adjusting the height, until the volume of each is equal. Then back off the neck pickup a little bit, to boost the

d.i.y.

Gibson pickup height		
Neck pickup	Factory	Mine
On the treble side:	3/32"	3/32"
On the bass side:	3/32"	3/32"
Bridge pickup	Factory	Mine
On the treble side:	1/16"	1/16"
On the bass side:	1/16"	1/16"

power of the bridge pickup. (At the bridge pickup's location, the string's elliptical vibration is reduced and has less power.) When depressing the two outer E strings at the last fret, and measuring from the bottom of the string to the polepiece tops, you should get the readings shown in the chart.

Fender factory specs Here are the setup specifications used at Fender to adjust most of their bass and guitar models during the "tune test," or final setup stage of production. These tune-test adjustments include:

✔ Bridge height (for tremolo guitars only—clearance between bottom of bridge plate and face of guitar)

✔ Relief (Fender refers to this as "neck bow")

✔ String height (clearance at the 17th fret)

✔ Nut height (clearance at 1st fret)

✔ Pickup height (with strings pressed at last fret)

Follow these tips to make Fender setups easier:

Sight the neck Even with strings removed you can get a good idea of how the neck is adjusted by flexing it and sighting it. Sometimes you can make an adjustment before you string up, and it'll be correct when you get to pitch.

Check the electronics At Fender, the very first check is to ensure that the guitar works when it's plugged in! A dud, or one that misfires, goes back to the starting gate.

The capo trick String height and relief measurements are made with a capo installed at the first fret to eliminate the nut as a factor when setting up. Also, when capoed at the first fret, the string becomes a straightedge when pressed at the 17th fret as well (leaving you a free hand to take measurements). This capo technique is useful for setting up up any guitar.

Preset the intonation Fender sets the bridge saddles to an approximately correct intonation pattern to make the final intonation adjustment faster. This insures that the strings won't be kinked in front of the saddles in case you have to move the saddles back while setting the intonation. For guitars or basses, set the treble E string so that the center of the saddle is at the exact scale length measurement from the front of the nut (25-1/2" for Strat and Tele, 34" for Precision and Jazz Basses, etc.). Then rough-in the other saddles by eye to the approximate the intonation pattern shown in the photo. Now you're ready to begin the setup adjustments.

8-step setup for a guitar or bass

1 String to pitch.

2 Install capo at the first fret.

3 Adjust relief at 7th fret by pressing down a string at the last fret so the string becomes straightedge (sometimes you'll get better results by measuring at the 9th fret, especially with basses). If your adjusting nut is at the fretboard end, expect to take the neck on and off a few times before you get it right. I prefer to adjust my neck almost perfectly straight at this stage and go on to setting my string height. Then if it's too buzzy, I'll loosen the rod and introduce relief gradually. At the factory they adjust in the relief, period.

4 Set the string height across the fretboard at the 17th fret (follow the factory specs). Raise or lower the strings by adjusting the saddle height. Use the proper tool: a .050" (4-40) Allen wrench for Strats and some Teles, or a small screwdriver for other Teles and bass models. Fender saddles have two threaded set-screws: raising one screw more than another will change the spacing between strings, while at the same time raising or lowering the saddle. Keep an eye on the string-to-string spacing. Use your radius gauge to set the bridge radius.

5 Remove the capo. If the string height at the nut is too high, you'll have to file the slots. If it's too low, you must raise the nut with shims, or replace it.

6 Set the height of the pickups (two outer polepieces) to the factory specs. Press the outer two strings at the last fret, and check their clearance over the pickups.

7 Play the guitar at all frets, checking for buzzes.

8 Using an electronic tuner, fine-tune the intonation, and you're done! Speaking of electronic tuners: these days I'm using Peterson's small Strob-O-Flip tuner, and I recommend it highly.

10-step setup for tremolo guitars

>d.i.y.

This is similar to the 8 steps above, but with additions for dealing with a tremolo. I learned this setup while visiting Fender. My tour guide was **Albert Garcia**, a long-time friend and Fender employee. Having set up thousands of Strats, Albert uses a few tricks on

Fender factory specs					
Model	Pickup Height *	String Height **	Bridge Height	Relief at 7th fret	Nut Action ***
Amer. Standard, Vintage, & SRV	1/8" bass side 3/32" treble side	4/64"	3/32"–1/8"	.012"	.020" (−.002")
Ultra, Plus, Beck	1/16" both sides	4/64"	3/32"–1/8"	.012"	.020" (−.002")
Burton Tele, '52 Tele	3/32" bass side 5/64" treble side 10-12/64" middle	4/64"	n/a	.012"	.020" (−.002")
Malmsteen	1/8" bass side 3/32" treble side middle flush w/pickguard	4/64"	3/32"–1/8"	.008"	.020" (−.002")
Clapton	1/16" both sides	3/64"–4/64"	flat on body	.008"–.010"	.020" (−.002")
SRV	1/8" bass side 3/32" treble side	4/64"	3/32"–1/8"	.012"	.020" (−.002")
Floyd Rose Classic	1/8" bass side 3/32" treble side 3/32" both sides for humbucker	1/8" use pivot screws to even out action	7/32" (±1/32") top of bridge plate to top of body (4/32" ±1/32") measured at pivot screws	.012"	.020" (−.002")
5 String Bass	7/64" bass side 5/64" treble side	3/32" (±1/64")	n/a	.014"	.020" (+.002")
Amer. Standard & Vintage Bass	1/8" bass side 3/32" treble side	3/32" (±1/64")	n/a	.014"	.020" (+.002")
Ultra & Plus Bass	1/16" both sides	3/32" (±1/64")	n/a	.014"	.020" (+.002")

   * Pickup height: the gap between the string and pickup when the string is pressed at the last fret
  ** String height measured at the 17th fret
 *** Nut action measured from bottom of string to top of 1st fret

d.i.y.

his own guitars that are not used at the factory. Before beginning, cover these four points:

✔ Be sure that the electronics are working.

✔ No springs are installed on the tremolo.

✔ The tremolo claw should be quite loose (1" from the rear wall of the tremolo rout) to allow easy spring installation later.

✔ The intonation is roughly pre-set.

1 String up lightly, but not nearly to pitch. Use .009s for the American Standard, and .010s for the Vintage.

2 Block the tremolo in the middle position so it can float in either direction. Use a hardwood block measuring 1" wide and 2" long that tapers from 1/4" to 1/2". Shove it in between the rear of the tremolo block and the guitar body until you get a gap of about 11/32". Now string to pitch, and the tension will hold the block in place.

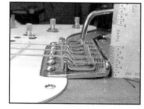

Shove the block in, or pull it out (re-tuning as necessary), until a gap of 3/32" shows between the bottom of the bridge plate and the face of the guitar. Once tuned to pitch, the bridge can't go anywhere—it's blocked.

3 Install a capo at the 1st fret.

4 Adjust the neck. In the playing position, depress one of the wound strings (I use either the D or A) at the 17th fret. Adjust the neck to the proper relief, or straight if you prefer it that way. (Both Albert and I prefer a neck to be almost straight, or maybe with just a little bit of relief—.004" to .006"). If you have a neck that adjusts at the body end, you may have to remove the neck a number of times to complete the adjustment. At the factory, they seldom have to take the neck off more than twice—they're good at it!

5 Set the string height. With the capo still on, adjust the string height at the 17th fret to match the specs in the chart. You can do that either of two ways: set the outer two E strings to the correct height and use the radius gauge to set the remaining bridge saddles; or use the ruler to measure and adjust the height of each string until it shows the same clearance all the way across at the 17th fret. The factory clearance is 4/64" for guitars, but Albert sets his bass E string slightly higher, to 5/64" and then blends that into the 4/64" height.

6 Remove the capo.

7 Lower the string height at the nut to match the factory specs. This is generally set between .022" and .020", but if you really want to be exact, there is a range from .018" to .022" depending on whether you're working on a guitar or bass. You'll notice in the chart a plus or minus symbol (+ -). The plus gives the measurement for the low bass string, the minus indicates the treble string setting. For example: .020" (-.002") means that you set all the strings at .020", but the treble E string could measure as low as .018" (guitar). Or, .020" (+.002") means that all the strings are set to .020", but you could leave the low E string as high as .022". It's always best to go with the tallest measurement, and fine-tune the nut by degrees.

8 Adjust the pickup height. Use the chart measurements and, fretting the outer two E strings at the last fret, measure the gap between the bottom of the string and the top of the E string polepieces. Albert prefers to set his pickups slightly farther from the strings than the factory does, to avoid overtones and possible intonation problems and to give that "clear as a bell" Strat tone.

9 Play the guitar and check for buzzes at every fret (you may need to dress the frets—or perhaps only one fret—on any guitar, at any stage). Albert sets his final intonation at this stage, while the tremolo is still blocked; it's quicker to do it now, before the tremolo springs and string tension get involved.

10 Install three tremolo springs and begin tightening the claw. For heavier strings, or a stiffer tremolo, use

more springs. Strats come with five springs if you want to use them all (Stevie Ray did). Since the claw is loose, nothing will happen to your setup because the springs won't pull on the tremolo block until they get close to the right adjustment. On most Strats, the tremolo claw is in the approximate correct adjustment range when you have around a 21/32" to 5/8" clearance between the claw and the cavity wall. Once the springs get to the right tension, they take control of the bridge and the wooden block loosens (no longer blocking the tremolo), and pulls right out. You're done! The block will loosen at the exact moment the springs come into play.

If you've done everything correctly, you should have a great-playing Strat! If you didn't fine-tune the intonation after step 9, do it now or play it the way it is (the factory's "rough" setting is actually quite close).

6-step setup for electric bass

The 8-step setup mentioned above applies to both guitars and basses, but here's some more setup info just for bass players.

1 Install the strings you prefer, and if the bass is new, play it awhile to get the feel of its action.

With Fender slab-style necks that have no headstock angle, install the strings with enough downward wraps to create good pressure on the nut. Basses with angled headstocks require fewer wraps to achieve good down pressure. Expect to go through several sets of strings until you find what's right for you. Begin with the manufacturer's string recommendation, and go from there. These basics may help you choose a set:

String tension is important. Equal tension from string to string gives a balance that feels right to both the fingering and plucking hands. For hard-to-adjust necks or those that tend to have up-bow, choose a light-gauge, low-tension string. Within a given gauge (regular, medium, light, etc.), flat-wound strings have the highest tension, half-rounds the second highest, and round-wounds the least tension.

Round-wound strings are bright in tone and easy to intonate, but of course they create more finger squeaks and fret buzz. Flat-wounds, being less bright, are harder to intonate. Half-rounds are a good compromise for intonation. Core-contact ("taper-core") strings have an exposed core that contacts the saddle rather than the outer string wraps. Some bassists feel that these are easier to intonate. If you're a 5-stringer looking for the optimum low B string, D'Addario's Jim Rickard, noted expert on all matters related to guitar design and construction, recommends a .145" gauge.

2 Sight the neck, looking for straightness or relief.

3 Make basic neck adjustments before adjusting the nut or bridge.

4 Adjust the bridge and nut together. String height at the nut is critical. If the nut's string slots are too deep or the nut itself is too low, the heaviest strings are sure to buzz against the 1st fret. With a little luck, after any neck adjustments are made, you'll still have a nut that's slightly tall, allowing you the option of lowering the strings a bit. But if the strings are too low at the nut, you'll need to shim the nut or make a new one.

Measuring between the bottom of the string and the top of the fret, low action at the nut would read: E, .035"; A, .030"; D, .025"; G .025". When I make a new nut, I stop lowering the strings at .050" on the E and at .030" for the A, D, and G. From that point I prefer to lower the strings gradually, with a customer's specific attack and playing style in mind.

Players with a strong attack, especially those using slap-style techniques that pull the string up and almost out of the nut slots, should use a fairly low-profile nut with string slots that aren't too deep. This way, the edges don't break off as the string is strained in its slot. From half to a third of a string's diameter is a good depth for the string slots. While bone is a preferred nut material for guitars and many basses, if your style is really hard-hitting, stick to resilient plastic, graphite, or phenolic materials, which have a reduced chance of breaking.

Bridge setup controls the height of the strings, matches the curve of the saddles to the fingerboard radius, and sets the intonation. Bridge adjustments aren't difficult, but they're time-consuming. Expect to spend several hours getting things right, and if your first attempts aren't perfect, keep on trying. A delicate balance exists between neck, nut, and bridge, and their combined effect determines your action. Here are the basics:

String height is raised or lowered at the saddle by adjusting small set screws with an Allen wrench or screwdriver. Matching the radius of the saddles to that of the fingerboard makes the action comfortable to both hands. Forward/backward saddle travel controls intonation. If a string notes sharp at the 12th-fret octave, move the saddle back away from the neck. If a note is flat, move the saddle forward toward the neck.

d.i.y.

d.i.y.

For low action and the least fret rattle, get the neck as straight as possible with very low action, and then eliminate any buzz by loosening the truss rod to add relief. You can also eliminate buzz by raising the bridge inserts. Remember that some buzz between metal strings and metal frets is normal, especially on basses.

5 Re-check the neck adjustment.

6 Adjust the pickup height to suit your tastes. Don't raise them so high that the strings slap against them, or get pulled toward the upper frets by the magnets (causing buzz).

String height measurements vary from manufacturer to manufacturer. I discussed bass setup particulars with a panel of experts: Michael Tobias, Ken Smith, Roger Sadowski, M.V. Pedulla's Brett Carlson, and Bob Malone at Alembic. All of their string height measurements are between the bottom of the string and the top of the fret, and here's what they had to say:

Michael Tobias: "We never measure, because each bass is different. But our setups start out with 1/8" at the last fret all the way across, following the fingerboard radius (15" to 17"). This gives a height of 1/16" to 3/32" at the 12th fret. When you press a string at the 3rd fret, it should clear the 1st fret by .010" or .012". No bass will play without some relief. As a measure, hold down a string at the 1st and 15th frets—you're using the string as a straightedge—and adjust the neck until, at the 8th fret, you can just slide a Fender thin pick in between the string bottom and fret top; that's your relief. Our stock strings are .040", .060", .080" and .100" gauges."

Ken Smith: "I use taper-core Ken Smith strings on all but the G string, in gauges of .044", .063", .084" and .106". You must have relief, between 1 mm and 2 mm at the 9th fret, even up to 1/16" at times. Really, all basses must be set up on an individual basis. I don't actually measure string height at the nut, but prefer an action where a player can depress a string without having to press hard, and with no buzzing on an open string. I consider a low height at the 12th fret to be 1/16" all the way across."

Roger Sadowski: "I shoot for a mostly straight neck with a little relief, and prefer a string gauge of .045", .065", .080", .105". My standard setup is for the string height at the 12th fret to be on the fat side of 5/64" for the G, and

3/32" for the E—measured from the bottom of the string to the top of the fret."

Brett Carlson: "We use relief, except on fretless models—with those we get the neck perfectly straight. Our relief, measured by holding down a string at the 1st and last frets, is set at .015". String height at the first fret is .025" under each string, and at the 12th fret I shoot for 3/32" under the G and 5/32" under the E. All our nuts are brass, so we don't have a problem with the string slots breaking. Our standard strings are D'Addario roundwounds in the .045", .065", .080" and .100" gauges." (Brett's .015", by the way is a slight relief.)

Bob Malone: "In a setup you can't go beyond what you have to work with. It all comes down to how straight you can get that neck. If you can get it straight to begin with, then your setup can go from there. I like a very slight relief, but I don't measure it; it's all by feel. For nut height, when a string is pressed at the 3rd fret, it should just barely touch the 1st fret. Alembic basses are built with brass nuts."

If you've followed these basic setup tips for guitar or bass, you've also encountered most of the potential problems, eliminating them as you went along.

Special thanks to **Jim Werner**, who was extremely helpful in steering me toward many of the repairmen and collectors contacted on the subject of Strats. If you're interested in Jim's list of Fender instrument serial number and neck dates, contact him at R.R. 1, Box 236, Letts, IA 52754. Jim works hard to preserve the past, and we can all thank him by sending him any information on Fender instrument serial numbers, neck dates, models, colors, and other pertinent features that help date an instrument to a specific era.

Setting up a Gibson flattop acoustic

Electric guitars have mechanical, easily adjusted hardware—especially bridges. Acoustic guitar bridge adjustments, however, are often difficult enough that they fall into the "repair work" category. You may need to refer to the acoustic bridge adjustment information in chapter 9 to help get your guitar ready for these setup specs.

These measurements apply to all Gibson flattops made from the 1930s to the mid-'60s, and for those made in Montana from 1990 until the present—the eras

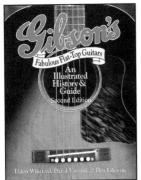

of Gibson making great flattops. I skip the late '60s, the '70s and '80s because those were not the best years for Gibson flattops, and many flattops made during that era did not, and could not, conform to these factory specs. If you'd like to understand why, and learn more about Gibson flattop history, read the book *Gibson's Fabulous Flattop Guitars* by Eldon Whitford, David Vinopal, and myself.

Gibson Montana, the company's acoustic guitar division, was established in Bozeman, Montana in 1989. There in Bozeman, Gibson is building even better flattops than they did during the glory year of the 1930s—and that's saying a lot! The following measurements came from **Ren Ferguson**, a master builder and head of

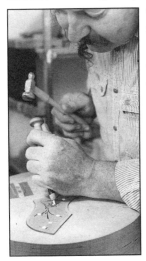

Gibson Montana's Custom Shop. Ren and his right-hand man John Walker are the builders responsible for resurrecting Gibson's flattop heritage. These factory specs apply to all good Gibson flattops. I've added my own specs are taken from an original but well-broken-in 1940 J-35, and reflect the lowest normal action you'd expect from a well set up Gibson flattop played by an acoustic, not an electric, player. Two acoustic specs that weren't needed for electrics are: 1) "saddle protrusion," or the amount of saddle height above the top of the bridge (because a good string angle over the saddle is important to achieve tone and power), and 2) the thickness of the bridge.

I prefer as straight a neck as possible—especially on flattops. That isn't to say *you* won't prefer relief, but start by getting the neck perfectly straight first. If there are no buzzes, and you like the feel, great. If you've got problems with buzz, slowly add relief until you're happy.

Factory specs for Gibson flattops

🔧 **d.i.y.**

Maximum neck relief at 7th to 9th fret	Factory	Mine
On all strings:	.012"	.004"

String height at 12th fret	Factory	Mine
On the bass E string:	6/64"	4/64"
On the treble E string:	4/64"	2-1/128"

String height at the nut

These measurements differ from Gibson's Nashville electric setups. The strings are left somewhat high so that final adjustment to suit the customer can be made by the music dealer after the sale. Measured from the bottom of a string to the top of the 1st fret with a feeler gauge, the strings are factory-set to .030". On my guitar, the treble side is .012", and the strings follow a radius to the bass side: .020".

Bridge saddle protrusion

The saddle should have from 1/8" to 1/4" showing above the top of the bridge at its highest point (the saddle will vary in height because of its radius). I consider 1/4" to be the absolute limit in saddle height for any acoustic guitar, and 3/16" is a better limit. My J-35 measures 7/32".

My observations on Gibson flattops

✔ For many of us, vintage Gibsons have become as highly prized as Martins. Be careful what jobs you attempt on them until you know what you're doing—less is better.

✔ The Gibson 12" fretboard radius is a good average between the vintage 7-1/4" Fender and the 16" Martin.

✔ For me, the short-scale Gibsons make better blues guitars than their long-scale models.

✔ Most older Gibsons (1930s until the late 1950s) seldom need neck resets.

✔ It's common for a Gibson to have loose braces, and as a rule the top and back braces of vintage instruments are not tucked deeply into the "kerfing," or lining which connects the sides to the top and back. Because of this, the braces often come loose, especially toward the ends (this allows the top or back to crack).

d.i.y.

✔ Gibsons don't normally have the severe "bellying" problems around the bridge sometimes found in other steel-string guitars. Instead, Gibson flattops usually have a graceful arch in the top until the early '60s (from the '60s until 1983, Gibson tops have shown a considerably higher percentage of loose bracing, and top problems in the bridge area.

✔ The interior structure, design and bracing of Gibson flattops made during the "bad" years mentioned above can be horrendous (huge plywood bridge plates, enormous braces, sloppy work, warped tops, horrible neck sets, impossible action and poor tone are just some of the symptoms).

✔ Most great Gibson flattops, with the exception of several models like the Advanced Jumbo and the SJ-200 (J-200), and certain Hummingbirds made during the 1960s, have short (24-3/4") scales. The short-scale "Great Gibson Flattops" I'm referring to include (to name just a few) the L-O, L-OO, Jumbo, J-35, J-45, S-J, J-50, and others. Although the bodies of the "Jumbo" or "J"-models are comparable in size to the Martin dreadnaughts, the string length isn't. So don't expect them to play like, or sound like, long-scale guitars. For playability, compare these guitars (if you must) to the short-scale (24.9") Martin 0, 00, and 000 models. Even then you can't compare the two guitars since the Gibson has a larger box! It's important to understand this when trying to relate to a customer, or if you're looking to buy an axe.

✔ Gibson is making better flattops now than ever before, thanks to the guys referred to previously.

Setting up a Martin flattop acoustic

It's not true that "Only A Gibson Is Good Enough." In 1961 I bought my first really good flattop guitar—a Martin 00-28 K. It was a lovely guitar made from Koa-wood, a type of curly mahogany that grows in Hawaii. Since that time I've owned at least 30 Martins, and loved them all. To this day I'd hate to have to choose between my Gibson J-35 and my old D-18. I just couldn't do it. They're different guitars and I play differently on each of them.

For playing some of the old country music that I love (tunes by the Stanley Brothers, Louvin Brothers, the Blue Sky Boys, and of course Bill Monroe), I prefer the long-scale, the tight crisp tone, the definite volume, and that certain country sound of a Martin dreadnaught. If money weren't an object, I'd own many different Martins (my dream is to someday custom-order a 12-fret OOO-45). As it is, though, I always seem to settle on a D-18. I like mahogany, I guess.

Martin factory specs vs. my specs

Maximum neck relief at 7th to 9th fret	Factory	Mine
On all strings:	.010"	.005"

String height at 12th fret	Factory
On the bass E string:	3/32" min - 7/64" max
On the treble E string:	1/16" min - 5/64" max

String height at the nut	Factory
Measured from the bottom of a string to the top of the first fret.	Bass E: .024"max Treble E: .016"min

Bridge thickness	Factory
	5/15", 11/32" or 3/8"

Bridge saddle protrusion	Factory
	3/32" min–3/16" max

Bridge saddle shape

The radius of a Martin bridge saddle is slightly flatter than the fretboard, and the saddle rises gradually in height toward the bass side to eliminate buzzes on the bass strings.

String inset	Factory
Distance between edge of fingerboard and the outside of both E strings.	3/32" ± .016"

Bridge pin height

All pins must be a uniform height above the bridge surface, and measured from bottom of the "ring," must be .032" min–.062" max.

String installation

Bass side strings passed throught the string hole with string wound halfway around post under longer portion of string, bent backward over string, and wound counter-clockwise 2–3 wraps around post toward headplate. Follow same spec for treble strings with 3–4 wraps clockwise around the post.

At Martin: Jim Trach recording in the repair log as Ellworth Bush inspects the interior.

Martin guitars are set up a little differently than Gibsons. If you're looking at getting into the guitar repair business and you happen to be a Gibson lover, or don't know much about Martins, don't ever set up a Martin like a Gibson (or vice-versa)—you'll lose a customer! Notice that the C.F. Martin factory has several actual checkpoints for jobs that Gibson either does by eye, or has no written measurement for (note also that Martin lists measurements differently than Gibson). Some of the following adjustments, such as bridge pin height, would never be incorrect on a new Martin because they're an integral part of final inspection. But you may need to make adjustments on numerous used instruments, especially if they've had a replacement bridge installed by an untrained hand.

My observations on Martin flattops

✔ The fretboard radius will vary from 16" to 20". A 16" radius is most common.

✔ The action will go lower than the factory specs if the frets are properly leveled.

✔ Because of the flatter fretboard radius, Martins may not feel as comfortable as instruments with more arch in the fretboard do when playing chords. However, many players feel that you can get more power without buzzing on a Martin than you can a Gibson, because of the flatter board.

✔ Models made before 1985 do not have an adjustable truss rod. Certainly the newer Martins with adjustable rods are easier to setup than the old ones. I still prefer the old "T"-bar Martins (pre-1969) for stiffness and tone.

✔ In my experience, Martins need neck resets far more often than Gibsons (especially vintage pieces of the same era). Because of this, too many Martins that should have had neck resets ended up with bridges shaved very thin, and with low saddles; a good number that were sent back to Martin had their fingerboards planed

heavily (Martin's alternative to neck resetting at the time). Do not try to account for an underset neck by planing the fretboard or whittling down the bridge on vintage instruments!

✔ Instruments made between 1969 and 1985, with hollow "square tube" truss rods, often develop more up-bow than the older instruments.

✔ A "bellied" top (an arch in the top around the bridge) is not necessarily bad. Most flattop guitars are supposed to have a nice gradual arch in that area since the top is built with an arch in it. Do not hasten to "flatten" the top, or let someone talk you into it.

✔ A slight "bubble," or rise in the top behind the bridge, and a dip in the front, is not uncommon with Martins. It isn't normally severe enough to warrant serious interior structural work such as bridge pad replacement—but can be in extreme cases. Severe kinks are often caused by loose bracing (especially the X-bracing in the bridge pad area).

✔ I think the Martin company is too generous to their customers by offering a lifetime warranty on an object made of wood. Many owners take advantage of the warranty by expecting Martin to repair problems that are caused by nature or neglect. Martin, however, is unfailing about taking care of their customers. Give them a word of thanks sometime—they deserve it!

Setting up an archtop acoustic

I've been lucky to have seen and heard a number of great archtop players and the guitars they play, including **Grant Green** (Epiphone Emperor), **Kenny Burrell** (Gibson ES-175), **Johnny Smith** (Gibson Johnny Smith model), **Mel Bay** (D-Angelico New Yorker), **Jimmy Bruno** (Sadowsky Jimmy Bruno model), **Homer and Jethro** (Henry "Homer" Haynes, Gibson L-5C). Way back when, some even let a young guy play a little on their guitars after the show. None of them had light strings and low action, especially not the big band players who used no amplification.

Over the years I've owned some exceptional archtops, including a 1930's Epiphone Triumph, 1940s Epiphone Emperor, 1958 Gibson L-5, and a late 1930s Gibson Super 400 — the only one I still have today is the Gibson L-5,

d.i.y.

d.i.y.

and it's set up to play like a friend's — big band jazz guitarist **Rod McDonald** from Ann Arbor, Michigan. Rod owns several vintage L-5s, which he plays unamplified in several big bands—the setting where the great archtops show their stuff. (To Rod, "amplified" means playing into a good microphone on a stand in front of his chair.) Here's Rod's setup:

The strings are heavy bronze-wound, and unless a periodic cleaning and maintenance is needed, I always change them one at a time to keep from upsetting the balance between string tension and neck tension; also, by keeping tension on the bridge it won't shift out of position. The gauges are: .014, .019, .028 (wound, of course), .038, .048, .060.

The neck is adjusted dead-straight (sometimes, if Rod's getting buzzes caused by fret wear, he'll loosen the truss-rod to gain from .004"—.010"relief until he can have the frets levelled and dressed).

The action at the 12th fret shows a string clearance between the bottom of the strings and the tops of the fret of a heavy 7/32" on the bass side, and a heavy 1/8" on the treble. Sometimes Rod raises his bridge to almost 3/16" in a venue where he knows he needs extra power to cut through the band. I can't handle action that high (I'd last about a minute).

The bridge height—from the guitar top to the top of the bridge saddle—is approximately one inch. If an archtop bridge is significantly higher or lower than that, the neck is probably not set at the optimum angle for that guitar and a neck-set might be in order.

At the nut, Rod likes the "thickness of a matchbook cover" clearance under the treble E string — about .014", and .034" on the bass side. The remaining strings are set to follow the fretboard radius between the two E-strings (my fretboard is a 9" radius).

When installing heavy strings on an archtop for the first time, do it by degrees — install a set of true medium strings (.013" to .056") and let them settle in for a few days or a week before installing the heavier gauge.

Since heavy strings put a heck of a load on the neck, before installing them, loosen the strings until there's just enough tension on them to hold the bridge in place. Then tighten the truss rod until the neck goes beyond straight and into a slight back-bow. Then once you put the heavy strings, let the neck (and the top) settle in for a day or so. With a back-bow things may be a little buzzy, but not when you loosen the truss rod to allow the neck to pull straight. (With heavy strings, it's much easier to loosen a slightly back-bowed truss rod to straighten a neck than it is to use the truss rod to straighten it against a heavy string load.)

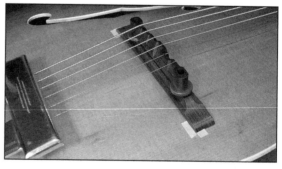

When you need to remove the strings (cleaning the fretboard, the peghead face, and the top under the strings), put low-tack drafting tape at each side of the bridge to mark its location.

Setting up a classical

Most of the setup techniques used here apply to adjusting a nylon-string "folk guitar," as well. Braced for nylon strings, these guitars typically have a wider, flatter finger-board than most steel-strings. Most American and European guitars made before the late 1920s fall into this category, and many of them have bridge pins. During the '50s folk boom, folk guitars were made by Goya, Favilla, Hagstrom, and other manufacturers from abroad. While these instruments are different from the modern steel-string, they aren't grand concert classical guitars, either. If you understand the setup of both classicals and steel-strings, though, you'll be able to handle the folk guitar.

I've set up my share of classical guitars, and once owned an excellent hand-made Yacopi. Like many of my peers, I learned Bach's *Bourrée*, studied the Carcassi method, struggled with Fernando Sor, and ended up playing the blues. So I'm no expert when it comes to the concert guitar, but I know experts. I contacted several of the best to get their opinions on setup: **William Cumpiano**, a student of **Michael Gurian** and the founder of Stringfellows in Hadley, Massachusetts; **Jeffrey R. Elliott**, a master luthier and mentor to a thriving community of guitar builders in the Portland, Oregon area; **Thomas Humphrey**, a world-renowned classical guitar builder from New York city who designed and builds the "Millennium" guitar; and **Richard Schneider**, who collaborated with **Dr. Michael Kasha** on taking the design of the classical guitar to new heights. (After hearing a new Kasha/Schneider guitar, Segovia wrote: "To Schneider, in whose hands is the future of the guitar.")

I lost a good friend when **Richard Schneider** passed away unexpectedly in 1997. Schneider's guitars incorporated the principles of the Kasha design, and his avant-garde instruments are hailed for their beauty, play-ability, and superior concert tone. Although he sat at the pinnacle of the guitar building craft, Richard was more likely to speak about design ideas or his students than about himself. He felt that his main achievement might be that he would one day leave behind him more students trained in his methods than any other builder in history. With students including such well-known builders as **Abraham Wechter**, **Gila Eban**, **Jeffrey Elliott**, **Mark Wescott**, **Gregory Wylie**, **Peter Hutchison**, **Charles Merrill**, **John Mello**, Italy's **Enrico Bottelli**, France's **Michel Geslain**, and Sweden's **Fredrik Gustafsson**, Richard Schneider reached his goal.

Relief and string height "Nylon strings have greater elasticity," points out William Cumpiano, "and therefore a greater vibrating arc than steel strings. To avoid string rattle, they require greater clearance all along the fingerboard. Fortunately, however, nylon strings are comfortable at a higher action setting, and they also intonate properly at a height where steel strings would play out of tune." Since proper classical setup requires a higher action, the need for relief is less than you might think. In fact, the relief necessary to accommodate the vibrating strings of a classical guitar usually occurs naturally from the string tension (90 lbs. of pull) exerted on a perfectly straight fingerboard. Relief is a very subtle measurement, and most makers expect to see from as little as .004" to as much as .040" when measuring the air space between the bottom of the strings and the top of the fret in the area in the 8th through 10th frets. According to Jeffrey Elliott, "Relief generally runs from a minimum of .004" to an average of .020" at around the 10th fret. More than .040" of relief is excessive, and too little relief can sometimes cause 'back-buzz,' where the string is laying on the frets between your fingering hand and the nut, causing a slight but annoying buzz."

"I like to see a neck as straight as possible," claims Richard Schneider, "but some relief is inevitable and perhaps a help. Too much relief can cause sympathetic string vibration on the short string length setup between your fingering hand and the nut. This is a somewhat rare occurrence and is different than the back-buzz that Jeff's talking about, but it's annoying when it occurs. The average relief would probably measure from .020" to .040"." As a result of string tension, most classical necks take a permanent "set" or forward bow of as much as .020". This doesn't go away even when the strings are removed, so don't mistake this for a warped neck! Again, the higher action is not a problem for the player because of the softer touch used with nylon strings. Some makers may build a slight relief into their necks, while others remove extra wood on the bass side, starting at the nut and running "downhill" to the end of the fingerboard in the Ramirez and Hauser style. All these methods are correct, and all of the builders questioned approached relief differently.

d.i.y.

The nut Bone is the preferred material for making a good nut or saddle for any acoustic guitar. There's no need to go deeply into making a classical nut, since the same techniques described in the section on nut making are used to fit the classical nut. Because nylon strings are so delicate, the correct angle of the string slot to the tuner and a perfectly round shape in the nut slot bottom are even more important than with steel strings. It's especially easy for the wound strings to hang up in a poorly shaped slot, and when they do, they unravel and sound awful—just before they finally break! The classical nut has a flatter top to match the unradiused fingerboard, and like the steel-string, when viewed from the side the nut and string slots must taper at a gradual curve from the back to the front (about a 10° angle).

Correct nut height can best be determined by eye, feel, and experience, but the novice can get close by measuring. Richard Schneider says: "The clearance, or air space, over the 1st fret with the string open and coming off the nut should be a little greater than the clearance over the 2nd fret with the string pressed on the 1st fret. A business card measures .005", so use three business cards to measure under the treble strings and maybe five or six business cards under the bass."

Of course, the overall action and height of the bridge saddle has a big effect on nut measurement. Use the same techniques shown in the nut making and saddle sections, balancing one end to the other and working the action down by degree. Another general rule for nut height that works for steel or nylon strings is to press a string at the 2nd fret, looking to see a slight clearance between the string and the 1st fret; as long as there is some clearance here, the open strings shouldn't buzz. The clearance should increase gradually from the high to the low E, because the lower wound strings must sit from .015" to .030" higher in the nut than the treble strings to avoid open-string buzz. Overall string height at the nut shouldn't get too low, since there's a strong tendency for nylon strings to buzz sympathetically between the fretted note and the nut behind where you're actually playing, just as they would from too much relief! Here's a final general rule for nut height: Measure the air space between the string and the top of the 1st fret, looking for a gap of 1/2 mm (.020") under the treble E and around 7/10 mm (.030") under the low E.

A traditional classical guitar fingerboard is flat from side to side, although some modern makers are introducing a very slight radius to make it easier to play barre chords: "This is a very gentle arch that's imparted with a plane," says Cumpiano. "It's not greater than a 1/32" offset at the fingerboard edge. It makes the instrument easier to play, and probably lets a player get away with a little bit less technique." The classical guitar's saddle should be flat, too, or match the shape of a slightly arched fingerboard. As with the nut, set the saddle action lower on the treble side, following the same 1/32" rise from treble toward the bass. Some makers taper and thin the fingerboard on the bass side in order to keep a more regular saddle height across the bridge (this creates a more even angle on the string which exerts a more even tension on the top). Other makers who feel that the bass strings need to break at more of an angle than the treble strings disagree with this technique, since it eliminates that option.

Action/string height To set the action, use a small ruler at the 12th fret. Measure the air space from the bottom of the string to the top of the fret. Different builders prefer different readings under the two E strings: Elliott's preference is 3 to 3-1/2 mm under the treble, and 4 to 4-1/2 mm under the bass, while Cumpiano favors 1/8" under the treble and 5/32" under the bass. "A high action for a classical," he adds, "would be 5/32" treble and 3/16" bass." Schneider describes: "When fretting the string at the 1st fret, measure 3 mm under the treble and 4 mm under the bass. A good concert player can handle this action, although some prefer to have the action higher. After adjusting the action to these parameters, I make two more saddles: a low one measuring 2-1/2 mm treble to 3-1/2 mm bass, and another one that's 3-1/2 mm treble to 5 mm bass. I also cut a second nut with the string spacing closer by 1 mm. These are put in a little walnut and rosewood box that I deliver with each instrument."

Traditionally, the classical saddle isn't shaped quite as round as a steel-string's, because of the nylon string's tendency to unravel or break when it meets a sharp edge. Instead, the saddle is often tapered smoothly towards the front edge (above) so that the string "takes off" gradually, with full support from the saddle shape to avoid string breakage. This method of shaping is only valid if the exact compensation has been calculated into the placement of the bridge; otherwise the peak of the saddle may have to be slightly altered to get the most accurate intonation. Many classical builders prefer to use a gently rounded saddle top; either method is correct. The saddle should fit snugly into the bridge slot and have a well-sanded and polished top surface for optimum tone. There should be no sharp edges or notches cut into it, although John Williams, a great classical guitarist, has been known to prefer a notched saddle.

Jeffrey Elliott points out that the builder can control tone and string tension by altering the saddle's angle and thereby changing the pitch of the string to the tie block. This subtle refinement is probably beyond the scope of our needs, but it's the combination of such little subtleties that make one guitar sound better than another. Jeff also states that the height of the strings from the top is extremely important; from the bottom of the string where it meets the saddle to the guitar's top should measure somewhere between 8 mm to 11 mm for most instruments.

Thomas Humphrey had this to say about setting up the classical guitar: "Dan, what you have to remember is that all guitars move a great deal between summer and winter, especially new guitars. All of the measurements given here are fine, but there are very few players who are going to accept a "factory" setup until they've had time to feel it for awhile. Before people are even out of the shop they want two saddles—a high and a low. They never leave it alone! So it doesn't matter how the maker sets up the guitar. As long as a classical guitar is setup within reason (an average setup) you're fine. Until a player gets the strings under their fingers, action setups don't mean anything. You have to give a lot of room to the player. The better the player, the more they'll want adjustments made.

"No two guitars play the same way—not even from the same maker. Each may require a slightly different setup. It depends on things like the shape of the neck in the back, the curvature of the fingerboard, and of course the scale length. Long-scale and short-scale guitars must be set up differently because of the difference in the string tension, and there is no scale length standard. 650mm is the most common scale length, 670mm is the longest I've heard of, and the shortest I've ever made is 620mm."

String recommendations What brands are good, and how often should they be changed? Cumpiano points out that a recitalist often changes strings every two or three days, and always before a performance. String deterioration has a dramatic effect on intonation, and sadly enough, classical strings are not only quite fragile, but expensive. Old strings lose pitch accuracy and tone. Cumpiano cites D'Addario Pro Arte Hi-Tension strings as a modern, well-built set, and he also uses Savarez Blues and Whites. Schneider prefers D'Addario Pro Arte, Savarez Crystal Solis, and GHS, which are all high-tension strings. "You might want medium- to low-tension strings for a recording situation," he adds, "because they're easier to finger, and some instruments do sound better with low tension." **Kurt Rodarmer** plays a Schneider/Kasha guitar and only changes his treble strings every six to eight months, since they get rock-hard and stay that way, creating the best sound. He changes the bass strings every other week during normal practice, and always two days before a concert. (I encourage string manufacturers to market sets of bass strings only, because everyone always has scads of extra trebles!) Elliott favors both high- and normal-tension D'Addario Pro Arte and Savarez Alliance in Red or Yellow, which, he says, "are made of a new material that is smaller in diameter than most others, has less tension, provides a good tonal variety and response, and is extremely accurate and clear sounding." **R.E. Brune**, a famous luthier based in Evanston, Illinois, has recently begun importing the excellent Hannabach brand. Many players have been extremely impressed with these strings.

Tom Humphrey's Millennium design incorporates a sloping soundboard and an elevated neck. These two

factors combine to create a greater string-to-soundboard angle, thus producing a different load on the soundboard (similar to that of the harp). According to Humphrey, "this angle also creates a more resonant sound, and is one of the features that make the Millennium so playable."

The other feature that struck me is the elevation of the fretboard from the soundboard. Because the player's hand is no longer obstructed by the body at the 12th fret, greater access is achieved and the instrument is more playable in the higher registers. Mr. Humphrey received a mechanical patent on this innovation from the U.S. Patent Office in 1987.

Low action and the blues

Low action without fret buzz is what electric players are after most. Somehow they get it into their heads that the strings should be close to the frets—real close—and they expect this low action without buzzing. Always a blues player, even when blues wasn't as mainstream as it is today, I've tried to convince customers that by having the action a little higher they could get better bends, more sustain, and make the guitar sing. But sometimes I'm sure they just think I can't or won't give them the low action they think they should have.

I realize there are many guitarists whose style requires low action in order to execute certain passages fast enough. And many hot country pickers that don't do much string-bending can have a slightly lower action than players that do bend. But more often than not, when you get the rare chance to play a top professional's axe, you'll find the action higher, and the strings stiffer, than you might have guessed. I believe that this is because more players today incorporate blues styles—in particular the singing blues bends made famous by B.B King and Albert King—into their playing. Where would Jeff Beck or Stevie Ray Vaughn's music be without the blues? What made Eric Clapton and Cream famous? How did Hendrix drive crowds wild? With certain traditional jazz guitarists as an exception, I don't know of many great guitarists who can't, and don't, play the blues; and players like Eric Johnson, Vernon Reid, and Steve Morse have taken blues to new heights. None of them are wimps, and neither is their action. With this in mind, I took advantage of every opportunity to check out the setups of some of the world's great blues players. Before we get into those interviews, let's look at the kind of setup that most blues players prefer.

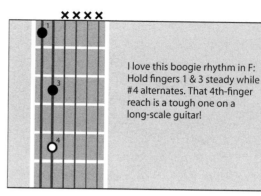

I love this boogie rhythm in F: Hold fingers 1 & 3 steady while #4 alternates. That 4th-finger reach is a tough one on a long-scale guitar!

Get ready for the blues A guitar that's out of tune or hard to play isn't "close enough for the blues," but blues setups *are* a little easier than most because the buzzing and dead notes caused by light strings, fretboard radius, and other factors aren't as apparent when the strings are raised—and most blues players like higher action. Here are some points to consider when setting up a blues guitar, electric or acoustic, that will help you play better and may also influence your next guitar purchase.

Scale length Scale length is worth considering when choosing any guitar. Understanding why it's important will help your blues playing—especially in terms of bends and left-hand reach. Most electric and acoustic steel-string guitars use either a "short" 24 -3/4" scale (Gibson), the "long" 25-1/2" scale (Fender, Gibson, and others), or something in between (PRS compromises with its 25" scale). Martin's short and long-scales are 24.9" and 25.4", repectively. With its reduced string tension, the short scale is easier to bend on, responds quicker to the touch, and enables small hands to span greater distances. Short-scale guitars—electric and acoustic— make the best fingerpicking instruments.

Because of its higher string tension, the long-scale is louder and more powerful, has better individual note separation and definition, allows for heavier picking attack, and offers brighter, tighter sound. But a long-scale is also harder to bend on, and long reaches are more difficult. According to Gibson's Tim Shaw, "When you play a chord on a short-scale guitar, like most of the Gibsons used for blues, the strings 'blend' well and sound like a family singing together, like the Everly Brothers. On the other hand, chords played on the long-scale sound more like hired professional singers—clean and perfect, but without the blend. As for hand size, when I

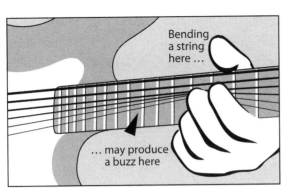

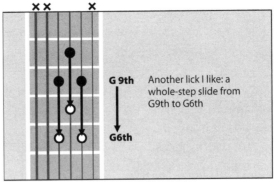

Bending a string here …

… may produce a buzz here

G 9th
G6th
Another lick I like: a whole-step slide from G9th to G6th

play the basic two-string blues shuffle rhythm in the key of F on a long-scale, my left-hand 4th finger barely reaches the 5th fret, but I can get it easily on a short scale."

Fretboard radius Your fretboard radius determines how close you can set your strings to the frets while still being able to bend the first and second strings without "bottoming out"—an Albert Kingism for a dead note. Most vintage Fenders used a 7-1/4" radius while Gibsons used a 12" measurement. Simply put, the more-exaggerated Fender radius follows the hand's natural curve and facilitates barre chords. The same tight curve, however, may cause the aforementioned problems when the bent string runs into the slope of the fretboard. Today, many Fenders have a flatter radius, but the company's vintage replicas retain the 7-1/4" dimension. Gibson's 12" radius has always facilitated blues bending with no bottoming out, even with low action. Martin's flatter 16" to 20" radius has never presented bending problems.

Fret size is very important if you bend a lot, and what blues player doesn't? Tall frets are much easier to bend on than low ones. Optimum blues fret height for unworn frets ranges between .035" and .055". Frets lower than .030" begin to give poor bending results, because they no longer hold the string far enough from the fretboard to prevent your finger from slipping off when it grabs and pushes. Fretwire for blues—and most modern guitar playing—falls into two size ranges: "thin," .078" to .090" wide and .040" to .047" tall (Fender, Martin, Gretsch, and some older Gibsons); and "wide," .100" to .108" wide and .040" to .047" tall (Gibson and most others). While .055" to .060" extra-tall wire is available in either width and is great for bending, you may consider it too tall for blues chord slides, like the famous "6th to 9th" that we all use from time to time.

Nut slots The depth and quality of a guitar's nut slots always affect its sound and playability. (For a guide to making a nut, see chapter 13.) Normally, string slots are cut no deeper than one-half of a string's diameter, so that the strings don't become pinched or "muted." A blues setup, though, may require somewhat deeper slots on the treble strings (G, B and E), since a first-string bend can cause the B string to pop out, especially when bending 2nd-fret F# up to G or G#. In this case, the short section of string between the fretted note and the nut is extremely taut, and you'll pop the string if you tend to slip your finger under the open B.

String gauge String gauge can affect your style a lot, so experiment with all the gauges—from ultralight to fairly heavy. But remember that each time you significantly change string gauge, you also change your setup. This will result in either spending some dollars at the local repair shop, or learning to do the job yourself. As a general rule, the heavier the strings, the better the resistance to pick attack, so you can play things such as bass-string boogie/shuffle rhythms harder, with more drive.

Gradually grow accustomed to a heavier string gauge. For instance, don't bend a .012" first string without first toughening up. Otherwise, you risk getting "split nails," where the flesh of your finger pulls away from the nail. Splits are common and take about a week to go away. I've made it through many a night's playing by super-gluing the split, but I don't know if this is medically sound. Stevie Ray constantly glued his split nails.

Albert King may have been the most-copied blues player in the world, so he had a good thing going. He tuned way below concert pitch, **C F C F A D**, low to high, which for years allowed him to use Black Diamond silver-wound heavy-gauge acoustic strings and still be able

deep

to bend. In later years Albert used this set: .009, .012, .024 (wound), .028, .038 and .050. If you're studying Albert's style, try his strings (he didn't seem to prefer a particular brand) and tuning. You'll be surprised. **Stevie Ray Vaughan** also tuned low, but only a half step. His strings measured a hefty .013, .015, .019, .028, .038, and .058; even tuned down a half step, you need extremely strong hands to do what he did. On an electric guitar, anything less than a .010" through .046" set is a little light for me, but I admit to occasionally using a .009" high E. For years I preferred Gibson E-340 L Sonomatics (.011" through .056") because Otis Rush used them in the early '70s. E-340 L's came with a .019" wound third that sounded great; you could bend it, but it broke all the time. Try substituting an unwound .020" for the G, and you'll have a good, fairly heavy set.

For the average acoustic player, light-gauge strings are best for blues, unless the guitar is very old and can't support them. Extra- and ultra-light strings won't strengthen your hands or draw out that "different" style of music inside you. Medium-gauge strings may be too heavy for the tops of many acoustics, so have your local repair shop check out your instrument before you take the plunge. Strong hands are a must for playing blues on medium-gauge strings.

Action Most guitars have adjustable bridges and necks, so setting action is relatively easy. As a precautionary measure, have a pro initially adjust your neck, and be sure to find out if the truss rod is working well. Necks are adjusted either perfectly straight or with "relief," a slight bow toward the strings' pull. Relief makes room for a vibrating string's elliptical pattern and helps avoid buzzing. You straighten a neck by tightening the truss rod, and relieve it by loosening the rod. There are hundreds of variations possible between straight and relieved necks, high or low string settings, and different string gauges, which is why you should learn to adjust your own neck and bridge. You may never know what setup is best until you've tried them all, so here are some helpful tips:

✔ Most of us like a neck that's adjusted as straight as we can get away with.

✔ You'll need a few simple tools, selected Repairs columns, one or two copies of this book, and at least a whole day to experiment.

✔ The heavier the strings and higher the action, the straighter you can adjust the neck.

✔ Light strings close to the fretboard need more relief.

✔ Short scales tend to buzz more easily if the strings are too low, so they need relief more than the long-scale.

✔ Fret buzzes not heard through your amp are okay.

✔ Straight necks and low action may work if you play with a light touch and a loud amp setting. Don't expect to bend notes very far with this setup.

✔ Gibson action can be adjusted more easily than Fender action because the entire bridge raises and lowers on two thumbwheels, whereas most Fender bridges—Strats in particular—have an adjustable bridge saddle for each string.

✔ Most electrics and acoustics should have relief that measures anywhere from .005" to .030" in the 7th- to 9th-fret area.

✔ Raising an acoustic's action at the bridge may require reshaping the saddle, which should probably be done by a pro. Sometimes you can simply shim or un-shim the saddle's height.

To set your own action, start with the neck straight and lower the strings at the bridge until they buzz badly. Next slowly raise the bridge or individual saddles until the buzzing barely stops, and see how the action feels—you'll probably have a medium-low action that buzzes with relatively firm pick attack. Now give the neck a little relief and recheck the action. The buzzes should stop. The action will be higher, and you may end up liking this setup. If the buzzing doesn't stop, add relief until either it does go away, or the up-bow is so ridiculous that it feels uncomfortable. If you have to start over by re-straightening the neck and re-lowering the strings, try raising the bridge until the buzzing stops. You might like this medium-high strings/straight neck setup.

Three typical blues setups

The measurements in the chart on the next page were taken from a long-scale '56 Fender Strat, a short-scale '59 Gibson ES-345, and a '44 short-scale Gibson J-45 acoustic. In each case, the guitars were lying on their sides in the true playing position when I measured them. Using a 6" steel "scale" and a set of feeler gauges, I

Guitar	1st fret	12thfret	Relief
	High E / Low E	High E / Low E	
ES-345	.010/.024"	1/32–3/64"	None
Strat	.014/.034"	1/16–3/32"	.009"
J-45	.013/.022"	3/32–7/64"	None

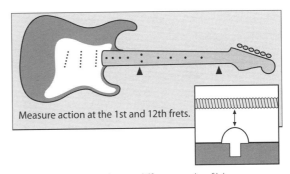

Measure action at the 1st and 12th frets.

recorded the distance between the bottom of the first and sixth strings (high and low E) and the top of the 1st and 12th frets.

I rate these setups like so:

1 The Strat is average to medium-high ("normal" Strat action), plays well, and the strings bend easily.

2 The ES-345 has a very low action. Since it was a brand-new fret job, I was able to get the neck perfectly straight without buzz.

3 The light gauge strings on the J-45 provide enough tension so that the neck can be kept straight. It has low to medium action and plays great.

Pickup preference varies greatly. Electric blues is played with humbucking or single-coil pickups and combinations thereof. **B.B.**, **Freddie** and **Albert King**, early **Eric Clapton**, and the **Allman Brothers** all have a humbucking sound characteristic of Gibson ED-series semi-hollowbodies, SGs, and Les Pauls. For the single-coil sound, think of **Buddy Guy**, **Otis Rush**, **Magic Sam**, **Robert Cray**, **Anson Funderburgh**, **Jimmie Vaughan** and **Stevie Ray**—theirs are Fender Strat sounds. A Tele-caster also offers an excellent single-coil blues sound (**Albert Collins**), but it isn't used as often. Some of the greatest blues guitars are the Gibson arch-top hollow-bodies used by **T-Bone Walker**, **Chuck Berry** and many '50s rockers, including the ES-295, the ES-300, the ES-350 and the ES-5 Switchmaster. Many of these early guitars were powered by "soap-bar" single-coil pickups and have a sound all their own.

As a rule, Gibson guitars—even with single-coil pickups—have more sustain, a fatter, thicker overall sound, and more output than Fenders. Strats are more percussive-sounding than Gibsons, but they have less sustain, unless you get them into the distortion mode.

Acoustic guitars draw a different style of blues performance from you, which is why they're so refreshing to play. To me, ideal guitars for playing acoustic blues have a shorter scale length, which leaves out most of the larger dreadnought style instruments. Of course, you can play blues on a large guitar—think of **Brownie McGhee**—you just have to work harder. The short-scale's lower string tension offers three advantages over the long-scale flattops:

1 It's more responsive to fingerstyle playing.

2 It's easier to bend on—even with light-gauge bronze strings, which are quite heavy compared with most electric sets.

3 It facilitates left-hand reach—an advantage if you're trying to play some of the nearly impossible things **Robert Johnson** did.

My favorite acoustic blues guitars are the early Gibson J-45, J-35 and the smaller L-0 or L-00 series, and all Martin 0-series models in either the 18 or 28 style (**Big Bill Broonzy** played an 000-28). To my knowledge, the only major company making short-scale guitars is Gibson, which is producing an excellent reissue of the J-45 and an improved X-braced L-1—sure to be a collector's item, since it is the model Robert Johnson played. A builder who makes custom short-scale flattops is **Bill Collings** of Austin, Texas. His guitars are expensive, but none are finer, and they sound as good as vintage instruments!

Vintage blues guitar expert **Dave Hussong** of Fretware Guitars says: "Some customers put the cart before the horse when they shop for a blues guitar; if B.B. used an ES-345 with an Ampeg Gemini II amp, they've gotta have the same equipment. But the great players can produce their sound on just about any guitar. **Hound Dog Taylor** did fine with an Airline. The style overrides the instrument. The best blues setup can only be had after

deep

your style has developed. If you're just getting into blues, don't rush out and buy a guitar until you've played for a year or so. Use what you have, unless you're worried about all the great vintage guitars getting bought up.

"Fretwire size has never made much diffence to me, but rosewood boards and big frets generally produce a big tone, and maple necks with smaller frets give you the brighter tone. I don't like low action and still subscribe to the Texas school of players like **T-Bone Walker**, **Lowell Fulson**, and others, which means that I use as heavy a string as I can handle. Right now I'm playing an .010" through .050" set.

"My two favorite blues guitars are a 1960 Shoreline Gold Fender Strat, which is on loan to me from Anson Funderburgh, and a 1982 Gibson ES-355 with the wide 1-11/16" neck. If you've been playing a Strat and then pick up the Gibson, it's like a ball player laying down his heavy practice bat as he steps up to the plate. You've got to fight the Strat more, while the Gibson is easier to play. But a Strat has a certain tone all its own. When you're out there playing, you're more committed on a Strat, which means your mistakes will be more obvious."

Setups for pro players

Stevie Ray Vaughan and Jeff Beck

Great guitarists have the ability to make their instruments talk. Doing so takes a special gift, a lifetime of practice, and a great guitar. Haven't you always hoped that the guitar had something to do with it? Wouldn't you guess that a great player's guitar is set up to play really well? If you're like me, you'd like to know just how their guitars are set up (and I don't mean simply with what gauge of strings, or whether the action is high or low). You wonder how their guitars might feel in your hands. Would you play better?

I had a chance to try out the guitars of **Jeff Beck** and the late great **Stevie Ray Vaughan** when the two played in Columbus, Ohio. I was anxious to see how their guitars would measure up to my expectations. Then I decided to do just that—measure them—so that you, too, would have a chance to adjust, set up, and compare the feel of your guitar to those of these top players.

Before the show, I spent time with Jeff's guitar tech, **Geoff Banks** from Witley, England (top photo at right),

PHOTOS: BRIAN BLAUSER, ATHENS, OH

and Stevie's tech, **Rene Martinez** of Denton, Texas. Geoff has worked with Trevor Rabin of Yes, Robert Plant, and most recently Jeff Beck, Phil Collins, and Genesis. Rene (left) honed his skills for years as a repairman for both Charley's Guitars and Zack's Guitars in Dallas. I was interested in the simple but subtle setup and action adjustments—the everyday stuff of being a tech for a guitar mogul. Of course, I was all ears for any other tips, tricks and secrets Geoff or Rene might divulge. Here's what I found out:

Jeff and Stevie Ray were traveling with nine guitars, all of them Strats. Jeff's four included a yellow Vintage reissue model made by Fender's **George Blanda** in '86, as well as three custom-ordered Strat Plus models recently handcrafted and set up by ace guitar man Jay Black of the Fender Custom Shop. The Strat Plus models are equipped with Wilkinson nuts, Lace Sensor pickups, and the American Standard Tremolo, and are actually prototypes of a Jeff Beck Signature Model. One significant change is the size and shape of the neck. Jay Black notes: "Jeff wanted the biggest necks he could get—like baseball bats—so I patterned them after a 1935 Gibson L-5. Each neck is big, but different in size, shape and feel. The seafoam green one, which Jeff favors, is an inch thick all the way down."

Plastic tubes protecting Stevie Ray's strings from breaking.

Stevie's guitars are all pre-'63 models, except for "Charley" (outfitted with the Danelectro "lipstick tube" pickups, it was made from kit parts at Charley's Guitar Shop in 1984). They all have names, too: Number One, Red, Butter Scotch, Charley, and Lennie. The only significant change from stock on these Strats has been the addition of 5-way switches and a good coat of shielding paint in the control cavities. Number One, the beat-up sunburst that we all know, is Stevie's main squeeze.

Neck adjustment With all the guitars, neck straightness is the first thing I checked, sighting down the fingerboard. A fingerboard should either be dead-flat or have a slight up-bow, known as relief, in the direction of the strings' pull. Stevie's guitar had approximately .012" of relief around the 7th and 9th frets, and then leveled out for the remainder of the board. Jeff's fingerboards are flat—adjusted straight as an arrow. Jay Black said, "I gave them a little relief, but .007" at the 7th fret would have been generous."

String gauge Stevie tuned his guitar to E♭ and used GHS Nickel Rockers measuring .013, .015, .019 (plain), .028, .038, and .058. On this particular day, Rene had substituted an .011 for the high E to keep down the sore fingers that blues bends can cause. Jeff performs his acrobatics exclusively on an Ernie Ball set gauged .009, .011, .016 (plain), .026, .036, .046. Both Geoff and Rene change strings every show for each guitar that gets played.

Fretwire If you're trying to evaluate action, it's nice to know what size and shape of fretwire is used. Number One's frets measure .110" wide by .047" tall. These frets would have started out at .055" tall when they were

new, and were probably either Dunlop 6100 or Stewart-Mac-Donald 150 wire. Jeff Beck's frets aren't quite as big. According to Geoff Banks: "Jeff went with the Custom Shop's recommendation of a .098" wide by .050" tall fret. Fender now makes this as a 'vintage' wire, although it's taller than the wire used in the '50s and early '60s."

String height I measured the distance from the underside of the strings to the top of the fret at the 12th fret on both E strings. Rene Martinez describes, "I set up all of Stevie's the same: 5/64" on the treble E string and 7/64" at the bass E." Geoff Banks: "Actually, I don't measure them. I do it by feel, and what I know Jeff likes." (I measured slightly over 3/64" on the treble side, and 5/64" on the bass. Later, Jay Black told me: "I set them up at 3/64" (treble) and 4/64" (bass), but I did this with the string fretted at the 1st fret; I like to eliminate the nut when making this measurement."

Fingerboard radius Knowing the fingerboard's radius can help in setting up a comfortable bridge saddle height and curve. Stevie's Number One was somewhat flatter than the vintage 7-1/4" radius. Rene has refretted the neck at least twice, and in the process the fingerboard has evolved into a 9" or 10" radius in the upper register. This isn't the result of a purposeful attempt to create a compound radius, which allows string-bending with less noting-out; it just happened. Jeff's custom Strats have a compound radius, too, starting out with Fender's currently popular 9-1/2" radius, but flattening out further on up the board. Jay Black hand-shaped them, and from about the 12th fret up they flatten out to an 11" radius.

Bridge saddles The bridge saddles on Jeff's green custom Strat Plus were set at the Fender Custom Shop to the same 9-1/2" radius as the fingerboard. The new-style Fender saddles are formed with a smooth groove to follow the string angle, and support it gradually up to the point where the string takes off at the saddle's peak. While these saddles aren't overly prone to string-breaking, Jeff did manage to break a D and high E string or two later that night. This was more a result of his exuberant attack, though, than evidence of any bridge saddle troubles.

Stevie's Number One, however, wants to break high E and B strings at the saddle every chance she gets. Rene

deep

showed me why the strings break, and how he takes care of the problem: As a string comes out of the vintage Strat tremolo block/bridge top plate, it "breaks over," contacting the metal directly; this causes a slight kink that weakens the string. With the bridge saddles removed, Rene uses a Dremel Moto-Tool to grind the hole's edge until the lip is smooth and gradual, and binding is eliminated.

Number One uses vintage replacement saddles (the originals wore out long ago), and they're not all alike—some have a shorter string slot than others. The high E and B strings may contact the front edge of this string clear-ance slot as they rise toward the takeoff point at the saddle's peak. The kink formed by the contact stretches onto the saddle peak during tuning, and breaks right at the crown. Rene elongates the slot, again by grinding, and then smooths any rough metal edges. Finally, he slides a 5/8"-long piece of plastic tubing (insulation from electrical wire) over each string to protect it from the metal break points. He uses the heaviest piece of tubing that still fits down into the tremolo-block hole. Even with this, the high strings still cut through the plastic quickly, and strings break—sometimes in only one set.

Nuts Jeff's Vintage reissue has a standard Fender-style nut. The three custom Strats are setup with Fender/Wilkinson roller nuts, like those used on the Strat Plus. Stevie's Number One, Lennie, and Charley have standard Fender-style nuts, but Rene makes them from bone. Stevie prefers the sound of bone, although for studio work he had Rene make brass nuts for Scotch and Red.

Stevie Ray used all five springs on his standard vintage tremolo.

Tremolo setup

Measured at the rear of the tremolo plate, Jeff's American Standard Tremolo shows a healthy 3/16" between the bottom of the plate and the guitar top. He uses three tremolo springs mounted in the two outer and one center hole in the tremolo block. The springs connect to the middle three fingers of the claw, and are tensioned so that when he plays, say,

the 3rd fret of the D string, it provides one whole-step if the bar is pulled up until it stops. His standard Vintage tremolo is mounted with all six screws and uses all five springs. It's tensioned so that the plate returns flat onto the top; I measured 7/16" between the spring claw and the cavity wall where the claw is attached.

Rene prefers the durability of the stainless-steel Fender tremolo bars. He puts a small wad of cotton at the bottom of the tremolo-block hole to keep the bar from over-tightening and becoming hard to remove if it breaks. He emphasizes the importance of lubricating all the moving parts of the tremolo system, preferring a powdered graphite-and-grease mixture (the grease holds the graphite in place where it's needed). He lubricates everything that moves: mounting screws/plate, all string breaks and contact points (including the saddle peaks) where the springs attach to the block and claw, the nut slots, and the string trees. Many other lubricants work: Vaseline, Magik Guitar Lube, Tef-Lube, etc.

Pickup height As a reference point, I laid a precision steel straightedge along the frets for making this measurement. Jeff's Lace Sensors have little magnetic string pull, and therefore can be set quite close to the strings; in fact, they work best that way. On the treble side, the pickups were all within 3/64" of the straightedge; on the bass side, they touched it.

Stevie's pickups were raised fairly high. I measured from the straightedge to the pole-piece tops: On the treble side, the bridge pickup touched the straightedge, the middle almost touched the straightedge, and the neck pickup was 1/16" away. The bass side measured 1/32" at the bridge pickup, 1/16" at the middle, and 1/32" at the neck.

Tuning machines We've covered about everything except tuners, and there's nothing secret here. Except for the yellow Vintage reissue, Jeff's Strats are equipped with either Sperzel or Schaller rear-locking tuners. Stevie Ray's tuners are the originals, and each has three full string winds for the best angle at the nut.

Well, that's the end of this story. You'll need an accurate 6" ruler to do the setups, and you can get one at any hardware store (General makes a good one). Don't be surprised if you go through a few sets of strings while you experiment. Good luck, and I thank Geoff and Rene for all of us! I had a lot of fun gathering this information, to say the least, and I hope you find it useful.

John Mooney's slide innovations

If you're into slide but have never heard **John Mooney**, catch his act if he comes near your town. One of the few guitarists to master the true feeling of Delta slide guitar, the "Moonman" comes mighty close to capturing the Robert Johnson sound. John spent his late teens and early twenties learning firsthand from Son House. Now, after living in New Orleans for 15 years, he plays "second line blues," combining the best of the Delta style with the infectious rumba boogie and funk rhythms made famous by Professor Longhair and the Meters.

I found that when it comes to guitars, John's a skilled do-it-yourselfer with some revolutionary ideas concerning slide setups for Strats. I wouldn't suggest these modifications for a vintage piece, but for newer Strats or the many copies, you could have some fun.

Onstage John uses two early-'50s National wood-bodied electric archtops, as well as two real Fender Strats (a white '65 and a seafoam-green '62 vintage reissue) and three extremely high-quality Japanese copies made by Artex. The Nationals have great tone, but at certain volumes they feed back too much (unusable feedback, that is, since John points out that some feedback is good for electric slide). He started using Strats because they're easy to travel with, they can take a beating, they make a great blues guitar, and they don't feed back.

Except for the '65, John has dramatically customized his standard vintage tremolo bridges. Using wood, bone, and fossil ivory, he either alters the metal bridge saddles or replaces them entirely. "The typical Strat sound is not what I'm after," he says. "Strats, with their metal bridge saddles, are just too tinny. There's not enough tone generated by the slide. I like a more woody sound. By using different combinations of wood and bone at the bridge saddle, I capture enough of the National tone to keep me happy. A wood bridge adds warmth and a physical presence to the strings' vibration that interacts with the slide to give the response and tone that I need."

One alteration is the filing of square notches into four of the metal saddles, into which hand-carved bone inserts are super-glued. John uses this setup on his standard-tuned Artex.

The complete bridge overhaul involves replacing all the metal saddles, springs, and adjustment screws with a hand-made, compensated wood bridge (some ebony, some rosewood) to mellow out the treble. Mooney

describes, "The ebony or rosewood bridge saddles removed too much brightness from the treble strings, so I capped the saddle with bone inserts super-glued under the E, B, and G strings to balance the brightness. When I make these wood bridges, there are no adjustment screws to save me if the bridge saddle height gets too low—it won't go back up. So I lower the action slowly, stopping at various stages to play it for a couple of days, until it's just right. Then I set the intonation. I fret notes too, so it's not like playing certain lap-steel styles where the strings never contact a fret and the fretted intonation is less important. "You'll notice that when I replace the standard metal saddles, I re-string through the bridge-plate holes that previously held the saddle's six length-adjusting screws. Stringing up through the tremolo block in normal fashion creates such a steep angle that the wood saddle would slide forward or fall over. This creates a different sound than stringing through the tremolo block, but I like it.

deep

"At first I tried using wood archtop bridges on the Strat. I'd use the top saddle part, cut off the ends, and shorten the height. But with my high, stiff action, I had a rough time getting these 'store bought' compensated wood bridges to play in tune—the saddle peaks reach correct intonation in a different spot. Now I'm carving my own, which is better. With heavy strings and the high pitch of open-E or open-A tuning, you get a good, strong note when you compare the 12th fret octave to the harmonic—it's much easier to hear than a low-action, light-stringed ax. I carve the saddle peaks close to the right intonation by ear, super-glue the bridge in place, then finish up using a tuner to tell me where to remove wood with a file."

Mooney "Deltarizes" his Strats by chiseling an increased "sound chamber" into the body wood under the pickguard and installing a solid mahogany pickguard. "I hear a big difference in sound with the solid mahogany pickguards," he notes. "Even acoustically, the sound is great." John's first Strat, a '63, had no pickups when he got it, so he chiseled the body out to accept a pickup from an old Present Company brand guitar. "I was a kid, you know, and I just wanted it to work. Later I put a mahogany pickguard on it, a Tele pickup at the neck, and a hum-bucker at the bridge—more chiseling. It sounded great! I realize now that part of the sound I liked was from the body being routed, so I'm trying to recapture that sound that I remember from a long time ago. I don't remove a lot of wood, but it makes a difference. The Artex factory routed out the two most recent guitars after they'd seen the one I chiseled out, but they took out a little too much, so I've been filling them back in with scraps of wood."

John keeps six guitars onstage in order to have a pair each in standard tuning, open A and open E. He sometimes has a seventh for G or D tuning as well: "I like to sing in G and D, but I prefer playing with the higher tension of the A and E tunings. If you play in five tunings and only have one or two guitars, you'll be tuning up all night. And a guitar properly set up for open-A tuning won't play just right if you drop it to open G. And the string gauges are a little different for each tuning." John uses bronze-

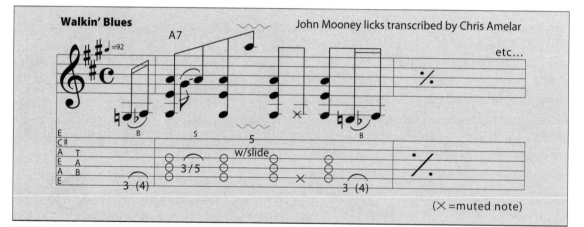

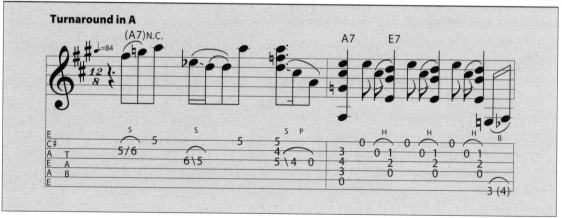

wound D'Addario mediums or GHS Boomers. For open-G tuning: .016, .018, .024 (plain), .034, .046, .059. For open A or open E: .016, .018, .024 (plain), .032, .044, .058. Standard tuning: .013, .016, .019 (or .020), .030, .044, .058.

All of them have a bridge saddle radius that's quite flat (ranging from 14" to 20"), even on the 7-1/4" vintage radiused Strats. To get good contact from one string to another with the slide (especially on treble strings), he flattens the radius by putting the high B string at almost the same height as the G string and the high E as tall as the B, so it's not as round as the fretboard radius would dictate. He flattens the bass side a little too. "The National steel has a fairly flat fretboard radius, about 16"—that's what I'm used to. So setting the high E and B strings a little higher than the radius calls for lets me hit them really hard and get better tone. And using a .016" for an E, you can really lay into some stuff. I think Bob Brozman uses an .018"! The .016" works for me. Even on my standard guitars, I set the high E up a bit because I hit it so hard." Mooney's fretboard/bridge radii on the National archtops are 10" board, 14" bridge. On the Fender Strats: 7-1/4" board, 12" bridge. The Artex: 16" board, 20" bridge.

All of John's necks have some relief, and he sets up his standard-tuned guitars a little lower than the sliders: "When you tune up to A or E tuning with fairly heavy strings," he points out, "the truss rod really has to work to keep the neck straight. In time, a neck can even take a 'set' from the string pressure—they all pull up into at least .010" of relief, and sometimes as much as .018". That extra up-bow gives good clearance in the middle of the fretboard for slide playing, without your accidentally fretting the string with the slide."

John's string height wasn't as high as I would have guessed, considering his clean tone. His heavy strings and high tunings create lots of tension. Measuring the gap between the string bottoms and the top of the 12th fret, I found that all of John's guitars measure about 1/8", give or take 1/64" in either direction. The National arch-tops are set the highest because they have the same 24-3/4" "short" scale as many Gibsons (Les Paul, 335, J-45, etc.), so their string tension isn't as stiff as the longer-scale Strats, which measure 25-1/2". John sets them up higher to make up for their lower tension. "Since I do most of my slide work on the treble strings," he adds, "I set the treble strings on the Nationals higher than the

bass. Scale length makes quite a difference in string tension." Mooney's nut is another reason his slide sound is so clean: "I like a good stiff nut height for slide playing—around 3/64" clearance between the string bottoms and the top of the 1st fret all the way across."

Mooney points out that since his playing style evolved on the National steel, he tries to recreate the National's action (and in many ways its sound) when he sets up an electric—the Delta sound is in his blood. He doesn't travel with the National because it's hard to amplify and doesn't take a beating as well as the others. He did have it along on this trip, however, and it looked like it sure had taken a beating—especially the wooden bridge saddle. John describes a repair he often performs: "With some National steels, it's common for the low E in particular to pop out of the bridge saddle slot. You can super glue matchsticks on top of the wood saddles to hold the strings and keep them from popping out. Several have broken loose and need to be replaced. Got any superglue?" (Are you kidding?)

Mooney keeps his white '65 Strat tuned standard. "This is my least-customized guitar," he explains, "the only one with a stock Strat bridge. I wired the pickup selector switch backwards, because I hit it when I play. That way, since I almost always use either the neck or neck/middle combination, I can just leave the switch pushed down out of the way of my picking hand. I've also raised the B-string's polepiece by pushing it up from the bottom. It'll move about a 1/16", and I set it even with the high E polepiece. I need that extra power on the B string to keep up with the higher-pitched .016" E string." *[This is a bad idea! It can cause the pickup to quit working entirely. It's better to custom-make pickups with the polepiece set this way.]*

For his slide, the Moonman uses a piece of brass pipe that came out of an old house in New Orleans. "It's different than the brass you can buy today—it's pitted, and the texture reacts to the string differently than smooth brass. Like Son House, I put the slide over the first two joints of my pinky. It just goes to the second knuckle. See, a big part of Son's slide style was damping the strings behind the slide."

deep

Albert Collins: talking with the Iceman

Albert Collins' unique Texas swing blues guitar was refreshingly different from Chicago blues. Albert's "simple" style, brilliant tone, and organ-like phrasing earned him the title "Master of the Telecaster" and made his patented licks a part of any blues player's arsenal— from Robert Cray to the Stevie Ray.

Albert's tour bus broke down as he pulled into the Columbus, Ohio, hotel parking lot. He drove his own bus and sometimes fixed it too, so my first in-person glimpse of the Iceman was of his black leather coat, pants, and boots sticking out from under his vintage Greyhound!

PHOTOS: BRIAN BLAUSER, ATHENS, OH

Who takes care of your guitars?

I take care of my own. There's only two, my original Telecaster and the new model Fender made for me, which is a copy of the old one. Changing strings, cleaning, or little stuff—it doesn't need much. Oh, sometimes my little E will rattle, stuff like that, and I'll adjust it at the bridge with the little Allen wrenches.

You've had some heavy-duty work done on your fretboard, including having a 3/16" maple "cap"

laminated over the worn neck from the end of the fretboard all the way to the 3rd fret.

That was done by Guitars R Us, which is down the street from the Guitar Center in L.A. But now the stuff on it—the neck finish—makes my hand break out with a fungus. It doesn't do it with my right hand, but it makes me break out on the left one. I guess it's from the type of finish used. It's been happening quite a while now.

Do you carry any special guitar tools?

Allen wrenches and stuff like that, in case one of my screws comes loose. Or I used to have the problem of where you plug it in at the input jack, and it would fall out all the time. The whole jack would fall out, so Guitars R Us fixed that for me.

Do you set up your own action and intonation?

Not too much. I just take it to a guitar tech—somebody who can work on it.

You must have had problems over the years with fret wear and buzzing. Do you ever adjust your own neck?

I don't ever really have that problem very much with my guitar. And the humbucking pickup was already on it when I bought it used in '68 or '69—it's a 1961 Telecaster. The first time I heard a humbucker in a Tele was on the one I got now—I liked it, and I got it.

Those big frets on it weren't available in '69. What made you choose them?

I wanted the big ones since I saw Stevie Ray —he had a guitar with the big frets on it. Stevie said, "Put some of them on there—it'll last longer," so I had them put in there in '82. And he was right. I used to wear them little small frets out. They didn't last me no time— I'd just keep wearing 'em down. You know, I used to put 'em in myself a long time ago!

No kidding! You did your own refrets?

Mm-hmm. I'd go buy my frets, they'd give me the stuff to put em in, and I'd set it like I want it. That was on a '59

Tele—that's the one that got stole from me when I first got to California. Yeah, I miss that one. I refretted it two times through the years. I'd just go down to Parker Music Company in Houston where I lived—I'm really fond of Houston—and he'd say, "If you leave the guitar, man, you can have it back in two or three weeks." I'd say, "No, I'll do it myself. I can't wait so long—I gotta play!" He gave me all the stuff [tools] to do it with. He basically told me what to do. I didn't have no problem.

During the past 10 years, have you had the big frets worked on?

Nope. I've just had the guitar strobe-tuned, and that's all. Nothin' on the frets. And I used to take the necks off. When I first started playing, it was on an Esquire; I couldn't afford a Tele-caster. So I went and bought a Tele-caster neck and put it on an Esquire. I did that myself too.

How does your old Tele, the famous one, feel to you these days?

It feels pretty good, but I want to redo it again just to make it look a little better. It's pretty worn in places.

How does your new Albert Collins model compare with the old Tele?

I need to break in the new one, and it'll be fine. Like all guitars, even though it's a copy, it's still different. I don't say better or worse—just different. I had both my guitars weighed, and the new one is heavier. Since that time the actual production Albert Collins model has been lightened to match the original.

Do you break strings very often?

Every now and then I break 'em when I get, like, a sweat on. So I change strings twice a week if I'm playing six nights. I'll break two strings at once sometimes—at the bridge, the middle of the neck—it don't make no difference. I break my little E string the most.

Can you recommend a brand of string?

Well, I've been playing the Fender Rock 'N Roll 150 set a long time. I use .010, .013, .015, .026, 032, .038. I used to play the Black Diamond strings. Man, they were so thick they used to make my fingers bleed. I've tried a .009, and I can't use them; they're too light for me.
[Albert tunes to an Fm triad: F, C, F, A♭, C, F, low to high. He often capos.]

Your high tuning and use of a capo must make it tough to bend strings.

Sure. My hand sometimes gets so sore I can't hardly touch them strings, but you gotta play anyway. We used to get that stuff you call "new skin" [mole skin] and put it on there. But some-times it would take the feeling out of my finger-tip—I couldn't feel it like I wanted to. Before I left home we hadn't been playing that much in about a year, and then we'd be playing every night. Them strings will make you real sore until you get tough.

Which pickup position do you use most?

Most of the time I'm in the middle. Sometimes I use the bridge position for a real hard sound. But I get the hard sound in the middle because I use my fingers, not a pick.

Do you have many other guitars?

I got a '67 at home, I don't carry it now here, but I'm gonna take it out next time and try it. It doesn't have the humbucker, but it could make a good sound.

Why is your sound called Texas swing blues?

They call it Texas swing blues because I use a horn section—it's just different than in Chicago, where the guys from Mississippi would migrate up. We didn't have no harp players or slide guitar players come out of Texas. I was raised up with [saxman] Illinois Jacquet and others. Where I come from, the bigger the band, the better

deep

it is—that's just the way it was. At one time I had nine pieces, and I carried that for about two years. But some of my favorite guys didn't work with a big band. Lightnin' Hopkins was a cousin of mine, so I was around him more than anybody. I remember when him and Little Sonny Jackson used to run around together, and I think they did some time together in prison. Lightnin' used to live in Dallas, and he was the only legend I ever knew well.

Vital statistics

String gauge Albert says he uses Fender strings gauged .010–.038, but the strings I measured read: .009, .011, .013, .025, .031, .037. It seems strings never measure out to be exactly what the package says, so it's a good idea to own a pair of dial calipers to measure different brands.

Neck width 1.553" at the nut, 1.920" at the 12th fret.

Fret size/height Approximately .108" wide by .047" tall—probably a Dunlop 6100 or Stewart-MacDonald 150 fretwire worn down from the normal .055" height.

Pickup height (measured from the top of the pickups to the bottom of a straightedge laid on the frets, with the guitar in playing position):

Pickup	Bass Side	Treble Side
Neck	1/16"	3/64"
Bridge	1/32"	1/32"

Nut height/string clearance (with the guitar in the playing position, measured from the bottom of the string to top of the 1st fret). The clearance between the bottom of the outer E strings and the top of the 1st fret for both guitars was .010" under the high E, .022" under the low E.

Neck relief (measured at the 7th and 8th frets with guitar in the playing position and a long straightedge laying on the frets): .003"—quite a straight neck!

String height at the 12th fret (bottom of outside E strings to the top of the 12th fret): Medium-low action measuring 5/64" at the low E, graduating to a little more than 3/64" under the high E.

String width at the nut (measured with dial calipers from the outside E to E): Approximately 1.281" to 1.310".

PHOTO: BRIAN BLAUSER, ATHENS, OH

Buddy Guy: "My guitar is almost like my love"

Ever since his first road trip in 1968, when he played out of this world on a '57 Stratocaster, Buddy Guy has been inspiring Strat players everywhere. These days his tone is better than ever, and there's arguably no finer blues player alive than Buddy Guy. We met to talk guitars, and then I took the setup measurements of Buddy's signature-series Fender Stratocaster and his trusty Guild Nightingale.

How does your Strat feel right now?

It feels great. My guitar's almost like my love.

Is the Buddy Guy model the only Strat you play these days?

No, no, no. Now they just sent me another one they made—the Stevie Ray Vaughan model. But I want to go back to as close as they can get to the original sound that those guitars had when Leo [Fender] first made them.

How do those Lace-Sensor pickups compare to the ones on your old Strat?

I don't have no choice. Let's put it like this: If you had an accident in a car now, would you rather have it in one of these new ones or one made in 1940? Because you could bump in 1940, and you wouldn't dent it. All that was stone chrome on those cars back like that. So there's just no comparison to that. I think it's the same thing with amps, but they did do pretty well with this new reissue of the Fender Bassman. And they're doing a tremendous job with the Fender guitar, but I don't think you'll ever compare to the old sound. I don't want to put the scam out on nobody, but when Fender went haywire there in the '60s and went out of hand, I think it was a

PHOTOS: AL BLIXT, ANN ARBOR, MI

come out, it's like you said, they had a switch for each pickup. Then we found that sound in between both of them [two pickups wired in parallel]. And that got back to Leo or somebody at Fender, so they decided to make that switch many years later. Now all of 'em got it made on the switches.

rat race for the look of the guitar—not the sound. They come out with all the different pretty colors and was just settlin' for the color.

Why don't you just put the old-style pickups in your guitar?

I don't have them! You can't find 'em. They can make the new one look like the old one, but it's not there. The engineers and everybody else know it's not there.

Do you work on your own guitars?

No, the only time I work on them is when I hook them son-of-a-bitches up—any other way, no. Oh, sometime if I have to adjust something on it, I know how to do that, but I won't fool with the neck or nothin' like that. But the bridge I would—especially on the Strat. Sometimes I have to fool with that. I never learned that much about fixing it. I put most of my time on learnin' how to play it better—each and every day, as I still do now. And when it needs some work I'd rather send it to someone else while I hold the other one in my hand and try to learn. If I knew how to play like B.B., I probably would learn some technique about adjusting and so on. About the worst thing I will do is the height of my strings. Sometimes I think I play them too low, 'cause I like to play with one hand, and the lower they are, the more you can get out of one hand. So that's the quickness and the snap that gets me to the frets. You snap, and it notes more clearly like that.

The Strat you used early in your career only had a 3-way switch, whereas Fender later decided to go with a 5-way switch.

No, no, no. We finally set that switch in between those two things and got that sound. Then they heard about it and came up makin' that switch like that. When they first

So on your old Strat, you used the in-between position?

A lot, a lot. Towards the front—between the front and the second pickup. That's what I was usin' when I went into Chess and started playin' a lot of sessions with Muddy and the rest of them. And that's what sound I used on the *A Man and the Blues* album. That was on my original Strat—the vintage which they call it.

Do you know what year that Strat was made?

I borrowed the money to buy that in '58, so I'm sure it was a '57 or a '56—at that time I don't think they was even keeping up with the years on the guitar. They kept up with the years on a car, but guitars wasn't as famous. But all of a sudden all the numbers and things started comin' out on guitar and things like that. When I first knew anything about a guitar, all that there was was a cutaway Fender. And I only knew two that was there—a Telecaster and a Strat. And then later on in the years they started doing the guitar like they do the automobiles. But I never go into that with a guitar because that number don't mean nothing to me if the guitar don't sound right.

Do you favor your shorter-scale Guild for a certain sound?

Ah, yes, when I want to sound more like B.B. And I got quite a few of those Guilds. When I first got one, B.B. came in and said, "I heard you got a Lucille." He came back in the dressing room and played it, and I just kept that with me at all times. And now, if I really want to imitate B.B. as much as I can, I'd have to go get that guitar. It's impossible to imitate him, but I do the best I can. That guy deserves way much more than he's gotten credit for.

He's doing okay, but I think B.B. should be as well known as Eric or Beck or anybody like that, man, because we all playing his licks. Nobody was squeezing that string until he came out. Then I got it, some-body heard it from me, and it just went on and on.

Do you keep in touch with each other?

Of course. I still got a key to his house in Vegas; I never took advantage of that, though. He can have mine, too! He can go in my house any time he gets ready. If I'm not there, he can go on and go to sleep. I'd tell my wife get out of the bedroom and leave him alone. Let him have the master bedroom.

Speaking of B.B., is it easier to bend strings on the Guild because of the short scale?

They are easier to bend on the Guild, and I guess that could be why. Because that's my style of playing, bendin'. I break more strings, I think, than any guitar player I know.

You break them on the Guild?

I break 'em on anything, if you give me time out there. Because I figure if you don't break 'em, you're not playing 'em. But I do feel embarrassed when I break too many in one night, and sometimes I do. I use a light string, and that even makes it worse. But if I get to the point where I'm making people happy, I don't care. Then I get a smile. I'm fortunate now to have enough guitars out there to not hold up the show, and I got a great guitarist with me, Scott Holt from Tennessee, so if I break 'em all, he can make you forget I'm gone!

Which string do you break the most?

The first one. And I break 'em everywhere, even the middle of the string. Sometimes I get to bendin' on a string, and I just don't have no end. I just don't think it should stop being bent. That's the feeling I get. I think I read somewhere where Eric made a crack where I was bendin' whatever's in it out of it [laughs]. I know I like to see the first and the last string touch one another sometimes.

As you bend, do you slide your fingernail under the neighboring string?

Aaah, no. Well, actually I don't even know, man. If it comes under, it's alright; if it comes over, it's alright. You know, I'm not a technical guitar player. I make a lot of mistakes. But when I do make a mistake, I try to come out of a mistake on time. I make a lot of mistakes, because

I never go home and practice. I don't think I could sit down and practice. I just go on the stage, and it comes to me and says, "Let's go, go, go, go." Like a rubber band— you stretch and stretch, and you know sooner or later it's gonna break.

Can you recommend a string gauge?

Yes, I'm an endorser for Ernie Ball, and normally I use a .010 or .011 on the number-one string, but on *Damn Right I've Got The Blues* my first string was like .015, which is a big one. I was trying to not break a string if I got a good solo while cuttin' the album. You know, a lot of times you get a groove making an album, and if it's good you may not never get another one that big, be-cause everybody gets too tense. They say, "Oh, we can do it better, we can do it better," but it looks like it gets worse, worse, worse. So by using the heavier strings, I was making sure of not breaking any. Stevie Ray Vaughan played a heavy string tuned down; Hendrix did too. They both tuned to E♭. And Stevie's guitar felt like barbed wire, like it was strung with hay wire. Strong hands—oh man, I don't know what that guy had in his hands. But like I was saying, on that album I used a heavier string, and I tuned down the guitar too for recording—first time. I said, "If they gonna tune to E♭, then I'm goin' all the way to D"— which I did.

Have you got many guitars at home?

I got every guitar I ever had in my life at home, except the ones that got ripped off.

Do you have any old Strats like the one you used to play?

No, those the ones they go after most. If they would break in the house and see the ones that's not Strats, I guess they'd say, "I can't get rid of that one" and don't take 'em. The Strats I got now is the ones they just made—an Eric Clapton, a Stevie Ray, and mine, the Buddy Guy. And I got another one from the '70s. The Buddy Guy model has got the same pickups that Eric's been using—that's the pickup that use the battery, which is fine.

Is the Strat your main guitar?

I favor the Strat because I went into Chicago with it, so I guess I made my little name with it. Plus, I'm not a guitar player of B. B. King's caliber. I was always a wild man with my guitar, and a lot of times when you play like that, the guitar has to be rough. And a hollowbody guitar is not rough. If you drop it in the wrong place, you through for the night—and I couldn't afford two guitars. So I said, "Give me the one that if I accidentally drop it off my neck, I won't break the neck off." I may break a string, a volume knob, or something, and I can replace that. But it'd be hard for me to replace the guitar. So I went after the Strat, and I've had it fly off the top of a car going 80 miles an hour in Africa. The case bust open, it fell out, and I went back and there wasn't but one key out of tune. If I'd have had a hollowbody, I wouldn't have seen anything but splinters on that highway.

How do you prefer your action?

Low, low on the Strat. Sometimes I think I keep 'em too low, but that's good for the one-hand playing. But the Guild has a higher action—on purpose.

Do you have any acoustic guitars?

Yeah, they gonna make me play it on my next outing. I got a Guild. You didn't hear the new album *Alone And Acoustic*. There's no band, and I'm playin' 12-string acoustic and singing with Junior Wells. I don't even have the album—I haven't heard it—but it's out there, and it's doing pretty well. Man, I cut it over 10 years ago, and they just released it this November.

What's the extent of your record collection?

I had more than I got now. My kids started going up there, and I started missing records. Then after you get pretty well known, friends come by and tell you, "You don't need it because you can sing it when you get ready." So a lot of my records disappeared like that— which I've changed now, because I'm back into collecting records. A lot of jazz, a lot of piano playing. I love great old piano players. I don't just listen to guitar players. When Bill Doggett's "Honky Tonk" came out man, the horn solos was like, "I gotta learn that." And I recommend to all guitar players: If you get hung up on just guitar players, you've missed something. I like to play piano solos, harmonica solos—if I can—and whatever. Don't ever get to a point where you just gotta be a guitar player. You hear something, go try to play that note and sound as much as like that as you can. And who wouldn't want to sound like the late Little Walter, man—oohhh!

Were you ever tempted to play slide?

I came to Chicago with a slide because I wanted to really do like Muddy Waters. And before I got a chance to get to know anybody, Earl Hooker shows up with this slide, and I gave him mine. On Muddy Waters' boxed set, if you search through there you'll find a cut with Hooker on it— somethin' about the birds singing—and I've never heard anybody take a slide and do that before in my life. I didn't want to even attempt at the slide after Earl, so I gave it to him. Every song that came out of the Top 10, whether it was country-western or what, and he could play the melody with a slide. And he didn't tune his guitar like a lot of slide people do—cross-tune to where it'd slide just right—he played everything in the regular tuning.

Do you ever use open tunings?

No, I don't even know how to tune it like that. I know how to drop my low string down to just an open D, but I can't play the open stuff like Bonnie Raitt and them do.

What amp did you record with in the early days?

I always had the Fender Bassman, except when I recorded at Cobra [in the late '50s], I didn't have no Fender amp. I went there with a Gibson with four 10s in it. I forget the name of it now, but I loaned that to a friend of mine and that disappeared. Damn near everything I had disappeared in Chicago, because being from the South I didn't know nothing about stealin' and takin'—but I learned that will happen to you in Chicago, because just about everything I went there with come up missing from me because I was kindhearted. I would loan it to people like the late Earl Hooker, the late Bobby King, and a lot of great guitar players at that time which didn't have guitars, didn't have amps. And they would come to me: "If you're not working tonight, let me use your amplifier," and so on. And I would say, "Okay, man, just make sure you play because I intend to hear you and steal some licks." So I was always loaning some amps. And if I let anybody have it for any time, they'd never return it. On a couple of cuts on *Hoodoo Man Blues* with Junior Wells we used the Leslie speakers for the organ. A lot of kids would ask me what was that when I had that little funny sound, but the rest of the album was all Fender Bassman. But let me take you back for a minute.

The first time I got an endorsement was from Guild. Guild was makin' amps then, and they came to me and said, "You come to the factory, and we're gonna' make you what you want." And they told me to bring my

deep

Fender Bassman amp in. And they kept it for two years, and then called and the engineer said, "You come and get it, because I can't reproduce that." They used to put it on the monitor, and every time I'd strike the guitar to show what the amp's doing, it was like a speeding automobile, hiding the needle, while those other ones was scufflin' trying to get it up to 60, 80, or whatever points they wanted on the monitor. So they never did reproduce the Fender Bassman that Leo had made. Maybe there was something in the transformer they never did get. And then now people tells me it was the material, the wood, and so on, and I believe that.

What amp are you playing through now?

A Fender Bassman. They reissued the Fender Bassman, and I'm very proud of that because to me, that's the guitar sound. Otis Rush had it. In the earlier days when I went to Chicago, Muddy Waters and Howlin' Wolf was giants in my book—there wasn't no Rolling Stones, no Beatles, there wasn't no super rock groups or nothin' like that. And we used to travel with the whole band in a car, because two guitar amps and a bass amp would fit in the trunk. And the little P.A. system with two speakers in it would fold up like a little suitcase, and all that went in the trunk along with your own personal microphone. And when you'd get there you set the two little speakers on each side of the stage and set your mike up. All the guitar amplifiers were so small, but when you played the blues you could hear it very well. 'Course we wasn't playing in as big of places as we are now.

And then came along the Fender Bassman, which was a little larger than the ones we had then. That stayed until the '60s, when the British got it and the amplifiers started getting larger and larger. And then you needed an extra man to carry your amp. [Laughs.] As small as I was, I couldn't carry the big amplifiers they was makin' so I had to have somebody really love my music just to follow me and help me carry—otherwise you stayed at home.

What are your stage settings?

On the Bassman everything's wide open but the bass—no bass at all. That amplifier don't have that much to open up no-ways, you know. It's simple, just like the old Strat guitar.

Do you still own your original Bassman?

I got my old Bassman saved. Actually, I would love to have it installed in the wall of my house, so if somebody do happen one day to decide to break in, they would say, "It's too much trouble to get that." Yeah, I've still got the same covering on it, but I don't play at home. When I sound good, I want somebody else to share it with me. I don't want it to sound good just to me. I want to bring my sound out there and look at the expression on your face and the other fans, and let them say, "wow!" Then I go home and feel good.

See, I don't say, "I'm the best guitar player" —I don't do that. If somebody else says it, fine, but I don't never say that. Because they got too many great guitarists, just like they got good-looking men, good-looking women all over the world. Every time I go to different country, I'm saying, "I thought I saw the best looking woman in the world." And it comes better and better wherever you go, every time you go somewhere, man. So I'm just happy living and looking and learning and watching all this from the music on down to the human beings. If everybody felt like me, wouldn't nobody in the world have a problem, because they would just listen to good music—guitars, pianos, drums, and everything. They'd just smile and say, "I want to come back tomorrow for more so I can smile again. I'm tired of being mad at the world."

Vital statistics

Buddy's Strat gets more play than the Guild, but you can't prove it by the hole worn in the Guild's top from strum-ming. Buddy had it filled with clear epoxy to protect the wood.

String gauge On both guitars, Buddy uses Ernie Ball strings gauged .010, .011, .015, .028, .034, .044.

Neck width Strat: 1.685" at the nut, 2.055" at the 12th fret. Guild: 1.703" at the nut, 2.070" at the 12th fret.

Fret size/height Buddy agreed that his Fender needed fret work soon, and he'll send it back to the Custom Shop. Since Buddy plays so much, bends like crazy, and covers the entire fretboard, his Strat frets were worn uniformly flat, creating a sharp burr at the front edge of each one. You could almost cut yourself. Normally, a fret crowning would do the job, but his frets are also worn so low that the instrument needs a refret. The Guild's frets are still quite round and have a decent height. Strat: .080" x .042" "vintage" wire measured .028" at the 7th fret and .032" at the upper frets—pretty low! Guild: .108" x .045" Gibson-style fretwire averaged .030" to .035" all over.

Pickup height (measured from the top of the pickups to the bottom of a straightedge laid along the frets, with the guitar in the playing position). Note: Being Lace Sensors, the pickups can get closer to the strings without the magnetic pull common to traditional Strats (this magnetic pull can cause "Stratitis"—a difficulty in obtaining true intonation in the upper register).

Strat:	Pickup	Bass Side	Treble Side
	Neck	touching	touching
	Middle	3/64"	3/64"
	Bridge	3/64"	3/32"

Guild Nightingale: I didn't measure these. They're EMG pickups, which can be very close without noise—and they were close!

Nut height/string clearance (with the guitar in the playing position, measured from the bottom of the string to top of the 1st fret): The clearance for both guitars was .010" for the high E, .022 for the low E.

Neck relief (measured at the 7th and 8th frets with guitar in the playing position and a long straightedge laying on the frets): Strat, .011" Guild: .016"

String height at the 12th fret (bottom of outside E strings to the top of the 12th fret):

Strat: E, A, D all 9/64"; G, B, E all 1/16"

Guild: E, A, D, G, B a heavy 3/32"; high E 9/64"

String width at the nut measured with dial calipers from the outside E to E: Strat: 1.437", Guild:1.421"

PHOTOS: BRIAN BLAUSER, ATHENS, OH

deep

B.B. King: talking about Lucille

B.B. King would sound like himself on any guitar, because it's the man and his music—not so much the guitar—that's truly important. But on behalf of those of us who've spent hundreds of hours listening to this great bluesman and learning his style, I thought it would be beneficial to actually play Lucille and report on the type of action and response that lets B.B. do his thing. Perhaps these measurements and observations will help other players—especially blues newcomers—find what's right for them. At first B.B. seemed a little apprehensive about answering questions about the guitar rather than music. He began our conversation with a disclaimer:

"I'm like a test pilot for the airplane—he don't know much about it, he just flies it. An amp and a guitar, I don't know much about 'em. I just play—or at least try."

Have you ever been a do-it-yourselfer, adjusting and setting up your guitars?

Not too much, but some. I've been pretty satisfied with the way they're made by Gibson. I have done some little things, like setting the bridge intonation.

Did you help design Lucille?

Yes, a few little things. The ES-355 is prac-tically the same thing, except that I wanted a thinline, semi-hollow, but also solid-body guitar with no f-holes, and they did that for me. So Lucille's like the big brother to the Les Paul. At one time I suggested that they narrow the neck a bit, and they did that for me. Also, the nut was a little different—I believe it was made of brass. With the current model they've returned to the usual white Gibson nut. And that's one of the things that's a little different.

How many Lucilles do you own?

Well, this is Lucille the 15th. I've given some of them away, and been ripped off for others —I mean, people have stolen them. Couple of times, they've come in the dressing room when I'd be talking to someone, and Lucille'd be in the next room. The last time, somebody went in that next room and got it. But luckily the sheriff was able to find it. A young fella had taken it home, and the funny thing was, when the sheriff came up to his house, he said, "Oh, did you come for the guitar?" [Laughs.] Yeah, that was the last time, but I've got about five or six of the Lucille model at this time.

Do you own any acoustics?

I've got two or three of them around home. One is an old National with the tin body and a resonator. I've got another one, but I can't think of the name now. The Gibson company is planning to give me one—at least one of the gentlemen there said they were going to.

One of the new flattops from Montana?

Mm-hmm, and that's what I want—one that's acoustic, but that you still can amplify. [Author's note: Ren Ferguson, the man credited for the excellent guitars being built in Montana at this time, is making B.B. a very special J-2000 with extensive abalone inlay. The flattop will be a soft-shouldered, round cutaway with rosewood back and sides and a spruce top. The scale length will most likely be 24-3/4", like Lucille. This new "Lucille" will have a bridge transducer pickup and on-board electronics.]

Do you play acoustic at home?

Not often, but I do. I would rather play it at home [laughs] than let anybody hear me trying to play it out.

Do you play fingerstyle at all?

Oh no, I'm not that good—always a pick. In the early years I didn't have a pick. You know, I'm not as talented as a lot of people are; they can take the plectrum or use their fingers. It's all I can do to use the plectrum. So if I try to divide the time between the two, I don't do so well! I see Chet Atkins and guys like that just go to town with it, but I'm not able to do that.

Do you travel with more than one Lucille?

Yes, but until about a year ago I always just carried one Lucille. Then my manager suggested that I carry two in case something happened.

Is there a favorite Lucille, or one that's the most broken-in?

No, not really. It's like if you were drivin' a car—say, a Ford or Volkswagen, what have you—and you had two of them. They're both the same thing; it's just that one maybe feels a little different than the other. But actually the guitars' necks are pretty near the same.

You played heavy strings for years. In the old days they didn't have the light rock and roll strings.

The only strings I knew about in the beginning were called Black Diamonds, and gosh, it seemed to me that the first E string would have been the size of the G that I use today.

Could that have been what made your left hand so strong?

I won't say it's what made my hand strong, but I can say it probably did help. Then all of a sudden 20 years later somebody said, "Hey, man, have you tried the slinkies?" I said: "What? [Laughs.] The slinkies?" A .009" set, you know. So I tried 'em once, and it was like I'm playing with toys, so I took them off because my hands had gotten used to a specific gauge. For another thing, I'm not the best with chords, but I like light jazz. And I like rock—you know, I like some of all of it—but I can't seem to get the sound of the chords that I want with a real light-gauge string.

Do you ever get sore fingers from bending?

Yeah, my fingers get a little tender, but I don't have corns [callouses] on my fingers, like most people. And the action's pretty high on Lucille, a little higher now than I usually like it to be. I prefer it a little closer. The only time that I'll have a corn is if I don't play for awhile and then pick up

the guitar—then I'll develop one. But usually my fingers stay very soft on the tips.

What fingers do you bend with?

A lot of people think it's only this one or that one, but I bend with all of 'em, and a lot with the third finger. The way I bend, I don't push it up or pull it—technically, you could say I'm just trilling. I bend with my little finger too. I guess, you know, I'm one of those guys that was never satisfied—never, never satisfied—so I was always tryin' to find something to add to what I was doing. So I didn't spend as much time practicing as I should have—still don't.

The Stratocaster is popular with all kinds of blues players. Have you ever messed around with one?

I had one of the first Fender guitars that came out.

The Strat?

If that's what it was [chuckles], I had one. You'll see a few of my early records with me holding it. But I believe it was a Telecaster.

When did you discover the semi-hollow body guitar?

About '58 or so is when I got the first one, with the long neck—I believe it was called the ED-355 at the time. I got one of those, and I have liked them ever since. But my first Lucille was a little black Gibson acoustic guitar, and I used a DeArmond pickup on it to electrify. And my first amplifier, the very first one I ever had, was a little Gibson amplifier with something like about an 8" or 10" speaker in it—one speaker.

What amplifier would you recommend for small clubs?

I love the Fender Twin. When they first made the Twin, I used it all the time, because I never found another

amp that satisfied me like it did. But when the company changed and went to a different type of amp during the '70s and '80s, then the sound somewhat changed too. So I started searching for something else, and that's when I found this Lab System, which is what I'm using now and which I like very much. Because with the Lab System I got a sound similar to the older Fender Twin, so I try to buy every Lab System I can find, because they stopped making them.

No more Fender Twins?

Oh, I still use the Twin too. Because with the Fender Twin, later on they returned to the old way of making them, and I again started to find the sound that I used to hear. You see, I didn't know much about the settings of those other amps, because I'm a three- or four-button guy, you know [laughs]. The volume, the bass, the treble, and reverb—and that's about me. So now, in my contracts, if they don't have a Lab System, which most often they don't, our contracts state that they must have a Fender Twin—and that's what I use all over the world. [Albert Garcia of Fender explains, "The Fender Twins that B.B. didn't like were models where they added things like master volume, gain control, and a more powerful output and power supply that upped the power from 85 watts to 100 and finally to 135 watts. I'm sure he couldn't get his sound with it, because it's too powerful, for one thing. But now we have the '65 Twin Reissue—just like the original—with more simple controls, two channels, reverb, tremolo and 85 watts."]

Do you adjust the knobs on your guitar as you're playing?

Well, as you know, the guitar has tone controls as well as volume. The two front controls are volume for both pickups, and the rear controls are treble and bass. I use these controls all the time—up and down—according to the sound of my ear.

How about the settings of your amp?

My amp is turned up to the maximum, usually, as far as volume is concerned. If you were to think in terms of 1 to 10, the volume would be about 10, or maybe 8 or 9—not always completely wide open. It's according to how much balls it's got. If it's really hot, then about 8 for the volume. Now, I don't like a lot of bass since I can't hear it so well. Generally the bass would be between 5 and 6

most of the time. I have the treble up all the way practically, unless it's very hot—too hot for me—then it would be like around 7 or 8. But I prefer a lot of treble because I can hear treble, and with a good amp it usually cuts through pretty well. I like reverb, but not too much—just so it's not flat. So reverb would be about 2. That's the way I like the settings when it's a good amp, but I'm pretty rough on amps because I play pretty hard and I wear them out.

You wear them out?

Well, with the volume up strong—and I like a lot of feedback from time to time—that's pretty hard on an amp.

How do you get feedback?

I can find ways of getting feedback, which I can't explain really, but there are certain positions in which you can stand. You don't necessarily have to face the amp or have the guitar toward the amp. With this solidbody Lucille I can pretty well control feedback like I want. That feedback's pretty hard on an amp.

Do you have a special repairman or tech who works on your guitars, or do they go back to Gibson?

To Gibson, every time. After I've kept it for about a year or two, I usually will send Lucille back whenever she's startin' to wear a little bit. I get them to check her out, especially the frets.

Have you experimented with different fret wires?

No, this is the standard one that comes with the Lucille model [the wide oval, see measurements].

How often do you need a fret job?

About every four or five years, usually. I don't know, even though I slide up and down the fretboard a lot, I don't seem to wear them down like I've seen on some guys'

guitars—I guess the frets are pretty good on them. I've known some guys to file their frets down to where the fret is just above the neck. You know, where it's just out enough to fret it. But I don't like that.

You can't bend on those, right?

Yeah, I could. I can bend on any of 'em. Man you get me one and I'll bend 'em [laughs]—I don't care what kind it is.

Your adjustable Gibson TP6 tailpiece has the individual tuning screws removed. Why?

I don't like 'em, because they easily come out of tune for me. I took 'em off and threw 'em out! For some they may be good, but for me to have to reach back here [points to tailpiece] and tune, no! The next guitar, I plan to talk with Gibson and see if they can't just keep 'em off of mine. Another thing I like is the old style of tailpiece that holds on like a trapeze, so you just put the ball end of the string in the hole, and there it is. I'd like something like that. But if you ask about moving the bridge saddles, I do adjust them when the guitar seems to be out of tune with itself at times. I always check them at the 12th fret.

Do you use Lucille's Varitone switch much?

No, I hardly ever use it. Put it on full and just leave it there. To me, I can get a better sound mixing it myself.

Which pickup combination do you use most?

I leave the toggle switch in the middle most of the time. It's supposed to be stereo right, so it's got two input jacks—one for mono and one for stereo. So generally the mono input jack is the one that I use most times with just a standard cord. It also has a stereo jack that uses a Y cord, so you can use two amps, right and left, and get the stereo sound with each amp working individually.

You mentioned that you like the long neck.

The guitar's got 22 frets on it. With the long neck joining the body way up, usually a guy with big hands like mine has no trouble going from here all the way down there to get it [slides from the nut up to the high D]. You got that D way up there on the 22nd fret, so you're all the way from here to there with ease.

What do you wipe your strings with when you're all done for the night?

Most times I'm kinda lazy, I don't wipe 'em down because when I come off the stage generally somebody else brings it off, and a lot of times I forget to do it when I get to my room. When I get to my room some nights, I'm so tired I put Lucille in one corner and I go in the other. But when I can think of it, the best thing to do is wipe the guitar down—then it won't corrode or rust. And my hands perspire so much, if I don't wipe 'em down they rust.

What brand of strings do you use?

I use Ernie Ball's light top/heavy bottom. I once used Gibson; I liked the Gibson strings, and I'm kind of a loyal guy. But then they started making the wound Gs, which I don't like. A wound G is nice if you're playing jazz, but I like to bend the strings somewhat. And the wound G doesn't get the sound, to me, when I'm bending. I can bend, but it's not the sound I'm looking for. My high E string is a .010", sometimes .011"—I like 'em pretty heavy. A .013" generally, for the B string, and a .017" on the G. For the D, a .030"—I prefer a .032", but the .030" usually comes in the set. The A string is a .045", and there's a .054" on the bottom E. That's what I use.

Do you change strings yourself?

Always.

No guitar tech to do it for you?

I can't afford it! No, it's me and Lucille. In fact, I broke a string onstage last night, but I'm pretty good with changing them. Usually I'll change before anybody really knows that I'm doing it.

Right while you're playing?

While I'm playing—never stop. I'll go into something that features somebody else, and if I'm playing a 12-bar thing, in 24 bars I've almost got it together—if it's a slow one.

Do you change strings for every show?

No, It's according to how much I'm playing. If I'm playing every night, about once a week. But if I break one, then I'll change the whole thing. It's like an old story about bears takin' corn out of the fields. If the bear had an armful of corn and he dropped one ear, he'd throw it all down and collect him another armful! [Laughs.] So that's the way I am about the guitar. I don't care if I changed last night, if I break one tonight, I'll take 'em all off and put a new set on.

You wind lots of string onto your tuners.

Again, I'm from the old school. We used to break strings so much, so you use it all! You wound it all up here [points to peghead], then if you break one, you still got

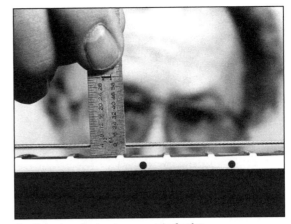

Lucille has lots of string clearance at the first fret.

more so you can pull it down and tie it on.

Do you run your strings through the post twice or have any special knots or ties?

No, I don't need to because I start to wind the strings from almost their beginning—for instance, like you take the average E string and pull it about an inch through—you can wind it about 12 times around there.

Maybe having that many windings is the key to staying in tune.

I don't know, but the tighter your string gets, the more it holds itself. My B string has about eight winds, about six or seven for the G string, and if I am in a hurry, I can put one on very fast. The only one that gives me trouble is the big E. Windin' it together up there gives me a little trouble. But at one time they had—and I liked it—keys with little cranks that you could fold out and wind the tuner very fast. I used to have 'em on the 355. I'm going to get them on Lucille [Author's note: These M-6 Gold Crank tuners are still available.]

Do you ever practice or play along to records?

I'm pigheaded. I've never learned that well that way. I read a little slowly, but if I really want to learn, then I buy the lead sheet on it and I sit down and play it. And nowadays I put it in the computer and let the computer play it. But that's the way I learn songs mostly. I've never been able to sit down and play a tune and learn it from that.

Like everybody has with your music?

Well, I guess. I don't have the knowledge of chord patterns like most people do. So, seeing is being—hearin' is deceiving! [Laughs.]

Lucille's vital statistics

Neck width 1.698" at the nut, 2.055" at the 12th fret.

Fret size .098" wide x .045" (leveled and dressed, the frets range from .038" to .045", averaging .040").

Polepiece height (with the strings open rather than pressed down): in the bridge position, 5/64" at the high E, 9/64" at the low E. The neck pickup's polepieces are 9/64" (almost 5/32") at the high E, 13/64" (a heavy 3/16") at the low E.

Nut height/string clearance (measured from the bottom of the string to top of the 1st fret): .015 for the high E, .038" for the low. The open strings don't buzz.

Neck relief (measured at the 7th and 8th frets): .030". This is a lot of relief. A more normal .015" could be accomplished by slightly tightening the truss rod a quarter-turn or less.

String height at the 12th fret (bottom of outside E strings to the top of the 12th fret): All strings measured 7/64" in height across the board—a stiff, high action!

String width at the nut (measured with dial calipers from the outside E to E): 1.425"

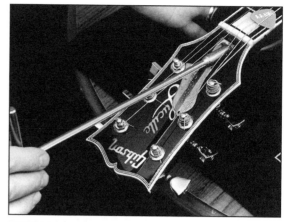

Alone with Lucille: I just know that B.B. King sound's gotta be in there someplace!

basic

Understanding compensation   63

---

d.i.y.

Setting intonation   65
Adjustable bridges (electrics)   65
Non-adjustable bridges (acoustics)   65

---

deep

Buzz Feiten Tuning System   66

Chapter 5

Intonation and compensation

basic

Repairmen are often asked: What's the reason for the different saddle positions on tunable bridges? Why are some bridge saddles closer or further from the nut? This is all about string-length compensation, which most players refer to as "setting the intonation." This is an essential part of setup for both acoustics and electrics.

Understanding compensation

To begin with, accept the fact that fretted instruments play in tune only to a point; they're not perfect and never will be. With its fixed-position frets, the guitar is known as an even-tempered instrument. The fret positions are a compromise that enables a guitar to play closely in tune in every key, but not perfectly in any. Many players can hear the out-of-tune notes in the even-tempered scale, and it drives them (and their repairmen) crazy.

At best, proper intonation is a compromise of many factors, and at a certain point guitarists must accept some degree of out-of-tuneness or give up the guitar. Too often, the repairman doing the setup is blamed for not getting a guitar perfect, and that's not fair.

Your repairman is doing a lot more than turning a couple of screws. He's checking to be sure that all other important adjustments—such as truss rod, action height, fret dressing, nut and bridge saddle shape, string gauge, etc., have been made before setting the intonation. That's important!

Understanding compensation and setting intonation is tricky, with many factors involved. I like things simple, so here are some basic facts regarding string-length compensation as I understand it.

String length, or **scale**, is the distance from the nut to the center of the saddle. A Strat, for example, has a scale length of 25-1/2". But the bridge saddles may actually measure as much as 1/8" to 3/16" more than that, depending on string height, string gauge, etc. This added string length at the saddle is known as compensation.

On non-adjustable acoustic bridges, compensation has been accounted for at the factory and is seldom a serious problem. Most acoustic guitars with problems suffer from sharpness and need to be compensated by adding to the string length. Occasionally, though, flatness caused by over-compensation is found on acoustics on which the bridge has been installed out of position. Don't expect the guitar you buy to have perfect intonation. Tweaking the intonation needs to be done to suit the the individual player's needs, governed by the factors mentioned here.

When setting intonation, we try to get a string to play the same note when fretted at the 12th fret as when played open, only an octave higher. In theory, the distance from the nut to the 12th fret is the same as from the 12th fret to the saddle. The 12th fret octave is the halfway point of the scale (scale length equals the measurement from the nut to the 12th fret, times two). In practice however, the string length must be increased to compensate for the sharpness that results when the string is pressed down during playing. The mathematical distance of the scale is based on a straight line from the nut to the saddle's center, but when you press the string down it becomes stretched, and goes sharp. This is a basic explanation of the need for compensation.

Add in the factors below, and you'll see why the seemingly simple job of setting the intonation can cause you to tear your hair out before you finally take the guitar to a repair shop, so they can tear their hair out!

The closer the strings are to the fingerboard, the less compensation is needed, since the strings go sharp less when pressed. However, guitars with lighter strings generally need more compensation than heavier ones, since as string tension decreases (going from heavier-gauge strings to lighter), the compensation need increases. Therefore, the lighter the strings and the lower the tension, the more need for compensation. So, perhaps one cancels out the other. Confusing, but you can prove it for yourself by trying this test:

Using an electronic tuner, check your guitar's intonation on the low E string at concert pitch. Retune the string to D. It will intonate sharper, which indicates the need for more compensation, or added string length. That's why the modern electric player, who uses .010 strings or lighter, often searches far and wide to find a repairman to set the intonation.

Wound strings need more compensation than plain ones. Because of their extra weight and slower, low-pitched vibrations, wound strings need more clearance from the fingerboard to avoid buzzing. The extra clearance is gained by raising the string height from the fingerboard for wound strings. This increase in height causes the strings to go sharp more than the unwounds when depressed. This is why bridge saddles slant toward the bass side on steel-string acoustics or electrics.

I like the term "speaking length" of a string. **Franz Jahnel's** comprehensive *Manual of Guitar Technology* refers to the mathematical string length as the "true" length (the measured distance from nut to bridge saddle), and the actual vibrating length as the "playing," or speaking, length. A string, especially a wound one, doesn't actually start vibrating, or speaking, until it gets a certain distance from the nut or the saddle. So, part of the string's length (in terms of sound) is always lost—another reason for compensation.

Notice that classical guitars have saddles with no slant. Why? The wound strings have a stranded core rather than a solid one, and sharp out at a rate similar to that of the solid nylon treble strings. Classical strings have a more even tension across the fingerboard than steel strings. Therefore, they require close to the same amount of compensation per string, and in general are more uniformly spaced from the fingerboard in terms of height. You may find saddles that have been slightly filed off-center (compensated) under the B and G strings on some classicals.

Instruments with longer scales need less compensation than shorter-scaled ones, because the longer string must be tighter to reach the same pitch. Thus the longer string is less apt to be sharp when fretted and needs less compensation (the higher the tension, the less a string goes sharp). The two most common scales are long and short. Long scales are 25-1/2" or thereabouts (these include Strats, all their clones, and many Gibsons; Martin uses a 25.4" and Guild a 25-5/8", but we lump them all together as long scale); short scales are 24-3/4" or thereabouts (Gibson Les Pauls, ES-335s, smaller Martins at 24.9", etc.). Classical guitars have long scales. There are many other scales, but only a few really common ones: a "medium" 25" scale is used on Danelectros and PRS guitars (I really love this scale); a "Three-Quarter Scale" (23") is used on the Gibson Byrdland and the ES-350-T, and Fender's Duo-Sonics, Mustangs and Musicmasters use 24" or 22-1/2" scales.

Setting intonation

Adjustable bridges (electrics) Setting the intonation on guitars with adjustable bridges (which even some acoustics have) is simple. All that's needed is a small Phillips or flat-bladed screwdriver or an Allen wrench. If a string sounds sharp at the 12th fret, move the saddle back (away from the nut) to increase the string length. If it sounds flat at the 12th, move the saddle forward (toward the nut).

Non-adjustable bridges (acoustics) Acoustic guitars tend to shrink over the years as their wood shrinks. Add to this the effect of the string's pressure pulling the nut and saddle toward each other, and you lose a bit of string length—measured in thousandths of an inch, perhaps, but it all adds up. Even solidbody electrics suffer from string tension compression on the neck and lose some string length over the years.

Differences in a string's gauge, quality, and physical makeup drastically affect intonation. As a string's cross section (diameter) increases, so does the need for compensation: hence the saddle slant toward the bass side

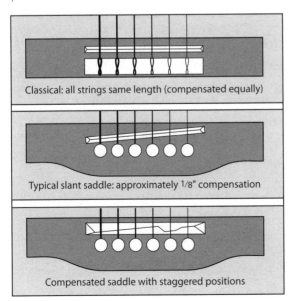

Classical: all strings same length (compensated equally)

Typical slant saddle: approximately 1/8" compensation

Compensated saddle with staggered positions

> ✔ If the string notes sharp, move the saddle back, increasing the string length.
>
> ✔ If the string notes flat, move the saddle forward, shortening the string length.

on steel-string guitars. A string's elasticity, or ability to return to its original position after being deflected, is also a compensation factor, and stiffer strings go sharp more when depressed. You'll have to try many brands and gauges before settling on the right strings for you. The sad thing is that by the time you find the set you like, your playing style may have evolved to a new level, requiring that you start all over again!

The standard factory-installed slant saddle on acoustic guitars is usually sufficient compensation to please most players. The saddle slants approximately 1/8" in a 3" length, toward the bass side. If the intonation doesn't please you, ask a good acoustic repair shop about a compensated saddle (where a wider saddle blank is inserted and then filed to staggered peaks under the different strings, as in the bottom drawing at left). If you're interested in compensating your own saddle, you're ready to go deeper than deep. More information on this subject may be found in **Don Teeter's** *The Acoustic Guitar, Vols. 1 and 2*, **Hideo Kamimoto's** *Complete Guitar Repair*, **Franz Jahnel's** *Manual of Guitar Technology*, data sheets from the **Guild of American Luthiers** and *Guitar Making: Tradition and Technology*, by **William Cumpiano** and **Jon Natelson**.

I hope this information helps you understand how even a top-quality guitar can play out of tune, and why it can be so tough to get it right.

When it comes to setting your guitar's intonation by compensating, the interrelation of many factors is complex, and the slightest change in any factor (especially string height) can throw the whole deal out of whack. Be sure to do a good basic setup before starting to set the intonation. An electronic tuner is a big help. The following approximate compensation is usually added to the scale length of any guitar:

✔ Most electrics and steel-string acoustics: 1/8"–3/16".
✔ Classical saddles: 1/16"–7/64".
✔ Electric bass: 1/8"–1/4".

Special thanks to **William Cumpiano** and **Dick Boak** from Martin Guitar's Woodworker's Dream—two expert luthiers who were very helpful with technical information. Woodworker's Dream has a great selection of rare hardwoods and guitar parts, and their catalog is a must for aspiring luthiers.

The Buzz Feiten Tuning System

I've been a firm believer in the Feiten System since I first played a Feitenized guitar. I heard the difference immediately! I have retrofitted several of my guitars to use the BFTS: my Firebird, Les Paul, and Strat—and now that there are aluminum nuts for Danelectros matching the Feiten specs, I'm Feitenizing my '56 Danelectro U-2.

I've heard comments like this from some players: "James Burton didn't have the BFTS, and you can't tell me he played out of tune," etc. That's no way to investigate something new, in my book (pun intended). I don't have a Feitenized acoustic, because my 1939 Gibson J-35 sounds so good that I won't mess with it. (The bridge is too thin, and the saddle is too low for Feiten adjustments anyhow.) I am saving up to buy a Martin D-18 Authentic, and I will Feitenize that right away.

Buzz Feiten joined the Butterfield Blues Band at only 19 years old. The young Buzz Feiten's recording debut was on the Paul Butterfield album *Keep on Movin'*, and he more than filled the vacated guitar seats of blues legends Mike Bloomfield and Elvin Bishop. Soon the word was out that there was a new voice on the guitar, right in the middle of the Hendrix-Clapton-Bloomfield era. Check out Buzzy's rig with the Butterfield Band (at right): a Gibson ES-345 with the stop tailpiece holes plugged, and a single, stop-bar/bridge combo—Buzz was experimenting already!

The Butterfield gig catapulted Buzz into a career as one of the world's great guitarists; and, after leaving the Butterfield Blues Band he became a much sought after session player, and remains so to this day. Feiten has recorded and toured with many artists—from Stevie Wonder and Aretha Franklin, to Bob Dylan and Rickie Lee Jones—as well as co-leading bands with keyboard artist Neil Larsen. Their debut album *Full Moon* is a highly prized collector's item, and one of the seminal moments in the development of fusion jazz.

With an unrelenting passion for anything having to do with making the guitar sound and play better, Buzz's laser-like focus eventually zeroed in on the fundamental problem of every guitar player: tuning and intonation. He discovered a new approach to guitar intonation, and along with his partner Greg Back, developed the Buzz Feiten Tuning System.

"I think it was 1992 when the light bulb went on," says Buzz. "I was on tour with Bette Midler, and had been struggling over the years with tuning problems like everyone else. I was sitting on stage during sound check, listening to Will Jennings, Bette's piano tech, tune the grand piano. He would tune only one note with the electronic tuner, and everything else he tuned by ear! Every night the piano sounded great. In contrast, I was tuning

only six strings with a very accurate, expensive tuner, and my guitars simply didn't sound in tune to me. It was so frustrating that I began to question the basic setup formulas. What if there was a better way to tune and intonate guitars?

"The result was a series of tuning experiments that I called 'intonation modeling'. I'd sit at Will's beautifully tuned piano, and adjust the guitar's intonation until it started to sound pleasing. This was a very methodical process; I started with the high E only, then added the B, and so forth. This process resulted in charts of numbers; one column for open string pitches, and one for 12th fret pitches. Gradually, we developed one chart for electric guitar, and different charts for a variety of fretted stringed instruments, and within each, mode charts for different gauges of strings.

"I'll never forget the morning that I was working on my kitchen table 'luthier's bench' trying to get the 1st fret F of my Ibanez Roadstar to play in tune. Finally out of sheer frustration, I took a hacksaw and cut the end of the fingerboard off. Right away, the guitar sounded better!

"I started doing detailed measurements of pitch and distance, and came up with an interesting observation. Every guitar I measured was at least 3 cents sharp at the 1st fret—even with a perfect nut dress.

"The first fret being sharp was due to the effects of end tension. End tension dictates that it's easier to press a string down at, say, the 12th fret, than at the nut, or 'end'. The increase in tension directly translates to pitch. The Pythagorean formula for fret placement, called "the Rule of 18", did not take end tension into consideration because when Pythagoras invented the Rule of 18 he simply stretched a string between two supports, and placed a moveable fret under the string. He'd pluck the string and move the fret along the string length to find the correct fret placement. He didn't use a fingerboard, and didn't have to press down on the string, so he never experienced 'end tension.' His formula was absolutely brilliant, and we all use it today, but it has that one little flaw that we have now corrected.

"At the time, Greg was completing his BS degree in Engineering at CSUN, which included the course Physics and Music. Greg performed the research on how end-tension affected the guitar fingerboard, the Rule of 18, and the Pythagoras Mono Chord. This research was nec-

essary to further develop our concepts and create the foundation for our patents.

"The Buzz Feiten Tuning System improves the intonation in two ways: 1) it compensates the end-tension by relocating the nut (so that those first three frets play in tune; 2) the bridge is compensated to reflect a very detailed, precise 'tempering' formula, which offsets the pitch slightly for each string. The result is that all the chord shapes sound pleasantly in tune, with no excessive 'beating' from a particular chord shape.

"After using this method for about a year we showed it to Steve Vai, Larry Carlton and other top players, and demonstrated it for Tom Anderson, and some other builders. Their positive reaction convinced us that we'd developed a system that could be duplicated and taught—important not only to me, but to other players as well."

When Feiten showed Tom Anderson the System in 1996, Tom—being as much a guitarist as a builder—loved the results enough to incorporate the BFTS in all his guitar models from then on. "I will be forever grateful to Tom for his courage and vision," said Buzz. "and also to Washburn and Larry English who showed a lot of guts in accepting the BFTS. All USA Washburn guitars and basses have had the System since 1997, and they're adding new models every year.

"D'Addario Strings has become a strong advocate of the Buzz Feiten Tuning System, they use the system in their presentation for their dealers. To be acknowledged by the largest and most respected string manufacturer in the world is very gratifying and important to me—the relationship is an indication that the Buzz Feiten Tuning System is not only becoming well received, but setting a new intonation standard as well."

Converting your guitar to the BFTS

Feitenizing your guitar involves precise modifications by a retrofitter authorized by the Feiten System folks. I talked with Buzz's partner Greg Back, a veteran guitar repairman who was the first Feiten retrofitter:

"We developed our own proprietary shelf nut that allows our authorized retrofitters to perform a completely non-invasive retrofit on guitars and basses. The shelf nut is recognizable by our logo, and makes for an efficient retrofit so the work goes faster and is less expensive. The

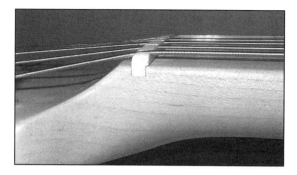

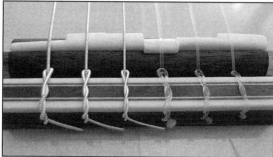

suggested price for a shelf nut retrofit is $139; we also have acoustic steel and nylon string saddles for acoustic retrofits."

I don't agree when Greg says the retrofit is not invasive: Feitenizing an electric guitar is reversible, but the nut is removed and replaced with their "shelf nut," which hangs over the end of the fretboard. This shortens the scale length and reduces the effects of end-tension in the first five frets (end tension is never eliminated entirely). The amount of shelf nut overhang is determined by the retrofitter after calculations taken from each instrument.

An acoustic steel string guitar retrofit involves a fair amount of structural change: the bridge saddle slot is filled with matching wood and re-cut to reflect the BFTS measurements. An acoustic nylon string guitar has both a shelf nut and shelf saddle with no wood removal at the bridge (so it's completely reversible).

lesson because the acoustic installation is not easy, and I wanted the info from the top. It's a two-day intensive training in all aspects of the system, including the specialized luthiery techniques, tuner technique and all the formulas. The training gives the students everything they need to retrofit acoustic instruments. (For example, how to fill an existing saddle slot, find the intonation points and make a new saddle that is tuned for the BFTS—it's an advanced technique, to say the least. The classic guitar saddle in this photo gives you a good idea of the hand-fitting involved.

Retrofit training The BFTS training program has expanded by authorizing luthiery schools such as Bryan Galloup's School of Luthiery and the Summit School of Guitar Building to train qualified students in the theory and application of the system. I signed-up for a group

Chapter 6

Tuning machines

basic

Tuner basics   69

d.i.y.

Installing tuners   71
Steinberger tuners   72
Tuner repairs   74
Damage from over-oiled tuners   75

deep

Rotted plastic knobs   77
Making new tuners look old   78
Reconstructing rotted knobs   80

basic

Tuner basics

A locking nut for your whammy-bar guitar, and an electronic tuner to tune up with — these are great things, but don't overlook the most fundamental purchase you can make for being in tune: tuners. Replacing old worn-out tuning machines that no longer hold their pitch might be what's needed most.

If you're considering new tuners, there are lots of good ones, and many of them are made to look like the older machines they're replacing (to save your guitar from a dorky "I just got a haircut!" look of shiny new tuners on a funky old axe).

When you turn the tuner knob, you're turning a worm gear that's meshing with a crown gear connected to the string post. The design of these gears determines whether your tuners have a 14:1 or 15:1 (etc.) ratio—the number of knob turns it takes to make the string post go around once. Higher numbers mean finer tuning (but slower, because you have to turn the knob more times). Electric bass tuners typically use a 20:1 or 24:1 ratio.

Judge a tuner's quality by its "backlash," the amount of free play felt when a peg is turned in an opposite direction before the string post starts moving (zero backlash is the goal). Also check to see whether the post moves— thereby changing the pitch—without the tuning key being touched. Backlash is especially noticed by players who bend strings or use a tremolo, since when the constant pressure of the string at the post is altered, the string may not return to the original pitch. A locking nut is a good solution to backlash and post movement, but for vintage guitars, I feel that the tuners should be replaced before a locking nut is even considered. Eliminate backlash, and you may solve your guitar's tuning problems. Other tuner flaws that become less apparent as you buy better tuners: end play (looseness of the knob shaft) and shaft wobble (looseness of the string post in the peghead face).

For years, all tuners were constructed with exposed gears or a stamped sheet metal housing. **Kluson**,

basic

Waverly and **Grover** were the big manufacturers. Kluson's **Deluxe** was the most widely used, and now it's most often the tuner needing replacement. The Deluxe were notorious for backlash because their gears were made on a screw machine rather than a specialized, more accurate tool known as a gear hobber. Also, they made the worm gear from brass, when steel would have worn longer (tuners today have a brass crown gear, but use steel for the worm). Klusons had a backlash the day they were born, but no one knew enough to complain. There wasn't anything better, so players put up with them until Grover came along with their **Rotomatic**.

The Grover Rotomatic was the first high-quality tuner. Its diecast housing enclosed well-machined gears that were completely sealed and lifetime-lubricated. In addition, a threaded bushing with extra length replaced the press-in grommet to better support the shaft. This tuner became the replacement choice of repairmen everywhere, and a factory-installed standard on many higher-end guitars. Years later the Rotomatic was copied, and then improved upon, by Schaller and Gotoh. Between Grover, Schaller, Gotoh and the lesser-known but equally high quality **Sperzels**, you'll find a size, shape and style to fit any guitar or bass.

Diecast tuners are the most precisely made and offer the least backlash, but they're also more expensive. And because of their larger size, you'll have to do some drilling in order to use them as replacements for the old-style tuners with a smaller string post diameter. They may not be a wise choice for a valuable vintage guitar or bass.

In the good old days, players had two choices for solving tuning machine problems: install a set of diecast Rotomatics or buy a new set of stamped factory replacements that were no better than the originals. Today's replacements for those old, low-priced Kluson Deluxe tuners are excellent. Modern Deluxe styles offer a 14:1 or 15:1 gear ratio, compared to the old 12:1, which means closer tuning capabilities. Also, the gears on all brands are accurately machined, with nylon washers added to reduce end play in the worm gear, thereby eliminating much of the backlash. That means you're safe using them as an exact look-alike replacement, and you won't have to deface a vintage axe by drilling for the larger diecast machines.

I seem to recall that the earliest Deluxe replacements had larger shafts than the vintage 1/4" style—and a larger bushing ("grommet") too. So those tuners wouldn't just "drop right in" the existing bushings since the shaft was too large. In that case the tuner bushing holes in the peghead face had to be enlarged to accommodate the new replacement bushing, which isn't preferred on a vintage axe! I believe that most of the manufacturers have taken care of this oversight, but be sure to shop around—I know that the Gotoh Deluxe replacements will fit vintage bushings. However, Gotoh's bushings still have a larger outside diameter than vintage ones by about .012" (.344" compared to .332"). These bushings will slide into some peghead holes but not others. It takes just a few minutes to file down the ridged teeth on the bushing sleeve until they fit, however.

Vintage Martin and Gibson guitars often used the Grover G-98. The perfect replacements for those pegs

are Waverly Guitar Machines (above) are pricey, but the Waverly is the best tuner I've ever used. This tuner fits the old Grover plate footprint (the imprint in the lacquer on the back of the peghead), and the mounting hole spacing on many Gibsons and Martins from the 1930s through the 1950s. If you're custom ordering a new guitar, ask the maker to use Waverlys and you won't regret it.

If your guitar no longer has its original tuners, and has oversize string post holes from a diecast tuner installation, Waverly offers vintage conversion bushings, so it's possible to revert back to vintage-size tuners with the right look. These retrofit bushings come in the Martin or Gibson hex shape, and the round Fender or Kluson Deluxe style.

If you want diecast machines and you don't mind enlarging the holes read this chapter's D.I.Y. section before attempting an installation. Or, since many guitars manufactured since the late '60s already have diecast tuners, replacing them is easy; the hole is already the right size, and no drilling is needed. But even diecast tuners wear out or eventually suffer from backlash. So if you're shopping for a new set, there are several points to consider. The first is size: Mini diecasts are available for headstocks that won't accept the standard ones (Fender, for example). You can also choose color—from black, gold and chrome to red and blue. Several other options are available, such as string locks—miniature locks that are actually built into the posts to help control string slippage. Sperzel offers staggered-height string posts for Strat style headstocks, which keep a good angle at the nut without using string trees; this is a real enhancement when using a tremolo without a locking nut. Perhaps you need Fender's slotted safety post and trimmed plate to fit a Fender. Also keep in mind that some sets are heavier than others, and try to find pegs that match the original shape and mounting screw holes. If properly matched, they'll drop right in, probably even matching the original footprints in the lacquer.

⊃d.i.y.∘

Installing tuners

Those are the basics of tuning machine construction —from costly diecast tuners to the less expensive, stamped variety. Almost any of today's well-made, inexpensive tuners are a good replacement value. Here are a few more tuner facts, with some installation tips.

Not only are diecast tuners accurate, but they also suffer the least from backlash. This doesn't mean that you can't tune well or won't be satisfied with stamped vintage replacements; you may well be. But diecast tuners are the best, which is why you see them on most top-of-the-line instruments. (Would you put two-ply tires on a Cadillac?) Now, even diecast tuners can develop backlash over the years: As the brass crown gear wears, the fit becomes looser. Another little-known fact is that if you tune a string too high—especially a wound string—and it suddenly breaks, the instant release of torque at the string post can loosen the screw that holds the crown gear to the post. This allows slop between the gears, and backlash can result. This explains why

one tuner may occasionally develop tuning problems. You can't repair this, because you'd damage the tuner by trying to get inside it. Your music store, though, can often order a single replacement. Most of the various styles are available from Grover, Schaller and Gotoh at competitive prices, and they are all equally fine tuners. And don't forget the Waverly W-16 if it's appropriate for your instrument!

While researching this chapter, I learned that Sperzel tuners are unique. Their construction features totally eliminate backlash, end play and shaft wobble. Not only are the machining tolerances extremely close, but the string post and crown gear are a one-piece, solid unit that is locked into the diecast housing by a cleverly machined collar (see previous page). Also, the bushing threads are outside the housing rather than inside, allowing an even tighter fit between the post and housing and further eliminating any play. Since the string post and gear are solid, there is no screw that can loosen. Sperzel has been able to drill up through the shaft, thread it, and install a unique string lock that is adjustable with a thumbscrew from the rear; this Trim-Lock is an option. Another option is staggered post heights for Strat-style guitars, allowing the removal of the string trees while maintaining a good angle for the string passing over the nut. Sperzel tuners are a little more expensive, but they're definitely worth looking into.

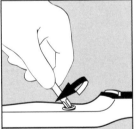

Replacing stamped Deluxe tuners is often simply a matter of removal and direct replacement. Installing diecasts, however, sometimes requires the enlargement of headstock holes. First remove the old tuners and mounting screws. Often the headstock grommets are quite snug, and you may have to rock them out, or at least loosen them by inserting a screwdriver shaft inside and gently rolling it in a circle until you feel it loosen. The grommet can then be pushed out from the rear with a blunt tool. Don't overdo the rolling motion, because you could crack the finish. Now measure the housing's diameter: It will usually be around .380" or close to 3/8", while the original hole will be around 11/32".

⊃d.i.y.∘

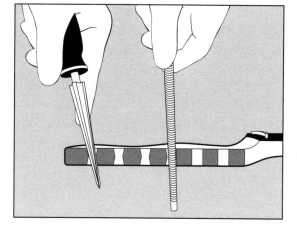

d.i.y.

This exact hole size would be important if we were going to use a drill, but we aren't; that's for pros or for people in a hurry. Enlarge the hole by using a tapered reamer (available from hardware stores and guitar shop suppliers). Ream halfway through from the front and from the rear, testing often with the new tuning peg until it fits. If the two reamed sides don't quite meet, leave a ridge in the center (above, right), removing this last bit with a rat-tail file. Be sure to hold the reamer at right angles, clean its blades often, and don't be in a hurry. Each hole may take you five or ten minutes. Wrap a piece of masking tape around the reamer's cutting flutes at the correct width of the new tuners to act as a depth stop.

Once all the holes have been cleared and the pegs slip in easily, install the tuners and tighten down the hex-nut bushing against the washer on the headstock's face. Now you can line up the tuners with the headstock shape in a fashion that both pleases your eye and allows the easiest turning of the keys. When the pegs look right, snug the hex nuts and drill the mounting-screw holes. Use masking tape on the drill bit as a depth guide to avoid drilling through the headstock's face! Be sure to use a bit that's smaller than the actual screw thread, so that the screw can bite into the wood. Thread each screw into the mounting hole to finish the job. The correct way to drill the mounting holes is illustrated and explained in the section on problems caused by over-oiled tuners.

You need to fill the old tuner holes to seal them from moisture absorption and to make the finished job look neat. Remove the tuners to make the job easier. A local

guitar shop or cabinet maker can provide small wood scraps (usually mahogany or maple) that match your neck. Carve or file small, round, tapered plugs that are slightly oversize to the hole for a snug fit. Glue them in with white or yellow glue such as Franklin Tite Bond or Elmer's; use super glue only if you're experienced with it. If you "dry fit" the dowels to each hole, you can see where to trim them to length before gluing them in. This makes cleanup easier and lessens the risk of damaging the finish as you trim. A pre-trimmed dowel should push down into the hole until it's flush with or slightly below the surface. Don't expect the color or grain to be a perfect match, and seal the finished plug with a drop of lacquer or super glue as a drop-fill (the section on dents, dings and scratches explains how). Of course, the plugged holes will be visible unless you totally refinish the headstock, but they should look good enough; besides, that goes along with the installation of diecasts as a replacement for the old-style tuners.

When the finish dries, reinstall the new pegs, put on a new set of strings, and go find someone to play with—you've earned it!

Steinberger tuners

I try to keep an open mind about trying new things—tuners, for instance. I saw the Steinberger gearless tuners when they first hit the market and thought they were not only too radical, but ugly. Still, my curiosity got me to try them out on my Gibson Firebird, which already had rear-adjust banjo-style tuners. I couldn't believe how well I could tune with them; with a 40:1 ratio, they out-tune anything else. Notice that I didn't say a 40:1 *gear* ratio: instead of gears, the Steinberger tuners use a machine screw post to pull the string down into a hole. The post has a locking capstan to hold the string. Some vintage lovers will freak out to find that I put Steinbergers on my 1939 Gibson J-35, but I couldn't help myself.

Changing strings with these tuners is a little bit slower, and a little more difficult than with other tuners.

How to install Steinbergers

1 Loosen the 2 hex set screws that hold the knurled tuning knob to the tuner shaft and remove the knob. Remove the white Teflon washer, the hex nut and the thick spacer from the shaft.

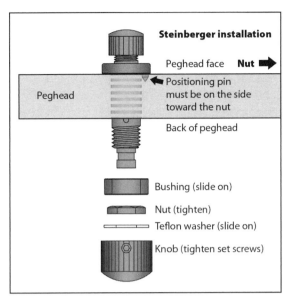

Steinberger installation

Peghead face **Nut** ➡

←── Positioning pin
must be on the side
toward the nut

Peghead

Back of peghead

── Bushing (slide on)

── Nut (tighten)

── Teflon washer (slide on)

── Knob (tighten set screws)

2 Insert the tuner shaft through the 3/8" (10 mm) tuner hole on your guitar from the face (front side) of your headstock. Note there is a pointed positioning pin on the lip of the tuner. This pin *must* be positioned towards the nut. Orient the pin and push down on the tuner to accurately make a small location mark on the face of the headstock next to the tuner hole.

3 Remove the tuner and drill a 1/16" pilot hole 1/8" deep. The fit will be snug, but will be pulled in tight when installation is complete.

4 Insert the tuner from the face side of the headstock, fitting the alignment pin into the pilot hole. From the back of the headstock, install the spacer and then the hex nut. Tighten the hex nut very carefully: use only enough force to pull the tuner flush to the peghead. The tuner body is delicate, and over-tightening will break it.

Install the white Teflon washer and knurled tuning knob on the shaft. Gradually tighten the two set screws that hold the knob (these screws fit in the groove at the end of the tuner shaft). Tighten one screw slightly, then the other, then the first—alternating between the two as you tighten. Wiggle the knob to be sure the screws remain in the groove, so the knob will stay centered on the tuner shaft. Don't overtighten the set screws; if they're too tight, the pressure will distort the shape of the shaft and prevent it from turning freely.

The tuners are lubricated. However, if needed, you can remove the knurled tuning knob and put a *small* amount of graphite lubricant on both sides of the washer.

Install strings Unwound strings *must* have steel or silk wrapping at the ball ends, or be soldered, or they *will detune* during severe string bends.

1 Unscrew the tuning knob clockwise all the way, so the string hole is fully exposed.

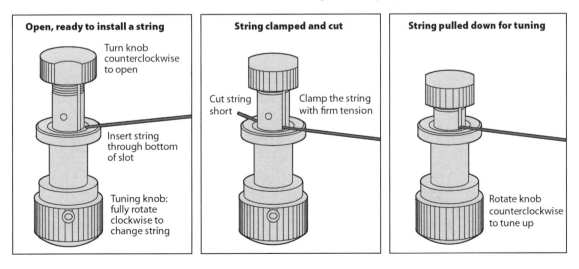

Open, ready to install a string

Turn knob counterclockwise to open

Insert string through bottom of slot

Tuning knob: fully rotate clockwise to change string

String clamped and cut

Cut string short

Clamp the string with firm tension

String pulled down for tuning

Rotate knob counterclockwise to tune up

2 Unscrew the clamping knob (smaller knob on the front of the peghead) counterclockwise until the string hole is fully open.

3 Insert the string through the hole in the tuner. Pull the string tight, and hold it tight during the next step.

4 Clamp the string in the tuner by turning the clamping knob clockwise as *hard* as you can by hand.

Tremolo guitars Because the high E string can stretch so much, tilt the tremolo forward a bit and pull the string tight before clamping (do this on the high E only).

The clamping knob should be *very* tight to assure stable tuning. (I tighten them more than finger tight, using a small Crescent wrench. Just a bit more snug is all you need; don't reef on it).

5 Cut the string approximately 1/4" from the tuner post. Sometimes the G, B, and high E string tuners will need to be de-tuned, the capstan loosened and the string pulled tight again to give you enough range for tuning. For this reason I don't clip the string end off until I'm sure that I won't need the extra length to pull on when retightening.

6 Tune the string with the tuning knob.

Tuner repairs

Extracting broken mounting screws

Everyone breaks off the head of a screw at one time or another—even pros. With guitars, it happens most often with tuner mounting screws installed into maple, since maple is hard and the screws are small— their heads twist off easily. If you follow the correct drilling technique for the screw thread and shoulder, you should never be faced with the problem, but never say never—I've snapped them off more than once when it seemed that

everything was going right. Here's a clever trick for removing them, passed on to us by my good friend Paul Warmoth of Warmoth Guitar Products. It's a combination plug cutter/screw extractor.

At the hobby store, buy a piece of hollow brass tubing large enough to completely surround the broken screw shank and some of the wood that it's embedded into. A 3/16" outside diameter tubing has a large enough inner diameter to straddle the screw because the tubing's walls are so thin. Clamp the tubing lightly into a vice and file small teeth into one end. I filed the teeth with a small feather-edge file that's used to sharpen the teeth of Japanese Dozuki and Ryobi hand saws, but any small, thin metal file will do. File the face and gullet of each tooth at slightly less than 90°, and the back or rake at any angle— you needn't be too specific—just so it angles back and away from the cutting edge to eliminate friction.

Chuck your new plug cutter into a hand drill, electric drill, or drill press, and drill slightly past the depth of the embedded screw. Then back the cutter out and wiggle the plug until it breaks off, or use the cutter, gently to avoid breaking it, to get the plug out. The plug that pops out will have the broken screw in it! Now all you need to do is plug the hole with a piece of wooden dowel, and here's how you do that.

The hole you're going to fill is 3/16" in diameter, so whittle and file down a 7/32" or 1/4" dowel. When you get in the 3/16" ballpark, be very careful to keep the dowel round; you'll probably have to try several times, but dowel sticks are cheap. If you have access to lots of drill bits, and preferably a drill press, there's a better way to size a wood dowel to keep it round and get a good fit.

Using a #9 drill bit, drill a hole through a 1/4" plate of steel or aluminum. The #9 bit measures .196", which is

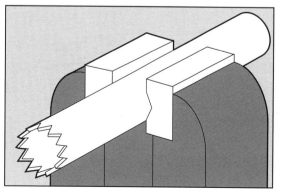

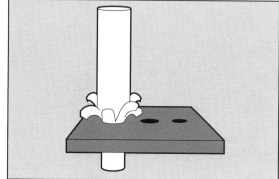

bigger by only 9/1000" than the 3/16" (.187") hole you wish to plug in the back of the headstock. File or sand a taper on the end of the whittled-down dowel (which is still slightly larger than 3/16"), and pound it through the hole drilled in the steel plate. The dowel compresses as it's forced through the sizing hole, allowing it to press-fit into the headstock hole when you tap it in. Then it will swell up tight if you glue it in with a water-base glue such as Franklin's Titebond or Elmer's Carpenter's Glue. Note: Whenever you drill steel, aluminum plate, or anything hard, clamp it down! Especially with steel or aluminum, and especially with a powerful tool such as an electric drill or drill press. When the metal binds to the drill bit—and it often does—it can go whipping around fast enough to cut your fingers off, at the very least! Speaking of drills and drill bits, here's some information you may be able to use:

A full set of drill bits (under a half-inch) is called a drill index, and has three types of bits: letter bits from A (.234") to Z (.413"), number bits from 1 (.228") to 80 (.013"), and fractional bits from 1/16" (.062") to 1/2" (.500"). These bits allow you to drill almost any size hole. Such a drill index was once out of reach for most of us, costing hundreds of dollars; we repairmen would buy just what we needed at a good hardware store. These days you can find the full set (of a lesser quality, but they're fine) for $49 in almost any mail-order tool catalog.

If you can get your hands on a full set of drill bits, try this old-time furniture maker's trick for sizing dowels: drill a series of sizing holes. In our case, start at just under a 1/4", with perhaps a "D" or .246" bit, and drill holes at intervals of 10/1000" until you get to the #10 (.193") size. The holes will actually shave the wood off as you drive the dowel through the plate, not just compress it!

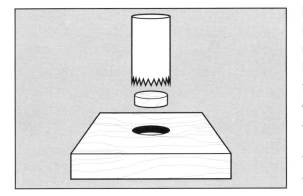

There's a method here for everyone, so for the well-equipped do-it-yourselfer or the serious professional, here's another way to plug that hole in the headstock if you have access to a metal lathe.

Make two plug cutters: one to remove the screw and its surrounding wood, leaving a 3/16" hole in the headstock (.187"), and the other with a .196" (#9 bit) inner diameter to cut the plug that fills the hole. The smaller cutter is made from 3/16" steel rod, and the larger one from 1/4" rod.

Chuck a 1-1/8" length of the 3/16" rod into the lathe, face it off square, and bore a hole 5/8" deep into the end, using a #25 (.150") bit. Remove the #25 bit, put a 3/32" (.093") bit into the drill chuck, and bore a clearance hole completely through the length of the rod. This is so you can push the plug out later; we used the smaller bit for the clearance hole so the plug cutter would have some strength. File the teeth, and this is your extractor. It will cut a .150" plug around the screw and leave a 3/16" hole in the headstock for you to fill.

Next chuck the 1/4" rod and drill a .196" (#9) hole clear through it (a smaller clear-through hole isn't needed here, because the 1/4" rod has quite a bit more strength). File the teeth, and this is your plug cutter—it will cut a tight-fitting .196" plug. The beauty of this method is that you can cut a plug out of side grain in any scrap of matching wood (maple, mahogany, whatever you have), and the match can be tremendous. Avoid burning your plug, especially in maple, by cutting slowly—these are somewhat crude, homemade bits (and they certainly aren't hardened)! And all this just from a little tool idea that Paul called me with one day.

Damage caused by over-oiled tuners

Something that's often overlooked when people are buying or caring for a used guitar is tuning gears that have been oiled too much. Most modern tuners are permanently sealed and lubricated, so they need no oil. However, I've seen hundreds of good guitars with tuners that have been oiled regularly, and this excessive oiling causes three common problems that can be expensive and aggravating.

The first problem is stripped mounting screw holes. The screws vibrate loose after years of playing, and when the owner tightens them, the soft, mushy wood no longer holds the screw's thread. Second, the finish lifts away around the tuners at the rear of the headstock or on the face of the headstock around the shaft hole. Finally, splits occur in the headstock wood itself. The oil seeps under the tuner, down the shaft hole and into the wood's end grain. This eventually causes the wood to swell and sometimes split, or it may simply rot. Often these problems can be caught in time and aren't too serious. Before you attempt any repairs, the work area on the headstock needs a good cleaning and degreasing.

Begin by removing the strings and then the tuners themselves. The holes in the headstock —both the shaft holes and the mounting screw holes—are often swollen and mushy. You can remove much of the grease by packing the large shaft holes with Kleenex or cotton balls. Clean the screw holes with a pipe cleaner. The round, tightly packed cotton wadding used by dentists is an excellent absorber. Soak up as much oil as you can, and then clean the larger holes with some lighter fluid applied with a rag, cotton, or Q-Tip; use a fresh pipe cleaner for the mounting holes. The lighter fluid helps degrease the problem areas. If you're not in a hurry, leave the holes exposed for an overnight dryout. Clean the tuner housings with lighter fluid also, so they aren't reinstalled in their oily condition. When you've cleaned and degreased these, you can begin any necessary repairs.

The worn screw holes can be fixed quickly and easily with some baking soda and water-thin super glue. After you have cleaned and degreased the worn or stripped hole, fill the hole one-third full of baking soda, followed by a drop of super glue into the hole and onto the soda. The glue and soda harden immediately, usually with a puff of smoke. Don't inhale the fumes or let them get into your eyes! Fill the remaining two-thirds of the hole in the same manner, a third at a time, making sure that the glue saturates all the soda. When you've filled the hole flush to the surface, you can redrill it and know that the

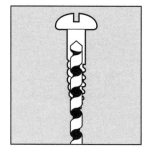

screw will hold.

It's important to use the proper size drill bit. It should match or be slightly larger than the screw's shaft, but it should not be as large as the outside measurement of the threads

themselves (left). Some screws have a shoulder that is larger than the thread. You may need two drill bits in this case—one for the shaft thread, and one for the shoulder if it extends down through the tuner housing and into the headstock. Take the screw to a hardware store and pick out the appropriate bits. Look for number bits as well as standard fractional bits; number bits are available in a much larger selection, graduated in finer increments. Numbered drill bits ranging from #51 (small) to #44 (larger) are commonly used for tuner screws. Hold the screw against a background light and compare the bit to the screw shaft. You want to see thread on both sides of the drill bit without being able to see the screw's shaft. If the screw has a shoulder, choose a second bit that is slightly larger, to allow for clearance.

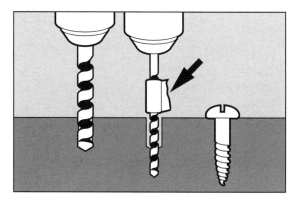

This super glue/baking soda technique works great on any stripped holes you are likely to come across, such as those for pickup mounting rings, truss rod cover plates, etc. When drilling a hole, wrap a piece of masking tape around the drill bit shaft as a depth guide as shown; this is to stop you from drilling too deep or even through the headstock.

To remedy the second common problem—finish that has lifted from the wood—let a small amount of lighter fluid seep under the finish where it has raised up. Allow it to evaporate and dry for at least several hours. Follow this with a drop of super glue. The glue will run under the finish as you touch the bottle's tip to the loose edge. Hot Stuff's thin, flexible applicator hose is perfect for this delicate work. Press the loose finish onto the wood, using any round, blunt object. If you wipe some wax onto this object, it will be less apt to stick to the finish or to any glue that squeezes out. Never use your finger! Don't use much super glue, and don't try to wipe off any excess.

When the glue has dried (usually in a minute or two) you can remove the bead that may have squeezed out at the edges by carefully chipping it off with a sharp, pointed tool; a needle or pin will do. You may be wise to practice first on yard sale specials or a piece of old furniture.

The final problem, splits in wood, should be dealt with by a qualified repairman. If you've noticed any serious separation of the wood at the headstock, get a pro's opinion. Regluing or filling a crack is usually inexpensive, and I advise you not to do this yourself.

To avoid these tuning-gear problems, use the proper lubricant. For the time when it is necessary to sparingly lubricate a stuck gear, use a powdered graphite or the new space-age lubricants such as Magik Guitar Lube, which have microscopic Teflon balls suspended in a solvent that evaporates quickly, leaving no oily film. A dab of Vaseline often works wonders. In most cases, the stuck tuner is an open-back, non-enclosed type. The gears are visible, so make sure that the parts aren't stripped or cross-threaded. If the gear looks worn or damaged, ask your local repairman for spare parts—most repair shops save boxes of old gears and can match parts easily.

Rotted plastic knobs

In the early 1990s I received a note from **George Gruhn**, warning of a problem that was just beginning to crop up: "We're now seeing an epidemic of deteriorating plastic tuner buttons, pickguards, and body binding on certain guitars built during the early '60s and before." So much for the notion that plastic is forever.

Some plastics used during that era are ticking time bombs with 30-year fuses. The parts most often affected are Kluson "Keystone" and white oval-type tuner buttons, pickguards on older Gibson archtops and mandolins, and the pickguards and body bindings on D'Angelicos, Strombergs Gretsches and some Epiphones. We are not seeing the same problems with Martin pickguards, for example, or on other instruments that apparently used different types of plastic.

The cause of plastic deterioration seems to be the long-term escape of the solvents and plasticizers used during the manufacturing process (without these, the plastic dries out and crumbles). At progressive stages of this deterioration, the escaping gasses cause fumes that can eat into finishes and wood, corrode surrounding or attached metal parts (turning them green), or exude a sticky, smelly mess that can ruin a clean case. Plastic deterioration may be accelerated by leaving an instrument in a case for long periods of time (not allowing the fumes to escape), by exposure to high heat, or by a combination of high heat and extreme humidity. Oddly enough, not every tuning-key knob on an affected instrument may turn bad.

Solutions for this problem range from complete replacement of the faulty part to repairing plastics that haven't completely disintegrated. **John Hedgecoth** has found that if the material is still all there for bindings and pickguards, super glues can be used to stabilize the plastic, which should then be sanded smooth and coated with lacquer to seal in the solvents. Bindings that are not too far gone can be masked off and sprayed with several coats of lacquer, since generally only the outer layer of binding deteriorates.

"At the time these instruments were made," Gruhn and Hedgecoth write, "there was no way that the manufacturers could have known that these problems would crop up in the future. With today's synthetics, who knows if we are going to face similar problems thirty years down the line."

Replacement of bindings would be major surgery, involving removal, replacement and refinishing. But replacing tuners with rotting knobs using exact retrofit look-alikes may just require small Phillips-head screwdriver! Here are two choices of exact, retrofit Kluson Deluxe-style tuners:

✔ Individual three-on-a-side Gotoh Vintage Kluson-style tuners with single-ring translucent Keystone knobs (as used on Les Pauls, SG's, ES-335s, etc.). These machines feature an improved 15:1 gear ratio and a nylon-bushed worm gear, and they have no name on the back of the housing. They're available from many guitar supply houses, such as **W.D. Music Products**, **Stewart-MacDonald**, **Elderly Instruments**, **ALLPARTS**, and **C.F. Martin's Guitarmaker's Connection**.

✔ ALLPARTS' Kluson Deluxe Replica 3x3 tuners have off-white plastic oval buttons, a 15:1 ratio, nylon bushings like the Gotoh, and "DELUXE" stamped on the back.

A third Kluson Deluxe-style individual replacement tuner is available from Schaller, but the grommet is not a retrofit (3/8" instead of 11/32"), and the Keystone buttons are too green for my tastes.

Making new tuners look old

You can make shiny new tuners look old and funky using "relic" techniques. My friend **Erick Coleman** did this in his shop, United Lutherie, which he operates with another pal, **Gene Imbody**. Their shop is a communal workplace for several local luthiers. Here's Erick:

"Dan, I started with a set of vintage-style tuners with the same shape and embossing as the originals. They'd fit right in on a cleaner guitar, but I wanted these to look old and nasty! The trick is something I saw online at the Les Paul Forum (*lespaulforum.org*), and what you need for the job is available at Radio Shack: etchant solution for printed circuit boards. This fluid contains ferric chloride, which eats into metal surfaces.

"Scuff-sanding is the first step. Before using the etchant, I scuff-sanded the tuners with 1800-grit Micro-

Mesh finishing pad to distress the plating a bit. I didn't go crazy with it, just enough to knock off a little shine and give the solution something to bite into. Then I'm ready for the etchant.

"The etchant is corrosive, so don't mess around: wear gloves and eye protection, and work in a well-ventilated place. It also works fast, so it's a good idea to test this on some scrap hardware first. You can control its working time by diluting it with water. I use 3 parts etchant to 1 part water. This does a nice job of dulling the tuner plating. A stronger mix will give a stronger effect, but it's easy to go too far. So I give it a light touch. I want it to look like something out of the '50s, not out of *Tales From The Crypt*.

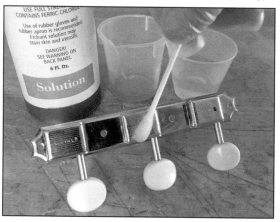

"I apply the etchant with a Qtip, and the process happens quickly — so be ready to move fast. Once I get the look I want, I give the tuners a good rinse in water to stop the etching. Most modern vintage-style tuners are packed with lubrication which will protect the gears. I simply dry these with a paper towel, then use a can of compressed air to blow out any water that might remain.

"The knobs still need to be aged. I've tried stains, tea,

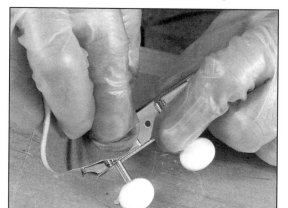

and coffee to yellow them, but didn't get the results I wanted until I tried good ol' brown Kiwi shoe polish. I rub it into the knobs with a soft cloth, let dry for 20 minutes, then take off the excess with a clean paper towel.

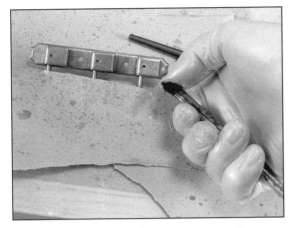

"As a final touch I tape off the tuner knobs and, with a toothbrush, spatter-paint the exposed metal with shellac mixed with a little ColorTone vintage amber stain. The shellac-speckling is icing on the cake; it gives 'em the genuine honkytonk look.

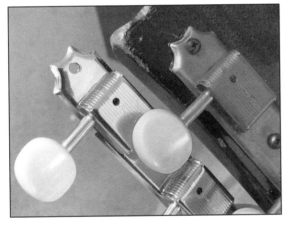

The result is subtle, yet convincing, and you can even see it in a black and white photo!"

What if you don't want new tuners? You can keep the tuners you have, and replace just the knobs, or sometimes you can even manage to repair the knobs and keep them. Keep in mind that often old tuners don't work well anymore—consider whether staying all-original is worth this much trouble.

The tuner knobs on this 1957 Les Paul Junior were rotting right off the posts. The old celluloid plastic is looking diseased, and the knobs are crumbling.

d.i.y.

Replacing rotted knobs Off with the old: a few gentle bites from my fret pullers crumbled the rotted plastic and they fell off the shaft easily.

Clean up the shafts With the dead plastic removed, the spear-shaped button shafts were green with corrosion — I use a cheap, stiff-bristled acid brush dipped in naphtha to clean and remove it. A wire wheel on a Dremel flex shaft is the perfect tool for getting down to bare metal in seconds.

d.i.y.

After cleaning the shafts, I heated them one at a time and pushed new plastic buttons on. For heat, I use a Weller 140/100 watt soldering gun, replacing the tip with two pieces of 3/32" dia. copper wire (the ground wire from a scrap of heavy-duty electrical cable). With the two wires placed against the tuner shaft, the circuit is complete, and the shaft gets hot fast. It takes 15-20 seconds to heat it enough to install the new knob. The buttons slide onto the heated shaft with ease — wear gloves, though! (You can also use this technique in reverse to remove buttons).

It's that easy! Plastic replacement knobs are available from at least two suppliers that I know of: ALLPARTS and Stewart-MacDonald.

Reconstructing rotted knobs

Sometimes you can repair crumbling plastic buttons. Here's how to do reconstructive surgery on Krumbling Klusons from the 1950s.

Crumbling and rotting knobs can often be stopped in their tracks with a bath of super glue. Remove the tuners from the guitar, but if the knobs are badly cracked and

As added insurance that the buttons will stay put, I run a drop of water-thin super glue into each button. Use a pipette to get a small drop of glue in the right spot.

crumbly, don't even detune them to remove the strings. Instead, clip the strings off (wear eye protection to do this), since the plastic knobs may crumble to pieces in your fingers.

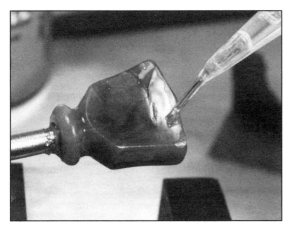

d.i.y.

Clean off all dirt, green corrosion and goo, with naptha (lighter fluid), and let the parts dry several hours or overnight. Dip the knob in water-thin super glue, immersing them just enough that the plastic is covered. Keep them there for several minutes, and be happy if you see air bubbles (the glue's getting into them). Remove and drip-dry, wiping away any big drop with a Q-Tip or pipe cleaner.

Once the super-glue has saturated all the cracks, further fill any other fissures with medium viscosity super glue. Let dry until hard.

This baking soda filler can be sculpted with files and sandpaper. Rejuvenated knobs can be given a final gloss-dipping of super glue, then wet-sanded and buffed.

For missing corners or chunks, build up layers of brown Fresco powder mixed with baking soda, saturating it with super glue as you go.

Some of these four tuners have new replacement knobs, stained to look old. The others are reconstructions of baking soda and super glue. All of them have a nice gloss to them, and look appropriately vintage for an early-50s guitar.

basic

The many Tune-O-Matics	83
TonePros and Pigtails	85
Steve Rowen on T-O-M hardware	87

d.i.y.

Slotting Gibson bridge saddles	91
Adjusting an ABR-1 bridge radius	92
Bridge posts and tailpiece studs	93
De-rusting metal bridge saddles	94

deep

Chapter 7

Electric bridges: non-tremolo

basic

Non-tremolo electric bridges are simple, durable, adjustable machines without a lot of voodoo—more like Henry Ford than Antonio Stradivari. The tricky stuff begins in the next chapter, when whammy bars are added.

Fender's approach to mass-producing a guitar bridge is metal stamping. Gibson chose diecast metals. Both are my favorite. The Gibson Tune-O-Matic design has triggered a minor industry of replacement parts with various kinds of modifications, and I've recently been researching these a bit. I'd like to use this basic section to take a little tour of your options if you play a T-O-M equipped guitar. (I'm not going to go all D.I.Y. on you, but there are a number of tweaks and tips sprinkled through this part, too.)

The many Tune-O-Matics

Gibson has offered five different Tune-O-Matic bridges since 1956, when their original ABR-1 was introduced. In addition to the original, there are: the Three Point, the Top Adjust, the Wide Schaller, and the Nashville. The Three Point and Top Adjust have been dropped for some time; the Schaller, Nashville and ABR-1 are still available, so those are the three we'll focus on here.

A wider bridge has more room for intonation

All three bridges adjust up or down, and have saddle inserts that adjust back and forth for intonation. Since the wider bridge offers more travel for the saddles, there's more latitude for setting accurate intonation when it comes to action height and string gauge. The Schaller is the widest, the Nashville in between and the ABR-1 is the narrowest. With the original ABR-1, if the bridge isn't mounted in just the right spot (as is sometimes the case), getting the correct intonation is difficult. The other two bridges offer more string length adjustment, so one way of correcting poor intonation is to mount a wider bridge in the same mounting holes used by the ABR-1. Another method is to first plug the ABR-1 stud holes, and then relocate and redrill the stud holes without switching bridge styles. Note: If you own a valuable vintage piece, think twice about doing this!

One of the most solid of all the bridge mounts, the Schaller was introduced in '72 as a stock item on SGs, and then on Marauders, L5- and L6-S models and other Gibsons. Its height-adjusting studs screw into heavy steel anchor bushings that are pressed tightly into the top. Older Schaller bridges can suffer from flaked plating and metal deterioration caused by sweat, and it's often necessary to replace the pitted bridge saddles and sometimes the entire assembly. The saddles appear to be permanently locked in by a machine screw with a slot-head on each end, but they aren't—one of the slotted ends is a threaded cap superglued in place; heat will break the glue-joint. Since you won't know which end is glued (it's usually on the backside, away from the headstock, but the one in the photo was the opposite), heat both bolt ends (one at a time) with a hot soldering iron and then try unscrewing the cap. **You must have two small screwdrivers** with tips that fit the screw slots perfectly; loose screwdrivers will mangle the slots, so you must file, sand or grind both screwdriver tips until they fit.

Replacement saddles for the Schaller come in a set numbered from 1 through 6—be sure to install them in the right order! Because its large size, looks, weight,

and material, I wouldn't choose the Schaller bridge for a guitar I was making; I prefer the ABR-1 style.

The Nashville bridge is the "new, improved" version of the ABR-1. It looks somewhat similar, but it has more travel since it's wider by 7/64", and it doesn't need a retainer spring to hold the saddles into the bridge body. (Neither the Nashville nor the Schaller require the thin wire retainer spring that the ABR-1 uses to keep the saddles from popping out; some players see this as a plus.) It mounts on threaded flanged inserts that are pressed into the body, although the inserts aren't the same as the heavier Schaller anchor bushings. If your guitar is equipped with the Nashville bridge, you may find that the body anchors pull out too easily; in some cases, they want to fall out! I prefer a tighter fit than this for good tone transmission. You can carefully line the hole in the body with epoxy, white glue or super glue, let it dry, and then refit the bushing. This tiny increase in the walls of the hole usually makes for a tight fit. If it becomes too tight, you need to scrape the walls slightly to remove excess glue. Working with glue—especially super glue—around a finish can have disastrous results, so be careful. A safer way to firm the bushing is to omit the glue, and instead wrap the bushing with Teflon plumbing tape before pressing it in; or increase the bushing's outside diameter by coating it with glue (instead of lining the hole with glue).

Here's a neat trick for Nashville bridge anchors, from my friend **Bob Pettingill** of Carrollton, Georgia. Besides being a top-notch guitarist, Bob's a machinist by trade. He put a short length of 10-32 threaded rod on a lathe and reduced the end of it down to .136" in diameter. He then threaded that section with a 6-32 die. Next, by measuring to the bottom of the anchor bushing hole

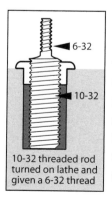

6-32

10-32

10-32 threaded rod turned on lathe and given a 6-32 thread

in the Les Paul body and carefully trimming the length of his new part, he got the new bridge stud to bottom out on the wood at the hole's bottom, while leaving the new 6-32 threads above the body surface. Now he can raise or lower his bridge with standard ABR-1 thumbwheels used on the turned-down 6-32 thread section. Going through the anchor bushings and down to the wood, the custom studs are very rigid, appreciably improving the tone and sustain!

Unlike most imported copies, all three Gibson bridges are available with saddles that aren't pre-notched. Be sure to **specify that you want them this way**. The replacement saddles have no notches, either. This allows you to individually notch the strings into the saddles for custom string placement. The imported ones—even Gotoh, which I like—come pre-notched, and this is less desirable. The saddles on this Tune-O-Matic have been

"deluxed" by me (smoothly rounded with good string exposure).

To say that the Nashville bridge is new and improved implies that something is wrong with the ABR-1, which isn't necessarily the case. In fact, when properly located for intonation, **I prefer the ABR-1**, because it's the bridge I grew up with, it looks "right" and it has a certain tone. To some, a major drawback of this original Tune-O-Matic is its nar-

rower string travel, and it does have a few quirks of its own. The ABR-1 retainer spring, which holds the saddle inserts into the bridge body, has a tendency to spring upward and buzz against the strings. You can correct this by pressing or "kinking" the spring downward in between the slotted screw heads with a small screwdriver tip.

Not all retainer springs cause problems, though, especially on vintage instruments. The old ABR-1s were built to more exacting tolerances, and the originals didn't need the retainer because the hardware fit so well. With the Nashville and Gotoh bridges, you will find some variation of a snap ring or spring clip holding the insert into the bridge body; these must be carefully pried loose before you can remove the bridge screw and saddle insert. This is actually a tricky job, and you need to apply downward pressure to both lips of the snap ring at once, pushing with two pieces of blunt steel. Be careful, since every slip can chip plating from the bridge parts.

Two manufacturers of bridge hardware actually do have substantially new and improved versions of the ABR-1 bridge design: TonePros, and Pigtail.

TonePros' specialty is locking hardware that not only increases sustain because of tight coupling, but locks in your intonation nicely. Their AVR-II (Advanced Vintage Replacement II) is a locking Tune-O-Matic style bridge that retrofits guitars manufactured with Gibson's original ABR-1, and many other brands (recently, the AVR-II has become stock hardware on many models of the Les Paul and SG directly from the Gibson factory). It has patented setscrews on each end of the bridge body that, when tightened against the threaded posts the bridge mounts on, make for great coupling. Also, intonation issues caused by a sloppy fit and movement are eliminated, because the AVR-II has a tighter saddle assembly than some other hardware (the saddles are brass). It also offers a little more saddle travel than the competition due to the size of the saddle pocket in the bridge body (a little bit goes a long way with regard to intonation).

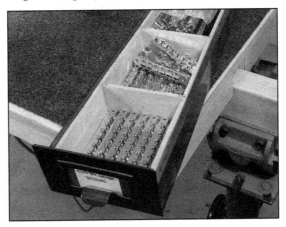

TonePros saddles are locked in and can't fall out, but a retainer spring is still used for looks only. I go through a lot of AVR-IIs with happy customers (that's my drawer full of 'em above), and it's my choice for an upgrade and setup using a reasonably priced T.O.M. bridge (It would be my choice if it didn't have the locking feature, too because of its build quality). TonePros offers the bridge without pre-cut string notches in the saddles, and that's the way I like them.

TonePros also offers a locking tailpiece—setscrews fasten against the tailpiece studs. And, if that isn't enough coupling for you, try their Locking Tailpiece Studs. The slotted heads of these studs are removable, threaded capstans; with these you can lock down on traditional stop-bar tailpieces and tailpiece/bridge combinations. In this photo, the slotted head is removed.

Last, not least, is TonePros' locking wraparound bridge—an intonateable replacement for vintage Les Paul Juniors, Specials, TV models, SGs, and the like, and another reason that TonePros has become a household word in guitar families.

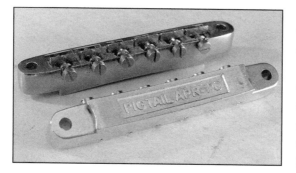

Pigtail's APR-1 (A Pigtail Reproduction #1) is an extremely high quality, especially toneful piece of hardware like no others. At $200, it's expensive—but you get what you pay for, and then some. It's the best example of a vintage-style ABR-1 that I've seen. Like the originals, the Pigtail doesn't have a retainer spring, and doesn't need one because the machining is so good; the saddles fit so well that you need to leverage them out of their pockets in order to replace them.

Pigtail has a version of an intonatable Wraparound too, made with the same aluminum casting method used on their APR-1. Similar to the TonePros unit, it's lighter. Made

of lightweight aluminum with plated brass screws and averaging 41 grams in weight, it weighs a third to a half as much as its competition.

Pigtail also makes the most authentic looking, lightweight cast aluminum stop-bar tailpieces and studs I've seen, and steel body anchors like the originals. Pigtail's complete back-end kit, when retrofitted onto new guitars, essentially equips the instrument with the finest new old stock components one could find (if only they were still available).

Pigtail owner/operator **Steve Rowen** is my go-to guy when it comes to knowing about vintage guitars and their hardware (plus he's a pro guitarist). After years in the trenches of the tool and die industry, he turned his talents to the things he loves: guitars. He designs guitar hardware, then does the machining and plating. He's an old-school craftsman, expert in all areas of metalurgy, diemaking, tooling, machining, and CNC work. For me, meeting Steve was like a bodybuilder meeting the Incredible Hulk—he's that strong in his field. Steve can describe well, and give reasons for, the tonal responses of the good vintage guitars. He's also a walking guitar history book.

Get yourself a cup of coffee and sit down with this detailed information from Steve Rowen. You'll know the inside story (literally) of this hardware we've all been taking for granted since we played our first C chord. Here's Steve:

"You gotta love what you're going to be a manufacturer of, I can tell you that" says Rowen. "The reason you like my stuff so much, Dan," he continues, "is because you appreciate the work that goes into the details.

"I have two versions of the APR-I. One is super-light-weight hi-tensile aluminum, with saddles machined from aircraft-grade aluminum. The other is vintage to the bone: a zinc bridge with yellow brass machined saddles, made from vintage-correct materials with vintage-correct methods that most guys don't have experience with anymore.

"The tolerances are tight, and the bridges are hand assembled and inspected by me, so I can substantially increase the contact area of the mechanical interfaces of the screw, saddle and body—making it more efficient than mass-produced hardware, which might have only a few sharp edges of contact. I've put the vintage style on late '50s–early '60s Gibsons; without fail, the owners tell me they get a good tone bump.

"I use the term "stored energy" to describe the makeup of an aluminum diecasting such as what I use for my tailpieces. When the mold cavity is filled, the outside wall takes a set to shape first, because the mold is quite a bit cooler than the molten metal flowing into the mold. This means the material in the center of the part is still in motion, and in an expanded state, since heat causes things to expand (whereas the outside wall has already begun to contract). The end result is when the inside solidifies, it's stuck inside this pre-formed shape, and wants to get even smaller, but it's difficult due to the fact that the crystaline structure wants to pull together with a strong magnetic-type attraction. That's why atomic weapons are so powerful, as they release that type of bond (it's not exactly the same thing, but you get the idea). Simply put, the inside of the walls of the part want to be smaller than the outside of the part, creating a metallurgical tug-of-war. That creates the stress and stored energy that makes the part kind of like a spring, or like tight guitar or piano strings. The results are a bridge that allows a maximum of string energy to pass through to the guitar body, with excellent harmonics and a great woody tone.

"Casting in light alloys is fraught with porosity issues that lead to plating problems. A way around these manufacturing issues is to use thick plating like you find on most modern guitar hardware. I chose not to sidestep the problem. I met it head-on: my plating is super-thin and lightweight. Plenty of times, plating issues are so much hassle that I feel like giving up—since heavy plating simply isn't my style!"

Wraparound style bridges "The use of the 50's casting for the wraparound bridge ended around 1962, but it was used as a stopbar until 1965. As we all started wanting to play the old guitars in the late '60s/early '70s, the wraparounds were getting tired, and would begin to generate unwanted "sitar" sounds. Using a later stopbar, like on a '69 Goldtop, wasn't too successful because there was no clearly defined string break on those units. The radiused top surface was too ambiguous, and it aggravated intonation problems.

"Enter the Leo Quan Badass bridge—a good idea, but with only a reasonable execution. In those days, making a molded product in an ergonomically abstract geometrical shape required much skill and effort. Probably for that reason, the Badass appears like something you could make on a Bridgeport milling machine. The Badass was also compromised by being made from diecast zinc as opposed to an aluminum, magnesium or light zinc alloy. This is because the zinc diecast machines that became mainstream in the '50s would run without an operator, but the light alloy machines need an operator to ladle each shot from a crucible located next to the machines. This made zinc parts cheaper, and even though casting cost was a small portion of the end cost of the products, economics won out over tonal considerations.

"The Tonepros is a good wraparound, and is definitely an improvement over the Badass in appearance and range of adjustment, but it's heavy. Zinc diecast tends to be sort of like hardened lead, while the aluminum alloys are essentially inert, and they store a great deal of energy."

"The intonatable bridge was needed, because, when you measure the distance from the nut to the center of the stud on an old LP Jr. or similar instrument, the length

basic

varies quite a bit. For instance, on the treble side it seems to run from about 24-5/16" to about 24-7/16". This means that the studs can be forward (toward the neck) or backward 1/16" to either side of true center (thus the theoretical center is moving around about 1/8"). Players needed a replacement bridge that's more adjustable—enough to work on a variety of instruments.

"Factor in the neck set issues in Gibson-style instruments, and how that relates to the bridge height. There was a need for a bridge with a significantly lower profile for under-set necks requiring the bridge to be closer to the guitar body. A vintage bridge is .490"–.500" from the bottom to the top, and the Tonepros bridge is .580". The Pigtail intonatable is .510" from bottom to top, but since its mounting ears are offset .040" upward, the Pigtail bridge will go an additional .020" lower than the lowest vintage bridge. To a machinist, and a good guitar tech, .020" is a lot!"

Pigtail wraparound "Early in 2000 I began working on an improved wraparound to market through Tonepros. The idea was to put a Tune-O-Matic in a vintage wraparound body, while taking into consideration the additional instruments using a vintage-style layout like Hamer and PRS. On the Tonepros bridge, I had a few vintage instruments to measure for design considerations, along with a PRS single-cut. Tonepros had tooling made and produced a good wraparound, but being diecast in zinc, it's a bit heavy as a result. When differences arose between Tonepros and myself, I decided to produce my own wraparound—cast in aluminum like my bridge and stop-tail. I decided in favor of tone over economics.

"When I made the initial production run of the Pigtail intonatable, Tom Anderson was developing the Atom guitar model. After building the initial prototypes of that instrument, Tom asked me to make some changes that we both agreed would substantially improve the product. The end result is wraparound that I feel is several generations improved over what I envisioned initially. It's made of material quite similar to the vintage wraparounds on '50s Gibsons, and only weighs about 8-10 grams more than a vintage tailpiece!

"The redesign issues are important, and there are two: 1) I was able to incorporate string tunnels that make re-stringing effortless, when compared to others, since the tunnel eliminates the need for getting the string to line up with the back hole (not a huge problem on the bench, but if you're trying to change a broken string right during a set, you know the hassle that I've eliminated; 2) I was able to lower the profile of the overall height of the bridge in excess of 1/8"—meaning it will work on any wraparound instrument built from mid-1953 forward—even mid-'50s Gibsons with the low neck set issues. TonePros and others aren't low enough for these guitars.

"As far as tone goes, with a number of instruments the heavier, greater-mass hardware seems to work better with particular random necks and bodies, as well as with certain types of wood or combinations of wood. In my experience, it's canceling undesirable anomolies that occur with those combinations, rather than adding to the instrument. It, in effect, is acting as a sink for the undesirables. For that reason, I am now doing small runs of my wraparound in zinc, with machined yellow brass saddles just like vintage ABR-1s. I think with guitars, there are things that work well in general, but there are always exceptions and anomalies. My design philosophy is to provide the player or luthier with components that allow them to push the instrument wherever they need to in the tonal envelope.

"Dan, earlier you used the word 'jingly' to describe the sound you get from my diecast aluminum stuff. Has it occurred to you that hardware coupling may act as a tone sink—sucking away the good stuff? That jingly stuff? Metal can absorb a lot of energy in a hurry—especially brass, which is what most studs and anchors are made of. My studs and anchors are steel, like the old ones were, not brass as we see today, and I also heat-treat the studs for further improvement.

"Who's to say that locking-down heavy hardware to the body—improving a certain mechanical coupling—gives a better tone? You can't say that. It's a different tone; and non-locked, lightweight parts have their different tone. Some players love a dense, heavy Les Paul for its dark tone and great sustain, and another player swears by a super lightweight for its vibrant response and jingly qualities.

"People sometimes forget that real vintage Gibsons are more jangly than their modern counterparts. Another thing: real good PAFs are most often 7K or slightly more, not the over-wound stuff that seems to be omnipresent. My customers who are real serious studio guys in Nashville or LA love the aluminum APR-1 because it gives them a bigger tonal envelope: not only bright and jangly, but by rolling back the tone control, thick as well. I find that, for the most part, pro players are the only ones that use their tone and volume controls effectively. The average hobbyist turns his or her guitar controls all the way up, sets the amp to a pleasing setting and stomps on a pedal.

"If a '59 sunburst Les Paul Standard, or an early dot-neck ES-335 is the benchmark that all Tune-O-Matic-style guitars are measured by, and most would agree they are, then well-constructed, low mass hardware that floats is the most likely to get that great vintage sound. Violin-type instruments have been made for something around 2000 years. In that vast time period, instrument makers have tried all sorts of things to improve the acoustic performance of stringed instruments. One thing has been constant for hundreds of years: floating, low-mass hardware with a good footprint (a hardwood bridge and tailpiece, in the case of a violin or cello); and although an acoustic instrument when compared with a solidbody electric guitar might not seem like apples and apples to you, I find it works about the same, with a little less efficiency being the main difference.

Remember your first car "I often remind others when asked about this to remember their first car. I remember driving an old Ford pickup over washboard gravel roads—the floating of the loose suspension, along with loose balljoints and steering knuckles, would

nearly jerk the wheel out of your hands. Think of that oscillating string as the wheel on the washboard bumps, and your hands as the connection to the body of the guitar though the floating hardware. The diecast hardware acts like a tuning fork with many levels of various overtones, and you get an amplifier of sorts. Now picture driving down that same washboard road in your father's new Thunderbird; you know the bumps are there, but you feel little direct contact with that topsy-turvy washboard surface. That's kind of what happens when you lock things down and snub them up.

"Here's and interesting little anecdote about Thomas Edison. As I've already explained a little about stress and stored energy, the issues with stress come up in other cast products like engine blocks and transmission housings. This stress also tends to have a harmonic focal point located geographically on the cast part. It has a lot to do with things like where the gate for the molten metal flows in, and the overflow area (also known as risers) of the cope and drag (names of the top and bottom halves of a sand-cast mold). Anyway, back in the late 1800s when engines, turbines etc. were being developed, someone (maybe Edison) figured out that if you could locate that focal point and drill a hole through it, and plug it, it would stop a good portion of the harmonic issues that would cause failures of anything, from bearings to mounting issues of the unit itself. As the story goes, one of the firms that began building power generating sets in the early days of commercially available electricity had these kind of issues with the generator set that they built. At that time, Edison had a more insightful understanding of harmonic issues than others. So they hired Edison to find a fix.

"They put him in a closed room with the unit operating, and he stayed there for a week listening to the unit through a wood dowel held up to his ear (and whatever other means he had to isolate the problem). He stayed there while food was brought to him and so forth. Eventually, he took a piece of chalk out of his pocket and made a mark. The appropriate individuals were then summoned, and he told them to drill a hole at that location. Upon doing so, the harmonic issues were resolved, and he invoiced them for $10,000. Upon receiving the invoice, the accountants for the firm wanted a breakdown of what he did for the $10,000. The end result was that

Edison revised the invoice to say, $.04 for chalk, $9,999.96 for knowing where to make the mark.

"When I discuss physics and mechanics with the builders and players that use my parts, they're mostly building a caricature of a LP, Strat or Tele. They do what they like, mostly based on some vintage legacy of materials and components, or ergonomic concerns. Most, even if they have some higher education in scientific principles, don't really tend to apply them to the end result they want. My stock in trade is knowing where to make the mark with the chalk. In marketing myself, and my products, I try to give enough information to establish that I know where to make the chalk mark. Then, if I can get folks to be a little more analytical, that's good.

Footprint = significant contact "Another thing is the footprint that you asked about, Dan. On a Tune-O-Matic style guitar, the footprint is in the posts and thumbwheels under the bridge, and the studs and bushings (anchors), but the bulk of the footprint is in the studs and anchors that mount the stopbar. Threads are for the most part, a 60° male shape that meets a 60° female shape in a helical inclined plane. If the two 60° forms are created as accurately as possible, and there's minimal clearance between them, then you'll have maximum contact area between the two parts.

"On the other hand, if you have poor geometry and excessive clearance between the two mating surfaces, you get contact through a few sharp edges. That's a small footprint. I fit my studs to the anchors as tightly as possible to increase surface area. With other hardware I see, the threads can be sloppy at best; when you lock down ill-fitting hardware, you create a U-shaped beam vs: a straight one, you've simply just fastened your hardware on, and little more. It will tighten in the anchor if you screw one side in far enough to take up the clearance, but still the surface area is a few sharp edges. The most popular way of plating today tends to collect material on sharp edges further aggravating the surface area or footprint problem.

"The way that something responds to bending and springing back is called the modulus of elasticity. For example, a 2-1/2" toothpick has a better modulus of elasticity than a 2-1/2" long piece of spaghetti. The reason that I go to the extra effort to make steel studs and heat treat

them is that steel has a better or more efficient modulus of elasticity than brass. Being cantilevered out of the body of the guitar (the studs have leverage sticking out of the body), the steel stud reduces losses, and transfers the string energy to the guitar body more efficiently. It's a leverage thing—think of trying to pry something up with a piece of lath vs. a 2x4 . That's how steel studs vs brass studs are! The modulus of elasticity is a key factor with the studs and bridge posts.

Brass is cheaper "The anchors that the posts fit in are the final part of the equation.The anchors that are zinc colored just have a thin coat of zinc over steel or brass, they are not made of zinc. From my point of view, the biggest problems with much of today's hardware is that manufacturers don't seem to know much about the materials they're making stuff from. For example, we see brass studs used with brass anchors a lot, or brass, studs with steel anchors. Why the brass, if it's a tone-sinking material? Again, it's a matter of economics; brass is a great deal more free-machining, induces less tool wear, and you can run a significantly faster machine cycle, and thus cheaper parts costs.

"Gibson uses steel anchors for the most part, but I suspect that they occasionally buy anchors from outside suppliers, as some customers with Gibsons have mentioned that their anchors have no magnetic qualities. I have some of those anchors, and they are zinc plated brass. They look the same as the zinc plated steel. As far as stress affecting the tone goes, there is some residual stress in round bar stock, but it's nothing like a diecasting has, so the stress and related harmonics don't come to bear here. The hardness of steel over brass seems to be the factor regarding anchors. Think of a mattress compared to a steel plate. Hold up a mattress and let someone hit it with a hammer and you'll hardly feel it on the other side. On the other hand, hold up a steel plate of appropriate size, and you'll feel the force of every blow, minus the force absorbed by the mass of the plate itself.

"All and all, I love a responsive, traditional-style instrument. I like to use a guitar and amp that fit the room, and that's what I mostly try to use when I do gigs. It's the best way for all these little nuance type things to come out, but if I have to use an overdrive like a Tubescreamer, because the amp's too loud for the room to get it's own overdrive, I turn it on, and leave it on. Then I turn the amp up to where I play solos, and set the gain so that I can back the guitar volume down to 6, and have a really clean sound. I can turn up to 8 to solo; and I make sure there's more drive and volume on tap if I need it to cut through the mix. Hobbyists assume, through the recordings that they hear, that the players were using more overdrive than they actually did. A great pick attack coupled with a good vibrato and a tasty choice of licks is the real ticket.

"And the last element, that gets passed over and I don't know why, is what type of music you're playing. If it's traditional blues, country, jazz or rock, you want a nice woody sound; if on the other hand, your playing style is

gained-out, you may want your electronics to control your tone more than the chunk of wood you're holding, In that case, hi-mass locked down hardware may be the ticket for you."
–Steve Rowen

Thanks for sharing your knowledge, Steve. I find all this super interesting. You've demystified what it is about the vintage hardware that we love so well, and have made me remember some great vintage Les Pauls and semi-hollowbodies that I let go and always remembered ('59 not-neck, '61 ES-345). Right now, those crystaline lattices are tugging away inside aluminum APR-1 on my '02 R9 Les Paul!

A wailin' pound o'sound? A digital scale tells what these various Clone-O-Matic bridge items weigh:

Wraparound bridges (intonatable)

Badass:	101.5 grams	(3.5 oz.)
Imported:	118 grams	(4.1 oz.)
TonePros:	95.5 grams	(3.3 oz.)
Pigtail:	42 grams	(1.4 oz.)
Hipshot Baby Grand:	51.5 grams	(1.8 oz.)

ABR-1-style

Gibson ABR-1:	49–54 grams	(1.7–1.9 oz.)
TonePros AVR-II:	50.5 grams	(1.8 oz.)
Pigtail APR-1:	27 grams	(0.9 oz.)
Gotoh:	58 grams	(2 oz.)
Imported:	44 grams	(1.5 oz.)
Schaller:	53.5 grams	(1.8 oz.)

d.i.y.

Slotting Gibson bridge saddles

Replacing worn saddles in a Tune-O-Matic bridge is pretty simple: the little screws holding them pry up and out easily in most cases. This was not so in the old days: I remember T-O-Ms that fit so tightly they were scary to try remove the first couple of times. Pigtail's APR-1 fits like those old Gibsons, and even tighter. Steve Rowen's

recommendation: "Get a little block of wood or metal that, with the bridge sitting on your table or workbench, is a bit too tall to slide under the heads of the screws. Lift up the bridge, rest a screw on the block, and push down on the bridge body. The screw and saddle will lift right out."

If you follow my advice when putting new saddles in, you'll be buying saddles without notches, and will need to create your own string notches. This is a skill that requires practice, and the right file(s). You might be able to get by with a single tiny needle file, but if you can, I recommend that you get a minimum of three gauged nut slotting files. Stewart-MacDonald offers them in 16 sizes ranging from .010" to .105" to handle both guitars and basses. The three I'd choose are .013", .024" and .042" (.013" for the treble E-B-G strings, .024" the D-A strings and .042" for the low E string. Slotting files have rounded cutting edges, so they create round-bottomed string slots, and you can cut a slot larger than the file's width by filing sideways to widen the slot.

I use nut slotting files even though metal saddles are tougher on the tools than bone or plastic nut material. My favorite tool for this is a diamond nut file. On a visit to Gibson Nashville, I noticed the production line setup folks notched bridge saddles by moving the strings around until the spacing was right, and then giving each string a sharp tap with a plastic hammer. Because the saddles are relatively soft metal, each string creates its own groove (the wound strings leave the imprint of the string winds in the notch). I don't know if this is the only way they do it, but it was the only way I saw them doing it. I don't think the strings are changed before

d.i.y.

shipping, which explains why I've seen a number of new Gibson electrics with crunched strings where they meet the saddle peaks.

On a Strat, the strings rise up and over the saddles at a steep angle, holding the string down tightly—so Strat saddles don't need to be notched like Gibsons. Tune-O-Matics need notches because, having a separate tailpiece, the string angle to the saddle is not steep, keep a string from moving side-to-side. Notch the saddles just deep enough to keep the string from shifting sideways as you pick—never be more than half of the string's diameter.

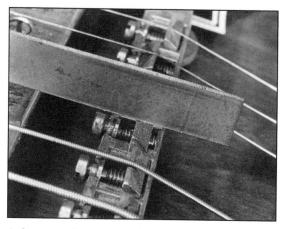

1 Start a small notch with your slotting file or razor saw.

2 Use different file sizes for the different strings.

3 "Ramp" the string slot, giving a slight taper toward the front of the saddle; don't just cut any old "notch"—shape it nicely.

4 Polish all edges with 2000-grit sandpaper wrapped around a file that's several sizes smaller than the string slot.

Adjusting an ABR-1 bridge radius

Adjusting the bridge saddle radius on a Strat or Tele-style guitar is a cinch because each saddle is height-adjustable. That's not true with the ABR-1, which has a radius machined into the bridge body by means of stepped saddle channels or "pads" (the area that the underside of the saddles rest on).

Gibson fretboards were intended to have a 12" radius, but they can end up with an actual radius of anywhere from 9" to 14" (I find 10" is quite common). This is due to the gluing, shaping, sanding, inlaying, grinding and other production operations that introduce stress or fatigue in a neck, and cause tolerances to be less than perfect. Any mismatch between the fretboard and the bridge saddles must be corrected when the string notches are filed into the saddles as described below. I've always thought that the ABR-1 saddle radius was 12", but the following information from Steve Rowen was a revelation to me:

"Something I found with the ABR-1 is that the saddles really aren't on a 12" radius. Of the many vintage bridges that I've inspected—on a granite surface plate with a digital height gage—is that the two E saddles are on a 16" radius from the theoretical center of the neck and bridge, and the A and B strings are on a 14" radius from that same theoretical center. For the most part, everyone copies the original ABR in the aftermarket, and that's one big reason why, along with the fretboards being mostly less than a 12" radius, you have to go through so much aggravation getting the string radius to match the fretboard. I'd bet that the original draftsman read his slide rule wrong when trigging-out the pad heights on the bridge. In the end the pads don't follow a radius, but make a kind of mustache—sort of like the Gibson peghead shape.

"So, to achieve the correct bridge saddle radius to match a given fretboard, you lower the strings by deepening the notches in the saddle until they match an understring radius gauge. When the notches get too deep, remove material from the top of the saddles to expose the strings for a clear sound. Because of this, and at your urging, Dan, I now make three sets of saddles that produce a true radius of 9", 10" and 12"—these can also be mixed and matched to produce subtle differences by a knowledgeable technician. They're available in vintage yellow brass, or heat-treated aircraft aluminum."

Traditionally, the ABR-1 came with the treble bridge saddles facing forward and the bass saddles facing back for the best intonation. I think that was because they used heavier strings and flatwounds back then. However, it's more difficult to shape the saddle peak that faces the rear because of its sharp edge, and I've found that when installing new saddles, I can turn them around on the bass side (sharp edge to the front) and notch them like the others. I still get good intonation, provided the bridge has been well placed.

Bridge posts and tailpiece studs

Some owners of vintage Gibsons equipped with the ABR-1 may notice a buzzing problem or strange action caused by a collapsed bridge—one that's sinking down, becoming concave and allowing the saddle radius to flatten. The problem is caused by metal fatigue under pressure—especially if the tailpiece is cranked down to the body—and also by a player pressing his hand heavily on the bridge while picking. Sometimes you can flatten out the warp as shown in these before/after shots, but

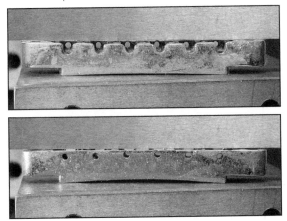

sometimes you can't. I don't recommend trying it yourself because you're very likely to break the bridge. An experienced repair shop or machine shop familiar with the metals and stresses involved can often manage it. With the bridge supported on each end, an arbor press or C-clamp can be used in the middle to gently press until the warp straightens out. (Or until you hear a cracking sound!) It's necessary to press the casting past the original point of flatness so it springs back to true flat—a tricky task. On a valuable vintage guitar I recom-

mend that you set the bridge aside for posterity, and get a replacement.

On older instruments, especially those that were played hard, the studs that support the ABR-1 bridge have a tendency to loosen, bend and lean forward. Here are some ways to fix worn stud holes, made possible because the ABR-1 mounting hole spacing is so close to that of the Schaller, Nashville and Gotoh replacement bridges—they're generally interchangeable. The hole-to-hole stud centers for the various bridge bodies are ABR-1, 2.891"; Nashville, 2.926"; wide Schaller, 2.891"; Gotoh ABR-1 copy, 2.891"; and Gotoh Nashville copy, 2.904". There are exceptions to every rule, so double check all measurements before making changes. You might have a little trouble getting the Nashville (2.926") and the ABR-1 (2.891") to interchange; it depends on the situation. If you're doing any drilling, tapping or parts-switching, do a mockup installation on scrap wood to be sure everything fits before digging into your guitar.

Fixes for wobbly bridge posts

Harden the threads with glue If the bridge is just a little wobbly, remove the threaded posts and coat the walls of their holes with super glue, epoxy or white glue. This decreases the hole size and hardens the threads cut into the wood by the post. Next "chase the threads" by follow them lightly with a 6-32 metal tap to recut them. Coat the new threads with super glue to harden them, then chase the threads one more time with the tap, and you should have tight-fitting posts.

You can also chase the threads with the bridge post itself, rather than buying a tap. I do this by holding the

post with a bridge post tool, which has interchangeable threaded brass inserts (6-32 thread for Gibson, and M4 x.75 thread for imports). Tighten the tool against the post's thumbwheel and hold the two together to turn the post in the threads.

Set the post deeper My favorite fix, which I've used often, is to make a longer post and set it deeper into the guitar body. I buy a 6-32 brass, flat-head machine screw

about 1-1/2" long and cut off the head, leaving a post about 1-1/4" long. After rounding and smoothing the cut end, I deepen the post hole and install the longer replacement. Steve Rowen now makes and sells longer posts like this (1-5/16" long, machined and plated like the real deal).

Use a dowel plug You can drill out the worn hole to enlarge it, fill it with a hardwood dowel, drill a fresh hole and install a new stud. Use a 6-32 tap or the post itself to cut threads in the wood. This drill-and-plug method is quite noticeable if you use a large dowel, unless you can do a very artful finish touchup.

Use a Nashville post You can stay with the original design by switching to the Nashville mounting studs (without the anchor bushing inserts that come with the Nashville). These posts have a larger thread (10-32) than the ABR-1 (6-32), so you can simply resize the sloppy original hole with a #21 drill bit, then rethread it with a 10-32 tap. This way you don't use a dowel plug, but your ABR-1 won't fit on the Nashville bridge post: you'll need to find someone with a metalworking lathe to downsize top part of the Nashville stud to fit the ABR-1 holes. The thumbwheel part of the Nashville stud may need to be reduced a little, too.

Use a Nashville bridge You can switch not only to the Nashville bridge posts (above), but use the Nashville bridge as well. I suggest that you don't use the Nashville anchor bushings—mount the new studs directly into the top wood with the appropriate drill and tap.

To get into these drilling, tapping, pressing and fitting modifications, you may want to buy a full drill selection with fractional, number and letter bits, as well as a good assortment of standard and metric taps and dies. You can instead buy bits and taps one at a time, as you need them. You'll need a pair of dial calipers, too—the inexpensive plastic kind will do fine. Ask your local hardware store for a drill bit set that lists the decimal sizes for drills and taps. If you choose to install the Nashville post anchor bushings in your guitar (rather than installing the post straight into the wood), note that a J-bit fits tight, while a 9/32" gives a nice press fit. For the wide Schaller anchor bushing, the 7/16" is a finger-press fit, while 27/64" is a pretty tight machine-press fit.

Fix for wobbly tailpiece studs

Here's a easy modification with results you can hear: get better hardware coupling at the tailpiece by giving the tailpiece studs something solid to tighten down against—filling the pocket of dead air under the studs with a short Allen setscrew.

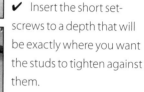

✔ Determine the perfect height for the tailpiece studs and record the measurements.

✔ Insert the short setscrews to a depth that will be exactly where you want the studs to tighten against them.

✔ With studs tightened down on the threaded inserts inside the threaded anchor bushings, the result is strong coupling. You won't see these studs lean or wobble! It's an easy mod with dynamic results.

Cleaning and de-rusting bridge saddles

At one time or another, most of us run into adjustable bridge saddles that no longer adjust becuase they're rusting, dirty and corroded. After years of sweat, wear and corrosion, some bridge parts may be beyond repair. But many bridges, saddles, screws and springs are junked unnecessarily when with a little care they could be made to work. Here's advice on breaking rust joints, removing caked dirt, and cleaning, degreasing and lubricating metal bridge parts in general. I'll use the Fender bridge as my example, since it is both height and length-adjustable, and has more parts to clean. But all electric guitars, from Gibson to Ibanez, are prey to the dreaded crud monster. These techniques for cleaning, rust-breaking and lubrication work on all metal electric parts (not just bridges), and won't harm a vintage piece when used with care.

Electric bridge saddles have two likely rust problem spots: the height-adjusting screws and the length-travel screws that set intonation. The bridge body itself, a stamped or diecast housing that holds the saddles, needs to be cleaned, too. This is much easier to do when you can remove the parts first.

Whenever possible, remove the bridge from the guitar (a Telecaster bridge holds a pickup, so you may want to clean Tele bridges in place to avoid having to remove the pickup first). Before trying to disassemble any parts, clean them with naphtha (lighter fluid). Pour some into a jar and apply a wet coat to the saddles, screws and springs with a small, stiff brush or toothbrush. (Remember your safety glasses, gloves and good ventilation!) You may submerge the whole bridge in naphtha if you wish. After the parts have soaked awhile, remove as much crud as possible with a dry toothbrush. An air compressor is a great help in blowing out dirt. Next, apply a mixture of naphtha with a little light oil in it—the two mix together, with the naphtha thinning the oil and helping it run down into rusted threads.

Before turning any screws, clean the slots in the screw heads. Remove as much dirt and rust as possible. I use the sharp end of a straightened-out dental probe to scrape the walls; a pin, needle or sharp X-acto blade also works. Straight slots are easy to clean, but the Phillips type require more work. Often the Phillips criss-cross slots are partially stripped from removal attempts made

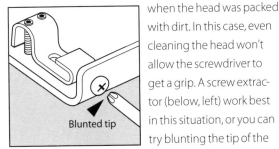
Blunted tip

when the head was packed with dirt. In this case, even cleaning the head won't allow the screwdriver to get a grip. A screw extractor (below, left) work best in this situation, or you can try blunting the tip of the screwdriver on a grinder. By shortening the sharpest part of the tip, the screwdriver can get a grip on what's left of the original slots. Don't fight the hardcaked dirt. Scrape a little out, and then soften the remainder with naphtha. If you're dealing with rust, dab a little Liquid Wrench or WD-40 onto the rusty area. Eventually you'll get the length-adjusting screw to turn, and you can back it out of the saddle.

The height-adjusting screws on Fenders—in particular the Allen-head type—may be frozen with rust and dirt. It takes a very small, sharp tool to scrape the dirt from the screw's six corner walls. Careful soaking and scraping will, nine times out of ten, finally allow your Allen wrench to slide in properly. Don't try to turn the screw until you're sure the wrench is in far enough that it won't cause stripping!

In some cases, even when the wrench fits the Allen slot well, the screw still won't back out. Try turning it forward instead—all the way through the saddle. If this doesn't work, don't get rough with it! If the saddle's off the guitar, apply a little heat with a propane torch; this causes the parts to expand and contract and often breaks the rusted bond. Do this gently, since overheating could cause premature cracking of the plating, although this has never been a problem for me. Hey, don't start a fire! Get all the solvents and explosives away from the area; be sure the part is completely dry. If the screw still won't budge, relax and try the following.

With a small pair of Vise-Grip pliers, grab the very end of the screw from the underside of the saddle. With the saddle clamped firmly, turn the threaded part slowly down and out of the saddle. If a small bit of thread becomes crushed from the grip, you can rethread it with a 4-40 thread-cutting die—or leave it alone and reinstall it later from the bottom up. This way the crushed thread won't get hung up in the saddle's tapped hole or cause damage to the saddle threads.

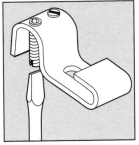

If the screw's head is so stripped or rusted that you can't get it to work, and you can't find/don't want a replacement (or have to play in an hour), try this: With a .010"-.016" nut-slotting file or a the smallest razor-saw blade (.012"), cut a screwdriver slot on the bottom of the screw. Use this new slot to, with a screwdriver, help remove the screw for cleaning. Then when you replace the screw, reinstall it upside down. This modification switches the Allen head to slot head, with the part now being adjustable with a screwdriver, like with Tele-style bridge saddles. This works great!

Once all the parts are disassembled, submerge them in naphtha. I like to keep all the parts from each saddle together, so they don't get mixed up. Try using a plastic ice cube tray for this, marking the separate compartments E A D G B E with an indelible marker. After a good soaking, dry the parts and brush them well with a toothbrush before reassembly. You probably won't even need to oil the parts to get smooth movement after cleaning, but if they're still a little stiff, lubricate the threads with sewing machine oil, Teflon lube, graphite, etc.

Sometimes a screw can become so clean that it will vibrate loose and allow the saddle and string to drop in height. This can happen even if you haven't cleaned the parts. If this is your trouble, adjust the saddle to the proper height and fingerboard radius, and then back each screw out slightly. Use a toothpick to put a drop of glue on the threads right where they enter the saddle itself. Then readjust the screw to the desired position and let it dry. While not actually a bond for metal to metal, the glue will set the threads and stop them from coming loose. A good product for this is Titebond or any carpentry white glue. I've also seen saddles that have a dab of clear silicon bathtub caulk spritzed on the underside around the loose screw. This is a sure-fire method, but it might dampen the tone.

Don't expect every bit of color or rust to disappear. Metal and plating that have been extensively corroded will never appear new. Just try to get the parts functioning again. Once you've reassembled all the saddles and reinstalled the bridge, put a very light coat on the threads, using any of the lubricants mentioned earlier. Brush the parts off periodically—say, every few months (depending on how much you sweat) or during a change of strings.

Chapter 8

Electric bridges: tremolos

basic

basic

Setting up your tremolo system 97

---

d.i.y.

Floyd Rose installation and setup 97
Kahler installation and setup 103
Fine-tuning a Strat tremolo 107
The Trem-Setter 111
Roller nuts 114

---

deep

String benders 117

Installing a tremolo and its partner, the locking nut, is difficult work for any do-it-yourselfer. If your guitar already has a Floyd Rose or a Kahler installed, this chapter contains the basics on setting it up; you'll find it in the D.I.Y. pages that follow, included with the installation process for these individual systems.

d.i.y.

Installing the Floyd Rose tremolo

Let's start with the basics of installing a stud-mount, knife-edge tremolo, then see how to install the locking nut, and how to set up and fine-tune the unit as a whole. If your tremolo is already installed, don't go away—there's something here for everyone!

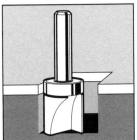

Routing templates and ball-bearing router bits make tremolo installation fairly simple. The body cavities are routed by using Plexiglas templates mounted to the guitar's top or back. These templates are screwed to a guitar's existing holes (pickguard holes, pickup mounting ring holes, etc.) or held on with double-stick carpet installer's tape. Specialized ball-bearing router bits follow the template shapes (see the illustration at the top of the next page). The bearing on the router bit is the same diameter as its cutting edges, so the cutter trims flush with whatever the bearing rolls against. Routing templates and ball-bearing bits are available from Stewart-MacDonald.

Typical installations involve either a modified rout for guitars with an existing standard Strat-style tremolo (the cavities need only to be enlarged in certain places) or a full rout for guitars that never had a tremolo, and for custom-built guitars and many kit bodies. The same rout depth, width and clearance measurements used for the full rout apply to the modified rout as well. We'll start by describing a full rout.

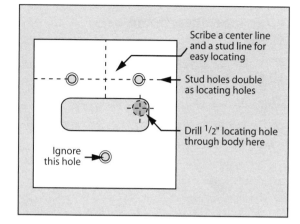

Scribe a center line and a stud line for easy locating

Stud holes double as locating holes

Drill ¹/₂" locating hole through body here

Ignore this hole

Full rout installation The clear Plexiglas top rout template illustrated above is most easily placed if you scribe locating lines on its underside. Scribe a line laterally, when looking at the guitar, through the centers of the two mounting holes (right), and then scribe a second line at right angles to it, centered exactly between the holes. This second (longitudinal) line will correspond to a center line taken from the neck and laid out on the body. To find center, use a finely graduated rule and mark the center of the fingerboard at the nut and the last fret. With a long (30") straightedge resting on those marks, transfer the line onto a piece of masking tape fixed to the top in the area where the tremolo will be located. A taut piece of string (and a friend to stretch it) will work if you don't have a long straightedge.

Now locate the template on the guitar top with line B on the guitar's center line, and with line A located the correct distance from the front of the nut. (Exact measurements for the bridge-stud centerline measurements are given at end of this section.) Mark exactly the two template mounting holes onto the guitar top; these should be 2-5/16" apart, or 1.465" to each side of the center line. Drill the mounting holes with a 7/64" bit, and use #6 x 1" drywall screws for fastening. The holes must be perpendicular to the top, since later they'll be enlarged and used for the pivot-studs.

Screw the top template onto the body and measure 1/4" from each edge of its top right corner, marking this location with a center punch. Remove the template and, using a drill press and brad-point drill bit for accuracy, drill a 1/2"-diameter hole here, right through the body. This hole aligns the front and rear templates (the modified rout skips this step).

Remount the template. You're ready to rout, using a 3/8" ball-bearing bit. Eliminate plunging into the wood by starting each routing pass with the bit in the 1/2" locating hole drilled earlier. Rout the front 11/16" deep, but go slowly—no more than 1/4" per pass. The first rout is deeper than the others since, for the bearing to contact the template, the bit's full 1/2" cutting length must make the first pass (unless you shim the template up 1/4" to get started, which is a good idea). Once you're 5/8" or more deep, remove the template (its thickness might keep the bit from going to 11/16"). The bearing will follow the routed wall just created. Tape paper over the finish to avoid scratches from the router base plate. Stewart-MacDonald offers long-shaft bearing bits that permit chucking more shaft into the router collet—a safety feature I like. Never rout with less than 1/4" of safely chucked shaft on the router bit!

The rear template mounts by aligning one corner over the pre-drilled 1/2" index hole (above). Square up the template lengthwise to the body. Drill mounting screw holes or use double-stick tape to attach it to the guitar.

Rout the entire inside shape of the template to a depth of 5/8". The rear rout will meet the front rout. Now the spring cavity is complete. Continue routing inside the template to a depth of 19/16" for good tremolo clearance. The rear template can now be removed. Center the tremolo-spring claw on the front wall of the rear cavity, with its two holes 3/8" from the back of the guitar (drawing at left). Mark the holes and drill them with a long 1/8" aircraft bit.

Return to the guitar top, and redrill the two mounting holes 1-1/4" deep with a #10 bit; this is for the threaded portion of the mounting stud. Next, drill the holes again with a letter I-bit, but only 3/8" deep. This hole gives clearance for the stud shoulder; it's a close-tolerance fit, since it supports the shoulder during use. Install the studs. Press-in anchor inserts with machine-thread pivot studs are available as a substitute for the original wood-thread studs. These eliminate wood fatigue and the loose studs that can occur with prolonged tremolo use.

The studs, tremolo, claw and springs could be installed now, but without the locking nut and strings, what's the use? Hold on until we get the nut on, and then we can play a few tunes.

Here are the mounting distances for five popular tremolos, measured from the nut's front edge to the center of the pivot-stud line. Figures for both long and short scales are given. A common installation error is to install the tremolo too far from the nut, causing the guitar to play flat, or the bridge saddles to hang over the unit's front edge. You'll be safe with these figures:

Tremolo	25-1/2" Long scale	24-3/4" Short scale
Floyd Rose	25"	24-3/16"
Schaller Floyd Rose-licensed	24-15/16"	24-1/8"
Ibanez Edge	25-1/16"	24-1/4"
Kahler Spyder	25"	24-1/4"
Gotoh Floyd Rose-licensed	25"	24-1/4"

Mounting the locking nut Now that you've installed the Floyd Rose stud-mount tremolo, continue by getting the locking nut on. Once you can lock the strings at both ends, your tuning troubles are over.

When we shot a videotape on Floyd Rose installation at Stewart-MacDonald, I was worried about how I'd teach the nut installation so that it could be done with simple tools such as a router. (I'd been doing my installations on a vertical milling machine.) I actually dreamed up the following method right during the shoot, and it works better than I would have guessed at the time! Stew-Mac now sells this jig, and if you plan to do more than one of these operations, or perhaps to get into the business, it would be a wise investment. It's inexpensive and comes with extremely detailed instructions, and you'd need a machine shop to build one as accurate. But for one-time do-it-yourselfers, here are the jig instructions in abridged form, accompanied by illustrations to help you fashion your own router jig.

The installation consists of cutting a ledge for the nut to sit on by removing a predetermined amount of wood where the original nut was installed. Then, holes for the

nut's mounting bolts are drilled and countersunk. In an experienced woodworker's hands, a sharp chisel could cut the ledge quickly and easily, but a novice should use a Dremel Moto-Tool to slowly machine it. You players who are serious enough about guitar repair to install a locking nut yourselves should welcome an excuse to add a Dremel router to your toolbox.

Installation with chisel or router requires that you accurately measure the depth of the ledge, so that the nut ends up at the right level with respect to the frets. Having it too low causes buzzing, while having it too high creates a stiff action. A pair of dial calipers that measure in thousandths of an inch are a real help. Plastic-bodied dial calipers can be purchased for around $20 —another invaluable addition to the tool chest.

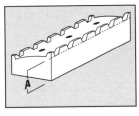

When the outer two E strings are .010" above the height of the frets as they sit in the bottom of the nut slots, you're in the right ballpark. This is an average, slightly stiff playing height. You'd seldom want a higher action, and you can lower the nut if it feels too stiff. To rout the correct depth, you need one measurement: the distance from the locking nut's string-slot bottoms to the bottom of the unit itself ("A" above). The nut described here is a Schaller R3 Floyd Rose-licensed model with an "A" measurement of .208". (Floyd Rose and Schaller designate neck/string spacing width with numbers ranging from R1 to R6; they're all slightly different at the "A" measurement.) Here's how to guarantee that the nut slot bottoms are .010" higher than the fret height.

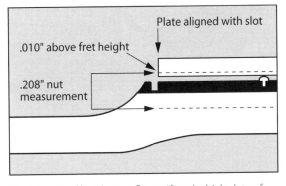

Making the jig Clamp a flat, uniformly thick plate of wood, metal, Plexiglas, etc., to the first two frets, with its front wall flush to the original nut slot (above). Now, the bottom of the clamped plate is level with the fret tops, so if you use dial calipers to measure .010" short of the bottom, that's where you want the nut-slot bottoms to end up. Next, add the one nut measurement we took (mine is .208", yours could be different), and you'll have the distance from the top of the clamped plate to the nut bottom; this is the ledge to be routed.

The plate is more than a surface to measure from, however. With its front edge in line with the nut slot, it acts as a "fence" to guide the Dremel router base, keeping it from cutting into the end of the fingerboard. And routing the end of the fingerboard would change the overall string length—a disaster! The locking nut's front should be flush with the fingerboard end, with the nut bottom at a 90° angle to it.

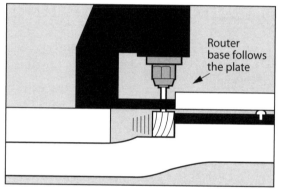

Router base follows the plate

Complete your installation jig by clamping a second platform of uniform thickness to the headstock face. This raises the Dremel Moto-Tool above the surface to be routed, allowing the cutter to be lowered into the wood by degree. You now have a usable facsimile of the jig I made, which is a single unit made of clear Plexiglas (the upper and lower plates are joined with threads and cap screws). The lower plate has a routing hole machined into it, and a built-in clamp holds it to the neck. There are two types of headstock: the straight, Fender style, and the angled, tilt-back Gibson type. With either, you remove the tuners in order to clamp on the platform (for the tilt-head, shim the table level with the fingerboard).

Routing The jig I made uses a #115 Dremel router bit for the cutting (a 5/16" diameter bit that cuts flush with the front edge of the router base I used). Rout no more than 1/16" per pass, and be sure that the bit cuts flush with the router's base edge. If the bit cuts more than flush, it could trim the fingerboard end. (If this happens, loosen the two mounting screws and wiggle the base into line, or put a couple strips of masking tape along the base edge to shim it away from the fingerboard).

Measure often from the top plate as you rout, and when the ledge is cut, lightly glue the nut body (with string clamps removed) to the ledge. Spray Hot Stuff accelerator on the nut bottom and put two small drops of Hot Stuff Special T super glue on the newly routed ledge. Thirty seconds of drying time will firmly set the nut. Then use it as a drill guide for a #30 drill bit. Using a layer of wax paper in between, place a hunk of modeling clay under the rear of the neck/headstock area and press the neck into the clay to form it. The clay supports the wood, allowing your bits to punch through with no splinters! Drill down through the two mounting holes, right through the neck—the nut will hold the bit square. Now tap the nut loose using a block of wood and a hammer. Enlarge the #30 holes with an 11/64" bit, again drilling from the top side.

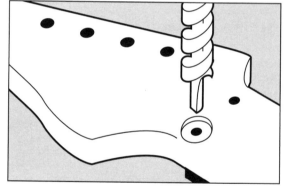

The countersunk holes are most safely drilled by using a step-bit. Stewart-MacDonald makes a step-bit with an 11/64" pilot to follow the 11/64" hole drilled earlier, and a 5/16" outer bore that drills a shallow flat-bottomed hole for the bolt heads. Extra care must be taken to avoid the bits' grabbing or tearing the wood by accident. From the rear, countersink the holes until three or four threads protrude through the ledge when the bolt is inserted. This is plenty to hold the nut tight—any more, and the bolt could come through the locking nut's top and touch the string clamps. Go ahead and mount the nut. If your nut ends up too low, it's common to shim it up to the right level. Good shim materials include 3M wet-or-dry sandpaper in fine grits, or mesh-like drywall sandpaper with a good grip (check your lumberyard).

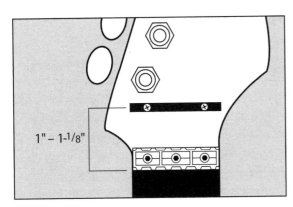

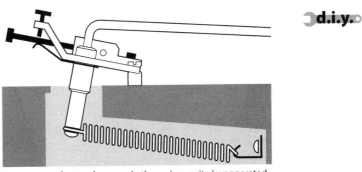

1" – 1-1/8"

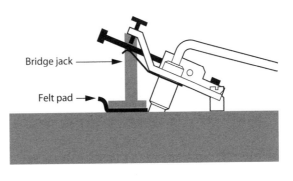

You may need extra clearance in the spring cavity (exaggerated here). Note the tapered back wall: the shallow end may be 5/8"–3/4" while the deep end may be 11/16"–13/16"

Last of all, mount the retainer bar. Locate it 1" to 1-1/8" from the front of the nut, and centered from side to side as at right. Drill the two screw holes with a 9/64" bit marked with masking tape —this provides a visual depth stop to prevent drilling through the headstock! Put your strings on, and check your work. You're done with the worst part. Now we'll troubleshoot any problems, cover setup and fine tuning, and look at the recessed top-rout made popular by Steve Vai and the Ibanez Jem 777.

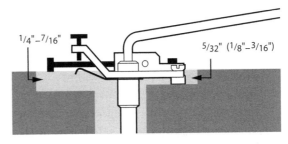

Bridge jack →

Felt pad →

Setting up the Floyd Rose

Setting up your tremolo is easy if you learn these simple setup basics: level the tremolo to the body by adjusting the springs and spring claw, set the string-to-fingerboard height by adjusting the two pivot studs, and adjust the intonation. Action and intonation are discussed in the earlier chapters of this book, so I won't bore you with repetition. I'll just skim through the simple stuff, making a few important points as we go. This will leave some space to take a look at the optional recess rout made popular by Steve Vai and the Ibanez Jem 777 series.

Leave the locking nut unclamped while you do the following work. First, level the tremolo parallel with the body by adding or removing springs in the rear spring cavity. Using a Phillips screwdriver, adjust the spring claw in or out until the unit is level. Most players use either two or three tremolo springs for string gauges beginning with .008 or .009, and usually three for .010 and up. Experiment until you get the right feel. Next, the string height from the fingerboard should be set before adjusting the intonation. Most players look for a low action that shows around 1/16" between the bottom of the strings and the top of the 12th fret. However, most players settle

1/4"–7/16"   5/32" (1/8"–3/16")

for a slightly stiffer action than this—say, 3/32". How low you can go depends on the adjustment of the neck and the condition of the frets.

Set the string height by simply raising or lowering the two pivot studs that the tremolo mounts on; this is much easier than with the individual saddle height adjustments common to Strats and many other guitars. Unless your tremolo uses machine-thread studs that adjust with an Allen wrench, use a flat-blade screwdriver with a sharp, well-ground tip that fits the stud slot snugly. This eliminates slippage that can not only mar the slot, but also cause the plating to lift away. As a general rule, most players adjust the tremolo so that the underside is from 1/8" to 1/4" off the face of the guitar; this provides plenty of forward dump and a fair amount of up-pull.

d.i.y.

Keep in mind that a tremolo set close to a guitar's face has little clearance in the rear for up-pull on the bar. A tremolo that's set high off the top may require shimming the bolt-on neck to keep the strings close to the fingerboard (for advice on neck shimming, see page 163). Also, a high-set tremolo may seem uncomfortable for players accustomed to resting their picking hand on or near the body (one solution, the recess rout, is explained later). And, depending on the cavity depth, a tremolo that's mounted high off the body may cause the springs to rub the bottom of the spring cavity. Ibanez and Kramer use a tapered cavity to solve this problem.

Floyd Rose saddles are made in three different thicknesses or heights. The tallest is used for the D and G strings, the medium for the A and B, and the shortest for the two outside E strings. This saddle-height combination creates a curve in the bridge saddles that matches the radius curve of most electric guitar fingerboards. Many players find that the "medium" saddle curve of the Floyd Rose plays comfortably with most necks. Custom-tailoring the saddle height is possible by shimming the inserts with thin metal shim stock available from most automotive suppliers, or by carefully grinding the bottoms of the saddles to alter their height. (Grinding is a tricky operation, and a grinding wheel is a tool that can cause serious injuries. Be careful, and definitely wear eye protection!) If you want to experiment, replacement saddles are available directly from Kramer.

Setting the intonation of the Floyd Rose bridge saddles works on the same principle as any other adjustable bridge—if a string notes sharp, move the saddle back away from the nut; if the note is flat, move the saddle forward toward the nut. Since the string is clamped into the saddle itself rather than into a separate tailpiece, the saddles tend to slide forward from string pressure when you loosen the Allen bolt that holds them in place. This can be annoying if your intention is to move the saddle back, since you have to loosen (detune) the string in order to do so. Try "dumping" the bridge forward and inserting a bridge jack (see drawing, previous page) to hold the tremolo up, keeping the strings slack while moving a saddle back or forth. I made my jack out of two scraps of hard maple and covered the bottom with felt as a protection for the finish. Of course, an electric tuner is a help

for setting the intonation. When your setup and intonation are correct, clamp the locking nut tight.

Here are a few tips on recess routs, which involve the removal of wood under the tremolo (below the surface of the guitar face). This allows the tremolo to sit fairly close to the top (1/16" is common) while still having clearance in the rear for up-pull. Also, many guitarists keep their palm, hand, or entire arm on or close to the top while picking, and the recess rout keeps the bridge closer to the body for this type of picking comfort. Recess-routing templates are available from some guitar shop suppliers. Most recesses are from 1/8" to 3/16" deep in the front portion of the rout, and deeper (1/4" to 7/16") toward the rear for up-pulling (above). Since you can always rout deeper, start with the shallower measurements and follow the ball-bearing routing techniques described earlier.

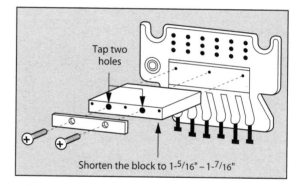

Tap two holes

Shorten the block to 1-5/16" – 1-7/16"

Recess routing may require shortening the tremolo block to keep it from sticking out of the guitar's back. The amount you shorten it depends on how close to, or deep into, the top you want your tremolo. The Ibanez Edge block measures 1-5/16", while Kramer's shortened block for their guitars with factory-equipped recess routs measures 1-7/16". I shortened the block on my Floyd Rose-licensed Schaller to match the Ibanez Edge tremolo. Here's how to do it:

With a 1/16" drill bit, deepen the five spring holes by the amount you plan to remove (up to 3/8"). Using a hacksaw, remove up to 3/8" from the block's bottom, and then file it smooth to a length of 1-5/16" or 1-7/16", etc. Drill and tap the two spring holes on each side of the center-spring hole to accept a machine screw; I used a 10-32 truss-rod tap that I had handy. Finally, make a 1/8" x 2" x 5/16" flat spring retainer bar (1/8" screen-door aluminum stock purchased at the hardware store and hack-sawed and filed to shape) with two clearance holes for mounting the bar to the tapped holes in the block. This keeps the springs from popping out when the tremolo's in use, especially on up-pulls where the springs go slack.

Kahler installation and setup

I chose the Floyd Rose tremolo to teach measuring, layout, and routing basics, not only because it's popular, but because it's the hardest to install. If you can mount a Floyd, you're good with a router and can definitely handle any other installations. The most popular and readily available tremolos on the market are the Floyd Rose, the Schaller-licensed Rose and the Kahler flat-mount. The last section covered installing the stud-mounted "floating" tremolos; now watch how you can apply those same skills to installing another excellent and popular tremolo, the Kahler 2300 series cam-operated, flat-mount tremolo. The 2300 series is the original Kahler tremolo that became popular in the early 1980s.

Several features set the Kahler apart from stud-mount "floating" tremolos. It requires a much smaller body rout (removing less wood, and therefore less mass) and the rout doesn't need to go clear through the body, since it doesn't use a rear-rout for tremolo springs. Instead, the Kahler achieves its smooth operation by way of two small factory-installed springs, ball bearings and a cam. Not having to rout clear through the body makes for an easy, good-looking installation on bodies that have never had a tremolo before, such as Gibsons, hand-made guitars, Teles, etc. Here's how the Kahler's installed, but first a word of advice before you turn on that router.

My friend and former apprentice **Charlie Longstreth** helped me compile this Kahler information, and he emphasizes a good point: "The first question that should occur to anyone about to install the Kahler or any other tremolo is: Should the installation be done at all? It'd be tragic to modify a pre-CBS Strat, and many Kahlers are mounted on Strats. If you're lucky enough to own one of those rare birds, pick up a newer Strat and put a Kahler on it—and even then, remember that Strats that are new now will be old someday. Maybe you should build a guitar from kit parts." Okay, let's begin.

While Kahler makes a version of its famous flat-mount tremolo that can be installed on the tailpiece studs of a Gibson ES-335 or Les Paul, we'll use a Strat-style guitar for this installation. First, be sure that your neck is lined up to

the body the way you want it, especially with reference to the bridge and pickups. Read the section on bolt-on necks carefully, and then remove any parts that could get in the way of your router, such as the pickguard, pickups, bridge, and the volume and tone controls. Next, lay a strip of masking tape over the six factory bridge mount holes, and lay out the center line of the body using the same method described for the Floyd Rose. Another way to find center is to use a straightedge long enough to lay along both sides of the fingerboard and extend out onto the body as far down as your masking tape. Mark the straightedge line on the tape and find the center between the two marks.

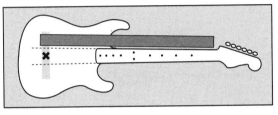

With each tremolo, Kahler supplies a heavy cardboard template for laying out the area to be routed and to locate the mounting holes. To ensure correct lengthwise placement and good intonation, this template is located on a line measured out from the nut and marked at right angles to the body center line. Note: This cardboard is not a routing template; it's only for locating the tremolo. If you're using a Plexiglas routing template the cardboard piece can be omitted, since the Plexiglas template will work for the layout as well as the actual routing.

The front two mounting holes in the baseplate of the Kahler flat mount 2300 bridge (and the layout templates) are intended to line up with, and screw into, the outer two mounting holes of a standard Stratocaster bridge. You can mount the bridge this way, but if you do, the roller saddles will not be centered with the centerline of the neck (and more importantly, the strings). The saddles will be closer to the treble side than they are the bass side because the centerline of the two mounting holes is not the centerline of the roller saddles! I'm unsure why Kahler designed it this way, and it's not way off, but there is a difference of a healthy 1/16" at the saddle. To avoid problems, lay out the correct centerline of the saddles onto the template and then center to the neck's centerline—ignoring the original Strat mounting holes. Here's how to do it right:

All the instructions I've seen for installing a Kahler recommend marking a centerline on the template between the two front mounting holes and then centering the template on the guitar. Ignore that incorrect centerline and make a new centerline on the template that is 1.132" from the center of the bass side hole—not between the two holes.

When you center the template onto the body's centerline, the original outside two Strat mounting holes will not line up. They'll be close, but not right, so plug the

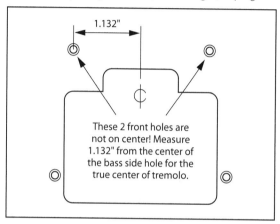

1.132"

These 2 front holes are not on center! Measure 1.132" from the center of the bass side hole for the true center of tremolo.

two holes and redrill them. (Or you can use the two rearmost holes at the back edge of the template to locate the bridge laterally, because they are centered to the bridge saddles). In either case you'll still have to plug the original Strat mounting holes if you want to be perfect. *[I had the wrong bridge centering information back in the first edition of this book, and my error was pointed out to me by Koenraad Strobbe, a repairman in Belgium. Thanks, Koenraad!]*

Three other considerations when trying to center the Kahler correctly on a traditional Strat are: 1) The pickguard may have to be trimmed on either side of the

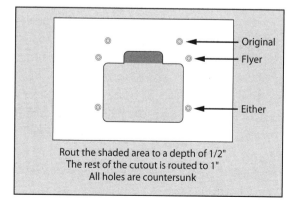

Original
Flyer

Either

Rout the shaded area to a depth of 1/2"
The rest of the cutout is routed to 1"
All holes are countersunk

tremolo. 2) When the tremolo is lined up properly, a small bit of the original tremolo rout may peek through on the treble side. 3) Really, the above centering information is the most helpful for those about to install a Kahler on new work—where there's no good reason not to center it correctly in the first place.

So on a Strat you can: 1) plug the holes, line the template on the body center line and redrill the holes, or 2) go with the two factory holes and ignore the center line you laid out. The safest way to guarantee an accurate placement is to ignore any pre-drilled holes and measure yourself. Here's some help:

To correctly place the Kahler in regard to the string length, measure from the nut's front (where it meets the fingerboard) down to the masking tape on the body, drawing a line at right angles to the center line. This new line is for lining up the two mounting holes of the template; later these holes will be used to mount the actual tremolo, since they're the same holes. If the original Strat tremolo mounting holes don't line up with this line, plug the outer two and redrill them. For a long Strat scale (25-1/2"), measure 25-1/4" from the nut. For a short Gibson scale (24-3/4"), measure 24-7/16". Once you've located this line, attach the routing template to the guitar body using double-stick tape, or screw the template to the guitar's face with wood screws. The Stew-Mac template that I use (above) has countersunk mounting holes and can be used for either the Kahler Flyer or the Standard flat-mount. The front two holes are for the Original, and the rear/front holes are for the Flyer; the back holes are the same for either tremolo.

Mount the template with wood screws that are smaller than the final mounting screws, and make sure their heads are recessed and won't interfere with the router. After the template is mounted, scribe around the finish along the inside edge with a sharp scribe or X-acto knife. You'll be routing right up to this line, so scoring the finish first helps prevent chips when you remove the template.

The overall depth of the Kahler rout is 1", although many of us prefer to rout only 1/2" deep on the front part (the shaded area at left, which gives clearance for the two springs) to avoid taking away unnecessary wood, mass and tone. When you've routed the cavity and vacuumed up the chips, lay a couple coats of clear lacquer on the bare wood to seal out moisture; you can even do this with a rag or a brush. If you want to get fancy, you can tape off the area and spray the new cavity with a matching paint. Sometimes I use black Magic Marker to darken the rout before the clear lacquer. That way, any part of the bare-wood cavity that you could see from the outside can no longer be seen. If your guitar requires a ground wire mounted to the bridge, run that wire now (on new work, you may have to drill a long hole from the tremolo rout to the control cavity, using a long 1/8" "aircraft" bit). You can get an adequate ground simply by screwing the tremolo base plate down onto a ground wire bent up the side of the cavity and wrapped over the edge. Keep this wire away from the workings of the tremolo! Go ahead and install the tremolo now, just to see how everything lines up, and then go on to the locking nut.

Kahler offers three 6-string nut styles, plus one for their 7-string tremolo. Two of them, the original Standard and the Deluxe no-wrench, flip-lever nut, are behind-the-nut locks that work together with a real nut. The third is called a Locknut and is similar to the Floyd Rose, which requires that a ledge be routed for installation. We've already covered the Floyd style, so let's briefly discuss installing the behind-the-nut style. It's easy.

With a Strat, the only real work involved is in making a shim to support the nut at the proper height for getting good string angle through the nut slots. As with any nut, too steep an angle causes string binding or breaking in the slots, while too shallow an angle allows the strings to flop around, causing buzzes. Kahler recommends a string angle of eleven degrees between the string lock and the real nut; check this angle with a protractor.

Make the shim from a hardwood such as maple, rosewood or ebony. Trace around the nut for the outside shape, mark the holes and then drill them before shaping the shim; this eliminates splitting the delicate shim once it's shaped. Kahler offers pre-shaped and drilled Polystyrene shims that come in two shapes: a flat shim .068" thick (part # 8450), and a curved-bottom one (#8460) that measures .068" at the thickest part of its center, but tapers quite thin at the edges of the bottom curve. In certain situations you may wish to stack different combinations of these shims together. The string-lock should be as close to the real nut as possible, while still keeping the right amount of angle to hold the strings

in their slots (about 1/4" to 3/8" from the rear of the nut). Too much distance between the lock and the real nut tends to store more slack than necessary. To keep from going clear through the headstock, use masking tape wrapped around your bit as a depth guide while drilling the four mounting holes.

If you pick with a strong attack and are looking for big sustain, you may be interested in recessing your Kahler into the body. John Suhr of Rudy's Music in New York City inlays, or recesses, a Kahler flat-mount 5/32" deep into the body. This allows you to raise the roller bridge saddles to their highest point in order to get a strong string angle over the roller (saddle), without having overly high action. As a general rule, Kahler recommends setting the bridge saddle roller height so that a minimum of .475" and a maximum .625" shows from the bottom of the outer two E strings to the guitar body. With the recess method you get the maximum height (and more if you want), but still retain a normal string-to-body relationship, avoiding the necessity of shimming the neck in the body to keep up with the high rollers. Raising the saddle rollers really high creates better response and tonal quality, but the trade-off is more variance in tuning because you introduce more friction to the rollers with the increased string angle. This doesn't bother most players, though, so try it!

Note If you recess the tremolo 5/32", you must move the bridge forward 3/32", since as the rollers are raised they also move backward—away from the nut—increasing the string length (just raise a roller saddle up and watch how much it moves). An alternate to recessing the Kahler is to raise the saddles high and then shim the neck to meet the strings; of course, the pickups have to be raised, too, and sometimes you just can't get them high enough. I should point out that Kahler doesn't recommend setting the saddles this high. There's nothing wrong with trying all these different setups and deciding for yourself; that's the whole idea of this book!

Kahler includes a pamphlet called *Adjustment And Setup* with each tremolo; it does a good job of teaching you how the tremolo works. They've also published a troubleshooting guide and *Service Tips And Adjustments*. Even if you're not experiencing any trouble, ask your dealer to get you copies of these pamphlets, because they'll come in handy some day.

d.i.y.

◑d.i.y.◐

Replacing a Kahler string hook

It's not uncommon for the cast metal string hooks on a Kahler to break. Replacements are available online at *kahlerparts.com*. Here's how to install one.

1 Unscrew and remove all six knurled thumbscrews. Notice that these are well bent from being unstrung many times and left to bend against the casting.

2 Since the pieces you need to get at are mounted to a spring-loaded block under tension, you may have to force the block upward. Find a friend to help you if you can't hold the spring tension with one hand.

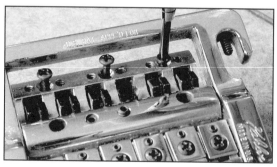

3 Unscrew and remove the three black machine screws; the fine-tuner bracket will lift free.

4 Drive the pin out as far as you can, using any sort of punch or nailset that's smaller in diameter than the pin (this photo shows the bottom side).

5 Use a pair of pliers to remove the pin, catching the string hooks as they come loose.

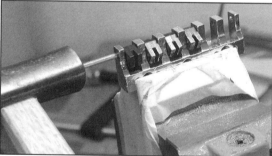

6 Insert the replacement hook and tap the parts back together.

7 Hold the upper part of the bridge housing down against the spring tension if necessary, and replace the three machine screws. You're back in business!

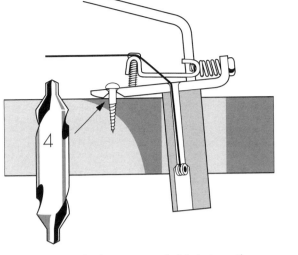

Fine-tuning a Strat tremolo

With its slab-style body, bolt-on neck and "automotive style" construction, the Stratocaster is easy to work on from the repairman's point of view—there's nothing to break! How often have you seen a Strat with a broken peghead? And even though the ten steps (page 29) are an excellent approach for basic Strat setup, there are still a few points I'd like to make about Stratocasters. Understanding Strat quirks and knowing a few tricks of the trade can be a great help in adjusting your guitar for maximum playability.

Tremolos really became mainstream in the early '80s, when Floyd Rose hit the guitar world with a locking nut and string-clamp "floating" tremolo system that eliminated most of the tuning problems long associated with tremolo use. Still, for many, the most desirable tremolo is that used on the Fender Strat—especially the two-piece unit made from '54 until late '71. Fender has introduced several Strat tremolo designs since then (most notably the "American Standard"), and when used with a properly set up nut, they all work well. So if you're a traditionalist not wanting to disfigure your favorite axe, you may wonder, "How can I keep my vintage Strat playing in tune, without installing a locking nut and modern bridge?"

The following modifications and adjustments will not only help the guitar stay in tune, but improve its sound, as well. And all this is possible without installing any of today's locking nut/bridge systems, all of which require alteration of vintage Strats. These tips will be a help to vintage Strat lovers trying to keep pace with the modern music world.

Smoother action, better sustain Before setting the tremolo, adjust the six mounting screws that fasten the bridge plate—if they're screwed down too tightly, the tremolo won't have the proper freedom of movement. It's a good idea to loosen the screws slightly, and then retighten them slowly until they just touch the plate. Sometimes, friction between the plate and screws causes jolting, catching and sticking. One way to track down that problem (and often it's just one or two screws) is to remove the four center screws.

Actually, the two outside screws alone are able to hold the bridge sufficiently for playing. Stevie Ray Vaughan sometimes used only two—proof of their strength, considering his high action, heavy strings and hard-hitting blues attack. Test the tremolo function with only the outer two screws holding the bridge down, and then by replacing the screws one at a time you'll find the problem. You can remedy this by carefully filing and fitting the holes to the screws.

With the bridge removed, inspect the six holes from the underside. You can increase the bevel by using a #4 counterbore (above). This increased bevel gives more of a knife-edge pivot point to the bridge where it rocks against the mounting screws, and therefore noticeably increases the sustain. Many bridges are beveled properly and need no modification, but it won't hurt to have a look. The bevels should be the same. Concentrate on the rear edge of the hole—the edge that bears against the screw. Bevel (countersink) the underside of the holes until the remaining rim is approximately 3/64" to 1/16" thick on each hole. When replacing the bridge, tighten all six screws snugly, and then back off each screw a quarter turn; this keeps the bridge plate flat to the body while allowing room for the tremolo to work.

A different approach is to hold the tremolo forward in the tilted position, and then tighten the screws against the plate, preventing undue pressure on the screws when the tremolo is in use. Use whatever method suits you. I've known some players who prefer using two mounting screws, yet would rather keep the middle four screws for looks. This can be accomplished by drilling clearance holes in the plate so that the screws aren't actually touching or holding anything. The instrument is altered, however, which could affect its value.

Spring adjustment Adjustment of the standard two-piece tremolo involves much trial and error. In the end you must please yourself, and there is no one way to do it. Some players prefer that the bridge come to rest on the body as a positive stop or return point after being "dumped" (pressed downward to lower the strings' pitch). These hard-hitting, string-breaking players often like a positive body stop, so that the remaining strings don't all go instantly out of tune from the difference in string pressure caused by a broken string. The standard factory setup, however, is with the tremolo plate raised slightly off the body at its rear (3/32" as mentioned previously), enabling players to cause the pitch to go slightly sharp by pulling up on the arm.

The tension adjustment of the tremolo springs depends on string gauge and desired tremolo action—a personal choice. Many players want the plate to return to the guitar's face after use, but keep more tension on the springs than is necessary. Here's a good test for proper spring tension: Pluck the open low E string and, at the 15th fret, immediately bend your top E string one-and-a-half to two steps. If the low E holds true, the spring tension is probably correct. If it goes flat due to the additional pressure caused by bending the top string, tighten the spring claw until the low E is close to remaining in tune. Experiment to find the springs that best suit your style. Not all springs are the same length, size or material, so shop around. Players using sets beginning with an .008 to .009 high-E should experiment with two or three springs; .010s and up play best for me with four springs. Properly adjusted springs should ring clear when plucked, with no dull, plunking sound. A good spring tension and tone are important to a Strat's unique sound, since they create a natural reverb chamber.

No absolute rule exists regarding the number of springs used and onto what claw hook and into which tremolo block hole they should be placed. Some guitarists who favor light-gauge strings beginning with an .008 use only two springs with the claw backed most of the way out; .009 players often use three springs with the claw still backed out quite a bit. Most players, however, end up using either three or four springs and adjusting the spring claw to get the desired tremolo feel and return point. Some use five springs with medium or heavier strings (Stevie Ray, for instance, used strings

gauged .012, .015, .019, .028, .038, .058). I feel that five springs are too much, and I don't like the way a tremolo plays this way. String gauge is extremely important when adjusting tremolos, and you should decide on a favorite gauge before making any adjustments.

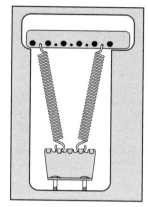

When experimenting with the number and placement of the tremolo springs, try two at first, placed on the second and fourth hooks of the claw and extending to the two outside holes of the block (left). If you want to add another spring—and most players do—place it in the center of the claw and block but relocate the other two springs to the outside hooks and holes. With four springs, simply omit the center one—the idea is to keep the springs balanced.

Here's a common tremolo setup trick that pleases most players: With the strings tuned to pitch, adjust the spring claw tension so that the bridge leans slightly forward, with the plate slightly off the face of the guitar (1/8" maximum). Fret an A at the 5th fret on the high E string, and pull up on the tremolo arm until the plate hits the body and stops. Adjust the spring tension until the note played at the 5th fret is B♭ when the plate hits the body. After this "half-step sharp" test is completed, you'll be able to pull up on the arm slightly. Of course, if you change string gauges or alter the number of springs, you have to start all over again.

Eliminating friction This information applies to any Fender instrument, but in particular to Strats with tremolos. If you eliminate the friction which causes strings to bind, you'll have a better playing axe—with or without a tremolo.

The nut is where many tremolo problems occur. That's why the modern locking nut/bridge system is so popular because it basically eliminates the problem of slack storage—string tension that "hangs up" at the friction points outside the playing area in between the nut and bridge. When you tune a string or run it through the nut and string tree by depressing the tremolo, the friction

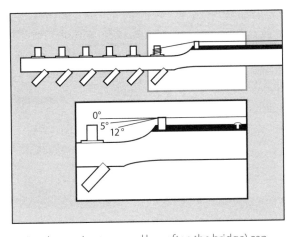

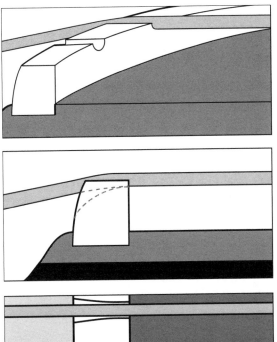

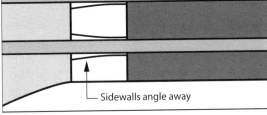

Sidewalls angle away

points (nut, string trees and less often the bridge) can make the string hang up, causing it to return sharp and throwing the guitar out of tune. The stored slack is held temporarily and usually releases the next time you make a bend or use your tremolo. If you retune this "sharp" string, it will be flat when it releases. Most slack storage occurs at the nut, at the string tree hold-downs behind the nut, and to a lesser degree at the bridge. If you eliminate these friction problems, your guitar will stay in tune. Start with the nut.

For nut-making, I prefer bone over man-made nut blanks of Formica, phenolic or plastic. Graphite can be a good choice for tremolo nuts, but I don't like the black color and it seems to wear quickly. The string angle, which comes from the tuner or string tree and breaks over the nut, should not be too steep when viewed from the side. A proper angle is between 5 and 12 degrees off the fingerboard plane—no more, no less (above).

The nut's grooves or string slots should be deep enough to hold the string and keep it from popping out when played, but no more than half the diameter of the string in depth. A nut slot should have a round bottom, and the slot sides should bear slightly away from the string, so as not to bind. On tremolo guitars, some repairmen prefer a slightly flattened bottom for the string slot so that the slot's round shape doesn't grip the string as it moves (below).

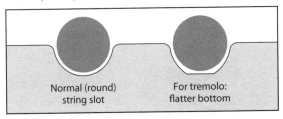

Normal (round)   For tremolo:
string slot   flatter bottom

Occasionally a repairman or manufacturer will hastily file nuts with too sharp a back angle. This puts all the load and friction at one very small point at the front of the nut. While the string should "take off" at the nut's front (where it meets the fingerboard and the actual string length begins), it should have some "meat" or backing behind it and gradually slope up to the front edge. The nut sidewalls should also be slightly dressed away from the string on the back side to allow free movement, and so that they don't pinch the string and keep it from returning to pitch (or cause a muting effect). Slots that are too shallow don't hold a string when it's bent from side to side; plus they can cause a string to pop out when least expected.

As a final step when you finish any nut—especially one designed for tremolo use—give a glossy polishing to the string-slot bottoms with (at least) 1000-grit wet-or-dry sandpaper; this relieves friction and improves tone. A little lubricant in the nut slot doesn't hurt either. Common nut lubricants are pencil lead, powdered graphite, Vaseline, Guitar Grease and GHS GraphitALL

d.i.y.

(GraphitALL was created by **Rene Martinez** — guitar repairman extraordinaire, and **Stevie Ray Vaughan's** guitar-tech and best friend). A well-fit and lubricated nut allows the string to travel lengthwise without binding.

String tree problems Eliminating the slack storage occurring at string trees can be done in a variety of ways, but the removal of them alone is not a solution, because then there will be insufficient down-pressure, or angle, at the nut, and the strings may pop out when struck. Also, without a decent angle at the nut, a great loss of tone occurs. Roller trees are available from a variety of sources (check your music store—Wilkinson makes several). These are an easy retrofit for the originals, allowing the strings to move smoothly when the tremolo is used.

All Strats have a string tree for the B and high-E strings; on models made after '59, this tree is supported by a plastic or metal spacer. Often players remove the spacer and screw the tree down to the headstock face—don't do that! The angle becomes too steep, and the spacer is an improvement. Be sure that the string tree is de-burred and polished, and use it. Strats made since '71 also have a tree for the G and D strings. The trees and spacers put enough angle on the nut to keep the string from popping out, but not so much that they cause the string to bind from friction and not return in tune. Combat friction at the trees with Teflon gun oil or Magik Guitar Lube—just a drop on the underside is a help.

With the four highest strings, two or three windings around the tuner maintains a proper angle between the tuner and string tree. If you remove the tree holding the G and D strings or own a pre-'59 one-tree Strat, experiment with the number of downward windings (toward the bottom of the tuner post) needed to achieve the correct string-to-nut angle. On the low E and A strings, any more than two downward windings causes too great an angle, and the strings will bind when the tremolo's in use. A neat trick is to wind the string up toward the top of the post, to let you control or alter the angle.

You can eliminate the trees entirely by using replacement tuners with graduated shaft heights. Sperzel and Schecter offer graduated shaft pegs, so check with your dealer to find what's currently available. Installing these pegs, however, involves enlarging the tuner-shaft hole. Instead of enlarging the holes, you can make a tapered

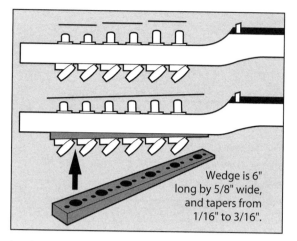

Wedge is 6" long by 5/8" wide, and tapers from 1/16" to 3/16".

hardwood wedge, drilled with clearance holes for the tuners and screws, and slipped between the tuners and the back of the headstock. This "wedge" solution works well, doesn't disfigure a vintage instrument, and is a simple way out if graduated shaft height solves your problem. At one time Wilkinson offered machined aluminum wedges which worked great. However, I couldn't find the wedge in recent searches — that doesn't mean it's not available. If you remove your string trees, expect to make an adjustment in your playing style, because the upper two strings may seem a little harder to bend; you may have to push further to get the desired note. You'll be pleased, though, that the string has a little more resiliency at the top of the bend. Also, this extra resiliency results in a lot less string breakage, since the strings tend to give more.

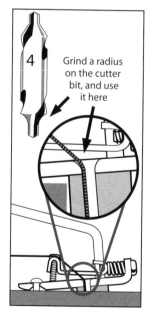

Grind a radius on the cutter bit, and use it here

String breakage occurs where the string angles over the bridge plate. You can radius (taper) these holes with a small file and sandpaper, or by grinding a radius on one end of the #4 counterbore mentioned earlier and using it in an electric drill to bevel the hole evenly. This type of counterbore is generally used by machinists and is available at most industrial supply stores; any machine shop can quickly grind a radius on it. Besides eliminating string breakage, this bridge-plate modification also helps eliminate binding that occurs at the same point. An easier solution is to do what Stevie Ray Vaughan did: Slide a piece of plastic wire insulation over the string at the point of contact at the bridge saddle. This must inhibit some tone and sustain, although you sure can't prove that by listening to recordings of Stevie Ray.

If you follow these tips, you should find that your guitar stays in tune nicely and has marked improvement in tone. The Strat tremolo's a great invention; it just needs a little understanding and care.

Tightening a loose Strat tremolo arm

In response to a Strat tremolo arms going limp and not staying in place, one player I know removed the center spring from a small die punch cutter and ground a 1/4"-long piece off one end. This spring is about 5/32" in diameter and very stiff. He then dropped the spring into the tremolo arm hole and screwed down the arm until it hit the spring (below). By tightening the arm slowly until it met with resistance from the spring, there was enough pressure on the bottom of the arm to hold it in place.

Being extremely stiff, this spring keeps the tremolo arm from being either too tight or too loose. The punch cutter was purchased from Holiday Steel Rule And Die in Greensboro, North Carolina, but you should be able to find one at any die-maker's shop. Or, see your Fender dealer — Fender learned the same trick and had a spring made for the job.

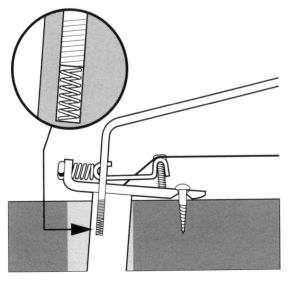

Lindy Fralin, the noted pickup maker and Strat-wielding guitarist firms up a tremolo arm with several wraps of Teflon plumber's tape. What could be easier than that?

The Trem-Setter

The Trem-Setter helps keep a full-floating tremolo guitar in tune (full-floating means up/down pitch changes, not just dive-only). They've been installed by repair shops as a custom add-on, and Fender's put them on their Strat Plus, Strat Plus Deluxe, and Ultra Strat guitars.

This adjustable spring-loaded device replaces the middle spring in your guitar's rear cavity. The standard 5-spring claw in the cavity is also replaced with two single outer spring claws, making room for the Trem-Setter. A brass rod connects it to the sustain block, and after you pull or push the tremolo the Trem-Setter's spring returns the tremolo block to the same spot consistently. It also keeps even tension on the tremolo so that bending or tuning a string doesn't cause the other strings to drastically alter their pitch.

Here are the benefits it claims, and it delivers quite well. At the end of this section, I've listed what my own experience with it says the Trem-Setter can/can't do.

✔ Returns the trem to zero point, in tune.

✔ Reduces "tremolo flutter" (a waste of string energy).

✔ Keeps other strings in tune when you're bending.

✔ Makes bending easier: the bridge doesn't sag forward when you bend so you don't have to bend so far

✔ Holds tune better if your hand touches the bridge.

✔ Helps make up for worn-out edges at your old bridge's pivot point.

One thing it won't do: it won't keep a guitar in tune if you break a string. It was never intended to. The amount of tension needed to compensate for a broken string would detract from the Trem-Setter's sensitivity.

I talked with **David Borisoff**, designer of the Trem-Setter, and he's got a good description of what it's all about: "A standard tremolo is like a bathroom scale— you can get on the scale twice and get two different readings. Or if you stand on the scale and shake, like shaking or bending a string, you'll make the dial flutter on both sides of your actual weight. This is what happens to a tremolo bridge when you bend notes, play certain notes with a strong attack or even hit certain open strings: You upset the balance, and the tremolo flutters back and forth. The Trem-Setter's like a car's shock absorber; it stabilizes the tremolo."

How much does the Trem-Setter change the feel of a tremolo as it's being dumped or pulled up? Fender's **George Blanda** responds: "Not too much, and not at all when you pull up, because the pull rod moves through the spring on an up-pull, without affecting the tension at all. The tension of the Trem-Setter's spring is comparable to that of a normal tremolo spring. But rather than the spring stretching when you dump the tremolo, it compresses. A factory setup for a Strat Plus uses three springs and usually .009"–.042" or .010"–.046" strings. A player who wants to use only two springs and .008" strings couldn't benefit from the Trem-Setter, since it's a three-spring system. Besides, we don't recommend using two springs on a tremolo in the first place. I should point out that all springs are not the same tension; springs used on locking tremolo systems are typically stiffer by as much as 15%. In a repair shop, extra springs end up laying all over the place, and if the wrong springs end up being used along with the Trem-Setter, the tension won't be right when you dive-bomb."

Sometimes I feel, or almost hear, a little drag when I press the wang bar on a Trem-Setter-equipped Strat Plus. "This isn't normal," Borisoff explains, "but it can happen. Over time we discovered that if too much grease was used on the brass pull rod, it actually vacuumed around the small stop-collar washer as it moved, creating a suction effect. Dismantle the Setter, clean off any grease, and when you re-assemble it, leave the washer dry or lightly lubricate it with WD-40. Be careful not to lose the washer when you take the device apart—the parts want to pop all over the place. We may switch to a fiber washer that not only won't vacuum onto the rod, but will also compress less, eliminating any possibility of slop.

"If you do take the unit apart, once the small slack spring that pushes against the stop collar is removed, you can see how the brass collar bears against the end of the threaded brass tube that the pull rod slides through." How much can the nylon thread nuts be tightened or loosened when the tremolo's tension is being adjusted? "You can tighten it a lot," says Blanda, "but you won't want it too tight. You'd never want to see more than 5/16" of exposed thread on the brass tube: experiment until

you find an adjustment that feels right. As for loosening it, by temporarily removing the lock collar spring as we mentioned, you'll see that loosening the nylon thumb-nut counterclockwise too much causes it to hit the brass stop collar—you don't want that bit shaft as a depth! The whole trick in setting up the Trem-Setter is to get the brass stop collar to make perfect contact with the washer at the end of the threaded brass tube when the tremolo is sitting at its balance point. Then any lowering of the tremolo arm puts the Trem-Setter into operation instantly. You can loosen the thumb-nut tension as far as you like as long as it doesn't touch the collar. Hold one nylon nut while you tighten or loosen the other; otherwise they'll just rotate together, and nothing happens."

Borisoff describes why he feels there's a tone improvement when a Trem-Setter is installed: "When the string's energy hits the bridge, you want it to transfer instantly to the body so that the sound comes from the bridge and body together. When a tremolo flutters at the balance point, the tremolo block and springs cancel out and absorb much of the string energy that you're working hard to get to your amp. The player puts a lot in, but not enough comes out. It's like running in sand, where half the energy just pushes sand behind you, with only half left to push you forward. Get on solid ground, and you can take off with a one-to-one transmission of energy and no waste." Blanda adds, "There's a better coupling between the tremolo block and the body, which produces a difference you can really hear."

One of the big questions, of course, is how well does the Trem-Setter work with a standard Strat tremolo? "Quite well if the guitar is set up right," insists Borisoff. "A vintage Strat has friction at the six mounting screws of the bridge plate, as well as at the nut slots, non-locking tuners, and string trees. Comparatively speaking, a Strat Plus looks pretty good with its roller nut, two-point pivot, and lack of string trees and locking tuners. So setup is crucial on a vintage Strat. All friction points must be smoothed and lubricated so the strings can't hang up and store any slack."

Trem-Setter installation tips

The installation and adjustment instructions supplied by Hipshot (and Fender with Trem-Setter-equipped guitars) are accurate, thorough and easy to follow. The installation is only slightly invasive to the guitar. Rather than going through the whole operation, I'll just add my notes to what you already have. The installation only takes about a half-hour, and the tools needed are an electric hand drill, a small ruler, Phillips screwdrivers, and such. Adjust your tremolo to suit your tastes before you begin the installation, and take the time to set your guitar up right.

Since the original five-hook spring claw is replaced with two individual outer spring claws, you'll be setting the tremolo balance point with two springs instead of three (you'll be tightening the spring claws closer to the end of the cavity than you would with three springs). The Trem-Setter has no effect, or spring tension, on the tremolo until you depress or lower the strings.

The hinge-clip has two mounting holes; the front hole (closest to the tremolo block) is located 3-3/8" out from the sustain block. The hinge-clip mounts at right angles to the block and in line with the center spring hole. Use a center-punch to mark the hole and help the drill bit stay on center. Use a #50 drill bit for soft wood and up to a #80 bit for hardwood (the bits vary depending on the type of wood—practice drilling on scrap to be sure it works for you). Drill only the front hole at this time. Then temporarily mount the hinge-clip with one screw, and not too tightly. Now put the Trem-Setter onto the hinge-clip and snap the brass pull into the center spring hole of the tremolo block. Since the hinge-clip is slightly loose, it will line itself up naturally with the tremolo block. When it does, mark it, remove the Trem-Setter and drill and mount the other hinge-clip screw.

The instructions call for drilling a 3/16" clearance hole in the end wall of the tremolo cavity (another invasive move), but they don't tell you that you really should use a long aircraft drill bit. (You can order such a bit through a hardware store.) The long bit can create the low angle necessary to allow proper clearance for the Trem-Setter's pull rod. The bit I use is 12"–14" long. I use a smaller 1/8" bit as a pilot, and then enlarge that hole with the 3/16", so there's less chance for the larger bit to run off course.

On some installations, the pull-rod hook and thumbnut nearest to it scraped the back cover plate when the tremolo was dumped. The instructions advised rebending the pull-rod hook if this happens, so that its angle matches the angle of the hole in the tremolo block (it

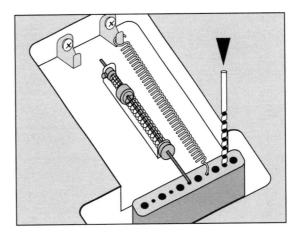

won't seat right if the angles don't match). I stuck a #50 (.070") drill bit into an empty hole so I could see the true angle of the tremolo block spring holes, and then bent the pull rod's brass hook to match (above). In one case this was the solution, but in another it wasn't—I found a different problem.

I was working with a replacement neck and body, an original Wilkinson roller nut (not the Strat Plus style), and a real American Standard tremolo that I got in a parts swap. By laying a straightedge across the back while working the tremolo, I could see just where it was rubbing, and that bending the hook wouldn't quite solve my problem. In this case the spring cavity was deeper than that of a real Strat (11/16" to 3/4" as opposed to 5/8"), causing the Trem-Setter's pull rod to rise at an angle where it hooked into the block. I used my Dremel tool

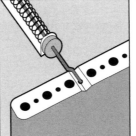 with an abrasive mesh wheel to grind a groove across the bottom of the block, so the hook would sit deeper and at less of an angle. I might have been able to shim the hinge clip up 1/16" to 1/8" higher to get the same effect, but I took this route.

One trick **Dave Borisoff** uses when the brass hook needs re-bending is to hammer on the hook with a center punch or nail set while it's in the trem block; the block acts as an anvil, shaping the hook to the right fit.

With the traditional Fender Tremolo (6 screws), a Trem-Setter is very helpful; they tend not to come back to the same "home" as easily as a 2-post knife-edge fulcrum bridge. Either bridge can benefit from a Trem-Setter.

To sum up, I like the Trem-Setter, but find that some players misunderstand it and expect too much from it. Here's what I think it can and can't do:

✔ It eases bending strings and when one string bends the other strings stay in tune.

✔ It does a good job of helping a tremolo return to zero. It isn't perfect, so you should know that before you start. The slight out-of-tune effect that may remain after dumping the tremolo can be straightened out by shaking the tremolo bar or hitting the bridge with the palm of your hand to settle it back into place.

✔ As for the improvement in tone resulting from a better string/bridge/body coupling, I don't hear it.

✔ String flutter or warble is something many players aren't aware of, or bothered by; but for those who are, the Trem-Setter is a way to eliminate it. It eliminates the need to "block" the tremolo (many players shove a hardwood block between the sustain block and the body to improve tone, eliminate flutter and stop the guitar from going out of tune).

✔ The improved stability doesn't do much to keep the bridge from moving if you rest your hand on the bridge while you pick or mute the strings. It might do a little to help, but when you press down on the back of the bridge, you're pushing in the direction that the Trem-Setter's spring has no control over (this is the only claim of the manufacturer that I disagreed with). But David Borisoff explains that if you slightly loosen the two tremolo springs and then tighten the Trem-Setter's buck spring a little, your bridge should have more stability in the string-raise mode, letting you rest your hand on the bridge more.

Roller nuts

The Wilkinson roller nut Many tremolo users don't want to hassle with a locking nut, and don't want to use a tremolo system that can only be tuned with fine tuners. To help guitars with traditional tremolos stay in tune (and help them return to pitch), Trev Wilkinson designed the Wilkinson roller nut. It uses steel rollers in the string grooves, or nut "slots" to help ease the friction that occurs during tremolo use. Wilkinson's roller nut is significant because he also made a variation of it for Fender (the Fender/Wilkinson nut) which was Fender's non-

locking alternative for tremolo players from 1987 until 1993—and standard equipment on many thousands of Fender's Strat Plus guitars during that period. Then, in the summer of '93, Fender switched to the LSR ball-bearing roller nut designed by Bill Turner. Here's some information on the Wilkinson Roller Nut.

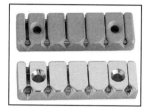

Like Floyd-style locking nuts, the Wilkinson nut requires some removal of wood to create the flat on which it sits. Also, the end of the fretboard must be shortened by 1/16" in length so that the nut's rollers are in the correct spot for intonation. So, while the wood removal necessary for a Wilkinson nut is minimal when compared to a Floyd-style locking nut, some routing is necessary, and the need to shorten the fretboard means you won't be installing these on a vintage axe.

The Original Wilkinson nut is 3/16" in width, which means you end up with a nut slot of 1/4" on a Fender or a Gibson. The nut comes with a separate "hold-down," installed behind the nut, to keep down-pressure on the rollers. Fender's Strat Plus nut has six roller hold-downs built right into the nut frame, and that's why it's significantly wider (1/2") than the 3/16" Original.

Both Original and Fender/Wilkinson nuts have a chrome-plated brass housing that holds six loose-fitting needle-bearing rollers at its front edge. The nut's six individual string slots measure, from treble to bass, .011", .014", .018", .028", .038" and .049". Deduct a half-thousandth (.0005) from each measurement for chrome plating, and you'll know what string gauges fit through the slots (a set of .010 – .046 works best, and an optional nut for .012– .052 strings was available).

The Wilkinson nut, at times, exhibits these problems: 1) seizing of the rollers; 2) too tight a string notch which would bind on some strings—not allowing them to return in tune; 3) and rattles or buzzing. Partly because of these intermittent problems, Fender retired the Wilkinson nut in the summer of 1993. According to **Dan Smith**, Fender's vice president of marketing:

"When we first looked at the Strat Plus, we knew we had a great unit in the American Standard Tremolo. We'd made 10 or 11 different tremolos over the past 15 years, and the American Standard was the best—it surprised even us. Taking advantage of this tremolo meant stabilizing what goes on at the headstock between the nut and the tuners. Trev Wilkinson happened along with his roller nut at just the right time. He redesigned it with exclusive, built-in hold-downs to do away with string trees on the headstock face.

"Our first model had rollers on the top three strings only. Soon, we installed them on all six strings to get better down-pressure on the wound E-, A- and D-string rollers. This eliminated any chance of open-string buzz caused by either inadequate string angle or from headstock deflection. It's a little-known fact that a headstock can deflect —or bend up—toward the strings. This changes the down-pressure slightly, but enough to cause a possible buzz. Some headstocks deflect, and some don't, even when made from the same tree. A traditional nut can work well with a tremolo, if everything's perfect and if it's made by a skilled luthier. But those 'perfect' nuts have only a short lifespan before wearing low enough to warrant replacement—another reason we wanted a roller nut on the Plus.

"We were happy with the Wilkinson nut, and of course there are thousands of Strat Plus models equipped with it—and an equal number of satisfied players. The fact is that less than 5% of those Strat Plus nuts had any problems. However, we never stop looking for ways to improve our products. We found that improvement in the LSR nut designed by **Bill Turner**."

Solving roller nut problems For those of you having problems with any version of a Wilkinson nut—the Original or the Fender version—here are some solutions:

First, eliminate any binding in the slot. A too-narrow string slot can cause a string to bind (usually the high-E), keeping it from returning to pitch or causing a buzz at the roller. The binding may be caused by a warp you could never see or measure, or it may be due to a bit too much plating. I use Mitchell Abrasive Cord to carefully de-burr the back edge of the string slot. These cords are coated with abrasive and come in a variety of sizes. You can also use "lightning strips," super thin diamond coated steel strips that your dentist uses to clean between your teeth after a filling—ask for one. I also use my .010"precision nut file, again on the rear wall of the nut housing. Don't scar the rollers!

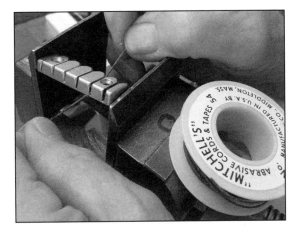

d.i.y.

Sometimes there's no binding trouble, but a slight buzz. Most likely, this sitar-like sound is on the high E. If a buzz isn't being caused by string-slot binding, it's generally intermittent and will go away by itself (especially if you try to show it to your repairman). But if it won't play itself out, try these remedies:

✔ Simply put on a fresh set of strings.

✔ With the strings removed, tap lightly on the problem roller with a sharp-pointed tool, like an awl or scribe.

✔ Remove the strings and blow out the nut with compressed air.

✔ Loosen the nut's mounting screws, let the strings line the nut up naturally, and retighten. Often, just moving it like this solves the problem! Don't overtighten the two small mounting screws—just make them snug.

✔ Lubricate the offending roller after it's been blown out with air. To avoid attracting dust, use a non-oily Teflon type of lubricant. A little dab will do you.

✔ Rinse out a dirty nut with a spray-type tuner degreaser followed by a blast of air.

✔ To alter the nut height, your Fender dealer stocks stainless-steel nut shims in thicknesses of .002", .005" and .010".

Removing and replacing the Wilkinson nut

Here's how **Roger Sadowsky**, of Sadowsky Guitars in New York City, solves problems with the Wilkinson Nut. Roger is in the big leagues of guitar repair and setup. His repair work is renowned, and so are the guitars and basses he makes. Roger offers this solution to problems with the Wilkinson nut:

d.i.y.

"I replace it when a customer experiences problems. The nut really only works its best with .009" strings. As soon as you use .010s, the problem of the string binding in the slot often shows up. And the intermittent buzzes may happen with any string gauge (or not at all). We replace the roller nut with the Floyd Rose Replacement Nut from ALLPARTS. This nut is made from Ebonal, a black, low-friction phenolic somewhat like Micarta, and was designed for players wishing to convert back from a locking-nut system.

"The truth is, I think most people aren't knowledgeable enough about guitar setup to complain. They don't know that it's not working right. I will say that if Trev Wilkinson himself installs the nut and sets it up, there won't be any problems. But most of us out in the field have met with some trouble. Here's how we take care of the problem:

1 Use a 1/16" spacer to add back the missing fingerboard length.

2 The ALLPARTS nut has holes for the Floyd nut-mounting screws, but they don't match the Wilkinson holes. We avoid plugging and re-drilling mounting screw holes in the neck by simply super-gluing in the nut.

3 Mount a string retainer on the face of the peghead, behind the nut.

4 Adjust the string grooves in the replacement nut and set up the instrument."

Fender's LSR roller nut The LSR nut is factory-installed on the Strat Plus, Deluxe Strat Plus, and Strat Ultra models. This innovative roller nut features rotating steel ball bearings that are precision set within a compact stainless steel frame. (This frame is smaller than the Fender/Wilkinson nut, about the size of the 3/16" Original Wilkinson nut.)

Each string rides over its own pair of ball bearings through string clearance slots that will accept string gauges from .008" to .056" (high E to low E) without touching the strings. The strings' only contact is with the the two steel balls, which they're centered on.

A neoprene pressure pad behind the ball bearings puts just enough pressure on them to eliminate ring, buzz, and rattle, but not enough to hinder their motion.

Fender offers the LSR nut separately for custom installations. This includes an adapter for easily upgrading models produced before the introduction of the LSR. If you have an older Strat Plus, Deluxe or Ultra, you can switch to the new nut without a problem. I'd say more about the LSR, but I haven't been able to find anything to fix on it! Being stainless it won't rust, and lubrication isn't even necessary according to **Dan Smith** at Fender. An occasional cleaning with a dry toothbrush is the only maintenance it needs.

String benders

When Fender Telecasters are mentioned, talk of the late Clarence White and his legendary Stringbender is never far behind. In 1967 Gene Parsons created the first String-bender for Clarence's Tele, and shortly thereafter Clarence immortalized it on the Byrds' *Sweetheart Of The Rodeo* album, with his buddy Gene on drums.

Beside the Stringbender, the other popular string-bending devices are the Glaser bender (used by Ricky Skaggs and Diamond Rio's Jimmy Olander) and the Hipshot (Hellecaster Will Ray's weapon of choice). All three devices create a "pedal steel" effect by raising a string's pitch (normally a whole step on the B string) when a lever is activated. Let's look at what's involved with installing these devices, starting with the original.

The Parsons/White Stringbender Since it involves removing wood from the body, Stringbender installation permanently modifies a guitar. It's available as a kit that includes an excellent 25-page instruction book, but the factory recommends having it installed by an authorized dealer/installation center ($550 installed). Do-it-yourselfers must have advanced woodworking skills, access to a router and drill press, and a good selection of hand tools. Here's why:

✔ A rear-routed cavity in the body houses the mechanism. The pull-lever connects to the guitar strap button at the neck end.

✔ Connected to the strap, the pull lever is activated by pushing down on the neck.

✔ The strap button on the pull lever travels 17/32" when depressed, creating a whole-step B-string bend, and it moves a string-pull "hub" on the guitar's face.

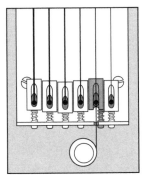

✔ The B string runs from the pull-hub to the bridge saddle through a clearance slot cut into the bridge base plate. Traditional three- and six-saddle Fender bridges require only the slot. Imported bridges (such as Gotohs)

with in-line flat saddles need additional machine work on the saddles. A new length-adjust screw is moved over in the base of the saddle. The area vacated by the adjusting screw is ground away so that the B string is able to run onto the saddle.

Randy Stockwell, a great luthier in Columbus, Ohio, installed two custom-machined rollers in the saddle shown below: one puts down-pressure on the string, and the other is for the string to roll over. With the down-pressure roller, there's no need to machine a slot in the bridge plate, since the string can run straight through the original hole vacated by the length-adjust screw. Randy no longer offers this service; he suggests you contact a local luthier with a good machinist's knowledge, and the proper tools, to make the alteration.

d.i.y.

Fender's Custom Shop offers a Clarence White Tele with a Stringbender. Asked how a Tele's tone is affected by removing wood from the body, Custom Shop Stringbender expert Fred Stuart replied: "I've installed the Stringbender on two of my own Teles, but not vintage stuff, of course. It may sound strange—and some people don't believe it—but it improved the sound of both guitars. These were guitars I knew, and it just opened them up and made them sound more dynamic."

The Glaser Bender Nashville luthier **Joe Glaser** made one of his earliest benders in 1979 for **Jimmy Olander** of the band Diamond Rio (that's Joe, left, and Jimmy in the photo below). Soon after, **Ricky Skaggs** made it famous on his Glaser-made "Mandocaster" and guitar. Joe's goal was to make a mechanism that could be installed without having too much of an impact on a guitar's looks or sound.

Joe doesn't offer a kit, preferring to install the bender himself, and he's only recently authorized installers in the field. Three new holes have to be drilled into the guitar,

removing roughly the same amount of wood required for a 9-volt battery installation.

A 1/2" square hole under the neck plate houses the pull-lever, which extends through a small hole in the plate and attaches to the strap with a StrapLok.

A 1"X 3/4 " oblong hole is milled into the face of the body under the bridge for the string pull, and a long hole is drilled through the length of the body. This starts at the heel, runs through the body and oblong bridge hole, and out the guitar's butt end, where the tension adjustment is installed (above).

Fine tuning is adjusted at neck's heel. The link stays invisible by connecting to the underside of the bridge where it comes through the bottom to the saddle's "pull finger", much like the pull lever of a steel guitar.

During a whole-step bend, the pull lever's travel, or "throw," is about 1/2" at the strap button. This is the factory-preferred setting, although it can be adjusted much longer.

Glaser prefers, and stocks, the Gotoh Tele bridge with six individual saddles, although his bender is compatible with a variety of bridges, including Fender's American Standard and the G&L ASAT.

The Glaser bender, like the Parsons/White, is a permanent installation, since wood is removed. However, with the exception of the tension hole on the butt end, it can be removed with no visible effect. On a Glaser, the strap attaches at the neck plate, whereas the Parsons/White connects at the shoulder button in the normal position. "By attaching at the neck plate," Joe says, "the energy of the down-push is efficiently converted. You're not fighting the direction in which the guitar hangs, since the strap pulls in the direction of the lever rather than at a 45 degree angle to it." The B string anchors under the bridge on a hinged finger, transferring all the string pressure to the bridge plate while maintaining original string tension, saddle height and sustain. The string doesn't slide back and forth over the saddle, thus eliminating friction and the possibility of squeaking. (With the Parsons/White and the Hipshot, the B string runs at a gradual angle to the saddle, which may weaken the tone of that particular string.)

Ricky Skaggs says, "I didn't start playing electric guitar in the band until 1985 when Joe made me my first bender guitar, which I still play. I've got five of them with his benders now: a '57 Tele, the new Custom Shop Tele, two Glasers, and a G&L that Leo Fender gave me when he first started making them. I set the bender for a whole step, and adjust the 'throw' to be a little on the stiff side, maybe stiffer than easy, because I don't want the weight to pull it down and out of tune when I'm standing still.

"Joe's a very creative guy with a real heart for music. He's such a great repairman, too. He does the work himself, and he takes care of all my stuff. Many people don't know the long hours he works to keep the Nashville musicians going. Joe teaches all the young musicians to appreciate a guitar that plays in tune and stays in tune."

Glaser's double-bender is a second string pull (usually the G string) housed within the same space as a single bender. Also exiting through the neck plate, the G-bender connects to a small cord that attaches to the player's belt loop. Pushing away from ones' body activates the second pull. The cost of two benders is $700. Joe doesn't recommend starting out with two, since the second can easily be added later.

Jimmy Olander is the master of double-bending (just listen to "Meet In The Middle" on *Diamond Rio*). Jimmy reports, "I have one of Joe's first benders—a complete Glaser guitar, actually—built in 1979. I also have double-benders in a Strat, three Teles and a bajo sexto from the Fender Custom Shop. I think differently when bending on a Strat—doing a more bluesy than country thing, and playing more single lines.

"With the double-bender, I set the G-string, rather than the B, for the down throw [pushing on the neck], and I use it the most. The tension on my G-string is set relatively stiff, and both of my pulls are set to a whole step. You can bend double stops in a whole step, or lower and raise the strings at the same time in whole steps. The double-bender was a trick to learn, but worth it! As for which brand of string bender to get, it's what you get used to. My Glaser is the first electric guitar I ever played. I came to Nashville as a banjo player ready to set

'em on fire, and nobody cared. So I picked up a guitar to make a living, and I'm glad I did!"

The Hipshot Bender You can install the Hipshot yourself in minutes, and it's not permanent, since no holes are drilled. Designed by **David Borisoff**, maker of the Tremsetter and the Trilogy Multiple Tuning Bridge, the Hipshot adapts to a Tele, Strat, 335, Les Paul and many other models. The weapon of choice for **Will Ray** of the Hellecasters (above), the Hipshot is easy to install:

✔ Temporarily remove the strap button on the butt end. Locate the clearance hole in the Hipshot's trapeze tailpiece over the strap button hole, and remount the strap button, which holds the Hipshot in place (above). It's that simple! A movement of the hip and/or a slight pull on the guitar activates the lever.

✔ For added strength, Will Ray drills two extra mounting holes through the tailpiece and into the guitar's butt end. This isn't necessary, but it does make the unit more stable. It's a good idea if you're not dealing with a vintage piece. (In the photo Will is using a "ring slide" for slide guitar effects.)

✔ The hip lever can be located anywhere along the tailpiece bar by loosening two snap rings and sliding it over—a nice feature.

✔ The standard Hipshot comes with a "toggle tuner" that drops the low E to D. It can be moved to other strings, or more can be added (with toggles on the low E, A and high E strings, for instance, you could instantly drop into G-tuning).

✔ A palm lever may be added as an option. The Max Hipshot setup is three toggles, the hip lever, and a palm lever (all strings are loaded except for the D).

Will Ray points out: "With the Hipshot, you can have benders on several guitars for the cost of one Parsons/White or two Glasers, or move a bender from one guitar to another. After using it for 10 years, I can install one in about 60 seconds; then I'll spend half an hour getting the lever in exactly the right spot. For smooth operation, lubricate the friction points —the nut, string trees, and B-string saddle—with Teflon gel. If you have roller string trees—my G&L has them for the E, B, G and D—you don't need the gel.

"I activate the lever by rocking the guitar, not by pushing my hip into it. I push the guitar with my right hand until the hip lever moves. The Hipshot's sensitive—I set it for whole step bends—but I can bend half steps too, by stopping halfway. It took a lot of practice, but that's the challenge of it."

My string-bending consultant for this section was **Mike McGannon**, guitarist with the Men Of Leisure band in Columbus, Ohio. A string bender since '78 and an authority on the subject, Mike offers this advice: "Installing a permanent string bender is an expensive proposition that can't be undone. Who you deal with to install it and the kind of service received from those people who take your guitar and 'make it more' is very important. Your guitar will come back as something different, so you must have a positive feel for both the installer and the manufacturer."

Mike recommends these albums for aspiring string-benders: **Albert Lee** on "Blue Memories," from **Patty Loveless'** *On Down the Line*, and "Settin' Me Up" on *Hiding*; **Mike Warford** on **Linda Ronstadt's** "Willin,'" from *Heart Like A Wheel*; **Marty Stuart's** "I'm Blue, I'm Lonesome," from *Tempted*; **Ricky Skaggs** with **Mark O'Connor** on "Restless," from *Nashville Cats*; *The Return of the Hellecasters* with **Will Ray**, **John Jorgenson**, and **Jerry Donahue**; **Jimmy Olander's** "Meet in the Middle" and "Pick Me Up" on *Diamond Rio*; and **Clarence White's** classic "Muleskinner Blues" from *Muleskinner*, and "Truck Stop Girl" on the **Byrds'** *Untitled*.

Chapter 9

Acoustic guitar bridges

 basic

No part of the acoustic guitar is more important than the bridge, because it transmits sound from the vibrating strings to the guitar's soundboard. If the bridge has problems, the guitar's tone and volume have problems.

This chapter focuses on acoustic bridge saddles and bridge pins. This information is "semi-repair." If you're doing an acoustic guitar setup, you may need to draw from this chapter. This is somewhat deeper material, and trickier work, than what's covered in Chapter 4. On the other hand, your guitar's bridge

ay have bigger problems than we cover here: if you're facing a loose bridge or unglued braces, you'll find the help you need in Chapter 10. Cracked bridges, warped tops, loose braces and other serious problems need to be repaired before you're ready for the adjustments described here.

basic

Fitting flattop bridge pins   121
Evaluating acoustic action   123

d.i.y.

Replacing a bridge saddle   124
Archtop bridges   127
Fitting an archtop bridge   128

deep

Fitting flattop bridge pins

Flattop acoustic guitars only sound their best when the strings are correctly installed and well seated in the bridge pin holes. The bridge has two functions: to hold the strings and to transmit their sound to the body. Any problem in either of these functions results in loss of volume and sweetness of tone. Every detail counts. For example, on a well-made bridge, the bridge pin holes should be reamed carefully so that the pin is snug, but not too tight. A string's ball end must fit firmly against the bridge pad on the top's underside. It should never be pulled up into the bridge pad, the top or the bridge itself.

basic

(Use a telescoping inspection mirror through the sound-hole to see the bridge pad.)

Bridge pins that pop out or creep up, string-end windings that pull up onto the saddle, or a dull, muted tone are indicators that things aren't right down below. Also, I prefer to see a slight chamfer (countersink) on the bridge top so that the head of the pin has clearance around it. This chamfer not only looks attractive and allows the pin to sit lower in the bridge, but it also lets you get under the pin's head to pry it out when changing strings.

Most bridge pin holes have a slight notch at the front edge for the string winding to pull into. The pin's job is to keep the ball end shoved forward into this notch when the string is tuned to pitch. Each string, being a different diameter, requires a properly sized notch in the bridge. For some builders and repair techs, a properly

Clean bridge pin hole compared to a worn one.

fit string, notch and bridge pin would often allow the complete removal of the pin with the instrument at pitch—leaving only the notch to hold the string—but there's no need to try it. I don't mind notches that deep if the guitar arrived in my hands that way, but I prefer more subtle notches in the bridge paired with a custom-sized slot in each bridge pin to match the gauge of the string it holds. These pin notches, or flutes, are small for the unwound strings, getting bigger by degrees to accommodate the bass strings.

String notches in the bridge were originally needed because bridge pins were solid—without flutes. Without notches in the bridge, the string and the bridge pin would pop out. In the '50s bridge pins became fluted, and smaller notches were needed in the bridge.

Most modern bridge pins are installed with their flutes facing the string, but on older guitars with worn, overly deep bridge notches, you may want to turn the pin 180° so the groove faces the rear. This simple pin rotation often keeps a bridge pin from falling out of a too-loose pin hole.

Many bridges (generally on inexpensive guitars) have only very slight notches, or none at all, and a skinny, fluted, cheap plastic bridge pin. For these I prefer to create or enlarge these notches until the string locks in

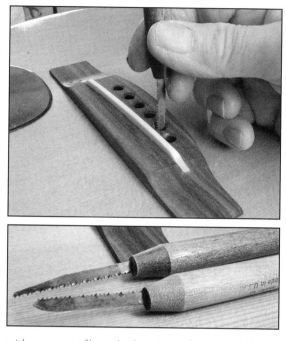

with a new set of bone bridge pins — fit and fluted by me. The improvement in tone on a cheap guitar is huge. I use a miniature, wooden-handled jigsaw blade for slotting bridge pin holes. I customized the saw by removing the blade, flipping it end-for-end, and regluing it in the handle so the teeth point upward and cut on the upstroke. This avoids the tendency to tear out bridge pad wood, which can happen on a saw's downstroke. After sawing, use a small needle file to smooth and radius the slot's top. The notch should be radiused toward the

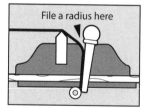

File a radius here

saddle where the string angles out of the hole. Slotting and filing bridge pin holes isn't complex, but take your time so the holes are clean and straight.

Bridge pad damage

Use your inspection mirror to look at the bridge pad—the pad of wood glued to the underside of the guitar top directly below the bridge. The bridge pad on an old guitar can be quite worn out. It may have six jagged holes where the ball ends of the strings have been wearing away at it, or it may have suffered damage when the bridge pin holes were first drilled through the top. (A hardwood block should be held on the inside to keep the drill bit from breaking wood from the bridge pad as it plunges through, but this step is sometimes omitted on cheap guitars or in work done by inexperienced craftsmen.) Your inspection mirror can tell you a lot in a hurry.

If these holes are fractured or worn out, the ball end of the string will pull up into the bridge pad and you may find that the string windings will end up reaching the saddle. Don't despair—the problem's fixable (page 148).

Here's a temporary solution for badly worn holes. It works well and may even add tone and sustain to lower quality instruments: slide a plastic, wood or ceramic

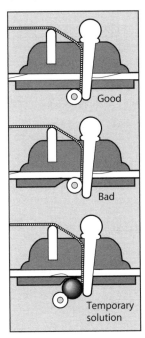

Good

Bad

Temporary solution

bead over a string's windings and up against the ball end. Now the bridge pin can properly hold the string and spacer against the bridge pad, as in the bottom drawing at left. I used to make myself fishing lures, and I still have a drawer full of small, cone-shaped brass weights used to make Mepps spinners. I slide the string through hole in the brass weight and string from inside. When the customer tires of stringing this way, it's time to repair the bridge pad.

Evaluating acoustic action

Here's a letter from a worried acoustic guitar owner, and his concerns are no doubt shared by many players:

Dear Dan:

I've been advised to get some work done on my steel-string, and I'd like a second opinion. The guitar is a good-quality ($900) import with a solid-spruce top and laminated back and sides; I bought it in 1988. The problems are that the action has gotten high and the strings buzz at the lower frets (up to the 5th). I took it to several repair shops without too much satisfaction.

Here's what happened: Adjusting the neck didn't solve the buzzing problem, so the frets were filed, but it still buzzes. A neck adjustment helped significantly with the high action

problem, but it was still stiff. The saddle was then filed lower to further bring down the string height, but the strings rattled slightly at the saddle since the angle had been lowered so radically. Then the repairman cut slots in the bridge behind the saddle to steepen and improve the angle as each string came out of its hole in the bridge. I have been told that this is normal and that nothing is wrong with my guitar, but in the future I may need to have the bridge shaved thinner to further lower the action. Now I have a guitar that has good action, but it still buzzes and has an ugly bridge. Are these techniques standard practice, or is all this work a compensation for poor construction? Why is the guitar still buzzing? And what about this bridge shaving?

P.S. I live in the Southwest, where the climate is very stable and supposedly good for guitars.

All guitars, especially new ones, need adjustments over the years to compensate for any or all of the following: climate; settling of the entire instrument; poor construction; a basically good construction, but with poor design in one area (perhaps the neck-set in your case); average wear and tear. You problems are common, so let's analyze the repair work that has already been done to your axe.

✔ Adjusting the neck can eliminate buzz if the frets are leveled correctly to begin with. Straightening an up-bowed neck (excessive relief) will significantly lower high action. But even a neck with perfect frets can be adjusted either too straight or with too much relief, and you'll end up with buzzes if you haven't matched the adjustment to your playing style and string gauge.

✔ Leveling the frets can help eliminate buzz, but if the frets only buzz up to the 5th fret, perhaps they have been worn much lower than the rest of the fingerboard (this is common if you play mostly in the first position). Instead of lowering the remaining 16 frets to the height of the first five, you might have to replace the five frets (a "partial refret") to bring them up to the height of the others. If you're still getting buzz, it could be coming from the bridge saddle. Also, remember that some amount of buzzing is normal for a steel string resting against a metal fret. Don't be too finicky!

basic

basic

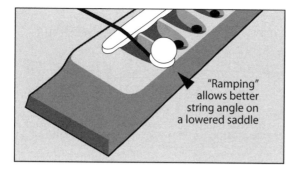

"Ramping" allows better string angle on a lowered saddle

✔ Cutting slots from the bridge pinholes to the saddle is one way of getting sound out of a low bridge saddle, since it improves the string's break-angle over the saddle. This is not a preferred method, however, and usually the saddle is only low because it's been sanded to improve an action that's too stiff, as in your case. The slotting technique you refer to—hollowing out wood behind the saddle—is often referred to as "ramping." Ovation uses this ramping technique in the manufacturing process. I don't think it looks good on guitars that weren't designed with it, but on Ovations it looks cool because the guitars are so modern in design. Cutting these slots is acceptable as an inexpensive fix-me-up, but not the preferred correction for a good instrument.

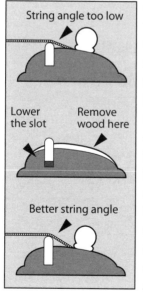

String angle too low

Lower the slot

Remove wood here

Better string angle

✔ If the bridge is 11/32" thick or more, it is okay to shave it to expose an almost-buried saddle. The process involves removing wood from the top and re-cutting the depth of the slot that holds the saddle (since it would be too shallow once the wood is removed from the bridge). For the record, the most commonly accepted steel-string bridge thicknesses are 3/8", 11/32" and 5/16", although you'll often see bridges shaved to 1/4", which makes me nervous. To many of us, even 5/16" is beginning to get a little skimpy.

✔ In your case, a neck reset may be the best way to lower the action without totally losing saddle height (as well as the guitar's volume and tone). Neck resets are more complicated and expensive than grinding down the bridge/saddle or slotting the bridge behind the saddle. Most imported neck joints I've seen don't reset as easily as Martin, Gibson, Guild and many other American-made guitars using the traditional dovetail joint and conventional glues.

But now for the crux of the matter. Your repairmen should have advised you to take the guitar back where you bought it so that the dealer could send it back to the distributor. Since many repair shops have little or no experience in retailing, they often don't realize how well most manufacturers back up their products. Often distributors of the more recognized imported brands such as Takamine, Alvarez, Washburn, etc., will even replace the whole guitar to keep a customer happy, especially with a higher quality instrument. Of course, it's only fair that you must be the original owner. It may not be too late to send it back to the maker, so at least give it a try. Good luck!

d.i.y.

Replacing a bridge saddle

Acoustic players who search for the utmost in tone and volume can't be particular enough about having a well-fit saddle. Made and installed properly, the saddle puts the finishing touch on expensive, high-quality instruments. The same attention to detail in fitting a saddle to a less-expensive model is probably even more important—it's amazing what a tone-sink a poorly installed plastic saddle can be.

The saddle is the final stopping point of a string's length, so its placement is essential in determining proper intonation. More important, it's the transmitter of sound from the vibrating string to (and through) the bridge, causing the top to move. This creates the sound, tone and volume that is unique to each individual guitar. In order of preference, my choices of saddle and nut material are: ivory or bone, Micarta and plastic. Bone is the best all-around material for saddle-making, since it's readily available, inexpensive and quite hard.

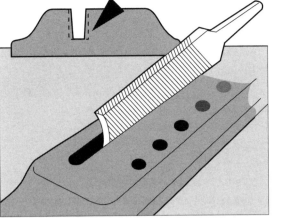

A saddle should be replaced when:

✔ It fits loosely in the saddle slot and can be easily moved with the strings removed. This loose fit may not only cause vibrations and slight buzzes, but it also seriously inhibits the guitar's ability to produce volume—not to mention tone.

✔ It has become pitted or grooved from years of use. To file or sand out these imperfections would lower the action—time for a new saddle.

✔ It is made from plastic, and the player is looking for more volume and better tone. In my opinion, plastic just won't cut it.

✔ The slot is too shallow, causing the saddle to lean forward and eventually develop a warp or crack. In this case the slot should be recut deeper before fitting another saddle.

Sight across the bridge from the side, looking lengthwise along the saddle. If it looks curved or warped or seems to tilt forward, most likely the saddle should be replaced (and the slot it rests in should be squared-up). Squaring the slot is important, since there's a huge difference in power and tone transmission when the saddle fits well. A saddle should be somewhat difficult to remove, due to its tight fit. In fact, you should be able to grasp a well-fit saddle with a pair of pliers and pick up the whole guitar with it—but don't try it! A snug fit is what you want, but a saddle that's too tightly forced into its slot could cause the bridge to split.

Practice on scrap If you feel like doing your own saddle work, don't start on a guitar that's dear to you. Find a clunker to practice on.

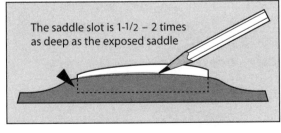

The saddle slot is 1-1/2 – 2 times as deep as the exposed saddle

Record the saddle's height before removing it. Make a mark on the front and back of the saddle with a sharp pencil at the point where it enters the bridge. This will help you remember the saddle height after you have installed the new saddle blank and are ready to set the

string height. Remove the saddle by gripping it with a pair of end-nippers or pliers, and gently rock it side to side slightly as you pull upward. Don't force anything, and remember that some saddles are glued in. If you have too much trouble, take the guitar to your local repairman. When the saddle is out, mark the bottom on the treble side with a small "X." This will help you remember which side was treble or bass when you're ready to trace it onto a new blank.

Before you can replace the saddle, you must be sure that its slot is well shaped and straight from end to end, with smooth, perpendicular sides that are square to the bottom. The slot should be deep enough to support the saddle well (one and a half to twice the saddle's exposed height above the bridge top — depending upon the bridge thickness). It's not uncommon to find slots with sides that are not perpendicular to the bottom or parallel to each other. Going slowly from end to end with a sharp, long-beveled chisel, you can pare the wood from these sides to square up the slot. A spark-plug file with the tip ground as shown above can be used as a scraper on the push stroke, filing at the same time. It's also great for smoothing and straightening a slot from end to end, as well as for cleaning up any chisel marks. If the slot looks good to begin with, try inserting a standard blank into it and don't mess with trying to change its size—I haven't run into this situation enough times, however!

If the slot is too shallow, allowing the saddle to lean or fall over, it must be made deeper. The best method is to rout it with a Dremel Moto-Tool mounted in its router base. This miniature routing tool is well known by professional repairmen and serious hobbyists. The base holds the router at right angles to the bridge, and with successive passes of 1/16" or so, you can quickly reach the desired depth. After routing, clean up any slight marks on the sidewalls with the chisel and file. Wear a dust mask while cutting or sanding bone or hardwoods.

Most saddle blanks are between 3/32" and 1/8" thick. While some replacement saddles drop right into the existing slot, most are thicker than the original by as much as 1/32", to account for the squaring up and consequent over-sizing of the old slot.

I prefer oversize blanks of bone, and usually size them

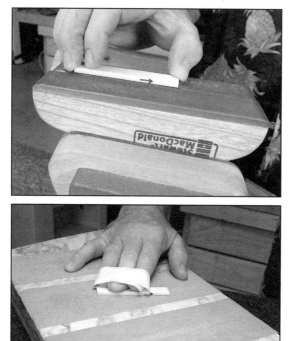

on a stationary belt sander. Accurate results can be achieved by hand: first smooth and flatten one side by rubbing the saddle against a leveling file. After measuring the saddle slot width, transfer the measurement to the new blank with a pencil or scribe, measuring and

marking off the good, flat side. Remove material from the opposite side until you come to the measured line. This can be done by rubbing on the smooth file, against 180- or 220-grit sandpaper, or by using a scraper blade. If you're sanding, wrap tape around your fingers (sticky side out) to hold a saddle that only needs light thicknessing to get the proper fit. When the blank begins to fit, trim it to exact length and round the ends to match the slot's dimensions.

Rather than just dropping in, a well-fit saddle "squeaks" when installed. Support the guitar under the bridge with your free hand while pushing the saddle in from above. A too-tight saddle might eventually cause the bridge to crack, or it may not go in at all. Once inserted, it's hard to remove for shaping and action work. Again, practice on inexpensive instruments as you learn to do your own work.

When the new blank fits into the slot, recreate the former string height and saddle shape by referring to the original, which you've marked with a pencil. If you didn't like the feel of the original action, shape the new saddle to suit your taste, raising or lowering the strings by degrees. In general, the saddle should follow the fingerboard's curve, but rise slightly and flatten out a little as it goes toward the bass side. In other words, the bass strings should be higher than the treble strings to avoid buzzing. While roughing in the saddle, always be sure that its top, or crown, is rounded, so you won't be breaking strings each time you string it up to check the action.

The correct shape for the saddle top is smoothly rounded and free of sharp edges. The saddle should be showing 1/8" to 3/16" exposure above the bridge. This ensures a string angle steep enough to produce good volume. A too-tall saddle exerts too much pressure on

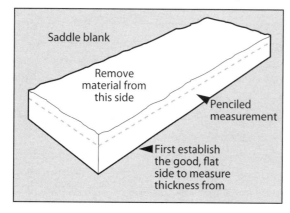

Saddle blank

Remove material from this side

Penciled measurement

First establish the good, flat side to measure thickness from

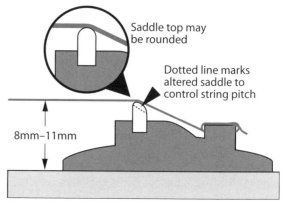

Saddle top may be rounded

Dotted line marks altered saddle to control string pitch

8mm–11mm

the slot, and can cause the saddle to warp. A height much less than 1/8" does not give the guitar's body enough chance to sound.

When you reach the desired action height, final-shape and round the saddle to a gentle curve and polish it with 400 or 600 paper. This final setting of the action is actually extremely tricky and requires much practice.

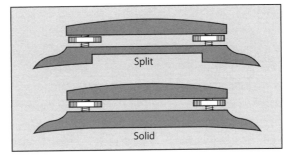

Archtop bridges

Archtop bridges often suffer from a poor fit of the bridge base to the guitar's top. The best fit can be achieved by hand, using a sharp knife such as an X-acto or a violin-maker's knife. It takes a great deal of skill to do this, however. As a substitute you can tape a piece of 120-grit sandpaper to the top and then slide the bridge base back and forth to contour it. An archtop bridge-fitting jig (below) exists just for this purpose. I like the results that a sharp knife produces, but it takes a knack developed over years. Good violin makers are adept at it; if you can find someone good at violin setups, see if they'll carve a bridge to fit your top—it'd be worth the effort!

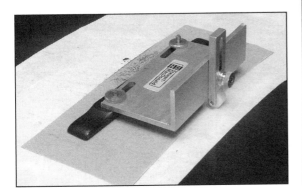

Some archtop guitars have a solid, unsplit bridge base, while others are split. In either case, check the bridge fit under normal string tension, since the top and base will flex somewhat. A perfect fit without string tension might be imperfect with the strings on.

I prefer archtop bridges that do not have metal Tune-O-Matic type saddles; the solid wood top pieces produce a better tone. These solid wooden "saddles" are often staggered for intonation compensation, especially on more modern instruments. The string notches should not be over one-half the diameter of the string in depth—just enough of a groove to keep the string from popping out when plucked. The notch should fit the string's shape and be rounded to a dull peak, not a sharp point, with all burrs removed. I polish the string grooves on rosewood or ebony archtop saddles with 0000 steel wool to burnish the wood and make it hard.

Archtop bridges should not be glued into place. They usually leave a mark in the finish, so you'll know where to reposition the bridge when you remove the strings while cleaning the fingerboard or polishing the instrument. If the bridge seems to pull to either the treble or

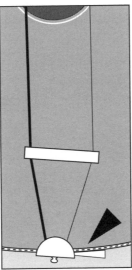

bass side and the strings won't line up with the fingerboard, the tailpiece may have to be moved slightly to either side. Have this checked by a qualified repairman, since the mounting holes may have to be plugged and re-drilled. But in many cases, this simple trick often solves the problem: loosen the tailpiece and slide a small shim of wood, paper, cardboard, etc., under one edge of the tailpiece bracket on the same side that you want it to move toward (see drawing). The shim forces the tailpiece into position—and it doesn't take much!

While there are some bridge problems that these pages haven't covered, you now know the basics and should be able to see how all the different factors relate. If you have bridge problems, think everything out before trying a repair yourself—and don't be ashamed to get professional help before doing any work that you may regret. For information on repairs under the bridge inside the guitar, see chapter 10.

Fitting an archtop bridge

Fitting a bridge on an archtop guitar can be a very time-consuming and frustrating job. Like a violin bridge, the underside of an archtop's bridge has to curve precisely to fit the top, but on a guitar you have a larger area with much more wood to remove. I use the bridge fitting jig to get this job done quickly.

2 Before unstringing, record the exact bridge location to make it easy to set up again later. The tool I use for this is called a Saddlematic. I also put relocating marks on small pieces of low-tack drafting tape near each end of the bridge; the tape is placed about 1/8" back from the ends, to make room for the sanding I'll be doing. These marks will also help me to keep the bridge centered while sanding.

I masked the area under the bridge with a low-tack paper mask called "sign-painter's tape." It's meant for taping off windows, truck sides, etc. when spraying artwork and lettering. The brand I use is TransferRite, which comes in several low, medium, and high tack. I use low-tack on vintage instruments with shellac or lacquer finish because it doesn't pull off finish when you remove the tape. Also, sign-painter's tape doesn't have the strong chemicals that masking tapes do to make them sticky—chemicals that leave an impression on nitrocellulose lacquer (especially on new finishes). Those marks show up as a rippled, shrinking look, and they don't go away without fine-sanding and buffing. On say, a "newish" Les Paul for example (a year old or less), masking tape can leave marks in minutes, and if tape is left on overnight you'll be sorry in the morning. This is important for all of us to be aware of.

1 The bridge on this Epiphone is the toughest kind to fit, because its entire length contacts the top, not just two feet with an arch in between as on many archtops. At string tension, an .008" feeler gauge slid easily under a large section of the bridge.

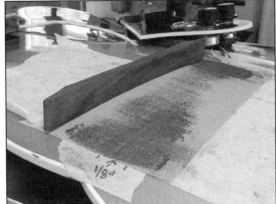

3 On top of the mask I used 120-grit Stikit Gold sandpaper for the job, because with a bridge that fits reasonably well as this one does, a more aggresive grit isn't needed. After marking the underside of the bridge with a white pencil so that I could monitor my progress, I went to work. As you can see from the dust on the sandpaper, the bridge fitting jig is removing wood from the ends first (the bridge was already high in the center).

5 This is where I stopped. The pencil marks are gone.

4 I have a rectangular, steel machinist's V-block that just happens to fit on top of the jig perfectly; its weight works as ballast, making the sanding both faster and more controlled.

6 And that's a real nice fit if I do say so myself!

Chapter 10

Acoustic body repairs

basic

basic

d.i.y.

Clamps and glues   132
Closing and gluing cracks   135
Gluing loose braces   143

deep

Reattaching loose bridges   144
Bridge pad problems   148
Neck resets   152

While most electric guitar bodies are just slabs of wood, acoustic bodies are constructed from dozens of wooden parts. Each part can warp or crack, and each glue joint can pop apart. Acoustics make up some of the toughest repairs you're going to meet.

If you're not a do-it-yourselfer, use this information to understand the troubles your acoustic can get into, and what the fixes are. You'll get a better feel for your guitar's care, and you'll know what you're asking for if you do have to take to a repair shop. And there's no getting around the fact that some professional repair shops are more experienced in electrics than acoustics, and they may want your business anyway. The more you know about acoustic repairs, the better you'll be at picking the shop to work on your guitar.

One thing that every acoustic owner must understand is how changes in climate affect a guitar. A change in seasons can take a guitar from dry winter air to damp summer heat. Just a trip across town can go from a steamy hot car to cold clammy air conditioning. Dryness sucks moisture out and makes wood shrink; dampness pumps it back up again. These repeated changes often result in cracks and glue separations. See "Dealing with humidity" on page 6.

d.i.y.

Before we start this d.i.y. section, you and I need to have a little talk!

You and I both know that by writing a do-it-yourself guide like this, I could be launching a platoon of eager beginners onto the fine guitars of the world, each one armed with brace clamps and titebond glue. The potential for mayhem makes me want to shout, "Leave the acoustic body repairs to the professionals," but I won't.

Every professional started as a beginner, so I don't want to discourage you. But I will say this: learn on cheap expendable guitars before trying your acoustic repair skills on an axe that really matters to you.

I'm a believer in yard sale specials — guitars I pick up

for a few bucks here and there. I've learned a lot this way. When these yard sale repairs are successful, somebody gets a birthday present. When they crash and burn, nobody knows but me.

So this chapter on acoustic repairs is the best place to emphasize the Golden Rule that every pro luthier has tattooed somewhere:

Practice on Scrap!

Clamps for acoustic repair work

Clamps are chosen for their throat (reach), opening, strength and weight. For working on guitar tops, a long throat is important so the clamp can reach the bridge or braces from the soundhole, and lighter clamps won't weigh down the top when you use several.

Cam clamps
The first widely produced wooden cam clamp was the Klemmsia brand, but the design has become a standard and now there are several brands available. Because of their wide 8" opening, they perform all sorts of guitar repair and woodworking tasks. They're available in three throat depths: 3-1/2", 5-5/8" and 7-3/4". They're fairly light at 1/2, 3/4 and 1lb., respectively. Cam clamps have shallow bottom jaws that balance and grip well. The large surface area of the cork-padded jaws spreads gluing pressure well, and even without cauls these clamps normally don't leave marks. With appropriate shop-made cauls to space around the braces, cam clamps make adequate bridge clamps, and they are excellent for leveling cracks, gluing bracing and many general shop tasks.

Camless clamps
are a recent innovation. They're a cam clamp without the cam: it's been replaced with a screw-threaded knob, which many find more convenient. This mechanism requires less space than the cams, which allows more clamps to be clustered together.

Mini cam clamps
are a design I came up with in my shop. They're traditional cam clamps, but are much lighter and skinnier. Five of these can fit into the space taken by three standard cam clamps.

Sloane clamps,
also known as Ibex clamps, are cast aluminum, with a 6-1/4" throat and a 2-1/4" opening. They have good grip and balance when clamped directly onto a brace or onto an interior caul (cauls are described below). Sloanes weigh 1 lb.

Pony clamps
are the strongest. These are the heavy-duty cast clamps that Martin uses for bridge clamping. A long throat model (6-1/4") is good for classical bridges, and a short one (4-3/4") for most other guitars. Martin uses only one Pony clamp per bridge,

relying on several styles of special cauls to do the rest of the job (left). Pony clamps have a 2-11/16" opening, and they weigh as much as 2 1/2 lbs. Because they're cumbersome and heavy, I don't prefer them for most bridge work. But for certain advanced repairs such as flattening a top, bridge pad replacement or Martin's approach to bridge gluing, their incredible strength is just what's needed. In my shop, sometimes I'll use one Pony and two Ibex clamps for a bridge job.

Soundhole clamps are long, lightweight C clamps with throat depths from 5"-11". Their frames are stamped steel instead of cast, so they're thin and strong. In addition to the long reach, this design has two features specifically for guitar tops: a threaded lower jaw lets the clamp reach over guitar braces without touching them, and an additional leveling screw in the middle of the clamp provides extra support and leverage. The shortest one is of course the stiffest, so I use that for bridge reglues. The longer ones are unusually agile for reaching braces anywhere on the guitar top.

Brace repair jacks are a different way to press braces into place. While clamps reach in from the outside, jacks are positioned inside the guitar and expand to apply clamping pressure. A typical brace jack is a turnbuckle with a caul on each end. The caul should have a groove in it to fit onto the brace.

Clamping cauls To keep a clamp from crunching the delicate wood of a guitar, we use a lot of homemade cauls. A caul is a scrap of wood placed between the clamp and the item being clamped. When clamping the braces inside a guitar body, cauls need to be hand-shaped to fit snugly onto the brace and stay in place. Cauls also increase the area of pressure applied by the clamp. This spreads out the pressure more evenly, while reducing the number of clamps needed to give even coverage on the piece being glued.

You'll usually make your cauls from scrap wood, and sometimes you'll cover them in waxed paper to keep them from sticking to glue squeeze-out. A sheet of clear acrylic (Plexiglas) makes great cauls for crack and brace work. It's flexible enough to follow a top's arch while still keeping both sides of a crack level. Its great strength, even in thin (1/8") sheets, protects the guitar top from clamp marks, and the ability to see through it is a plus when positioning the clamp over a crack. Also, the acrylic doesn't stick to most top-repair glues.

Cauls jigs and gizmos for keeping a brace where you want it while clamping—these are all part of the craft. It can take many dry runs to find the right setup for a clamping situation. A good rule for acoustic guitar work: never use any clamp without a caul.

Glues for bridge and brace repairs

For the novice, Titebond is the best all-around top-repair glue because it allows the most working time before it sets, and it is not as permanent as epoxy. But every glue has its advantages.

Fresh hide glue is used by many experts for all vintage top repairs, not just because it's historically correct, but also because it dries clear and brittle (like the finish surrounding it). This enhances tone, especially on bridge reglues. Hide glue swells wood less than Titebond, and is thin enough to work easily into cracks. On the downside, it sets into a gel very quickly as it cools, so you must work fast to use it! The best hide glue is mixed fresh from dry granules, and used hot in an electric glue pot.

Bottled hide glue Ready-to-use hide glue such as Franklin's Liquid Hide Glue has a shelf life, meaning that it must be used before it gets too old. The chemicals that keep bottled hide glue from going rancid, and give it more working time, also cause it to lose the ability to dry once the shelf life has expired. Always test bottled hide glue on scrap to make sure it will dry before using it. I've had some nasty experiences with bad hide glue, so be careful!

Titebond, because of its high water content, causes cracks to swell—so you must be prepared for that, and work quickly. The swelling goes away after the glue is dry and the moisture has evaporated. Titebond is good for bridge regluing, and cleans up easily with warm water.

d.i.y.

d.i.y.

Epoxy, used correctly, is great glue for joining cracks and for splints (pieces of wood inlayed into cracks). Never use epoxy for regluing bridges or loose braces, or anything that you might want to take apart sometime. Certain structural repairs can be done with epoxy, but it can be messy and tricky. I don't recommend it for novices.

Super glue is great for tiny cracks that don't need to be aligned during the gluing operation, but it sets so quickly that don't recommending it for most situations. That said, the fact is that many of us use it all the time for quickie repairs (and sometimes as a substitute for the glues mentioned above). This only works because we've become so experienced at gluing that our technique is very fast and accuate. Don't use super glue for body repairs until you feel that you're a seasoned pro.

Basic gluing technique

Clean before gluing Before regluing a separated glue joint, clean it thoroughly. Even the tiniest particles will prevent the joint from closing tightly. You'll probably wind up with a coffee cup on your workbench, filled with your cleaning tools: dental probes, skinny little brushes, pokers, reachers and whatnot. Never use a tool that's too thick to fit comfortably in the gap, unless you are purposely "wedging" the joint open to clean it.

Be careful not to force crud into a corner or under something where it can't be removed.

If you clean a glue joint with sandpaper, sand with the wood grain, not against it, to avoid cross-grain scratch marks. To clean under a brace before regluing, I reach inside the guitar body and work sandpaper into the gap. Then, with my fingers on each side of the brace, I sand with the grain. I use this same technique to apply glue

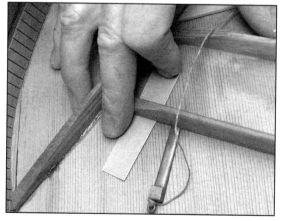

under the brace: thin metal feeler gauges work like palette knives to push the glue in, giving good coverage and penetration. Don't use the sandpaper to push the glue in, it will swell up and possibly tear inside the glue joint.

Repeatedly vacuum out the joint, or blow it with compressed air. Do this one last time before gluing.

Applying glue When you're gluing interior braces, lay rags or paper inside the guitar body to protect against glue dripping onto the opposite surface (top or back). As mentioned above, don't use sandpaper as a palette knife to apply glue. It becomes soggy and may tear and get stuck in the glue joint.

A hypodermic syringe makes a great glue applicator. Slip a piece of heat-shrink tubing (used for electrical

work) over the needle, leave a bit of the tip uncovered. This serves as a depth-stop to let you know when the needle tip is into the glue joint, and how far it's in.

Always do a dry-run of your gluing and clamping procedure without any glue—until you can do it quickly without fumbling.

Clean off excess glue After clamping, use your joint-cleaning tools for cleaning the glue squeeze-out. Tape damp or wet pieces of cloth to the ends of your reaching tools to clean up difficult areas. Work quickly to get rid of the glue while it's wet.

Most interior repairs can be done with little or no glue smear showing. This takes careful planning, taping-off areas not to be glued, careful application, speed and sometimes skinny arms (to get into the soundhole). The best repairers are the ones who don't try the first technique that comes to mind. It may be necessary to think for days about the right way to approach a loose brace, crack or crunch. There is almost no excuse for a sloppy interior glue job!

Gluing reminders

✔ Don't use glue until you know that the clamping setup is correct.

✔ Consider training someone smaller than yourself (a child?) to be your helper—applying glue or cleaning in an area that you can't reach.

✔ Use protective cauls at both points of clamp contact to prevent damage and to spread the clamp pressure evenly.

✔ If the clamp won't reach, find one that will (that 11" soundhole clamp will reach most anywhere). If can't find one, make one! Don't ever "go for it and hope for the best." Wait until you have a plan.

Crack gluing techniques

Cracks are among the most common structural problems afflicting hollowbody guitars. Many a player has rushed to my shop, expecting me to read the last rites over his pride and joy just because of a simple split. While a split on the top, side or back is certainly not to be ignored, if it's caught soon enough, it can be easily and inexpensively repaired—and quite invisibly, too. Guitars are, after all, made of wood, and wood splits. Of course, a mistreated guitar is bound to suffer damage. Too few people realize that lack of humidity can split even the best of instruments, causing as much of a crack as a sharp blow. In both cases, a simple hairline crack is easily repairable, often without the need of a professional repairman.

Hairline cracks These may be very hard to see; often you can only spot one when holding the guitar at a certain position in the right light. Hairline cracks can be mistaken for checks or crazes, which are finish cracks that should be left alone and are nothing to worry about (besides, they cannot be repaired without serious finish work that could hamper a guitar's tone and value). Many of us love a checked or crazed finish and feel that it adds to a guitar's charm and character.

Here's a simple test for determining whether a crack is actually in the wood: Using the ball of your thumb or fingertip, press very gently along the edge of the crack and watch for any movement of the wood. Avoid pressing your fingernail against the wood, since this could leave a mark. If the wood is actually cracked, you will see a slight

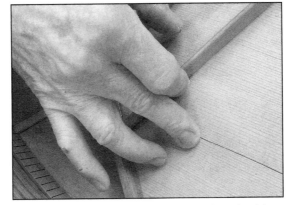

movement of the wood—most likely on the side of the crack that you're pressing on, since the pressure won't transmit across the split line. If you can reach through the soundhole, remove the strings and apply pressure from the inside. If you can reach it, get your fingertip right under the crack and press dead center. This should gently force the split open while you're looking from outside. Remember where you pressed, so that you can repeat the process later while gluing.

For gluing cracks, you'll need a bowl of warm water, some small pieces of clean cloth (3" x 3", some dipped in water and some dry), and good-quality masking tape that has lots of stretch. Squirt a dab of glue onto the fingertip of either hand, and then quickly use your free hand to move the crack in the same direction as you did earlier, only this time work the hide glue into the open crack. Work in enough so that when you release the pressure, a slight bead squeezes out. Wipe off excess glue with a damp rag, and then wipe the entire area dry in preparation for clamping.

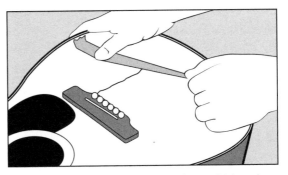

Tape clamping At a right angle to the crack's length, apply masking tape by rubbing/pressing with your thumb two or three inches from one side of the crack. Stretch the tape up and over the crack—without actually touching the tape to the crack—and press it down again about two or three inches on the opposite side. If the tape is fresh and stretchy enough, the crack will close as the tape attempts to shrink back to size. Practice the taping operation with a dry run (no glue) until you get a feel for the tape's stretching qualities. Use as many pieces across the crack as necessary (sometimes I cover a crack completely for good pressure). If there's a glue squeeze-out each time you apply a piece of tape, wipe it off with a damp rag and re-dry the area so that the next piece of tape will stick. Let the glue dry at least 12 hours.

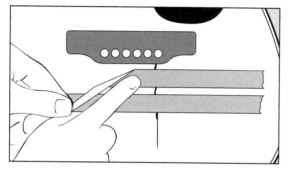

When the glue has dried, remove the tape by pulling it off at an angle. Peel it very carefully, since it's possible to remove small pieces of finish, especially on older instruments with thin, checked finishes. If you see finish coming off with the tape, rub the tape with your fingertip slightly ahead of the point where the tape is releasing from the body. This helps break the surface tension and allows easier removal of sticky tape. If you cleaned the glue bead well when it was still wet, you're done once the tape is removed. However, if there are still any dry glue beads that squeezed out, pick them off carefully with your fingernail or a sharp tool such as an X-acto knife. Buff the area with a soft, dry cloth and add any good guitar polish (Martin offers one).

Bar clamping, Martin style

Instead of using tape, you can clamp a crack together if you also use cauls to protect the guitar and its finish. When possible, it's good to use a second clamp from top to bottom to keep the crack aligned. Here are four photos that show **Milt Hess Jr.**, head structural repairman in the C.F. Martin repair shop, clamping a crack. Milt offers this advice:

"With hairline cracks on the top, sides or back, push on the crack from the inside to open it up, and saturate the crack with water. This "pre-moistening" of the crack causes the glue that follows to be drawn deeper into the wood for better glue penetration."

1 The crack will close up (the bridge is taped off to protect it from glue and water).

2 After the water, work plenty of glue into the crack, from the outside, until it penetrates thoroughly (look inside with a mirror). Be generous with the glue (Milt generally uses a Titebond-type glue).

3 Clean the excess glue off with a damp rag, and using cauls and a long bar clamp, gently squeeze the crack together. The bar clamp rests on a 1/2" thick clear Plexiglas caul. The Plexiglas keeps the crack level and gives the clamp something to rest on.

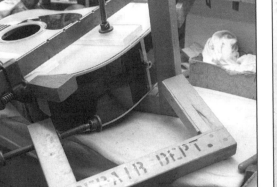

4 A second clamp (like the one in the foreground) and the Plexiglas caul keep the two sides of the crack level.

Supergluing cracks

Small "fissure" cracks often look like tiny splits in the finish but are actually in the wood (usually from a lack of humidity in the guitar's environment). These kind of cracks don't really move (you can't wiggle them or open them up), but they don't go away either! They're most common in the sides about 1" from the top or back

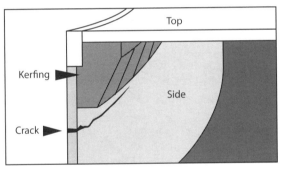

(where the kerfing that holds the side to the top or back stops and the wood is free to move). Wood movement at this point can cause a crack. If the guitar has a healthy lacquer finish, these cracks (and the finish) can be filled with super glue—several coats at a time, letting each coat dry—then sanded smooth, lacquered over, and buffed out. Here is the procedure used by repairman **Dan Shook** at the Martin repair department.

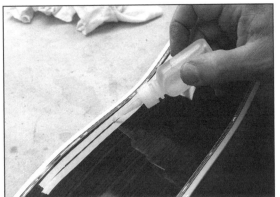

1 Tape off each side of the crack.

2 Run superglue deeply into crack until it builds slightly above finish—let dry (above).

3 Remove the tape. The crack is more than filled with the superglue—it's slightly mounded up.

4 Scrape the mounded superglue to bring it down flush with the surface of the finish.

d.i.y.

5 Scuff sand with 220-grit into the surrounding finish.

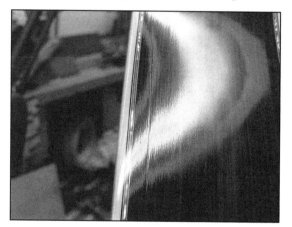

6 Spray fresh lacquer over area. These coats of lacquer have melted into the original finish (one of the nice things about lacquer—it dissolves itself!) and can now be wet-sanded and buffed. You'll never even see the finished crack.

Splinting cracks that won't close

Many cracks won't close easily (or at all) and cannot be repaired using the gluing method for hairline cracks just described. An open split that you can look into may need to be filled with a piece of matching wood. This process, called "splinting," should be done by a professional. Often, but not always, a large crack will close up in the spring as humidity increases, and then it may be glued with little trouble and no splinting. In fact, if the crack was splinted when the humidity was low, the fill might be "spit out" by the wood as it attempts to close and return to normal. Therefore, let a professional determine whether a large crack should be splinted during the dry season, left until spring to swell shut and then simply be

glued, or glued and splinted in the spring or summer (moist months).

Those cracks that are wide, stable and no longer swell shut in summer should be splinted with a sliver of matching wood (spruce, rosewood or mahogany on most guitars). Some cracks only need a small thin sliver of wood, while others require a fairly wide insert. Spruce tops are splinted more often than rosewood backs and sides, and are the most difficult to match because of the lighter shade of wood. Most spruce splints are made from the soft wood, which occurs between the darker hard grains, since the crack occurs when soft wood splits away from the hard grain.

With the narrower cracks, before gluing in a splint, I use a "crack knife" to clean dirt from the crack and make its edges parallel. It also tapers the walls slightly, to keep the spruce fill from falling through. This crack knife was designed by the Martin repair department. I discovered it on page 48 of Irving Sloane's excellent book *Guitar Repair* (most of the photos in Irving's book were taken in the Martin repair department). It's a wedge-shaped piece of steel that can enlarge and shape an open crack to a wedge, or "V" shape.

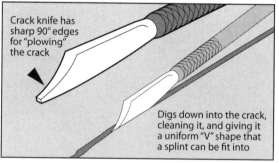

Crack knife has sharp 90° edges for "plowing" the crack

Digs down into the crack, cleaning it, and giving it a uniform "V" shape that a splint can be fit into

I made my crack knife from a worn Swiss needle file by grinding off the teeth on the sides and bottom, and shaping it as shown above. After grinding the sides of the file smooth, and to a wedge shape, the angular "face" is ground at a 35° to 45° angle and sharpened on a stone, leaving sharp 90° edges to the sides. The knife can be used in two ways: 1) On the push stroke the sharp edges of the face will actually cut both walls (or either wall alone) of a crack at once—creating shavings much like a chisel, and shaping the crack's sidewalls to a wedge shape by removing wood. 2) Once the right amount of wood has been removed from the sidewalls to make the crack even in width, the knife can be drawn in the opposite direction along the crack's length, to smooth the "V" groove and slightly compress the wood outwards so that it can swell up when the splint is glued in. For more on this technique, see Irving's book—a very important reference book for all of us.

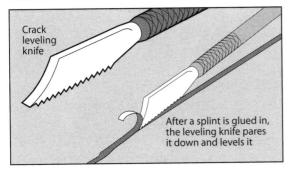

Crack leveling knife

After a splint is glued in, the leveling knife pares it down and levels it

An offshoot of the crack knife is a crack leveling knife created by my brother-in-law **John O'boyle**, repairman for Sam Ash Music in Tampa, Florida. Again, John's is a re-shaped Swiss needle file. The face is ground just like the crack knife except that it comes to a distinct chisel point, and the sides are not ground to a wedge shape. The teeth on the bottom edge of the file/crack-knife are not ground away—but left alone. What you get is a small, thin chisel with a sharp edge that meets the teeth of the file. With it, and depending on the angle at which you hold it, you can pare down the top of a wood fill, or splint, and file it smooth at the same time! John came up with this tool when working as my apprentice in '72, and we've used it ever since.

The items at top right are handy for acoustic body work: a telescoping inspection mirror and a long narrow inspection mirror help you see inside the body, reflecting the braces above. This battery-powered tube light works great inside the body (a discount store find).

d.i.y.

Now you've cleaned and tapered the crack walls, and chosen a splint of wood, matching the area around the crack in color and grain pattern. Your splint should be slightly wider than the crack: it will then be gently compressed so that it slides in easily. The wetness of the glue can swell both the crack and the splint, making insertion difficult—the compressed splint goes in easily and then swells up to full size. Once dry, a splint is pared level with (or sometimes lower than) the finish and carefully touched up with lacquer. This can be almost invisible when done by a pro.

Speaking of pros, one of the finest crack and touch-up men I know is **Tom Marcell** of Islip, New York. Tom spent many years studying with the great **John Monteleone**, and he's now a much-sought-after vintage restoration expert (when he's not building classical guitars—very talented fellow). Tom taught me this method of splinting wide cracks, holes or punctures:

1 Enlarge the crack on each side of a grain line following the grain's lengthwise pattern.

2 Measure the crack's width at 1/2" intervals and shape the splint to match any variations (some spruce is per-

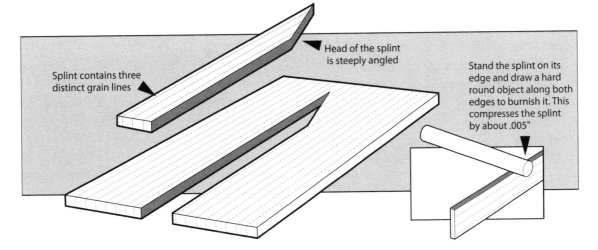

Splint contains three distinct grain lines

Head of the splint is steeply angled

Stand the splint on its edge and draw a hard round object along both edges to burnish it. This compresses the splint by about .005"

fectly straight-grained and easy to match). Leave the splint wider than the crack by .005" for compressing later.

3 The splint is shaped as in this drawing. The splint is pre-finished with several light coats of lacquer to help with color matching the refractive quality of spruce. The finish, which also keeps glue and color off the new wood, is wiped off with thinner after the splint is in, and a proper touch-up is done.

4 Glue the splint in with epoxy colored with a fresco powder to match the lighter-shaded softwood.

5 Paint surrounding grain lines over the beveled "head" of the splint.

6 French-polish, drop-fill or spray lacquer to blend the finish in.

Save those busted guitars! Martin guitar repair-man and vintage guitar expert Dave Musslewhite makes splints and patches from old Martin guitar tops and leaves the finish on. This guarantees a good color match and the correct vintage look. Once the patch has been inlaid into the top, and is flush with the surrounding

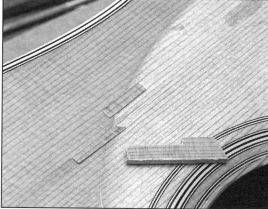

finish, French-polishing or a lacquer "melt-in" make the touchup complete.

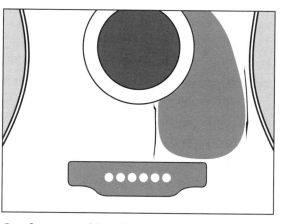

Cracks caused by shrinking pickguards

Another dryness-related problem that affects acoustic guitars with solid wood tops is the shrinking and curling of the pickguard and the damage it can cause to the wood underneath. Martin guitars are especially prone to such troubles, as are most would-be Martin competitors. Here's a list of common pickguard problems, along with their symptoms and suggested repair methods.

Martin pickguards shrink because they're made from either nitrate (until '76) or acetate ('76 until present) plastic. Both are notorious shrinkers, with the older nitrate being the worst. But along with their good looks, these plastics were chosen because they sound good, too—and Martin's tried them all. The shrinking plastic wouldn't be a problem if it didn't take the wood with it. That's why Martin switched to pickguards backed with double-stick adhesive in late 1987; this modern adhesive allows the wood to move.

Wood needs the freedom to shrink in the dry winter months and swell during the humid summer. Up until 1987, the backs of Martin pickguards were brushed with a solvent to melt the plastic, and "glued" directly to the bare wood before the finish was applied. These glue

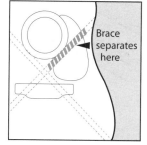

joints don't move well with the wood, and as a result problems occur: cracks at the pickguard's inner or outer edges; curling of the pickguard and the top wood, sometimes causing the top to pull away from the main X-brace or the pickguard to fall off.

Shrink cracks along the pickguard's edge take years to get very big. Some aren't even visible, and lie just out of sight, soaking in moisture, sweat, grime and guitar polish, all of which make any problem worse. Caught early, a small shrink crack can be sealed with lacquer or glue; this keeps it small and prevents it from absorbing moisture until it stabilizes. The most common pickguard cracks are the ones shown in the drawing on the opposite page. If these cracks are wide, stable and won't close up, they must be splinted as mentioned above. But usually, if the crack is caught in time, it will reglue nicely, as described here:

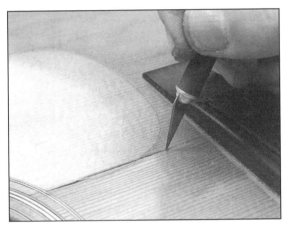

1 Clean any lacquer chips or dirt from the crack with a sharp knife.

2 Saturate with water to swell the crack shut and draw in the glue.

3 Pressing the crack open from the inside, work in lots of Titebond from the outside with your free hand.

4 Use a caul, made to fit over the bracing, on the inside.

5 The Plexiglas caul, backed with a rubber block, flattens the crack as it dries.

Curling pickguards are upsetting Even mild cases look scary. Severe curling may create a concave dip in the top, pulling the wood loose from the main X-brace (indicated by the arrow on the drawing opposite). By the way, loose braces should be fixed before using the crack-splinting techniques just mentioned. When appropriate, the pickguard can be removed to let the wood relax and flatten before being reglued to the brace. Removing the pickguard without pulling up spruce is tricky, so have it done by a professional shop with prior experience.

The mildest problems are pickguards that come either partly or completely loose of their own accord. The relief of stress often prevents any cracks, curls or loose braces, so it's nice if nature does the job for you. A pickguard that's only loose around the edges can be reglued (at least temporarily) with white glue or hide glue and then clamped in place to dry. Don't use a permanent solvent-type glue such as Duco or super glue. Usually, it's best to take a pickguard off, then reglue or replace it.

When a pickguard is off, any glue residue should be removed from the top, and the bare wood should be sealed before any remounting is done. I generally seal the bare wood with a coat or two of lacquer or shellac. Once dry and sanded smooth, the hard surface gives future adhesives something to cling to rather than the wood itself. As for the proper remounting glue, follow Martin's lead—use double-stick adhesive, or buy a real Martin pickguard. If you make your own pickguard, mount it with a spray adhesive such as 3M 77 or use double-stick adhesive carpet tape. And don't mount it on the bare wood!

Repairing a cracked end block

When a guitar gets dropped on the butt-end, it will probably split through the block if there's a strap button installed. We see this often in a repair shop. The end block will usually split in one of two ways, depending on the grain structure of the individual block: a straight split, or an angled split.

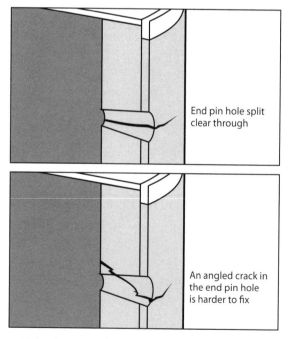

End pin hole split clear through

An angled crack in the end pin hole is harder to fix

It's harder to get glue into an angled split. In either case, it's important to glue all the way throughout the break. The best method I've found is very similar to what caused the break in the first place: driving a wedge into the end block hole.

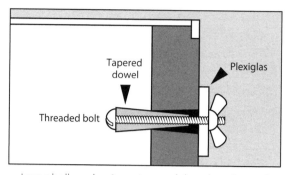

Tapered dowel

Plexiglas

Threaded bolt

I use a hollow aluminum tapered dowel as a "spreader," inserted from the inside and through the end-block hole. A simple 1/4-20 machine bolt runs through the dowel and is long enough that a Plexiglas caul can be slipped over it on the outside. Tighten the bolt and the spreader slowly opens the crack—just enough to make it easy to insert glue with a feeler gauge or with a syringe.

Clamping a long crack in the side

Simple cracks in the side are easy to spread open and work Titebond glue into, and can then be clamped with spool clamps (shown below). Some cracks in the sides, however, run along one side all the way around (and through) the end-block. Take your time aligning this type of crack, and practice the clamping procedure many times before getting out the glue. You may need someone else to help you align the clamps on such a long crack.

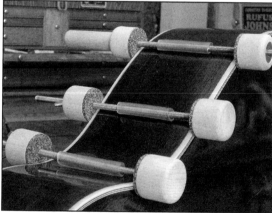

Gluing loose braces

With all acoustic guitars, and especially flattops, problems can arise that are related to the top's construction and its reaction to the pull of the strings. Aside from accidental damage (punctures and serious breaks) and the normal cracks discussed above, loose bracing is one of the most common structural problems with the acoustic guitar. A good repair shop can take care of most loose braces, and knowing a little about these repairs will help you choose the right shop. I don't recommend that you attempt brace regluing on any good guitar—leave that to the pros because often it's a one-shot deal.

Throughout the 1930s and early '40s, the highly desirable Adirondack, or "red" spruce was used exclusively for tops and for braces—until the end of World War II. The war effort used a tremendous amount of spruce for airplane propellers, ship masts, rigging and the like, so that at war's end the supply of red spruce was depleted. Gibson and Martin switched to sitka spruce at that time (and they continue using sitka today). Repairs on these vintage instruments should be done with red-spruce if they're to look right (another reason shops save smashed instruments—especially vintage ones).

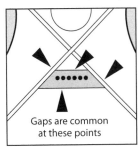

Gaps are common at these points

The two main X-braces, in the bridge area, are the first place to look for looseness. Before beginning your inspection, vacuum the interior of the guitar thoroughly, and follow by blowing it clean with compressed air. Try to avoid blowing dirt into a glue joint, however. Vacuum and blow—repeating the operations several times. Then use a mirror and an interior light to check for a gap between the top or back and any brace (this should be done with the guitar tuned to pitch). A loose brace will show as a dark shadow. The best mirror is the 2-1/4" round Telescoping Guitar Mirror which extends to 11". It's really a good idea to inspect your guitar's bracing from time to time.

A good inspection light can be made with a porcelain fixture, and a low-wattage bulb. I scrounged my parts at an electric supply store—they're probably refrigerator replacement parts or something. You can rig up a similar

one by asking a few questions at your local electric shop. I plug the light into the on/off footswitch that I use for my Dremel Tool router. The footswitch leaves both hands free to work, and the bulb (which does generate heat) is only on when I'm actually looking with the mirror. Caution: If you make a lamp, be sure it's insulated at the terminals to protect against shock, and properly grounded.

Gibson flattops up until the late '50s were constructed much the same as in the '30s—with thin, light bracing that wasn't tucked into the lining very deeply. Because of the light construction, it's more common to find loose or cracked brace ends on a Gibson (photo above) than on a Martin. Cracked brace ends on any brand of guitar are usually the result of a less-than-perfect piece of wood being chosen for the brace (not well quarter-sawn).

Until the early '60s, Gibsons and Martins were constructed with hide glue, and their braces can be cleaned and reglued easily. Sometime during the '60s manufacturers began using white glues; these glue joints can be cleaned and reglued too, but they're a little more difficult than hide glue. Another nice thing about hide glue is that it can be reconstituted with warm water or fresh hide glue; so if you haven't cleaned the glue from a joint perfectly, what's left inside will soften and help reglue the joint (Titebond doesn't do this as well even though it too is water-soluble).

It's best to remove as much of the old glue as possible from the bad glue joint (the brittle hide glue removes the easiest). I use a variety of spatulas, feeler gauges, thin saw blades, sandpaper strips and scrapers to remove dirt and glue from between a brace and the top or back. The "Sandplate" files, which are toothed and act like "steel sandpaper," make great cleaners if you remove the self-stick backing with lacquer thinner. Sometimes you must fashion a wooden, plastic or metal "arm" just to reach a loose spot on a particular guitar. Attach the cleaning tool to the arm with superglue or masking tape (later any arm you fashion can be used to apply glue and to hold a cleanup-rag afterward).

⌐deep

Loose bridges

My cousin David once glued the bridge back on his old Silvertone acoustic by stacking volumes A through F of the *Encyclopedia Britannica* on it, and leaving the books there for a month. Not a bad repair job, either: that bridge stayed on after that. Loose bridges are one of the more common problems confronting owners of flattop acoustic guitars.

Actually, the term "flattop" is a misnomer. Most flat-tops have a slight curve built into the top. Vintage Martins and Gibsons (especially Gibsons) have a graceful arch in the bridge area. This is normal, and the curve becomes more pronounced over the years as string tension pulls up on the bridge.

The problem is that the sometimes the bridge becomes separated from the top. It's easy to see why, since a stiff flat bridge won't stay in good contact on a curving surface. Some of the thinner bridges (commonly Gibsons) will curve right along with the top. They may become loose, but their shapes match the top, so gluing them back is easy.

But thicker, stiffer bridges (commonly Martins) will keep their flat shape as the guitar tops bow up underneath them. These are tougher to fix.

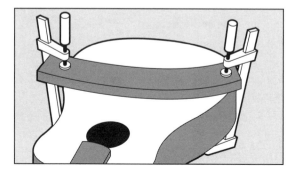

If you've got a loose bridge, hopefully you'll be able to simply glue it back on, leaving the curved top as it is. You may need to shape the bottom of the bridge to conform to the curve of the top (pictured below, left). There's a good chance that the loose bridge isn't your only problem: often a curving top is the result of the main X braces coming unglued immediately beneath the bridge. In this case, the loose braces need to be repaired before you can fix your bridge.

Sometimes on these guitars, the bridge pads have obvious gaps, too, or they're made of thin, warpy plywood instead of a proper hardwood. A combination of gluing the braces and replacing the bridge pad can flatten a humped top and help lower high action at the same time. A horribly warped or severely kinked top can be flattened by using a flat, or even a reverse-warp board or a caul during gluing. But these are extreme cases, and last-ditch measures.

If your vintage Martin or Gibson has a bowed top, don't let anyone try to flatten it. Instead, fit the unglued bridge to the warp. Generally, I only flatten tops on cheaper guitars, and often part of the reason is to bring down a too-high playing action. On vintage instruments, the proper way to lower the action is to remove and reset the neck at a different angle, or perhaps do some clever fingerboard leveling and refretting.

Bridges that are cracked, warped, loose or poorly positioned have a detrimental effect on your guitar's intonation, tone and playability. They need to be removed and reattached. This work is difficult if you're doing it, and expensive if you're hiring it done, so before attempting or authorizing any repairs, consider all of these common mistakes to watch out for:

✔ Damaging the top wood around and under the bridge during removal. (Refer to the drawing about spruce grain on the next page.)

✔ Gluing the bridge on crooked.

✔ Mounting it too far toward the bass or treble side, so the strings pull off the sides of the fingerboard.

✔ Not recognizing when a bridge should be replaced entirely rather than simply being reglued.

✔ Trusting that the factory mounted the bridge in the perfect spot (professionals always measure it for themselves).

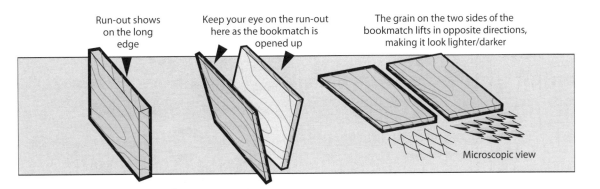

Run-out shows on the long edge

Keep your eye on the run-out here as the bookmatch is opened up

The grain on the two sides of the bookmatch lifts in opposite directions, making it look lighter/darker

Microscopic view

deep

✔ Failure to check inside the body for loose braces, etc., before installing the bridge.

✔ Not letting the glue dry long enough. *Allow a minimum of 24 hours for Titebond or hide glue— two or three days is best.*

✔ Not understanding the grain direction of the top wood (usually spruce) in order to remove and replace a bridge correctly.

If you've had success with repairing cracks, you might feel ready to try a bridge repair on a guitar you can afford to experiment with. But keep in mind that a messed up crack repair just looks bad, while messed up bridge repair may mean an unplayable guitar. Everybody properly scared? Okay, let's see what bridge repair is about.

Regluing without removing the bridge Is your bridge just slightly loose? If you can just slide the flap of a guitar string envelope under the bridge, it's loose and needs attention. By acting soon, you can avoid having to remove the bridge before gluing. Bridges that are only slightly loose at the back edge can often be reglued by forcing glue into the gap and clamping the bridge in place to dry. A thin metal feeler gauge or an artist's palette knife are good tools for getting the glue into this tight spot.

Removing the bridge

To avoid damaging your spruce top, you really need to understand spruce grain. If you know how the grain "runs out," you can keep from scarring your guitar top as you work the bridge loose. Start by reading this little lesson from Martin repairman **Dave Musselwhite** about bookmatched spruce:

Determining grain orientation "Bookmatched spruce tops are split, opened like a book, and the two edges are glued together. This glueline becomes the centerline of the guitar top. On one half of the centerline the grain often looks darker than on the other. This

is normal; the darkness is caused by a small degree of natural 'run-out' in the spruce. When the top gets book-matched, the run-out then goes in opposite directions along the centerline.

"When your light source catches the end grain of the run-out it looks darker, telling you which way the grain is going. Which direction the light's coming from, and the direction you're looking, determines which side, the top is darker. My light source is behind me and I look at the top with the peghead toward me. So if the dark grain of the spruce is on the treble side, I'd attack the bridge from the rear on the treble side, and from the front on the bass side. If the dark wood is on the bass side, the reverse is true. This way you will be working with the grain, not digging into it.

"With the grain lifting up in opposite directions on either side of the centerline, considerable damage can be caused by pushing your palette knife under the bridge if you go against the grain. You'd be pushing into and under the grain, rather than over and with the grain. It takes experience to develop your eye, but it's important in order to get a clean separation of the bridge from the top.

"Unfortunately, this won't work on every guitar top. Some tops have so little run-out that both halves look the same from any direction. It's hard to know where to enter with the knife. In these cases, it doesn't matter as much, because with no run-out, the grain doesn't lift. Bridges on such soundboards leave a perfect surface when they're removed.

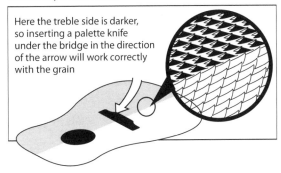

Here the treble side is darker, so inserting a palette knife under the bridge in the direction of the arrow will work correctly with the grain

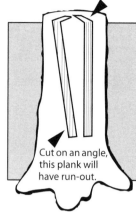

This plank is cut vertically, so will have little or no run-out.

Cut on an angle, this plank will have run-out.

deep

"The wood fibers of a tree grow upward (this is the lengthwise direction of the grain). Some trees have straighter grain than others, and spruce is one of the straightest. All spruce has at least some run-out, by nature of the way it grows. Run-out can also be a result of how the planks are cut."

Dana Bourgeois, another wood specialist, describes bookmatched spruce like this: "If the two halves reflect light the same way you have a top with very little run-out and you can come either way with your tool. There's no such thing as wood with a perfect level grain matrix; it will always run-in and run-out a little.

"I've removed bridges on tops which reflected light the same in all directions, but still lifted—because right in the bridge area there was localized run-out that I couldn't see. When I can see the darker grain, I antici-pate an easy bridge removal because it's so obvious! And Dan, be sure to point out that understanding grain orientation is just as important if you have to remove the bridge pad—maybe more important."

Bridge removal techniques

When a bridge is removed, the goal is to break or loosen the glue joint between the bridge bottom and the top wood (usually spruce, cedar or mahogany). This isn't as simple as it sounds; lots of care is required to avoid dam-aging the guitar top. Like any of these deep body repairs, go through your learning phase on yard sale specials (probably with plywood tops) before trying your hand on a guitar you care about.

Here are three accepted bridge removal techniques used by professionals:

Heat Use heat to warm and loosen the glue joint. A bridge heater has a metal block that can be warmed on a hotplate and applied to the bridge (also for use on fingerboards). You can also heat a bridge with silicone rubber strip heaters made by the Watlow company of St. Louis, Missouri. These strips can be custom-made to the shape of the bridge, fastened to a metal caul, and

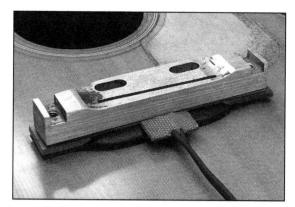

controlled by a rheostat. Either way, when the glue joint is softened, the bridge lifts off easily with a thin, wide round-nosed palette knife. (This same knife can is used to loosen the fingerboard tongue over the body during a neck reset.)

Impact You can strike the glue line between the bridge and the top with a wide chisel so the impact shears it off. (Now that's a technique you'd want to perfect on yard sale specials first!)

Routing Use a router to pare away the bridge a little at a time (after carefully rigging a way to protect the guitar top!). Reduce the bridge to a paper-thin layer, then warm the glue and peel away the remains of the bridge. This may sound extreme, but when done expertly, there's little risk of damage to the top. Obviously, this method is only appropriate when a complete bridge replacement is necessary, and it takes a lot of experience to pull this technique off!

Don't use a hot knife Bridges shouldn't be removed with hot knives. This method often scorches and scars the finish. There's just no way you want or need to have telltale marks left over from a bridge reglue.

Shaping the bridge

Scraping If the bridge hasn't curved to match the shape of the top, I'll reshape the bottom of the bridge to match the top curve before regluing it. This shape is a very subtle arch, so it doesn't mean removing a lot of wood—but still this technique only works when the bridge's thickness will permit it. If you reshape a bridge that isn't thick enough, you'll grind away too much wood from the thin tapered "wings" at the ends of the bridge. This loss of mass weakens the bridge which can cause

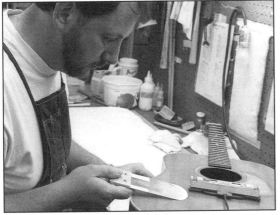

Dave Musselwhite using a palette knife for bridge removal.

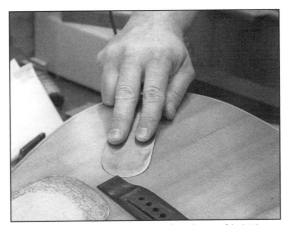

With the round-nosed knife, he's working from the rear of the bridge.

the bridge to split in some future dry season.

Shaping the bottom of a guitar bridge is a slow process, even for an experienced worker. The bridges on archtop guitars often sit on small wooden feet, and in these cases it's possible to put sandpaper on the curved top and move the bridge on it until the feet conform to the curve. That's not practical with these large flat-top bridges: there's just too much wood to remove. The answer is to hold the bridge in a vise, bottom side up, and shape it with cabinet scrapers. These simple tools are flat pieces of spring steel, sometimes rectangular, sometimes curved, that are pulled across the wood in a scraping motion. The cutting edge is microscopically small: just a tiny burr that takes off a little wood with each stroke. Remove wood by scraping the bottom of the bridge, frequently checking to see if you're getting the curve right. Be patient as you scrape/check, scrape/check your way to a curved-bottom bridge.

Before you shape your bridge, read about X brace problems on page 143. It may be that you have two repair jobs in order to fix this bridge separation. If your X braces are okay, and you've got the bridge shaped, you're ready for clamping and gluing.

Bending Warped bridges can sometimes be soaked in water and clamped into the proper shape to dry before regluing, but this at other times this doesn't work— these bridges can seem to have a "memory" that returns them to their original shape. When you've reached this point, it's best to treat the bridge for what it is: a piece of warped wood. Throw it away and make a new bridge.

Regluing the bridge

The gluing surfaces must be free of old glue and dirt. A small scraper, or the back side of a chisel, is good for cleaning the bridge area on the top. Cheap guitars may have finish under the bridge (which helped cause the bridge to pull loose). In these cases, remove the finish for wood-to-wood contact in regluing. Carefully mask the bridge's "footprint," and remove the finish using a small scraper or chisel. You may need to use tiny amounts of gel-type stripper on an artist's paintbrush. Scrape in toward the center, so no stripper gets outside the footprint of the bridge. For an invisible repair, leave about 1/16" of finish untouched all around, which the bridge will cover when you reglue it.

Use cauls to spread clamping pressure and protect against clamp marks. Make cauls curved to match the bridge shape, so you get solid pressure without creating dents. Don't forget to protect the guitar's interior with cauls, too—especially the braces! The size and shape of

deep

your cauls will determine the number of clamps needed, but plan on using at least three. I often use more, but on the other hand Martin uses just one! (They have developed a very sturdy and uniquely shaped caul to make this work.)

Too much glue is as bad as too little. Over-gluing or under-gluing weakens any wood joint. A thin even layer applied with a glue brush (like the flux brush used for soldering) is a good method. Spruce absorbs glue into the grain; practice on scrap to develop your gluing technique.

After gluing the bridge on, keep an eye on it for at least 15 minutes, looking for any excess glue to squeeze out along the edges. With a damp rag, clean along the glue line until there's no squeeze-out left; you may have to clean the line four or five times.

Here's a unique bridge gluing caul used by Gibson Montana: it doesn't require a clamp. Half of this metal fixture goes inside against the bridge pad and the matching half is outside on the bridge. Two bolts pull the two halves together to apply pressure.

Splits in the bridge

Minor splits occur in a bridge, running through the bridge pin holes or the saddle slot. These can be filled with a mixture of sawdust glue, or a slip of wood. This is usually a good long-lasting repair. I recommend it if you have a vintage instrument and want to keep the original bridge to preserve the guitar's value. A skilled repairman can make you a perfect duplicate of the original bridge, without splits, and you'd never know it had been replaced.

Improper saddle location

Some vintage guitars have poor intonation due to a misplaced saddle. A replacement bridge is an opportunity to fix this by correctly locating the new saddle. An alternate method of correcting a misplaced saddle slot is to fill the slot with wood and re-cut it in the correct location. (I do wonder if filling and re-cutting the slot hampers tone, however.) Don't be afraid to have a vintage bridge replaced entirely by a good repairperson.

Adjustable bridges aren't tone-friendly

On many acoustic guitars with adjustable bridges (some of the low-end Gibsons from the '60s and '70s, and many imports), I find a tremendous improvement in sound from filling the holes in the top and replacing the bridge with a solid-saddle, non-adjustable model. Since these guitars' bridge plates can usually be replaced relatively easily, a repairman can remove the bridge plate and thumbscrew hardware, plug the holes in the spruce top, replace the bridge plate with new wood and custom-make a standard bridge with bridge pins placed closer to the saddle. This gives a better string angle over the saddle, and improves power and volume. In this drawing, the dark areas indicate where the new bridge pin holes are located, while the lighter areas show the origi-

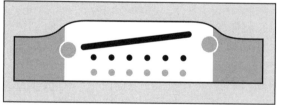

nal holes to be plugged. I don't recommend replacing all adjustable bridges—some vintage Gibsons would lose their value if altered this way. But the tone of adjustable bridges doesn't match that of traditional designs.

Worn out bridge pin holes

The bridge pad—also known as the bridge plate—is the reinforcing piece of hardwood glued inside the top of a steel-string acoustic to support the bridge area. The string ball ends pull against it when strung to pitch. Years of wear, poor drilling during an earlier repair or in manufacturing, and sloppy string installation may cause chips, splintering, wear, and tearing on the pad's underside.

Some symptoms of a pad in need of repair are:

1 String slots at the front edge of the bridge pinholes that are overly deep, and too close to the saddle slot.

2 String ball ends that no longer hold against the pad, allowing the string windings to reach onto the saddle.

3 A top that's bent, kinked, warped or collapsed in the area of the bridge.

4 The feeling that your guitar should have better tone, volume, and sustain —especially if the nut, frets, and saddle have all been properly fit and adjusted.

Avoid bridge pad problems by installing strings carefully (it helps to use an inspection mirror as you do this). Push each string into the hole and see that the winding and ball end are at the front and pulling into the slot as you put the bridge pin in. Install one string at a time and tune up slowly, watching with the mirror to see that the ball end settles in. And if your bridge pins are bent or worn, replace them. The strings shown are installed correctly — a snug fit in front of the bridge pin,

tight against the pad, and clean as a whistle. Notice that the ball ends nest at a slight angle into the bridge pin flutes.

In years past, the two most common solutions for bridge pad problems were replacing the entire pad or gluing a thin veneer over the damaged pad. This is tricky work that should only be done by someone with a lot of repair experience.

BridgeSaver repair technique

I've come up with a better method: a tool called the BridgeSaver that goes inside the guitar and cuts a round, dome-shaped scoop out of the bridge pad. On the outside, it can cut the same scoop in the top (if the bridge is removed). A second tool creates matching dome-shaped plugs of wood to fill these holes (spruce for the top, rosewood or maple for the bridge pad). This way,

the worn area of the pin hole is quickly replaced with all new wood.

This tool makes the old bridge pad repair techniques unnecessary in most cases. When you use the Bridge-

The tool's center shaft keeps it centered on the hole while the cutter does its work.

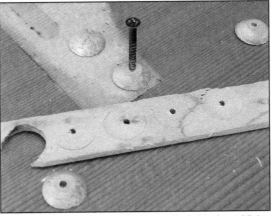

Maple plugs for the bridge pad of an Alvarez. The hole in the middle lets me pull the plugs into place using a small woodscrew as a handle.

This plug is wet with glue, and is about to be inserted into a bridge pin hole. This way the damaged area is replaced with solid new wood.

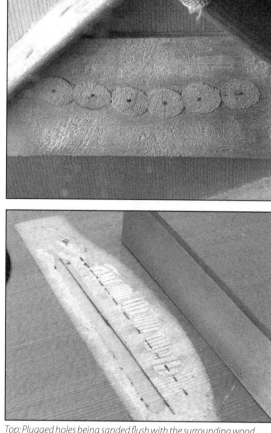

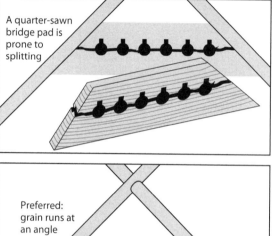

Top: Plugged holes being sanded flush with the surrounding wood.
Bottom: Six holes plugged in spruce.

Saver to put new wood on both the inside and the out-side, the damaged area is "new" again so you can drill fresh clean pin holes — and even relocate them to allow for saddle relocation due to intonation issues.

Repairing the bridge pad

Removing and replacing the pad is not always an easy task. The same type of Watlow silicone rubber heating pads mentioned earlier for bridge removal are also used to heat the bridge pad. The glue softens enough so that the pad can be pried loose. A variety of spatulas, hooks and scrapers are often needed to coax the stubborn bridge pad out.

A bridge pad removal tool (above, right) has a long bent handle that allows you to move the spatula blade from side-to-side while at the same time pulling it into the heat-softened glue joint. A real knowledge of spruce grain is needed to keep the tool from cutting up and through the delicate spruce top.

The best replacement wood for a bridge pad is maple or rosewood (Brazilian rosewood, if you can get it). In general, the bridge pad should be replaced with one that matches the original—particularly on a vintage instrument. There are times when a somewhat larger pad is needed to flatten a warped top or give more sup-port (especially on plywood-topped guitars). Tradition-ally, bridge pads were made of quarter-sawn (vertical-grained) wood that ran at right angles (cross-grain) to the length of the top. The only problem with this design is that if the bridge splits through the bridge pinholes, the bridge pad splits right along with it! Because of this, I prefer to use a grain that runs at an oblique angle to the top as in the drawing below (it can be flat-sawn, quartered, or in-between). On good guitars, the pad shouldn't be too thick: anywhere from .090" to .125" (.100" is the average).

When replacing a bridge pad, never use epoxy! I prefer hide glue: I think it enhances tone, although I use Titebond often (depending on the age and history of the guitar). And, before you drill new bridge pin holes through the pad, a backer block should be clamped inside to keep the holes clean and un-chipped!

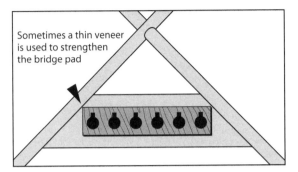

Sometimes a thin veneer is used to strengthen the bridge pad

Veneering the bridge pad Another accepted repair method for a worn out bridge pad is to veneer the underside of the original pad with a reinforcing piece of wood. This piece only needs to be big enough to add strength, and to give the strings something to pull against. It should definitely not be too thick or it may dampen the tone. A good thickness is from .030" to .070". I generally use Titebond glue for these "veneer" jobs.

Simple auto body filler technique A third, and 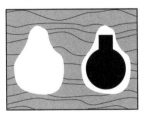 simple "quickie" method is to work a Bondo-type filler (represented by black, at right) into the worn or chipped holes. Use a rubber squeegee and wear a rubber glove. Once dry, remove the excess filler with small scrapers and sanding blocks, and seal the plate's repaired area with several layers of medium viscosity super glue. Then carefully re-drill the bridge-pinholes with a backer block inside, and create the string notches using the miniature jigsaw and an upstroke to keep from pulling the new filler out of the holes.

Complex auto body filler technique And here's a fourth and somewhat trickier way to repair just the worn areas of the existing pad—the method I used on my own 1944 Gibson J-45. The original small maple pad was ter-

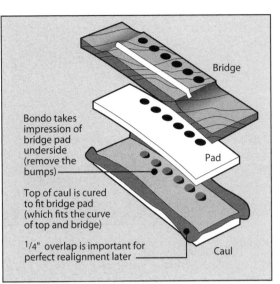

Bridge

Bondo takes impression of bridge pad underside (remove the bumps)

Pad

Top of caul is cured to fit bridge pad (which fits the curve of top and bridge)

1/4" overlap is important for perfect realignment later

Caul

ribly worn, but it was still well glued even after 50 years and had warped gracefully along with the top. I felt that removing and replacing the pad might harm the guitar's tone. (The best time to repair a bridge pad is when the bridge is off—the case with my J-45—but this method can be used with a bridge in place if you're very careful).

✔ Make a bridge-pad-shaped caul of 3/8" thick pine or soft wood band-sawed to conform to the inside curve of the top. Make the caul wider than the pad by 1/4" on both long edges.

✔ Fasten a layer of wax paper to the underside of the pad with double-stick tape.

✔ Spread a "frosting" of Bondo on the caul and clamp it inside against the wax paper-protected top until the Bondo squishes up against the pad. Clamp it lightly so as not to flatten the top's arch at all. The caul being slightly wider than the pad lets the Bondo flow over each edge, and the "impression" taken guarantees exact realignment of the caul later. Note: Spread a rag inside the guitar to catch any Bondo droppings!

✔ When it dries—about five minutes—remove the caul and file off the high spots of Bondo where it molded into the holes of the pad. You'll have a perfect imprint of the underside of the pad with six hollow areas, or "pockets," where you removed the high spots.

✔ Wax the face of the new Bondo caul, let it dry, apply double-stick tape over the face, and stick a sheet of waxed paper to it. The wax insures that the caul won't super glue to the pad later.

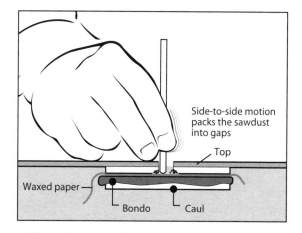

Side-to-side motion packs the sawdust into gaps

Top

Waxed paper

Bondo   Caul

✔ Clamp the caul inside the guitar against the pad.

✔ File a block of whatever wood matches the bridge pad (usually rosewood or maple) to get a pile of fine sawdust.

✔ Sprinkle sawdust down from the top through the bridge pinholes and with a small, blunt, round bottomed tool, pack it into the pockets (above). Don't tear the waxed paper!

✔ Compressed air blown into a hole with a rubber-tipped blowgun will further force the sawdust down and out into the pockets.

✔ Use a pipette to drop water-thin super glue down the hole in a pool and watch as it wicks into the sawdust. Don't fill the hole so deep that the super glue gets out and onto the spruce top, since that could inhibit a good bridge reglue later.

✔ After all the holes are filled, drip a little accelerator into each hole to guarantee a cure. Better yet, let the fills dry several hours—the glue-saturated sawdust may need extra time.

✔ Remove the caul and check your work. The wear spots should be smoothly filled, so smooth them if they're rough.

✔ When the holes are repaired, use the caul as a "backer" when you re-drill the holes to keep the pad from tearing out again. The filled area will be as hard as the surrounding wood and can be renotched as if it were new.

The drawback to this last method is that the superglue saturates the top, pad and bridge— "welding" them together (this could make it tough to remove the pad later). I chose this method for my guitar because it "felt right,"

and I knew I could get the pad out if I ever had to. Because of this "welding," I'm not recommending this for your guitar (nor would I use it on a customer job without due notice), but it suited me fine!

Neck resets

If you own an acoustic guitar with a stiff, hard-to-play action, or if it isn't as loud as it should be, don't be alarmed if your guitar surgeon prescribes an operation called a neck reset. The life of your favorite guitar may depend on your understanding the basics of this common yet difficult surgery. This is not a "how-to" for beginners, but a description of the neck resetting process as I know it.

The need for a neck reset is a result of the settling of an instrument's wood and joints. This movement of the top, sides, back and neck block, coupled with the constant pull of string pressure, can cause the strings to gradually rise further and further from the fingerboard. Other reasons for a reset include improper fit to begin with (causing poor action that becomes more noticeable and unbearable with age) and glue failure at the neck joint (often due to dryness). If the guitar has great action but isn't putting out the volume it should, it could be due to a low bridge saddle. If there's no saddle height left to remove, it may mean a reset. Resets are also performed just so a luthier can raise the saddle height and drastically improve a guitar's sound.

A new guitar with any of these problems may be a candidate for a warranty repair, but in general don't blame the maker, especially with older guitars. These problems due to wood joints settling are often unavoidable in a delicately made wooden instrument. If it's a favorite guitar, a reset is worth the cost. Have it done by a skilled repairperson with whom you can discuss the instrument. Use the following information to help you in that discussion.

Is a neck reset needed? A neck needs resetting if, when strung to pitch, a long straightedge resting on the frets meets above or below the top of the bridge. A straightedge long enough to reach the bridge should just meet the bridge top. If it hits below the bridge top, the neck is "underset," and needs to pitched back. If it hits above the bridge (less common), the neck is "overset," and needs to be pitched forward. Removing wood at the neck joint is how the neck angle is changed. In the photo below, the straightedge is in the foreground with a lighter-colored ruler measuring the gap between it and the bridge. This neck needs a reset.

Here's how to calculate the amount of wood you need to shave off the heel of the neck in order to reset the neck at the correct angle. The numbers in this example happen to be from a Martin D-18; replace them with the numbers you find by measuring your guitar.

Measure to find the distance from the plane of the frets to the top of the bridge, then use this difference in calculating this formula: **x = (Difference x B) / A**. "A" is the distance from the neck/body joint to the center of the saddle slot. "B" is the height of the neck heel. Here are the numbers from my example guitar:

A = 11.375"   B = 3.687"   Difference = .125"

Plugging them into the formula gave me :

x = (.125" x 3.687")/11.375"

So in my example, x = .040". I need to shave .040" off the

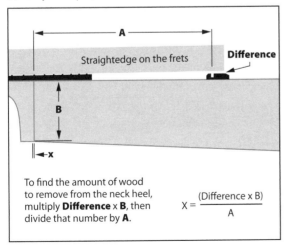

To find the amount of wood to remove from the neck heel, multiply **Difference** x **B**, then divide that number by **A**.

$$X = \frac{(\text{Difference} \times B)}{A}$$

bottom of the heel, gradually removing less and less as I move up the heel, until nothing is removed where the fingerboard joins the neck.

For an absolutely correct measurement, use a prop inside the guitar under the bridge to simulate the amount of soundboard pull-up that occurs when the guitar is tuned to pitch.

Removing the neck

First, we must determine the best method for separating the neck/body joint. Usually this is a dovetail joint. The preferred method is to first loosen the fingerboard tongue from where it overlaps the top. This is done by heating the tongue until the glue releases. Next, the neck joint is loosened by injecting it with steam. This is

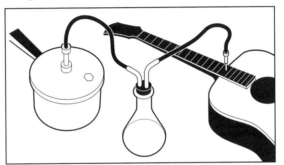

done by removing the fret just past the body joint, drilling a small hole in the slot, and injecting steam into the joint below. This generally works for Gibson, Martin, Guild, Gretsch, Harmony, Kay and most traditional American guitars. Some of the joints and glue used on the less-expensive imports, however, have surprised more than one luthier, myself included. Prior experience and quick decision-making are needed for good results. My first neck steamer was an old pressure-cooker. Later, I added an Erlenmeyer flask from a chemistry lab with two glass tubes in the rubber stopper. The wet, boiling steam enters the flask and leaves much of its moisture

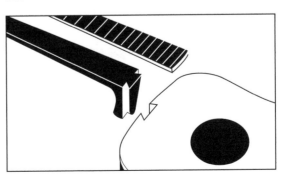

behind as it exits as "drier" steam on its way to the neck joint. Nowadays I use a Mr. Coffee espresso maker; it does the same job as the flask, but better and faster. Another recent development is that neck-steaming needles are now readily available from lutherie suppliers.

If you're picking a luthier to reset your neck, see if they're using a moisture trap. Without it, the job produces unnecessary swelling, and even can lead to finish problems around the repair.

After steaming, the neck is carefully pulled up and out of the dovetail socket. Excess glue is quickly removed while it's still wet, and the neck/fingerboard assembly and top/neck block assembly are allowed to dry. I gently clamp these parts while they're drying to insure that they don't come unglued.

Once the wood is thoroughly dry, a small portion of the neck heel is trimmed away with an extremely sharp chisel, changing the neck-to-body angle and bringing the strings closer to the fingerboard. Much experience and a keen eye are needed for knowing how much wood to remove during this heel shaping. If you're assessing a shop to do this work, see if you can play a guitar that they've done a reset on.

When I visited the Martin repair department I paid special attention to how they go about neck resetting. **Milt Hess, Jr.** does most of the neck removing, and then he jobs out the neck re-fitting to **Dave Bosich** or **Dave Musselwhite**. Bosich is the foreman of the neck setting department for production—he's incredible to watch.

Here are the 10 steps they follow at Martin:

1 An infrared heat lamp loosens the tongue/top glue joint.

2 The bridge removal spatula is used to pry up the tongue (below).

3 A pressure cooker, mounted under the workbench, provides the steam.

The pressure cooker is attached to a strong rubber hose connected to a bicycle-pump needle that is inserted into a hole drilled at the 15th fret to steam the joint, and the neck is worked free.

4 The glue is cleaned from both parts immediately, and the neck and body are left to dry.

5 Lacquer thinner, painted along the heel, softens the finish so that it won't chip when the heel is trimmed.

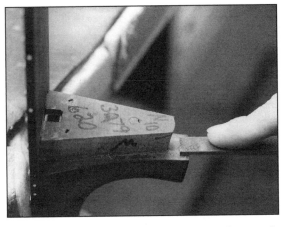

6 The "cheeks" of the heel (where it contacts the guitar's side) are trimmed down with a file or a chisel.

7 The dovetail itself is trimmed, or else a shim is placed in the female portion of the joint.

8 An aluminum template rests on the fretboard and indexes off the neck—letting **Dave Bosich** know when the set is right.

9 After a final dry-fitting the neck is glued in.

10 It's left overnight to dry.

After a neck reset, fret work is often required—sometimes even a total refret. The need for fret work can usually be anticipated beforehand, but when wood is heated and steamed apart, the swelling can lead to loosened frets, and fret work is always part of fine-tuning a guitar's playability. Finish damage caused by escaping steam is also a possibility, and may require touch-up.

The easier resets are the older guitars constructed with hide glue, which requires little heat and steam. The toughies are guitars built with modern glues and those with wide, thin heels that have more glue area (some Guilds and Gibsons). Wide heels tend to swell and crack from the steam, too. Guitars with fingerboard binding require special care to avoid burning or melting the plastic during the reset process. Neck resets aren't simple!

A variation for neck resetting involves removing the fingerboard tongue to reach the neck joint, rather than removing the neck and fingerboard as one. When this method is used, the fingerboard should be cut a few frets up the neck—not at the body joint—to keep a strong wood joint. Another method is to loosen only the fingerboard and "slip" the neck by bending it back and regluing the board. The back, side and neck-block joints can sometimes be loosened to allow you to shift the neck heel. These last two "slip 'n' squeeze" methods should only be used on inexpensive quickies.

The principles governing flattop acoustic guitar resets also apply to archtop acoustics and electrics. These guitars don't require resets as often, thanks to their adjustable bridges. Exceptions are old Les Pauls with trapeze tailpieces or shallow neck angles, some mid-'70s SGs and some semi-hollowbody ES models—especially those with non-Bigsby tremolos. On most of these Gibsons, neck-set problems are solved by slightly grinding down the bottom of the bridge. When you find a Gibson solidbody that does require a reset, expect to lay out some dough, since they aren't easy, even for the factory pros. Early Gretsch guitars are often found to have loosened at the dovetail and fingerboard extension. But once the neck problem's fixed, these old Gretsches are hard to beat.

A neck reset will probably last 20 years or more—maybe even a lifetime, if the wood has truly finished settling. To get a less-than-perfect flattop to play and sound its best, neck resets are sometimes the only way.

basic

Fender guitar neck shapes   158
Fender bass neck shapes   159

d.i.y.

Installing bolt-on necks   161
Fret buzz in the high registers   166

deep

Broken pegheads   166

Chapter 11

Necks

basic

Fender guitar neck shapes

If you look around the industry you'll find that every manufacturer copies the depth, width and "feel" of Fender necks. (Many would copy the peghead shape too, if they could get away with it!) Understanding the cross-sectional profile of Fender necks is useful in discussing new or used instruments.

In the early 1990s I visited the Fender factory and Fender Custom in Corona, California. On that visit, I finally understood the terminology used to describe Fender neck profiles. These shapes, plus front-to-back thickness and fingerboard width determine whether or not the guitar feels good to your hand and style.

Many different terms, such as "boatneck," "V," "oval," and A, B, C, and D designations, have been used to describe Fender necks. Custom Shop master builder **Jay Black** helps clear up the mysteries:

"The letters A, B, C, or D that were stamped on the end of necks from the early '60s until around 1973 refer to neck width at the nut—not shape. So when people say they've got a 'C' neck—referring to its shape—they're wrong, although early '60s Fender necks are somewhat C-shaped in profile. But we call that 'oval.' The only letters we use when talking shape are 'U'—the shape of that real early '51 to '53 Tele—and 'V' for the triangulated shape. Neither of these letters were ever stamped anywhere on a Fender neck. The corresponding nut widths for the old letters are: **A=1-1/2"**, **B=1-5/8"**, **C=1-3/4"**, and **D=1-7/8"**. Currently, all production vintage necks have the **B** nut width, while the **American Standard** is slightly wider, between **B** and **C** at around **1-11/16"**. In the Custom Shop, we'll make anything you want.

"Boatneck, an archaic term used for describing certain neck profiles, is a misnomer because it's been used by too many people in too many ways. As Jay explains, "When Fred Stuart, one of our master builders, uses the word boatneck, he's referring to the older Martins, Washburns and many big V-necked guitars, so we're trying to drop the word from our vocabulary. But if you have to

use the word boatneck, you'd be talking about a #4 or a #1056 neck."

Five basic neck shapes

Due to the use of less-sophisticated machinery and subsequent hand-shaping, old Fender neck profiles are so subtle in their differences that it would be virtually impossible to reproduce them all. So Fender has agreed upon five basic "generic" neck shapes based on specs from the '50s and '60s. "Today's production necks are made from specific templates on machinery that is very consistent," Jay Black explains. "This is helpful with production models because the neck on any new SRV model will be identical in feel to Stevie's 'Number One.'

"Right now the Custom Shop will shape any neck that a customer requests, but most players want one of the five basic shapes. By using these generic shapes as a reference point, we can cover everything from 1950 all the way up to '62. Anything other than that is usually made from an oversize blank and hand-shaped to what the customer wants, using the five shapes as a means of communicating with the customer. Some players have a qualified local luthier measure a favorite neck and send us the specs to work from."

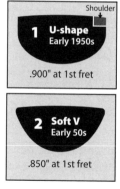

No. 1 Essentially a round, chunky, '53 Tele shape—the "U" shape, with lots of shoulder.

No. 2 Also called the "54" or "soft V," it has some shoulder, but less than No. 1. It's not quite as deep from the top of the fingerboard to the back of the neck, but it's still a fairly chunky neck. Vintage '54 necks varied quite a bit. Eric Johnson's '54 Strat has one of the smallest front-to-back dimensions Jay's seen.

No. 3 The 1960 and '62 "oval" shape. Thinner, front to back, at the 1st fret than at the 12th, it has a very oval (or you could say "C"-shaped) bottom. "We can alter the No. 3 to produce the '63 or '64," says Jay. "This is a slightly beefier version of the same shape, except the 1st-

fret dimension becomes thicker by .030" or .040"."

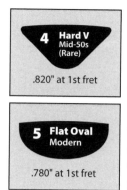

No. 4 Different from the large, soft No. 2, this is a "hard V" that's .030" thinner front to back. You'll find this neck on Strats from late '56 and '57.

No. 5 The contemporary "heavy metal" style neck. Not used too often, it's similar to the '80s necks on Jackson, Charvel, Ibanez and other models. It's a much flatter, very non-traditional neck, and its shape changes as the trend changes.

No. 1056 (not pictured) is patterned from a "10-56" neck (referring to October, 1956), this is a very big V neck. '56 necks generally had a small V, but they made plenty of chunky ones too. "If anything could be called a boatneck," says Jay, "it would be this."

At Fender's Custom Shop: Art Esparza, Steve Boulanger, Ralph Esposito, Fred Stuart, me, Jay Black, Yasuhiko Iwanade, Larry Brooks, John Page.

Fender Custom Shop builders **John Page**, **Jay Black** and **Larry Brooks** answered some of my questions:

Q: Are most Fender Strat necks based on one of the five basic shapes?

John Page: "Yes. With modern machinery and setup techniques, we can alter the patterns slightly to make one model quite different from another—consistently. So one pattern can be responsible for a variety of shapes. Our most popular Custom Shop neck shape is the #3, and most production necks are based on that pattern too. Our model "1962" Strat has a neck based on the #3 pattern, but with a slight alteration in dimension from top to bottom to make it thinner and different-feeling from the American Standard or SRV models, which are also made from the #3 pattern. The American Standard

Strat, designed by Dan Smith, is a #3 variant that's wider at the nut and has a little more shoulder (the area from the fretboard edge to about a third of the way down either side of the neck)."

Larry Brooks: "The 'Stevie Ray' also starts with a #3 pattern, but we flattened the fretboard radius from the vintage 7-1/4" to a 12" curve, which removed some of the fretboard's thickness and changed its feel. And we added a little more meat to the shoulder to fatten it up—more like a '63 or '64 vintage Strat. Stevie wanted a Custom Shop Strat to take the place of "Number One," which had been broken too many times. The neck shape was critical, especially the "round-over" (edge of the rosewood fretboard in the shoulder area). It had to be smooth, polished, and as worn-feeling as the original."

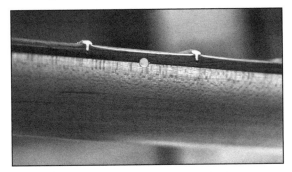

Rounded-over edges on Stevie Ray Vaughan's Number One.

Q: Do production SRV necks have round-over edges?

Brooks: "They are machine-shaped like Number One's worn shoulder, but without the hand-shaped and polished vintage round-over along the fretboard. Not every customer would want that worn, vintage round-over, since it removes wood and reduces the neck's dimension and longevity. I did shape it on Stevie's, though. You could take a new SRV model to a good luthier and have the edges smoothed and rounded-over quite easily."

Q: Why did Stevie want a 12" fretboard radius, when Number One was made with the 7-1/4"?

Brooks: "Rene Martinez, Stevie's guitar tech of many years, had re-fretted Number One so often that the fingerboard evolved into the flatter 12" radius, a result of minor sanding and levelling of the board when the frets were removed. A flatter radius means less noting-out during bends, and Stevie liked that. And Stevie had played—and enjoyed—Bonnie Raitt's brown Strat,

which also has a 12" radius. So he requested a 12" radius and the tall Dunlop #6105 fretwire. Rene sent the guitar back to us after Stevie's death so that we could get the production model exactly right."

Jay Black: "The Eric Clapton model's neck shape combines the #2 and #4 patterns. It's as large as the #2, but with a little more "V" like the #4. It has a 9-1/2" radius for easier blues bending and is fretted with a thin vintage-style wire measuring .085" wide by .045" tall—much like Stewart-MacDonald's #148 fretwire."

[Author's note: All Custom Shop and American Standard products feature a 9-1/2" radius fretboard. The only Fender guitars currently being built with the old-style 7-1/4" radius are the '62 and '57 vintage Strats and the '52 vintage Tele. In fact, Jay Black says that over the past four years and 500 guitars, he's only had three customer requests for vintage 7-1/4" radius necks. The 9-1/2" radius is a nice compromise for most players.]

Q: I've played fatter '50s necks that seemed to have more shoulder on the bass side, and almost none on the treble.

Black: "Because of the amount of hand-shaping done back then, you'll find some old Fenders with an asymmetrical shape. That extra shoulder gives good support to some hands. It's often a real help to sufferers of carpal tunnel syndrome. A hard "V" on the bass side doesn't please a player with carpal tunnel, whereas the chunky shoulder supports the hand."

Four basic bass neck shapes

A bass neck's profile is as important as good fretwork in determining whether or not a bass feels good, plays well and suits your playing style. To better understand Fender bass shapes, I called **John Page** at Fender's Custom Shop, and he directed me to the neck specialists on his staff: senior R&D engineer **George Blanda** and Custom Shop master builders **Jay Black**, **Mark Kendrick**, **Fred Stuart** and **Yasuhiko Iwanade**. Yasuhiko, in turn, introduced me to his friend and "bass mentor," **Albert Molinaro** of Guitars R Us in Hollywood. Among the seven of them, there's not much about the Fender bass that isn't known!

Fender recently specified four basic neck shapes for bass, based on specs from the '50s and '60s. Any Fender

basic

neck, whether it's vintage, production or custom-made, relates somehow to these shapes. Jay Black reminded me that "the four shapes didn't exist during the vintage years, but we realized that the neck builders in both production and the Custom Shop needed to be speaking the same language. And since the Custom Shop will make almost any neck you want, it was even more important to set shape standards for communicating with our customers. So we selected the four most popular neck shapes, ones that would cover everything from the '50s through the '60s—the necks made later were simply variations. The satisfaction of our bass-playing customers proves that we chose the right shapes."

Yasuhiko Iwanade (Yas) handbuilt the '51 Precision re-issues made by the Custom Shop in 1991, a short "production" run of 82 instruments. He even hand-wound each pickup! Word is that it couldn't have been done better by anyone, and that Yas is an acknowledged expert on Fender history—basses in particular.

Yas got to know Leo Fender himself before Leo's death in 1991, and he told me what the company's founder explained to him about the early days. "Even though the same cutters were used to shape both guitar and bass necks, the shape of guitar necks and bass necks made even on the same day in 1954 would be quite different from one another," Yas notes. "This is because P-Bass necks are wider than guitar necks, and the machine's cutter couldn't reach as far toward the center of the back of a bass neck. Therefore it carved them differently.

"Of the four generic profiles" continues Yas, "the neck shapes that most Fender bass players talk about are the round or U-shape, the soft V and the oval. I've seen only a few hard-V bass necks, but you should ask Albert Molinaro about them."

Albert has a collection of 75 vintage Fender basses, so I checked in with him next. "Fender set the standards for neck shapes that bass guitar manufacturers worldwide would follow," notes Albert. "As they went through the '50s, the necks evolved from big, round and chunky to flat, wide and smooth—possibly to accommodate the changes in music. There definitely were hard-V necks on basses, although I haven't seen many. I have two of them, both made in 1957. I don't like the feel of them too much, though—they're too skinny."

Yas and Albert compared notes to decide what to call two other profiles that were used during the '70s and early '80s. "Both shapes are simply variations of the round, or U, profile," explains Albert, "with the later bass having a sharper round-over." *[These are the last two shapes shown on the opposite page.]*

Still handmade "Handmade" is a term often used to describe a quality musical instrument. With the use of more sophisticated machinery and the four standard shapes to control consistency, I wondered if the handwork that made the old necks special had become a lost art. George Blanda works closely with production, so I asked him: George, is there any hand-shaping on production necks today?

"In essence," he responded, "our necks are handmade, when you get down to the details. The machines remove everything but the critical few thousandths of an inch that are still done by hand. All transitional areas, such as the peghead, butt and fretboard wrap-around—any place where a machine cutter enters or exits the wood—are still finished by hand. In other words, the things that really give the neck its feel are done by hand. In fact, neck-shaping is one of the most important positions in our guitar factory. We use the most experienced employees; many have worked here for 20 years or more. The machinery just gives these skilled people a more consistent piece to start with.

"Currently all production P-Basses have the B [1-5/8"] nut width, except for the Vintage Precision reissues, which have the C [1-3/4"] width. And Yas is right about the oval profile being the most popular shape—it has now become the standard shape for all production bass necks, including the Vintage Precision reissue. The Jazz Bass, whether a Vintage reissue or contemporary, still has the A [1-1/2"] width, and it never strayed from the oval shape, even in the '70s and '80s, when the Precision changed. A player wanting the old U, V or other shape can contact the Custom Shop. "

Bass futures I asked George Blanda and Fred Stuart about the future direction of the Fender bass. "The Urge (Stuart Hamm model) represents our current thinking on bass design," said George. "It began as a Custom Shop project; as it developed, there was a lot of excitement, and production got involved.

"It's good for us to do new things. It was always true that if you could have only one bass it had to be a Fender, and we'd like to keep it that way. We recognize the requirements modern music places on electric bass, and we're offering instruments to fill that need. Take the P-Bass and J-Bass Plus instruments—these basses are reminiscent of their predecessors, but with 22 frets, downsized bodies, and Lace Sensor pickups. We knew players who didn't play our traditional basses tended toward smaller instruments, so we responded to that."

Fred Stuart has made lots of basses at the Custom Shop. "Most of them have been left-handed ones," he says. "The typical left-handed bass player is buying a Fender for the historical significance: perhaps he had a P-Bass back in the '60s and wants to recapture that. Being a lefty makes it that much harder to find a bass on the vintage market, and Fender isn't offering the Vintage P-Bass or J-Bass re-issues for lefties. We've gotten so many orders we even have a standard price for a left-handed bass ordered through the Custom Shop.

"The Jazz Bass and Precision have their own sounds—and that's what many people are looking for. When they think of a contemporary bass they don't always think of Fender, but perhaps they should. I guess it's just a matter of time—we need to let people know what we've got and that we're serious about it. At this point, we've got a lot of the elements in place for reaching a new market, so a first-time bass player who doesn't go for the Jazz or Precision can still start out with a Fender bass. There's something special about that!"

The evolution of the Fender bass neck

Fender has changed the shape of its bass necks five times over the years. Here's how Yasuhiko Iwanade of the Custom Shop charts the development:

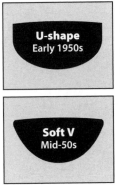

Early '50s: U shape. Round and chunky.

Mid-'50s: Soft-V shape. A more rounded V than the hard V, which had a pronounced ridge down the center. Some hard-V necks are found on basses from late '56 and into '57, but they're quite rare.

Late-'50s to Mid-'60s: Oval shape. These were the widest of all Fender P-Bass necks: 1-3/4" at the nut. The depth (thickness) was reduced considerably, so they feel very flat and wide. Although the Jazz Bass, which first appeared during this era, shared the same oval shape, it feels more like a U in the lower positions due to its narrow (1-1/2") nut. The oval is the most popular of all Fender bass necks.

Late '60's through '70s: A variation of the original U shape—narrower than the '60s oval necks, not quite as chunky as the early-'50s U shape and with no hint of a V.

Early '80s: Very similar to the '70s U variation just mentioned, but sharper on the fingerboard edge, or "round-over." The early '80s necks became very wide again, reminiscent of the early '60s P-Bass but with a different shape.

1985: All bass necks returned to the oval shape—still used in production today.

d.i.y.

Installing bolt-on necks

What's the most indestructible electric guitar ever built? I'd say it's the Fender solidbody with its bolt-on neck. When's the last time you saw a Strat or a Tele with a broken peghead or a cracked body? These guitars outlast their owners! However, the neck-body joint can be a troublesome spot, since its alignment controls the instrument's action and playability. Attaching a neck to a body by means of four screws sounds simple, but by understanding a few key adjustment techniques you can get your guitar to play its best. If you're putting together a solidbody guitar, read this section before assembly, since the biggest problem you'll face is getting the neck set into the body so the action feels right.

Pulling the neck into alignment The most common adjustment made on bolt-on guitars is the re-alignment of the neck. This becomes necessary when the strings are falling off either edge of the fingerboard, sometimes even when you're playing simple chords. Looking at the guitar from the front, the two outer E strings should line up equally to an imaginary center line, neither being closer to the fingerboard's edge than the other. Because Fenders are designed with fairly wide bridge spacing and a fairly narrow fingerboard, the outer two strings are quite close to the fingerboard's edge to begin with. If the neck is even slightly out of alignment, the high- or low-E string will lean too close to the edge.

To correct this problem, slightly loosen the four mounting screws. Then hold the guitar in the playing position with the side edge on a table, gripping the body between your chest and one arm. With your free hand, give the neck a slight sideways pull in the direction that you wish to move the strings. Because the screws are only slightly loosened, enough grip should remain to hold the neck in its new position while you retighten the screws. If the neck still remains out of place after you shift it and retighten, you may have to use force to hold it in position while you tighten the screws (this can be tricky if you have only two hands). Some necks can be shifted without even loosening the screws—simply give the neck a quick jerk in the right direction.

Often, lightly sanding the finish on the underside of the neck heel and on the bottom of the neck cavity, de-glossing the lacquer will keep the two parts from shifting (use 220-grit sandpaper for just enough bite).

Another way to keep a neck in alignment is to slip a piece of metal screen-door mesh (or drywall sandpaper) between the neck and body. The mesh embeds itself into each surface's lacquer, creating a friction that makes it hard for the parts to shift. This slightly raises the neck's height in the body cavity, so you'll have to readjust the bridge and pickup height.

If the fit between the neck and body is so tight that there's no gap on the side you're shifting toward, you won't be able to move the neck without removing a small amount of wood or excess finish from the body

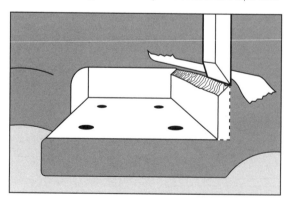

cavity. Go slowly and carefully to avoid chipping the finish, removing too much wood or removing wood in the wrong place. Lay a strip of masking tape on the body beside the neck, with just the amount of body/finish showing that you feel should be removed. The arrows in the drawing above show where wood may need to be removed to make room for the neck to move.

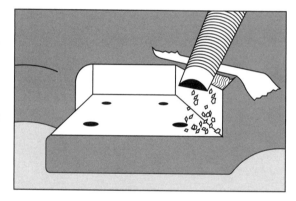

After removing the neck and pickguard, use a smooth file held at an angle to file the paint back to the tape line.

When you've filed to the tape, stop. Switching to a sharp wood chisel held at right angles to the body, pare away small bits of wood until you've removed the proper amount. Use the tape as your guideline as you chisel away the obstructing wood. Avoid touching the paint with the chisel, since paint chips easily. If you have a tight-fitting pickguard, you may have to file a small amount off that, too, before the neck will fit.

A bolt-on-neck guitar's string height and action is controlled by adjusting the height of the bridge inserts. It's not uncommon to find a guitar with strings too high, even though the inserts are as low as they'll go. You may also find one that has strings that are too low, despite the bridge pieces being in their highest positions. In either case, the neck needs shimming. Begin by setting your bridge pieces at the center of their height adjustment and at a radius that conforms comfortably to the fingerboard radius. This way, you'll still have room for fine-tuning the inserts' height after shimming the neck angle.

Shimming involves slipping a piece of thin cardboard, wood, or plastic between the neck and cavity. Very little thickness makes a drastic effect in the action. Time-proven shims have been fashioned from playing cards, matchbook covers and flatpicks. I once even found the tooth of a comb used as a shim. If your strings are too high, making playing uncomfortable, put the shim at the end of the neck that's closest to the inside end of the body cavity (this is where shims are most likely to be needed). If the strings are too low, place the shim towards the front of the cavity, just ahead of the two forward mounting screws. Proceed by trial and error—put in the shim, refasten the neck (holding the guitar as level as possible to prevent the shim from sliding out of place), and tune to pitch. It's best to start off using a matchbook cover; one thickness usually works, and two thicknesses are usually too much. Experiment, and remember that screen-door mesh not only keeps the neck in place, but makes a good shim, as well. You should have a comfortable action when done.

Many Strats made during the '70s have a three-bolt neck mount with an adjustable tilt mechanism. These are more difficult to get snug, and keep snug. This is especially true when the tilt mechanism is engaged, because when it tips the neck up, the contact between the underside of the neck and the neck cavity is broken. Even de-glossing the finish won't help then.

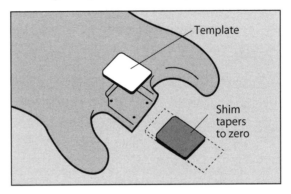

Full-size shims The small neck shim described earlier leaves an air space in the joint. This gap may cause an upward kink in the neck. And many players feel that they suffer a loss of tone unless firm contact is maintained between the neck and body. For these two reasons, a full-size shim that fills the entire gap is often preferred. I make these full shims out of mahogany, which is soft enough to shape easily and hard enough to transmit tone. Before making the full shim, first shim the neck with a small sliver of wood as described earlier. This gives you the proper thickness of the new shim at its thickest part. Measure this test shim with a pair of calipers that read in thousandths of an inch, or use a feeler gauge. Next, trim and fit a piece of cardboard to fit the cavity. Hold it in place and mark out the four holes from the rear, using a 3/16" drill bit. Use this cardboard template to mark out the mahogany shim.

Start with a piece of wood that's 1/8" thick and slightly larger than the cardboard template. The grain should run lengthwise with the body. Trace around the template onto the wood, drill out the holes and file, whittle or sand to shape. Use a few strips of double-stick carpet tape to fasten the shim to a piece of hard, flat wood that's as wide as your shim and about 6" longer. This will be your backing support while sanding, with the extra length serving as a handle. Before sanding, lay out the taper of the shim with a sharp pencil, matching the thickest measurement that you made earlier at one end, and tapering the other to nothing. This line is your sanding guide. Hold the support block with the attached shim in one hand while using your free hand to press it against a belt sander equipped with a medium- or fine-grit belt. Although it may take several tries, you'll end up with a sliver of mahogany matching your thickest measurement at one end and feathered out to zero at the other end—very fragile!

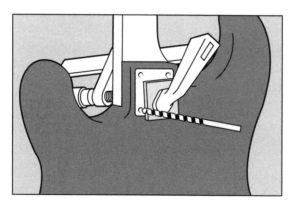

Neck mounting screws Replacement or kit necks often arrive without the four mounting screw holes already drilled. I prefer ordering them this way, since it allows me to really line things up properly before drilling the holes myself. Set the neck into the cavity and clamp it while you install the two outside E strings for alignment. When the strings are in line with the fingerboard's edges, run the proper drill bit (3/16") through the hole. You'll feel when it touches the neck. Rotate the bit with your fingers to make a mark for starting the holes; then remove the neck and change drill bits to a #30. Finish drilling the holes, using the starter marks as a guide.

Most neck-mounting screws are standard-size, and the hole they thread into is smaller than the outside of the thread, which leaves enough wood for the screw to bite into. Use an electric hand drill or a drill press and be

sure you drill perpendicular holes. If you measure the amount of screw showing through the cavity with the neck plate in place, you'll know how deep to drill without going through the fingerboard. Wrap a piece of masking tape around the drill-bit shank as a depth guide. After drilling the holes, pre-thread each hole with a mounting screw used as a tap. Rub the screw against beeswax, paraffin or paste wax to lubricate it before pre-threading each hole. Now mount the neck with the backplate and all four screws. It should line up with the strings.

If the four mounting holes in a neck are stripped, try coating them with super glue to provide grip for the screw thread. Use a toothpick in each hole to spread the glue around, and let it dry for an hour or use accelerator to speed up the cure. Repeat this operation several times, then you can rethread the holes with well-waxed mounting screws. This usually solves the problem.

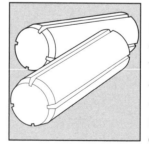

If the holes are too stripped, you need to drill each hole oversize, plug it with a hardwood dowel, and redrill from scratch. Most worn holes may be plugged with a 3/16" wood dowel. To ensure a snug fit, you need to drill the hole in the neck slightly smaller than the wood dowel; a #13 bit is a few thousandths smaller than the 3/16" dowel. Whether you use a drill press or hand drill, remember that the neck is usually hard maple and may cause the drill bit to run off line, causing the hole to be drilled oversize or out of round. Always clamp an object that you are about to drill, especially maple.

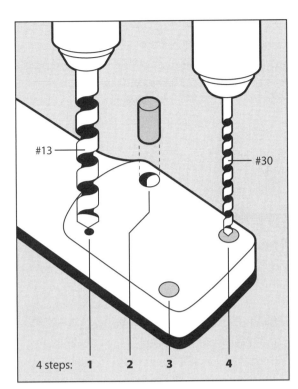

4 steps: **1** **2** **3** **4**

This mod makes it possible for him to disassemble and reassemble the neck and body as often as wants. For example, Bill takes the neck off of his famous Telecaster when he traveled overseas. He'd unbolt the neck and put it and the body (with the strings still on) in a briefcase, and carry it on the plane—safe-keeping for his favorite Tele, and instant access. Arriving in London he'd go directly to soundcheck, bolt the neck on, tune up and come out playin'. The amazing thing is that he has absolutely no trouble being in tune, while most of us would freak out if we'd just slapped our guitar together and had to step on stage, right? This is not a job to try without plenty of experience drilling, tapping and keeping things square, because if an insert is installed even slightly off center, the bolt won't fit.

Bolt-on neck installation in my shop is something we take pretty seriously. We start by making sure the neck is level and square to the drill bit (first photo, below). Then we start tapping the drilled hole with the tap in the drill-chuck, finishing it by hand once the tap is well-started and square to the work. The neck is never removed from the initial clamp-up until all the inserts are installed.

After drilling the holes, cut four pieces of 3/16" maple or hardwood dowel (use a larger wood dowel and corresponding drill bit if the hole is really bad) approximately 5/8" deep, or whatever depth you have drilled into the back of the neck's heel. Coat the holes with super glue or carpenter's glue, and tap the dowels into the holes, one at a time, with a small hammer. When the glue has dried, trim the dowel ends if they aren't flush, and then clamp the neck back into the cavity and proceed with drilling the screw holes. If you've been careful with your work, the neck will tighten home snugly.

If you really want a solid, no-shifting, neck mount, do what **Bill Kirchen**, the Telecaster master, did. A founding member of Commander Cody and the Lost Planet Airmen, today Kirchen's band Too Much Fun keeps him busy and traveling constantly. To make traveling easier, Bill had four threaded steel inserts installed in place of his Tele's neck-mounting holes and uses four 10-24 oval-head, Phillips stainless-steel machine bolts to hold the neck fast.

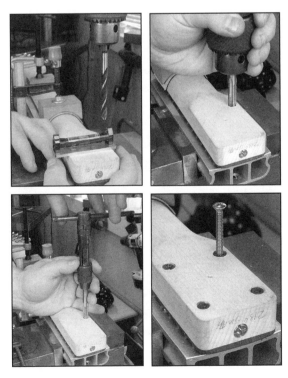

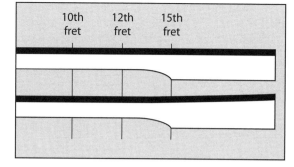

| 10th fret | 12th fret | 15th fret |

Fret buzz in the high registers

Buzzes in the high registers are often caused by a swelling or hump that begins somewhere past the body joint. Many bolt-ons have a kink where the neck joins the body, due to the length and slimness of the neck, which is fastened abruptly to the body and placed under constant up-pressure from string pull. Sometimes these forces are more than the truss rod can correct. Also, the neck absorbs moisture through the four mounting-screw holes, as well as through the end-grain of the maple at the body edge. While lacquer is still my favorite finish for the neck and body, it doesn't impede the absorption of moisture as well as some other finishes. This moisture absorption can cause a slight swelling, noticed more often with rosewood fingerboards because of the extra swelling of the glue joint between the maple and rosewood. I've encountered fewer humps, swelling, or rising tongues on the old, pre-'59 maple necks.

I mentioned previously that a shim placed under the neck to change the tilt can cause kinks, too. The thin strips of fill material that are commonly used as neck shims create an air space that allows the pressure of the four mounting screws to act as a clamp, forcing the fingerboard tongue to rise up. Combined, these forces—string pressure, moisture absorption and neck shims—can cause the last six or eight frets to be higher than they should be. These problems can be corrected with a fret dressing, or by a partial refret in which those last frets are removed, the rise is scraped/sanded from the fingerboard and the frets are reinstalled. Sometimes the original frets can be reused, sometimes not.

This rising tongue can be detected by placing a 12" straightedge on the fingerboard alongside any given string. The guitar should be strung to pitch, resting in the playing position, with the straightedge running from around the 10th fret to the fingerboard's high end. When viewed from the side, the fingerboard should appear flat, with the frets level with each other. If you see any gap or relief on this portion of the fingerboard, the tongue is probably high. The drawing at left shows two necks: the upper on has a flat fingerboard and the lower has this rise. Lay a small straightedge over the two drawings and see for yourself.

Broken pegheads

What's the scariest thing that can happen to your guitar? I think it's a broken peghead. When your guitar's head breaks off, you feel like that's the end! But it isn't. Read on.

Leaving a small bandstand at the end of a performance can be a tight squeeze—stepping over cords and cables, while at the same time snaking between drums, cymbals, mic stands and amps. Sooner or later, many guitarists watch with horror as their instrument springs from its stand and ends up on the dance floor with a broken peghead. The three most common breaks are hairline cracks, heads that are totally snapped off, or those that are cracked severely but still hanging on by the peghead veneer. You also occasionally find one that has been broken in the past and then repaired, with a new break on or near the area of the old break.

In almost all cases, a broken peghead can be made like new again, but it's tricky. My advice is, take it to a pro who's done this a lot. Unless you have a great deal of woodworking experience, the best thing to do is to loosen the strings immediately and place the instrument in its case (where it should have been in the first place!). If the head is completely snapped off, clip the strings near the tuners and carefully wrap the head and severed neck end in newspaper; your repairman will want these slivers and fragments of wood to be as clean and untouched as possible.

Many peghead breaks are initially ignored because they are mistaken for simple cracks in the finish. Although these cracks are hard to open, the wood is usually broken. If the repair is not done soon, sweat, grease and polish will find their way into the joint and the inevitable repair will be much more difficult and expensive.

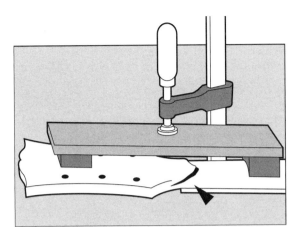

These breaks can be carefully spread open with a clamp and cauls as shown above. Then it's easy to inject glue deep into the break.

Some pegheads snap off cleanly, leaving a long, slanted wood surface showing. While these are easy to glue because of their large surface area, they can be tricky to align because the two pieces may want to slide once clamps are applied. These pieces need to be pinned temporarily during the gluing to align the two surfaces. I have seen many pegheads that were glued on crooked, and they seldom hold for very long.

A peghead that's broken cleanly and hanging by the peghead veneer is easier to repair. Usually this case involves plastic peghead veneer, because wood veneer generally breaks when the peghead does. This plastic veneer helps hold the two parts in alignment during clamping. Still, this is a very tricky repair.

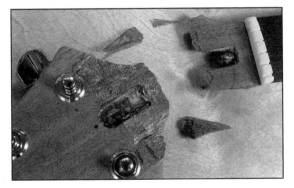

The most difficult repair is the clean snap with a very short break line, as on this PRS repair. This is a re-break of a neck that was previously repaired. Often the wood is extremely short-grained and inherently weak—the two parts have fingers of wood that slide back together like a locking puzzle. **Resist the temptation to slide these puzzle pieces together!** If you're not doing this repair

yourself, don't try to fit the two parts together. Leave it to whoever's going to do the repair, because there may be just one opportunity for a good fit, and test-fitting the parts will probably blow that chance. It's necessary to very carefully remove even the tiniest pieces of bent or loose wood before fitting the puzzle together. After years of experience, I seldom even try mating the parts at all before actually applying glue. I can usually tell which ones will mate well, and after applying the glue I often drive the head home with a hammer tap.

Re-breaks sometimes happen on an old glue line that wasn't repaired properly. In these cases, all the old glue must be carefully scraped away down to bare wood, since new glue applied over old glue seldom holds. New wood can be added in at least two ways:

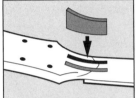

Splines These are pieces inlaid through the break for reinforcement. Splines should run well past the break into solid wood— from 1" to 2" on both sides of the break line. Splines should run deep into the neck and peghead, running with the neck's length and grain, and they should be of matching wood.

Sandwiched around the break. In my shop we often (not always) add new peghead overlays onto the peghead face, and/or cover the whole back of the peghead with a "backstrap"—a veneer of wood that covers the back surface of the peghead and even runs out onto the neck. This is a common building technique for fancy banjos and certain higher-end guitars. By putting new wood on the front and back of the peghead, you can sandwich the broken area, with or without splines. In the example that follows, the top laminate is 3/16", and the bottom is a bit over 1/4", mahogany on mahogany.

This repair can be as strong or stronger than the wood itself. The first repair is the important one, and choosing the right repair method is important. Follow these rules:

✔ On new breaks, a simple regluing and minor touchup is often all that's needed, and it's the best approach.

✔ Resort to reinforcement techniques on rebreaks, and breaks that are horribly shattered.

✔ When the situation calls for it, we sometimes fashion a

basic

new peghead and graft it onto the neck somewhere between the 3rd and 5th frets (hard, but doable by a pro).

✔ Sometimes the best idea is to replace the neck entirely. This is the easy on newer American-made guitars for which parts are available. Vintage pieces may require a custom-made reproduction neck using the original parts (fingerboard, binding, peghead overlay, etc.). This may cost several thousand dollars or more, but there are craftsmen capable of the task.

These techniques take an experienced touch and lots of practice. A repairman should be glad to discuss any technique with you beforehand. Obviously, a fair amount of finish work has to be performed before the job is complete. Most pegheads can be artfully touched up so that few people would ever know that the job has been done. Shop around, because not every repair shop can handle this job.

There is no one best glue for repairing pegheads. The glue depends on the situation, and any of several glue types are acceptable. In my order of preference, they are:

Hot hide glue is good for any kind of clean break, from simple splits to complete breaks. However, you must have experience using hot glue because you don't have much "open" time to clamp before it cools and sets. We always heat the parts to be glued to extend the working time.

Epoxy is good for the same tasks as the hide glue, if the right epoxy is used. I use a professional epoxy made by RBC Industries of Warwick, Rhode Island. It's a 24-hour cure glue, and when mixed, it becomes very thin and able to penetrate as deeply as hide glue. As with hide glue, heating the parts to be glued extends the working time.

Superglue has its place — especially for impossible to penetrate breaks. It's really a worst-case scenario glue choice; if the break is accessible and clean I wouldn't use superglue.

Aliphatic-resin, or white glues (Titebond is the most widely recognized) will work, and I used these for years until I discovered hide glue and my favorite epoxy. I don't trust white (or yellow) glue not to move or creep over the years. I use Titebond for lots of woodworking projects, but not broken pegheads.

With this PRS repair, most of the wood fibers we'd like to have had been dulled, compressed, and flattened. We pinned the peghead together with dowels to keep the parts aligned as the glue set (24-hour-cure epoxy).

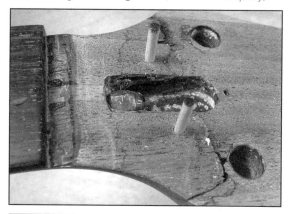

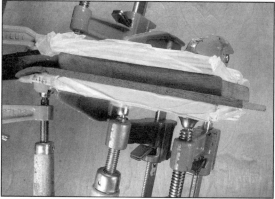

We clamp the new pieces one at a time; in the photo above, the backstrap's being glued on.

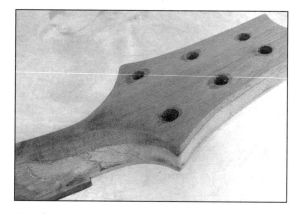

A mahogany sandwich If you look closely at the old break area you can see the dark lines that indicate how many pieces were glued up the first time (that didn't hold — wrong glue, or not well done).

basic

What to expect from a fret job   169

d.i.y.

Loose frets   170
Fret files   171
Compound radius fingerboards   174
Fret dressing   177
Refretting   184
    Choosing your fretwire   190
    Hammer-in method   194
    Compression fretting   196
    Martin bar style fretting   199
    The glue-in method   201
    Bound fingerboards   207
Vintage Fender fretting   209
Fret slots and tang size   213

deep

The neck jig   214
The Plek machine   216

Chapter 12

Fretwork

basic

If your guitar needs fretwork

Fretwork isn't basic level activity—it's a D.I.Y. thing. It has everything to do with how your guitar plays and sounds, and is worth all the time, attention and skill you can muster. If you're not a do-it-yourselfer, than this chapter at least can give you an overview, and help you know what sort of work your guitar needs.

For the purposes of this chapter, let's break fretwork into two categories: installing and dressing. Installing might be a complete refret, a partial refret, or brand new frets in a guitar you're building. Once those frets are installed in the fingerboard, they need to be leveled, shaped and made ready to play: we'll refer to these activities as dressing the frets.

What should you expect from a fret job?

If you've experienced action problems from a warp in the neck or humps in the board, a fret job probably will let you set your action much lower without undue buzzing. But remember that a certain amount of clean, metal-to-metal string buzz is normal for any guitar, especially if one plays with a medium or heavy attack on light strings (.010s and under). Keep that in mind if you take your guitar to a repairman; they're a sensitive breed that becomes offended when, after doing a painstaking fret job and then taking half a day to set up a guitar, the customer picks it up and whines, "It buzzes!" Any new fret job takes some time to break in, so be patient. It may take as long as a month for playing and fret wear to make things feel normal again.

If the prices you find for professional fretwork seem high, let me take this chance to speak up for my fellow repair techs—the many skilled men and women doing this work. Few customers appreciate the careful and tedious setup involved with fret work. Often the nut must be replaced or shimmed to accomodate the new, taller frets. Bridge heights and truss rods must be readjusted, and often intonation must be set. This labor must be included into the price of the fret job itself; there's no way around it. Action and setup to involves truss rod adjustment, bridge intonation on electrics, string-height adjustment and the final fit of the nut. For many acoustics, the saddle has to be refit or replaced by hand to accommodate the subtle action changes after a refret. To be a really skilled luthier takes years of experience and training, all of which benefits your guitar and the enjoyment you'll get from playing when it's right. If you can't afford a first-rate refret, save your money. Price is important, but a botched fret job is much worse than no fret job at all.

d.i.y.

Loose frets

Before you can dress your frets, you should make sure that you don't have a fingerboard full of loose frets. It's hard to level and re-crown frets that are loose because they press down as the file passes over them, and pop right back up after it goes by. Loose frets are common, even with good fretwork on great guitars. A lot of fret buzz is caused by loose fret ends, which are hard not only on the ear but also on the fingers. Sometimes a complete fret job is needed to correct fret buzzes, but just as often the problem is solved by gluing down the end of the one fret that has lifted. In the old days, the resetting of a raised fret end was difficult and time-consuming, but that was before super glue. Now the average guitar player can easily and safely solve this problem.

A fret end can rise for a variety of reasons. The fret slot may be too big, or the fret tang (the part that's driven into the fingerboard slot to hold the fret in) could be too small. Rising fret ends may also be caused by insufficient glue, or wood that has shrunk: some frets are held in with glue as an aid, while others are hammered in dry, letting the small beads on the side of the tang do all the holding. Dirt, grease and oils may have loosened the glue or softened and weakened the wood that holds the fret. Here's a quick and easy technique for tamping down

those high fret ends:

Find a wooden dowel at least 1/4" in diameter and 6" long. File a notch in one end. This dowel is used for pushing the fret end down

flush onto the fingerboard while you wax the fret and its surrounding fingerboard area (to keep glue from sticking where you don't want it). The stick also holds the fret in

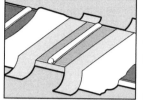

place while the glue sets.

Next, lay a sheet of paper on each side of the bad fret and tape it down to within 1/2" of the fret. Use enough paper to cover all of the fingerboard except the fret you're working on. Wax the exposed fingerboard and fret edges, going over the side of the fingerboard or binding, as well, in case any glue might run over onto the neck. Use a Q-Tip to apply any sort of paste wax, such as Turtle Wax. Don't load the Q-Tip with wax; twirl it in the wax and wipe off any lumps. When you've finished waxing, release the fret. It should pop right back up, with no wax having gotten under the fret where you want the glue to do its work.

If you have more than one loose fret end (and often you will), don't try regluing more than one at a time. Use a water-thin superglue that is able to penetrate deep within the fret slot and tang area. You'll also need a bottle of accelerator to speed up the drying time and cause an "instant" cure. The reason we covered the rest of the fingerboard with paper is so that all the frets don't become activated by the accelerator's effect, which lasts about 15 minutes.

The guitar shouldn't move while you're working, so block the neck with some books or something firm for it to press against. Apply a drop of glue to each side of the loose fret along the fingerboard edge as far back as your eye tells you it's loose, and watch it disappear as it runs deep into the problem area. With a soft rag or tissue paper, remove any wet glue that doesn't run under.

Immediately follow with a squirt of accelerator on each side of the fret, and then quickly but smoothly peel off the tape and paper. While the glue is accelerating, it's wise to have your wooden stick in the other hand, ready to press the fret down. While pressing the fret flush to the

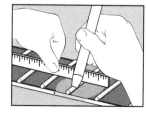

fingerboard, you can use a straightedge or flat object to help judge when the fret is level with its nearest tight fret. The glue should set within 30 seconds. Don't press the fret lower than the frets on either side, since this will result in a fret that's too low and subject to buzz. The actual gluing and accelerating must be done swiftly and efficiently, so first practice the operation in a dry run. Follow this sequence: apply glue and clean up excess (5 to 10 seconds); squirt accelerator (2 or 3 seconds); remove tape (2 seconds); press fret down and level with straightedge or block (5 seconds).

In less than a minute the fret should hold, sometimes leaving a small bead of squeezed-out super glue showing along the fret/fingerboard edge. Remove this glue with a sharp-pointed tool (pin, X-Acto blade, chisel, etc.). Any glue that might remain on the waxed area of the fingerboard should be removed by scraping lightly (lengthwise with the fingerboard rather than across-grain) with a razor blade, and then polish with 0000 steel wool. If you still have a slight buzz, you may need to slightly level the fret with a smooth mill file or block of wood wrapped with #320-grit sandpaper.

If you have any trouble getting the fret level or if you feel that you didn't glue it properly, use a soldering iron to loosen the glue bond and try again. Heat breaks a super glue bond in the same way that it loosens most any glue, including epoxies. Be careful: the heat causes some glues to vaporize. Do not breathe the fumes or let them get in your eyes! The second round of gluing on the same fret may be more difficult because the hardened super glue is now under there. Don't use too much glue, and be especially careful not to let the glue run onto the neck. If it does, wipe it off immediately with some lighter fluid, which you should keep handy.

Wear safety glasses when using super glue, and remember that it can bond your fingers together. A short while back, a fret sprung up on me when my push-stick slipped, spitting super glue onto my prescription plastic-lens safety glasses. The glue hardened instantly and permanently. I had to buy a new pair of glasses, but my eyes were spared. Of course, avoid splashing a guitar's finish. Buy a bottle of solvent for cleaning glue from your fingertips and to help separate them in case of accident. Never use this solvent to remove glue from a lacquer finish, since it dissolves lacquer. Practice with the super glue and accelerator on objects that you don't care about before trying a repair. This will give you a feel for the setting time and show you how quickly it runs.

In extreme cases (with much sweat and oil worked under the fret), this method may not work, but it's worth a try; if it doesn't work, a partial or complete refret may be needed.

Fret files

Here are the specialized files used by most repair shops: leveling files that even out the fret tops, crowning files that re-shape the frets and dressing files for the final shaping.

Leveling files are used to make the fret tops flat and level with each other. You'll want two fret leveling files, approximately 3" and 6" long. These are the leveling files that will be used to rectify high or low frets and hump or rise, as well as to create fall-away at the high end of the fingerboard. These flat, fast-cutting files are available commercially with comfortable wooden handles. When I got started years ago I had to make my own, by grinding notches across smooth mill bastard files so they'd break into short pieces (as shown in the illustration).

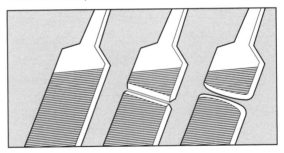

Working with a grindstone that way is just plain dangerous (a friend of mine was badly injured this way). I suggest you just buy your fret levelers instead.

Rounding files come in several sizes to accommodate frets of different width. Their cutting surface is concave to accommodate a fret's rounded shape. Some have teeth, some are diamond-plated. It's best if a rounding file is larger than the fret size so that it fits easily over the fret crown. When a rounding file is much smaller than the fret it's working on, the edges of the file contact the fret rather than the middle of the file. This puts scars in the fret. Some files have both a narrow and a wide groove on opposite edges; others have the same size groove on both edges. Over the years, I've purchased every fret file there is: call me compulsive, I don't mind.

Rounding file being used with a stainless-steel fret protector

Toothed rounding files The cut made by a rounding file is round, of course. This file rounds off, or recrowns, the fret after it's been filed or sanded flat during leveling. The quality of the file's cut depends on the make of file and how it's used. New toothed rounding files tend to chatter and leave hard-to-remove marks on frets, especially on the fret ends. A few tips for fret rounding:

✔ Avoid excess pressure with rounding files.

✔ Clogged metal in the teeth causes scratching, so clean them often.

✔ Wipe a stick of paraffin over the teeth to act as a lubricant and help eliminate clogging.

✔ Practice on scrap to check the cut of a new file.

A toothed rounding file sits over the fret, but the curve of its teeth isn't deep enough for the file edges to scratch the fingerboard; this could happen with an extremely worn or low-crown fret, however. Sometimes it's effective to use a rounding file with a radius that's *smaller* than the fret width for rounding just one edge of a flat-topped fret on either side of center, but be careful that the edge doesn't cut a groove into the fret top by mistake. These edges of the file where the teeth run into the smooth side walls are often sharp; grind or sand them smooth along the entire file length to avoid gouging the fingerboard on each side of the fret as you're working.

Diamond rounding files don't have teeth. Instead, the concave surface is covered with industrial diamond abrasive (coarse and fine grits are available). These files don't leave scratches, and they cut in both directions! Even dyed-in-the-wool "triangle filers" love this file once they give it a chance. I seldom use toothed files anymore, unless I really need to hog away a lot of metal.

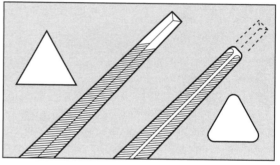

Triangle or **3-square files** Another great dressing tool is a 6" to 8" slim-taper, three-corner "triangle" file with its sharp edges ground smooth. I learned to use one during my visits to the Gibson plant in Kalamazoo in the good old days. At the time, I had a beautiful flame-top Les Paul, and because I never trusted myself to work on it, the frets were dressed more than once at the factory. (In those days, you could make an appointment to have service done while you waited. I learned a lot by wandering around and watching.)

The triangle file can be used instead of, or along with, a rounding file to round or crown the fret tops left flat after the leveling operation. It is also used to round over the frets' ends and remove any jagged burrs along the fingerboard's edge. You must remove any trace of a cutting edge on all three corners of the file with a grinder or belt sander (here's a look at the file before and after). Also, blunt and round the tip, or nose, of the file. A poorly

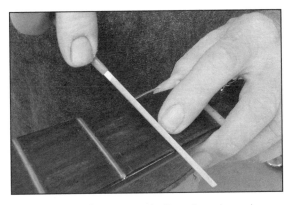

edges of this file directly on the fretboard surface for support (you don't have to balance on the fret as with other files).

ground triangle file can scar the fingerboard wood on either side of the fret you're working on, even though you have taped off the fingerboard.

A second triangle file is the small extra-slim triangle file from StewMac. Unless I'm hogging metal, I prefer this file because it has a finer cut, is more delicate, and can shape fret ends better since it can get in closer.

When you shop for your files, pick up one sheet each of wet-or-dry sandpaper in 320-, 400-, and 600-grits, as well as some 0000 steel wool and a file-cleaning brush (also known as a file card). My favorite file card has small metal bristles on one side and fiber bristles on the other; buy one if you can find it. Even better than a file card is a brass-bristle mini-file cleaner; they're great for cleaning small, fine-cut triangle files.

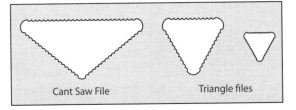

Cant Saw File   Triangle files

Cant saw file A third style of triangular file is the cant saw file, used in Texas by **Michael Stevens** and **Rene Martinez**. Michael Stevens co-founded the Fender Custom Shop along with John Page, and now operates Stevens Electrical Instruments in Alpine, Texas; Rene Martinez was Stevie Ray Vaughan's guitar tech and best friend (see section on Stevie Ray's setup). The Cant saw file is a variation of the Triangle file, and is similar in cut to the large triangle file, but cuts even faster.

These are also available at hardware stores and should be ground to look like the cross-section shown in the illustration: smoothed on all three corners. When the fingerboard is taped off, you can rest the smooth-ground

Fret end file Last but not least is the Fret End File used to shape the fret end bevels. It's ground smooth and round on one edge to do the rounding without cutting into the fingerboard or binding; the other edge is ground flat—leaving sharp corner edges that can knock-off any sharp burrs.

I've been criticized for having too many files for fretwork, but I don't care. Not having a wide selection of files is rather limiting (especially if you're in the business of working on frets). I often have quite a selection of specialty files laid out as I work.

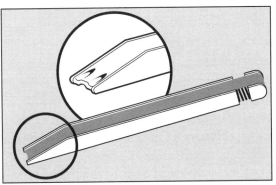

Sanding stick An even better fret burnisher is the Fret Dressing Stick, an inexpensive handheld sander with a spring-loaded abrasive belt. I file three slight grooves into the plastic—two on one side and one on the other—which hug the fret's rounded shape. I use three "Sand-Sticks" during dressing: 320-, 400- and 600-grit.

Sanding block A good tool for sanding and steel-wooling frets after leveling and rounding is a rubber squeegee from the 3M Company. This should be available at any automotive store selling finish supplies. Buy the smallest rubber squeegee available, and grind or file a groove along one edge of it. Eventually, you'll wrap the steel wool or sandpaper around the edge of this "fret burnisher" to do your polishing (see page 6 for an illustration of how to shape the squeegee).

Sandpaper Finally, pick up a roll of masking tape for taping off the frets while you file and sand them. You should have light-tack draftsman's tape (from an art supply store) as well as standard masking tape.

Take the time to find and prepare the proper files, and to buy the sandpaper, steel wool and squeegee—and finish reading this chapter before starting! The next part about fingerboard radius will give you a better understanding of the fretwork you're about to get into.

Compound radius fingerboards

On vintage Strats, bluesy bends that note out or buzz with a low action setup are caused by the very curved 7-1/4" radius of the vintage fingerboard. Many players like the feel and comfort of the curve when playing barre chords, and country and jazz guitarists find less need for far-stretching blues bends. Most blues and rock players, however, run into bending problems—especially on the high-E and B strings, and usually in the upper register (10th fret and higher). Sometimes the easiest solution is to have metal dressed off the frets in the tongue area under the second and third strings—where the high-E and B strings end up when bent to their peak. But often this dressing solution is barely acceptable at best. The real answer lies in having a complete refret by an extremely good repairman experienced in tapering the fingerboard radius, gradually and subtly flattening it out as it goes up the neck and ending up with a 12" or 16" radius at the fingerboard's end. This is known as a compound radius.

On a 7-1/4" radius fretboard, take a good look at a whole-step bend on the first string. The string is moving at an uphill angle toward the middle of the fingerboard radius, so it *has* to buzz! If you need proof, remove the strings and set a straightedge on the fingerboard at the angle of the bent string: it will rock on the spot that causes the buzz. Since the strings rise at an angle up and away from the fingerboard toward the bridge, the fingerboard's radius needn't be flat to be buzz-free, but

7-1/4" is pushing it. This is why Fender started using a 9" and 12" radius in recent years (only the vintage models still have a 7-1/4" radius). So, if you want to play the blues on a vintage Strat, your action mustn't be too low.

Understanding the difference between a cylinder-shaped and a cone-shaped "compound" fretboard may be the most subtle and important fretting task you'll face. Using this knowledge during fret work separates the novice from the pro, and the clean playing note from a buzz, yet I've never seen it explained!

In my opinion, radiused fretboards are more comfortable for playing chords than are flat fretboards because they follow the natural curve of the hand. A flatter fretboard radius offers fewer problems to string benders: Gibson's traditional 12" radius has always been good for blues-bending, and Martin's 16" too. But the flatter you get the radius, the less chord-comfort you have. So an "in-between" radius, like a 9" or 10", may be just right.

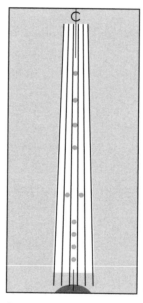

For some, a combination of radii—the compound radius—is the answer.

Most fretboards are uniformly radiused from end to end—like a section out of a cylinder. When the fingerboard is cut to the tapered width of the neck it's much narrower at the nut than at the very last fret. Looking down from above, notice that the outer two E strings follow the taper (profile) of the fingerboard; they're not parallel to the fingerboard's centerline. The remaining four strings follow the same taper but come closer to parallel with the centerline.

Imagine this shape on a perfectly straight neck. A straightedge following the paths of the strings, especially the outside E strings, will rock from end to end because the only way a straight line can be in full contact with the surface of a cylinder is when it's parallel to the center. (Set your straightedge on a length of pipe; it sits flat when it's parallel, but at even a slight angle it rocks on the pipe.)

On a fingerboard, this becomes even more pronounced when you start bending strings—you're increasing the angle, getting further from parallel with the center. You're going to hear fret buzz for sure.

The way to avoid this is to shape the fretboard into a cone. This simply means that the curvature at the nut will be greater than at the last fret—the fingerboard radius will flatten gradually from end to end. In repair shops we have been compounding fretboards for years to give customers low action with blues-bending capabilities and little buzz. Some manufacturers that have offered a compound radius are Warmoth, Jackson, Collings, Taylor and Martin.

Vintage Martins were compounded this way. They started out with a 16" machine-shaped cylinder fretboard that became tapered to 20" at the end because Martin hand-leveled the board in "the lie of the strings." Martin guitars made after 1993 have cylindrical fretboards with no taper because they changed their fretboard preparation technique (they realized that for a 16" or higher radius, a compound fretboard wasn't too great an issue, especially on an acoustic guitar). As a general rule, the radius of an average compound fingerboard flattens out about 3" or 4" toward the end of the fingerboard.

When preparing the fretboard for a fret job you will sand, file or scrape the surface until it's straight from end to end across the radius of the board. If you check your progress with a straightedge resting in the six individual string lies (which is the most common method), you are shaping a slight compound taper into the fretboard. In the case of a refret on many factory guitars (Fender, Gibson, Guild, Martin after '93), you're altering the machine-made cylinder, which was never intended to have this tapered profile.

A quick fix for vintage buzz The quickest fix for vintage Fenders that buzz when you bend, is to re-level the existing frets until the straightedge sits flat where the top three strings lie (E, B, and G). You don't need to worry about the bass side because the strings are heavier, higher, and you don't bend them much. You'll be removing the most metal on the edges (E and B strings) where the string taper is greatest. The first and last few frets will hardly get filed at all because they aren't part of the

"hill" in the center causing the problem. You're creating a slight compound radius on the fret tops themselves.

After compounding, some frets will be taller than others, but if the frets were fairly tall to begin with the lowest ones usually aren't uncomfortably low. Coupled with the traditionally higher action normally accepted with a vintage Strat, you can now get the blues bends you're after. This solution is only worthwhile on a vintage axe that still has plenty of fret to work with, however, and that's not too common.

A better solution is to put the compound radius into the fretboard itself—prep the board's surface that way. Now the tops of the newly installed frets will touch the straightedge (after a normal light fret leveling) because the frets will follow the compound radius from end to end and the fret height will be uniform. This compound leveling is common during a refret, and I fretted guitars like that for years before realizing that what I was doing had a name: compound radius. You can't compound a vintage maple neck without removing most (or all) of the finish however, and neither can you re-shape thin veneer rosewood boards on some Fenders (there's not enough wood to remove). In all cases, you have to take inlays and fingerboard side dots into consideration.

It's easy to run into side dots, especially on Fenders. Since Gibson usually starts out at 12" you have less chance of hitting side dots, but it's still possible. Because of side dots, inlays and the fretboard thickness, a partial compound job may be the answer. You don't need to go all the way in following the formula given below in order to benefit from a somewhat flatter board.

I generally read a fretboard, and prep it, with my straightedges resting on the lie of the strings. This creates a cone, and I wanted to know what radius I should look for at the fretboard end, and what's the projected radius when it meets the bridge saddle? I asked my good friend **Don MacRostie**—head of R&D at Stewart-Mac-Donald. Working with two other interested luthiers, **Gila Eban** and **Dana Bourgeois**, Don worked out the three basic fingerboard radius formulas shown here.

The purpose of these formulas is to keep us from removing more wood than necessary while attempting to get the straightedge to sit flat on the fretboard during a refret. The amount of wood to be removed is subtler than some realize, and is determined by the fingerboards' taper (width of the nut and 12th fret), scale length and starting radius at the nut. With it you can find out what the radius must be at the end of the fingerboard, at any point along the fingerboard (for checking your accuracy with radius gauges as you work), and determine the projected radius at the bridge saddle. It's very useful information!

Formula for determining the radius at any point on a fretboard

Here's Don MacRostie:

Anyone doing a fret job without understanding the difference between a cylinder and a cone is working blind. Straight lines that run lengthwise on a cylinder and are in full contact with its surface must be parallel, and could never be tapered to each other as guitar strings on a fingerboard are. I have drawn out three formulas for dealing with the phenomenon of string spread over a curved surface. Whenever straight lines eventually converge on a point (the fingerboard tapering from the body toward the nut), and those straight lines lie in full contact with a radiused surface, then the shape of that surface must be conical or some portion of a cone. First we must determine where the lines (strings) converge. I've defined the following:

X = Distance from the nut to the Origin (focal point)

T = Distance from the nut to the 12th fret

Sn = String spread at the nut

St = String spread at the 12th fret

Rn = Fingerboard radius at the nut

Rd = Fingerboard radius at **D** (certain distance from nut)

D = Arbitrary distance from nut

1 Using the spacing of the two E strings at the nut and 12th fret, extend the lines until they converge (illustrated at the bottom of this page). Measure from the point of convergence to the nut and you will have **X** or the focal length. **X** is then used in the remaining formulas. This is the formula marked #1, below.

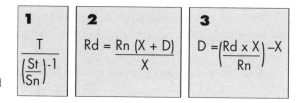

$$\textbf{1} \quad \frac{T}{\left(\dfrac{St}{Sn}\right)-1} \qquad \textbf{2} \quad Rd = \frac{Rn\,(X+D)}{X} \qquad \textbf{3} \quad D = \left(\frac{Rd \times X}{Rn}\right) - X$$

2 The second formula (above) assumes that you have already determined **X**, the location of the origin of the cone. This solves for the radius at any point along the fingerboard represented by the value **D**.

3 The third formula, to find point **D** where the radius equals a known value is written as #3 above. This formula can be rearranged to solve for any of the values.

All of these formulas are linear and relatively easy to solve and rearrange.

Thanks, Don. I should have put this in the Deep section of this chapter! You don't need to do these calculations in order to do fretwork, and we're ready to start dressing frets now.

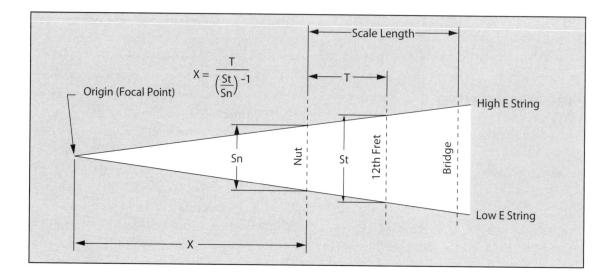

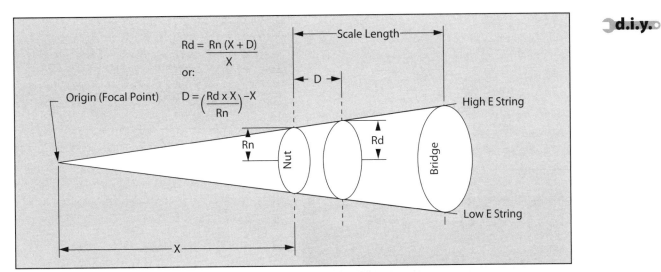

$$Rd = \frac{Rn\,(X + D)}{X}$$

or:

$$D = \left(\frac{Rd \times X}{Rn}\right) - X$$

d.i.y.

Fret dressing

Fret dressing is one of the most common reasons a guitar ends up in the repair shop. Before you start any fret work, be sure to read and understand neck evaluation and truss rod adjustment in chapter 3. And don't start filing your frets as you read: finish this chapter completely so you understand the whole process. This way you can determine whether a partial or complete fret job is needed.

Fret dressing refers to leveling out any high, low or worn spots on frets, and re-rounding ("crowning") the fret tops. When the tops of all the frets are not level, you get buzzes and "noting out" (notes that don't play cleanly). Basically, fret dressing is a three-stage process:

1 Leveling is done with a smooth, flat mill file, followed by 220-, 320- and 400-grit sandpaper for smoothing.

2 The fret tops left flat by the leveling operation are re-rounded with a small triangular file or a fret-rounding file. Any jagged fret ends along the fingerboard's edge are rounded now, too.

3 Finally, a good polishing with fine sandpaper and steel wool gives smooth, buzz-free frets that are a dream to bend on.

Many new guitars come from the factory with the frets leveled, but only a cursory job of crowning has been done. This is often why some factory-fresh guitars play less than perfectly. Fret dressing is time-consuming manual labor, so a deluxe job at the factory would

raise the instrument's price. Crowning is necessary though, since frets with flat tops have extra surface area for the strings to buzz against as they vibrate. Flat frets also cause intonation problems, with the strings playing sharp or flat because they're not noting on the dead center of the fret. Also, flattened frets are harder to bend strings on due to the increased friction.

Guitars that have been played for a while can develop grooves or pits in the frets, especially in the first five frets. If the grooves are too deep, you don't want to file all the good frets down to the level of those few bad ones for the sake of flatness and a level fingerboard. When a pit or groove has been worn much lower than a third of the fret's full height (and definitely if the wear approaches the fret's halfway mark), the fret's going to need to be replaced. If you show it to an experienced repairman, he may recommend replacing only the worn frets using matching fretwire (a "partial refret") or it may be necessary to refret the instrument completely. It's a judgement call based on experience, and something you might want to get a second opinion on.

In this chapter, I'm going to tell you how to do this work. Not having your guitar to look at, or an example of your skill with tools, it's hard to say whether you should go for it and work on your own frets. If you do, you should (and forgive me if I've said this before) practice on a guitar you can afford to make mistakes on! (I know I keep saying that, but we all learn our skills the hard way, and it takes some mistakes to get good at fret work.)

Frets that are worn down and too flat can be found on any guitar—from inexpensive imports to the finest American-made models. Rather than being pitted, the tops of these frets are extremely low and flat (above). This can be caused by years of playing or by a poor fret job that someone tried to correct by leveling without taking the extra time to crown. You may eventually need a refret, but often these low frets can be rounded with a lot of work.

Loose frets, or a fret that's taller than those around it, will also cause a string to note out—meaning you can't hear the intended note at all because the string is actually fretting at a higher fret. Usually this is caused by the fret working loose (above); it needs to be reseated. It can probably be fixed with super glue as described above.

The opposite of a too-tall fret is, of course, one that's too low, causing the string to note on the next-higher fret. I see this often on cheap guitars. It's usually caused by a fret that was driven into the fingerboard too hard, or by a mismatch of fretwire height. These frets should be pulled up to the proper height, or new frets should be installed. This is tricky for a newcomer, but for an experienced repair tech this can be an instant repair.

Jagged fret ends along the fingerboard edge are uncomfortable because they catch your hand as you slide up or down the neck. They're usually caused by the fretboard drying out and shrinking over time. You can use a flat-leveling file to re-bevel these fret ends, and a triangular crowning file can round and deburr any jagged corners. Occasionally, frets will even fall short of the fingerboard edge (above). Don't try to bevel the rest of your frets to match these; either have the troublesome frets replaced or do your best to de-burr the ends and make them feel comfortable until the guitar's refretted.

Let's get started First check the fretboard radius; if it measures the same at the nut as at the last fret, you have a cylinder-shaped board (Fender and Gibson). If the radius is flatter at the last fret than it is at the nut, you have a compound radius fretboard. Below are two ways of leveling the fret tops with a file: one for a cylinder-board, and one for a compound. Using either method, the file stroke is always lengthwise with the fingerboard.

Adjust your truss rod to remove any relief. Get the neck straight from the 1st fret to the 12th, using a metal straightedge for reference. Then duplicate this straight, or "leveling," position with the strings removed. Lay a towel or pad on the tabletop, covering it and the entire work surface with newspaper to catch any metal filings. Rest the guitar's body on the padded part of the work surface, and cradle the back of the neck on a stack of books or anything else that can serve as a support (I like the "rock-n-roller neck rest" used by repairman **Pete Towers** in Chesterton, Cambridge, UK).

Any neck support should be padded, and covered

with paper as well, because filings will scratch the lacquer on the back of the neck. (To avoid scratching, vacuum or remove the filings often). Check with your straightedge again to be sure that the neck support hasn't altered your neck straightness. If it has, move the support to a different part of the neck and/or make a slight truss rod adjustment.

Even with the strings removed and the truss rod loose, some necks may tend to back-bow slightly. These necks gain relief from string tension alone. In this case, support the headstock, not the back of the neck, and later you may either put slight pressure on the body or pull down on the neck's heel to straighten the neck as you file.

A better way than pulling down on the heel to get the neck straight was shown to me by Rich Starkey at the Martin repair department. For simulating string tension on a neck—whether re-fretting or dressing—Rich supports the peghead and then sets two 6 lb. weights on either side of the fretboard on the shoulders of the guitar. For a non-flat top (like a Les Paul), use a sandbag or sack of buckshot. The weights add just enough pressure to get the neck into the perfect leveling position.

Following are two lists of the tools used to level and crown (round) the frets. The "must have" shows the beginner the minimum number of tools needed to get by; the other list describes the tools that Im likely to use during a day spent dressing frets.

Short list: the must-have tools

Straightedges—a long one for checking general levelness, and a couple of short ones to test individual frets by rocking on a high spot.
10" leveling file, or substitute a 2" X 8" carborundum whetstone
1 rounding file (diamond, triangle, cant saw, Gurian)
Sanding block 1" wide X 14" long
Wet-or-dry sandpaper 320-, 400-, 600-grit (self-stick, or use double-stick tape). The 320-grit is for leveling, the other two are for polishing out marks after filing.
Small file cleaning brush with brass bristles
Steel wool 0000 (extremely fine)
Masking tape

My list: the tools I use

Leveling files 3", 6" and 10"
Carborundum stone
Steel leveling block (for sandpaper)
Wet-Or-Dry sandpaper 220-, 320-, 400-, 600-grit (3M Gold self-stick)
Triangle files small and large
Cant saw file
Diamond rounding files coarse- and fine-grit
Mini-file cleaning brush with brass bristles
Sand-sticks three, with 320-, 400-, and 600- grit belts
Steel wool 0000 (extremely fine)
Variety of tapes draftsman's tape, masking tape, and heavy brown binding tape
Small flat file StewMac Fender nut-seating file for removing burrs, and cleaning up individual fret ends
Straightedges long, short, notched and a set of fret rockers in 1-1/2", 3", 4" and 5" lengths

Protect the guitar at all times With masking tape, protect any part of the guitar that can be scratched by your files or sandpaper, especially around the fingerboard tongue and the pickups (which, if not protected, will magnetically attract and retain metal filings and steel wool dust). To insure that the tape won't pull off delicate vintage finishes when it's removed, I lay down one course of the less-sticky drafting tape directly on the finish and then, with regular masking tape, I tape thin (.018") pickguard material onto it as a protector.

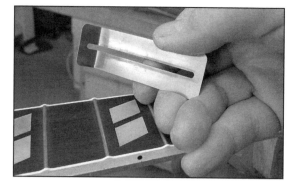

A good way to protect the fretboard is with a stainless steel fret protector with a slot that lies over the fret and protects the board while you work. I make an almost right-angle bend on one end of the protector so that it locates on the bass edge of the fretboard.

Remove the nut In theory, the leveling file must pass over the nut slot if the file is to hit all the frets equally. In practice, you can stop your file stroke at the nut as soon as the tops of all the frets have been hit. If the nut can be removed and replaced easily, or has to come out anyhow for replacement and if vintage isn't an issue, remove it—you'll level the frets more effectively. First, carefully score around the nut with a sharp X-Acto knife to break the lacquer. With a block of wood and a hammer, gently tap the nut to knock it loose.

Highlight the fret tops I use blue Magic Marker to color the fret tops before filing. This lets me see instantly what's being removed, and is especially necessary if you're doing the tricky "sideways" leveling mentioned later. Since the file is flat, a number of successive passes are needed in order to cover a radiused fret's width. The blue magic marker shows how much fret the file is con-

tacting on each stroke. **Caution:** Tape off the fretboard to avoid getting marker on the wood—especially on binding and light rosewood. You shouldn't use marker at all on a maple neck!

Get rid of any hump at the body joint First, check out the fretboard extension: many necks straighten easily with a truss rod adjustment, and have no hump or rise at the neck/body joint or out on the tongue (fretboard extension over the body); with these necks, you really won't have to do much filing—you'll only be kissing the tops. However, if you have a hump, or high frets on the tongue, level those frets first so that they don't cause the straightedge to rise up while you're checking for flatness on the main portion of the board.

To remove a hump or rise, use the short leveling file to work down any small, isolated problem frets. Check your progress constantly—a small amount of filing can make a lot of difference. **Note:** Many necks are not set at an exact 90° angle to the body, and a straightedge resting on the main fingerboard from the 1st fret to the neck/body joint may be on a different plane from the tongue, with the tongue naturally falling away because of this angle. This is normal, and should not be confused with a hump, which is actually due to a swollen glue joint or high, loose frets. Usually, the most annoying problem on the tongue is a rise, where the last few frets are higher than the ones preceding them. Sometimes this takes a fair amount of filing to rectify, and in extreme cases it will leave the last few frets quite low and hard to round.

When you feel that you've eliminated any high or low spots on the tongue, restring the guitar to pitch, readjust the truss rod accordingly, and check the relief and/or straightness, and fall away as described in the neck evaluation section. Once any tongue problems have been eliminated, the straightedge will give you a much more accurate reading on the main fingerboard (1st through 12th frets).

Level the main part of the board Use the longer (10") file—this file must be the flattest one you can find! Your goal is to create an accurate, smooth plane across the tops of the frets, so that no fret is higher or lower than any other. You want to expose new metal, or a fresh "flat," on each fret. With the longer file, begin where the tongue filing ends and file in long, even strokes from the body towards the headstock, applying light pressure. Always file lengthwise with the fingerboard, and because a mill file only cuts in one direction (we use the forward push stroke), don't file back and forth. In theory, the file stroke should continue right off the fingerboard at the peghead end (out into space) so that all the frets get filed the same amount. You don't always have to do this however, and if you do, be careful not to dip the file and hit the shafts of the tuning keys! I usually stop filing when the tool has passed about halfway over the 1st fret. Then I back up and make another pass, continuing in this fashion until I've covered the width of the fingerboard from end to end.

Many repairmen prefer to use a carborundum stone to level the fret tops—especially if the fretwork was well done and there isn't much metal to remove. The Martin repair shop, and the fretting department, recommend a Crystolon fine bench stone, #FJB8.

Compound or cylinder For compound radius boards, the file stroke should follow the 6 individual string lies created by the fretboard profile. Then smooth the flats together using the file in a sweeping arc across the fretboard, working lengthwise and across the board at the same time (do this from the treble side toward center, and then the bass side toward center). The only "straight" file stroke is between the D and G string area which is perfectly straight, or parallel to the center.

On cylindrical (uniform radius) boards, the file always remains parallel to the centerline. If you start filing on center, part of the file will be "filing on air" as you approach the fretboard edge. If this feels uncomfortable, you can begin on the edge, going lengthwise, but moving the file sideways, toward center, while you're moving lengthwise. This is a tricky stroke, but it works great!

Cylinder-shaped boards can easily be compounded during a refret (sometimes by accident), depending upon which of the two methods listed above are used on the fretboard.

Remove the leveling marks After leveling with a file, I use 320-grit Stikit Self-adhesive sandpaper to smooth the fret tops and remove any harsh file marks. Either wet-or-dry (black), or else the gold metal-cutting sandpaper works best for leveling frets. The free-cut (gray) lacquer-

sanding paper doesn't work as well on frets as it does on finishes or wood—it breaks down too quickly on metal. One or two passes length-wise is all you need for each sanding grit: don't overdo it. The wet-or-dry black and gold sandpaper cuts fret tops like butter. In fact, when the frets only need a light leveling, you can level the frets without files at all—using just sandpaper

For compound fretboards, my leveler is a steel block that measures 1-3/4" x 1" x 14". I use the 1" edge, which is ground perfectly flat and faced with self-stick paper. The weight of this chunk of steel makes for instant, controlled leveling, but a block of wood or plexiglas would work too if it's flat (the weight of the steel is nice, though).

On cylinder-shaped fretboards, I use radiused sand-

ing blocks (with the same self-stick sandpaper) instead of the heavy flat block. But they can only be used for sanding on cylinder-shaped boards! If you level the frets in the compound manner, the radius blocks would just "erase" your work since they can only create a uniform radius. Don't mix up the two methods of leveling.

Leveling without files (just sandpaper) If the frets are in good shape and don't need heavy leveling, you can skip using files entirely and level the frets using just the flat block—or the radius blocks—and sandpaper. Whether you're filing or sanding, use different pressures if you need to blend one section (for example, the 1st through 10th) into another (the 10th through 15th). If you know there is a high fret or a cluster of them, use your 3" or 6" file to work down that area. Follow with the long file to feather it in. A beginner should string to pitch often and readjust the rod to see how the feathering-in affects relief, leveling out and fall away. You can always get the neck back into the filing position if—when you begin—you put a mark on the truss rod nut as an index and return to it every time. The approach just described for leveling compound and cylinder fret tops is also used to level the wood of a fretboard during a refret, but with some tools other than files.

Texas luthier **Mike Stevens** has this advice: "When all the level-filing and length-wise sanding is done, I use a 5-3/4" x 2" wood block wrapped with 320- or 400-grit sandpaper strips. Cut the sandpaper into strips less than the 2" width of the block, and long enough to wrap lengthwise on the block to stretch it tight—it doesn't sag that way. Go sideways (in the direction of the fret) with the sanding block to remove the final marks. From this point on, all your work will be in the direction that you bend strings—just to add that extra edge."

Cleaning up the fret end bevels Now, feel the fret ends. Sometimes they'll stick out beyond the fingerboard edge because the wood has shrunk while the metal fret hasn't. You can smooth the ends until they're flush with the wood by using the 6" leveling file held flat, but lightly, against the edge of the fingerboard. Avoid filing the finish any more than you must. If the fretboard edge is straight the file will ride smoothly along the finish and cut only the fret ends. If the board's edge is irregular, use the 3" file; its shorter length lets it follow the contours. If you find it difficult to get the ends without damaging finish on the fretboard edge, use the small "touch-up" triangle file mentioned earlier.

If you start to remove finish, stop. Then lightly sand any dulled finish with 1000- to 2000-grit wet-or-dry sandpaper, using water as a lubricant, and return the original gloss by polishing with Mirror Glaze # 7 to finish the job.

Normally during a fret dressing, you won't have to do much beveling on the fret-ends, since they were beveled during the original factory fretjob. But while you're cleaning up the fret ends hold the file at the angle of the bevel and kiss them too—being careful not to over-bevel them (you'd remove playing area)! Watch carefully until you see the file just touch the sharp edge of the fretboard and stop! I use a white mat on the bench and a strong backlight to help me see the sliver of light disappear as the file contacts the fretboard.

Rounding the fret tops My workbench has a repair vice on the two front corners facing me. I work with the peghead to my left (treble side of fretboard away from me); I consider this working "right handed." For all the frets clear of the body, I do the fret tops and the treble side fret ends in the right hand position. When I reach the fretboard extension (tongue), I do half of the fret tops, from the center toward the treble side, and the treble fret ends. Then I turn the guitar 180° ("left handed") to do the bass side fret ends and the other half of the frets on the tongue. Since I have two repair vises I usually clamp the neck firm while I dress—at least I always did until I discovered the cantaloupe-shaped rock'n'roller neck rest.

I have a small pad to protect the part of the guitar body that contacts the bench, and I lay fresh clean paper on the bench top, under where I'm filing, to catch fret filings and sanding dust (I empty this constantly). I lay the tools out to the rear of the guitar being worked on, or I'll lay a protective pad over the guitar and use it as a tool caddy.

Using the triangle file Starting at the 1st fret, hold the triangle file between the thumb and second and third fingers with the index finger on top, using the other hand's index finger to guide the file on the fret. With a forward stroke, apply light pressure, rolling the file to center as you push it across the fret's length. Switch from one side of the fret to the other, rolling toward center. You are removing the square edge and rerounding the flat top that you made while leveling.

The triangle file I use most is a small slim one. My fretwork is accurate enough that I don't need a larger file to hog metal. But if I'm working on existing fretwork, where the frets are low and need considerable rounding, I'll use the larger triangle file or the cant saw file.

Using rounding files You don't have to roll to center with a rounding file—they shape the whole fret at once. You can use a rounding file instead of, or along with, the triangle or any other file. Since the diamond rounding file came along, I seldom use a toothed version anymore. If the fret tops aren't very flat—just a sliver of metal—the fine-grit diamond file is best (the coarse-grit diamond file removes metal pretty quickly). The rounded end of my diamond file is an advantage: by lifting up onto that the rounded tip you can focus on one particular area.

Low frets (under .030") are more difficult to round, and if you're using a rounding file don't let the file edges mark the board—they can even cut through masking tape.

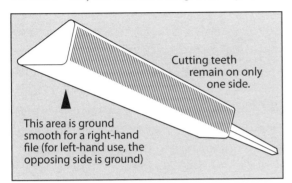

Cutting teeth remain on only one side.

This area is ground smooth for a right-hand file (for left-hand use, the opposing side is ground)

Using the cant saw file These files are Mike Stevens' weapon of choice. He grinds away all the teeth on one beveled side so that he can lay the file directly on the fretboard and file only one side of the fret; he grinds two files this way: a right and a left. Stevens uses the right hand file most, for the easily accessible frets clear of the body. He files all the frets from the body to the nut on his right hand side only, then he turns the guitar around to do the other side with the same file. "I'm ambidextrous," he says, "so I could switch to the left hand file and not flip the guitar. But I prefer to see the fret top with the file in my right hand as I'm looking down."

On the tongue frets over the body Mike dresses from the center out (just as we do) toward the treble side, and flips the guitar again to go toward the bass side. But he actually does the frets in four passes with the right and left hand files: first from center out with the right hand file, then the same frets with the left hand file, then turn the guitar around and repeat both steps. For this left hand filing, he uses his left hand (he's a showoff).

If this seems like a lot of trouble, it's not—I've watched Mike work, and we all have to flip the guitar around a lot during a dressing anyway. The cant saw file is what he learned on, and what he likes. You can't teach an old cowboy new tricks!

Filing the fretboard extension Here are three files that can round the all the frets on the fretboard extension (the "tongue") over the body in the right handed position, without having your knuckles hit the top. From

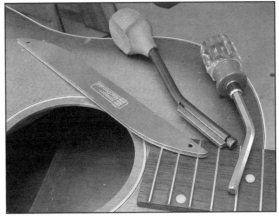

left to right in this photo they are: the offset diamond fret file, the three-in-one fret file and the dual-grit diamond fret file. They all have offset handles that keep your knuckles up and away from the top.

Filing the fret end bevels Novice fret workers often over-bevel the fret ends; the results of over-beveled ends are too narrow a string spacing at the nut, too little playing surface overall and strings that fall off the fingerboard edge. An exaggerated bevel isn't necessary as long as the fret ends are filed smooth and don't catch the hand. A smooth, nicely rounded end is what you're after.

Be aggressive on the first file strokes, because the fret ends are so rough after nipping that the file gets caught on them and will barely move. When it does move, it wants to run up onto the new frets, so keep your fingertips against the neck as a guide. To rough-in the bevel I like the coarse-cut of the StewMac 6" fingerboard leveler. As soon as the file is riding smoothly, and getting close to the wood (or finish), switch to a smoother cut. The 3" or 6" fret levelers have a perfect cut.

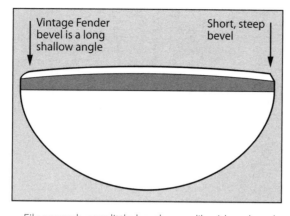

Vintage Fender bevel is a long shallow angle

Short, steep bevel

File as much, or as little, bevel as you like. A long bevel (most Fenders) has little drag on your playing hand, but it takes away from playing area. A short steep bevel gives you more fret to play on but will catch your hand. Always use a white backlit surface so you can see what you're doing. Keep filing until the file just contacts the edge of the fingerboard and finish. The sliver of white light (which you can see between the file and the neck) disappears at the same time that the fret end bevel is finished. To finish the final rounding, shaping and polishing of the fret tops, follow the directions given in the fret dressing section.

Shaping the fret ends You'll see the flat top getting smaller as you work. "Round and roll" until the tiniest flat is left on the center of the fret. If you marked the fret tops earlier with a magic marker, it's easy to see when you're ready to stop rounding. When you get to this stage, leave the small flat showing and do a final cleanup on the fret ends with the the fret end file, and/or the small triangle file, using a downward stroke that follows fret's beveled end, and then rounding over the ends. One light downstroke should polish the bevel, followed by a series of downward strokes, rolling to the center to round the end and remove any burrs.

You can round all the fret tops that are clear of the body working right handed, but you can only get the fret ends that are away from you because a downstroke is required. So on the bass side, you must turn the guitar end-for-end or walk around your bench to get the fret ends. Also, when you're rounding frets on the tongue just do one half, working from the middle towards the fret ends away from you—then turn the guitar around to shape the other side. It's hard to get the correct filing

angle otherwise, since the knuckles of your filing hand run into the top (unless the fretboard extension is elevated, as with some arch-top guitars).

Another great tool for fret ends (not pictured) is a tiny 1/8" nut-seating file intended for shaping Fender nut slots. This file removes the annoying burr sometimes created during fret-end leveling. It has a smooth side that can be held against against the fretboard without harming it (mine had some sharpness where the smooth side met the toothed side, so I smoothed that away on my belt sander.

Final polishing With the tape protecting the fingerboard on either side of the frets, wrap 400-grit wet-or-dry paper around the 3M squeegee fret polisher with the groove side down—or use the sand-stick, which is even better. With a series of back-and-forth strokes, polish the fret top and sides to remove any marks. Switch to the 600 paper and repeat the polishing process.

Now, wrap a thin layer of 0000 steel wool around your fret polisher or your thumbnail, and bring the fret to a high polish. Do this for each fret. When you're through with the polishing, remove the masking tape, peeling it carefully from the outside edges of the fingerboard towards center; this helps you avoid pulling finish away from the fingerboard's edge.

When all the frets have been rounded and polished, blow or vacuum off any metal dust and steel wool particles, and remove the tape protecting the body and pickups. Caution! On any guitar with an old, brittle finish, be *very* gentle in removing the tape to avoid pulling away the finish. As you peel the tape, rub gently with a fingernail on the tape's back just ahead of the bonding point to break the surface tension. String the guitar up to pitch, readjusting the truss rod if you need to give some relief once again. If you use a straightedge now, be very careful not to scar your fine, shiny frets. You'll now have the best-playing guitar you've ever touched!

Refretting

If you keep a guitar long enough and play it often, someday you'll be faced with getting it refretted. Most players get very nervous about letting just anyone pull and replace the frets on their favorite axe, and with good reason: except for accidental damage, a poor fret job is

Head of the Martin Fretting Dept., Ben Locicero (left) with Dennis Kromer from the nut-making deptartment.

the surest way to ruin a good instrument. Don't try learn to refret on your pre-war Martin or '50s Strat—stick to junkers until you develop your chops.

If you decide to hire somebody to do your refret (that's what I'd recommend), this chapter will educate you on what they'll be doing and help you judge whether the shop you've found has the capability you're looking for.

A refret is an opportunity to correct many of your guitar's action and playability troubles. Abnormal buzzes caused by worn, high, low or loose frets can be eliminated. High action resulting from too much relief, up-bow or just plain old neck warp can also be repaired by actually scraping the wood of the fingerboard itself once the frets have been removed, rather than filing the fret tops. Perhaps a guitar's frets have been over-beveled, causing not only cramped string spacing at the nut but also a tendency for the strings to slide off the fingerboard during play. New frets that are less beveled make better use of the fingerboard's full width.

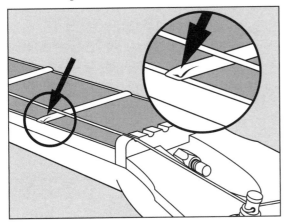

Hard string-bending, overall stiffness and sore fingers resulting from frets that are too low indicate the need for fret work. Many players will have a guitar refretted not because it plays poorly, but because they're after a different type of fret shape or size to accommodate a certain playing style (tall frets are easier to bend on, jumbo frets have more sustain, etc.). Frets can be installed in a variety of ways, but the three most common methods are hammering, pressing or gluing them in.

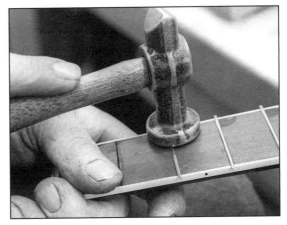

Traditionally, frets have been installed by carefully hammering them into the slots with a smooth-faced chasing hammer (this method is still being used today, even in many factories). Eventually, to increase production, some factories began using a large overhead press to squeeze frets in (and some of us smaller operations use inexpensive "arbor presses" to accomplish the same task). The most incredible factory method I know of was the "sideways" technique used by Fender until about 1979 (page 209).

Since the mid-70s, another common fretting method (especially for repairs and refretting) is the glue-in method pioneered by Don Teeter: The repairman removes the frets, slightly widens the fret slots and then gently presses and glues the frets into place with finger-pressure only—the glue holds them in. The glue-in method is well explained in Don Teeter's important repair book *The Acoustic Guitar,* but we'll give a nutshell version here. I also have my own variation, which I'll call "the new glue-in method" (page 203).

So there are several ways of going about refret work, and no one method is right. I never fault fret work if it's done neatly and the guitar plays well. I do, however, have flaming fits when I see fret jobs done by so-called "repairmen" who do nothing but yank 'em out and pound 'em in, paying no attention to the fingerboard's prefret preparation. The prep work separates the pros from the amateurs.

Fretboard preparation

No matter what fretting style you plan to use (sometimes I use them all on the same guitar), fretboard prep is basically the same. The basic rule is, do as little as possible to alter the fretboard in any way. The hardest part of a fret job is getting the neck adjusted into the right position so that once the new frets are installed, the neck remains straight (neither back-bowed nor up-bowed) with the ability to loosen into relief when needed.

I use a tilting-table neck jig for all fret and neck work, so I'm able to control the situation quite well. But I fretted guitars for years without it. This neck jig is discussed on page 124, and just understanding how and why it's used will help anyone do a better fret job, even without it. Refer to the neck evaluation and truss rod adjusting information given elsewhere in this book, so you can read a neck correctly to do the best job.

Here's how to go about any style of fret job:

1 Start by determining the customer's complaint with the frets as they are, listening to his or her opinion about what's wrong before forming your own opinion. Pay special attention to the player's style and string gauge. Choose a fretwire shape and crown size that the customer agrees to beforehand.

2 Evaluate and inspect the neck and fingerboard, looking for any problems such as warp, humps and dips in the surface. Before estimating a fret job's cost, you must adjust the truss rod (when possible) to its maximum looseness and tightness in order to get familiar with the neck. By checking the action of the truss rod, you determine if a neck has the ability to adjust perfectly straight, yet still offer relief when the rod is loosened. In my opinion, a "perfect" neck is one that can be adjusted perfectly straight under string tension, and yet pull gradually into relief when needed by loosening the truss rod. Finish this evaluation by leaving the truss rod adjusted so the neck is as straight as it will go with the strings on.

Instruments without adjustable truss rods (especially vintage Martins) are often fretted with too much relief on

purpose, knowing that the cumulative effect of the fret tangs will straighten, and stiffen the neck; or the opposite may occur (a neck is fretted with a back-bow planed into the surface because it's known that this particular neck will pull straight under string tension). This method, known as "compression fretting," is discussed separately. But in truth, that section and this section are inseparable—they go hand in hand. I only separate compression fretting to keep from confusing you during the traditional hammer-in method coming up. Compression fretting is also used to "help" an adjustable truss rod neck that isn't working well. The neck evaluation that follows is how I go about checking non-adjustable truss rod necks (Martin) for stiffness —but I use the same test on all guitars (adjustable or not).

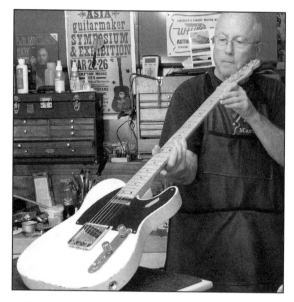

String to pitch, then rest the instrument's body on the workbench, and while supporting the neck by holding the peghead in one hand, pull down in the center of the neck to see how much "give" or flex there is. You may find that the neck is quite stiff, or it may be rubbery. While at pitch, set the instrument gently on its side (the playing position) and measure the relief at the 5th and/or 7th fret by sliding feeler gauges between the bottom of a long straightedge and the top of the fret (or use a notched straightedge and measure the gap to the fretboard itself). Record your measurements.

With the strings removed, repeat the above evaluations (neck flexing, and then measuring the relief in the playing position), and record those measurements too.

The difference between the neck at pitch and when it's relaxed tells you a lot about its stiffness, and it helps determine how much, if any, wood you'll remove from the fretboard (and where you'll remove it).

The full effects of truss rod adjustment often take several hours (sometimes even days) to appear. After adjusting, be sure to allow enough time for the neck to settle before any frets are removed and replaced. Also allow time for settling after the refret is done, and before the final setup prior to going out the door. There are times when a job must be done overnight for a pro on the road, and occasionally these may need a little redressing after the guitar has settled.

3 If you're fretting a bolt-on neck you should remove it from the body so that it's easier to adjust (vintage-style) and so that you can work on it without damaging the body. Tape off the top around the fretboard of glued-on neck guitars with draftsman's tape, etc. (see the Fret Dressing section for the correct procedure). Remove the strings. If the truss rod was adjusted to keep the neck straight with strings on, the neck will probably be back-bowed—leave it that way since the frets will pull out easier because the back-bow "opens" the pressure slightly on the fret slots.

4 Use a soldering iron to heat each fret before pulling it out with small flush-ground end nippers. This important step helps to avoid chips in the fingerboard by "boiling" oil and moisture out of the wood and onto the fret, lubricating it as it's being removed. The inevitable small chips along the fret slot edge are easily glued back or filled in, but heating the frets does help to avoid chipping. Sometimes large chunks will pull up, the result of poor wood or hasty work. Keep your soldering iron's tip tinned (just as if you were doing electrical work), and the heat will transfer instantly. For a quick heat transfer, it doesn't hurt to put a little solder right on the fret, but be careful on maple fingerboards!

Vintage Fender fretboards are chippier than others (check out the section on Fender sideways fretting, page 209). Pay close attention to the quality of the wood as you remove the frets. Is it hard or soft? Chippy or solid? Vintage ebony and Brazilian rosewood fretboards are much denser, harder and stiffer than modern boards. Frets remove more easily from vintage boards, and you

can fret them with a smaller tangled wire because they hold a fret better. You need this information later when you select a fret. If you're having fret work done, be sure your repairman is familiar with heating frets.

5 We discussed getting the neck into the leveling position in the fret dressing section, but here's some more advice: You're trying to remove the least amount of wood, and to do that you must get the neck as close as possible to where it was under string tension and then remove any high or low spots. On adjustable truss rod guitars you'll most likely have to loosen the truss rod to get the fretboard back to the same degree of straightness it had under string tension, since now the strings are removed and it will be back-bowed from the compression of the truss rod.

It's easiest to duplicate string tension on glued-on neck guitars because you can rest the peghead or the back of the neck on a padded block and the weight of the body will put some tension on the neck. Or you can press down on the body if the neck won't return to its string-tension-straightness with the truss rod loose. Sometimes I pull down on the neck's heel while the peghead is propped. Propping the peghead is also a good way to treat non-adjustable necks, such as those on vintage Martins.

Rich Starkey of the Martin repair department says, "We put a padded 6 lb. weight on each front shoulder of the guitar top, with the peghead end propped up. This puts the perfect average string-tension on the neck so that we can see exactly where to take wood off when necessary, while leveling the fretboard. It also puts the fretboard in the string tension position for leveling the frets. And of course some necks are stiffer than others; with the really weak ones you need the larger fret tangs to stiffen them up. Propping the peghead and using the weights is a perfect, and instant, way to check the neck-stiffening progress as we hammer in the frets."

Vintage Fender necks, and many of their clones, must be removed from the body for a truss rod adjustment to avoid gouging the pickguard, the pickups or the body. For this reason we generally remove them for fret work. But once a bolt-on neck's removed from the body, it's harder to duplicate the string tension than it is with a glued-neck guitar. If your bolt-on neck is adjustable at

the peghead end, you may choose to leave it bolted into the body—although it's very hard to fret, nip frets and file fret ends in the upper register without damaging something. I use a "surrogate body" for bolt-ons. I've made them in a number of shapes, all blocks of wood that the neck bolts on top of—not into—so I can work on the frets easily with all my tools. The surrogate body also bolts into my neck jig. My current-favorite surrogate body has upper and lower "bouts" so that I can easily hold the guitar in playing position while sitting to check the frets and the action.

Even without a neck jig, a surrogate body is handy (and much easier to make than a real guitar body). With your neck bolted into a surrogate body, you can prop the peghead and weight down the body in the same way that Martin does.

In general with a bolt-on neck you loosen the truss rod completely, and then tighten it a little bit so that you have some tension on it as it's being fretted (you'll still be able to loosen it later for relief). But this isn't always true. Where to leave the truss rod adjustment on any neck is

tricky, but with a bolt-on it's trickiest. That's why I like the neck jig (page 214).

Michael Stevens, who's fretted hundreds of Strats and Teles, says: "The ideal Fender neck would have a little tension on the rod, and still have some 'negative' (relief) that the fret compression doesn't quite remove when they're installed. Then I can take that last bit of negative out with the truss rod, to make the neck perfectly straight. (And loosening the rod gives back the relief).

"But too often the neck is straight with the rod completely loose—you can't tighten it, or you'll end up with back-bow for sure. In that case, if there's not a finish you can sand a little negative into the board. Sometimes you've got a finish, like on a maple neck, and you can't sand. Then you've got to fret with the rod loose (the nut might even be rattling), and hope you don't get a back-bow. Or you can work down the fret tang so it doesn't compress the neck so much. So, if you have some relief on a Fender neck don't sand it flat—use it! And if you're removing wood on a vintage rosewood fretboard, to give back the dark polished look of age and finger oil—use Watco's Black Walnut Danish Oil."

6 Remove fingerboard imperfections with files, scrapers and sanding blocks.

At this point, just as with leveling the frets, you must decide if you're shaping a cylinder or a cone (compound radius).

Prepping a cylinder For working on uniform-radius fretboards, my favorite sanding tools are fretboard radius-sanding blocks. Available in seven different radii, in several lengths, and made from either wood or aluminum (inexpensive, and expensive, respectively), these are available from StewMac. Also an adjustable radius block of molded plystyrene, the Handee Fredder, is available through Luthier's Mercantile. Choose your weapon! I use Stikit Gold Self-adhesive sandpaper to hug the block's contour. The most common cylinder-shaped fretboards you'll work on are Fenders and Gibsons that have not been refretted since the factory.

Prepping a compound radius Except for vintage guitars (especially maple necks, where I don't want to touch the finish), my fret jobs are at least somewhat compound. This is because I read and level in the lie of each string. When I'm prepping a board with a compound radius, instead of radius-sanding blocks I use either of two long, narrow, flat surfaces that contact most, or all, of the fretboard at once. One is a 1" x 1 3⁄4" x 15" steel block that I like because of its weight, and the other is a 1" x 3" x 24" maple block, that I like for its length. I use self-stick sandpaper on the 1" edge. With either one I work the board lengthwise, in the six individual string lies, connecting the six "flats" together with a tapered sweep of the sanding block.

You can't perfectly sand the six flats together with a radius block because the radius block doesn't recognize the tapered profile of the fingerboard—it just shapes a cylinder from end to end. By trying to smooth a cone with radius blocks, you'll only erase the flats you worked so hard to get. You can use a progression of radius blocks to remove the flats, but you'll still have to finish up by hand with a flat block.

Wanting to know how much the high spot, or difference between a cylinder and a cone would actually measure on a given set of neck dimensions, I again turned to **Don MacRostie**. Don calculated the difference between a cone-shaped and a cylinder-shaped fretboard (with all other specifications being equal), and found that on a cylindrical fingerboard the high spot in the lie of the outside E-strings would measure a maximum of one and a half thousandths (.0015") on a 7 1/4" radius, and only a half thousandth (.0005") on a flatter 16" board. This isn't a lot, but it is the amount that a radius block would remove as it re-shapes a cone into a cylinder. This small high spot could mean the difference between buzzing or not buzzing, if you have extremely low action. Taking it into account is important if you hope to gain every bit of accuracy possible during a refret.

Most factory-made guitars (Martin, Gibson, Fender, and many others) have fretboards with a cylinder-shaped radius. When their action is set too far below factory specs, which many customers seem to want, there's more likelihood of fret buzz than if the fretboards had a compound radius. The lowest action without buzzing, with or without bending strings, can be had on cylinder-shaped fretboards with a very flat radius (16" or flatter, like Martin), on compound radiused fretboards and especially on compound fretboards beginning with a fairly flat radius.

So, if you're creating a compound radius during a refret, you might as well be aware of it and work with that in mind. Choose between fretting either a cylinder or a cone, and approach the job in that fashion. You do, of course, have the option of removing the .0015" high spot on a cylinder board by filing down the fret tops—this is often the best way to avoid removing material (be it wood, inlay or lacquer) on a vintage fret-job. Remember: that .0015" high spot is theoretical—actually, you've got to be damn good to flatten a fretboard within .002" or .003"; add .0015" to that and your high spot really measures .005", which is much more typical of what we really run into with strings buzzing on a cylinder fretboard!

As you prep, check the work's progress often by comparing the board to very accurate straightedges. Inlays, especially custom pearl-block types in badly affected areas, must often be removed to avoid being sanded too thin. They're replaced later just before final leveling.

When the straightedge sits flat on the board—either in the lie of the strings (compound radius), or parallel to the lengthwise centerline of the fretboard (cylinder radius)—I usually add from .002" to .004" of "fallaway" into the tongue (the last few frets over the body). Fallaway is discussed as a part of setup in chapter 3. You're done when the board is flat from end-to-end, or has a little fallaway (but never a rising tongue)!

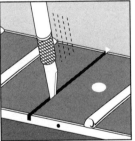

7 When the board is properly leveled, clean any residue from the fret slots. One good slot-cleaning tool is the back edge of a #11 X-Acto knife blade held vertically and used to scrape the crud out of the slot. Some fret slots will have dried glue in them that scrapes out easily. Vintage Fenders and Martins didn't use glue, while Gibson and some others fretted with hide glue.

My favorite slot cleaners are the fret slot cleaning tool and the refret saw. The slot cleaner has a hook-shaped blade, .019" thick, with a ground edge that effectively

"claws'" wood chips, dust, grime and old glue from the slots. The refret saw has two short blades (each cutting the opposite direc-

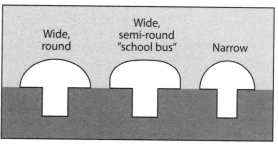

tion), and can excavate hard-to-remove crud even on bound fingerboards. The short blade length keeps the saw from cutting where I don't want it to (inadvertently scarring or widening the slot. They're available in three different thicknesses: .015", .020" and .025".

8 Once the slots are cleaned and you're sure of the proper depth, lightly re-sand the fretboard surface to remove any burrs on the edges of the fret slots. Next run a diamond- or V-shaped file across the fret slot to slightly chamfer (bevel) the edges. This helps the new fret go in, eliminates chipping and facilitates removing the fret in years to come.

Choosing your fretwire

Fretwire shapes and sizes A customer with an old Les Paul "fretless wonder" asks, "Am I really missing anything by using a guitar with short frets?" Another wonders, "Will tall frets cause poor intonation?" The answers depend on the feel that you like and the sound that you want. In the uncomplicated old days, most acoustic and electric guitars came with little variety in fret styles; but today dozens of different fretwires—thin or fat, short or tall, soft or hard—are used for guitars. Generally, a thin wire is used for most acoustics, while a wide, or "jumbo," wire is common for electrics. I like "medium-tall" fretwire that measures from .045" to .050" in height, and from .084" to .100" in width. These wires offer a better sustained note, are easier to bend on, and level and dress easier than low fretwires.

Looking at a cross-section, the most common, and popular, fret shape is either round or oval. You may have seen a rectangular and extremely low fretwire on a Gibson Les Paul or early SG. These guitars were nick-

named "fretless wonders," which they nearly were. This fret offered very low action with little drag on the fingers when moving up and down the board; sustain, tone and easy bends were traded off for that action, however. Round or oval-shaped wires (which have different heights, widths and advantages) are far and away the most common, and therefore the most deserving of our attention here, although I do use a pyramid-shaped wire when a customer asks for it.

Tall fretwire ranges from .050" to .065" in height above the fingerboard (about the thickness of a dime). Not many tall wires are available. Here are some advantages: Tall frets are easier for string bends, since the fingertip has less contact with the fingerboard. They also offer more sustain, due to the greater mass and because the string isn't damped by as much finger/fingerboard contact, which draws away some tone, volume and sustain. While tall frets don't offer the same advantages as the radical scalloped fingerboards described later in this chapter, they lean in that direction more than a short fret does, so you'll get better hammer-ons and pull-offs. They also outlast low frets and withstand more fret dressings between refrets. Some disadvantages: Poor intonation could result from pressing too hard, but this can be corrected with a gentler touch. Until the left hand relaxes, the frets may feel like railroad ties when you slide up or down the fingerboard, and the neck may "feel" slightly thicker, but this is minor.

Regardless of width, medium-height fretwire is the standard that has commonly been used for the last 40 years. Some very wide, medium-height wires are called "jumbo," but this refers to the width, not the height. This wire ranges from .036" to .050" in height. Pros: With jumbo frets, the player can more easily achieve accurate intonation (again, this depends on touch), since the fingerboard wood stops the fingertip, not allowing the string to be pressed too deeply. Barre chords and slides are easier, and the guitar's tone is softer, since the finger has more contact with the fingerboard. Cons: To enjoy medium-height fretwire at its best, the fret work must be done accurately, to ensure that you don't lose precious height during dressing. Medium-height wire wears out sooner than tall wire, and it allows fewer dressings between refrets. You'll still get years of playing out of medium wire if the fret work is good to begin with. Hammer-ons, pull-offs, bends and sustain are not as easy as on tall wire, but most of us have been playing on medium wire for years and enjoying it; again, it's my favorite.

Except for the squared, low fretwire on the "fretless wonders," you probably won't run into low wire (.020" to 034") on a modern instrument. Expect to find low wire on used guitars that have seen much use and are simply worn out from years of playing and fret dressings. They're ready for a refret. While low wire is good for easy slides and fast action, it's not conducive to hammer-ons, pull-offs, string bending and good tone and sustain. I don't enjoy playing on low wire.

A fret's width, regardless of height, affects playability and tone. Here you'll have to decide what you like. The increased mass of a wide fret offers a more "heavy metal" sustain than a narrow fret of comparable height, and wide frets wear longer than narrow ones. However, wide frets must be dressed more accurately than narrow ones to avoid poor intonation and buzzing caused by the string making contact off center, causing poor intonation or flopping on a too-wide flat. Note: I dress a wide fret in two ways: rounded accurately to center, or semi-round like the top of a school bus. The school bus shape is often preferred by my rock customers, and it wears longer. Narrow frets offer a unique sustain, due to a cleaner contact point between string and fret crown, as well as the most accurate intonation. They don't have any disadvantages that I can think of, except that thinner frets have a crisper sound—clean, like breaking a glass—due to the accurate contact made between string and fret. This clean sound is sometimes misinterpreted as buzzing, and may take getting used to. The choice of fret width can only be decided by you.

Fretwire hardness A fret's hardness is determined by its composition. Usually the choice is 18% nickel/silver (hard), or 12% (soft). Stick with the hardest wire you're offered—it wears longer. Some classical builders prefer the softer 12% wire, though, feeling that it is gentler on nylon or gut strings. The most commonly used fretwire for steel-string acoustic or electric guitars is 18% nickel/silver. Harder wire produces more sustain, but a greater advantage is its resistance to string wear. In most cases, the harder wire is the preferred choice (although, from a repairperson's standpoint, soft wire is easier to hammer in, and having less spring tends to stay down better than harder wire).

Relative fretwire hardness is a source of controversy in the guitar repair business. I've heard repairmen complain about customer remarks such as: "My guitar was refretted just a year ago, and the frets are grooved already. My friend's '61 Strat has original frets that still play okay, with few worn spots. Are you guys selling us soft frets so you can get more work out of us?" Believe me, luthiers don't want their customers back in a year complaining of worn frets or expecting free remedies—fret jobs just ain't that much fun!

I checked with the fret manufacturers and found that they haven't changed their alloy specifications (as some of us have wondered). In the U.S., a 12% wire is considered soft wire, while the industry standard, 18% wire, is comparatively hard. The percentage—12% or 18%—refers to the amount of nickel in a given wire, not silver (fretwire looks silver, but it's made of copper, nickel and zinc—with no silver at all). The alloy mix for an 18% wire is 65% copper, 18% nickel and 17% zinc.

Fretwire is still made as it always was. It begins as a semi-hard round wire that is heated to anneal (soften) it, and it's then allowed to cool. It becomes "work-hardened" from being drawn through roller dies that compress the wire into a shaped fret. Once drawn, there's no practical way, at the manufacturing end, to increase fret hardness (in experiments, manufacturers found that rolling a too-hard wire, or wire with a nickel content over 18%, caused breakdowns in the machinery).

I sent old fret samples (saved over the years from vintage guitars), along with new ones, to a lab for the Vickers hardness test for precious metals. The results ranged from 184 to 205 points on the Vickers scale, with the

d.i.y.

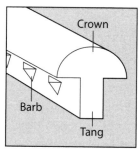

Crown

Barb

Tang

modern wire being hardest in each case. The tests showed that large wire was harder than small wire. In the process, I began thinking about how hard copper gets when bent and unbent (those who have run copper water lines know what I mean) and ended up making what, for me, is a significant discovery. By running the fretwire through a Fret-Bender, over-radiusing it, and then straightening it and rolling it again (repeating the process several times), the fret hardness gained from 14 to 20 points on the Vickers scale, which is appreciable. I was able to work-harden a smaller, Strat-size wire until the hardness matched that of the jumbo wires used in the lab test!

If modern fretwire seems to wear faster than "vintage" wire, it's because modern players are more aggressive than those in the '50s and '60s, utilizing considerable single-note playing, string bending and a heavier attack, all of which cause more fret wear. Today's harder string windings tend to wear frets faster, too. Also, many of the vintage guitars with original frets "still in good shape" were played with flat-wound strings—which aren't as hard on frets, perhaps accounting for the perception that frets aren't what they used to be. The real key to fret wear is playing time. It doesn't matter how old a guitar is; what's important is how much it gets played. Leave it in the case, and the frets will never wear out! Today's guitarists, though, play and practice more than ever.

This basic information should help you understand the different types of frets. If you're shopping for a new guitar, ask the salesman to explain what size, and type, of fretwire has been used. Or if you're looking for a refret, see to it that your repairman uses a hard wire; it lasts longer (a soft wire is fine for classical guitars, though, since the nylon strings won't wear grooves as easily).

Here are some of my favorite fretwires:

Standard wide frets (vintage "wide oval" Gibson): Dunlop #6130 and Stewart-MacDonald #149 (.103" wide x .046" tall)

Extra-tall and wide (modern heavy-metal wire): Dunlop #6100 and StewMac #150 (.110" wide x .053" tall)

Thin wires for electric or acoustic guitars (vintage Fender, Gibson and Martin): Stewart-MacDonald #0148 and Dunlop #6230 (.084" wide x .039" tall)

Medium width and medium height (Fender 'Stevie-Ray' size): StewMac #0141 (.095" wide x .045" tall)

Big Medium width and height (new size): StewMac #0152 (.092" wide x .048" tall)

Vintage Martin refret wire: CF Martin & Co: All sizes, including bar-style.

If you're serious about fretwork, you should buy samples of any wire that arouses your curiosity, and check it out for yourself.

At this point, the fretboard prep is finished. Choose your fretwire. Measure the cleaned-out fret slot with a feeler gauge. Fret slots vary from .018" (1930s) to .025" (modern imported guitars), but most slots are about .020". I say "about" because the use of feeler gauges to determine fret slot size (or for any measurement) is a subjective art that requires training, experience, and the ability to know when enough is enough. Since the sense of touch determines your opinion—what feels to me like a .020" tolerance fit, you might squeeze (or force) a .023" feeler gauge into! So let's assume that we could be "plus or minus a thousandth," as they say. The wire you choose is one of the factors that determine the outcome of the fretwork. Experience is the only real teacher, but here are some pointers.

Two big questions Only the manufacturer of a particular guitar knows the answers for sure (and I suspect that some of them don't know). First, if the fret tang is the same size as the slot (enough to hold the neck in proper compression so that it can't warp or up-bow because of the weakness caused by 21 fret slots, how large must the barbs be to hold the fret down without back-bowing the neck? Second, did the builder calculate the amount of stiffness (or possible backbow) the fret tang barbs give to the neck?

Some answers You must learn to match available wires to the existing fret slot in order to get a fit that will hold the fret down without causing over-, or under-compression problems that were never a problem at the factory. Factories fret hundreds of "test necks" in order to determine the perfect ratio of fret tang size versus fret slot size for production. During these tests they determine how much relief to leave in the fretboard so that it will be straight—not back-bowed—when the frets are in. On a refret, you only have one attempt. (OK, maybe two or three. Fretting mistakes are repairable, but you want to avoid them).

These hassles, by the way, are one of the big reasons that Don Teeter developed the glue-in method. With Don's method, fret compression (fitting tightly in the slot) does not determine whether or not a fret will stay down, and back-bow or up-bow because of fret compression is eliminated too.

One problem with fretting a neck today that was made in the 50s (or 30s, or 40s), is that modern fretwire is different than what was used back then—most modern fretwires have a bigger tang than those vintage wires did. If you pull the frets on a '56 Tele, and simply replace them with larger ones, you'll often back-bow the neck (from the over-compression of the frets being forced into the slots). And I've pulled frets on 1930s Gibsons that had .016" tangs, very small barbs and an equally tiny fret slot. I had to enlarge the slots in order to fret it with modern wire. Another solution for is to resize the fret tangs with a fret-fitting pliers that crimps or mashes the tang's width.

However, if the fret tang (not the barbs) is exactly the same size as the slot or less, and the barbs are about the same as the original fretwire, you won't back-bow the neck; the frets will go right in because the original frets compressed the wood of the fret slot downward and to the side as they were driven in. But now, since this is a refret (the second time around), the new fret may not stay down unless you use a wire with a slightly heavier tang, larger barbs or both, because the wood of the fret slot walls has lost its integrity.

The wood of the fingerboard (normally ebony, rosewood or maple) also determines what size fret you use for a refret. On a wood-hardness scale, ebony's the hardest, followed by rosewood, and maple can be almost mushy in comparison. So a larger fret may be needed to hold in a maple board (Fender) than would be needed for ebony or rosewood. Refer to the notes you took while removing the frets.

While your notebook's out, review your thoughts about neck flexibility versus stiffness and check your relief measurements. If the neck was really up-bowed (too much relief) and rubbery, you need a fretwire with a larger tang to stiffen the neck (at least to be used at certain frets). C.F. Martin offers replacement fretwire in eight different tang sizes, while the crown remains the same at about .078" wide and .036" tall. These wires are invaluable for choosing a fret several thousandths thicker in the tang, so that it will hold into a worn slot and keep an up-bowed neck (too much relief) straight. Martin wire, being somewhat narrow and not too tall, won't please every player, however; nor is it suitable for many electric guitars. If you're using Martin wire, use the slot-to-tang ratio listed below (or use the same ratio for any fret/fingerboard slot combination). Read about Martin compression fretting for straightening a neck on page 196.

Fret slot/tang ratio by type of fretboard

Ebony Use a tang .001" larger than the slot.

Rosewood Use a tang .002" larger than the slot.

Maple Use the same tang that you'd use for rosewood (perhaps a little larger), but on a vintage Fender, check into the other problems mentioned under Fender sideways fretting on page 209.

All the methods used in this chapter apply to new fretwork too—with the exception of fretwire selection. If you're fretting an instrument you made, run some tests (hopefully you'll have scraps of the actual fretboard, or at least wood from the same, or a similar, batch). Decisions must be made: are you fretting the board before you install it, and if so, how much back-bow can you deal with? Or will you fret it after the board is installed? (I prefer the latter method). On some new work you may want a fret tang that is slightly narrower than the slot to avoid back-bowing the new wood due to fret compression.

Other considerations

✔ Frets that are pressed into the slots seem to compress or back-bow a neck less than the hammer method (this is my feeling, but I've never proven it). So the method of fretting helps you decide which size fret to use.

✔ Does the neck have an adjustable truss rod? A rod can straighten a neck with too much relief. Or would you rather straighten it with the fret tang, and then loosen the rod to get relief? In the case of Martin guitars made before 1985 (when they started using an adjustable truss

d.i.y. rod) the best way to straighten them is with over-sized frets.

✔ Shape and size are important when you're doing vintage work. Many players want non-vintage wire installed on a vintage axe—I don't have any big complaint with that because the work is reversible if it's been well done. Fretwire shape, size and hardness were discussed earlier (but I always go for the 18% nickel/silver content).

✔ Martin offers a fretwire with 8 different-sized tangs (the crown stays the same) for neck-straightening. For vintage Martins with too much relief, this is the best wire to use.

✔ If the neck is stable and can be adjusted nice and straight (even into a back-bow), and can definitely be loosened into relief, choose a wire with a tang matching the fretslot, and just enough barb to hold it — perhaps using glue as a helper.

The hammer-in method

The fretboard prep is done, you've selected a fretwire and you're ready to start. I clean and degrease the fingerboard with naphtha just before fretting, so that it dries while I'm preparing the fret wire. As long as the naphtha's out, use it to clean any oil from the fret wire (clean the wire several times—until any trace of grease is gone). Even if you don't use glue in the fret slots, why introduce grease to the wood? I'll keep referring to compression fretting—you must become familiar with it since you'll use as much, or as little compression as the neck calls for with any fret job. Some compression is a byproduct of all fret jobs except for Don Teeter's glue-in method.

Cut the frets to length, leaving about 3/16" overhang on each side. Then pre-shape them so that they have a radius more curved than the fretboard itself. I use my FretBender, but a pair of fret pliers will do just as well (pliers with a notch in one jaw to hold the tang, and a groove the other jaw to hold the crown without marring

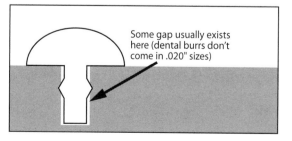

Some gap usually exists here (dental burrs don't come in .020" sizes)

it). Store the frets in the same order in which they'll be installed. In the photo above, notice that I've notched each end of the pre-bent fret to fit within the binding. I do this with a fret tang nipper.

For neck support as you hammer, you want something solid to act as an anvil. Good fret anvils can be made from thick cloth or leather bags filled with buckshot or sand, or curved padded cauls resting on a section of railroad tie, I-beam or steel.

Bob Taylor of Taylor Guitars says: "I've tried every kind of neck support there is, including opening up a bag of shot and re-making my own bags, big and small. The best neck support is a 25 lb. bag of buckshot left in its original canvas bag, period. Rest that on your neck support. It's what we use in the factory."

Hammer-in a short test piece (3/8" long) to get a feel for the fit—don't use a whole fret. Start the over-curved fret on both ends. Don't drive the ends completely home, but almost. Now, since the fret is arched more than the fretboard, it is also longer than the board is wide. Since the fret ends are already held quite fast, when you hammer the remainder of the fret home, it straightens lengthwise, pushing its barbs sideways through the wood. This helps the fret hold in (and down on the ends) much better than just hammering in a fret that isn't over-arched, or one that hasn't been tacked down at both ends. Some fretters hammer the fret in evenly from the center out, some hammer from the outside in. The Martin factory hammers from one edge across to the other.

Since there's plenty of excess fret length overhanging each edge, if a fret end isn't staying down, give the overhang a tap to snug it down. You may even want to float a little superglue underneath the end for insurance.

My two favorite fret hammers are a combination brass/plastic version, and a shorter, heavier, brass

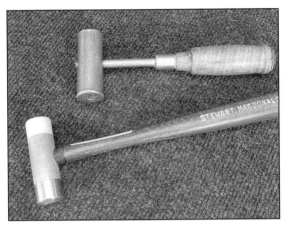

hammer that I made from brass bar-stock. You can also use a 16-ounce carpenter's hammer if you're very careful!

The neck area where you're installing a fret should be supported to give resistance to the hammer blow. Use good supports that conform to the neck's shape, such as the buckshot-filled bag mentioned above. Don't just support the headstock and then pound away at the un-supported fingerboard!

Pounding too aggressively or too hard in one spot will cause dents or flat spots in the fret as you're going across the board. If this happens, you must remove the fret and either straighten or replace it. Likewise, not pounding hard enough leaves frets that aren't seated against the board. As a general rule, frets that pound in too easily and won't stay down may need to be glued or replaced with frets with over-size tangs. On the other hand, if you're pounding away and the fret isn't going in, don't keep at it. Either the slot isn't deep enough or the fret tang is too wide. Back up and review the situation.

On an acoustic guitar, the hardest area to fret is the tongue over the body, since there isn't a solid surface to hammer against. Set the back of the guitar (in the area under the neck block) on your buckshot bag. Here it's essential to hold a metal block or a sandbag inside the guitar under the fingerboard area. It can be very tough to get the frets well seated over an acoustic body. One solution is to use the "glue-in" method only in this area (where fret compression isn't too important). This is yet another reason many of us use the glue-in method!

Bob Taylor's "fret buck" (above right) is the best tool for supporting the shoulder area under the fretboard tongue. It slides in through the soundhole, rests on the shoulders, and supports the tongue from underneath—

enough so that you can hammer frets in normally! You should still support the guitar body on the buckshot bag.

Glue? The decision to use glue to hold in the frets is up to you; even large manufacturers do it different ways. Some repairmen consider gluing frets to be a bad joke to play on a future repairer. I don't feel that way, though, since frets should always be heated prior to removal to break any glue bond. You don't need glue on a perfectly good piece of wood that wants to hold a fret, although the glue's lubrication sometimes helps a fret go in easier. The most common glues for holding hammered-in frets are Titebond, hide glue and shellac. While not really a glue, fresh shellac does a great job of bonding metal to wood, especially frets. It was commonly used by guitar builders long before any of us were born.

The last time I visited the Gibson company in Kalama-zoo, they were wiping hide glue into all the slots at once, quickly wiping off the excess with a damp rag, and then hammering-in the frets. At the Martin company, they wipe the fret slot with water to lubricate the fret as it goes in and to swell the slot around the fret. I generally use either hide glue or Titebond, but I've used shellac too. You can't use 'em all at once, so experiment! If you use glue, let it dry overnight before clipping or filing the fret ends.

Clip the ends until they are almost flush with the fin-gerboard edge (leave a little for final filing of the wood, or you may get nipper marks on the bare wood or finish). Frets that are hammered in without glue have a tenden-cy to pop up on the ends, so if that happens use a larger fret or check out the section on loose fret ends earlier in this chapter. With or without glue, use a downward pressure as you clip, being sure that you have sharp, flush-ground end nippers. To avoid fret ends popping up, use a downward motion to clip the fret's crown first, and then the tang.

I like to pre-cut the fret tang to length (but not the crown overhang) with the Waverly Fret Tang Nipper. Then I have less filing to do on the fretboard edges, and the clipping motion doesn't twist the fret as much.

The handles of the ready-made fret nippers are too short for clipping fret ends on the fretboard extension over the body, so you may want to grind a longer-handled 9" pair just for that area (save them just for that job, and they'll last longer). It's hard to get the proper grasp on the short handled ones if your knuckles are banging into the top.

Once the frets are in and the ends have been clipped, smooth the rough fret ends and file the fret-end bevels.

Compression fretting

Compression fretting goes hand-in-hand with any hammer-in or press-in fret job. **It's not a method of fretting, it's knowledge you use while fretting.** I tend to think of Martin when compression fretting comes to mind (it was the Martin repairmen who developed this important technique), but any guitar will benefit from this. Compression fretting refers to situations in which the fret tang width matches, or is greater than, the size of the fret slot. Here's some background on how compression fretting works on vintage Martins without adjustable truss rods, and it will help you with any other type of neck.

The amount of fret compression you need, and in what area of the fretboard you need it, depends on the neck construction (which is related to the guitar's vintage). In general, Martins from the mid-1930s through the '50s and into the '60s have very stiff necks.

There was a period during the war years in the early '40s, when Martin and Gibson suffered from wood and metal shortages. Martin used their old-style ebony neck support during that time, and Gibsons of that period also have no adjustable truss rod. So necks during that era are not as stiff as before and after. According to luthier T.J. Thompson: "I know they made necks with the old-style ebony filler during that time because I've had them apart from as early as 1939—and during that time Martin did different things on different models."

Excepting the war years, Martin's neck-reinforcing T-bar was very deep—these necks from the '30s–'50s are the stiffest. With them, only slight compression fretting, or planing a drop-off to the nut, is required (if it's required at all). In the unusual cases where compression is needed on these instruments, it's usually in the area of the first five or six frets (near the peghead where the string pull is greatest).

During the '60s, the T-bar was shallower. Those necks aren't as stiff, but they're still pretty good. Refretting them is not a problem, but the need for compression, and planing a little drop-off toward the nut, is more common.

In the late '60s, Martin began using the "square hollow tube" neck rod. The square tube was used until it was replaced by the current adjustable rod in 1986 (this new truss rod, by the way, is quite rigid). But the necks with the hollow tube can be far too flexible. Give them a flex test and you'll see a sag in the fretboard and a hump at the body—no rigidity. Whether you're a player or repairer, you want to know about the square tube neck because 80% of all Martins ever made were built during that era. Luckily, straightening these necks is commonplace and nothing to worry about.

It must have been early in the '70s that Martin developed the many different sizes of fret tang to stiffen and straighten these necks. These square tube necks require the most compression in the area from the 5th to 10th frets, and commonly need as much as .015" drop-off (back-bow) planed into the fretboard from the 5th fret to the nut, so that under string tension the neck is almost straight. Both compression and drop-off may be required. Most square tube necks that have been properly straightened will remain quite straight when they're first strung to pitch; then within six months or a year they'll pull into a little relief. So if you have a few buzzes with a newly-fretted guitar, give the neck a chance to settle in.

Dana Bourgeois, Joe Konkoly and T.J. Thompson

I learned compression fretting from Irving Sloane's excellent book *Guitar Repair,* where the method is explained quite well (the book is another must-have for the serious repair person). But I never fully appreciated this fretting technique, nor neck stiffness in general, until I came to know **Dana Bourgeois**. After hours of phone conversations, when I thought we'd exhausted the subject, Dana pointed me to **T.J. Thompson**—describing him as the "repairman's repairman," and master of the bar-style fret job.

T.J. learned the basics of compression fretting as Dana's apprentice, and then refined the technique during his years as head of the repair shop at Elderly Instruments in East Lansing, Michigan. When T.J. left Elderly to build Schoenberg guitars, he'd already trained a successor in **Joe Konkoly**. These three men, Dana, T.J. and Joe, are traditionalists when it comes to fretting, and they share their opinions with us here. Here's how Dana Bourgeois explains fret compression and judges the stiffness of a neck:

"When you strike a string it drives what's on either end of the neck—the peghead as well as the body. When the peghead is held rigid at the end of a stiff neck, it reflects the energy back up the neck to drive the top. A neck which is too flexible allows the peghead to flap around, which actually absorbs vibration. So flexibility in a neck is not good for tone, volume or sustain. When compared

with compression fretting, the Dremel fret job is more likely to cause a loss of neck stiffness and result in a fretboard that may be flat (straight) and well fretted when strung to pitch, but has no rigidity. Many fretboards are flat under string tension thanks to a truss rod adjustment and careful leveling of the board, but will have too much give if you apply the 'flex' test. Try this:

"Put the end of the guitar on the bench surface, and sight down the neck. Hold up on the headstock and pull down in the middle of the neck. Look, and feel, for the give. A neck should have very little give, so if you sight a neck and it flexes easily, you know you're losing some tone, even though the fretboard is straight under tension. As a tonal consideration, the stiffness of a compression fret job is distinct from flatness! When fretting, I flex the neck after every fret to check for stiffness. I can watch those weak necks stiffen right up. But you can only get as much stiffness as a given neck, or piece of wood, will allow.

"I've seen glue-in fret jobs where flatness (straightness) was obviously the only consideration. Stiffness is equally important! Flatness can be achieved by compression fretting an up-bowed neck and improving the tone, or by tightening a truss rod, which does little for the tone. Of course, both methods often require at least spot leveling of the fretboard itself. If stiffness can be retained when using the Dremel method, I have no problem with it. This is possible with careful matching of the slot to the fret, and properly mixed, good-quality glue."

Two ways to approach compression fretting

1 To maintain stiffness and straightness in a good neck;
2 To add, or return stiffness and straightness to a weak or fatigued neck. Use these compression principles with any fret job, refret jobs in particular.

To maintain straightness and stiffness, measure the wire you took out, and consider following Martin's recommendation for the correct replacement size: use the next size bigger tang for ebony, and two sizes bigger for rosewood so that the fret will hold down (the fret slot has widened some from the force of the original fret being driven in and pulled out). All you're doing is keeping a stiff neck stiff. You need a selection of Martin oversize wire for this job. Martin fret slots measure between .020" and .022" so when replacing a fret, the "next size up" means a half-a-thousandth since Martin wire comes in half-thousandth sizes (.0185", .0195", .0205", .0215", .0225", .0235", .0245", .0275"). The ability to work in such subtle increments gives you a lot of control. The heavier .0275" is only used in soft fretboards or at select locations on the fretboard, to add a lot of stiffness quickly. You wouldn't fret an entire Martin neck with the big wire too often.

When removing up-bow, as Dana pointed out, there's a limit to how much stiffness you can add to a given neck by increasing the fret size. Sometimes you can remove from .010" to .020" of relief from a fretboard by increasing the size of the fret tang alone, but beyond that you must remove wood from the fretboard surface to get it straight, and then rely on the compression of the tang to keep the neck stiff. So with Martin necks, it's common to scrape, sand or plane a certain amount of back-bow into the fretboard , so that when fretted and strung to pitch, the neck is straight, or has a slight relief (but not an unwanted up-bow).

Variations on compression fretting

✔ I've seen Martins that were compression-fretted too straight, even bordering on back-bow (and I like straight necks). I think that on some stiff vintage necks, by going to the next size tang to keep the fret down, you're adding more tang than you need (when you really only want more barb). I'm willing to use the same size fret (1:1) and glue to keep the fret ends down if I think the neck will benefit.

✔ An alternative to the above is to plane relief into the neck so that by using the next larger tang (for holding pressure), you get a straight neck when you're done. It's more difficult to give a fretboard the correct relief before fretting than to give it back-bow or drop-off however.

✔ Many times it's beneficial to use a neck heater or a heat-lamp to warm the glue joint between the fretboard the neck, and to clamp the neck into straightness or back-bow as it cools. Heat-straightening is used by many

to remove excess up-bow. While I don't think it's a permanent cure in most cases (the neck usually goes back into an up-bow), it's a great way of getting a neck where you want it temporarily so that you can keep it there with compression fretting. By heating a neck straight before fretting you can often eliminate the need to remove wood from the fretboard surface.

Typical Martin "T" fret installation

Here are a few words from Joe Konkoly on refretting Martin guitars: "When the strings are off, I like to see a slight back-bow in the neck—so that a straightedge would balance in the middle and drop at each end. This particular D-18 we have is a 1943 model with an ebony filler strip in place of the metal T-bar for neck reinforcement (the metal was needed for the war effort). With the strings on I measured .027" relief, and even with the strings off it was .014"—a difference of .012". It would be uncommon to find this much give in a Martin neck made before or after the war until you get to the square tube necks of the '70s. I'd like to see a back-bow when the strings are off (not relief). Under string pressure, the maximum relief should be .015"—that's the Martin spec. I like less, or almost none. After judging the stiffness of the neck and the density of the ebony fretboard I knew I couldn't simply fret the neck straight with oversize tangs: I had to remove some wood from the fretboard, too.

"Since there was a .014" up-bow without any string tension on the neck, I had to remove that much from the wood right off, just to get the neck straight, then back-bow it to remove the .012" difference between the original two measurements (the bow with the strings on and the bow with the strings off). I very rarely just pound in oversize frets to "straighten" the neck—they're used to keep the neck straight. I planed and sanded a .010" drop-off between the 4th fret and the nut, figuring that under string tension the neck would pull into at least the .002" of relief I didn't plane off, and probably another .002" on its own—giving me an almost straight neck under tension. If it came out perfectly straight (no relief), I'd be happy, too. Straight, or a little relief, that's what I'm after.

"So this neck, which is pretty typical of 1940s necks, looked like this after I prepped the board:

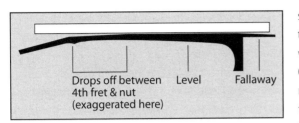

Drops off between   Level   Fallaway
4th fret & nut
(exaggerated here)

✔ A little drop-off from the 4th fret to the nut

✔ Flat from the 4th to the body

✔ From the 14th to the 20th fret: a drop-off of .002"

Of course all the areas are blended in—there aren't any distinct marks where one joins the other, and I re-cut the slot depth where I took off wood.

"The slots measured .022" and it was a hard ebony board, so I used the .0225" wire (the next size up). I put the first fret in at the 11th fret to get the feel in an area that doesn't affect the compression much (the most compression occurs between the 3rd and 9th frets). By testing a fret in a non-compression area I won't have to remove it if it doesn't feel heavy enough. It wasn't heavy enough, so I switched to .0235" and used it from the 10th fret to the nut. When I got to the 12th fret I switched back to the .0225" for the tongue.

"As a rule I use a half-thousandth over on the tongue in rosewood or ebony, and on the main fretboard I use 1-1/2 thousandths over on ebony, and at least 2-1/2 thousandths over on rosewood. Sometimes rosewood is so soft you'll use the big .027"!"

Joe wisely sticks several rags in the sound hole to deaden the sound, and wears ear protection!

Martin bar-style fretting

Bar fretwire is the old-style solid wire that was used on guitars until the modern "T" fret came along. Unlike the "T" fret, bar fretwire is rectangular in profile, meaning it doesn't have barbs or beads. It ranges from .045" to .055" in thickness, and is quite tall (about .160"). Most of its height, however, remains below the level of the fretboard—most bar fret players like a fret height of .040" to .055". Bar frets add great stiffness to a neck (and consequently improve the tone of the guitar), but they are difficult to install. Here, Dana Bourgeois describes his bar fretting method:

"Most bar-fret Martins that we see are 12-fret guitars, and usually have wide necks, short scales and a short

span, meaning there are 12 frets clear of the body rather than the later 14. Fret compression isn't as important with the shorter necks as it is with the long-necked OM. OM refrets are really hairy because they have a narrow neck, the longer scale, 14 frets clear of the body—and they only have wooden (ebony) truss rods. And they all had bar frets! Therefore you have to rely on fret compression to keep your neck straight, and the fitting of every fret is crucial.

"Using compression, you can flex a neck too far backward, or not using enough can cause forward, or up-bow. The typical OM has to be fretted in such a way that it's slightly back-bowed in order for it to be reasonably stiff under string tension. A plus with the bar fret job is that because the height is somewhat variable on bar frets, you do have the option of slightly adjusting your height if you've misjudged the compression versus flexibilty ratio (you can take off more metal from the fret tops if you need to). But the bottom line is that refretting an OM is like standing in a boat in rough sea, and shooting at a moving target."

A highlight of the Symposium '93 repair video from ASIA (Association of Stringed Instrument Artisans) is watching T.J. Thompson calmly pulling bar frets out of a 1931 Martin OM-45 in order to straighten the neck. He wasn't even nervous! T.J.'s into bar fretting—he frets his Thompson OM-style guitars, as well as the Schoenberg OM-28 and OM-45 reissues, with bar frets. T.J. knows that bar frets produce the most rigid neck and that their tone is unsurpassed—the guitars he builds prove his point. Here are some pointers on bar refrets:

Because of the massive depth and thickness of bar frets, they exert an even compression on the fretboard and neck (no barbs are involved). If you pull out a couple of bar frets, say at the 4th and 8th fret, you'll see the relief increase. Drive a couple of thick bar frets into a tight-fitting slot, and the opposite occurs—just as with oversize Martin wire, but quicker. So the perfect fit of the fret width to the slot is most important.

When Irving Sloane's book *Guitar Repair* was written in 1973, Martin no longer produced bar wire, and what they had on hand was saved for Martin customers. For this reason, the book recommends filling the fret slot with wood and recutting the slots to accept standard "T" frets. I disagree with that method, although I've done it.

Martin again offers two sizes of bar fretwire: .051" and .057". These will take care of any vintage refret, although you must do considerable filing on the flat sides to match many slots in situations where you don't need extra compression. I have a roll of newer Martin bar fretwire that measures .046", but Martin doesn't advertise it. Perhaps they no longer have it, I'm not sure (but it's mighty handy, and I try to use it sparingly). Vintage fretboards were fretted with wire ranging from .045" up into the mid-.050"s, and it's not uncommon to carefully pull up (or remove) the old wire, straighten and re-radius it, then re-use it by not driving it in as deep. Here's a brief rundown on how T.J. goes about a bar fret job.

"I use bar frets in two situations: refretting old work, and for the initial fretwork on my own instruments. With this particular OM-45 we have here, there's too much forward bow (about .015")which I will straighten by removing frets 4 through 9 and replacing them with larger wire.

"Use a hot soldering iron to heat the fret before pulling it with your nippers. With the frets removed, ever so lightly sand the fretboard surface just to clean it (400-grit).

"I'm cleaning the slot with a straight-sided Dremel burr—but not widening it. These particular fret slots are .050" wide, and I don't intend to widen them because I have a feeling that about a 054" fret will be perfect for the compression I'm after. So in this instance I'm just making sure that it's deep enough for the new wire, and clean. And often, when I take the frets out, I clamp the peghead back to open the slot's compression on the tang and make removal easier. (Sometimes I'll reverse the process to put them in.)

"Sometimes I will widen the slot slightly to get closer in size to the wire I intend to use. I grind new dental burrs to different diameters to suit my fret slot needs. You need a wide selection of cutters ranging from .002" smaller than the thinnest fretwire you intend to use, on up to .002" wider than the heaviest gauge (and everywhere in between). The .002" undersize bit is used to cut the fretslots in the middle of the neck (maybe frets 4 to 8), and the oversize cutter is used on the fretboard extension over the body where fret compression is undesirable. On the extension you can lightly hammer the frets in, or press and glue them in (the only instance where I use the Teeter-style fret job).

"You don't need a lot of compression per fret (usually .002" is plenty). It's the sum total of all the frets that give you the desired effect.

"OK. Back to this 'yard sale special.' The replacement wire measures .160" tall, and I want to leave a fret height of .050" above the board. So I set the cutter bit close to the .110" difference in depth so that when driven home, the new fret height will be only a few thousandths over .050" (for leveling when I'm done).

"Bar fretwire is rolled on its flat side for storage and is somewhat curved on its flat side end to end— it needs to be straightened. The FretBender does this perfectly—run the wire, on its side, backwards through the rollers and it straightens beautifully.

"I want the frets to be .054" wide, so I'm filing the flat side of the .057" down to .054" (I could be routing the slot wider, but I don't remove wood from the fret slot walls needlessly). I'll check the fit often by pressing the end of the wire into the slot. It shouldn't press in easily; if you tried to press the whole length in, you couldn't.

"Next, cut the wire to length with a little overhang on each side, and file the ends clean and square. It's good that we have this bound fingerboard, because the ends must be notched to overhang the binding, and that's an important step that I couldn't show you on an unbound board (otherwise the actual fretting is the same).

"Before notching the ends, curve the wire to match the fretboard radius. I lay the fret on this steel block with a piece of hardwood to support it. I hammer the curve into the wire because the Fret Bender was not really intended to radius the heavy-gauge bar fret. I hammer against the wood to keep from marring the top of the fret (even though I plan on dressing it down anyhow). We hammer the bottom of the fret.

"To notch the ends, grab the fret with your nippers so that they're a binding thickness from the end, and the height of the exposed fret (once installed) from the bottom. Hold the wire firmly with the nippers face down on a steel block. File until your file hits the steel-block 'stop'.

"The rest is easy. Hammer in the fret until the notches stop on the binding, and the crown is uniform across the width of the board.

"Don't bevel the ends at a 45° angle as you might other fret jobs—leave it perpendicular and flush with the edge of the fretboard. I shape the ends with a flush-bottom file which has one safe edge (no teeth), against the board. Don't remove as much metal, or shape the ends as round as a 'T'-fret often is.

"To dress the tops, lay a piece of venetian blind on one side of the fret, and a piece of heavy tape on the other side in case you slip.

"With a triangle file (or whatever you like) shape one side of the fret to center at a time, then reverse the Venetian-blind "protector" and the tape. Take your time. If this part of the job doesn't seem like it's working, and seems like it's taking forever, you're probably doing it wrong.

"Sand the fret tops with 320- and 400- grit paper to knock off sharp edges. Follow with steel wool. That's it!

"In closing I'll say this: Bar fret wire went out of fashion in the 1930s when steel neck reinforcement came in. This important detail is often overlooked. It's incorrect to say that the early guitars had no neck reinforcement—the frets keep the neck straight! If the frets are too loose, the neck bows forward; if the frets are too tight, the neck bows backward."

After watching T.J.'s demonstration, I still had a couple of questions: Would bar frets be good in a Strat or Les Paul? And what's kept more people from using bar frets? Here's T.J.'s answer:

"One half of the reason I use bar frets is to keep the neck straight—and the necks you mentioned have adjustable truss rods to keep them straight. So half the reason would be wasted—unless the owner was only interested in the tone bar frets might produce (because the other one half of the reason for using bar frets is to produce tone). The guitars that I build, and the vintage Martins which I specialize in repairing, do not have truss rods, but they have straight necks, and great tone!

"Most customers wouldn't want to go through the trouble and expense of a bar fret job on something like a Les Paul, that didn't need it for straightness, because they'd be experimenting on it in a very non-traditional way. And perhaps I make bar fretting sound simple, but it's actually a manufacturing nightmare—what Dana said about standing in a boat is right. And of course I wasn't there at the time (at least not in this life), but I know that Martin had very good reasons for switching to T-frets from a manufacturing point of view."

Thanks T.J.! And I'd be remiss not to point out that T.J. would ask, in his firm, yet gracious way (and he has all of our support), to please leave the vintage instruments to the professionals. Many times poor work—especially fretwork—is done to a vintage instrument that can never be undone. Don't cut your teeth on something you shouldn't—don't ruin guitars which are our national treasures! (When it's vintage, even if you own it, you don't really own it.)

The glue-in method

If you're serious enough about fretting to have read this far, then you'll thank me when I suggest that you buy Don Teeter's first book *The Acoustic Guitar, Volume 1*. The fretting section shows the original glue-in method in great detail, and the rest of the book is an incredible guitar repair education for the professional. There are few of us that haven't worn out at least one copy of Don's book. There'd be no sense in me teaching you Don's method—I certainly couldn't out-teach him. But I will point out the bare bones of his method and show you how I altered it to suit my needs. The glue-in method uses the same neck preparation as any fret job, which means following the steps starting on page 186. We pick up here with a new step 8 to start the glue-in method:

8 Widen the slots with small dental burrs and a Dremel tool mounted in the accessory router base. Widen the slots enough so that the frets will push in with finger pressure, or with a very light hammering. Only the outer edge of the fret tang barb should kiss the slot walls; the tang itself shouldn't touch at all.

9 With a Qtip and paste wax, wax off the area in between the frets. Wax up close to the slot, but leave a little dry clean wood (the width of the fret crown) on each side (and don't get any wax in the slot).

9 Tape off the fretboard with masking tape so that only the fret slot is visible. Then use a thin bladed spatula to pack 24-hour cure epoxy glue into each slot (Don Teeter uses Elmer's 601 epoxy exclusively). Mush the glue into the slot until it squeezes out, and remove the excess.

10 Remove the tape and carefully press the pre-radiused (no over-radius for this method) frets into the slots. The frets can be cut to exact length, or left with an overhang that you can clip off later. You will get some glue squeeze-out but this can be chiseled off when it's dry—the waxed board makes cleanup easy.

11 Clamp the frets to dry overnight, using a dowel rod on each side and a block of wood as a caul.

12 Remove the clamps, chisel off the glue squeeze-out, clean up the rough fret ends (or overhang) and then level and dress the frets in the normal way.

Glue-in variation In the '70s I used the glue-in method a lot because it guaranteed better results than I was able to get with a hammer (straightness-wise), helping to avoid the backbow and up-bow problems caused by fret compression. For me it was a great fret method to use while I slowly learned how to handle fret compression. It's an excellent way to deal with worn out, rotten fingerboards that won't hold a fret, and especially useful on the fretboard extension over the body (the tongue) where hammering is difficult and dangerous. I developed my own variation with a couple of differences. They are:

✔ I use five-minute cure epoxy and fret two frets at a time. While two are drying at the nut end, I go to the body end and install two more—going back and forth from one end to the other until done.

✔ I only wax off around the two frets that I'm doing so that I won't inadvertently drag wax into a clean slot.

✔ I use a different gluing caul. With Don's caul, the pressure applied to the top board with the clamp is crucial—too much pressure can make the fret rise in the center. I use a caul with 1/2" thick Plexiglas on the top, two 3/16" plexi-dowel rods, and a 1/8" Plexi-sheet on the bottom. The Plexiglas is super-glued at three points —the top of both dowels to the 1/2" block, and on the bottom of one dowel to the 1/8" sheet. This leaves one edge of the sheet loose so the caul can "flex"—curving to match the fretboard radius, and holding down the center.

✔ Several neck and body cauls are needed to facilitate clamping in the area of a curved neck heel.

There are as many variations to Don's original glue-in method as there are luthiers using it. You must read Don's book to fully appreciate his method before you experiment with your own. Now here's the new glue-in method, which is the evolution that I often use today.

The new glue-in method

The only reason I call this a glue-in method is because I do use glue, and because it evolved from my use of (and variations on) Don Teeter's original method. But it really incorporates all of the fretting methods described so far.

The three major developments are: 1) I generally don't rout the slot at all; 2) I often alter the size of my fret tang to match a particular fret slot; 3) I don't push frets in with a fingertip, nor hammer them—I press them in. Just as with the other fretting methods, follow the fretboard prep up until step #7.

It's important to me that the fret tang is the same size as the slot—without a gap. I may want an oversize tang (like the Martin compression method), but only in rare cases would I want an undersized one. I can live with a gap of .001" to .002" (which the glue fills) if I must, but I prefer not to have even that. To accomplish this, I may widen the slot to the tang size by using the different gauged saws.

Sometimes I will rout the slot with an extremely thin dental burr, but I'm enlarging it just enough for the tang, not for the barb as with a finger-press method. I widen the slot until it's the same size (or perhaps .001" to .002" smaller) as the tang of the modern fretwire that I'm using. I'm looking for the same fit required for a hammer or arbor press fret job.

I use glue, although I'm constantly switching between Titebond, 5-minute Epoxy, superglue, hide glue, and shellac. When the fit is tight (no gap) the type of glue is less important, but I'm still trying to learn. If I have to pick a favorite glue, I'd pick the System Three company's Quick Cure five-minute epoxy. This was recommended to me by Steve Anderson—famed builder of archtops, flattops, and beautiful mandolins. This epoxy dries hard and brittle—a quality I prefer for transmitting tone.

A significant tang barb is needed for hammer fretting to compensate for recoil from the blow of the hammer. But when the fret tang matches the slot, and you press in the frets with glue, the barbs don't have to be so large to hold the fret down (particularly at the ends). For this reason I will sometimes remove a fair amount of the barb with my fret tang sizer and de-barber (now available as the Fret Barber tool, upper right) to get the right fit in the slot. Here's how I made my original version of tool:

1 Cut a StewMac No. 864 fingerboard leveling file into two 2-1/2" lengths;

2 Clamp the faces (tape protecting the teeth) and grind the edges smooth and a bit rounded from end to end;

3 Space them apart with a feeler gauge and clamp them in a vise;

4 Insert the firewire between the files;

5 Draw the wire against the cut of the teeth. Switch feeler gauges every .002" to pare a .034" barb down to the bare tang on three lengths of fretwire in a minute!

With good fret compression and glue, I don't need much of a barb to hold the fret in (and superglue will hold in a fret that has no barb at all). It's as if I were fretting with Martin's old style bar fretwire, only I have a "T-head", or crown on the fret. This technique gives the best of both worlds: 1) The compression to retain stiffness; 2) The perfect seating of frets that are pressed in (not hammered) without the barb over-compressing. When the slot is clean, test a 3/8" sample length of the chosen wire for fit.

I'll often give the fret ends a slight over-bend. This helps to hold the fret ends down, especially on the rolled-over edges of vintage Fenders and some others. To create the over-bend, I clamp the fret into a small vice with the end hanging out, and gently tap the fret end with my fretting hammer (photo, next page).

Just as with the hammer-in method, before installing the frets I normally clip the fret tang to length (But not the crown overhang) with a fret tang nipper. Then I have less filing to do on the edges of the fretboard, and when I clip the overhang the clipping motion doesn't twist the fret as much.

Sometimes I over-bend the ends and clip the entire fret to exact length before installing it so there isn't any overhang. The overhang may not be necessary, depending on how the frets are going in and holding down.

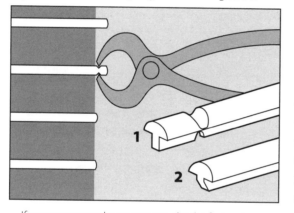

If you use an overhang, you can clip the fret ends anytime they become an annoyance. The longer you wait the better. Sometimes I re-clamp with a caul, to keep the fret from twisting as I clip (especially if the fret tang—not the crown overhang—wasn't nipped to length beforehand). Press downward on your nippers as you clip.

Another clipping variation, if you haven't clipped the tang ahead of time, is to clip the fret crown first, and the tang second. This, too, helps you avoid twisting the fret and making the ends pop up.

From this point on my method is much the same as the original glue-in. I put glue in the slot and press the frets in, but with my method your fingers can't press the fret in, and a medium-pressure hammer-tap isn't enough either. I could use normal hammer pressure to get them in, but I'd rather not hit the frets when I can avoid it (and I don't like to hammer in the neck jig).

For glue, if I use epoxy I wax the board and use the five-minute cure. I can squeeze Titebond or hide glue into the slots using a syringe, and have minimal cleanup with a damp rag (I don't have to tape off the board).

Arguments for and against glue-in fretting

Glue-in fretting has created controversy over the years. Some say that using epoxy is a poor trick to play on a future repairperson; others worry about hurting correct intonation by altering the fret slots, and the question of the vintage market comes to mind. I don't feel that the glue-in method is the right way to refret a valuable vintage guitar, but there are circumstances when it's the only way to go (rotten fingerboards that won't hold a fret, and on the fret extension over the body of acoustic guitars where hammering is dangerous).

If you rout the slot and press in the fret, an air space or clearance "gap" usually exists between the tang and the fret slot walls. With a finger-press fit, the very edge of the barbs are just touching the walls as the fret is pressed in. A medium-press (hammer) fit forces some of the barb to drag through the wood. With either of these press fits, the tang is not touching. That's why we use glue—to fill the gap, and hold down the fret. If a gap is left, and not filled with glue, poorer tone transmission showed in my tests. So the amount of gap, and the type of glue used, becomes the issue (and at times it has become most controversial between many of us). Here are the main problems pointed out, and some solutions:

Problem Those against the glue-in method feel that by routing the slots you create a weak "rubbery" neck, even though the playing surface may be perfectly level (especially on adjustable necks where you can control the neck's straightness with ease).

Solution Don't use the method, or don't rout the slots too wide, or perhaps not as wide as Don recommends. Don is very scientific, and has run many tests. He says that the epoxy he uses (Elmer's E-601) makes the neck stiffer than the wood itself—stiffer than before the slots were enlarged and the neck refretted.

Problem It's my opinion that over-widening the slot does cause a neck to lose stiffness in some cases, especially on adjustable neck guitars. If a neck loses its stiffness, tone will be harmed even if it plays well, but I don't believe that epoxy is the culprit.

Solution Study fret compression, hammer the frets in or use the new glue-in method described above.

Problem Glued-in frets can be a nasty surprise for future repairers.

Solution Use heat. The frets come right out.

Some suggest that epoxy is a tone-sink, and that fretting with it is like setting the fret into a shock absorber. Using a tool which measures sound transmission, I ran extensive tests, and found that not using glue, even with a traditional hammer-in fret job, produced a poorer metered response than using glue on any fret job. I used hide glue, Titebond, 5-minute epoxy, and four different 24-hour cure epoxies for my tests. Wide-slot glued-in frets measured lower than tight-slot hammered in frets with glue, but not significantly.

Epoxy seemed to match hide glue, shellac and Titebond as a fret-holding glue in tight-fitting and loose-fitting slots. I then measured hardened glues by themselves, and epoxy was lower on the list: actually in the same response category as nylon and plexiglas as a sound transmitter. Therefore, I would not want to use it as a bed for my frets with a finger-press, or a medium-press (hammer) fit, regardless of what the fret tests showed me.

You can use superglue to hold a fret in with the glue-in method, but I don't think it fills the gap well enough to ensure a tight fit and good tone (unless you fill the slot with slow-curing glue and wait forever for it to dry).

Harry Fleishman suggests mixing sawdust that matches the fretboard wood into the epoxy to stiffen the neck and improve the tone. This didn't produce any measurable effects in my tests, but it makes sense. Tests on sound, at least the kind that I'm qualified to make, didn't prove much really. So much for science.

Fret presses

Earlier I mentioned arbor presses, benchtop pressing devices often used for fret work. For my work, I've found that I prefer to bring the press to the guitar rather than the other way around. I use several handheld presses.

Jaws I squeeze the frets in with Jaws, a unique Vice-grip I converted into a fret press. I made several iterations of Jaws, and eventually we put in the development time at StewMac to make them available. It's a professional tool,

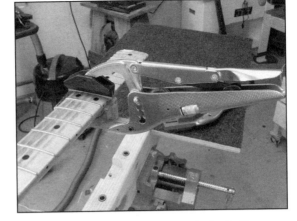

for sure. The radiused "shoe" presses the fret in. Since most of my fretting is done with the guitar in the neck jig, Jaws is the only type of press I can use to get in there and get the job done. You can use a drill press or arbor press to install frets on slab (bolt-on) necks, but it's hard to do a D-28 or Les Paul because the body and the tilted-back peghead are in the way. Often I use two pairs, and

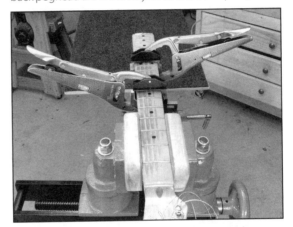

leap-frog down a neck. I can get quite close to the heel of an acoustic and then take over on the fretboard extension with a hammer, or use my Jaws2 or Jaws3 variations.

I have radiused brass pressing shoes for Jaws in these sizes: 6", 7-1/4", 9", 10", 12", 14",15",16" and 20". They are interchangeable so that on a compound fretboard I change them every two or three frets. On a cylinder board I use one shoe all the way up.

A drill press makes a nice press, if you're fretting a bolt-on neck. A version of the fret press caul used in Jaws is available for drill-press installations.

Jaws2 This version of Jaws is based on a Bessey clamp, and is designed for clamping on the fretboard exten-

sion over the body — either through the soundhole, or from the outside. Through the soundhole, it can reach the last few frets on some guitars that it couldn't reach from the outside. Jaws 2 can fret right through the neck heel/body joint area with ease, an area where the regular Jaws doesn't excel. You can fret the entire neck with Jaws2, but I prefer to use each Jaws model on the areas it's best at.

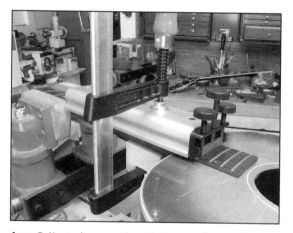

Jaws3 (Just when you thought it was safe to go back to the fretting!) This version frets through the neck body joint (or anywhere on the neck), but with a different feel. While it has great power, you can also squeeze the frets in gently with it.

Jaws is a professional's tool, but you can approximate it with radius sanding blocks. If you have the wooden ones, coat the face with thin sheet steel so they won't be dented. The typical orange Jorgensen clamp isn't strong enough. Get the stronger Bessey clamp. A Bessey used with a radius block caul can press frets into a slot that neither a finger press nor a medium press fit could.

If you do use radius-sanding blocks to clamp in the frets, you may need a slightly looser fret slot (or a de-barbed tang) on some rosewood or ebony because a radius block isn't as strong as the three-thumbwheel press used for Jaws3. Note: When the fret's height (average of .040") is added to the fretboard radius, the radius has increased (whereas the radius of the block hasn't). So there is a slight mismatch when you use the block as a gluing clamp or caul. But the difference is so minimal that you can ignore it. The ability to use a radius-block as a clamp is one reason you might choose to prepare a cylinder-shaped fretboard.

With regard to the radius mismatch of the sanding-blocks: If you really want to be exact, add a layer of .040" shim stock (or whatever thickness matches the fret height) to the bottom of the radius block before you sand the fretboard. Then remove it to use it as a press.

Let the glue dry ten minutes while you bend two more frets at the other end of the fretboard. Also wax and tape-off two more slots. By the time these two frets have been installed, you can remove the clamp from the two that are drying and begin the process over.

Remove the clamp, and with a sharp chisel pare away the epoxy squeeze-out on each side of the fret. The wax makes this job easy, although many glue-in fretters don't bother with it. Watch out! It's easy to cut into the fretboard with your chisel. As you work, keep the edge of the chisel that's away from the fret slightly above the fretboard's surface ("floating" is as good a word as any).

Repeat the process until you're done. Using this method you may run into a problem fitting a caul and clamp around the neck joint, and will need to rig up a caul under the neck.

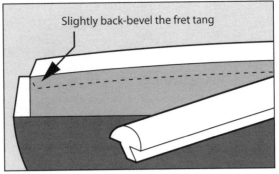

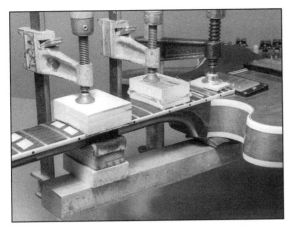

After I've pressed in a set of frets, I'll often clamp a radius block on them while the glue dries and I go onto the next pair of frets. Sometimes the frets press in so well that no caul is needed — you can just tell.

Bound fingerboards

Bound fingerboards need special attention. There is seldom a reason to remove fingerboard binding when refretting, yet it's done often, perhaps in an attempt to save the "nibs" at the fret end, as pictured above. It's almost impossible to save the nibs during a fret job. It's best to pull the frets, level the board as if the nibs weren't there and then fret it by either the hammer or glue-in methods. Also, removal of the binding involves much touch-up finishing, so don't be talked into doing it. (A rare vintage guitar can be fretted with its nibs left intact, but the job is so time-consuming and delicate that you'd best be sitting down when your repairman gives you an estimate.)

The frets can be installed so that the crown overlaps the plastic (at right), as with most bound-fretboard Martins, or they may be trimmed flush to the binding and then beveled. Players getting a refret on a guitar with nibs (Gibson, Jackson, Gretsch, etc.) may prefer the fret/binding overlap, since it takes the place of the missing nibs and retains the feel. In the case of the overlap, the fret's tang is notched and filed smooth before installation. The tang is also beveled slightly inward to avoid pushing the binding out. The fret end is then finish-beveled and rounded to the player's taste.

Some binding considerations

When nipping the fretwire for the overlapped-binding method, fret nippers are a great time saving device that eliminate most of the filing on notched fret ends.

Frets trimmed flush to the binding should have the tang slightly back-beveled with a file to avoid pushing the binding out. On flush-to-the-binding fret jobs, the ends of the frets must be filed at the same taper as the fretboard width.

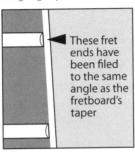

These fret ends have been filed to the same angle as the fretboard's taper

If you're hammering in frets flush to the binding, don't over-bend the radius

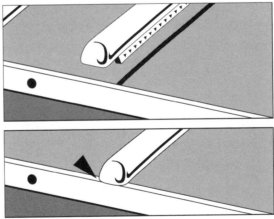

as much as you would for an un-bound board with fret overhang. It's hard to guarantee where the fret ends will end up as the fret seats, finally straightening out to its full length. You could end up with a gap on one end, and pushed-out binding on the other.

Overlapped binding is the easiest when a notched fret hides the tang. You can leave the tang a tiny bit short at each end with no danger of hitting the binding.

Question "I'm restoring a late-'50s Gretsch 6120. Everything's original, even the frets, but for some reason there's no fingerboard binding! When re-binding, what's the best way to shape the fret-end nibs, and where can I find the little red dots for the edge markers?"

Answer Create binding nibs by tracing the profile of the fingerboard and frets onto your plastic. Then cut it close to shape on a band saw. Finish the job with a scraper once the binding's installed. Also, drill your red-dot holes (.055" diameter) in the new binding before you glue it on—it's easier than drilling after the new binding is installed, especially on the fingerboard extension.

As for edge markers—recently, on a similar Gretsch binding replacement, I lost two of the red dots saved from the original binding—oops! The sharp tip of a red drawing pencil, dipped in super glue, stuck into the hole and sawed off, solved the problem—you'd never know which dots are fake.

Question "The original frets on my SG Les Paul 'Fretless Wonder' are so low that it's impossible to bend a note, so it needs to be refretted. The neck is wide, but the strings are really close together at the nut because the frets stop short at the binding. To get more playing area and wider string spacing, I'd like new frets that could lay out over the binding (similar to a Martin), but on my guitar the binding is all rounded over where it meets the fretboard, so I doubt you could overlap a fret onto it. But a friend says that the binding must be removed for refretting anyhow. Is this true? If so, could you put on thicker binding and then fret out onto it? Thanks!"

Answer Binding is not normally removed during refretting—this is a common misconception! You'd appreci-

ate a refret if you like to bend strings because "Fretless Wonder" frets were notoriously low, even when new. On your Les Paul the binding was over-rounded when the guitar was built, and you're right, there's nothing to fret over (which is something to fret over). This over-rounding isn't "wrong," it's just the way a particular Gibson craftsman chose to file and round off that particular neck on that particular day. I've seen other guitars just like yours that made good use of the neck's width without the binding being rounded over. I prefer to leave as much of the neck/fretboard/binding width as possible so that the string spacing can be comfortably wide. Why not replace the binding so that the guitar can be refretted the way you like?

In the case of this particular instrument, it would be okay with regards to the guitar's value as a vintage instrument to replace the binding, since the finish on the back of the neck is in rough shape—even worn to the bare wood in areas. Also, the guitar has been refretted, but with the same low "Fretless Wonder" fretwire—that's why he thought it was the original fret job! During that refret the binding was filed on and removed even more, as evidenced by the fact that there are no plastic "nibs" on the end of each fret, which there would be if the frets were original. With the removal of the nibs that had once "capped off" the fret ends, the replacement frets had to be slightly beveled and rounded-over. This makes the fret's actual playing width even more narrow than it would have originally been.

Another reason that it's OK, vintage-wise, to re-bind the fingerboard is that the neck has already been sprayed on and touched up (again, Phil was probably unaware of this because the work was done so well). But looking carefully at the rear of the peghead, I can see different colors of white, yellow and creamy white from the layering of different paints. My guess is that the instrument had a broken peghead that was well repaired and expertly touched up. The best way to see such finish repairs is to look at the instrument under black light—when you do, finish defects, spot touch-ups and hidden repairs to the wood that are not visible under normal light show up instantly. Using black light as a means of "reading" a finish is a trick passed on to us by the violin trade. Just having a black light doesn't mean you know the clues the light's revealing. You need an experienced refinisher to look under a black light with you and explain the clues that show up on your guitar.

So new binding could be installed and the neck finish could be touched up so that it still looks old and worn, with the different layers of color showing as they do now, and nobody would be the wiser. Then the frets could be notched to hang out over the binding "Martin" style as we've just seen. The total neck width of the guitar is 1-11/16" (1.687"), while the string spacing of the original nut is 1 13/32" (1.406"), measured between the centers of the two outer E strings. With new binding that is only slightly rounded, and with the frets installed with the overhang method and then correctly beveled, the guitar would end up with a new nut-string spacing of 1-15/32" (1.468"). The overall difference—.062" (1/16")—is a huge amount!

When I followed the above advice, it worked out well. The guitar ended up playing beautifully, with comfortable, wide string spacing at the nut, and nice, tall, rounded frets that are a joy to bend on. Finish-wise, it's hard to tell that the job was done. While I wouldn't recommend such drastic measures for all guitars, in this case it was the right thing to do.

Vintage Fender fretting

You can use any of the methods we've looked at to refret vintage Strats and Teles. I'll just add a few pointers here. The one difference with Fender fret jobs is that until 1982, Fender slid their frets in from the side. Knowing how they were installed will help you remove frets with less chipping, and do better fret work on guitars made before 1982. Haven't you always wondered why Fender, although they didn't use glue, never had loose fret ends? Here's a little history on Fender's sideways fret-job:

The sideways fret job

I'd heard about the sideways fret job for years but never truly believed it (nor unstood it) until **James Rickard**, **Wayne Charvel**, and **Bob Taylor** finally set me straight. James Rickard visited the Fender factory in the early '70s with **Wayne Charvel** as his guide. James was working for Ovation at the time, and Fender was "jobbing-out" certain custom finishing work and some refrets to Wayne's shop, so Wayne had the run of the place. Here's what Jim and Wayne told me:

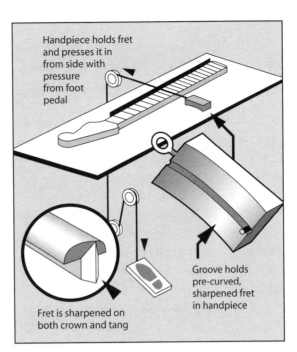

Handpiece holds fret and presses it in from side with pressure from foot pedal

Groove holds pre-curved, sharpened fret in handpiece

Fret is sharpened on both crown and tang

d.i.y.

"The neck blank was profiled (tapered from the nut to the end), but still unshaped at the rear. The fretboard surface had been radiused, slotted, 'trued' end to end and was ready for the frets. The neck lay flat on the worktable, and was very stable because its backside was still a flat slab of wood. The table was bare except for a pile of frets and an 8" long piece of angle iron, bolted to the rear of the table, that served as a 'fence' for the neck to be shoved up against. The angle iron was wrapped with a thick rubber band (about .090" thick) that acted as a cushion, and also spaced the neck just far enough off the fence so that the sharp fret ends could overhang the fretboard edge.

"The operator installed the frets from the bass side by working an under-the-table foot lever that pulled down on a cable. The cable was connected by pulleys to a steel hand piece. The handpiece was 3" to 4" long by 3/4" wide; the underside was radiused to match the fretboard (7-1/4"), and had a groove to hold the crown (head) of the fret. The fret tang was exposed. The machined groove that held the fret was stopped at the operator's end by a hardened steel dowel pin that drove the fret into (and across) the slot. The handpiece was covered with a smooth wooden 'shell' that protected the operator's hand.

"The secret to the operation was that the end of the fret away from the operator—the part that got pulled

d.i.y.

through the slot—was sharpened on a special jig. The tang edge was sharp as a knife, and the head (crown) was curved up like a ski so it couldn't catch on the fretboard surface. The barbs or 'beads' on the tang created their own groove (like a 'T'-slot) as the fret was pulled through!

"The operator would pick up a pre-sharpened, pre-radiused fret in his left hand, slap it against the underside of the hand piece (into the groove), and hold it in place with a finger. Then he'd slide the sharp fret end into the end of the fret slot and stop. Next he pressed the foot lever while holding the radiused hand piece bottom against the fretboard surface. The cable pulled the hand piece across the board, and pulled the fret into the slot. The hand piece was pressed firmly against the fretboard to help keep the fret down. After each fret he'd slide the neck along keeping the treble side up against the fence.

"Once the fret got started, the fret would sort of hold itself down as the beads 'broached' their own groove into the walls of the fret slot. The fret really couldn't come out because the wood above the beads, which would normally be compressed downward and sideways by a hammered or pressed-in fret, was still there—the fret had never entered through it. The end result was as if the fret had been pushed sideways into a T-slot, except that the fret broached its own T-slot.

"The frets were all the same size, and extra long—leaving plenty of overhang which was rough-band sawed and then trimmed flush on a pin-router. No glue was used during the fretting operation; however, when all the flush-trimming was done, the neck went under a small press with a radiused shoe that would squeeze the frets down tight, two or three at a time, just for insurance.

"I timed the installation several times. The worker we watched could install 21 frets in 27 seconds! Of course he was putting a show on for us, and the job wasn't done (they weren't trimmed or finished). But nobody could fret a guitar with a hammer or a press that fast. It was a crude process compared to Fender's very sophisticated techniques of today. But the old Fullerton plant was a monument to how much you could do with very little."

Jim Rickard passed away some years ago, and I know he'd rather be remembered for his knowledge and love of music, guitars, wood and woodworking than as the metalworking engineer and machinist who built machines that can take a freshly-made guitar string and wrap it, package it and store it in a box in 5-1/2 seconds. As manager of engineering and quality control for Ovation from 1968 until 1986, Jim was one of the creative forces behind the Ovation guitar, and he invented the under-the-bridge saddle pickup that made Ovation famous. Jim was a problem solver.

Next, I went to Fender's **Dan Smith**, Vice President of Marketing, to find out what year they quit the sideways method: "We quit sliding frets in from the side in '82—I was on the committee that did away with it. It required a lot of skill, and went beyond the limits of what we could reasonably expect someone to do, especially if the worker was encouraged to produce a high volume of work. It was one of the contributing factors to the poor fret jobs that sometimes occurred during the '70s. If you pressed too light the fret would be raised above the surface; too hard, and it would cut right into the wood. Each fret could have its own individual height! It was almost impossible to get perfect fret jobs unless the operator was really adept."

Then I asked **Bob Taylor** of Taylor Guitars if he knew anything about Fender sideways fretting (Bob seems to know how everything is done), and Bob said, "Oh yeah, I saw it! That's the way it was. In fact, I finally figured out that you can drive the fret out sideways—they come right out! I'll tell you Dan, when you try it, you're in for a pleasant day!"

Then I asked **Wayne Charvel** to add to the picture: "I talked with Leo Fender a number of times. He was a wonderful man who loved to talk shop. Did you know that the reason Fender switched from maple necks to rosewood fretboards was because Leo was watching a band on TV—all playing Fenders—when he suddenly realized that the finishes were starting to wear through on the fretboards? He thought they looked terrible! They got rid of maple necks in a hurry.

"A lot of people don't know how Fender fretted. Of course, how could they have known (who'd have guessed) if they'd never seen it? It's nice to be aware of it when you're pulling frets on Fender guitars made before—what year did you say they quit—'82? With a vintage maple neck, when you pull the fret up and out of the slot with your fret nippers, you get a line of small, evenly-spaced chips on each side of the fret slot—these represent the wood displaced by the fret barbs. If the fret had been pressed in, the barbs would have compressed the wood downward and to the side, and then could have been pulled out with less chipping.

"The chips are larger and more severe with rosewood boards because most of them were 'slab', or 'flat'-sawn. They really want to chip if something under the surface—such as a fret tang—is being pulled up through it. If you're experienced with vintage maple necks, you'll notice that the removal chips are very small, and actually become hidden by the new fret. But with the rosewood boards, they really chip—often in long V-shaped pieces much larger than the beads themselves.

"When I pull frets from vintage Fender necks—either maple necks or the rosewood fretboards—I dampen the fret and the fret slot with a 50/50 solution of water and rubbing alcohol. It softens the wood enough to let the frets pull out cleaner, and the alcohol seems to help the water evaporate fast enough to keep from over-swelling the wood. We were always afraid to use a soldering iron to heat the frets before pulling them (as you might on frets installed from above), because the heat makes the fret expand and chip the wood even worse, especially on rosewood boards.

"I'll tell you Dan, way back I tried what you and Bob Taylor are talking about—removing the frets sideways. They came out, but it made me nervous, so I didn't pursue it. I probably should have. I'll tell you though, a novice could really cause some damage that way. On thick-finished necks especially, be careful of the finish

along the fretboard edge on the bass side—you can pop a chunk out easily. Most of those thick-finished necks have chunks just waiting to pop loose at the fret ends because of neck expansion and contraction. You've given me confidence though, and I'll try it on the next original factory Fender vintage fret job that comes in—one fret at a time."

Thanks, Jim, Bob, Dan and Wayne! Now that I understand how the frets were installed on the majority of vintage Fenders I've worked on, I wish I had them all back (but that's water over the dam). From now on though, we all may consider a different approach to removing them. You have several choices:

1 Use a soldering iron and fret pullers.

2 Dampen the wood with the alcohol/water solution before using the fret pullers.

3 Combine the above methods (a soldering iron and moisture—I don't think you need to worry about watered-down rubbing alcohol catching fire, but to be safe omit the alcohol, use water, and "steam" them out).

4 Drive the frets out sideways, the same way they went in. The difference between a vintage fret pulled out sideways and one pulled up the normal way (on the same fretboard) is shown in the photos above. Here's how you can do it:

Grind a small notch or hole in the top of the fret on the treble side (I used a small dental burr in a Dremel tool)—just enough of a groove to catch whatever tool you use to knock it out with.

I'm using a small machinist's scribe that I press into the groove and tap with my fretting hammer. After it begins to move you can pull it out with fret nippers if you'd

d.i.y.

rather. Once the frets are loose you can slide them in and out like drawers!

I've been removing frets sideways (toward the bass side) with great results. When you tap out the frets, the top of the fret slot is perfect! You'll have to heat most of the '70s thick-skin polyester maple neck frets before they'll move, but you need less heat than if you were pulling them out the normal way, so there's less risk of burn marks on the maple.

Soon I'll try removing the frets out the treble side, since that's the direction the wood grain is pushed. There are two ways to think about hammering frets out: one idea is that removal is easier out the bass side because the fret is retracing the path it cut on entering the slot. The other thought is that removal is easier out the treble side because the wood fibers are already going that way and won't "reverse" and grab the fret as they might with the bass side removal. I suspect it will be more difficult (but possible) going out the treble side. I just don't have piles of vintage necks lying around to practice on! If you can drive frets out to either side, you can go to the side away from the player's eye (treble side for a right handed player, and vice-versa). If you did get a little chip, it wouldn't be noticed until after you'd gotten paid for the work! (Just kidding.)

But take Wayne's warning to heart. On all necks, especially the thick-finished ones, be especially careful of the fretboard edge on the bass side. Use heat, a sharp X-Acto knife, and a sharper eye to keep the exit of the fret under control. After the first tap, stop and check if either the wood or the finish are pulling outward in the direction of the removal (if so, do something about it and then finish removing the fret). I'm already thinking about a little fixture to keep pressure on the edge of the fretboard, around the fret-slot edge, as the fret comes out.

The small compressed groove below the surface of the fretboard ("broached" by the fret), is not actually cut or broached, but pressed—and I can't see it with a 10x lens. But because I know it's there, I wipe a drop of water into the slot (not too much) so the wood can swell back to where it had been in 1956, or whenever.

About fretting maple necks

Because of the lacquer finish, refretting a maple neck is more troublesome than working with a rosewood fretboard. Many maple necks are so true and the finish is in such good shape that you just pull out the old frets and stick in the new—the preferred method. Other necks are worn nearly bare, especially on the fretboard. Dealing with the finish on these necks isn't a problem, either, since you can't lose what you never had (some players want to have finish put back on and some prefer the feel of bare wood). Other necks may need to have the fretboard surface leveled before they'll play right, and then you're forced to deal with the finish.

We commonly see vintage Strat necks with some, or all, of the original lacquer, along with plenty of nice gray-brown wear spots. Unfortunately, these great looking necks often have the typical hump, or "rising tongue," at the last six frets. If the hump is bad and you want a great playing guitar, you'll have to remove the hump in order to get that portion of the neck surface level with the rest of the fretboard. Since these vintage boards are cylinders, I use a 7-1/4" radius block and sandpaper to keep the original fretboard contour. Here are some tips on maple neck refrets:

✔ If the neck's true, remove the frets and refret it, but don't touch the lacquer except to clean it. If you sand, don't use anything coarser than 2000-grit paper.

✔ Many maple necks from the '70s and '80s have a hard polyurethane finish ("thick-skin" as Mike Stevens calls it). There's less chance of harming this finish during a refret, but removing it is a chore if you need to level the board. Also, many of these finishes were too thick, and removing the frets without chipping can be tricky. You may have to cut the finish along the fret, or heat each fret slightly before you can remove it (especially if you plan to drive the fret out sideways).

✔ Don't sand out the wear spots. Wear spots are cool.

✔ Bare wood on the fretboard should be lightly dampened with naptha to raise the grain. When it's dry, any wood fibers that "fir-up" should be sanded or scraped off. Do this before you refret, since it's a little hard to sand later in between frets. You'll want to re-spray the lacquer over smooth wood.

Fret slots and tang size

✔ Carefully clean the fret slots with an X-Acto saw blade that's thinner than the slot. If you're careful not to deepen or widen the slots, they'll hold the replacement frets and look original. Blow the dust out of the slots. A

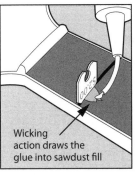

chipped fret slot can be filled with sanding dust (similar wood) and a drop of water-thin super glue. Use a piece of plastic to keep the slot open.

Wicking action draws the glue into sawdust fill

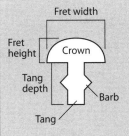

✔ Degrease a dirty board or slot edges by wiping with naptha or lighter fluid (in a well-ventilated place). Don't use lacquer thinner!

✔ If you had to remove wood from the fretboard surface, you may have to slightly deepen the slot to accommodate the fret tang. Don't overdo it.

✔ Save the old frets and compare with the replacement wire. Try to match the original fretwire in all dimensions. Two wires that nicely refret a vintage Strat are Dunlop 6230 and StewMac's #148. Refretters sometimes widen a fret slot for a press fit and use glue to hold the new wire, but not on a vintage Strat. You'll be tapping or pressing-in the new frets, so match the size as closely as possible.

✔ If the new tang is too deep for the slot, you can grind it shorter so that the slot doesn't have to be deepened.

✔ To avoid creating a back-bow or warp, it's important that both the tang and the barbs are not too large.

✔ If the neck was refretted before, the frets may tend to be loose in the slots. In this case, you want a wire with an oversized tang and barb that will hold.

✔ Glue may be needed to hold down the new frets or fret ends. Use an aliphatic glue such as Titebond or Elmer's Carpenter's Glue; don't use epoxy or super glue. Fender didn't use glue when they installed the frets, but you may have to.

✔ Overbend the fretwire radius to hold springy ends down in the slots.

Scalloped fingerboards

Even though the '80s speed-at-all-costs fetish has faded a bit in recent years, some players are still looking for advice on scalloped fingerboards. Should they perform this modification? What does it have to offer? Is it reversible? Does scalloping a neck cause problems in the future? John McLaughlin and Ritchie Blackmore used scalloped fingerboards years ago, but I think that speed-metal phenom Yngwie Malmsteen brought it mainstream attention.

Scalloping involves dishing out the wood between frets so that the fingertip has no contact with the fingerboard. It's difficult to do well. If you're thinking of doing the job yourself, be sure to finish this chapter before you start—and you might decide to have it done by the very best repairman or builder that you can find. Expect the scalloping job to be expensive, and don't be surprised if you have to refret your guitar at the same time—this is not an absolute, but a good possibility. Factory-scalloped replacement necks are available from some of the suppliers, which gives you the option of leaving your original board stock—a great idea where vintage pieces are concerned!

When playing with a scalloped fingerboard, you have to develop a whole new touch in order to keep from pressing the strings too hard and going out of tune. I found that this light touch was easy to get used to. My fingering hand became so relaxed that I was able to play much faster and smoother, since my fingertips were no longer fighting the fingerboard wood in order to press the string onto the fret. This seems to be in direct opposition to Yngwie's view that "it's much harder to play fast with a scalloped fingerboard because the string action has to be much higher." I don't know why he says this.

Since the guitar is a very personal instrument, the "benefits" of scalloping are subjective. Playing on one, I noticed the following changes in my playing: My fingering hand was relaxed, allowing me to play faster. Hammer-ons took less pressure in the attack, enabling faster trills and hammered chords. Pull-offs became easier, since the finger's flesh can reach deep down and really catch hold as you pull away, creating a distinctive percussive sound. A pitch bend (pushing straight down with the finger towards the fingerboard) could easily

d.i.y.

accommodate a semitone, and with a little practice, whole-tones and minor thirds can be done. Using this technique, you can imitate a pedal steel, for example, or even bend whole chords —I can't do that without a tremolo on an un-scalloped neck, and then the sound isn't the same.

Upside Due to the lack of pressure needed to hold down a chord, scalloping allows you to "rake"—or sweep—arpeggio passages, since your hand is free to move with the chord. This is an essential aspect of Yngwie's style. Bending blues notes has never been easier, since the finger can really get a good grab on the string with no slipping. This makes the wide, full-string vibrato of Yngwie or Ritchie Blackmore easier to achieve. Two-handed tapping techniques are also made easier, especially for the right-hand fingertip that is now able to pull off the string without first hitting the fingerboard. The violin-type finger vibrato also takes on a new sound since you can alter its pitch with a gentle pressing of the string. With scalloping, I find a more even, clear sound on all the strings in any position, probably because there is no longer any muting effect from the fingers touching the wood and drawing off some of the sound. Sounds good, huh? Now for the other side of the coin.

Downside I wouldn't suggest that you scallop a vintage guitar if you have any interest in retaining its market value—you'll ruin it forever. Scalloping could considerably weaken any neck (aside from one you may have had custom-built with a scalloped board in mind), since the fingerboard is an integral part of the neck's straightness and stiffness. After scalloping, a neck might twist or warp, but frankly, I think any good repairman could compensate for this by adjusting the truss rod accordingly or making up for the problem with accurate fret work. Also, since the scallops must be quite deep, the position markers may need to be removed and re-inlaid. This is easy for dots, but if you have pearl-block or large, ornate inlays, you may have to settle for dot replacements or foot a very expensive re-inlay bill. The side dot markers may have to be moved or eliminated as well.

The scallop is non-reversible. You cannot change your mind if you don't like it; the entire fingerboard has to be replaced. The tone of the guitar is going to change somewhat, too, and nobody could advise you as to what

to expect there. I'd worry about this more with an acoustic guitar than a solidbody electric, yet even with electrics, I suggest scalloping a bolt-on neck at first. Buy yourself an extra kit neck and scallop it or have it scalloped, leaving the original intact. (Or surf the Web. I found lots of scallops out there.) And if you're used to playing on strings that begin with a high E gauged .010 or heavier, be prepared to switch to .009s in order to gain the scallops' benefit. I found that my newly relaxed left hand compensated for the switch to lighter strings, and even though I don't enjoy playing on lighter strings, I really didn't notice a difference. (The strings I played on were .009, .011, .013, .022, .032, .038). Since standard truss rods curve up towards the fingerboard at each end of the neck, the scallop depth must be controlled accurately in these areas. Finally, scalloping is expensive and comes with no guarantees.

Recently a salesman in a music store tried to tell me, "Scalloping ain't no big deal; tall frets will do the exact same thing." This is simply not true.

deep

The neck jig

The neck jig is the most important tool in my repair shop. Although only the most serious fret worker would actually build this tool, its basic concept will help you understand more about neck repairs and fret work. When I wrote the first edition of this book the neck jig was a work in progress, taking several forms. I've refined it since, and have been using it in its current form for years. It's even commercially available now.

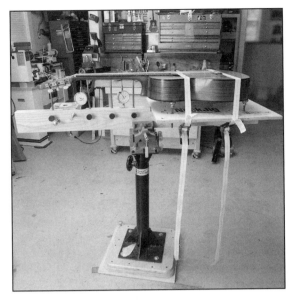

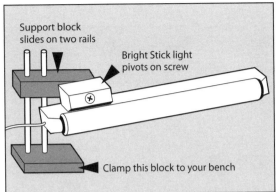

deep

Although I currently use this neck-stress jig for all my fret work, it was originally designed to help correct problem fret jobs: necks with twists, warps, humps and rises, or truss rods that don't work well. I wanted something that would duplicate the pressure of a fully strung guitar, so that as I worked on a neck, it would be under the same stress and in the same posture as when it was being played at normal string tension. I realized that because of gravity, the neck's straightness and relief when being held or hung from a strap in the playing position is different from when it's lying on its back with the strings removed. By using the neck jig, it's possible to gain a greater degree of control over any normal neck, and more important, it's easier to salvage the problem necks that are often found on rare and valuable vintage guitars.

Here's how it works The guitar is tuned to pitch, and the body, resting on padded levelers, is strapped firmly to the jig. At this point, the neck is suspended freely with ample space for stringing and unstringing. Now for the most important part: the neck jig, firmly clamped in a tilting vise mounted to a rigid floor stand, is tipped forward into the playing position — almost a 90° angle relative to the floor (I use 83° to 86°). Now the neck is analyzed from the side, using a good straightedge while looking for the proper amount of straightness or relief, depending on string gauge and action height. I use a fluorescent Bright Stick as a backlight. The light rides up and down on two rods, tilts to align with the fingerboard, and bolts to my rotating table top, following the work wherever it goes.

The tilting table eliminates the gravity factor, making it easier to adjust the truss rod, which controls the fingerboard's shape lengthwise. Note: With a properly working neck, there's always some pressure on the truss rod. With the strings in place, loosening a rod (turning counterclockwise) gives a straight neck relief, while tightening it (turning clockwise) removes excess relief, or "up-bow." Of course, tightening the rod too much causes a backbow away from the strings. Most players prefer a straight neck or one with a slight, controlled relief.

Once the neck is adjusted correctly, the two dial-indicators, lightly touching the back of the neck, are set to zero. Then the strings are removed, leaving them attached at the peghead (tuner) end. With no string pressure, the neck back-bows and the dials go crazy; then a small "peghead jack" pushes the neck back up into the playing position, returning both dials to zero. Now three neck support rods are brought into play. These steel rods with plastic protective caps are set into holes in the beam. First the rods are slid up to touch the back of the neck, and are locked in place with set screws. With the rods set, the neck jig is tipped back into the horizontal working position, and now gravity doesn't affect the neck's shape—the support rods and peghead jack are holding it in the same posture as when it was strung up. The neck jig eliminates the guesswork in fretting and allows me to control the truss rod, especially in problem cases.

Many fine vintage guitars have problem fingerboards. A great guitar can still have humps, rises, warp, twist, up-bow or back-bow. These are caused in part by the nature of the wood itself, but especially by years of playing with heavier strings and a tight truss rod. Remember that during the '50s and early '60s, light strings (beginning with a .010 high E and under) were not available, and most players used what today would be considered medium or heavy gauge strings. (Aa rare few used banjo strings to get those bluesy bends.) Many of these necks have taken on a definite "set" after years of stress. This isn't necessarily bad, but a fret dress or refret must be done carefully in order to avoid needless planing, sanding and scraping of the fingerboard. To me, the neck jig is a necessity in these cases.

Imagine the following situation: I received a '62 Fender Jazz Bass with severe problems. The neck was extremely back-bowed, which in itself is unusual, especially since the truss rod was completely loose. Worse still, the owner had tried to correct the problem in exactly the wrong way: by tightening the truss rod and breaking off the end of the rod along with its adjusting nut. I managed to replace the truss rod with one that worked, which got me back to the guitar's original problem: a back-bow with a loose rod. Here's where the jig helped greatly in solving the problem.

By stringing the bass up to pitch with the table tilted, I could see that the neck would become almost straight, but with none of the relief that most basses need. I supported the neck in this position, yet knew that with the strings removed, I couldn't loosen the truss rod to let the neck back onto the jig's rods. After removing the frets, I ran a guitar string through the empty fret slot at the 7th fret and tied it in a loop. This I hooked to a turnbuckle so I could tighten the neck down and hold it onto the jig's support rods. I was then able to scrape a little here, sand a little there, and by working carefully I managed to gain a little relief when stringing back to pitch. Next, I put

some pressure on the truss rod by tightening it slightly. The neck was now straight, and I rejigged it without the loop of guitar string.

This time around, I could set the neck back onto the rods by releasing the truss rod. I then scraped and sanded again, mostly in the middle of the fingerboard, but also a bit on the tongue and some at the 1st and 3rd frets. The next time I strung to pitch, I had good relief with no rod tension, slight relief with some rod tension, and a straight neck with good truss rod tension. At that point, I was able to proceed with a standard fret job. To me, this minor miracle could only have been accomplished with the neck jig.

The Plek machine: Look ma, no hands!

Something really new in the fretting world is the Plek fret dressing machine (*plek.com*). This is a CNC machine built just for guitar fretwork. It analyzes the condition, height, width, and accuracy of the frets and fretboard and stores the information. Depending on how the operator reads the information, upon his knowledge of fretwork, and his skill with running the machine, the Plek dresses the frets while the operator does something more fun and less tedious, than leveling, rounding and polishing twenty-plus frets.

The Plek was designed by **Gerhard Anke**, of Berlin, Germany; Gerhard and his partner **Michael Dubach** are the managing directors. In the US, the Plek is distributed by **Joe Glaser** (top photo, facing page), of Glaser Instruments in Nashville, Tennessee. Joe has been with Plek from early on, and has used, and studied it like a mad scientist.

"To me," says Glaser, "the Plek machine is like a guitar tuner. Today, I can't imagine living without a guitar tuner, and now I can't imagine not being able to see what's really going on with the neck. The Plek measures each fret relative to the fingerboard, then when the strings are removed, it levels and shapes them perfectly, regardless of the effect of the tension release.

"All of those things that I've always taken into account hand-dressing frets are still done, but once the parameters are programmed into the Plek, the actual work is turned over to the most accurate and consistent employee in the shop. That's the result of technology gone

right, to say nothing about the benefit of doing the hyper-accurate analysis scans with the neck at full string tension."

There are two versions of the Plek: the Basic, which performs the fret dressing mentioned above; and the Pro—which can also rough-shape a nut blank, cut the string slots it and leave a relatively small amount of finish

work for the operator.

After Joe, the next person to get on board the Plek train in the US was **Gary Brawer** (above), of Gary Brawer Guitar Repair in San Francisco, California. Gary told me, "By scanning a guitar before doing any fretwork, I can see exactly what the neck relief and fret alignment issues may be. Then, by doing a 'virtual fret-mill' on the computer — while the guitar is strung up and tuned to pitch — I can see the end result before beginning any work. I love being able to distribute the smallest amount of relief over any fret area I choose. The results are clearly documented, repeatable, and they help me decide whether the guitar needs new frets, or only a leveling

and dressing.

"If a refret is called for, I remove the guitar from the machine to do the work (often in my neck-jig) — then the guitar goes back in the Plek to scan and evaluate the refret, then perform the final mill, rounding and polishing as needed. The end result is a lower, even feel with less buzzing."

In the US, along with a half-dozen or so repairshops, several manufacturers have installed the Plek machine in their setup departments, including Martin Guitars, Heritage, John Suhr and Gibson.

Where to go for more on fretting

For those of you who aren't intimidated by the complex nature of fretting work and would like to learn more, these books are invaluable: Don Teeter's *The Acoustic Guitar, Vols. 1 and 2*, Hideo Kamimoto's *Complete Guitar Repair*, and Irving Sloane's *Guitar Repair*. Also I recently produced a three volume DVD series on fretting: *Fret Basics; Advanced Fretting Volumes 1 and 2*. Neck jig techniques are covered in detail on these DVDs. Also check out the photo-illustrated book I wrote for Stewart-MacDonald, *Fretwork Step-by-Step*.

Chapter 13

Nut replacement

basic

About nut replacement   219

d.i.y.

12 steps for replacing a nut   220
Tools   220
Removing the old nut   221
Roughing in the blank   222
Cutting slots, finishing up   222
String spacing   223

deep

basic

My first fix for a nut slot that was too low and causing the string to buzz on the 1st fret was putting a small, folded, piece of foil from a gum wrapper under the string. I was 17 or 18, and in my first band The Spiders. The guitar was a 1956 Danelectro U-2, and I still have it.

Later, when our band was playing at a fraternity party, it started buzzing again. I didn't have any gum, so I tore off a piece of matchbook cover, peeled it apart to thin it, and put that under the strings. It was a little muted, but not much because I was careful not let any paper hang off the front edge of the nut—that would have deadened the strings. It wasn't long before I realized that I could remove the nut and put a shim under it; I was becoming a do-it-yourselfer.

The point is, anything's better than nothing, and don't be afraid to mess with your first guitar, or otherwise you'll never learn. Now let's look at some better nut repairs…

d.i.y.

Nut replacement

The nut is one of the guitar's most important parts, affecting action, sound and playability. It's worth your while to learn to make perfectly-fitting nuts, but you might not achieve it on your first try. Don't quit: with patience and practice you'll be making beautiful looking, perfect-fitting nuts. You'll need a few specialized tools, but not many. And like always: practice on somebody else's guitar first — No, wait: I meant "Practice on yard sale specials first!" (Son't wreck a good one while you learn.)

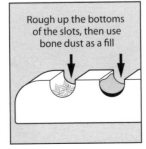

Rough up the bottoms of the slots, then use bone dust as a fill

You might avoid a nut replacement with this trick: if a slot's too deep, fill it with bone dust (created by sanding) and harden it with water-thin superglue. This is much like new bone, ready for refiling the slot.

d.i.y.

Nuts need to be replaced for a variety of reasons: the string slots are too low and cause buzzing at the 1st fret, the string spacing is irregular, or too wide, or too narrow to suit your taste, or the guitar just isn't producing a strong, clean sound (this is most often caused by plastic nuts). Maybe you've found a used guitar with a chipped-out slot on the nut. If your guitar plays well on fretted strings but annoys you on the open ones, the nut's probably worn out. If you were happy with the nut's general shape, you can remake it, copying the old nut's string width and spacing as closely as possible—simply leave the strings higher than before to eliminate buzz.

12 steps for replacing a nut

1 Remove the old nut.

2 Clean nut slot of glue and residue, and square it up.

3 Choose new nut material and rough-in the blank to fit the cleaned slot.

4 Lay out string spacing.

5 Rough-in the string slots, without going too deep.

6 Trim off excess nut material from the top as the slots get deeper.

7 Lower and shape the string slots, moving strings side to side, if needed.

8 Trim off excess material, rough edges and overhang.

9 Final-sand and contour the nut's shape.

10 Polish with a soft rag and rubbing compounds (especially the bottoms of string slots).

12 Final-check the string height and shape, then string the guitar to pitch.

13 Glue in the nut, with strings on for clamp pressure.

Tools

The right tools help make the job easier. You can make many of them yourself, and specialized items can be

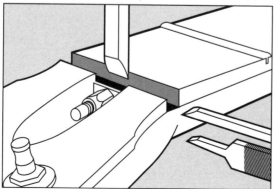

found at the luthier supply stores listed in the back of the book. Other items are available from hardware stores or woodworking suppliers.

A **sharp chisel** is great for shaving and scraping glue off the fingerboard's end; I like a 3⁄8" or 1⁄2" bench chisel for this job. A 1⁄8" chisel that's ground slightly thinner in width is also good, especially for getting into a Fender-style nut slot. You'll find a smooth mill file handy for shaping the nut, cleaning away old glue and helping with squaring-up. A small (6") mill file is also quite handy, since it's thin enough (.115") to file inside a Fender slot for squaring up, and the file's tang becomes a great scraper, chisel, etc. when sharpened on a grindstone (note the tang-sharpened file in the drawing). Specialized nut-seating files are also available in sizes to fit Fender, Gibson and Martin slots.

A set of **feeler gauges** is a help when measuring action height from the string's bottom to the top of the 1st fret. If possible, buy the kind that you can take apart by loosening a screw. In fact, feeler gauges are a must around any guitar shop, for all sorts of uses.

Small **razor saws** are often used to start nut slots, and in some cases to do the actual nut slotting. X-Acto makes a great razor saw set with three interchangeable saw blades of .012", .013" .014" thickness. Gauged saws are also available in sizes from .015" to .040". They take over where the X-Acto saws leave off. Saws are great for roughing in a slot depth in a hurry, but I prefer to finish up with rounded nut files.

Specialized **nut-shaping files** are available from Stewart-MacDonald, Luthier's Mercantile, and the C.F. Martin company. Custom-made for getting into nut slots, these rounded files have smooth sides that allow you to cut the nut slot bottom, without cutting the slot's sidewalls.

These precision nut files have accurate, well-shaped, round cutting edges, and cover sizes from .010" to .058". Full sets of files aren't cheap, but they're worth the money if you get serious about nut-making. You can also buy them one at a time; these three sizes make a good starter set: .016", .025" and .035".

A diamond nut file is one whose edges are coated in industrial diamond abrasive. Having no teeth, it doesn't run off the intended line as toothed files will.

An **X-Acto knife** with #11 blades is also a must. It's used to score the finish around the nut during removal.

6" stainless-steel rule that will read in 64ths of an inch is essential. The hardware-store variety made by General fills the bill; everyone should have one. Also check out the string action gauge from StewMac: it has a variety of scales. Having fractions converted to decimal equivalents on the back side is handy for string spacing. A dial caliper is always nice to have, but certainly not a must. Even the inexpensive plastic kind is plenty good enough for our needs. Nut spacing templates, with the string spacing already laid out are also available, and described below.

Whenever you're making or adjusting a nut, remember that string height at the nut is directly affected by the height at the bridge. You may need to work back and forth a bit from the nut to the bridge, by either raising or lowering an electric guitar's adjustable inserts or by filing, shimming or replacing an acoustic guitar's saddle. You should be basically satisfied with the action and playability of the guitar as it is (with the exception of buzzing from nut slots that are too low) before making a new nut, so that you don't discover at the job's end that the bridge was too high or low to begin with.

Removing the old nut

Before removal, score completely around the old nut with a sharp X-Acto knife or razor blade. This way, if the finish starts to chip upon removal, the chip will stop at the scored line. Most often the nut comes unglued after being tapped with a block of wood and a hammer. Firmly but gently tap from the front (fingerboard side) of the nut, and then tap from the rear. Do this back and forth until the nut rocks out of the slot. Once loose, grip it with your fingers and pull it out carefully. I can't overemphasize the need to watch out for chipping the finish! It's a risk you'll have to take. Many imported guitars with thick polyester finishes are hard to score, but not impossible. Wear safety glasses while scoring the lacquer or polyester and while knocking the nut loose. With Fender-style guitars, you'll have to grip the nut with some end nippers or pliers after gently loosening it by tapping, and then pull it out like a tooth!

Here's a nut-removal method from **Flip Van Domburg Scipio**, head of the Mandolin Brothers repair shop in Staten Island:

"When removing a nut from a guitar with a bound peghead, or one with a deep nut slot or heavy lacquer, I occasionally need to 'collapse' the nut instead of trying to knock it or pry it out. Saw through the nut with a fret saw until close to the bottom and then you can squeeze it together—pulling it away from delicate binding, finish or wood."

I took a pair of my flush ground fret nippers and ground the sharp jaws flat and dull. This works great as a "crusher" for removing the collapsed nut, and as a gripper for pulling saddles too. Once the nut's out, clean

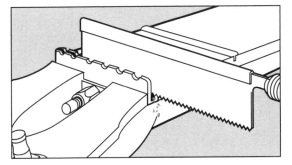

d.i.y.

any glue or residue from the nut slot (the groove that held it in the neck). Even on cheap guitars, the nut slot is generally uniformly shaped at the factory, but it needs to be scraped clean of residue for a good-fitting blank. Common nut thicknesses range from 1/4" to 3/16" (for Martin, Gibson, Guild and their acoustic clones) down to 1/8" (for Fender-style electrics). A variety of files and tools will fit in the slots for cleaning. I use a sharp chisel to remove any glue from the fingerboard's end grain and to trim any sticky stuff from the front edge of the headstock overlay. Held vertically and used with short strokes as a scraper, a chisel can be great for cleaning the bottom of the nut slot, too. The nut-seating files described earlier work the best. If you file the bottom of the slot, be sure to lightly file the lacquer's edge first, so that it won't chip as you begin to file the wood. To avoid pushing a chip of lacquer off the neck, always file in from each side toward the center.

Roughing in the blank

I prefer bone as a nut material, and no longer use commercial ivory, which necessitates the slaughter of elephants and other mammals with tusks. Don't even mess with sellers of "legal" ivory—they're lying. Bone makes an excellent nut, and synthetic Micarta is also good (Micarta's good to learn on because it's cheaper than bone).

Start with a blank that's bigger than the actual slot height, length and thickness, and slowly bring it down to size. Use the saddle-making techniques described in chapter 9 as a guide for squaring up the stock and getting it to fit the slot. (Quick repeat: Flatten one side against a smooth file, mark out the desired thickness and then sand, file or belt-sand the opposing side to uniform thickness.) Be sure the bottom is shaped exactly like the slot; Martin nuts, for example, have an angled bottom.

Leave a 1/8" overhang on both treble and bass ends to allow the nut to be shifted from side to side as you're laying out and filing the string slots. That way, if you happen to get a bit off on your string spacing, you can tap the whole nut towards treble or bass and relocate the string slots.

The nut should press into the slot and fit snugly. Viewed from the side or end, the blank should be gradually rounded toward the front edge (note the dotted line in drawing below). If it pleased you, copy the shape of the old nut. When the blank fits, trace the fingerboard's radius onto it from the front side by running a pencil over the fingerboard surface. Remove the blank and finish laying out the nut in pencil by adding the thickness of the frets (say .035"), the height of the strings from the fret top, the thickness of the string itself and a little extra for good measure. Most players prefer an action that's higher on the bass side than on the treble. (This treble-to-bass rise is illustrated in the previous two chapters.) Use care when taking the blank in and out, so you don't chip the lacquer or wood as a result of the tight fit.

Cutting string slots and finishing up

Before proceeding any further, lay some masking tape over the headstock face and on the fingerboard between the nut and 1st fret to protect the wood and finish from an accidental slip of the file. Use as many layers as possible without getting in the way of your work. On older guitars with brittle finishes, it's best to use low-tack draftsman's

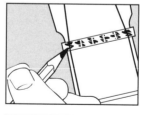

tape, which won't pull off the finish as aggressively.

Install the two outside E strings as far in from the fingerboard's edge as you like for spacing (I like

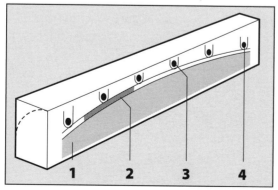

1   2   3   4

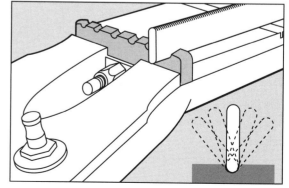

the outer edge of the E strings to be about .055" in from where the fret top meets the fret-end bevel) . Do this by looking down from directly overhead. Mark the outsides of the strings on each side of the nut with a pencil and file starter notches to hold the strings. The best tool for this is a thin X-Acto razor saw; it's also perfect for the actual filing/shaping of the slots for the high E, B and sometimes G strings. In general I use a specialized set of nut files that cut only on the thin edge and leave a round-bottomed slot. If a full set is too pricey, start with three files: .016", .025" and .035". These can cut most nut slots if you roll the file for extra width as you cut. This "roll-filing" action is the way to file slots. By using a file slightly smaller than the intended notch width and rolling on the forward stroke to widen the outside walls, you have more control and the file won't stick in its own notch.

A traditonal way to lay out string spacing on a nut is this: Once the outer strings are set in position, measure between their centers with the 6" rule or a dial caliper. Divide the distance by five to get an approximate equal spacing between all six strings. Use a calculator, because you'll be dealing in decimals—it's rare to find a nut width that's divisible by fractions. For example, if the outer E strings measure 1-3/8" center to center, the decimal conversion is 1.375 divided by 5, which equals .275 from string to string. I refer to this measurement as approximate because the lower wound strings, being fatter, would actually be closer to each other than the unwound treble strings when spaced exactly evenly. Use the exact measurement only for the initial layout, file very light starter slots, and then put on the remaining four strings. Now adjust the final between-string spacing by eye, as you file and lower the strings into the nut blank. Note that dividing by five gives equally spaced string-to-string centers, which is only a starting point.

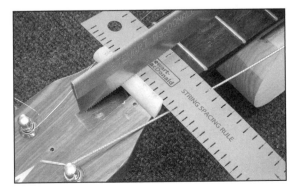

String spacing

The **string spacing rule** (below, left) is a new development that I think makes the traditional method a waste of time. The string spacing rule was designed by guitarmaker Kevin Ryan. It lays out the spacing dead-on, adapts to any nut width (saddles too) and positions strings proportionally so the fatter strings get the extra room they need.

When the string slots have all been started, just deep enough to hold the strings so that you can check them by eye, switch to your nut files, X-Acto saw blades and/or a fine-toothed hacksaw blade that's been ground down to cut a tiny slit. File at a angle sloping back from the nut's front edge, allowing the strings a good downward angle toward the string post. To play in tune, the string's actual contact point should be at the very front of the nut. On guitars with angled-back headstocks, which are the most common, you follow the angle of the headstock itself. With slab-neck Fender-style guitars, you won't file

as steep a back angle, so just file the appropriate angle needed for each string-post.

File the slots one at a time, starting with the high E. Loosen the string and lift it out of the slot as you file. Then replace the string, tune it to pitch and check your work. Expect to go back and forth from treble to bass several times before the slots get close to their final depth and shape. You'll need to keep filing the nut's top down as your strings get lower into the blank. In general, you want the strings to sit in round-bottomed slots, filed to the shape (diameter) of each string, and no deeper than one-half the string's diameter.

Here's a method for knowing when the strings are dropped enough in depth—using the feeler gauges described in the tool list given in the roughing-in section. You need to remove the protective masking tape from the fingerboard to do this:

1 Measure the height of the first two frets, from the fret's top to the fingerboard, by laying a straightedge across the two frets and sliding different combinations of feeler gauge blades under it until they just touch the straightedge. Record this measurement (let's say .035" for an average, somewhat worn fret height).

2 Add to this from .005" to .010" or any figure you come up with after experimenting. New total: .040" (.035" frets, plus .005").

3 Stack up a number of feeler gauges that equal the total measurement (.040"), and hold them against the front edge of the nut while you file at a normal backward

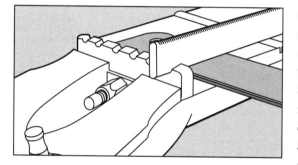

angle down to the metal. When your razor saw, nut file, or homemade hacksaw blade file contacts the hardened steel—you'll feel it instantly—it's time to stop.

The nice thing about this method is that you can control the drop of the string and avoid accidentally going too low. Also, when you find a good measurement for high E and B strings that is low and comes close to your final action, you can increase this amount by .002" or so for each string as you go across the radius of the board toward the bass side, slightly raising these strings more than their treble-string counterparts. When you find good average measurements, record them as a guide to use some other time.

When the string slots are well spaced and deep enough, do the final shaping and finishing. Using a very sharp pencil, mark the excess nut blank overhang and trim it off with your razor saw (file or sand if you prefer),

leaving a slight bit of the pencil line showing so that you can file and smoothly sand it away without chips. For the final time, sand down the top to eliminate any too-deep slots, finish rounding and shaping the nut to look like your original or the picture in your mind's eye, and sand off any scratches using 320-, 400- and 600-grit wet-or-dry sandpaper, in that order.

If you have any really deep scratches, you may find it easiest to remove them with your smooth mill file. Then buff the nut on a soft rag smeared with a buffing compound (I use ColorTone's #2 Medium). I like to high-polish the slot bottoms with 1200-grit Micro finishing sandpaper wrapped around my nut files or razor saw. Finally, dry-buff the nut surfaces on a clean dry rag. Care should be taken when sanding, smoothing and polishing the nut. Stay on the exposed surfaces and lay off the bone that actually fits into the nut slot—too much buffing here can create a loose fit when it comes to the gluing-in.

To be sure you have the action the way you like it, string the guitar to pitch before gluing the nut in. Recheck your string height and the relationship between nut and bridge. Don't be surprised if you have to take the nut in and out of the slot (stringing to pitch, as well) as many as a dozen times while you're learning. Expect some string breakage, too, from the constant tuning down and up to pitch. Most pros usually have a nut in and out of an instrument at least four times before completion, so don't feel bad.

If the final fitting meets your approval, glue the nut into place using a couple of light dabs of hide glue or white glue. I don't use super glue here, because its instant setting time won't allow you to move the nut from side to side when lining it up. Apply the glue lightly to the front wall and underside of the nut, set it in place, and quickly snug up the strings to hold it. After the glue has set (one hour for a white/yellow glue such as Titebond, and three or four hours for hide glue), you can tune to pitch and you're back in the business of making music.

Chapter 14

Bindings and pickguards

basic

d.i.y.

Loose bindings   225
Shrinking Strat pickguards   227
Regluing an acoustic pickguard   229

deep

d.i.y.

Fixing loose binding

One of the most common problems seen in a busy repair shop is loose binding. Bindings come loose along the fingerboard's edge, at the back or top edges where the sides join, on the peghead face and around the soundhole ring of an acoustic. Most bindings come loose because the wood shrinks in one direction (across its width), while the binding shrinks in the opposite direction (lengthwise). This shrinkage, combined with dry glue and sometimes improper gluing during construction, causes the bindings to come loose and catch any shirtsleeve that passes by. While most modern guitars are bound with celluloid, you might own a guitar with wooden binding. These bindings require a bit more experience to repair or replace, and although many of my tips also apply to wood bindings, this section deals with the more common plastic ones, which can be reglued easily with few tools.

Plastic bindings generally are glued with glue that's an acetone based, plastic solvent. Often this melts the plastic into the wood. Usually, such melted bindings won't come loose, but if they do, a bit of wood may come with them. If you need this type of problem repaired, have it looked at by a professional. More often, the plastic pulls loose with a clean separation—although if the joint has been loose for years, there may be a lot of dirt wedged into the gap. Obviously, this dirt should be removed before the regluing.

Cleaning the binding and the channel it sits in is easy. When the section of binding is completely separat-

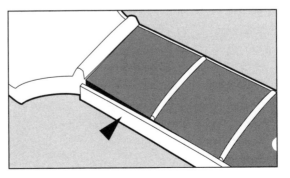

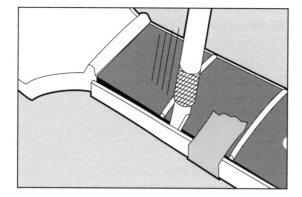

ed, gently remove any grease or dirt with a lint-free rag dipped in lighter fluid (I always wear disposable rubber gloves when I'm handling strong solvents). With a sharp X-Acto knife, you can cut, chip or gently scrape away any hard, caked-on dirt. Use the back of this blade as a scraper for pulling dirt from a crevice or from binding that is only loose in a section, with the main portion still glued tight (previous page). The idea is to remove foreign matter and grease. In the case of a binding that's loose for only a small area—say, from the 1st to the 5th fret along the fingerboard's edge—stretch masking tape across the point where it's still glued. This way, you can gently peel the plastic away from its glue channel to clean it without further loosening the section that is holding well (above).

Binding at the guitar's waist or any area where a sharp curve has to be dealt with, such as a cutaway, is difficult to reglue. So is the fingerboard binding over the tongue. The binding at the waist can shrink and pull away from the body, and because it has shrunk so much, the piece cannot be forced back to its original position. Carefully applied heat can soften the plastic and allow it to stretch into the original shape to cool—not a task for a beginner, though. Heat won't always work, either. Often the binding must be cut and a patching piece fitted into the resulting gap. This patching-in requires some experience, as well as a supply of different binding pieces for a proper match. The fingerboard tongue is somewhat difficult to clamp and requires specialized tools. Don't work on these areas if you're just starting out—leave them to someone with experience. Most other areas are easy to glue, and all you'll need for clamping pressure is a roll of masking tape (or preferably drafting tape).

Low-tack drafting tape perfect for clamping loose bindings on a peghead, fingerboard (though not over the tongue), and most body bindings. You can apply it near the loose areas on the guitar's side, top, back, peghead face or back of the neck. For best results, stretch the tape as you go around the guitar's edge. The stretched tape tends to pull the binding into its channel. Caution: On old, checked, thin-finished vintage instruments, be careful not to pull off finish when removing the tape after the glue has dried. Remove masking tape slowly, pulling at a slight angle to the tape's length.

Instead of tape, long rubber bands are an excellent way to hold bindings being glued, and they don't have adhesive to pull at old finishes. They can be used with, or instead of, masking tape. Made just for this purpose, these are called rubber binding bands. Always, always, do a dry run to make sure your parts fit, and your tape/bands/clamps are ready and you're familiar with where to put them. When you've got actual glue setting is no time to be figuring out your plan!

Titebond, carpenter's glue and hide glue are good glues, especially for a beginner. When the loose area is properly cleaned, these glues do an adequate job of holding the plastic in place—if left to dry overnight. White glues are water-soluble and offer the advantage of neat, easy cleanup. They usually run into cracks easily, but if you have difficulty, spread the crack with your knife tip and push glue in with a finger. Note: I usually do plastic binding repair with Duco Cement or super glue, but these glues should not be used by the inexperienced. Duco cement actually will bond by melting the binding itself, creating a real mess, and super glue sets too fast to allow enough working time for somebody who doesn't do this all the time.

Don't be alarmed if the binding is a little too short to fill the original gap. Remember that the plastic has shrunk from end to end. In order to stretch binding, you must use the Duco-type cement mentioned above. It actually softens the plastic on contact, allowing it to become somewhat flexible (the brand I use is Weld-On). However, this softening is the reason that I don't advise you to use this glue without experience. Don't try it on your old Les Paul or Martin D-28.

The usual problem with loose soundhole binding is that it pops up and out of its channel, often where two pieces butt together. While holding the piece up with your knife tip, work white glue in with a finger or by blowing it into the groove. Next, push the binding into place, wipe off the excess, and apply a small C-clamp for pressure. Use a piece of Plexiglas (lightly waxed so it won't stick) as a caul to hold it flat while drying (above). Protect the inside of the guitar from the clamp's jaw with a piece of wood or stiff cardboard. If you drill a few holes into the Plexiglas, the glue area will dry more easily. Leave the clamp on at least four hours. The proper-size clamp shouldn't cost more than a few bucks.

Be sure to study the problems mentioned here before attempting any repairs, and certainly don't do anything if you lack confidence. If you're at all in doubt, take your guitar to a qualified repairman and pay the small fee that these jobs usually cost. Most repairmen enjoy having a customer to talk shop with—someone who can appreciate the trade.

Shrinking Strat pickguards

Here's a note from a fellow who probably thought he was alone in the world with this trouble. I thought I'd share his problem, along with a solution:

"I have a '63 Strat that I dearly love. It's chipped and worn, and ugly to some, but it plays and sounds great. One thing worries me, though. The front pickup is almost touching the strings when I fret the high notes. I tried to lower it by loosening the two pickup height screws, but they move stiffly and the pickup goes nowhere. The pickup and screws seem to be stuck in the pickguard. Also, the pickup sort of leans at an angle. I'm afraid to take the pickguard off, but if I did, what difficulties might I run into?"

I've seen the problem you're describing, and some even worse. First of all, if you're unable to find professional help for your guitar or if you're afraid to mess with the pickguard, shim the neck slightly. This requires the consequent raising of the bridge inserts. The shimming moves the strings up and away from the pickups, and helps the fretted string clear the rhythm pickup's plastic cover. If your neck is already shimmed and the bridge inserts are as high as they'll go, or if you simply don't like the idea of a shim, you can fix the problem without too much trouble. You'll have to remove the pickguard, though.

If you decide to tackle the problem yourself, the heart of the matter is the celluloid/nitrate material from which the pickguard is made. Nitrate has a tendency to shrink and warp, while the wood body and metal shielding plate remain their original size (a plastic less prone to shrinkage was substituted for nitrate by about 1965). The nitrate's shrinking may cause the following annoying problems, some of which are correctable:

1 A mismatch between the mounting-screw clearance holes in the pickguard and the metal shield. Pulled by the shrinking plastic, the mounting screws slant toward center, often becoming hard to take out or put in. I prefer to leave these as they are. Trying to move or enlarge the holes in the pickguard could harm the guitar's value, and the slanting screws aren't really hurting anything, as long as they'll go in.

2 It sounds like your pickups have become squeezed by the surrounding plastic and are hard to move up or down, and that the height-adjustment screws are stuck in the metal shield clearance holes. These are off-center to the pickup height-adjustment holes, which have in turn shrunk and moved. To seat the pickups smoothly in their holes and make them adjustable again, you need to enlarge the holes in the metal plate as I'll describe.

3 The pickups tilt out-of-square to the strings as a result of the combined warpage and shrinkage. I've never had any success straightening out the warp, and don't recommend trying it on a vintage pickguard. The tilting pickups, however, will straighten up if you get rid of the squeezing plastic and clear out the shield-plate holes as mentioned earlier.

d.i.y.

Here's what you can do

You can remove the squeeze and relieve the tension. When the pickguard mounting screws are removed, lift the pickguard/shielding plate up gently, and turn it carefully over onto its face. Have a soft rag handy to place over the body cavity to protect both the finish and the pickguard face. The pickguard often sticks around the heel of the neck and at the bridge surround, so you may have to pry gently.

To make disassembly easier, the entire pickguard assembly can be removed by unsoldering the black (ground) and white (hot) wires at the volume pot as shown at right. Or, if you're careful, you can work with the pickguard still attached, but it's tricky. (The reason I stress taking your guitar to a pro is that experience minimizes the chances of accidental damage to the delicate copper windings.) In order to do this work, you need to remove the pickups and the tone controls from the pickguard and shield.

With a sharp Phillips screwdriver, remove the pickup height-adjustment screws. They may be stiff, but firm pressure will get them out. Be gentle when pulling pickups (still in their cover) out of the pickguard. You may have to wiggle them out. Keep the pickups inside their covers to protect the delicate copper windings, and handle them carefully. When the pickups are out and lying on the clean rag, remove the volume and tone controls. Now your pickguard and metal shield are free, and can be cleaned and worked on separately.

To enlarge the holes in the metal shield: From the underside, look at the mounting screw holes in the metal shielding plate. Because of shrinkage, they probably are no longer lined up with the holes in the pickguard. Use a small round needle file to file the holes slightly inward

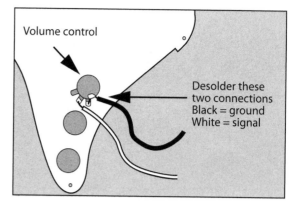

Volume control

Desolder these two connections
Black = ground
White = signal

towards the pickup (drawing, below). Or, you could also simply snip out a section of metal with small wire snips or scissors.

To clean the plastic that surrounds the pickup: scrape or file the slightest bit off the sides of the pickup hole. You'll find that it's mostly caked-on dirt, perhaps mixed with a vintage spilled pop or beer. To clean or alter the cutout's round ends, use a 1/2" wood dowel wrapped with 120-grit sandpaper. Sand small amounts from the rounded ends of the mounting hole; once again, it's mostly grime. It won't take much filing and scraping to get the pickup moving through its hole again. It doesn't even have to move smoothly—just enough to raise or lower. Don't overdo it.

You may also have to enlarge the pickguard's height-adjustment holes ever so slightly by filing outward, away from the pickup. Remember that shrinkage has caused these holes to creep a little closer to the pickups than is desirable.

When you replace the pickups, be as cautious as you were during disassembly. If you've worked carefully, there should be no visible change when all is back together. The pickups will now adjust up or down and sit level, since the rubber grommet or compression spring

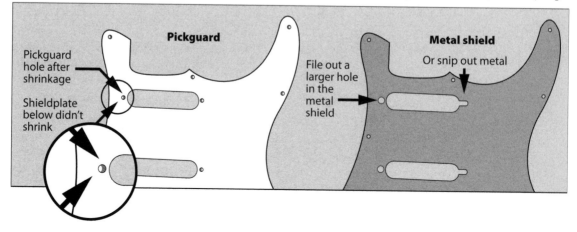

Pickguard

Pickguard hole after shrinkage

Shieldplate below didn't shrink

Metal shield

Or snip out metal

File out a larger hole in the metal shield

is able to do its job (pushing the pickup down, eliminating the tilt and allowing the pole pieces to sit level with the strings). Once again, do this work only if there's really a problem. Otherwise, just play the guitar and don't take a chance with its vintage value.

Regluing an acoustic pickguard

My friend **Frank Ford** is one of the great guitar repairmen. Frank and I have lots to talk about: both the same age, both love teaching our trade, both love fixing guitars, both love machinery, both getting bald and so on. Frank's website, *FRETS.com* is one that anyone reading this book will love to visit. Frank partners with **Richard Johnson**, owning and operating Gryphon Stringed Instruments, in Palo, Alto, California. It's one of the leaders in sales and repair of acoustic instruments.

I asked Frank to show you how to remove and replace a shrinking, warping pickguard on a flattop — a very common repair on the black-guard Martin guitars of the 1960s-80s. He's done this repair a hundred times or more. Here's Frank:

"Solvent or solvent glues are the customary way to get celluloid to stick really well to itself or to wood. Martin used solvent to adhere celluloid pickguards from about 1930 to 1985. The backs of the pickguards were coated with solvent and the pickguard was placed on the top of the guitar and weighted until the solvent dried. Then the guitar was finished right over the pickguard.

"Later, as a result of age, heat exposures or just bad luck, the pickguard began to shrink. Often the pickguard pulled loose and began to curl up at the edges. Sometimes the glue held so well that the pickguard caused the top to become concave in that area. The stress of shrinkage is so great that cracks in the spruce are fairly common at the edge of the pickguard when it shrinks.

"Bear in mind that Martin is not the only company to glue pickguards in this way, they're just the oldest and most consistent brand. Gibson and Guild pickguards are frequently very similar, and present more structural problems only because they are often larger.

"When I first became a warranty repairman for Martin, the accepted procedure for repairing the concave top was to laminate spruce underneath to make it more rigid. Turns out, however, that with continued shrinkage, the top would just sink again. One must not underestimate the "skin effect" of shrinkage or expansion in laminated materials!

"I figured that releasing the tension would be preferable, and worked on developing a more conservative approach to the problem. Quite a number of years ago I came up this system to reglue pickguards, and I've had very good success. Even though the reglued pickguard is somewhat smaller from shrinkage, it looks very good when reglued neatly. Here's how I go about it:

"The patient is a standard D-35, and the pickguard is obviously curling at the edges. As I press down at the very edge, it takes quite a lot of force to mash it down. Most people assume it's too strong to be glued.

"My first job is to loosen the pickguard and release it from the top. I'm being very careful not to let my knife drift downward into the grain of the top. Now is a good time to "read" the top grain. If I feel resistance while I'm pressing one direction, I may turn and try another.

"By watching my progress in reflected light, I can really see and feel what's going on under there.

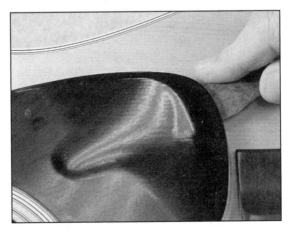

"The pickguard is especially tightly glued to the soundhole rings. I've even seen the soundhole rings lifted right out of the top by a curling pickguard. I'll take advantage of the strong bond by leaving at least half of the ring attached to the pickguard. That way I won't actually lift the guard off entirely, and I'll have no trouble keeping it in exactly the right position for regluing.

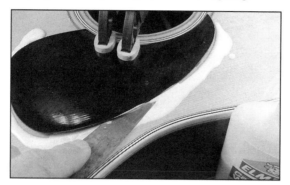

"When the pickguard is released from the wood, there are tiny wood fibers adhering to the surface of the celluloid. Although it wouldn't have worked for the original gluing operation, I now can use aliphatic resin, or regular carpenter's wood glue. I'll just smear some under.

"I hold the pickguard tightly at the rings so I don't lose that precious connection while I load up the underside with glue. I've thinned the glue just a little, say five or ten percent, with water.

"I'll iron out the pickguard by pressing it down with my fingers to squeeze out all the glue that I can, then wipe with a damp rag to clean it off the surface.

"It's time to clamp up. I need to apply a lot of clamping pressure to flatten this unruly pickguard. This is the caul I've made to go inside—it's as big as I could make it and still get it inside. It's cut away to fit over the top braces and spans an area just a bit larger than the pickguard. Made of two layers of 3/4" plywood, this thing is rigid.

"I have a top caul the size and shape of the pickguard made of 3/4" hardwood with a 1/4" acrylic clamping surface, and an ebony lamination to take my heavy clamp pressure. I lay on a sheet of waxed paper to avoid gluing my caul to the pickguard. I really load on the pressure! I can get four strong clamps on a dreadought pickguard.

"I'll jam a rag under the waxed paper and get as much squeeze-out wiped off as I can, but there will still be a lot of squeezed out glue left. After cleaning up as much glue as possible, I let it dry overnight.

"The next day, with the clamps and cauls off, I pick off the waxed paper and clean up: aliphatic resin glue cleans up slowly, but well, with water; I use water with a little detergent so it gets sudsy and can sit on the surface for a while to soften the glue. Repeated squirting and wiping gets all the glue off the surface without loosening the pickguard, if I don't let it sit there too long.

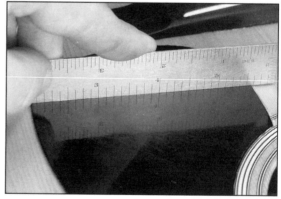

"All done! The pickguard is now tightly reglued and it is *flat*. This technique leaves the instrument in the most original condition possible, it's not particularly difficult or dangerous and it can be done again when the pickguard shrinks some more (and it will)."

Chapter 15

Guitar electronics

basic

d.i.y.

Tools and supplies for electronics	231
Soldering technique	234
Using a multimeter	235
Caps and pots	235
Switches	237
Shielding	238
Acoustic guitar amplification	240
Semi-hollowbody wiring	250
Pickup replacement	251
Pickup repair	256
Rewiring, modifications	260
Wiring diagrams	262

deep

Wind your own pickups	264

d.i.y.

With the exception of rare, vintage instruments, guitar electronics is one area of repair where someone operating at the basic level usually can't do much permanent damage. Sloppy solder joints can always be done over, and most burned-up parts are easily replaced.

To excel in guitar electronics, you must be able to take guitars apart and put them back together with your eyes closed. That means paying close attention the first time around, and the second and the third. Sketch out what you see before you dismantle it—make your own schematic. I do this all the time—at least for every new experience. Removing control cavity cover plates, pickups, pickguards, bridges, tailpieces, potentiometers, selector switches and the like is common—even for the simplest repair. Use an ice-cube tray as a parts organizer, since losing parts is the nemesis of many an otherwise well-meaning repairman. And if you don't know guitar parts well, draw a map of which parts went where. Disassembly/assembly tools are the basis of an electronics tool box, and you may have many of them already.

Tools for electronics work

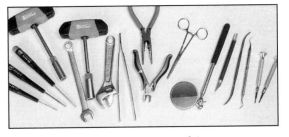

Common tools (not electronics-specific)

Small screwdrivers Phillips and flat-blade, in a range of sizes from 0 to 2.

Wrenches Sockets, open-end wrenches and nut drivers in the 1/4" to 1/2" range (metric sizes are useful, too).

Pliers and cutters Needlenose pliers, wire cutters, small wire snips and hemostats.

Inspection mirror Handy for finding a problem without removing anything.

d.i.y.

X-Acto knife with the #11 blade helps in cutting insulation lengthwise before stripping.

Curved-bottom file to remove plating or oxidation from the back of potentiometers that won't take solder; 220-grit sandpaper also works.

Probe Some sort of electronics probe or sharp, fine-pointed dental tool is needed to fish wire through holes, separate braided shielding, etc. The curved dental type can grab around potentiometer shafts and snake them through mounting holes.

Screw extractors to remove screws with stripped heads (left). You'll love this tool if you've ever tried to remove miniature screws with slots that are rusted, filled with dirt, stripped and mangled, or a combination of these problems — especially Gibson's Phillips-head pickup mounting ring screws!

Specialty electronics tools

Switch-nut wrench This uncommon but valuable tool is used for removing the knurled nut on a toggle switch. Most repairmen have seen lots of vintage switch nuts mauled by slipping pliers or Vise-Grips.

Soldering iron I generally use an Ungar 45-watt pencil type with small and medium chisel tips, and an insulated stand to set it in while hot. With most guitar electronics, you want to get the parts on and off fast, so usually the little 15- or 20-watt pencils don't

cut the mustard (but they are handy for some delicate parts like transistors).

Solder-sucker or desoldering tool, is a mechanical device that cocks like a dart

gun and creates a vacuum when you release the trigger. It's used for sucking molten solder away from parts. Another type uses a rubber squeeze-bulb; this one looks like an ear syringe, but it's Teflon-lined so the solder

doesn't burn through.

Soldering jig also known as a third hand, has a weighted base and adjustable arms with alligator clips that keep delicate parts aligned for soldering.

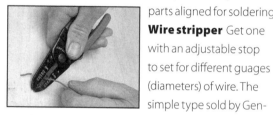

Wire stripper Get one with an adjustable stop to set for different guages (diameters) of wire. The simple type sold by General works fine.

Heat sinks clip temporarily onto the leads of delicate parts being soldered or de-soldered. These clips absorb the heat, so it doesn't move up the wire and burn nearby components. The small (1" to 1-1/2") brass, copper or aluminum alligator clips sold at Radio Shack work well.

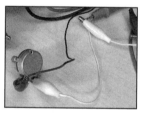

Jumpers Small lengths of wire with alligator clips at each end, these are used for temporarily checking a wiring plan before soldering it together.

Tuner cleaner and lubricant is used to flush out and lubricate "scratchy-sounding" and stiff or sticky volume and tone controls. DeoxIT is the brand I use.

Multimeter Also known as a VOM (volt-ohm meter), this is the most important tool. It's used to diagnose most of a guitar's electrical ills. A good meter doesn't cost much—from $30.00 to $50.00 buys a nice one. Choose one that reads DC resistances of at least 500,000 ohms.

Tester plug This is a 1/4" plug with its leads soldered to alligator clips. Plug it in, turn up the volume, and get a quick reading of a pickup's DC resistance.

Those are the basic tools; use this as a shopping list as you add to your toolbox. Now, let's look at supplies such as wire, shielding materials, potentiometers, capacitors and switches, and then spend some time working at the bench.

Supplies

Solder Use 60/40 resin-core solder (60% tin; 40% lead), which melts at 374°.

Wire One of the best all-around wires for guitar electronics is tinned, stranded copper wire. Being stranded, it bends easily without breaking, and the tinning (which turns the copper to a silver color) means the wire's ready to solder with no additional tinning necessary. Choose a wire to suit your needs from the following list. Except for the last one, they're all tinned, stranded copper

Single-conductor with plastic insulation (usually black, red or white) is your basic hookup wire; shielding isn't necessary. Some versions use Teflon insulation, which isn't melted by the soldering iron's heat.

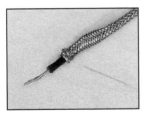

Coaxial Coax is a single-conductor wire with an insulating sleeve wrapped in a braided shield that protects the inner core from interference. This wire is used as a ground in many situations. Some coax types have a plastic outer jacket, while others have only the wire braid. Most Gibson pickup leads are this type of wire, having a stranded core, black cloth insulation and an outer braid that's used as the ground. Coax with Teflon features non-melting Teflon insulation.

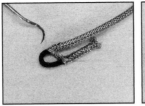

Use your dental probe to reach into a braided sleeve and pull out the inner wire.

Four-conductor wire has a foil shield plus a fifth stranded ground wire all in a plastic jacket. This "multi-lead" wire is used for four-wire humbucking pickup conversions. The foil shield is the best shielding you can get: 90% effective.

Push-back wire is a vintage style with a cloth insulating wrap that doesn't need to be stripped away; just push it back to reveal the conductor.

Small hookup wire It's convenient to have small (22 to 25 gauge) hookup wire. Usually this is solid copper single-strand wire, in red, white or black insulation. This makes a good jumper for short runs such as terminals on mini switches, etc. It also makes a good, strong ground wire.

Shielding I use two types of shielding: conductive copper foil, and conductive shielding paint. The foils comes in 2", 3/4" and 1/4" widths.

Heat-shrink tubing This insulates and encloses wire connections, shrinking to a snug fit when a flame is put under it. I use it in sizes ranging from 1/16" to 3/8".

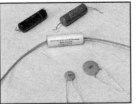

Capacitors known as caps, are rated microfarads (μF). You may find many different ratings used, but commonly .05μF caps are used with single-coil pickups (many Fenders), .02μF caps are used with humbuckers (many Gibsons).

Potentiometers Pots are used for volume and tone

d.i.y.

controls. They're a resistors that are variable, increasing/decreasing their resistance as you turn the knob. With a few exceptions, the control pots used in guitars are "audio taper" pots, not "linear taper." Pots are rated in kOhms, which we'll abbreviate as "k".

500k pots are typical in Gibsons, and a push/pull (switched) variety is also available.

250k pots are what you'll find in Fenders (push/pull versions also available).

Blend pots are for panning from one source to another.

25k pots are used for volume/tone controls with active pickup circuits (push/pull versions also available).

1mg pots (1000k) are used infrequently.

Soldering technique

Replacing a pot is pretty easy, when you can get at it. Teles, Strats and Les Pauls have easy access, but getting at the pots in a 335 semi-hollowbody can be a toughie. Before desoldering anything, make a drawing of which wires and parts went where.

Most pots have delicate wires and many have a ceramic capacitor wired to them. Protect these parts by clipping heat-sinks to the leads before de-soldering. This operation is made easier if you use a solder-sucker, so the metal can't reflow and harden as soon as you remove the iron. When the pot's free, remove it and throw it out—you don't want to start saving them!

When you solder in a new pot of the same rating, tin the connections first. This means adding solder to the lugs and to the metal case before re-installing the wires (any wires or capacitors are still tinned from the original installation). When parts are tinned before soldering, the actual connection goes much more quickly. Touch the soldering iron to the part, let it heat up, and then flow the solder to the part—not to the iron's tip. A good solder joint looks slippery, shiny and silvery—not dull, grayish and dry. Solder spits, so wear protective goggles, button up your shirt collar (and no shorts or short-sleeved shirts!) and protect any good finishes nearby (your guitar, the table top, etc.).

Use a soldering iron rated anywhere from 15 to 45 watts. The lower-wattage iron has less chance of burning up a part, but then again a higher-wattage iron gets on and off the part fast. I often use a chisel-tip 80-watt

Weber iron—it's great for adding solder to the back of a pot for a ground. Or, if I want to break a solder joint that's an obviously clean connection (stripped wire poking through the hole in the pot's lug, and not wrapped around it), the 80-watt is still my favorite. It's not uncommon to own soldering irons of several watt ratings. The 45-watter is my favorite all-around iron, although it's a little hot in some delicate situations.

I use a "soldering station" iron that has a variable temperature. It gets hot fast, so I keep it on idle at about 300°. It goes up to 900°. The melting point of rosin core 60/40 solder (the type we use in guitar electronics) is 370°.

Keep your iron's tip tinned (shiny with solder) from the moment you first turn it on, and clean it often during use by wiping it on a damp sponge. A tip that doesn't get tinned the first time it's used may burn up and never do a good job of soldering.

Don't forget to use heat-sinks on delicate work.

Insulating with heat-shrink tubing

Heat-shrink, or "spaghetti tubing" as it's known, will be in constant use in your shop. By sliding it onto one of two wires to be joined (or one wire to be insulated from another) before soldering, you can do away with sticky electrical tape. (Don't ever use masking tape; it turns stiff, yellow and crumbly.) Heat-shrink tubing insulates wires that shouldn't touch, and its stiffening effect strengthens connections. Plus, it makes even sloppy work look professional.

Choose heat-shrink in a size that not only slides over a given wire, but will fit over the solder joint you're going to make. You'll want to have it on hand in sizes ranging from 1/16" to 3/8". Use the smallest size you can get by with, and slide it far away from the connection while you solder. Wait until the solder cools before sliding the heat-shrink over the new joint (so it doesn't shrink before you can get it over the joint). Then heat it with a match and watch it shrink and compress tightly around the wires. Rotating the wire as you heat the tubing creates a uniform contraction (professionals use heat-shrink guns similar to small hair dryers). Multiple wires going to a common terminal point can be bundled together with heat-shrink tubing, making it easier to thread them through holes.

Using a multimeter

You'll use a multimeter *constantly* to troubleshoot problems and test parts. Buy one that has a digital readout (a needle/scale combo is hard to read, especially on an inexpensive meter). You also want one that's "auto-ranging," which means it finds the correct range automatically. I use the Fieldpiece LT83A Digital Multimeter. The four settings I use are DC voltage, AC voltage, ohm scale (for reading resistance) and continuity. You won't be needing the AC voltage range for guitar electronics, but the other three settings are used all the time. This meter comes with a removable magnetic belt clip (for climbing phone poles or something). I suggest removing it—you don't want magnets around an electronics work area.

The DC voltage scale is handy for checking batteries. A guitar with a preamp, active pickups or active circuitry needs its batteries checked often. Put the meter's black lead on negative and the red lead on positive for an instant battery check. Any 9-volt battery that reads less than 7 volts should be replaced.

Continuity testing's easy, and if your meter has a beeper, which mine does, you can see and hear continuity. In the meter's continuity setting, touching both probes to any conductive surface or surfaces (ends of a wire, copper-foil or conductive-paint shielding, pickup-cover to ground bridge to ground, etc.) lets you know if there's an uninterrupted connection or a dead short.

Use the ohms function to check pickups: the pickup's output wires will include a hot lead (usually white) and a ground lead (usually black). These may be two separate wires, or a coaxial wire with single-conductor center (hot) and a braided shield used as ground. Touch one test probe (red or black, it makes no difference) to the hot

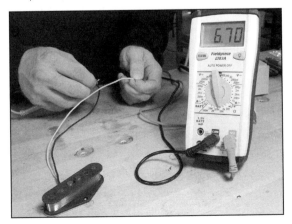

wire and one to the ground wire. This gives you a reading of the pickup's DC resistance in ohms. A Strat pickup, for example, should read from 5.5–6.75k ohms, and a standard Gibson humbucker should read from 7.2k to 8k ohms (new ones are 7.6k ohms). Some hot humbuckers, such as Gibson Dirty Fingers and DiMarzio Super Distortion, read twice that—12k to 14k ohms. Since it has two coils, the humbucking pickup is generally more powerful than a single-coil, but not always. A modern 4-wire pickup has four leads coming out of it, and each coil can be read separately; they should read the same. Pickups or coils with weak ohm readings or none at all are defective and must be repaired, rewound or replaced.

Caps and pots

Capacitors play an important part in your guitar's tone. They act like filters or gates, allowing only very high frequencies to pass through them. With this capability in mind, they're wired into circuits at locations where a simple piece of wire would result in a short circuit (no sound). The cap instead allows only the very highs to short to ground, removing them from the tone. The reason this is controllable is that they're connected to a pot that determines how much of the signal gets to the cap. If you turn the knob to let all of the signal get to the cap, you get a bassier tone. If you only let a little bit, or none, of the signal get to the cap, you keep your bright highs in your tone. That's a simple tone control.

Older guitars have the "Tootsie Roll" type with multi-colored rings to denote their value, while more modern instruments use either thin ceramic disks, square or rectangular plastic-dipped types or foil-wrapped versions encased in a plastic housing. Most single-coil pickups (Strats) use a .05μF capacitor, while humbuckers (Les Pauls) use a .02μF.

As former Gibson engineer **Tim Shaw** points out, "Gibsons have darker-sounding pickups and need smaller capacitors to cut off fewer highs. Our usual guitar capacitor value is .02μF. Fenders, on the other hand, have more top end and traditionally use larger caps to be able to roll off more highs. Fender's guitar caps are usually .05μF. Basses can be .05μF, or even .1μF. These values are for high-impedance circuits only. The lower the impedance, the higher the capacitor value. EMG pickups, for instance, use much higher capacitor values in their tone controls."

d.i.y.

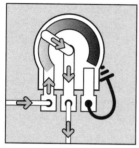

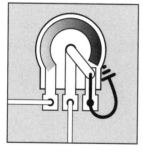

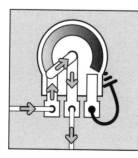

d.i.y.

Changing to a cap of a different value has an immediate effect on your sound, and is a harmless way to experiment, since you can always get back to your starting point by reinstalling the original cap. I like to measure a cap before installing it—especially old caps salvaged from radios, amps and other capacitor junkyards. To measure a capacitor's value you need a Sine-ometer; a regular multimeter doesn't have that funcion.

Potentiometers are variable resistors that turn various functions on, off and in between. Here's a simple illustration of a volume pot.

The signal enters the input lug, and exits through center output lug. To do that, it travels across the horseshoe-shaped band of resistive material to the metal wiper, which is fastened to the control shaft. Rotating the wiper, you determine how much of the resistor the signal has to get through. You're dialing in more or less resistance.

Notice that the lug on the right is soldered to the pot's casing. This grounds that end of the resistor, so if the wiper is turned to the very end of its rotation the signal goes immediately to ground and is silenced. That's an Off state; the amp hears nothing. Notice that this Off isn't due to the resistor blocking the signal, as is commonly believed; it's due to a deliberate short circuit to ground.

At the other end of the horseshoe, there's no resistance for the signal, so that's full volume.

Cleaning pots

Due to wear, dirt, dust, or spilled drinks, a bad pot might not work at all (no volume or tone change), or might have a scratchy, dirty or intermittent sound. In most cases, simply spraying a pot with contact cleaner cures its symptoms. (DeoxIT is a good brand of pot and switch cleaner.) Stick the cleaner's hose tip into the opening in the side of the pot's case, and spray liberally. Tilt the pot so the cleaner can run back out, flush away dirt while you turn the shaft. If your guitar has sealed pots with no hole to spray into, remove the knob and pull up lightly on the shaft. You'll see a little movement. Squirt here, and the very thin cleaner usually finds its way to the problem. Contact cleaners are available from radio/TV service shops. Don't forget to wear safety glasses, and be sure to protect the guitar's finish from the cleaner.

Here's a neat pot cleaning tool I saw being used on a visit to the Gruhn Guitars repair shop in Nashville. It's a round piece of brass 2" long x 1/2" in diameter. It's drilled and tapped to thread onto a potentiometer shaft, and on the opposite end is a small hole that fits the plastic tube of a spray pot cleaner. This way the cleaner is forced into the pot, and you can clean a pot from outside the guitar without having to remove it. The photo shows the tool on the left, and a version you can make yourself on the right: a plug in a piece of plastic tubing.

Testing a Pot's Resistance

If cleaning doesn't cure a pot's ills, test the pot with your multimeter: Set the meter to the ohm scale and practice on a pot that isn't wired into a circuit. Using both probes, touch one to each of the outer two lugs for a true reading of the pot's resistance. Now, if you put the test

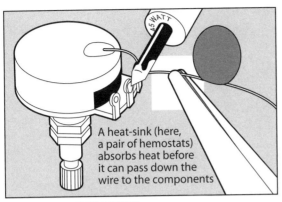

A heat-sink (here, a pair of hemostats) absorbs heat before it can pass down the wire to the components

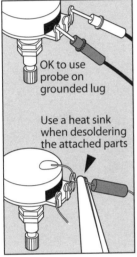

OK to use probe on grounded lug

Use a heat sink when desoldering the attached parts

Switches

Mini switches are as important to guitar electronics as capacitors, potentiometers, shielding paint and the like. These little toggle switches control most of the hot-rod and custom wiring options you're likely to try ("dual-sound," pickup phasing, coil cutting, series/parallel, etc.). Because of their small size, you can fit one or more of these switches into most control cavities without having to use a router to enlarge or re-shape the cavity walls; and for mounting, you only need to drill a 1/4" hole for the small shaft. You can buy double-pole or single-pole mini switches. Double-pole switches have two sets of three terminal lugs, while single-pole have only one set. I stock double-pole, because even though they're a little bigger, they do anything a single-pole does, and more.

probes on an outer lug and a center lug, the resistance will vary from 0 ohms to the true rating of the pot (250k, or whatever) as you turn the pot's shaft.

You can test a pot that's wired into a circuit using this method, but note: for a pot with a pickup wired to one lug and an outside lug grounded to the case (as is usual), you must de-solder one of these two connections. Detach either the pickup or the grounded lug before you can get the pot's reading. Without de-soldering, you simply get a reading of the pickup itself. If there is no pickup wired to a pot, the bent-back/soldered lug poses no problem, and you can test the pot normally. If a pot's good, re-solder the parts you disconnected, and you're back in business. Consider replacing a pot that isn't within 20% of its rating.

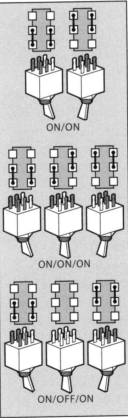

ON/ON

ON/ON/ON

ON/OFF/ON

The three most common double-pole mini switches are on/on, on/off/on and on/on/on. **On/on** controls pickup phasing, coil-cut (or two pickups coil-cut at once) or series/parallel. **On/off/on** puts a single-coil pickup in-phase, out of phase or off, and may be used for pickup selection. **On/on/on** can work like a Gibson Les Paul toggle switch (lead pickup, both pickups, rhythm). It can give series, single-coil and parallel selections for a humbucker, or act as a pickup selector switch for three pickups at once. The drawings show which terminals are hot when the lever is thrown.

With double-pole switches, each side (or pole) has three wiring lugs. Each side is independent of the other side, although they can be used together. In fact, it's common to "jump" from one pole to another, like the cross-corner terminals used during phasing, for example (as in the drawing, next page).

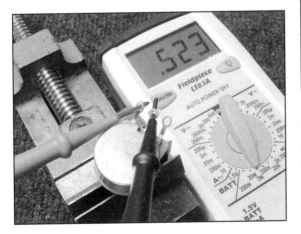

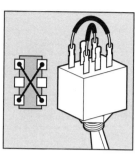

For short jumpers on mini switches, try this combination: Remove the plastic jacket from solid-copper wire and the Teflon jacket from a stranded wire, and then slide the Teflon over the solid core. This kills three birds with one stone, since the solid core easily pokes through a terminal's hole, it won't fall to pieces like a short strand and its Teflon won't melt on the crisscrosses and cause a short. When wiring a mini switch, don't rest your iron too long on any one lug, because most switch bodies are made from plastic. In the next section we'll use a mini switch to control the wiring options of a four-wire humbucking pickup.

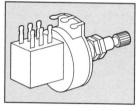

If space is tight or you don't wish to drill a 1/4" hole in your guitar for a mini switch, consider replacing a tone or volume pot with a push/pull potentiometer. These are normal pots with a piggyback mini switch that operates separately from the pot. Your tone or volume will still work as usual, but you have the option of controlling another function with the switch.

Megaswitch There are four different versions of the Megaswitch: **P** (for 2 humbuckers), **S** (5-way Strat style), **T** (3-way Tele style), and **E** (for 3-pickup combinations of single coils and humbuckers). The Megaswitch E allows wiring arrangements you can't get with a standard 5-way guitar switch, including automatic coil tapping and special hum-cancelling connections.

Super Switch This switch gives you a whole lot of possiblities. Coil cuts, series/parallel combinations, phase reversal and more can all be done with a Super Switch. The switch has a total of 24 solder terminals (lugs), divided into four separate circuits, or poles,

and each pole has six lugs, a common with five others. Many lever switches use the common lugs as outputs only, but with the Super Switch this is not necessarily going to be the case. The commons of this switch can be used to connect pickups together—an important concept to understand when designing custom wiring for this switch. There are so many possibilities with the Super Switch that I've included a chart of them in among the wiring diagrams. See page 273.

Shielding

Shielding your guitar's wiring helps give you a hum-free signal. Using shielded wire wherever possible is a good bet, but you can further eliminate hum by shielding the body cavities, wire channels and the pickguard with conductive shielding paint or copper foil. The paint is laced

with nickel, which creates a conductive barrier that AC hum and radio signals can't penetrate. Shielding paint is easy to use. Here's how:

✔ Work in a well-ventilated area, with eye protection.

✔ Use cheap, throwaway acid brushes to apply it (the kind found in plumbing supplies).

✔ Build up two coats, and test your work using your multimeter as a continuity tester. Touch various areas to make sure there's continuity.

✔ The shield is conductive, so it must not touch any part of the circuit other than the ground, or it could short the circuit.

✔ When you're finished shielding, run a wire from the shield to ground. The more carefully you shield, the cleaner your signal will be.

Copper foil is also a great shield. Shielding a surface such as the back of a pickguard is easy with foil, and it's cleaner than paint. But doing a body cavity is a different story. Shielding foil comes in rolls or sheets with a self-stick back; you peel away the protective layer, and it sticks to almost anything (mostly your hands). Shielding a cavity with foil is like making a slip cover for a couch or chair: You cut different pieces to shape (the bottom, sides, etc.) and then "paste" them in place with the self-stick. Let one piece overlap the other by 1⁄4", and then solder each joint—this is the ultimate shield!

Shielding definitely cuts down on 60-cycle AC hum, but along with the unwanted hum it removes certain qualities associated in a positive way with a Strat's sound. Ex-Fender Custom Shop master builder **Fred Stuart** said: "It was always my observation at Fender that when you shield the control cavity, you lose some noise, but you also lose some of the sparkle".

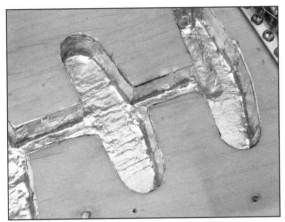

I had the pleasure of re-fretting two of **Carlos Santana's** Strats this year—a '65 sunburst and a '63 Lake Placid Blue. The shielding on the '65, installed by **Larry Craig**, was as good as I've ever seen. The Lake Placid Blue had a split in the body near the neck cavity, and to fix it I needed to remove the pickguard with its electronics to fix it. I didn't want this old pickguard to shrink or change shape while I was working, so I screwed it down to another Strat body to keep it stable.

I finished the fret job right before Christmas, and I sent it back to Carlos with this photo of me about to go to a holiday party. He got a kick out of it, and replied with a friendly thank you note, a vase of flowers and with some Santana artwork signed by the man himself.

BPSSC System: single-coil sound without noise!

Hats off to **John Suhr** and his Backplate Silent Single Coil System (**BPSSC**)! Finally, after over 50 years, I'm getting a true single-coil sound without the noise. I've always accepted noise as a "necessary" artifact that couldn't be eliminated without compromising the tone. It's even one reason that I didn't stick to playing a Strat more. The system eliminates the noise but keeps the sonic character of pure single-coil pickups. The noise is gone but the sparkle, the chime and the low-end response that we love in single-coil pickups is still there.

This is a medium-easy installation, if you know how to solder and make heat-shrink connections. The only invasive modification to your guitar are the solder connections. A pro player willing to ignore vintage guitar prices might install it in a really old Strat, but most of us wouldn't risk that—but still leaves loads of Strats that'll benefit from this.

You remove the current backplate on your guitar, solder the wires from the BPSSC to your guitar's electronics, then screw the BPSSC on the back of your guitar. That's it—you're done. I installed it in my Strat in an hour and a half—but I take it slow on stuff like that.

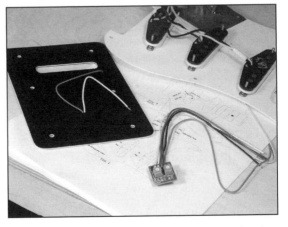

The BPSSC is optimized to work with single-coil pickups with the DC resistance ratings between 6K Ohms and 8k. It requires the middle pickup to be the same polarity and the same winding direction as the bridge and neck pickups. A reverse-wound reverse-polarity middle pickup won't work with the BPSSC.

I'd heard about the BPSSC, and wanted to try it, but at that time John was only using the system on his own line of guitars. Now he's taken it public, and I'm glad he did!

Acoustic guitar amplification

Finding a good amplified acoustic sound used to be a lot harder than it is today. Back before there were so many options, my first attempt (and I liked it) was to simply *tape* a P-90 pickup into the soundhole of my Gibson J-200! You can see it in this photo from an early band I played in called The Jeweltones. That was back in the late 60s, and we were the first band I'd heard of with a female bass player, Vivian Shevitz. There's Vivian with me, our singer Don Bolton and drummer Richard Dishman.

Today's acoustic players share the stage with drummers and electric guitarists, and they're actually being heard—without feedback, without rumble and with a relatively true sound—thanks to pickups made just for acoustics. And it's common for acoustics to have factory-installed pickups. Let's take a look at how acoustic pickups work, and how to install them. A piezo's installation is as important to the final sound as the transducer itself.

Here's a little piezo history Before the late 60s, when the first under-the-saddle pickup came along, there had been a variety of contact pickups available, but they weren't too great. DeArmond made one of the most popular. Then in '68 Baldwin introduced the first under-the-bridge-saddle transducer, but you had to buy the guitar with it and the guitar was none too great. About that same time, Barcus Berry introduced their

first pickup, which fastened inside to the bridge plate or elsewhere on the top. Barcus Berry seemed intent on making an improvement over the DeArmond top-sensing pickup, and was probably unaware of the Baldwin pickup (which was the first to produce the sound of the string rather than the top).

Observing all this was Ovation's **James Rickard**—one of the great guitar builders, repairmen and inventors. Aiming to please Ovation-endorsee Glen Campbell, Jim designed Ovation's now famous under-saddle pickup. It was second to Baldwin's chronologically, but first musically. This is the pickup that really made it possible for players to take their acoustic guitars onstage with an electric band—the same pickup Ovation still uses today, and the pickup that made Ovation guitars famous.

Mr. Rickard says: "The way it happened was, we'd just gotten our greatest endorsee—Glen Campbell. It was in '68 or '69. And then one night Glen shows up on the *Johnny Carson Show* with Jerry Reed and a matched set of Baldwin guitars—the ones with the earliest transducer. I saw Jerry give Glen the poison apple. Glen probably didn't like the guitar too well, but he liked that amplification. We freaked out, afraid of losing Glen—and we probably would have lost him if we hadn't acted as quickly as we did.

"So at Ovation, we looked at both of those pickups—the Baldwin and the Barcus Berry. We were very concerned about having a balanced output—getting an even response from string to string. We had to please a real player in Glen Campbell. Glen covered the fretboard from one end to the other, and he was very conscious of dead spots (low output) and hot spots (good, or maybe too much, output). This lack of balanced output was Glen's complaint with amplified acoustic guitars—including the Baldwin. We gave him what he wanted: the even, balanced output of all six strings equally—and not so much from the top. I'd found that the output from top-sensing pickups like the Frap or Barcus Berry was louder on some resonant frequencies than on others, and that's why some notes, or clusters of notes, had more or less output than others did.

"Where you place a top-sensing-pickup is a problem because there's no 'right' spot. All you do is move the pickup in and out of a guitars' natural hot-spots. A guitar top is full of tonal areas that produce one frequency better than another, but a single pickup can't sense them all at once—there's no place where a pickup can give you the whole spectrum. That's why we went to a pickup that sensed the string. Baldwin had the right idea with their pickup, but the design wasn't as practical as ours.

"Under-saddle pickups, which sense the strings, are top pickups as well—they do sense the top. Top-sensing pickups, however, sense only the top, never the strings. Under-saddle pickups, with the piezo element sensing sound from above and below, are therefore louder because they have output from both the top and the string. They don't feed back like a top-sensing pickup does because the string sound can be loud while the top sound is at a lower volume which doesn't induce feedback.

"Luckily for Ovation, the other companies didn't take us seriously at the time. We produced 30,000 pickup-installed guitars annually for many years before they realized we had something going! Our detractors would say, 'Ugh! A plastic bowl for a back' (actually, it wasn't the back that people first noticed, it was the soundhole rosette and the peghead shape). But the musicians responded to Ovation because we gave them a pickup that allowed them to go onstage and not feed back."

Barcus Barry then designed the Hot Dots (the rage of the late 70's), which being installed in the bridge body, were still "top-sensors." Finally Barcus Berry introduced an under-the-saddle transducer strip—Martin's First Generation Thinline—that was readily available over the counter. Along with a competitor, the Shadow pickup, the Thinline was very popular, but Ovation still had the best sound onstage.

Takamine soon got into the act with a very good sounding system that was much like Ovation's. Takamine came along in the 70s, around the same time as the Barcus Berry Thinline strip. Like the Ovation, the Takamine was a functional road guitar that was ready-to-buy. They became very popular, and one reason was because they were less expensive than an Ovation.

In the early '80s L.R. Baggs and **Larry Fishman** each produced under-the-saddle transducer strips which were much improved over the original Barcus Berry Thinline. From around '85 until '92 Baggs and Fishman lead the field, and twenty-plus years later Baggs and Fishman are still the two names that pop up in my mind when I hear the words "acoustic pickups". Currently, however,

there are a number of saddle transducers being manufactured—and choosing between them isn't easy.

Piezo construction and design

Under-saddle transducers are all quite similar in construction, although different brands vary widely in sound. There are two types: one has six pressure-sensitive pieces of piezo ceramic that are linked by wire and held together in a strip by various bonding methods (encased in foil, silicone rubber, a brass channel, etc.); the other is a ribbon of piezo film, rather than a series of piezo elements. An advantage gained with piezo film is that the exact placement of the elements under each string is no longer a factor, since the film sensor is continuous. Because of this, the balance of the string ouput is said to be better.

Both these styles of under saddle pickups transmit sounds by translating the pressure of the plucked strings on the saddle above them into electrical signals. The underside of the piezo elements also sense sound from the guitar top, so in that sense they are "top sensors."

Just a few companies that offer a ribbon transducer are: Fishman (Matrix and Martin Gold Plus), EMG (AS-93 and AS-125), Highlander (iP-1) and L.R. Baggs (RT System).

The pickup's material makeup, size, thickness and bonding method all contribute to each maker's individual sound. The manufacturers haven't invented any new technology at all. It's their different 'recipes'—the blend of physical and electrical proportions—that produce the different sounding pickup.

What this recipe talk means is that since each maker's pickups sound so different, you have to do some research to find the right sound for you. Check with your dealer or local repairman for information. Perhaps you can find out which customers use which pickups, and then call those people to see if they'd mind giving you a quick demo. And many stores have new and used guitars with factory-installed piezos.

Over the years, I've known many guitarists who have experimented with piezo pickups, only to quickly give them up, complaining of a poppy, "Donald Ducky," crackling sound that's often joined by unruly overtones, feedback, excess body noise and unbalanced string response. These discouraged, would-have-been acoustic players weren't aware that these problems could have been caused by impedance mismatch, lack of a preamp, or the wrong amplifier. Last, but not least, is the possibility that the guitars they tried were equipped with incorrectly installed saddle pickups.

So, before passing judgement on a pickup system be sure that your saddle/pickup installation is correct, and keep these five rules in mind:

1 The piezo strip must be located in the slot so that all six elements are under their respective strings.

2 The saddle must be made from the right material.

3 The saddle must be a slip—or "sliding"—fit, and in some cases split in two. Also, the piezo strip should be close to the same width as the saddle, and it should sit directly under the whole saddle.

4 The bottoms of the saddle and the saddle slot must be a perfect match.

5 The best sound is produced when you have a 50/50 installation—50% of the saddle is in the bridge body, and 50% is exposed.

Installing piezo saddle pickups

Now that you understand the basics of how the piezo pickups work, let's begin the actual installation procedure. Installing most under-the-saddle pickups is easy in theory and a little tricky in practice. And it requires certain specialized tools. If you're in doubt, leave the work to a pro; otherwise, here's straightforward advice for do-it-yourselfers.

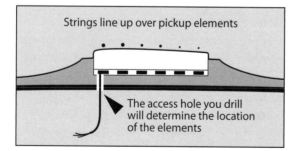

Strings line up over pickup elements

The access hole you drill will determine the location of the elements

Location The transducer must be located with its piezo elements directly under the strings, as shown below. First, the string spacing from E to E must be taken into account. Martin guitars, for example, have a string spacing at the saddle, from center to center, measuring 2 1/8". Their pickup is made accordingly. Most conventional steel-string acoustics have string spacing similar to Martin's, and the various pickup brands are made to match.

But if your guitar varies more than .050" from 2 1/8", you should check into having piezo elements custom-installed to match your spacing. Most of the manufacturers I spoke with do some custom work, although some welcome it more than others.

Actually, the location of the piezo elements relative to the strings is really determined by where you drill the hole for the output wire (because the six elements are wired together). This hole is drilled in the bottom of the saddle slot, down through the bridge, top and bridge plate on its way to the output jack that's usually installed in the end block for added strength. Each manufacturer's installation instructions will tell you the exact location of the clearance hole in the bridge, so just measure carefully. If the hole does get off towards one end or the other, you can enlarge it slightly to compensate.

If your pickup is a piezo film, location of the pickup under the individual strings isn't critical.

Saddle material I prefer bone for acoustic saddles, but piezo manufacturers recommend synthetic materials like Micarta and TUSQ as being the best material for transducer installation, since it's more homogenous (even in texture throughout). It's also more flexible than bone, and it moves with the top, bridge and piezo when a string is plucked. Bone or ivory may offer a stronger acoustic sound when the pickup is not being used, but (allegedly) it won't normally sound as good as the synthetic when you're plugged in. I've done many installations with high quality bone of uniform density that sounded great, however.

The fit To begin with, the piezo strip should be close to the width of the saddle slot, so that the whole saddle sits on it for even pressure. If it is too much narrower, it could end up close to the front or rear edge, or sitting at a cross-angle to the saddle. Any of these situations is less than optimum in terms of sound.

While most repairmen suggest that a saddle fit quite snugly, this is not true for piezo transducers. The saddle should slide or slip in without force. It shouldn't be loose, wiggly or falling over, but it mustn't be tight. Admittedly, this is a judgment call that's hard to describe on paper, but you'll get a feel for it after a couple of installations. A too-tight saddle won't exert the proper pressure down on the ceramic, and may cause the following problems:

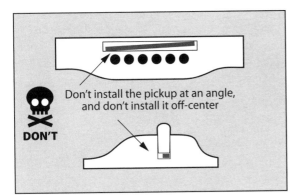

Don't install the pickup at an angle, and don't install it off-center

DON'T

no sound at all, unbalanced string response (i.e., sound on some strings and not others, or some strings louder than others), unwanted overtones, lowering of overall output and 60-cycle hum.

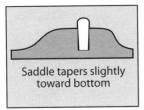

Saddle tapers slightly toward bottom

In general, the saddle sides should fit the slot walls with a slip-fit tolerance of, say, .002" to .005". Some professionals recommend shaping a slight downward taper on a saddle to guarantee that it reaches the bottom. This is smart if you're unable to get a perfect slip-fit. The saddle bottom should mate with the slot bottom with the same accuracy as the sides. Often it's best to rout the slot bottom to get it flat, and then shape the saddle bottom flat to match. This technique, along with a jig you can make yourself for doing the job, will be explained shortly.

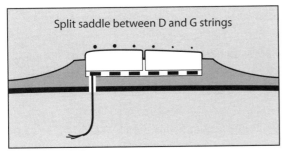

Split saddle between D and G strings

Perhaps you've seen installations where the saddle is split in two between the D and G strings. This is the proper method for some piezo saddle pickups, most notably the Barcus-Berry 1440 and the Shadow 1110. These systems utilize balanced phasing, which polarizes the pickup into two halves, like a humbucker. The E, A and D strings face up (north), while the G, B and high-E face down (south). If the saddle isn't cut, the D and G strings

read each other's plucked string signal and cancel each other out. This can cause a lot of dead notes and bad sounds when the saddle is left in one piece on double-pole transducers.

The Martin Second Generation 332, the L.R. Baggs LB-6, and the Barcus-Berry 1440 SP do not require saddle splitting. The need for splitting the saddle should be considered before installation. Perhaps you simply don't want your saddle cut in two. It's also harder to make a perfect-fit split saddle, since you're sort of making two saddles—and one is hard enough! Note: The L.R. Baggs Saddle Replacement Pickup comes with the Micarta saddle already bonded to the piezo bottom. In this case the routing and installation fit is the same as the others, except that rather than making a saddle, you shape the saddle that comes on it. Unless you're really sure of yourself, have this pickup installed by a professional, since if you go too far on the Micarta, you're in trouble.

Installation of under-the-saddle transducers generally involves some light routing of the bridge saddle slot—sometimes widening it and often deepening it. Most important, the routing is done to ensure that the bottoms of the slot and saddle match perfectly. The transducer sits between the saddle and slot bottom and must contact both evenly, so shaping both flat is the easiest method for guaranteeing a good contact. Curved bottoms are okay when well matched, but it's easier to be sure of a fit if both are flat. It's best to use a transducer strip that's close to the same size as the saddle, so that it sits directly under the whole saddle—not cross-slot or under one edge.

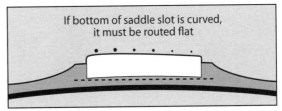

If bottom of saddle slot is curved, it must be routed flat

Most flattop guitars actually have a slight upward arch built into the top. This effect increases over the years from string pull on the top, causing the guitar to visibly "belly up". This is not necessarily bad; it's just a fact of guitar life. Realize that the bridge has slowly become curved to match the top, and therefore the bottom of its saddle slot is bent into the same slight curve. Even with the strings removed, the top and bridge remain some-

d.i.y.

what curved, having taken a "set." It's best to re-rout the saddle slot to create a flat bottom within its curved shape. It won't take much, and in so doing, you might also find it necessary to widen the slot, as well, so that the transducer drops in without force.

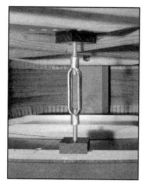

Recreate the top arch

Because the top becomes even more arched under string tension, I use a prop or jack inside the instrument to recreate the top's arch when the strings are removed for saddle slot routing. By holding the top in its true curve, the saddle routing operation is even more accurate. I recommend laying a board or caul over the back braces as a support for a jack or prop, and to spread the load across a large area of the back. With the strings on and tuned to pitch, you can install a prop-stick until it's just snug and no longer falls over in the same way that a sound-post is installed in a violin.

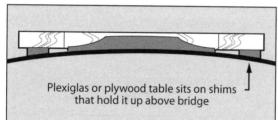

Plexiglas or plywood table sits on shims that hold it up above bridge

Using a Dremel Moto-Tool and a 5/64" bit, flatten the slot's bottom. Make a routing table cut from 3/8" or thicker Plexiglas or plywood that sits taller than the bridge and gives the router a flat surface to ride over. The table is shimmed level where needed, and lightly taped to the guitar's face with duct tape so that it doesn't move. If you also don't move while routing, you'll get a flat bottom. Clean up any router marks, and square up the sides with a sharp chisel, following the saddle-making techniques described on page 124.

The serious transducer installer will be interested in this saddle routing jig. Because it's adjustable, it aligns easily with any saddle slot, and then makes use of the Dremel Moto-Tool for pinpoint routing of the slot. It provides a flat, stable surface for a Dremel router to ride over, which ensures a flat bottom for the saddle slot and eliminates the need for clamping a makeshift routing table around the bridge. The jig's adjustable fences entrap the router baseplate, guiding it in a straight line during the routing.

If you're making the saddle slot a little wider than you started with, measure carefully and keep the walls parallel with each other. It's very tough to work on a saddle slot without widening it a little bit, so expect to replace the saddle with an oversized blank that is filed down to fit. Micarta, bone or ivory saddle blanks come in thicknesses ranging from 3/32" to 1/4", and they must be final-shaped by hand. The Martin Second Generation Thin-Line, Shadow's 1110, and the Barcus-Berry 1440 and 1440 SP fit into a 3/32" slot, while the Fishman AG-125 and the L.R. Baggs require close to a 1/8" slot. Ovation transducers require close to a 5/16" saddle slot (their non-electric guitars, however, use a 1/8" saddle slot, as do Guild, Seagull and some others).

There are many repair situations where it's advisable or necessary to widen the saddle more than 3/32" (compensation, warped slot, etc.). Some repairmen and builders prefer a wider saddle in general. The Fishman AG-I 25 and the Baggs LB-6 are well suited to these situations.

It's better not to install a thinner pickup (3/32") in a wider slot. Doing so might cause the piezo to become off-center or run at an angle to the bottom of the saddle.

The correct saddle depth, according to Fishman's **Rick Nelson**, is "A 50/50 ratio. That seems to be the magic number. We've found that optimum sound results when one half of the saddle is in the bridge body, and one half exposed. Too deep a slot can produce balance problems which we call "ghosting"—where one or more strings have a weaker output than their neighbors. If you have too much saddle in your bridge, and not enough showing on top, shim up the transducer strip from beneath with a piece of hardwood. If too much saddle is out of the slot, rout the slot a little deeper."

When the pickup fits the slot, you must drill a small hole through the bottom of the slot—down through the bridge, top and bridge-pad. This is for the pickup's output wire. The manufacturer's instructions tell exactly where to locate this hole. Next comes a tough part: drilling-out, or enlarging, the strap buttonhole in the end block to house the output jack (combination output jack/strap buttons are usually installed in the end block).

Installing an endpin jack

I've been installing endpin jacks in acoustic guitars since they first came on the scene, and I'll admit to chipping

the finish on a few before I developed a technique. Of course this was way back before tools like the endpin jack reamer, endpin jack socket wrench and the thin, flat output jack wrench were available (so that's my excuse).

The hardest part of installing the output jack is drilling the hole through the end block (you'll see some jacks mounted in the side of the lower bout, but this method isn't as strong without clever reinforcement).

Most end blocks have a hole for a strap button — either a relatively large hole for a tapered endpin, or a small hole for a wood screw if the endpin is the screw-on type. Either of these holes must be enlarged to 1/2" to accept an output jack. I do this with a specialized endpin reamer that starts with a tapered cut and gradually steps

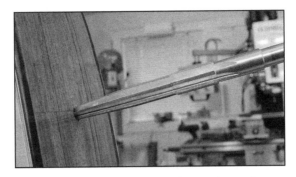

up to non-tapered cutting edges that produce a clean 1/2" hole through the end block.

You can use a common hardware store reamer as well. Hardware store reamers are about 1/2" at the widest end of the taper, and may be used straight from the shelf to do the job. They'll make the hole slightly larger than necessary, though, since the outside diameter of the thread on the endpin jack measures .469"—that is, .031" (1/32") smaller than the .500" (1/2") hole that the reamer makes. This slight bit of extra clearance presents no problems, but if you want a snug-fitting jack, stop reaming before the reamer passes through the hole and finish the job with a rat-tail file.

Either reamer needs a 1/4" pilot hole in order to enter the workpiece; but that's well inside the final 1/2" diameter hole it will ream—so out of squareness, or chipping at the edge of a drilled hole are not issues.

If you choose to drill a 1/2" hole instead of reaming, don't use a common twist drill bit; twist drills, especially as big as 1/2", are hard to center, and tend to grab the work and "hog out" the hole. Instead, use either a Forstner bit or a brad-point bit—both have points that center well on a small starter hole, and they cut sharp and clean on the outer edges. Use an awl or center punch to make a starter hole for the drill bit to center on.

Unless you're using a drill press and the work is clamped to the table, drilling a hole within a hole is fraught with accidents because there's nothing for the bit to center on. So, when a guitar has a tapered endpin hole for a strap button, I cut off the button part and leave the rest of the button in the hole; then I center-punch that and it keeps the drill-bit centered.

Once the jack fits easily through the hole, and before you install the output jack, measure the thickness of the end block so that you know where to adjust the inner hex nut on the threaded body of the jack.

Of course, it's easiest to use a digital caliper: just place a block of wood inside, and slide the end of the caliper up to it to measure. You don't need a caliper though. A small piece of brass bent into an L-shape can measure the thickness of the end block. Poke it through a piece of foam rubber, and you have a depth gauge. Hook the L on the inner surface of the end block, and slide the rubber up against the guitar. Lift it out, and measure the thickness you're dealing with. Now you can wire in the jack.

Even the Switchjack, which tightens from the outside, still has a washer and hex nut on the inside of the guitar, needing to be tightened. So be sure you slip the interior hex nut and washer over the wires—in that order—before you run the wires through the endpin hole for soldering! I've soldered up more than one jack without remembering the nut and washer, and it makes you feel kind of stupid.

Of the hundreds of ways to pull a wire through a hole, I poke an electric bass string through the end block hole and into the guitar. Then I stick the loose wire ends into the large ball end, pull them through the hole and out where I can solder them. An alligator-clip soldering jig makes a good holder for the work.

Solder the insulated lead wire to the jack's hot lug (for the tip of the guitar cord), and solder the bare ground wire or braided shield to the outer ring lug. Don't strip off any more of the wire shield than is absolutely necessary.

If you remove too much shielding, the exposed section acts as an antenna for picking up 60-cycle hum from fluorescent lights, dimmer switches, etc.

Once the jack is wired in, pull it back inside the guitar and out the soundhole to thread the inner hex nut and washer(s) onto the threaded exterior of the jack. Use the end block thickness measurement to locate the interior hex nut. Locate it so that when the outside hex nut is tightened, the inner hex nut and washers snug up tight against the end block. A double-ended output jack wrench is made for this: it's only .075" thick, as thin as the nut being tightened. Here, I've poked a scribe through the jack to keep it from turning while I tighten the nut.

The last step is to screw on the strap button. Fishman's instructions say to finger-tighten it, but I've found that these buttons tend to work loose. My buddy Frank Ford gave me a tip that works well: he uses a pair of wire crimpers to grab and tighten the strap button. The blunt jaws nestle down in the recess where the strap goes, and they don't leave a mark (even if they did, it would be hidden down deep in the strap groove). You can also wrap the button with a strip of leather and grab it with Vise-Grips.

A jack that tightens from the inside is tough to install without an endpin jack wrench—a hollow-shaft, deep-socket 9/16" nut driver with a slot milled through one wall of the hex and into the hollow shaft. The slot allows the tool to slide onto the wires and follow along them, over the jack's soldering prongs and onto the hex nut, making it easy to tighten the hex nut (drawing, next page). You might want to discard an endpin jack that requires this tool, and use the Switchjack instead.

A threaded endpin jack is another option: it tightens from the outside, and it requires no mounting hex nuts

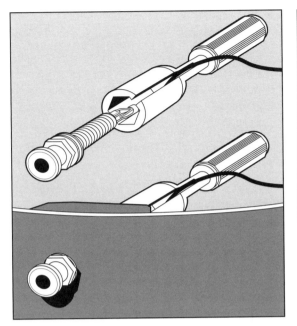

d.i.y.

or washers because it threads into the wood of the end block hole. It requires a 1/2" hole, and you need a 9/16"-12 tap to pre-cut the wood thread (both the jack and the tap are available from *stewmac.com*).

Onboard preamps Some manufacturers install a preamp with volume and tone controls in the side of the instrument near the neck block on the bass side. The routing, drilling and sawing required is complex and invasive, and differs for each product. My suggestion is to choose a system that mounts the preamp through the soundhole and fastens to the back.

Which acoustic pickup to choose?

With so many acoustic guitar pickups on the market, most players end up buying/trying more than one system, and figure that's just part of the deal. Quite frankly, it's hard to recommend one pickup over another because they sound so different, and you can't A/B them easily. I've installed plenty, but don't get to keep them long enough to make a fair opinion and know where to begin in choosing one. When I'm no expert, I know experts.

So I called my expert, **Frank Ford** at Gryphon Stringed Instruments in Palo Alto, California. Owned and operated by Frank and his business partner Richard Johnson, Gryphon is recognized worldwide as a major dealer in acoustic instruments, and as a major repair center for

them. Frank (at right, above) put me in touch with his pickup expert, **Brian Michael** (left), who does most of the pickup installations at Gryphon. Here's Brian:

"We have several flattop instruments with pickups installed so that customers can A/B them and decide which one works for them. We put in as many as we could fit," said Brian. "I can definitely help you narrow the field, Dan, at least from the Gryphon point of view. We don't carry every pickup made; we carry what we like and what our customers ask for the most—and those we have plenty of experience with.

"The two most popular brands that we sell and install are from Fishman and LR Baggs, and customers choose both of them about equally. By category, the pickups that we carry are:

Soundhole In the higher price range, we like the Seymour Duncan Mag Mic SA-6 and the L.R. Baggs M-1 is an excellent mid-priced model. In a lower price range, Seymour Duncan's Acoustic Tube, and the Fishman Neo-D sound great for the price.

Under-saddle That'd be the Fishman Matrix, L.R. Baggs Element Active and the Highlander IP-2. Everyone here likes the Highlander a bunch. The Highlander element is round, not flat, and piezo crystals react in a 360° field rather than only on one axis.

Under-saddle/mic combination Fishman's Ellipse-Matrix Blend is popular here, and Martin uses this system. From Baggs, it's the Dual Source and iMix—one reason we like these, and the Ellipse-Matrix, is because any onboard electronics don't need to be side-mounted. (We don't like drilling/cutting holes in good guitars with solid wood sides. If it's plywood we'll do it.)

d.i.y.

Soundboard-sensing We sell two top-sensors—the L.R. Baggs iBeam, and the Trance-Amulet system. We install other top-sensing pickups when customers bring them in; we frequently install Fishman SBTs in ukes—they work great in smaller instruments.

"The **iBeam** is not as consistent as an under the saddle pickup; in some guitars—the more heavily-built ones—it sounds really great. In a lighter, more-responsive guitar, however, sometimes it seems that the iBeam promotes overtones and nodes.

"The **Trance Amulet**, at around $450, is at the upper end of the price range. It's a wonderful system, however, and it sounds more like your instrument than any other pickup system.

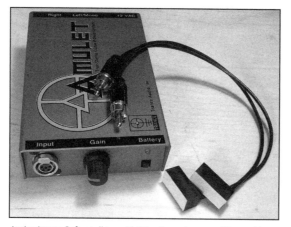

Author's note: Before talking with Brian, I wasn't aware of Trance. It's a small company that hand-builds each pickup, and they aren't interested in high production. There's a waiting list for their Amulet system. Frank Ford rushed me one of the precious few Amulets he had in stock—even including a fresh tube of Barge cement for the installation; that's how strongly he and Brian felt about the spreading the word on this great acoustic pickup. Being a non-invasive installation, I installed the Amulet in my favorite guitar—a 1939 Gibson J-35. It sounds great! Now back to Brian from Gryphon.

"Most of the pickups I've seen have instructions that are adequate for a do-it-yourselfer with the necessary tools. Some require professional installation by a qualified luthier or the warranty is voided.

"For any installation, always inspect inside with a mirror to be sure that what you're installing will fit. For example, the iBeam won't fit in a 00-size guitar because the X-braces aren't spread wide enough.

"Also, when you're drilling an access hole—don't drill through a brace! Measure, don't guess. With a mirror inside, you can use a bridge clamp through the sound-hole as a locator; clamp on the bridge right where you

want to drill and check the clamp's bottom foot—if it's resting on the X-brace, stop and think it over.

"Little rare earth magnets are also handy for locating braces (one on the inside, one on the bridge).

"The double-stick foam adhesive supplied with the iBeam is great stuff. (We've tried using carpet tape on some installations and had the pickup come loose). Also—and you'd think it would be the opposite—I think the foam acts as a buffer, and helps resist feedback.

"We use the **Fishman SwitchJack** on everything that doesn't include its own jack, because it's easy to install (tightens from the outside), and it's high quality.

Internal mics make a great addition to some pickups, but can be difficult to deal with on their own due to feedback problems and boominess inside your guitar. Some people don't realize that the sound inside your guitar isn't the same as the sound outside the guitar!

"One last thing, Dan: a Canadian company, Schatten, makes great affordable pickups for virtually any acoustic instrument—most of which could be installed by people reading this book.

—*Brian Michael, Gryphon Stringed Instruments*

Thanks, Brian, and thank Frank for me!

Frank Ford and I have been friends since we first met around 1992, and we're two peas in a pod when it comes to stringed instrument repair. We love our trade, and never quit studying it. We also love teaching the next generation, and have done numerous tandem repair presentations at the GAL and ASIA yearly conventions—sort of like Click and Clack. Twice a year Frank teaches a repair class at the Roberto-Venn school in Phoenix, Arizona.

Frank is also a technical advisor and tool designer for Luthiers Mercantile International (LMI), a luthier supply

company in California. A recent Frank Ford design is this clever gripper that keeps an output jack from turning while you tighten the hex nut. I'd say LMI is lucky to have Frank on board.

The rod terminates in an eccentric shaft, with an ec-

cedar, select the soft-growth wood in between the hard grain lines (or use poplar since its grain has no differentiation between spring and summer growth). The cedar should be quartersawn.

The acoustic guitar amp I use

I don't know why the term "unplugged" was coined to describe acoustic guitar amplification, because the last link of the chain—your amp—is as important to your sound as the pickup and guitar are. I have several great guitar amps in my shop for testing electric guitar pickups, but it wasn't until recently that I added a good amp for acoustic guitars. A friend steered me to Fishman's Loudbox 100. When it arrived at my shop, I called on **Adam J. Fox** to give it the once over. Adam is a songwriter/producer with a highly developed sense of hearing. He flipped out over this amp, so I knew I'd picked the right one.

"Like many acoustic guitar players," says Adam, "I've been disenchanted with every kind of amplified acoustic guitar sound—it just doesn't compare to the real thing. The Loudbox surprised me.

"It's ultra clean and extremely loud (114dB). It has a tweeter and an 8 inch woofer which are bi-amplified like studio monitors. This gives the amp studio-like accuracy and balance throughout the sound spectrum. The amp is dynamic—extremely musical—it moves a lot of air, and has a really wide axis that radiates lots of energy. The speakers are killer!

"The amp's tonal balance makes for a full, true, acoustic-electric sound. Most acoustic transducers produce boomy lows and shrill, splatting highs with few frequencies in between—played through this amp, those gui-

centrically drilled knurl on the end. Turn the rod in either direction, and the hardened steel knurl bites right into the side wall of the jack while you tighten away.

For recessed, or cup-mounted jacks, a second tool comes into play. It has a clearance hole drilled through its square-milled end. The square sides fit a 1/2"-drive socket, and Jack the Gripper slips right through and does his job.

Trouble with unbalanced output

The most common problem with under-saddle installations is unbalanced output. If one string is louder than another, and you're not getting even string response, you probably have a poor fit between the saddle bottom and the bridge bottom.

Another solution is placing a thin strip of cedar or spruce between the saddle bottom and the piezo strip. The wood acts as an "equalizer"—eliminating the difference in contact pressure between the individual strings. **Eric Aceto** at Ithaca Guitar Works tried the cedar strip trick and still had a hot string. He looked at the cedar under a microscope and found a piece of hard grain that he hadn't noticed. This hard grain was sitting under the string that was too loud. Eric changed to a piece of poplar which has the same amount of give but had no differentiation between spring and summer growth and the problem was solved. The moral? If you use spruce or

d.i.y.

tars would have midrange produced by the amp.

"The Loudbox's highs are smooth and silky, and the mids are very present. Having rich, dynamic, punchy mids gives you a fuller, meatier tone.

"It's got bells and whistles, too: two inputs, so stereo blending is always a possibility. (Both channels have effects sends/returns, and D.I. outs for further routing and blending of effects and dry signals).

"Each channel has a highly functional anti-feedback notch filter to tune out a wide range of resonances. Each channel has on board digital effects that are properly voiced for acoustic instruments. There's a tweeter level control, a tuner output jack and a foot switch input to mute the amp. If Dan won't let me borrow his, I'll be getting one for my studio."

Ground your amp Shock protection should be of concern to anyone using an amplifier. Using electrical equipment in a poorly wired building or a wet environment is no joke. I've heard of players getting shocked, and sometimes killed, onstage. Use that three-prong cord on your amp to ground it. Never remove the grounding prong! And if you use an adapter to put your three-prong plug into a two-prong outlet, understand

that you're not grounded. A jolt of electricity won't be safely drawn to ground, it'll be drawn to you!

Even when an outlet has three prongs, don't depend on the grounding. For a few bucks, buy an outlet tester at the hardware store and keep it in your guitar case. Check any outlet that you plug into. The lights on the tester tell you if you're properly grounded.

Adrian Legg's book *Customizing Your Electric Guitar* suggests adding a safety feature between the strings and the ground: Wire in parallel a 220k ohm resistor and a .001 capacitor with a minimum voltage rating of 500 volts. Twist the wires together and solder them as shown. This can be done out of sight inside the control cavity, and it only lets about 40 volts through to

your strings if a shock is headed your way. The normal string ground still functions, too.

However, with this safety device you'll still get it if you touch metal knobs, jacks or guitar cords. You can be safe from volume or tone knob shock if your pots have nylon shafts, such as Fender used to use.

Semi-hollowbody wiring

Much of guitar electronics is simple—cleaning pots, switching capacitors, etc.—as long you can get at the parts to work on them! Here's advice for Gibson ES-335 owners faced with having to remove the electronics for cleaning or replacement. This can be quite a puzzle; how the heck to you get the wiring out of the guitar?

There's no secret. If you simply want to clean the pots, loosen their hex nuts and washers, let the pots fall down into the body and spray them with a contact cleaner (most aerosol contact cleaners are equipped with small, flexible tube applicators for pinpoint spraying). If you're sure you need to remove the controls, I'd bet they went in through the *f*-holes, although they shouldn't have.

Gibson ES-335-style guitars have a solid wood block glued between the top and back, which runs lengthwise through the guitar's center (hence the name "semi-hollowbody"). This block not only gives structural support, but considerably enhances the guitar's sustain. From the 335's inception in 1958 until 1961, the center block was truly solid, and the wiring harness was installed or removed through the *f*-holes. After 1961, the factory machined a good-sized notch in the block (the shaded area in the drawing opposite) under the bridge pickup, which helped in the installation and removal of the electronics. A good picture of this type of construction is on page 143 of **Tom Wheeler**'s book, *American Guitars*.

Being of more recent vintage, your guitar should have the notched access for the electronics, but if it doesn't, perhaps the block was accidentally flipped over during gluing. This would put the notch on the bass side (look through the bass *f*-hole to see). You'll have to fish the controls through the *f*-hole as if it were a pre-'61 axe, de-soldering the pickup leads as the pots are pulled through the *f*-holes. As you can see in the drawing, the wood wall left by the notch isn't too thick (about 1/2"). A skilled worker could cut through the block on the treble side to give easier access for control removal.

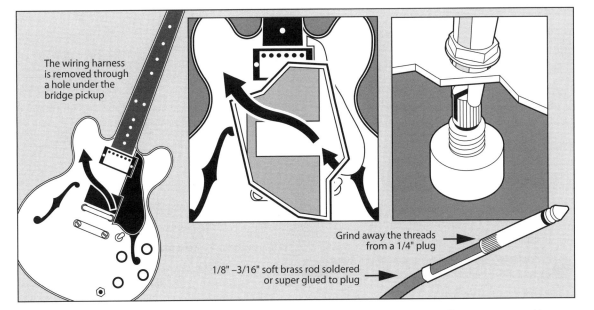

The wiring harness is removed through a hole under the bridge pickup

Grind away the threads from a 1/4" plug

1/8" –3/16" soft brass rod soldered or super glued to plug

d.i.y.

Here are some other helpful tips for working on the electronics of any *f*-hole electric guitar. Before removing the volume and tone controls, take off the knobs and mark the top of each shaft as an aid for later replacing them in the right order. Also, you'll have to remove the ground wire from the tailpiece in order to pull the parts out. Unscrew the tailpiece, and you'll find the wire—it may need unsoldering. For a stop-tailpiece 335, unsolder the ground wire as you remove the pots.

If you're replacing the whole harness after the guts have been removed, make a paper tracing of the empty control and toggle-switch holes on the guitar's face. Transfer these to cardboard and drill them out. Flip the cardboard over to duplicate the holes as they'd be on the inside of the guitar, and do your wiring with the pots and switch held in this wiring jig. It makes a great holder for the parts and assures a perfect fit upon reinstallation.

Whether you have access through the rear pickup or the *f*-hole, you still need to slide your parts carefully— and in the right order—back into the body. Keep from twisting or crossing any wires that later might touch a bare contact and cause a short. I've found that a pair of hemostats work great for reaching through a hole in the top and pulling a control shaft into place. Put the washer and hex nut on the hemostats before reaching through the hole (above) and tape them in place. Then you can drop them right onto the threaded shaft while holding it with the hemostats (you'll wish you had three hands).

Gibson R&D engineer **Tim Shaw** suggests making a tool for getting an output jack into the mounting hole in a guitar's face or side. This would be worth making for those who plan to do this job more than a few times. Solder or super glue a 12" length of 1/8" or 3/16" soft brass to a 1/4" plug. Bend the tool gently, and run it through the jack hole and out the *f*-hole or rear pickup notch, and plug it into the jack. Now you can pull the jack into place, dragging the rest of the wiring harness roughly into place at the same time.

Tim Shaw also pointed out that when Gibson installed the electronics in those early ES-series semi-hollow guitars such as the 335, 345 and 355, they kept cans of touch-up lacquer of the proper shade (usually cherry or sunburst tones) right at the bench to touch up the *f*-holes afterwards. Don't be surprised if you can't get the pots in or out without some degree of scratching—a little masking tape in the right places would help. Good luck with your work.

Easy, right? Actually, it sounds easier here than it really is. Be patient, and you'll get the parts out and back in. You know one thing for sure: Those guitars weren't wired from inside the guitar! Someone had to do it.

Pickup replacement

Installing a replacement pickup Wiring a direct-replacement pickup is generally simple: following a wiring diagram, you just unhook one pickup and wire in the other. But there are plenty of pitfalls, too, and you can avoid them by considering the following points before buying a pickup or tearing apart your axe.

Some older two-lead (hot and ground) humbucker pickups can be rewired as four-wire pickups. If vintage isn't an issue, perhaps you can rewire the pickup you have to get what you're after.

What sound are you after? If you add to existing pickups, will the mix be compatible? A well-stocked and knowledgeable music store can help you choose, and **Bill Foley's** book *Build Your Own Electric Guitar* includes an extensive chart that suggests which pickups sound best for different musical styles. For example:

Heavy metal rhythm/neck position	
Alembic:	SAE, HB assembly
Bartolini:	1HC, VHC
Dimarzio:	X2N, PAF, Super II, (2) HS2 or 3
Duncan:	Jazz Neck, Invader Neck, Seymourizer II, JB
EMG:	85, 58, SA assembly w/presence control
Lawrence:	M58, XL500 neck, (2) L-25 XL
Schecter:	Monstertone assembly

Do the polepieces match the string spacing?

Is the alteration permanent? Will you need to rerout your pickup cavity, or make other changes that can't be undone? Switching from single-coil to humbucking—or humbucking to single-coil—can require routing the body cavity. This is done with router templates, just like installing the Floyd Rose.

A direct-replacement pickup should drop right in with no additional routing, an important consideration with valuable vintage instruments. With careful disassembly and measuring, you can know if it fits before it's too late. Replacement pickups often have more depth than the original, so don't be surprised if you have to rout or drill the cavity to gain clearance.

Would routing a pickup cavity endanger the structural integrity of the instrument? For example, I've seen old Gibson SG single-coil guitars with a humbucker added in the neck position. There wasn't a lot of surface area in the neck/body joint of these guitars in the first place, so

when you add some over-zealous routing, the neck's not hanging on by much.

Several pickups offer a single-coil pickup that drops into a humbucker cavity. Seymour Duncan's SPH90 Phat Cat P90, Gibson's P-94, Kent Armstrong's P90, TV Jones' TV'Tron are four examples.

Universal routing is popular with many kit body manufacturers. These routs accept either single-coil or humbucking pickups, but you still have to enlarge the hole in the pickguard, especially when replacing a Strat-style single-coil with a humbucker. This, too, is done with a router and pickguard cutout templates.

Will you have to add other parts? Does the new pickup offer functions that the guitar's wiring system can't operate, such as phasing, dual sound, etc.? In other words, will you have to add mini switches, pots and such. Is there room for them? For example, If you're going active, you'll need someplace to put a battery.

Single coil = hum, two coils = humbucker

A pickup is made by coiling wire around a set of magnetic polepieces that are held in a bobbin. The vibrations of the metal string over them is picked up by the polepieces, which induces a very small electrical charge within the coil of wire. This electrical signal is received by the amplifier and… well… amplified. This single coil of wire is a single-coil pickup. Single-coils tend to pick up interference from AC current, which creates hum.

A humbucking pickup is a combination of two pickup coils under one cover. These two coils are wired together in series and out of phase to eliminate hum. They're also charged magnetically opposite to each other by turning the magnet around in one coil so that the two coils actually end up being electrically in-phase. This describes the traditional humbucker designed by Seth Lover for Gibson in the late 1950s. Seth applied for a patent on his discovery that two single-coils can be connected together in a certain way with a common output and ground to make up a hum-canceling pickup. This is the sought-after "patent-applied-for" (PAF) pickup.

"In series" means that one coil connects to the other end-to-end. This combines the resistances of both coils and gives us the famous humbucking power. The series link always joins matching ends of the coils: the finish wrap of one coil to the finish wrap of the other, or the start to the start. Most often it's the two finish ends of the coils that are used for this series link. Each coil's wire is wound in the same direction on its bobbin, but because the end of one goes into the end of the other, this is considered out of phase, hence the term in series/out of phase.

While series linkage combines two components by wiring them end-to-end, **parallel linkage** combines components side-by-side. If you're using these terms with regard to pickups or their coils, you're linking resistances. When two equal resistances are linked in series (i.e., the two coils of a humbucker), the result is the sum of the two; the series sound is powerful and bassy. When the same two resistances are linked in parallel, the result is one-quarter of their combined values. Parallel sound is weaker, but very bright and clean. The two "in-between" Strat settings on a 5-way switch combine the pickups in parallel, not "out of phase" as it's so often referred to. The series or parallel wiring options are what gives today's versatile four-wire humbuckers their distinctive sounds.

At the same time, the coils of a humbucker are also magnetically out of phase to each other because the two rows of polepieces are on opposite sides of a common magnet. This gives one row of polepieces a north polarity, and the other a south polarity, which causes the wire of each coil to induce the current (signal) in opposite directions. This phenomenon not only allows the hum of one coil to cancel the hum of the other coil, but it returns the two out of phase coils to being electrically in-phase after all! It's the relationship of the north and south polarity and the particular way the two coils are wired together that gives the pickup its hum-canceling ability, its power and its name. It must be pointed out, though, that the two coils don't have to be in the same cover. Any two single-coil pickups can be wired or switched together to make a humbucker. A Fender P-Bass pickup is humbucking, for example, even though it's split and sitting at different places under the strings.

Color-coding and start/finish wraps When a coil is wrapped, obviously there's a starting end and a finish end of the wire. The start is wrapped against the center of the bobbin, while the finish is the outermost wrap. Knowing which wire is the start and finish allows you to wire it with-

out regard to factory color-coding and without needing a diagram. Some manufacturers use the same colors but not in the same order, so you can't use a DiMarzio diagram to wire a Duncan pickup! It's no big deal, but each time you discover the start and finish to a certain pickup, keep a record of it. Here are the colors of the start/finish wraps for two-wire pickups from three manufacturers:

	Finish	Start
Seymour Duncan	Red/White	Green/Black
DiMarzio	White/Black	Green/Red
Schaller	Green/Yellow	White/Brown

Identifying a 4-wire pickup's leads You can also use your multimeter to determine the functions of four hot leads plus a shielding lead. Here's how (I learned this on page 51 of **Donald Brosnac's** book, *Guitar Electronics For Musicians*. Just as a writer needs a dictionary, an electronics do-it-yourselfer needs Brosnac's book. It has a lot of theory, and after studying the chapter on switches, you'd be able to choose the parts needed to do any of the conversions mentioned here.

1 If one of the leads has a zero ohms reading to a metal bottom plate, magnet or polepiece that is the ground; it shouldn't be connected to any of the other four leads.

2 Hold the black probe on one of the four leads and touch the red probe to each of the other three leads. Two leads will give an infinite ohms reading, and one will give a DC resistance reading in ohms.

Color codes: 4-wire pickups

Poles:	South (screws)		North (slugs)	
	start **S** finish		start **N** finish	
	start	S finish	start	N finish
Anderson	BLK	WHT	RED	GRN
Bartolini	GRN	WHT	BLK	RED
Benedetto	GRN	WHT	RED	BLK
Bill Lawrence	WHT	GRN	RED	BLK
DiMarzio	GRN	WHT	RED	BLK
Fender	RED	BLK	GRN	WHT
Gibson	BLK	GRN	RED	WHT
Gotoh	GRN	RED	BLK	WHT
Jackson	BLK	RED	GRN	WHT
Lawrence	GRN	BLK	WHT	RED
Lace	ORNG	WHT	ORG/BK	WH/BK
Lindy Fralin	WHT	GRN	RED	BLK
Schaller	WHT	GRN	BRWN	YELL
Seymour Duncan	GRN	RED	WHT	BLK

Four wires give you more options

If your guitar has a modern four-wire humbucking pickup, this means that instead of the coils being permanently wired together inside the pickup with only two leads coming out (a hot and ground), the start and finish ends of each coil are brought outside the pickup casing in a four-wire coaxial cable with a separate ground (either a separate strand or braid of wire). The two coils can be wired together in five combinations: 1) in series/out of phase (a normal humbucker); 2) parallel/out of phase; 3) in series/in phase; 4) parallel/in phase; 5) either coil by itself (a coil-cut). Of course, many more options become available as soon as you start combining two pickups together.

The five pickup functions are normally controlled with

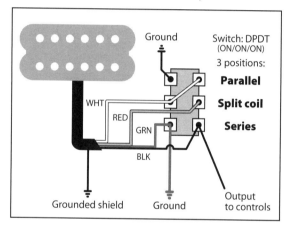

a mini switch (often supplied with the pickup) or a push/pull pot. Here's a simple Seymour Duncan diagram for using one humbucker three ways with a mini switch: in series, parallel or split-coil. This is a DPDT on/on/on mini switch. **DPDT = "Double pole, double throw."** Two poles (two sets of three lugs) on a switch that can be thrown two directions.

The best way for you to understand the different wiring options is to hear them. Install a four-wire humbucker in the bridge position, and bring the pickup wires out where you can twist (not solder) the leads together in the five different pickup combinations. Then solder two wires, a hot and ground, to an output jack and connect their free ends to two alligator clips. By connecting the alligator clips to the twisted ends of the colored wire combinations, you can plug a guitar cord into the jack and hear the sounds straight from the pickup to the

amp. Once you've heard the pickup sounds, you'll be more confident when using a wiring diagram to install the mini switches that allow pickup options to be neatly switched with the flip of a lever.

The following list shows how to wire finishes, starts and ground to get the five pickup combinations mentioned above. Remember, the pickup has five wires in all (two starts, two finishes and a ground).

Installing a humbucker in a Strat

Here's how to replace the rear (bridge) single-coil pickup of a Strat-style guitar with a humbucker. This is a tough job, requiring the use of a router and routing templates, but doable by a patient and careful do-it-yourselfer. You can eliminate the hassle of re-routing the pickguard simply by buying a pickguard with the rear humbucker cutout already made. These can be purchased from most guitar parts suppliers, and they allow you to save the original for posterity.

If you'd rather rout your own pickguard, here's how: lower the bridge pickup until it drops down, so that you can lay out the humbucking outline onto the pickguard. If you have a plastic pickup mounting ring, use that as a template. Otherwise, the usual humbucker rout is 1-1/2" x 2-3/4" with a 3/16" radius in the corners (you could make a cardboard template for tracing). Better yet, use a plastic routing template to lay it out; you'll soon be using it to do

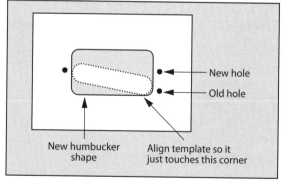

the routing, anyway.

With most Strat-style guitars, the rear rout is slanted, and you can use the original mounting hole in the pickguard on the bass (low-E) side for mounting the humbucker. You'll have to drill a new hole on the treble side, though, leaving the original treble hole showing. These days most bridge-mount humbuckers are installed at right angles to the guitar's centerline, and they're easy to lay out. The routing template has six holes drilled in it: the two center ones are for locating the height-adjustment screws, and the four corner ones locate the screw holes of a pickup mounting ring (as used on Les Pauls, 335s and many others). If you plan on using a mounting ring over the pickguard, you can use the four corner screws to mount the template. If not, use double-stick tape, since you wouldn't want the holes to show in your pickguard. Screwing down a template is the most solid and safest way to mount it; using double-stick tape works great, but you must be careful not to pull finish when removing the template. To avoid this, don't cover the entire template bottom with tape.

Place the template onto the pickguard with the bass-side holes for the height-adjustment screws lined up. Then align the template until its rear edge just touches the original single-coil cutout (as shown in the drawing, below, left). Mark lightly on the pickguard in pencil, unfasten the pickups, toggle switch, and volume and tone controls and remove the pickguard from the body. Now use the pencil marks to align the template as you stick it down to the pickguard with double-stick tape. You're ready to rout.

To do a perfect job, you should lay out and drill a 3/16" hole in each of the four inside corners of the area to be routed. This is because the smallest ball-bearing router bit is 3/8", which can't cut close enough to the four inside corners for the pickup cover to fit through the hole. The 3/8" bit will cut a proper size hole for a humbucker without a cover, however, since the corners don't need to be as tight. If you have trouble drilling the lower right corner because there's not enough plastic left from the original single-coil rout to hold the drill's tip, radius the corner with a small rat-tail file. You can do all the corners with a file, if you wish. Go ahead and rout. Routing templates are quite thin (3/16"), so be sure that the ball bearing is contacting the Plexiglas as you cut, and that the bearing can't slide up the shaft! If the bearing vibrates up the shaft, the router bit could cut an oversized hole. I use a length of 1/4" Teflon tubing slid over the router bit shaft to hold the bearing in place. When the pickguard cutout is routed, replace the pickguard and use the new hole as a template to mark out the body rout.

Routing the body cavity is much the same as routing the pickguard, but you need a different template be-

cause the mounting bracket or "tabs" extend beyond the length of the pickup. The hole in the pickguard is smaller and just allows clearance for the upper part of the pickup or its cover. The hole in the body is slightly bigger to accommodate the pickup frame. Install the new pickup into the pickguard and measure its underside to find out how deep the body rout must be. Note: You don't need to make the whole rout as deep as the mounting brackets, as you'll see if you study the situation or look at a factory rout on a Gibson Les Paul. You only need to rout or drill an oversize hole at each end of the cavity for the brackets and height-adjusting screws to fit into; these holes are usually routed slightly oval in shape.

Watch out for too-strong Strat magnets One famous quirk of Strat pickups is that if they are adjusted too closely to the strings, the magnets' strong fields can hold a string's vibration in a vertical pattern, not letting it vibrate freely in the normal elliptical pattern. This causes the low-E string (and sometimes the A and D) to go crazy, producing **unwanted harmonic overtones** that may be perceived as "double notes" or dead notes, and makes the proper intonation practically impossible. You may also notice a general out-of-tuneness on the bass strings, especially as you play up the neck. A pickup that's too close may also cause buzzing on the upper frets, because the magnets actually drag the strings down and against the frets, especially with light gauge sets beginning with .008s or .009s. This buzzing shouldn't be confused with a kinked neck, rising tongue or worn frets. Before setting the intonation or string/action height, you should lower the pickups a few turns to eliminate their pull, especially on the bass side. Later, when all the action and intonation adjustments have been completed, you can slowly raise the pickups to find that most of your bad-note problems have been eliminated.

You'll find the right height by experimenting. The overtones described above are found mostly on the bass strings, especially the E, and usually further up the neck. Simply keep raising the pickups until the overtone phenomenon begins to happen, and at that point back off a hair. By not getting too close, you'll find a cleaner sound with no bad notes, and eliminate potential buzzing in the fingerboard's upper register. Properly set-up Strat pickups are closer to the strings on the treble side

d.i.y.

than the bass; they actually slant downward across the body. And often the neck pickup is further from the strings than the bridge pickup.

Pickup repair

A P-90 potted in place I love soap bars (Gibson P-90 pickups). They have a killer sound. In working on them, I've wrecked two of them, out of ignorance and my sometimes too-curious nature.

I'll always regret taking out my first soap bar pickup to really get at the dirt while cleaning the guitar. I removed the two screws that held it down, but it wouldn't budge. Imagine my surprise when, as I pried out the pickup of my '55 Les Paul, I found that several hundred feet of very thin copper wire unwound right along with it—all over my lap! I managed to scrounge up another pickup, but these days an authentic vintage replacement would be hard to come by.

Normally, Gibson P-90 soap bars come out fairly easily, but you'll find some that are really tight. If it's just the cleaning that you're worried about, I'd say leave the pickups alone and clean around them as best you can.

P-90 pickups aren't glued in but they can feel like it. And it's usually only the dirty guitars that have hard to remove pickups—it's all the beer, pop, food and ozone that's been spilled onto them in the honky-tonks where these great guitars have paid their dues.

Sometimes pickups stick to the lacquer upon which they sit, especially in humid weather. Perhaps the wood around them has swollen a bit. To loosen the pickups, raise the polepieces above the pickup surface and use a Vise-Grip to grab them (use thin strips of wood to protext the polepieces from the jaws). Go easy! If the polepieces are rusted and frozen too, you'll need to make a strong, thin, L-shaped hook/probe to reach under the pickup base as a pry bar.

Don't just grab the pickup by its cover and pull—this is what caused my catastrophe. Those pre-'55 P-90 coil forms were glued together rather than machined of solid stock like the post-'55 models, and when I pulled the pickup cover, the top plate of the bobbin stuck to it while the rest of the pickup remained snug in the cavity.

Whoops!

Now a guitar like the '57 Les Paul Junior shown here that uses a P-90 mounted with metal tabs and "dogear"

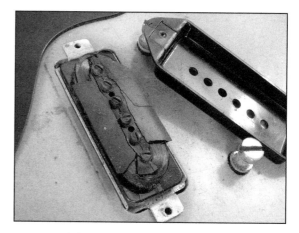

covers is a different story since the only contact made between the cover and the pickup is at the top of the bobbin—and the cover is more likely to lift free easily. Still you must be careful, and you don't know what you'll find. When I lifted the cover of this Junior I freaked —the top was crushed something awful, and there were even pieces missing.

I gently re-installed the cover without touching it further and I checked to see if it had any output by touching the hot probe of my multimeter to the lug that the pick-

up's hot wire is soldered to and the ground wire on the pot. The pickup worked! It measured 8.14K. I called my pal **Lindy Fralin** for advice.

"Dan, I'll bet you can leave it alone and it'll sound great for years and years. Especially since the plastic's just broken, not rotted.

Sometimes we see P-90s that no longer work, with decaying plastic and corroded coils. Those bobbins need to be rebuilt or replaced.

"But, because this pickup works, and because the coil has kept its original shape, and not expanded, it's a candidate for the repair I describe here. By expanded I mean when the plastic bobbin has cracked and fallen away—no longer supporting the coil, and the coil expands upward into the areas where the plastic had been.

"Light a candle, and dribble hot wax over the exposed copper wire. Mask off around the pickup by cutting a pickup-shaped hole in a piece of paper. Don't tape it down; tape and dry old finishes don't mix. You can slide

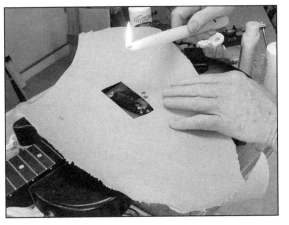

the paper around with one hand so that it's always protecting the area where you are waxing. Don't use potting wax or beeswax because it's too hot. You don't want to get the parts hot. Candle wax melts at a much lower temperature.

Don't worry if the wax cools fast and is lumpy. You can smooth it with a low-wattage soldering iron—just like frosting a cake. Touch only the wax, and not any part of the pickup; the wax will respond instantly, you'll see.

I was nervous about the soldering iron, and afraid I wouldn't have Lindy's skill at this, so I used a palette knife heated over an alcohol lamp instead. I bent my knife a little to give it a slight "spoon" curve (upper right).

Lindy was right: the wax smoothed out, and the cover fit back on perfectly. Here's a good little trick: put a piece of clear plastic tubing over the screwdriver shaft, and it holds the screw for you.

So, the pickup covers may or may not come free of the pickup easily, and in most cases there's no reason to ever take them off. Also, plastic covers shrink over the years and grip the pickup tightly. The plastic of both the covers

and the pickup are probably brittle from age, and may easily crack or break. Therefore, you should leave the covers on original P-90s if you can.

Soap bars made before 1968 had Alnico II magnets that demagnetize over time and lose power (we used to buy these magnets from Gibson and recharge our pickups with them, but they're no longer available). Ex-Gibson design-engineer Tim Shaw suggests having your old magnets re-magnetized at an automotive or bicycle shop that services speedometers. Ask them to saturate the magnets. This restores much of the original power and sound. If you remove the magnets, mark them so that you can replace them exactly as they came out. You can also re-magnetize P-90 magnets with "guitar repair magnets" as described on page 278 by passing the flat P-90 magnets between two fixed repair magnets. The great thing about re-magnetizing is that you can increase your output without doing anything to damage the integrity of a fine vintage instrument—always the best solution!

Back in the day I had more than a few Gibson Les Pauls in several models. One was a double-P-90 Gibson Les Paul Special that I bought at a pawn shop without even plugging it in, I wanted to get it out of there so fast. When I got it home I found that the bridge pickup was almost dead. I "knew" this because, when I tapped on

the polepieces with a screwdriver the bridge pickup was as loud as the neck; yet when I plucked a string it was real quiet—almost nothing came out. It seemed obvious to me that I needed to get another pickup.

This was before I realized that this situation is repairable, and before the time that it was easy to come by spare parts. We'd drive from Ann Arbor, Michigan up to Gibson in Kalamazoo, and buy what we needed. So I pulled that pickup out and put in a new one. Today, I realize my mistake—and it was **Seymour Duncan** who put me straight:

"Dan, if you can tap on the polepiece with something metal and get a loud, strong signal—but you hear almost no sound from the strings, one of the two magnets at the bottom of the coil has been reversed. Notice, however, that you only get the loud signal when you're holding the screwdriver sideways, at a right angle to

the polepieces. The magnetic field travels up through the shaft of the screwdriver and out over half of the coil, creating a horseshoe magnet effect and a strong signal when the screwdriver touches the polepiece. If you hold the screwdriver vertically and tap the polepiece with just the tip of it, you'll break the field and get the weak signal again.

"When you take a P-90 apart (two screws on the bottom hold it together) the magnets will fall out easily because Gibson assembles them with like poles (South to South) facing center—this makes them repel each other and "jump" right out! If you weren't paying attention, you wouldn't know which way they came out,

so it'd be easy to replace one—or both—of the magnets incorrectly. This could mean either of two things with vintage P-90s: 1) That mismatched North and South edges are facing center, causing a weak signal; 2) That two North edges face center causing both pickups to be out of phase when used together. There are clues for finding the South edge:

"On really old P-90s, the South edge of the magnet was machined smooth to butt against the center spacer, but the North edge remained in the slightly rougher state produced by the sand-casting process used in manufacturing. Gibson workers could identify North just by the rough-cast edge, but as a safeguard Gibson also marked the magnets' North poles (edges) with black-inked lines.

"Later, Gibson began using magnets with both edges machined smooth, but a black mark still identified North. Then, probably around '68 when a lot of pickup stuff was revamped, Gibson began putting the North edge (with its black mark) toward center on P-90s (where it remains to this day).

"Mismatched magnets (North to South) cause the signal to become weak, as you describe. Simply take the pickup apart and reverse one magnet, and you'll have a loud pickup again (and a more valuable guitar)—but if you happen to put North to North, instead of South to South, the pickup will regain its power, but it will be out of phase with the other pickup (obvious from a loss of power and a tinny, hollow sound when both pickups are used together in the middle toggle-switch position).

"Re-phase the pickup by reversing both magnets so their South edges face center. Or, I prefer to leave the North edges facing in, and re-phase the pickup by reversing the "start" and "finish" ends of the copper wire wrapped around the coil form. You don't just reverse the obvious braided shield (ground) and black cloth-wrapped (hot) output wires—you must go back to the small black and white plastic-coated wires coming off the coil, and wired at the base of the pickup. By rewiring the leads, instead of reversing the magnets, the pickups will be in-phase, but with "reverse-polarity"—making them hum-cancelling when used together in the middle position!

"Handle old P-90s with extreme care—they're delicate, so athough reversing the magnet is easy, and the rewiring isn't too difficult, have an experienced repair technician do either job.

"I wonder who ended up with that pickup and what they did with it, don't you, Dan?"—*Seymour Duncan*

At the time that I talked with Seymour I also talked to **J.T. Riboloff**, then with Gibson USA's research team in Nashville, Tennessee. After verifying the information presented here, J.T. added: "Today, we don't just reverse the magnets on our current P-90s. We wind the coil so that the start is positive, and the finish is ground—just the opposite of the old P-90s, but with the same polarity. If you use a new P-90 with an old one, together they're hum-cancelling just like Seymour described earlier."

Learning the hard way

I encourage you to try things out and experiment, but it's risky. Here's a case where my experimenting got me in trouble.

Along with the pickup, and good, detailed instructions, the Baggs iBeam comes with a great installation tool. I made a couple of modifications to the tool to adapt it to the X-bracing pattern of the guitar at hand. The tool locates on the two outer E string holes in the bridge—one of the post holes is oblong so that you can slide it sideways to match the particular string spacing of bridge. It's an elaborate jig.

I needed to trim off some of the jig's plate to fit it forward of the bridge pin holes without bumping into the X-braces. The bridge was slightly off center to the top and the X-bracing; I needed to enlarge the non-oblong hole a little with a rat-tail file to move in the direction I wanted, but even after the above mods, I couldn't quite get the iBeam enough forward of the bridge pin holes.

So, I filed and sanded off a little on each end of the pickup until it fit. **That's where I made my mistake.**

The pickup now fit nicely, but the it no longer worked. I called Baggs and they emailed me a diagram that showed exactly how much you can remove from the pickup and where. I should have checked this out in the first place, of course. Live and learn!

Whatever you gotta do to make it work

Here's an oddball little job: recently a friend tried to install a Seymour Duncan Acoustic Tube pickup in the soundhole of his Alvarez concert-size flattop (00-size). When he couldn't get it to fit he brought it to me.

At 3-3/4", the soundhole was too small for the pickup. I measured a 1950s 00-18 Martin, and it was the same (and a good number of smaller guitars are patterned after the 00-size, so be sure to measure before you buy). The pickup fits soundholes from 3-7/8" to 4-1/4" in diameter (like Martin dreadnaughts and Gibson Jumbos and L-00s). I could almost get the pickup in the soundhole, but not quite. I could have carved away a little wood (plywood) but he didn't want that. So, I modified the Tube.

With nippers I cut off the rolled-over lip on each end, then filed off the razor-sharp edges left by the nippers.

A wrap of black electrician's tape hides the work.

And it fit just right, like a good do-it-yourself job oughta

Remagnetizing

If a pickup has a good DC resistance, but is still weak, the magnet(s) may have lost their strength. If you don't have a gauss meter or magnetometer it's difficult to know how strong a magnet is. However, if you have similar pickups in your shop, and one seems to pull on the tip of a screwdriver harder than the other, you can guess that the magnet is weak. A polarity checker is a must for deciphering polarities. This is a simple little device containing a magnet that flips its North or South side up when placed against a polepiece.

Another reason for remagnetizing a pickup is to swap the magnetic polarity of a single-coil, so it will act as a humbucker when combined with another single-coil. Note: the coil must also be reverse-wound for this pickup to have the proper phase relationship and noise canceling humbucking properties.

To recharge a dead or weak magnet, use two strong Neodymium Boride magnets (I use my shop "guitar repair" magnets) held just far enough apart for the pickup to be held and guided between them. The magnets should be aligned so the attracting flat surfaces are facing each other (the magnets are pulling toward each other). You may wish to make a simple holding fixture in the shape of a "C" to hold the magnets (see an example on page278). Then you can hold the pickup steady with both hands as you move it through the magnetic field. Use your polarity tester to take note of which side is North and South polarity in your magnet-holding fixture, and what the top polarity of the pickup should be.

To swap a pickup's polarity, simply run the pickup between the two magnets a few times with the top aligned with the new desired polarity.

Rewiring, modifications

Rewiring a Strat for more options

Here's how you can wire a 5-way switch to use three pickups at once, or the front and rear in combination. I learned this from my friend and fellow repairman, **Mike Koontz** of Koontz Guitar Repair in Ferndale, Michigan. Mike's an ace repairman at all levels and a whiz at guitar electronics, and he always seems to find an easier way.

A simple way to get all possible pickup combinations is to install a single-pole/single-throw on/off switch between the neck pickup contact at the 5-way switch and the hot lug of the volume control. This way, the neck pickup is still controlled normally by the switch lever. But since it's also wired directly to the volume control through the on/off switch, you can cut it in or out at will. This lets you use all three pickups at once, or the front and rear together. You can wire in the bridge (rear) pickup instead of the front and get the same combinations.

The drawing on the next page is a wiring diagram for a Strat. Notice points "A" and "B"—you add the switch between these. But instead of drilling a hole in your pickguard and adding a switch, replace the rear-most (middle pickup) tone control with a "push/pull pot." This is a regular pot with a DPDT switch built into it. The push/

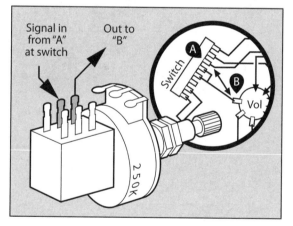

pull pot still serves as the normal tone control, but also acts as the new switch when you pull up on the knob. The rear tone control is the easiest to wire, since you wire in the new pot just like the one it replaces. Then run a wire from "A" at the 5-way switch into the new piggyback switch and out again to "B" of the volume pot (left). You only use one side (and two lugs) of the push/pull switch.

Also see the Megaswitch E wiring options chart on

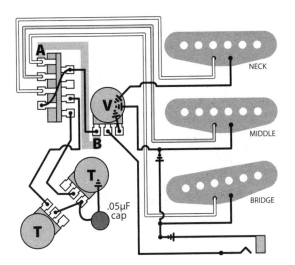

page 273. On the outside, this versatile switch looks a standard Fender toggle, but check out the many pickup combinations it makes possible.

Another option is to install three mini switches—one for each pickup. This involves drilling three holes in the pickguard. Each switch controls one pickup, so you can have any combination you wish. I've seen many guitars with this setup.

Rewiring a 3-pickup Les Paul Custom

Phil Henderson of Foley, Alabama writes, "I have a 1961 Gibson Les Paul Custom 'Fretless Wonder.' It's a white, three-pickup, SG-type that I understand was the transition between the Les Paul Standard and the SG. Its pickup selector switch allows three combinations: neck, middle, and middle and rear. Frankly, this doesn't give me the sounds I'd like. Can it be wired like a Strat with a 5-way position switch to get each pickup individually and the neck/middle and middle/bridge combinations? Can this be done without drilling any holes or harming its value too much (even though I'd never sell it)?"

First of all, Phil, remember that anything you do to alter a "factory" guitar will affect its value on a very finicky vintage market. But sometimes you just gotta do what you gotta do. I've never tried rewiring a three-pickup Gibson the way you want, but electronics expert **Mike Koontz**, of Koontz Guitar Repair in Ferndale, Michigan, has. Mike faxed me the solution to the question almost before I'd hung up the phone!

The wiring option he sent me is on page 267, labeled **Gibson Les Paul modification**. It gives you a

5-way Strat-style pickup selection—without drilling any holes—by converting the neck tone control to a middle pickup volume control. This leaves the remaining bridge pickup tone control as a master tone for all three pickups. This modification allows you to operate your guitar like a standard two-pickup Les Paul, with the option of "fading-in" or adding the middle pickup to any combination of the selector switch. Or, by turning down either the neck or bridge volume control in its respective switch position, you can use the middle pickup by itself.

The circuit's also useful for anyone planning to drop a third pickup into a two-pickup Gibson, since it uses the standard toggle selector switch that comes on a two-pickup Les Paul, which differs from the toggle switch used on a three-pickup Les Paul. The three-pickup switch has an extra lug, or "leaf," that you'll notice is not used in the modified schematic. All hot wires must be shielded, of course.

Wiring diagrams

On the following pages I've gathered together three dozen wiring diagrams that have been useful in my shop, and I think you'll use them too. Over the years I've saved piles of diagrams like my Danelectro drawing below, done on the back of an envelope. This one's also the first diagram on the next page, but since my scribbles are hard to follow, they've been cleaned up for you! This selection will help you with most of the guitars and modifications that you'll come across. If you want more, you'll find a lot at **SeymourDuncan.com**. And the free info section at **stewmac.com** includes more than diagrams: you'll also find instructions for wiring and electronics. But before you head online, take a look through these pages; you'll probably find what you need.

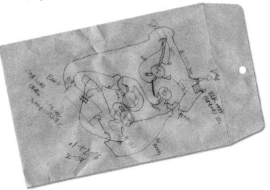

Danelectro U2

I love my Danelectro. I even posed with it for the back cover photo. Somebody rewired it before I got it, however. It sounds so killer as-is that I'm afraid to touch it, but I've always wanted to know how it originally was wired. I've never found a diagram that seemed right, until this one: it's copied from a Silvertone brand version of my Dano (like the one **Jim Weider** uses for playing slide). This guitar was built by Danelectro, and had an untouched wiring harness wrapped in folded copper foil. I unwrapped it and drew this from it.

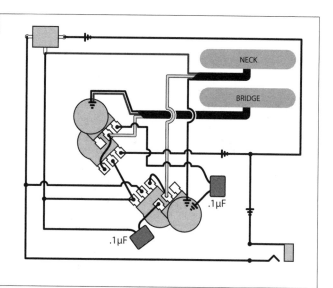

Fender Esquire

The first Esquire I remember seeing was in the hands of **Jeff Beck** on the album *Having a Rave-up with The Yardbirds* — and the sound of the guitar on *Mister You're A Better Man Than I*. I thought it was a Telecaster. (That was the famous one he gave to **Seymour Duncan**.)

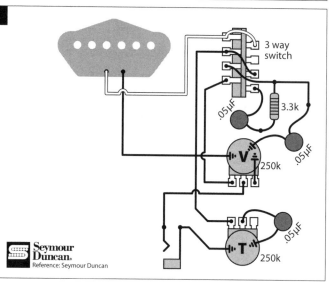

Fender Broadcaster with blend

The first significant production Fender. The Esquire prototypes that came before were the parents, the Broadcaster was the baby, and the Tele was grandchild (the "NoCaster" was the bastard child). Only about 200 Broadcasters were made. With two controls , volume and "blend", and a 3-way switch, the Broadcaster has these control options:

Neck alone With a pre-set bassy sound.

Neck alone Natural sound, no tone control.

Bridge and neck Blended together by means of the second "tone" control (not a true tone control yet).

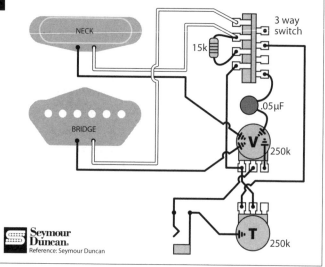

)d.i.y.o

Fender Telecaster 1953

Leo added a real tone control, not a blender. Now the pickup options were:

Neck alone Pre-set bassy tone.

Middle Neck alone, with a tone control.

Rear Bridge alone, also with a tone control. This lasted until around 1967.

A butterscotch color, black-guard '53 Tele makes me think of: **Keith Richards**, **James Burton**, **Roy Nichols** (Merle Haggard & The Strangers) **Albert Lee**, **Ray Flack** and the list goes on…

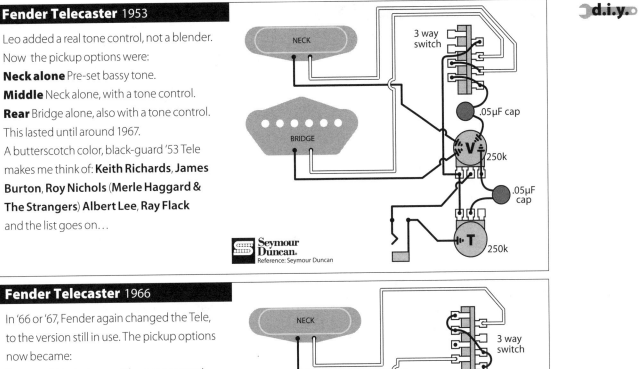

Seymour Duncan®
Reference: Seymour Duncan

Fender Telecaster 1966

In '66 or '67, Fender again changed the Tele, to the version still in use. The pickup options now became:

Forward Neck alone, with a tone control.

Middle Both together with a tone control.

Bridge Bridge alone, with tone control. These are the almost see-through blonde, white pickguard versions. **Buck Owens**, **Don Rich**, **Steve Cropper** and **John Hiatt** come to mind. This is still the most popular wiring.

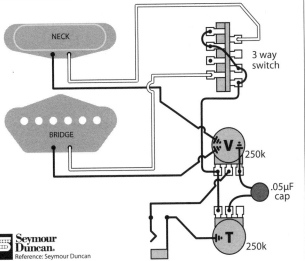

Seymour Duncan®
Reference: Seymour Duncan

Fender Telecaster w/4way switch

The same as the '67 with the additional option of both pickups in series for some real twang!

P1 Forward position: neck alone.

P2 Both pickups, parallel.

P3 Both pickups, in series.

P4 Bridge alone.

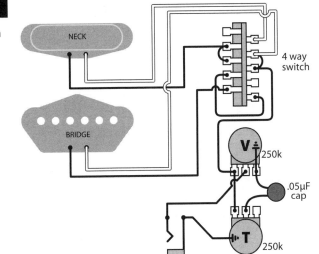

d.i.y.

Fender Stratocaster

The original Strat circuitry. Think **Buddy Holly** and **Buddy Guy**—who sold me on a Strat in 1967 when he played in Ann Arbor the first time out with his own band. He played the beat-up and beautiul '57 Strat that he was known for then, using the in-between switch positions to get his signature out of phase sound. It wasn't always easy to get the 3-way toggle switch to catch this way between the neck/middle, or the middle/rear position.

Forward Neck and tone control.

Middle Middle and tone control.

Rear Rear pickup, no tone control.

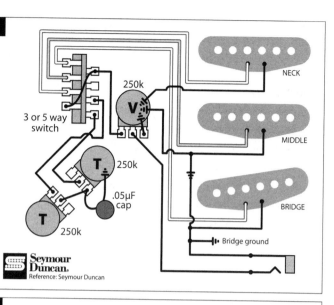

Fender Duo-Sonic

The Duo-Sonic was a Musicmaster with a second pickup in the bridge position and a selector switch to go with it. My first and only Duo-Sonic was a '59 with a gold anodized pickguard. Right in the middle of the 'guard was a doorbell with a white pearl button, used as a kill switch. Some do-it-yourselfer installed this long before Eddie Van Halen or Buckethead had hit the stage. It was a great effect (and good for ducking-out instantly if you hit the wrong chord). I let the little beauty go out one night and she never came back.

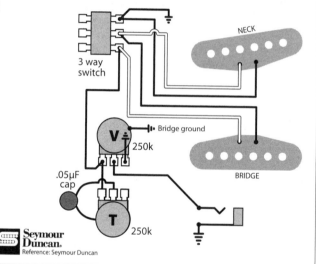

Fender Mustang

Fender's Mustang was a step up from a Duosonic or Musicmaster. The same two pickups, a volume and tone control, *plus* a pair of 3-position slide switches and a tremolo. Short of owning a Tele or Strat, the Mustang was the next choice for Fender players. Each pickup has a slide switch that operates the same: in the middle position, the pickup is turned off, and the two outside positions change the tone. Both pickups share the same volume and tone controls.

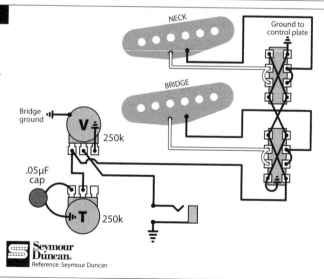

d.i.y.

Fender Jazzmaster

I bought my first Jazzmaster in '64 because there were two of them in the same store. My brother Michael got the other one. At the time we both played guitar in the Prime Movers, an Ann Arbor, Michigan-based band.

The Jazzmaster has master volume and tone control pots in the normal place, but it also has a second tone circuit activated by a slide switch in the upper side of the pickguard near the neck. This lets you pre-set the thumb roller volume and tone wheels for quiet, mellow, "jazzy" rhythm work.

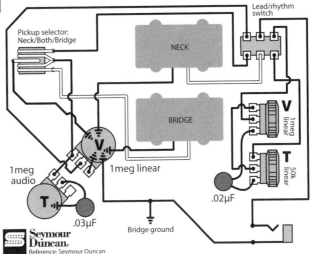

Fender Jaguar

The Jaguar is like a short-scale (24") Jazzmaster with bells and whistles. Like the Jazzmaster, for bells it had pre-set volume and tone with a switch on the upper horn to activate it. But, it also had whistles: three slide switches on the lower horn. One was a tone modification switch, and the other two were pickup on/off.

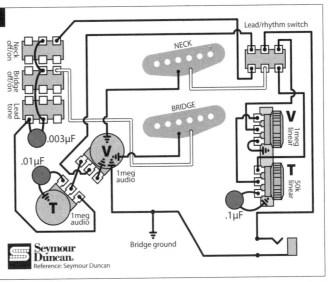

Fender Precision Bass

The first Precision Bass had a Tele-shaped body and peghead, and a somewhat Tele-style pickup that wasn't split in two. In '57 the body got a Strat-like body and peghead, and became the P-bass we know today. That's when it got that staggered-coil pickup, too. The two coils were wired in humbucking mode, but Fender didn't advertise that since Seth Lover's humbucking pickup patent hadn't yet expired. When I think of the P-bass, I think of **Donald "Duck" Dunn** and **James Jamerson's** Funk Machine. It's an easy wire: 1 volume, 1 tone.

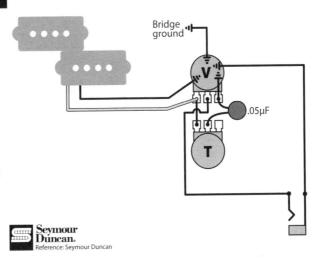

Fender Jazz Bass stacked knobs

The original Jazz Bass was introduced in 1960 with two single-coil pickups and two stacked-knob pots that provided individual volume and tone for each pickup. Rather than using a selector switch, you blend the neck and bridge pickups together.

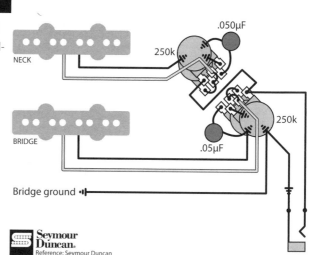

Fender Jazz Bass modern

In 1961, the stacked knobs on the Jazz Bass were replaced by standard control pots (a volume knob for each pickup), and a third pot was added for overall tone control. Still no selector switch.

This is **Jaco Pastorius'** Bass of Doom, the one whose fingerboard he yanked the frets out of and coated with epoxy.

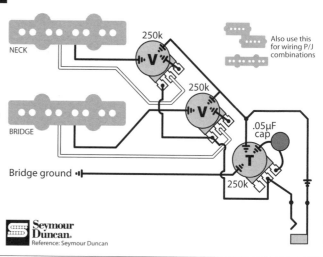

Gibson Les Paul and ES-335 1950s

My first Les Paul was a '59 sunburst. In 1967 I traded it to my hero **Mike Bloomfield** for the '54 goldtop he'd played on the Paul Butterfield Blues Band's *East-West* album. Before long I went back to a '59 burst. (Once again, I wanted to play what Bloomfield played). Had I not traded guitars with him, however, I might never have learned to appreciate P-90s. The ES-335 had the same wiring. My first "good" electric guitar was a brand new '63 cherry red ES-335. I loved it, but I "couldn't keep up the payments and the man he took it back" as Freddie King sang.

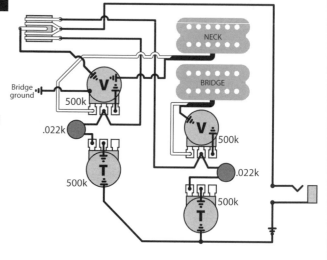

d.i.y.

Gibson Les Paul and **ES-335** modern

This is the wiring diagram for a modern Les Paul. It's just a modification of what came before.

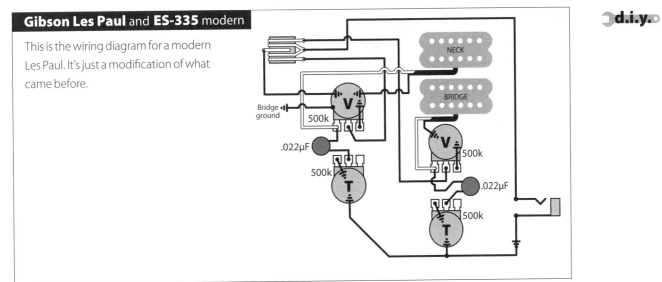

Gibson Les Paul with 3 pickups

In 1957 Gibson started offering the Les Paul Custom with the option of a 3rd humbucker in the middle position. These models were often used by players such as Keith Richards and Sister Rosetta Tharpe. The rhythm and treble settings are the same as the 2-pickup model. The middle position combines the bridge and middle pickups out of phase for a variation in tone.

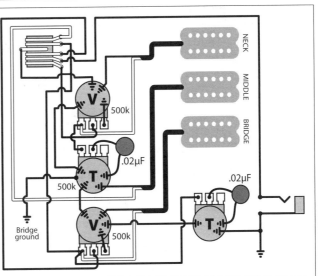

Gibson Les Paul modification

Here's a modification of a 3-pickup Les Paul: the diagram **Mike Koontz** created in answer to a question on page 261. This gives you a 5-way Strat style pickup selection. The neck tone control becomes a middle volume control, and the bridge tone control becomes a master tone for all three pickups.

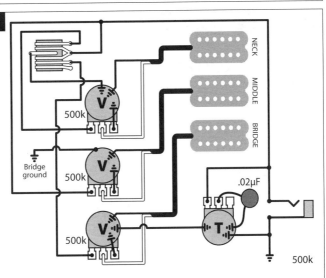

d.i.y.

Gibson Les Paul Junior 1950s

Back in the day, a Junior was "trading stock." I could find them easily, and cheap. Never happy with the sound of a single P-90 in the bridge position, I wasn't inclined to keep, or play, a Junior. Today, I wish I had kept them all, of course, because their stock has gone up thanks to such players as **Leslie West** of Mountain.

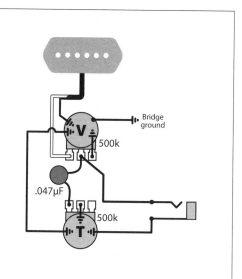

Gibson ES-345/ES-355 stereo, varitone

The ES-345 and -355 are fancier versions of the E-335, adding a 6-way rotary "Varitone" switch with caps of different values to act as a notch filter. Each control position shifts the notch higher or lower. I'd seen **Elvin Bishop** play his cherry red ES-345 many times, starting with the Butterfield Band, and of course there's **Lucille** on the cover of **B.B. King's** *Live at the Regal* album. When I saw **Freddie King** play his signature cherry red ES-345 at the Ann Arbor Blues Festival in 1970, that did it: soon I had one, too.

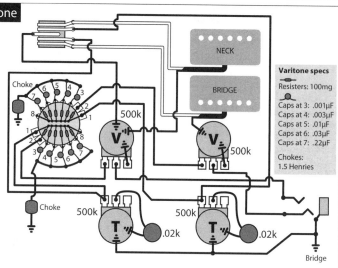

Varitone specs
Resisters: 100mg

Caps at 3: .001µF
Caps at 4: .003µF
Caps at 5: .01µF
Caps at 6: .03µF
Caps at 7: .22µF

Chokes:
1.5 Henries

Gibson Flying V and Explorer

I knew what a Flying V was because of **Lonnie Mack**. Then, probably in 1969, **Albert King** played at the Ann Arbor Blues Festival and I saw my first V in the flesh. I drew plans of Albert King's '59 Flying V so I could build him a custom version, which I did, and delivered about a year later. I still hadn't seen an Explorer yet, and wouldn't for a few years.

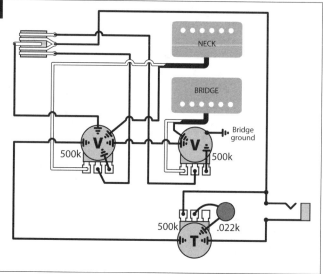

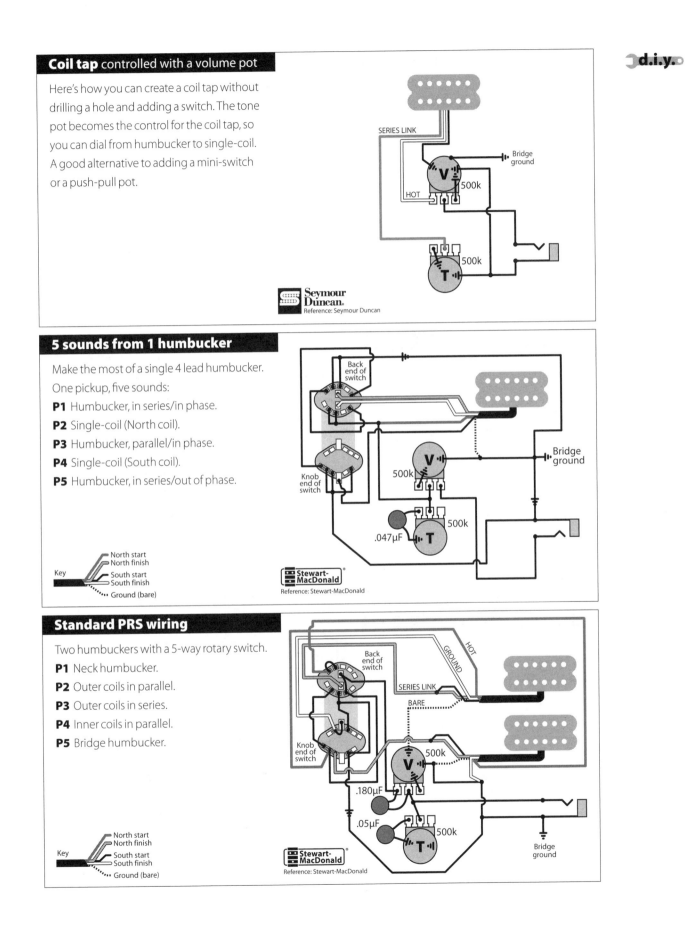

Coil tap controlled with a volume pot

Here's how you can create a coil tap without drilling a hole and adding a switch. The tone pot becomes the control for the coil tap, so you can dial from humbucker to single-coil. A good alternative to adding a mini-switch or a push-pull pot.

SERIES LINK

Bridge ground

V 500k

HOT

500k
T

Seymour Duncan.
Reference: Seymour Duncan

5 sounds from 1 humbucker

Make the most of a single 4 lead humbucker.
One pickup, five sounds:

P1 Humbucker, in series/in phase.

P2 Single-coil (North coil).

P3 Humbucker, parallel/in phase.

P4 Single-coil (South coil).

P5 Humbucker, in series/out of phase.

Back end of switch

Knob end of switch

Bridge ground

V 500k

.047µF

T 500k

Key
North start
North finish
South start
South finish
Ground (bare)

Stewart-MacDonald
Reference: Stewart-MacDonald

Standard PRS wiring

Two humbuckers with a 5-way rotary switch.

P1 Neck humbucker.

P2 Outer coils in parallel.

P3 Outer coils in series.

P4 Inner coils in parallel.

P5 Bridge humbucker.

Back end of switch

GROUND

HOT

SERIES LINK

BARE

Knob end of switch

V 500k

.180µF

.05µF

T 500k

Bridge ground

Key
North start
North finish
South start
South finish
Ground (bare)

Stewart-MacDonald
Reference: Stewart-MacDonald

d.i.y.

d.i.y.

2 humbuckers with a 3-way switch

Found on a huge number of guitars, including
B.C. Rich, ESP, Ibanez, Samick and many more.
It's basically like the 1966 Tele diagram, but
with humbuckers.

P1 Neck pickup.

P2 Both pickups.

P3 Bridge pickup.

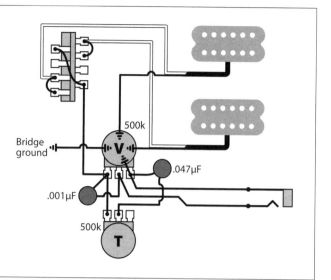

2 humbuckers with a toggle switch

Similar to the diagram above, but using a
toggle switch (think Epiphone).

P1 Neck pickup.

P2 Both pickups.

P3 Bridge pickup.

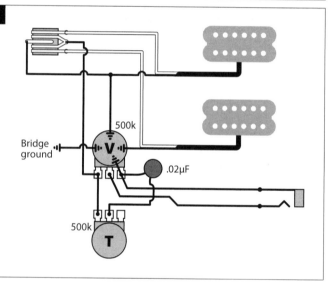

Fralin blender

Lindy Fralin's known as a Strat player, but he's
also a great player who's able to get the soul
of the sound of any guitar model. He has great
ears, and knows how to make pickups that
capture the sounds you describe. His blender
pot is real nice. It mixes the neck and bridge
pickups without affecting the 5-way switch.
With it you can control the volume of each
pickup and even get all three. The middle pot
becomes the master tone for the whole guitar.

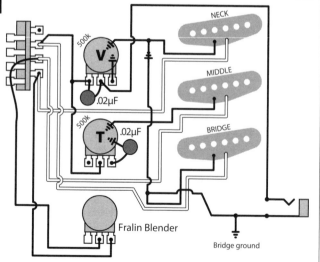

d.i.y.

H/S/H coil splitting with a 5-way switch

Commonly known as the Ibanez Steve Vai JEM wiring. A clever way of getting coil cuts from a standard 5-way switch, coil-cutting the humbuckers in the 2nd an 4th positions.

Key
North start
North finish
South start
South finish
Ground (bare)

Bridge ground

500k
.05µF
500k

Stewart-MacDonald
Reference: Stewart-MacDonald

S/S/H coil splitting with a 5-way switch

The wiring modification shown by the dotted line gives you the option of coil-cutting your bridge humbucker in position 4, giving you a single-coil Strat sound.

(Optional automatic coil cut of bridge pickup.)

5 way switch

NECK

MIDDLE

BRIDGE

Bridge ground

250k
250k
.05µF cap

Stewart-MacDonald
Reference: Stewart-MacDonald

2 humbuckers with a Super Switch

P1 Bridge humbucker.
P2 Bridge humbucker, inner coil.
P3 Bridge and neck humbuckers.
P4 Neck, inner coil.
P5 Neck humbucker.
The option indicated by a dotted line lets you tap the outer coils instead of the inner coils

500k

Optional: to split the humbuckers to the outer coils, connect this wire this way instead.

500k
.047µF
Bridge ground

Key
North start
North finish
South start
South finish
Ground (bare)

Seymour Duncan
Reference: Seymour Duncan

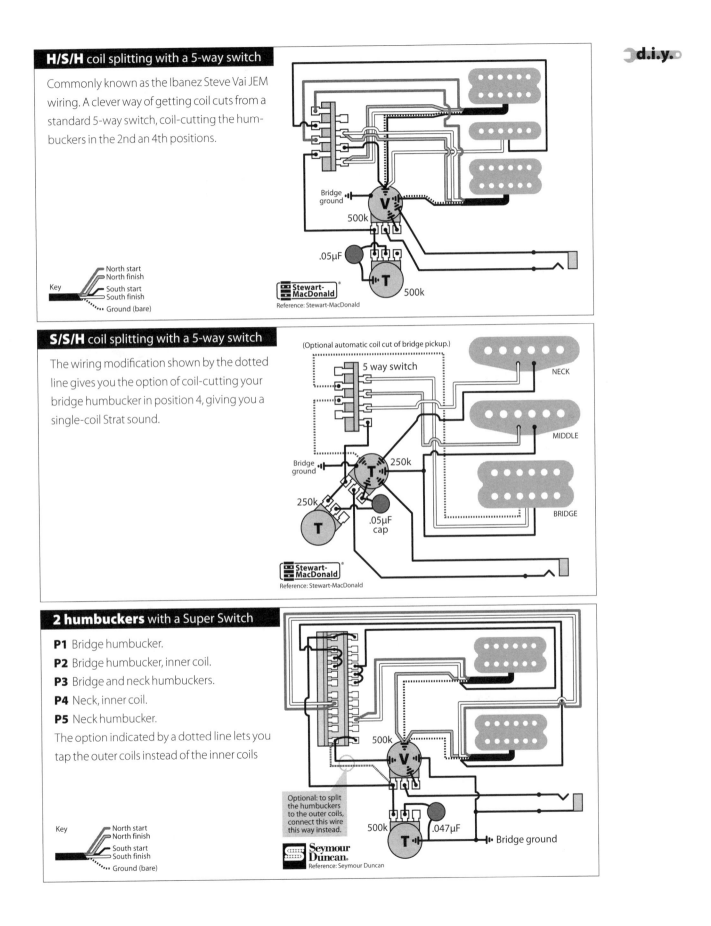

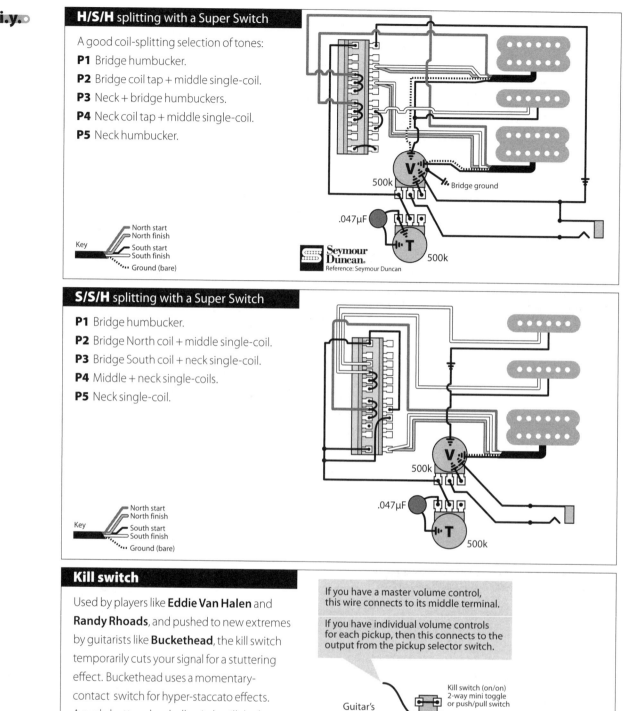

d.i.y.

H/S/H splitting with a Super Switch

A good coil-splitting selection of tones:
P1 Bridge humbucker.
P2 Bridge coil tap + middle single-coil.
P3 Neck + bridge humbuckers.
P4 Neck coil tap + middle single-coil.
P5 Neck humbucker.

Key
North start
North finish
South start
South finish
Ground (bare)

500k

.047µF

500k

Bridge ground

Seymour Duncan.
Reference: Seymour Duncan

S/S/H splitting with a Super Switch

P1 Bridge humbucker.
P2 Bridge North coil + middle single-coil.
P3 Bridge South coil + neck single-coil.
P4 Middle + neck single-coils.
P5 Neck single-coil.

Key
North start
North finish
South start
South finish
Ground (bare)

500k

.047µF

500k

Kill switch

Used by players like **Eddie Van Halen** and **Randy Rhoads**, and pushed to new extremes by guitarists like **Buckethead**, the kill switch temporarily cuts your signal for a stuttering effect. Buckethead uses a momentary-contact switch for hyper-staccato effects. A push-button doorbell switch will do the trick. Pete Townshend gets this effect on Les Pauls by turning the neck pickup's volume to zero, then moving the pickup selector from the middle to the bridge position, cutting the output. It's rough on the switch, though.

If you have a master volume control, this wire connects to its middle terminal.

If you have individual volume controls for each pickup, then this connects to the output from the pickup selector switch.

Guitar's main ground

Kill switch (on/on) 2-way mini toggle or push/pull switch

Seymour Duncan.
Reference: Seymour Duncan

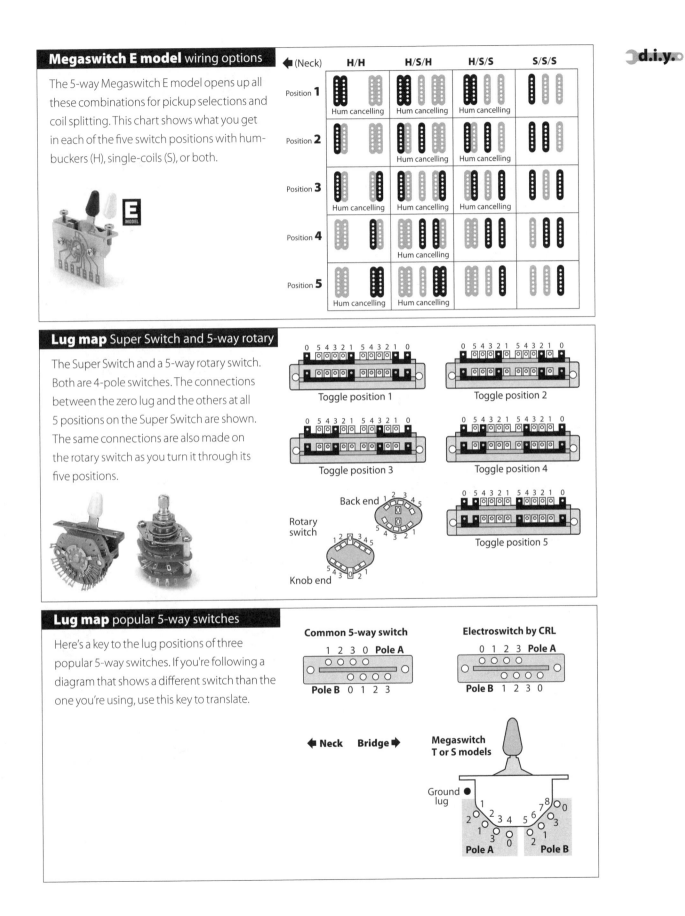

Megaswitch E model wiring options

The 5-way Megaswitch E model opens up all these combinations for pickup selections and coil splitting. This chart shows what you get in each of the five switch positions with humbuckers (H), single-coils (S), or both.

Lug map Super Switch and 5-way rotary

The Super Switch and a 5-way rotary switch. Both are 4-pole switches. The connections between the zero lug and the others at all 5 positions on the Super Switch are shown. The same connections are also made on the rotary switch as you turn it through its five positions.

Lug map popular 5-way switches

Here's a key to the lug positions of three popular 5-way switches. If you're following a diagram that shows a different switch than the one you're using, use this key to translate.

Wind your own pickups

One of the most fun things I've learned to do in recent years is making and repairing pickups—something I'd probably never have tried if an affordable pickup winder

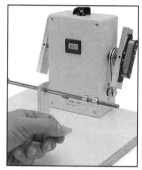

hadn't become available. With a built-in counter and a variable speed control, the Schatten Pickup Winder is a remarkably good tool for $350. To get an idea of a professional rig, here's TV Jones' highly sophisticated winder:

I'm lucky to have met and befriended many of our most prominent pickup makers: **Seymour Duncan, Lindy Fralin**, **JM Rolph**, **Jason Lollar**, **Kent Armstrong, Steve Blucher** (DiMarzio), **TV Jones** and **Joe Barden**. They've all encouraged me to try my hand at winding. Once I did I was hooked.

It's easy to daydream while winding a coil; while watching my hand and the spinning coil, I'd wonder how I might have built a pickup when I was a kid—back in the days of Erector sets. I decided to find some ways for someone to wind pickups when they don't have the cash for a professional winder.

The first one I made was the "Flintstone Winder"— built of plywood and dowels it looked like a Tinker Toy project. It's hand-powered by spinning the wheel. It took a while to fill a coil, but I wound several with it.

Then I took a cheap fishing reel, and fashioned it into a winder—driving the shaft of what had been the reel's hand-crank with an electric drill. I turned the spool

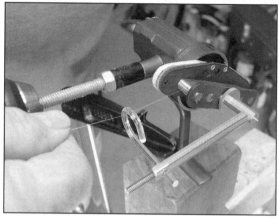

winder—the part that pumps in and out while laying the fishing line back and forth across the line spool—into a "limiter." This was great fun!

So was this one—powered by my electric drill.

Whether you make your own winder or buy one, here are uses you will find for it:

Rewinding dead pickups

✔ Rewind an entire pickup to original specs.

✔ Peel a pickup to find the problem, then rewind from the problem out.

✔ Rewind a pickup to custom specs (overwound, underwound, tapped output, etc.).

Modifying pickups

✔ Make higher output pickups out of standard pickups.

✔ Make a "tapped" single-coil.

✔ Add wire to an existing coil.

✔ Reduce the output of overwound pickups by peeling, tapping the coil and rewinding. This gives the customer more tone options from one pickup.

✔ Add to one coil of a humbucker to get slightly mismatched coils (credited for some players' unique tone).

Make pickups for specialty instruments

✔ Make replacement components to replace damaged pieces of an existing pickup.

✔ Design and build your own pickups.

Pickup rewinding requires patience and study. Don't dive into rewinding on valuable vintage pickups. Start with some el Cheapo pickups first. Most repair shops have collected a pile of dead pickups over the years—they're perfect for practicing. Remember the luthier's golden rule: Practice On Scrap!

Troubleshooting

To troubleshoot pickup ailments, isolate the pickup by unsoldering it from the guitar so that other electronic components don't affect your tests.

Weak output What is the DC resistance of the pickup? Normal DC resistance for a single-coil pickup is 6-8K Ohms; humbuckers are normally around 8-13K. If the pickup's DC resistance seems normal but the output is low, the magnets could be weak. See "Remagnetizing" on page 260.

A low DC resistance could indicate shorts within the coil windings. A typical cause is corrosion of the coating on the magnet wire, causing the coil wraps to short out against each other. This can drastically reduce output, making the pickup a candidate for rewinding.

No output Is there DC resistance between hot and ground, or is there a dead short? If there Is a reading for DC resistance, and it appears to be normal or close to

normal, the magnets may be dead, or there could be a poor solder joint, which has oxidized where the ends of the coil wire connect to the output wires.

If there is a dead short, then inner coil corrosion could be shorting out to ground, or there is a break in the coil wire. Before you do anything drastic like completely peeling or cutting the coil wire off of the pickup, make sure that the output wire solder connections to the coil wire are not corroded or broken.

Pickup peeling

How a pickup has been manufactured and potted (coated with wax, lacquer or epoxy) will affect how easily a coil can be peeled. Often, no matter how careful you are, a coil cannot be removed wind-by-wind. Age also can make the wire difficult to remove in one continuous piece. If you're not trying to retain the original wire or determine the number of winds on a specific coil (which would take forever), the quickest and easiest way to remove the coil windings is to cut through them with a sharp hobby knife.

Pickup winding

Read through these tips to get good idea of how pickup winding works before you start.

When you disassemble and peel a pickup be sure to make notes on how the coil attaches to the lead wires. Quick sketches or a photo are very helpful in recording how a pickup comes apart, and more importantly, how it will go back together!

File or sand any dings or nicks in the coil's flatwork. They should be smooth so they can't catch the coil wire. Make sure that there are no nicks in the edge of the wire spool or the traverse bar to snag the coil wire, so it comes off the spool cleanly.

Pickup wire isn't meant to feed off a rotating spool. It's too thin to take the strain of turning the spool. Instead, let the wire feed off the end of the spool. Position the spool horizontally, at the same height as the coil being wound, and about three or four feet away from it.

Be sure the pickup coil is well attached to the winding arm and that it runs true. Before attaching the coil wire, start the winder and see if there is a wobble or if the flatwork isn't spinning true and straight. Start the first 6-10 wraps by hand. This ensures that coil wire won't be

deep

pulled off of the bobbin when you start the motor. Start the winder slowly, then increase the speed. Use your fingers or a doubled-over piece of felt to pinch and guide the wire along the traverse.

Traverse end-stops limit the side-to-side travel of the wire. Position them so they're just inside the inner faces of the pickup's flatwork pieces.

Variations in tension and how the wraps align with each other are just two of the ways to affect a pickup's tone and response, so experiment to see what works for your needs.

The term "scatterwound" refers to pickups wound by hand rather than by a machine (i.e. the winder is used, but the wire is distributed onto the coil by hand—instead of by automation. Machine wound pickups have a very even winding pattern, and a "distributed capacitance" (the capacitance between each successive turn and layer of a coil). Scatterwinding lets you control the space between your winds and layers, therefore changing the distributed capacitance. Many feel the reason hand-wound pickups sound better and have more harmonic content than their machine-wound counterparts is because of scatterwound coils.

Don't wind a pickup too loose, but don't wind it too tight either! A loose coil will be microphonic and sloppy. If a coil's too tight you can actually deform the bobbin and it's even possible to cause the pickup to implode.

A former master builder at Fender, **Fred Stuart** gave this excellent description of scatterwinding: "My father was an engineer, and I remember riding in the car with him one day, and asking him why, after every third or fourth pole, the big, high-tension power lines that ran parallel to the road would cross over one another. He said to minimize "coupling" that if you run wires parallel to one another over a long distance, you get resistance in the line and you'll lose energy along the power line. In a pickup, when you wind those wires parallel to one another (as in machine-winding), the first thing you lose are the highs. When you hand-wind a pickup, I don't care how meticulous you are, it's almost impossible to get all the winds to line up parallel to one another. A machine, on the other hand can wind a coil with a huge number of parallel lines, and it's brutally precise; it will follow exactly the same path. When you look at the old Fender pickups you'll see these bumpy, lumpy, wound coils and that was

not an accident—Leo knew electronics.

"Something I do to my instruments, and I originally found this with old Fenders, is to twist the hot and ground going to the output jack in a barber pole fashion. You're wrapping the ground around the hot and giving it some degree of shielding. The same thing was done in old radios and amplifiers. It wasn't done to make it look pretty, it's functional." — *Fred Stuart*

You can wind until you reach a certain number of turns, or until the coil has the mass of wire you want or until you reach the desired DC resistance. You can check the DC resistance during the winding process by gently scraping off some of the protective coating on the coil wire with an X-Acto knife. Touch the "start" of the coil with one probe from your meter and touch the other probe to a portion of scraped coil wire just off of the coil (don't cut the coil wire!). When holding the VOM's probes on the wire, don't let your body's resistance affect the readings—there are VOM probes that have delicate little clips for clamping onto thin wire, and they are ideal for guitar electronics. If you need more wraps, put a drop of lacquer or nail polish on a paper towel and wipe a thin coating onto the bare portion of coil wire, let it cure for a few minutes and continue winding.

When you finish winding, carefully cut the wire and solder it to either the solder lugs (single-coil) or lead wires (humbucker).

Pickup potting

Potting a pickup means drenching it in a liquid that will solidify on it. This helps eliminate unwanted microphonics. Some pickups are not potted from the factory. While it's not necessary, potting is generally a good idea. Here are the common pickup potting materials.

Wax works well for most pickups. It's non-toxic, easy to deal with, cheap, and you can undo it if something goes wrong. Wax has a traditional appearance, and it works great for humbuckers with metal covers.

If the wax is too hot it can warp or melt plastic bobbins, and if it's way too hot you have a potential fire on your hands! Make sure that the wax never smokes— that's an indicator that it's getting too hot. Never try heating your wax on the kitchen stove or in a microwave oven because hot paraffin, and especially paraffin vapors, can ignite. It's best to wax pot outdoors until you have your methods refined and have eliminated any fire hazards.

To wax-pot a pickup after winding, suspend the pickup in canning paraffin mixed with 20% beeswax, heated to 145-150° Fahrenheit. After ten or fifteen minutes all of the bubbles should have risen out of the pickup, and all of the voids within the pickup should be filled with a coating of wax. Pull the pickup out of the wax and suspend it over the wax pot letting the excess wax drip back into the pot. Lay it on a paper towel and allow it to cool to touch. Carefully remove excess wax with a paper towel before the pickup completely cools to room temperature.

For potting, I use the same electric pot that I use for hot hide glue. It has a thermostat designed to heat hide glue to about 145°—just perfect for potting pickups, too (I keep a separate aluminum inner pot for wax of course). Keep the pot at least 2/3 or 3/4 full. It can operate with less liquid, but the wax may get too hot.

Lacquer is good for plastic bobbins that may melt during wax potting, but it can react with some plastic bobbin materials. Lacquer doesn't stop microphonics caused by metal covers on humbuckers, however, and it's difficult to peel a lacquer potted pickup. Lacquer has to be applied while winding, which slows down the process. To do this, use a small brush and add a thin coating of lacquer every minute or so. You must wait a few minutes before you start the winder, or you'll fling lacquer all over the place.

Epoxy is a virtually bulletproof potting material, and won't degrade in damp or harsh conditions, but it's difficult to get epoxy to penetrate deep into a pickup's windings, and practically impossible to repair an epoxy-potted pickup. I don't recommend epoxy potting.

A good case for making your own pickups

Here's a perfect example of why pickup making is so cool: a Fender Mustang being returned to its original state, undoing some unfortunate modifications. This is the same guitar seen in "Faking an aged finish" on page 304. Its original pickups were long gone, but my shopmate **Erick Coleman** had an idea for some custom pickups that would also have a little more ooomph than the original Mustang pickups.

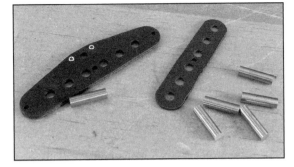

Since the shape of a Mustang pickup is the same as that of a Strat pickup, Erick used Strat-style pickup flatwork. However, instead of using polepiece magnets of staggered lengths, as a typical Strat has, Erick used six of the longest ones. He hammered the polepieces into the bottom flatwork, then hammered the top flatwork onto the magnets—leaving all the polepiece ends flush with the flatwork (like an original Mustang pickup).

The long polepieces and flush flatwork produced a tall coil that was able to accept more winds than a normal Strat-style pickup. This is why Erick chose long polepieces. Also, he used 43-gauge wire, which is smaller in diameter than the 42-gauge wire normally used on Strats, resulting in more winds and more power. All this added up to powerful pickups, which at 8.73k are even stronger than P-90s—which are about 8.3k.

Erick wound the two pickups in opposite directions (reverse wind) so that in the middle position the pickups canceled out any single-coil hum. With the pickup mounted on the winder, he's using the top-mounted rheostat to control the winding speed; operating the rheostat with one hand while guiding the wire onto the coil with the other.

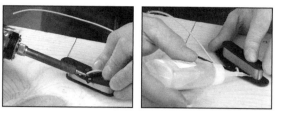

After winding each coil Erick threaded the black-and-white leads through the eyelets and soldered them in place. To protect the delicate start/finish wires, they're tacked down with super glue (medium viscosity).

The last step was to charge (magnetize) the polepiece magnets. Erick used rare earth magnets (which I call "repair magnets" in my shop because I there are so many uses for them). The idea is to hold the magnets in place so that as they get close to each other they can't snap together. To do this, one magnet is screwed to the bench-top and the other to a chunk of plywood clamped above it with South facing in on one jaw, and North facing in on the other. When the uncharged pickup is slid between the two magnets, it becomes magnetized.

s, who did the body and finish repairs on this Mustang.

If you want the tops of the pickup polepieces to be South, the bottoms of the polepieces must pass over the South magnet, and the top of the polepieces must pass over the North magnet. For this guitar, one pickup was charged South, while the other was North (reverse polarity). Coupled with the reverse-winding mentioned earlier, he produced a set of pickups we refer to as "reverse wind/reverse polarity."

This little Mustang is looking vintage again, even though now it's hot-rodded with overwound, hum-cancelling pickups. Not off-the-shelf stuff. For me, this is is what makes pickup winding so much fun!

Chapter 16

Finishing and finish repairs

basic

A basic finishing schedule

basic

d.i.y.

A basic finishing schedule 279
    Step 1: Wood preparation 279
    Step 2: Stain 280
    Step 3: Washcoat 283
    Step 4: Grain filler 283
    Step 5: Sealer 284
    Step 6: Color coats 284
    Step 7: Clear topcoats 285
    Step 8: Wet sanding, rubbing out ... 285
Spraying necks and bodies 287
Finish repairs 292
Supplies for finish repairs 294
Fixing chips 295
Fixing dents 301
Fixing scratches 301
Touching up color 302

deep

Faking an aged finish 304

First we'll describe each step and the various finishing products needed to complete it. Then we'll go through the actual steps for some common finishes. Not all finishes require every step, so skip those that don't apply in your case. Just don't change the basic order, and practice every finish operation on scrap wood. Put a complete finish on scrap before tackling the real thing!

Step 1: Wood preparation

At this stage, major work such as rough sanding, shaping, binding, scraping, hole drilling, etc. should be complete. All problems in the wood surface are corrected, final sanding is done, areas not to be sprayed are masked off and the instrument is well cleaned.

Pre-assemble all parts to make sure everything fits and lines up (neck/body, bridge, tuners, tailpiece or tremolo, etc.). This helps avoid drilling or last-minute "construction" after the finish is on (which often damages the finish by accident or causes lacquer to lift around newly drilled holes). Go ahead and string the guitar up. If the nut is to be finished, install it now. Continue by dressing the frets, especially their ends. You don't need to wire the guitar.

Fixing dents and chips

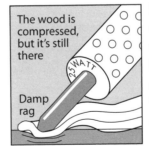

Dents or dings in the raw wood can be drawn out with steam, since the wood is still there. Wet the dented area with warm water, let it sit a few minutes, and steam it out using a damp rag and soldering pencil. Use stainable, waterbase wood dough to fill small chips. Its ability to accept stain is helpful if you're doing a natural finish, or it can be pre-colored with powdered fresco colors before the fill. Larger holes can be inlaid with wood or filled with auto-body filler (but body fillers can't be stained).

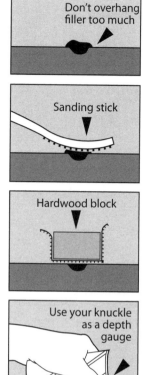

d.i.y.

Don't overhang filler too much

Sanding stick

Hardwood block

Use your knuckle as a depth gauge

If slowly added to the chip in layers, super glue makes a hard, clear fill. When dry, super glue does not take a stain, nor will a stain penetrate it. So do your staining beforehand, and confine any fill material to the damaged area, keep it off the surrounding wood. Level a dried fill with a homemade, curved sanding stick surfaced with 80- or 120-grit paper. When close to level, switch to a sanding block for smoothing.

Scraping with a cabinet scraper removes scratches in side grains, in end grains, and in the cutaways. A scraper is also perfect for removing colored overspray from plastic binding.

Sanding Some kit parts are so well sanded that they're ready to spray. Most, though, need final sanding to remove marks left by the factory. You can do your own sanding, following these rules: Raise the grain by lightly dampening the wood surface (don't soak it, though). Use a clean rag that's been soaked in clean water and well squeezed-out. When dry, the wood fibers will be raised or furred-up, making it easier for the sandpaper to cut them off. Dampen the wood, and let it dry, between every sanding to get a really smooth surface. Always wear a dust mask when sanding.

Don't use a sandpaper grit coarser than 120. Use either Fre-Cut silicon carbide or garnet paper. Start with 120-grit and progress through 150 or 180 to 220. A 220 final sanding will satisfy most of us. If not, continue sanding up to 320-grit. Sanding much finer can make a wood surface so smooth that lacquer has trouble adhering. Sand with the grain to avoid crosswise scratches. Block sand flat surfaces by wrapping the sandpaper around a flat-bottomed wood block. This spreads out the sanding pressure, so you won't create hollows in the wood from the roundness of your fingers. Keep moving, or you'll end up with an uneven surface. Don't use electric sanders until you have become proficient by hand. Blow off or vacuum the wood often to remove sawdust.

To remove the invisible sweat or oils left by handling, wipe the instrument with a naphtha-dampened rag before going on to Step 2. Wood preparation is the most important step of finishing, since the finish can only be as good as the wood, or "substrate," underneath. It's far more difficult to fix a substrate problem after finish is on it than fixing it right from the start. Learn to see those problems early!

Step 2: Stain

Coloring is the most complicated part of finishing new work, or repairing old work. We're discussing stain now, at the bare wood stage, because some of the world's most beautifully colored guitars (especially during the "Golden Age" of the 1930s) would have been stained at this point—directly after wood preparation and before wash-coating and grain-filling. If you want the color into, or directly on the wood, stain it now after reading the advantages and disadvantages mentioned. Otherwise go on to the wash-coat stage.

Your options at this bare-wood stage

1 Leave the wood bare and go on to the wash-coat stage to protect the wood from stain or filler.

2 Stain open-grain wood, and then seal in the color with the washcoat—before using grain filler. This keeps the stain in the wood, but leaves the filler only in the open pores (a terrific look).

3 Stain close-grain wood (birch, maple, spruce), skip the washcoat and filler stage (filler isn't needed if there are no open pores) and go directly to sealer (a Gibson ES-345-type "cherry" finish comes to mind).

4 Stain the wood, skip the washcoat and go directly to the wood filler (filling the bare wood). Much of this "base" stain, used before wood filler, will be sanded off when you level the filler, but not all of it. Later when the wood has been filled and sanded you stain it again for a "double-stained," subtly different look.

Stains used in guitar finishing

Electric and acoustic guitars can be finished completely natural (no coloring), in a solid opaque color, or with a variety of transparent stains. The most common stains were red, brown, black and yellow—usually sprayed in a sunburst—until Paul Reed Smith came along. Using brilliant shades of pink, green, blue and purple, PRS created a whole new appreciation for coloring guitar woods. There are many types of colorant, a number of ways to apply them and even more ways to screw them up. As your interest in finishing grows, experience will be your real teacher, and you'll come by knowledge naturally. I'll do my best to give you a head start:

Dye stains Some guitar finishes are crystal clear natural with no color added at all. You'll see this most often on the spruce or cedar tops of acoustic guitars, for example. More often, clear-finished guitars have some color in the finish, or on the wood (if only from the wood filler used to level the pores of open-grained woods like mahogany and rosewood). Usually any dark wood is enhanced with stain, and often brilliant stains are used on maple or other light woods to give dramatic effect (PRS colors, Gibson's Les Paul cherryburst or cherry red ES-345, etc.). Unlike pigments, dyes are transparent—you can see through them to the wood. These colors, which let you see the natural wood, are called transparent dyes, stains or dye stains, and are used often in guitar finishing.

Powdered aniline dye stains Before the advent of off-the-shelf stains and pigments manufactured in guitar-friendly colors (ColorTone brand for example), most of us made our stains from dry powdered aniline stains mixed into the appropriate solvent. These stains can then be used directly on the bare wood, or put over the wood by adding them to the clear finish. Powdered aniline stains are available in many colors, and in three distinct solubilities: water, alcohol or lacquer/oil (oil solubility is with mineral spirits). I haven't needed to mix my own colors from scratch in a long while, and see no reason for going back to doing so.

You need red, yellow, brown and black to produce traditional stained or sunburst finishes, but orange, blue and green are also handy for altering the tone of a particular shade. Most colors have a name—like "scarlet red" or "brilliant green." Scarlet red in water will look different than scarlet red in alcohol or lacquer thinner, and that's one reason a finisher might choose one particular solu-

Very important safety information

Finishing products have safety precautions printed on their labels. Please read them. Many experiences over the years have taught me to take these things seriously, and I want you to take them seriously too:

✔ **Wear rubber gloves** when handling these products.

✔ **Use a respirator** approved for organic vapors (available at an auto supply store),

✔ **Spray in a well-ventilated area**, like outdoors (just watch the bugs).

✔ **Wear eye protection** always.

✔ **Don't smoke** around spray products and don't spray around gas flames or pilots, hot light bulbs, or electrical appliances, including fans that aren't explosion proof.

✔ **Don't leave damp lacquer rags** lying around the shop—the smallest spark can ignite them. Let them dry outside. When they're dry, throw them away.

✔ **Don't pour chemicals down the drain.** Pour all unused finishing products into an empty can with a good lid, and mark it "Used." When it's full, make sure that it goes to the proper chemical waste disposal station (check with your city hall or a school's chemistry department to find out where).

bility over another. The solubility of the stain you choose depends on the application, but repair shops need those colors in all three solubilities: lacquer/oil, alcohol and water.

Lacquer/oil-soluble stain Because they bleed so readily, lacquer stains aren't commonly used for direct staining on bare wood, but rather for the transparent coloring of lacquer, and some mineral spirit based polyurethanes (creating "shaders"). Since you can also color lacquer with alcohol stains, you can get along without lacquer stains if you like the color of a similarly named alcohol stain.

Sometimes these anilines, used for their oil-solubility properties, are mixed into colored wood filler to give it a "bleeding" quality. Used without a washcoat, the filler not only fills the pores, it also colors the wood simultaneously—and the color springs to life under lacquer because it is also lacquer/oil soluble. I believe Gibson used this time saving technique on some mahogany SG finishes in cherry-red, and on mahogany bodies and necks of other models such as the Les Paul.

Alcohol stain (NGR) A supposed advantage of alcohol stains over water-soluble stains is that they are non-grain-raising, or NGR for short. They also dry faster than water stain; helpful if you're coloring bare wood with it and you're in a hurry. Alcohol stains are often used for staining bare wood, but they have a tendency to "disappear," not only soaking into the wood, but also evaporating at the same time. You may think you don't have enough stain on a piece and therefore apply too much. Later, when you spray on the first coats of lacquer, the solvents in the lacquer (alcohol is one them) cause the stain to pop to life. The color may even bleed out of the wood pores, and onto the binding or finish. To combat bleeding, add a touch of fresh shellac or clear lacquer to an alcohol stain (perhaps a capful per cup). This will keep it from soaking in too quickly by giving it body.

You can't dump huge amounts of mixed alcohol stain into lacquer, but you can generally add enough to produce the transparent shader you're after. A rule of thumb is no more than 10% alcohol stain should be added into un-thinned lacquer (one part alcohol stain to nine parts unthinned lacquer).

Water-soluble stain I like water stains better than alcohol for any bare wood situation (you can't add it to lacquer to make a shader, though). I don't worry about it raising the grain, since I raise the grain several times before staining anyhow. Water stains are generally more lightfast than alcohol stains, meaning they don't fade as easy as alcohol. They're also safer to use and clean up after, they don't leave lap marks because they stay wet longer; they come in brighter colors and they don't bite into shellac, lacquer, finish or bindings.

Should you apply stain directly on the wood?
Transparent colored stains are often sprayed or wiped directly onto the wood and then covered with clear finish. You look through the clear finish at the colored wood, with the wood grain showing through. Done properly, this technique gives wood the most beautiful look, and can even make plain-looking wood look exceptional. But it's tricky to do. Stains are hard to use on bare wood because it's easy to get streaks, blotches and an uneven look — especially in end-grain areas where the stain soaks in more than on the flat grain. If time isn't

an object, learn to use stains on bare wood.

Shader Lacquer-soluble dye (or alcohol-soluble) is often added into the clear finish to produce a shader: a transparent colored lacquer (think of Fender's two- and three-tone sunbursts, or Gibson's Les Paul sunbursts). When shaders are used, the unstained bare wood is first protected by several coats of clear sealer, and the shader coat is sprayed on top of that. You're looking through the color at the unstained wood below it. Excellent pre-mixed colored shaders in red, blue, yellow, gold and brown are available. Applying color this way can hide the wood grain.

Shader is quicker to apply than staining the wood, and it won't streak or blotch. If you sand through the colored finish accidentally, you only break into the clear sealer underneath, not into the wood. Sand-throughs to clear sealer aren't too hard to reshade, but sand-throughs to bare wood are tricky.

Combinations of stains and shaders are common. Often a dye stain is used on the bare wood as a color base, sealed with clear lacquer for protection, then sunbursted or highlighted with shader coats before receiving final topcoats of clear.

Spraying stain is considered by many to be the most uniform way of applying color. Professional spray equipment will do the best job, but Preval, an inexpensive aerosol spray gun with removable jars does an adequate job. Preval units are self-loading, meaning that you can add more or less thinner, stain or lacquer at will. Any aerosol propellant will get cold if you use it too long, and cold aerosols become clogged, so watch out for the spitting this can cause! It's a good idea to stand aerosols in a pan of warm (not hot) water.

Hand wiping is a good, quick way to get a base coat on an entire instrument (picture a red or brown Gibson SG). Yellow bases for sunbursts are often applied by hand. Water stain is the easiest to apply by hand without getting lap marks because it stays wet longer, allowing successive passes to dissolve together. Alcohol stains evaporate so quickly (called "flashing off") that successive passes can leave overlapping marks. Retarder added to alcohol stain slows down its drying and helps eliminate lap marks as stain is applied. The traditional sunbursts of the early days were hand-applied, very beautiful, and have a different look from the sprayed-on type.

Pre-soak the end grain with the appropriate solvent because end grain soaks up more stain than side grain. Pre-soaking wets the wood so that it can't take in as much stain, helping to avoid a blotchy appearance. Pre-soaking in the right places and right proportions guarantee good results, however. Like most finishing tasks, it takes practice.

Whether they're sprayed or wiped, liquid aniline stains can be applied straight from the jar, or thinned with the appropriate solvent to weaken the color. If you do use an alcohol or lacquer stain straight, you're begging for a color bleed into the clear topcoats. Water stain, even used straight, won't bleed into lacquer or other non-water based finishes, but it will bleed into the new water-base lacquers.

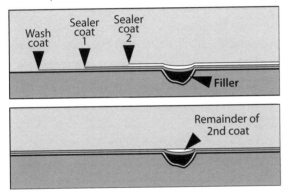

Step 3: Washcoat before filler

Close, tight-grained woods like maple and alder don't have open pores and therefore don't need to be grain-filled (the step coming up next). But many finished parts of a guitar (especially backs, sides and necks) are made from woods such as mahogany and rosewood that have large open pores. Finish applied over unfilled open pores will have a pitted look if the pores aren't filled first.

One could fill the pores with repeated coats of clear finish, sanding off what remains on the surface each time, and eventually the pores would be level with the surface wood. But this is a slow process that would wastes lacquer and pollute the environment. And the finish would shrink more than wood filler over the years, showing up as sinks in the surface.

Wood filler, packed into the grain and sanded level, is a better solution. But wood filler is not invisible. It's normally colored, generally dark brown (sometimes stained

to exotic shades). Even "natural" filler has a light butter-scotch color, which changes the color of bare wood.

Stained or natural, open-grain wood is often sprayed with a light "washcoat" of well-thinned shellac, lacquer sanding sealer or clear lacquer to keep the paste filler's color from over-staining the piece. Sprayed very thin (three–four parts thinner to one part lacquer), a wash-coat will follow the wood surface—into and out of a pore—without filling the pore. The washcoat acts as a barrier between the wood and filler. One of the best washcoats is vinyl sealer, sprayed in one thin coat. It's compatible with the nitrocellulose lacquer topcoats we'll talk about later. Martin prefers the vinyl sealer because it does the best job of keeping the natural oils in rosewood from bleeding into the clear finish and onto white binding.

There are times you don't want a washcoat; when you want the color of the filler to enhance the wood. Some very dark burgundy or cherry SGs got much of their rich-ness from red stain and cherry-red filler applied to the bare wood. In that case, if you wash-coated the wood before filling, the end result wouldn't be dark enough.

Step 4: Filling the grain

Paste wood filler is used to fill open-pored woods such as mahogany, walnut, rosewood and ash. It eliminates dust and air bubbles under the finish, and creates a flat surface for finishing by keeping the lacquer from shrinking into the pores as it dries. Filler isn't needed on close-grained woods like maple or alder, or on tonewoods such as spruce or cedar. Paste wood filler is available in either oil-base, or waterbase. Oil-base is easier to use because it dries slowly (allowing plenty of working time); but because of the oil, it takes at least several days to dry before you can spray over it without the finish lifting.

You'll use natural wood filler on light wood, and dark filler on dark woods. Or, you can start with natural filler and color it to match any wood shade in between by using fresco powders, Japan colors or compatible universal tinting colors (UTCs) of the type used in the paint coloring carousels at auto-parts and paint stores. If you're using waterbased fillers, ColorTone Waterbase pigments can be used. Stir the filler until it's mixed to about the consistency of thick cream. If necessary, thin oil-base filler with naphtha in a well-ventilated area; waterbase fillers can be thinned with water. Next "paint" the filler uniformly onto the wood and wait for a haze to form— your signal that the filler is dry enough to be rubbed.

When the haze just starts to form, quickly remove the excess from the surface with burlap or cheesecloth by rubbing across the grain. The trick is to keep from pulling filler from the pores when wiping, so don't fill too large an area. Do just the back, neck or one side at a time, since filler that's dried too long is hard to remove (if this occurs, wipe the area with naphtha and start over—you may even have to sand it off). Try to remove as much filler from the surface as possible, without pulling it from the pores.

Protect areas not receiving the messy filler (spruce or maple tops, etc.) with paper and masking tape. Allow 3 days to a week to dry before lightly sanding the filler residue from the washcoated surface with 320 Fre-Cut paper (waterbase filler can actually be sprayed over the same day, but overnight drying is better). After this light sanding, filler should remain only in the pores. Filler shrinks about 10%, leaving very slight dips over the pores that will later be filled and leveled with sealer coats.

I highly recommend the section on wood fillers in *The Woodfinishing Book* by Michael Dresdner.

A note on finish selection I may talk about other finishes in this chapter, but mainly I'm thinking of the **nitrocellulose lacquer** that's the most commonly used finish in guitar repair shops, and the woodworking trade in general. You can use automotive acrylic lacquer, and in fact that's an easy way to get any solid color you're after, as well as many transparent "candy" colors. If you go with acrylic, use *all* acrylic—including the sealer (primer) coat. Don't mix nitrocellulose with acrylic. It can be done, but may cause incompatibility problems.

Step 5: Sealer

Sealer is simply a clear primer for nitrocellulose lacquer. It's whatever you spray as your first topcoat. It's used to seal in the grain filler, stains or sunburst and when sanded it creates a level surface for the final topcoats. Thanks to its high solids content, lacquer sanding sealer builds the finish thickness quickly and acts as a bridge between the wood and the topcoat, giving the lacquer something to cling to. The best sealers are shellac, vinyl sealer, lacquer sanding sealer or clear lacquer used as its own sealer. Many professionals prefer to use clear lac-

quer at every stage—even the sealer stage. The result is a clearer finish. So lacquer can be used as a sealer, but it takes longer to sand. Sealer was developed to make the finishing process faster and easier.

Sealer that's been sprayed and sanded correctly leaves a smooth matte finish, with few or no shiny specks indicating sinks or dips over the filled grain. Two coats of sealer (don't count the washcoat) sprayed by a pro using an air compressor and professional guns is plenty. Too much sealer (four or five coats) can cause cracking in the harder topcoats and can add a slight milkiness to the clear finish. (But if you use the aerosol cans, they don't transfer as much lacquer per coat, so you may need three or four coats to get a good build.) Sand sealer coats with Fre-Cut 320-grit paper until the small dips over the filled grain are gone. Any remaining shiny spots indicate an irregularity or depression in the finish surface. Try to get most of these now, or they'll come back to haunt you when you're rubbing out the finish! Sealer actually leaves a fairly thin finish, since most of it is sanded off during leveling. Always be careful when you're sanding on sealer sprayed over colors: you don't want to sand through and remove color!

Primer: a sealer for solid colors Primer, usually white, brown or gray, is the "sealer" coat for opaque acrylic lacquers. There's no need for them to be clear since you won't see them anyhow. If you're using acrylic automotive lacquer, use primer as a sealer now and follow the advice given above.

Step 6: Color coats

Nitrocellulose lacquer is easy to find in clear, black or white; but it's hard to find in other colors, especially good-looking ones. If you're after a custom color like Fiesta Red or Surf Green you want a pigmented finish, or paint. These finishes are opaque. A Sherwin-Williams paint store can mix you a pigmented nitrocellulose lacquer in some colors, or an automotive store can mix up acrylic lacquer in a variety of automotive colors.

You can produce pastel shades like Surf Green, Daphne Blue, Seafoam Green and Fiesta Red by starting with white lacquer as your opaque base, and tinting it with the appropriate ColorTone pigment (transparent dye can also be used to color a white base). Or, for mixing a strong, brilliant color such as orange, red, white or black, add ColorTone pigment to clear lacquer.

Pigments are also available in semi-transparent wiping stains, but these are more often used in the furniture business (products like Minwax). The closest thing we use to a pigmented wiping stain is paste wood filler, which has a pigmented stain in it, so it colors the wood much like a pigmented stain would.

Solid colors in acrylic To achieve bright opaque colors, it's much easier to use automotive acrylic primer, color, clear topcoats and thinner—skipping nitrocellulose completely. Just use acrylic primer at the sealer stage (Step 5). Also, get yourself a tube of acrylic "spot putty," which is like an easy to use version of Bondo body filler. It makes any imperfections in the wood disappear. Spot putty's colored green or pink, so you can only use it under opaque colors. Again, if you use acrylics, stick with the entire system; don't mix acrylics with nitrocellulose wood lacquers.

Clear coats over color Some finishers use just enough color to cover the primer or sealer, and then switch right to clear. Some finishers put on lots of color (4 to 6 coats) and rub out the color coats (no clear topcoats). Using clear over color gives more depth, and I think a better look. With clear over a thin coat of color, you mustn't sand until you've built enough lacquer to avoid sanding through—this takes two to three coats.

Shading, toning and sunbursting At this stage a number of things can happen. It's the time to correct any mistakes or sand-throughs into color that may have been applied earlier to the bare wood. An airbrush (miniature spray gun) is good for touching up sand-throughs. Sunbursts or color coats applied earlier to the bare wood can be improved now, by "toning," or highlighting areas with shading lacquer. And some finishers will tint the binding for an antique look at this time. If you're using a colored transparent finish like a vintage cherryburst, or a Paul Reed Smith type, spray it now, just before the clear topcoats are applied.

Sunbursting Most modern sunbursts and transparent colors are sprayed at this time, over the clear sealer and under the clear topcoats. One way to imitate a Les Paul cherryburst, for example, is to spray a shader coat of clear yellow lacquer over the clear sealer applied in Step 5. Then spray a coat or two of clear lacquer over the yellow

to seal it from the red sunbursting shader about to follow. Then follow over the sealed yellow with your red and/or reddish-brown shader to create the sunburst.

By sandwiching the yellow in between the clear sealer coats, you have double protection: the bare top is protected from the yellow shader, and the yellow shader is protected from the red sunburst in case of a sand-through.

Whether spraying a sunburst, or simply toning the sides, lay down a number of lighter color coats, one at a time, until you get the desired color build. Don't try to lay all the color on in one pass, it doesn't look as good that way. Experiment with using more than one color, putting one over the other, to get great depth and color in the finish.

Step 7: Clear topcoats

If possible, avoid sanding on any color touch-ups from Step 6. Unlike sealer, you can lay on the clear lacquer; from six to twelve coats of lacquer is standard (depending on how much the lacquer is thinned for spraying). Allow a three-hour minimum drying time between coats, and spray no more than three coats a day. To avoid breaking into the color coats, don't sand until after a two- or three-coat buildup. Even then, sand lightly. Whether you sand between every coat is up to you— some do, some don't—so experiment. Don't sand on sharp, exact edges; un-sanded, they'll build up the extra lacquer needed to rub out nicely with the final finish.

Because of its thin viscosity, lacquer sprayed from pre-loaded aerosol cans builds more slowly than lacquer sprayed from spray guns or self-load aerosol units such as Pre-Val (where you control how thick the lacquer is by adding thinner). In general, follow the manufacturer's thinning directions; usually a 50-50 mix (a ratio of 1:1) of thinner to lacquer is required for lacquer to spray smoothly. In humid climates, a dash of retarder should be added to the lacquer to help minimize blushing (the nasty white haze caused by trapped moisture).

Step 8: Wet sanding and rubbing out

When the final coat of lacquer has dried at least a week (a month is better), sand the finish to a dull, satiny patina prior to rubbing out. Once again, you want to remove dips. A felt-faced block makes a good backer for the sandpaper. If you have a flat, level finish, start sanding with 800-grit Gold Fre-Cut sandpaper; on a pebbly, orange-peeled finish, you may need to start with 600-, or even 400-grit, and then work your way through 800-grit dry. Then switch to wet-sanding with 1000- and 1200-grit Micro Finishing Paper designed to be used with water as a lubricant. (Water-sanding papers should be immersed in clean water overnight before using). Rinse the paper often in clean water to wash away any clogging particles.

For a final gloss, hand rub with a soft, clean rag and the appropriate grade of compound. If your final sanding was with 800-grit, start with ColorTone's coarse compound, and follow with their fine. If you sanded to 1200 grit, go directly to the medium compound — that should give you a good gloss. If you want more gloss, finish up with ColorTone fine compound. These compounds are formulated to give hand buffing much the same results as the Menzerna compounds used with pedestal buffers.

For hand buffing (hand rubbing) use a piece of clean,

worn, linen with a cotton ball in the center to give it body. Load it well by smearing it in the compound, then break it in and warm it on a smooth hardwood board before going onto the finish. Rub with the grain, and in a circular motion (mix it up). When you've developed a good, even shine, either quit, or follow up with Color-Tone swirl remover.

In professional shops, two kinds of power buffing machines are used: the large, free-standing "pedestal" buffers used by Gibson and Fender, and the hand-held right-angle circular automotive buffers, with lamb's wool

bonnets, used at the Martin factory. Each of these buffing methods leaves its own distinctive look—the downstroke of the pedestal wheel, versus the swirls left by the circular machine. If you wanted to be picky, you couldn't get the "right look" on a Martin finish using a pedestal buffer, for example. Lots of practice is needed with power buffing to avoid going-through a finish—especially on corners, edges and cutaways.

Pedestal buffers, with large (12" to 18" diameter) flannel buffing pads, are the most common. The width of the buff is controlled by how many 1" pads are stacked on the arbor. The face of the flannel buff is loaded with the appropriate grit of the bar-style Menzerna buffing compound — coarse (reddish-brown) for a 600- to 800-grit sanding, medium (tan) for an 800- to 1200-grit final sanding and fine (light tan).

Until recently pedestal buffers haven't been within the reach of small shops. The buffer shown above, from Stewart-MacDonald, is affordable and does a tremendous job, giving a professional "Gibson" look in a hurry.

The circular buffers at Martin are heavy-duty industrial machines with a lot of weight. Martin uses two compounds, on lamb's wool pads, for buffing: 3M #05955 Polishing Compound for the initial cut, and 3M Imperial Hand-Glaze #05590 to remove the swirl-marks. Martin finishers, by the way, don't wet-sand the final sprayed coats, but instead go directly to the buffer!

Buffing pads An acceptable "machine-rubbed" look can be obtained by using a variable-speed electric drill equipped with a foam polishing pad (above, right). Using the same compounds used for hand buffing, these foam buffers have less chance of burn-through than conventional lamb's-wool bonnets, and give you a factory look.

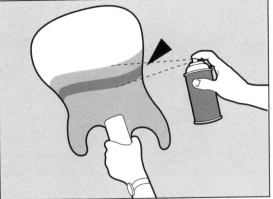

No matter how hard you try, you'll have some problems on your first jobs. The fun of solving these problems is what keeps me interested, and learning.

Spraying necks and bodies

We just looked at the different steps of lacquer finishing and the nitrocellulose-compatible products needed for doing them. Now here are basic spraying tips and safety measures, along with some specialized spray fixtures that you can make yourself. We'll start spraying with two simple finishes—a basic clear lacquer job for a bolt-on neck (both rosewood fretboards and "maple-necks"), and a solid opaque color on a kit body.

I like to compare finishing to cooking. The novice cook carefully follows recipes that guarantee success, while an experienced chef is more creative, instinctively adding a dash of this and a pinch of that while interpreting a recipe. Practice will allow you to experiment with your finishes, but for now let's stick to our cookbook.

Whether you use a spray gun or an aerosol can, overlap the spray pattern of each successive pass from one-third to one-half the size of the pattern. The finish material thins out toward the edges of a spray pattern, so overlapping ensures an equal coat build and a uniform color. When you spray the next coat, spray at right angles to the direction of the first coat for more even coverage. Spray with the can or gun held between 8" and 10" away from the instrument, and tilt what you're spraying away from the spray gun—don't hold it at a perfect 90 degrees. This tilting helps keep the spray from bouncing off the object, and directs the overspray ahead of the spray pattern, so it's covered by the next wet pass.

At times it's an advantage to spray down on an instrument that's lying flat. The lazy susan pictured below is easy to make and frees both hands to do sunbursts and touchups. You can turn it as you spray, which is great for spraying along the sides and in cutaways.

A length of two-by-four and a scrap of two-by-two make a portable spray hanger that can bolt, prop, or

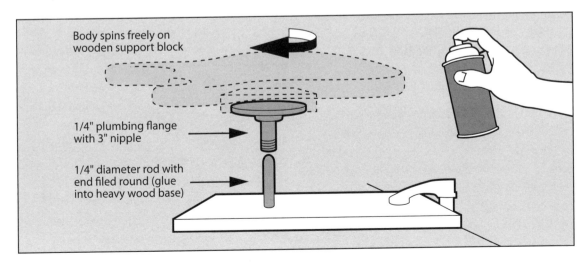

Body spins freely on wooden support block

1/4" plumbing flange with 3" nipple

1/4" diameter rod with end filed round (glue into heavy wood base)

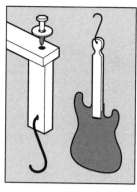

d.i.y.

clamp anywhere. A clearance hole in the two-by-four allows the lag bolt to spin freely, along with the short two-by-two that it's tightly screwed into. A length of 1/4" steel rod that's bent into an "S" hook holds the hanging stick for a solidbody, or it can be slid through a tuning machine's hole on a peghead for hanging. An instrument can also be hung from a screw eye placed in the butt end's strap buttonhole.

Maple neck with rosewood fingerboard

Spraying a clear finish on maple is the easiest to do, since there's no need for stain or filler. Here's the finish schedule for a maple neck with a rosewood fingerboard:

1 Wood prep if needed. Tape off the fingerboard to protect it from overspray.

2 Optional: For an aged look, stain neck with a weak wash of yellow-brown NGR stain. Pre-soaking end and side grain with reducer keeps these areas from absorbing too much stain. Experiment.

Skip steps **3**, **4** and **6** (which were given in the finishing schedule a few pages back), since no filler is needed on maple, and you're not using a solid color.

5 Seal the neck. This calls for two light coats of shellac, vinyl sealer or lacquer.

7 Spray four to six coats of clear lacquer that's thinned by a ratio of 1:1. Wet- or dry-sand as needed.

8 Dry one to two weeks. Dry-sand with 600- and 800-grit Gold, then 1000- and 1200-grit Micro Finishing Paper wet. Rub out by hand as described earlier. Carefully remove the masking tape from the fingerboard.

Spraying a maple neck

This question from **Al Valusek** of Ann Arbor, Michigan, brings up the subject of spraying a maple fingerboard:

"What kind of finish can I put on my late-'60s Strat's maple fingerboard after refretting? My repairman advised me that the fingerboard would have to be planed in order to remove some trouble spots, but he didn't want to take on the job because he's had poor luck finding the proper material

with which to redo the wood (the original finish would be removed in the fingerboard-trueing process).

Please help—I need a fret job!"

There are loads of clear lacquers, polyesters, enamels, etc. used to finish maple necks. I use plain old lacquer, like Fender always did, and spray right over the frets; depending on the "build" of successive coats, I may scrape the lacquer from the frets once or twice during the work. I don't worry too much because the lacquer will chip off during the fret dressing later. The secret to finishing a maple fingerboard is not to spray on too much lacquer. Use just enough to soak into the wood, and then build a gloss with three or four coats. If the finish is too thick, it will dent and mar, and not feel right.

Getting a vintage look on maple

Here's the answer I gave my friend **Jim Peat** of Laguna Beach, California, when he wrote asking,

"Dan, I have a birdseye maple replacement neck with a rosewood fingerboard. What's the best way to get that ambered 'vintage' look while bringing out the birdseye? Should I put amber into my clear lacquer?"

I recently had extremely good luck matching the color on a '61 Strat that needed only the peghead refinished. The neck's golden amber finish was original up to the nut, but someone had stripped the peghead's front, back and sides, polyurethaned it, and stuck on a bootleg decal. All that kept the owner from being proud of his piece was the neck's ugly head, which was whitish compared to the rest of the neck. The method I used to get the aged color is good for both refinishing a vintage neck or making a new one look old.

To get the vintage color, you have to stain the wood, not the finish. Apply waterbase stain to the bare wood, then use clear lacquer over it. Occasionally I'll add color to the lacquer, but only if the stained wood didn't look right after clear lacquer was sprayed on. (Since clear lacquer shows what stained wood really looks like, first practice on maple scrap.) I use ColorTone Vintage Amber Liquid Stain mixed in water for a vintage maple neck. I may or may not tint it with a tiny amount of Medium Brown, which has a hint of red in it. The mix ratio of Vintage Amber (and Medium Brown, if I use it) isn't scientific, I do it by eye. When you think it's right, test it on some maple. But remember, it won't look right until it's sprayed with clear lacquer.

As mentioned earlier, adding color to lacquer is called making a shader, but I prefer getting the correct color on the wood in the first place. When using shaders, it's easy to sand through a layer of color, which causes a patchy, uneven spot. These sand-throughs are very hard to touch up, even by an airbrush expert, so if you go the shader route, be sure to put lots of clear coats over any color coat. On the contrary, with water stain on wood, if you mistakenly sand through the clear lacquer and remove color, recoloring it with the same stain is remarkably successful: just wipe some more stain on the bare patch that you sanded into. Shaders have a tendency to hide (rather than enhance) the grain, especially on figured wood. They make the wood harder to see by laying a colored film over it. However, shaders are good for hiding repair work or creating certain sunburst finishes.

The mix ratio of yellow, red and brown water stain for "vintage maple" isn't scientific. I did it by eye, and ended up with about two ounces of stain, which is more than enough to stain one neck several times. Start with full-strength yellow (1/4 oz.) and thin with water (1-3/4 oz.) until the color isn't too strong when wiped on scrap maple. At this point it should cry out for amber. Then add tiny drops of full-strength red and brown to amber it. If maple scrap is at a premium, test as you go by putting the color on white pickguard plastic; don't test it on paper, since it will just soak in. When you think it's right, test it on some maple. But remember, it won't look right until it's sprayed with clear lacquer.

Highlighting bird's-eye grain is definitely worth the work. One method is to stain the wood and then sand most of it back off. The bird's-eyes will hold the color while the surrounding wood sands back to natural.

Sometimes this is done with black or silver stain to really make the grain stand out, and you can enhance it several times for a more pronounced effect. Then, when you wipe on your final coat of stain and don't sand it off, the pre-stained birdseyes jump right out at you!

You can wipe stain on with a clean rag or by spraying; it goes further by wiping.

Staining tips

✔ Water stain will raise the grain, so before staining slightly pre-dampen the wood to raise the grain on purpose. After it dries, sand off the "hairs" with sand-paper that's 200-grit or higher. Damp sanding like this is a common technique for many types of finishing.

✔ To avoid streaks and lap marks, quickly wipe length-wise (with the grain). Stain usually darkens end grains

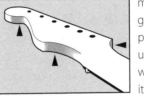

more than either side grains or flat grain, so pre-soak the end grain using a rag dampened with water. This keeps it from absorbing too much more color than the rest of the neck.

✔ The stained wood should dry at least several hours before lacquering.

✔ Wear gloves, or your hands will be yellow for weeks!

Lake placid blue metallic finish

I've found that the lake placid blue lacquer used on a small number of custom-color Fender Strats in the early '60s is still available at my automotive store in acrylic lacquer (Dupont Lucite 2876-L). If you'd like to try this vintage metallic finish, you'll need one pint each of color, clear topcoat and primer/surfacer, as well as a gallon of thinner (all acrylic-lacquer products). Spray the primer and color with self-load aerosols (like Preval), and the clear with self-load or pre-filled aerosol cans. (Of course the best job can be had with professional spray guns and an air compressor.) I saw an original lake placid blue Strat with the peghead face painted to match the body—it really looked great.

1 Prep wood as normal. Use acrylic spot putty for filling dents; this is available at an automotive supply store.

2 Skip this step—no stain needed.

3 Give a washcoat to ash or other open-grained wood. Alder needs no washcoat or filler.

4 Fill if needed; let dry a week or two.

5 Skip sealer. Prime the body with two-four coats of white or gray primer. Sand after the first two coats and after the last two. Allow three to four hours between coats, and let final coats dry three days. Sand the finish level.

6 Spray two–four coats of lake placid blue, or enough to cover. Allow four hours between coats and dry overnight. Lightly sand with 320 grit to remove dust. Touch up with blue if you sand through.

7 Spray four–six clear topcoats. Wait three hours between coats, and only do two coats a day. Sand as needed after the first three coats are down.

8 Dry two weeks, wet-sand, and rub out.

Fender candy apple red, circa 1964

Here's the answer to a call for help from **Malcolm Coombs** of Westville, Republic of South Africa:

"Dear Dan, I am keen to restore my 1963 L-series Fender Strat, which is in pieces, to its original state. Could you help me locate the missing parts? Also, the body was poorly sprayed in metallic red. Is candy apple red a vintage 1963 color, and if so, how can I attain it?"

Fender's vintage reissue Strats use parts identical to your '63, and these may be ordered through an authorized Fender dealer. Custom builder and repair expert **Michael Stevens**, who co-founded Fender's Custom Shop and now lives in Alpine, Texas, had this to say about the finish: "I've seen a '64 candy apple red that I know was real, and most likely it was available in '63. So it would be correct, vintage-wise, to restore the guitar to candy apple red." Here's how:

1 Color the alder body with a yellow waterbased stain or a yellow lacquer sanding-sealer washcoat. This duplicates the yellow Fullerplast dipping solution used by Fender in the early '60s as a base for the three-color sunburst (solid colors got dipped in it too).

2 Seal over that with a white primer, sanding sealer or lacquer. Sherwin-Williams Opex White Primer works well. Sand these white coats smooth and level.

3 Spray a coat of the same gold that you'd use for a Les Paul goldtop (gold bronze powder dissolved in a little thinner and added to clear lacquer). A Sherwin-Williams dealer can order the powder—ask for Crescent Bronze Powder #255 in a 1 oz. jar.

4 Don't sand the gold. Instead, spray over it with a couple coats of clear lacquer to set it.

5 Next spray a good coat of transparent red lacquer.

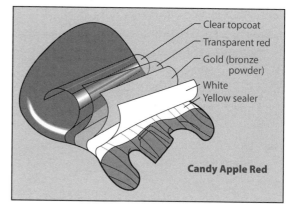

Candy Apple Red

6 Spray four to six clear lacquer topcoats over that, and you're done. After it dries, wet-sand and buff it.

By following the steps in the correct order (yellow, white, gold, red, etc.), any finish wear such as chips, dings and worn spots will expose the layers of paint in the proper vintage order.

Advanced finishes and sunbursts

You're never done when it comes to finishing—there's always lots more to learn. Perhaps you've experimented with some of the different finishing materials and have begun to develop a feel for them. Now you can really put yourself to the test by studying the schedules of two expert builder/repairmen: my cousin, **Mark Erlewine** of Erlewine Guitars in Austin, Texas, and **John Suhr** of Rudy's Music in New York City.

Creator of the Automatic, Lazer and Chiquita guitars, Mark Erlewine does a great vintage cherry sunburst that imitates the faded finish of a 1960 Gibson Les Paul. Mark was the first builder I know of to feature binding and carved tops on Strat-style guitars. John Suhr, besides handling the day-to-day repair needs of his customers, also finds time to create the Pensa-Suhr guitars for which Rudy's Music is famous. John sprayed the finish described here on a guitar made for **Mark Knopfler**.

These two finishes deal with instruments with a mahogany body and flame-maple top. You can do the same type of finish on other wood combinations, such as ash or alder bodies with maple tops, by staining the lighter wood with walnut stain (alcohol aniline) to imitate mahogany during Step 2 —otherwise Step 2 is omitted for mahogany. Both of these finishes require the careful taping and scraping of binding, as well as grain filling. They also involve careful, step-by-step planning.

I chose them for this reason, figuring that if you can do these, you can do anything.

Mark Erlewine's vintage cherryburst

1 Prepare the wood, mask binding and protect the flame top with a paper cutout held in place by masking tape (tape the paper up to, and right over, the binding masking tape). Protect the peghead, fingerboard and neck binding the same way.

2 This applies to alder or ash bodies only. Stain the back and sides of the body a brownish red, with brown being predominant. Use alcohol stains.

3 Washcoat the mahogany neck and body with lacquer mixed 1:3 (one part thinner and three parts lacquer).

4 Fill the grain with brown-red filler and let dry three days. Spray two coats of clear lacquer to lock in the color.

5 Color the filled mahogany with transparent lacquer shaders. Spray two coats of red transparent lacquer (made with cherry red liquid stain) mixed with a little brown and a touch of yellow on the mahogany. When these shader coats are dry, seal them with two coats of clear lacquer to help stabilize the color—this isn't the sealer step yet.

6 Expose the flame-maple top, and mask the mahogany with paper. Run the paper right to the edge so that the tape sticks to the binding, rather than the cherry shader you just sprayed (the shader could pull loose, since it's uncured). Hand stain the maple top with alcohol aniline stain mixed eight parts yellow, two parts brown and one part red. It looks dull when it dries, but don't worry. It will make the figure of the curly maple bolder, and it comes to life when it's hit with lacquer. Seal this color with two coats of clear lacquer just as you did the mahogany in Step 5. By sealing these colors from each other, you get less bleeding between the colors. More coloring to do: when the two clear coats are dry, spray two coats of Wolf Lemon Yellow transparent lacquer (thinned 1:1) over the top. Now watch the flame pop out! When this dries, seal and melt it with one coat of clear gloss lacquer.

Now for the burst Use the cherry red shader described earlier. Sunburst the edges of the top with your spray aimed off the instrument. Use a small pattern, and hit only the edges while sunbursting—don't spray toward center! Spray this first pass no more than 3/4" in from the edge; this creates a fairly strong red. Then, mix the same red with equal amounts of brown transparent lacquer. Spray lighter, but go in 1-1/2" to cover a larger area. Next, use just brown transparent lacquer to lightly mist the entire burst going in 2 -1/2" from the edge (this must be done lightly to duplicate the fading of this famous type of sunburst). When this dries, shoot one coat of clear over the burst to set the colors. Remove the tape and paper from the body. Scrape the binding to remove any color that may have bled under the masking tape.

If your peghead is already black (some peghead overlays are black fiber or plastic), remove the masking, and seal it along with the rest of the instrument in Step 7. If you're going to spray it black, do it now. Tape off the neck around the peghead face and spray enough black lacquer to cover the face. Let it dry, and scrape the paint from the pearl inlays.

7 Seal the entire instrument with two or three coats of clear lacquer (of course, mask off the fingerboard).

8 If you want the aged look, color the binding with some top color that's been lightened with clear and has a dash of brown and red. An airbrush does this best. Don't overdo it, or it'll look fake. I use a homemade lazy susan to rest the instrument on while antiquing. It also comes in handy for spraying sides and sunbursts. There are many times when it's helpful to spray one side of a piece while it's lying flat, especially for avoiding runs. If you do get a run or "sag" in the finish, wet-sand it out with a Finesse block or 400 wet-or-dry sandpaper wrapped around a small Plexiglas sanding block with rounded corners. Rock the block on the bump to "feel" it and sand it level.

2 Spray from four to six clear coats of lacquer.

10 Sand and rub out as usual.

John Suhr's Pensa-Suhr finish

When **John Suhr** lived and worked in NYC, he told me how to do this finish, which he used on a guitar he built for Mark Knopfler—a mahogany body with a flame-maple top and ivoroid binding. The bolt-on neck is made of maple with a rosewood fingerboard that's also bound with ivoroid. The binding runs around the peghead, as well, which calls for quite a lot of scraping. And it's got a unique twist—the Watco Danish Oil. Watch how John's methods fit into the schedule.

1 Prep wood as usual.

Skip the usual step **2**.

3 Skip washcoat, but wipe one coat of Watco Danish Oil onto the curly maple top. This keeps the filler from coloring it, and brings out the grain. Rub it on, and wipe off the excess.

4 Fill the mahogany with brown paste wood filler—no washcoat—and let dry three days. Clean the binding with a scraper afterwards.

Skip steps **5** and **6**.

7 Seal the whole body with one wipe-coat of Watco Danish Oil to mellow out the filler. Wipe one coat of Watco Oil onto the maple neck, too. Let both dry for one day, and then spray one thin coat of clear lacquer over the body and neck. This melds the Watco with the lacquer. Dry one day, and then finish sealing with clear lacquer mixed 1:1 with thinner. (As a rule, John's thinner is made up of two parts thinner to one part retarder; this is more than the manufacturer suggests, so experiment first.) Spray five or six coats of clear; after three coats, sand between coats with 400 Fre-Cut Gold sandpaper, which John says outlasts many others. Final sand until the finish is level. This ends the sealer stage.

8 Mask off the binding and top with newspaper and 3M Stripers tape (a pale green, latex-backed tape that is perfect for this type of work). Mask the fingerboard and neck binding, too. Spray the mahogany back and rims with a transparent red and brown shading lacquer mixed three parts red to one part brown and thinned 1:1 with thinner (add some clear lacquer to this if you want a weaker color). Spray two or three coats. A good way to spray a body is to screw a holding stick in the cavity in place of the neck, and make a hanger as shown earlier. This allows you to rotate the body by hand while spraying or to spray with the body hanging. Let dry two hours, and then scrape and clean the binding. If you let lacquer sit too long (four hours or more), it becomes too chippy,

and if it's not dry enough, it drags with the scraper. Two hours is right.

Now for the golden see-through top. Mix a transparent shading lacquer using mostly a transparent Vintage Amber-colored shader, with a little Lemon Yellow and Medium brown to suit. Extend this with one-fourth clear lacquer, and thin the mixture 1:1. Mask off the sides of the binding, but don't bother trying to mask off the thin top of the binding, since it's easier to scrape that edge. Spray no more than two or three coats for the right color. Wait two hours, and then remove the tape and scrape the binding's top edge. Spray the same golden color onto the maple neck.

Now we lightly shade the binding. Pour off some of your top color, and add clear lacquer and a little lemon yellow. Spray the body and neck binding lightly. You don't have to worry about the slight overspray on the surrounding finish, so an airbrush is handy for this. This completes the coloring. Let dry overnight.

9 Shoot clear lacquer, thinned 1:1, over the body and neck. Sand after three coats, and then as needed every coat after that. John sprays 10 to 15 coats of lacquer. You probably won't need that much, since your brand of lacquer may not be as thin as John's to start out with.

10 Let the finish dry one month before wet-sanding and rubbing out.

Both of these finishes involve, among other products, the use of clear lacquer that's colored with ColorTone liquid stain. Clear colored lacquer has always been part of traditional sunbursts, and has only lately become popular in creating see-through tinted finishes over highly figured woods.

For more information on finishing, check out *Guitar Finishing Step-By-Step*, written by Don MacRostie and myself. Don and I also produced two finishing videos for StewMac: *Spray Finishing Basics,* and *Sunburst Finishing.*

Finish repairs

Repairing a finish is more difficult than putting on a new one. You must know a lot about finishing materials in order to proceed correctly, and that's why I saved finishing repairs 'til last. Unlike many structural guitar repairs, you can learn finish repair work by practicing on junk you find at any garage sale: epoxy-finished clocks, ceramics, furniture, fishing waders, you name it. You can get quite good before you ever touch a guitar. (I'd never advise you to learn how to touch-up on a valuable guitar). Here's a brief description of the three most common guitar finishes.

Since the advent of modern spray techniques, lacquer has been used by many makers, the most notable being Martin, Gibson, Fender (until the late '60s), Gretsch and Guild. Many modern guitars, especially electrics, are finished in "poly"—polyurethanes, polyesters, epoxies, etc. These finishes don't redissolve or "melt in" like lacquers and are hard to rub out, but you can do a lot with them. It's important to know about these finish types and to consider which instruments you should or shouldn't work on yourself.

Shellac or varnish is often used on expensive hand-made guitars—especially classical and flamenco instruments. Shellac, applied with a "French polish" technique, was used on most American guitars made prior to about 1930. Although French polishing is an important technique for finish repair, it is beyond the scope of this book, and I won't go into it in any detail. I don't advise you to work on shellac finishes—they're hard enough to clean, harder to work on. No do-it-yourself repairs allowed on vintage guitars.

Lacquer finishes are found on most acoustic, and many electric, instruments made since 1930. Martin, Gibson, Gretsch, Guild, Harmony, Kay, Rickenbacker, Fender, and many other guitars have been finished with lacquer. In general, more recently-lacquered guitars have thicker finishes, and are easier to work on than vintage finishes which are thin, dry and brittle (and take very little sanding before bare wood is exposed). All lacquer finishes dent, chip and scratch more easily than polyester because they are more delicate.

Lacquer is the easiest to repair because it will redissolve itself; the fact that successive coats or drops of touch-up lacquer melt in completely (even years after the finish was applied) is a real advantage. Always be careful around lacquer finishes because they melt when touched by super glue, lacquer, shellac, alcohol and lacquer thinner (any of which may be used to repair a lacquer finish).

If the finish on your guitar looks as if the instrument has been dipped into a vat of liquid—thick and glossy—

most likely it's some type of polyester, polyurethane or urethane enamel. These surfaces are found on most imports and many American electric guitars made after the late 1960s. Once these finishes have cured, no solvent that I know of will soften them—which means that lacquer, super glue or "poly" itself won't melt in. This inability to melt makes invisible repairs next to impossible on these finishes. For touch-ups on these, use super glue.

Chips, dents and scratches

When you accidentally knock your axe into a foreign object, like a chair arm or a microphone stand, you wind up with a ding: a dent, chip or scratch. Finish dings on the peghead, body binding, fingerboard edges and the back of the neck are easy to touch up, because you can work on them without touching much of the surrounding finish, and they don't show sanding and rubbing in the way that a larger, flat area such as a guitar's face or back does.

Some professionals will buff the entire surface in order to make even a little teeny chip go away—the finish will no longer look original. You wouldn't want to do this to any of my vintage guitars, buddy! I'd rather have a touched-up chip or no repair at all in most cases. So to start out, I'm telling you that many dings just aren't worth messing with!

Chips and nicks are the result of contact with a sharp object, and leave bare wood showing. Repair is easiest on a clear, natural-wood finish, but stained wood is usually no problem (in either case, simply apply clear finish over the nick). Some clear finishes, though, have color in them, and these are harder for the amateur to fix because the repair must match the original color.

Dents are small pockets in a finish that result from the wood hitting a blunt object—the original finish remains, but is dented in. Sometimes the dented finish still adheres well to the wood, and sometimes the finish has separated from the wood. Some dents are smooth with no cracks in the finish, and others leave the finish not only dented, but cracked.

Scratches occur when a small amount of finish is removed by some sharp object, neither denting the wood nor totally chipping away the finish to bare wood. Scratches come in all shapes and sizes and may leave an

d.i.y.

opaque white mark. At other times they are perfectly clear, like V-grooves engraved into the finish.

All chips, dents and scratches are easiest to repair when they occur in inconspicuous areas. Beware of those that are away from the edges and out on the main body area—these can be tough to fix without showing.

Supplies for finish repairs

Many professionals have an extensive array of chemicals for finish repair, and know how to use them. We'll keep it simple, using only a few materials for filling in a ding that has been made in a clear topcoat (most colored guitars are usually top-coated with a clear finish of some sort, so you'll usually work with clear only; dealing with solid colors is explained later). All you need is lacquer, shellac or superglue. The lacquer should be used on traditional lacquer finishes (choose either nitrocellulose or acrylic lacquer), shellac on very old finishes and the superglue should be used on the catalyzed or "hardened" finishes.

Lacquer Since guitar lacquers and other lacquers come in quarts or gallons, and you only need a small amount, you might ask your repairman or local furniture doctor to sell you a small amount of clear, un-thinned lacquer and thinner. Clear nail polish is almost like lacquer, and could be used in a pinch as a substitute for a minor repair.

Naptha (lighter fluid will do) is good for cleaning and de-greasing any finish (including lacquer) before attempting any finish repairs.

Super glue is a generic term for cyanoacrylate instant glues. There are many good brands available — I use StewMac's #10, #20 and #30 (water-thin, medium, thick) because it's good, it's convenient, and I know it's fresh (freshness matters). For the type of gluing we're concerned with here, you'd choose one of the following consistencies:

Water-thin super glue penetrates the fastest and deepest. However, it is also the most dangerous because it sets instantly! Setting time: one to three seconds.

Medium viscosity super glue has a consistency more like honey. It's more controllable and sets more slowly—10 seconds to two minutes. If it's thin enough to penetrate where you need it, it's your best choice.

Thick viscosity super glue is used in jig-making and certain types of woodworking. It can also be used as a drop fill for finish repairs, filling more, and deeper, than the thinner glues without "cratering" (but you'll still need to use several applications).

Be sure to get some superglue remover, and some accelerator to speed the cure. Thin plastic pipettes are tiny and useful squeeze-bulb applicators.

Shellac is a wonderful repair tool, but I won't go into it in any detail since figuring out when and how to use it takes years of experience. Shellac is used to touch-up antique French-polished finishes, and is often used on vintage lacquer finishes. It also makes a great sealer coat under lacquer. The only shellac I recommend is made fresh from dry flakes; don't use off-the-shelf shellac because it has a notoriously short shelf life. Sometimes shellac is the perfect choice (especially for its color) for touching up vintage finishes.

Colorants There are a wide variety of colorants available, including the stains described on page 280.

An auto parts supplier is a good source for **wet-or-dry sandpaper** as well as **rubbing and polishing compounds**. While you're there, pick up a **spark plug file** to level a drop fill with (you'll need it later). Finally, you'll need **clean, soft rags** for polishing and wiping. My favorites are baby diapers or soft cotton flannel available at yard goods stores (buy plain, untreated flannel).

Since most dings create a low area in the finish (a spot where the finish is actually removed or dented in), your job is to fill in the hole, let it dry and then level and polish it to a smooth finish. Learn by practicing on the edges of old furniture, inexpensive yard sale guitars, clear objects like chipped ashtrays and even a marble—use your imagination. Be extremely careful with cyanoacrylate glues! Wear safety glasses and latex gloves, since these glues stick flesh to flesh.

Try to determine what type of finish you have before attempting a repair. To test the finish on most electric guitars, remove the plate covering the control cavity and test under it. With an acoustic, remove a tuning machine from the rear of the peghead and practice on the exposed area. If lacquer thinner or alcohol soften the finish, you have either shellac or lacquer. If nothing touches it, you have one of the polys.

Fixing chips

Drop filling is the technique of replacing missing finish by placing drops of finish into a chip or dent until they build level with the surrounding surface. Usually more than one drop is necessary. Then you sand and rub out the drop fill.

Before beginning, clean and degrease the area with a rag dipped in naptha, allowing a few minutes drying time. Use flammable chemicals only in well-ventilated areas, and never near heaters or open flame.

Drop fills on poly finishes Use superglue, clear lacquer or epoxy on these catalyzed finishes. Because nothing dissolves these finishes, don't expect a poly repair to look as invisible as one done in lacquer. A clear "crater" will always show after polishing (imagine a drop of clear vegetable oil floating on clear water—that's the look).

Use a toothpick to pick up small amounts of glue and drop them where you need them. I especially like the angled plastic drop fill toothpicks shown in the photo.

Experiment by filling in some practice chips with super glue of different viscosities. First fill a chip with repeated light coats of water-thin super glue, letting each layer air dry for 20 minutes or so. Then try a different chip with medium viscosity superglue. The longer you let the layers of glue dry, the better (and clearer) fill you'll get.

Try spraying accelerator on some spots before you apply the glue. Let the accelerator evaporate and dry for 15 minutes, and then add the superglue—it will dry from below thanks to the accelerator. If you over-use accelerator the drop fill will foam or turn milky.

Use small squeeze-bulb pipettes to apply just a small drop of glue. These are handy when precision is needed, but sometimes even with pipettes you'll have trouble controlling the flow of glue. In these cases, touch the tip of a toothpick to the dent and apply the glue to that, letting the liquid run down into the hole. This works for lacquer drop fills, too.

Another way to control superglue flow is to turn the bottle upright, squeeze out some air, and with the bottle still squeezed, turn it back over. The back-pressure from the squeezed-out air will hold back the glue, and allow you to control it drop by drop.

If you're using super glue for a lacquer drop fill as I often do, you don't have to use any thinner to melt the edges of the finish as you might with lacquer (below). Super glue does its own melting as it cures with lacquer.

When using drop fills to repair a chip on an area such as the binding or the back of the neck, position the guitar so that gravity won't cause the applied finish to run onto an adjacent area while setting.

Drop fills with lacquer On a lacquer chip touchup, use a brush to apply a small drop of thinner to a chip, both to clean the area and to help the lacquer melt in. The lacquer will work its own way into the finish, but thinner speeds it up and makes for a better melt-in; I generally use just one application of thinner, but I will add more sometimes to melt micro-bubbles or pockets of air trapped below the finish. It's easy to accidentally introduce air into a drop fill, and the time to remove it is during the application because you can push the bubbles out of the lacquer. If you miss an air pocket and the fill has dried, touching thinner to the area softens the lacquer and allows you to move the bubble to the edge of the drop fill and out. Follow with a drop of unthinned lacquer as a drop fill, letting it dry four to six hours before a second application.

Lacquer drop fills may require as many as six applications over two days, and overnight drying on the final fill until hard; clear nail polish should also dry overnight. When using a brush to apply finish, don't paint the finish on. Instead, use the brush to set a drop of finish into the

d.i.y.

hole; it may take several applications to get a build. If the drop fill doesn't flow smoothly into a dent, use a toothpick to spread the liquid around evenly.

Professionals often use a form of lacquer retarder, instead of normal lacquer thinner, to improve the melting-in process of lacquer. If you get seriously involved with finish touch-up, you might want to shop around for some Butyl-Cellosolve, which is a very "hot" ingredient of lacquer retarder. It is quite toxic however, and not to be used in a home shop.

Heavy-bodied lacquer Lacquer left open to the air evaporates and thickens as the solvents escape; this makes a great drop fill because, with a good deal of solvent having already evaporated, it won't sink and crater. I put a small amount of lacquer in a plastic mixing cup and let it evaporate in a separate, closed room used for finishing. It gets thick in a day or so and then I can cap it off and keep it for quite some time.

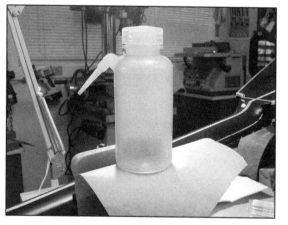

Using accelerator fumes The two photos at upper right show a super glue drop fill over small wood plugs in unwanted tuner mounting screw holes. I used accelerator on the plugs before adding the drop fill. For a safe, non-foaming fill I puff accelerator fumes using a Nalgene siphon bottle; I drop several cotton balls into the bottle, pour in enough accelerator to saturate them (but not enough to leave liquid accelerator in the bottom), and gently pump the fumes onto the work. Since it's such a mild application I don't wait before setting the super glue fill on the area, as I know that the fumes will help cure the glue from below without overdoing the cure. Just applied, the super glue is wet-looking. A couple minutes later I squirt fumes over the still-wet fill — the

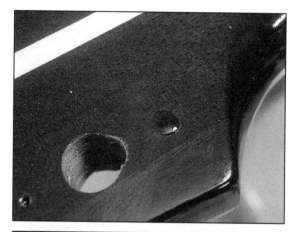

super glue congeals right before my eyes. After only a couple of minutes, the fill is ready to level. This hastens the process and works great.

Leveling the fill Here are some ways to level the tops of drop fills. I'm using super glue here, but the same techniques are used with lacquer fills.

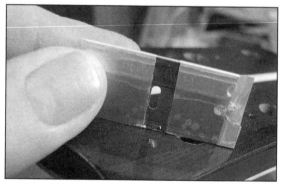

1 Wrap cellophane tape on a single-edge razor blade, on each side of center, leaving only enough blade exposed to scrape the fill when the blade is drawn over it. Hold the blade perpendicular to the work. With this technique you can level the fill down to the thickness of the tape (about .002"-.003").

2 When the razor blade can no longer scrape finish, switch to sanding.

3 Cut Gold Fre-Cut sandpaper into strips just wide enough to cover the fill area, and about 4" long. Use 320- ,400-, 600- and 800-grit.

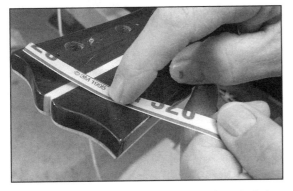

4 Strip-sand, pulling these strips over the fill with slight pressure from your fingertip on the sandpaper directly over the fill. One or two pulls is all you need with each of the grits. After you've "run the grits," switch to micro-finishing sandpaper in 1000-, 1200-, 1500- and 2000-grit (these are wet-or-dry papers, and we're using them dry here).

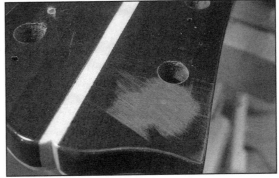

5 As the fill becomes leveled, extend the sanding area for about an inch around it, feathering the grits into the surrounding finish.

6 I'm halfway through the dozen fills on this peghead!

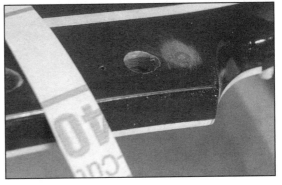

7 Here's a good example of a 400-grit Gold sanding. This won't get sanded again until all the holes are filled the same. Then it will be a general flat-sanding of the back of the peghead with 400-grit. matching the smaller sanded areas. Switch grits sooner than later, don't wait until you know it's time to go to a finer grit—you can always back up.

d.i.y.

8 Level-sand with felt blocks, rubber blocks, wood blocks, whatever. Always take the time to cut the sandpaper to shape with scissors or a razor knife, then stick it to the block with double-stick tape.

9 If a fill is mounded high, you can file much of it away, even before using a razor blade. This is where you can use that spark plug file I recommended earlier; they're rounded, and somewhat smooth on the non-cutting side edges. A file gets you where you want to go in a hurry, saving lots of time. The trade-off is the chance of filing too far or scarring the surrounding area, however. Here I've laid a piece of wide sign-painter's tape (mildly adhesive paper tape). A hole reveals the spot I'm filing, and the rest protects the finish from the file.

Here's a chip in lacquer, on maple This is a curved surface, so the area being drop filled must be kept level!

1 Bare wood, "puffed" with accelerator.

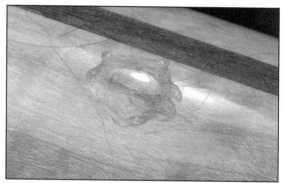

2 A big drop of medium-vicosity super glue left to cure from below for 10 minutes, then "puffed" and left to dry overnight.

3 A few careful file strokes (filing on a curved surface is both easy and hard — you can see in good light where the file is touching on the convex surface and guide by it. Or, you can absent-mindedly file a flat into the curve.

4 After filing.

5 After smoother filing.

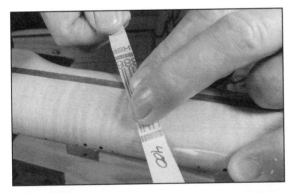

6 Strip-sanding.

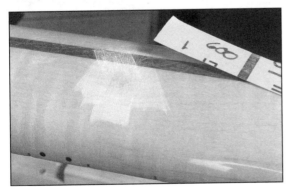

7 Feathering out with 600-grit.

8 "Block-sanding" with a rubber block wrapped with 2000-grit micro-finishing paper, and used wet with water. Keep the paper wet.

9 I keep my sandpapers clipped together, in order, until they wear out.

10 A little hand-buffing with a swirl-mark remover.

Keep warm water at hand in a low, wide bowl. As the paper loads up with finish, dip it often and wipe off the particles with your thumb. Feather the spot away from the damaged area; if you just sand right on top of the fill, you'll get a dip. Sand to as fine a grit as you feel like. A little known fact is that wet-or-dry papers should be soaked overnight for them to work properly. Wet-or-dry paper that isn't pre-soaked loads up, and wears out,

d.i.y.

almost immediately. Pre-soaked paper doesn't load up because the finish particles rinse out easily. I can almost use one small piece of pre-soaked micro-finishing paper to sand out an entire guitar, while the uneducated finisher would use up several sheets! The papers should be left in water when not being used, and it will last a week or more before it falls apart. Last of all, buff and polish to your preferred gloss.

✔ Even with fine sandpapers and the right compounds, you can usually tell a finish has been worked on because the sheen of the finish is altered around the repair. This is particularly true of older finishes. Think very carefully before working on any finish—you could ruin a vintage piece that a more qualified person would have done right (or might have left alone).

✔ I use lacquer drop fills on traditional lacquer finishes. Sometimes I may use lacquer on hardened poly-type finishes, but seldom the other way around (there are some cases when I drop fill superglue on lacquer).

✔ Lacquer fills, in lacquer, will re-dissolve the surrounding finish and become invisible, or nearly so.

✔ Superglue fills, especially in hardened finishes, will always show when held up to a light (you'll see a faint edge around the filled area).

✔ Superglue drop fills in lacquer will sometimes be invisible, but not always.

Guitar dentistry?

The new and best way I've found to fill chips in catalyzed finishes is with a clear liquid bonding agent used by dentists that cures under ultraviolet light and sticks to your teeth. It occurred to me while sitting in the dentist's chair that this stuff should work on bone (teeth are bone, I figured, and I was right). I invested in the equipment, and I can do some cool repairs with this technique. For example, when we remove and replace a nut on a guitar with a spanking new finish, we can replace the finish immaculately using the bonder, and it scrapes, sands and buffs easily — better than any other drop fill. Here, my shopmate **Erick Coleman** "puts back" the finish on the ends of a bone nut installed on an imported Epiphone.

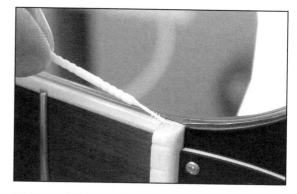

With a small plastic applicator bonding agent is dropped, not stroked, onto the end of the bone nut.

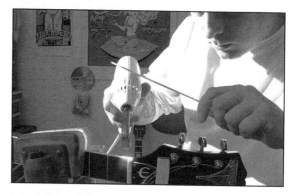

In his left hand, Erick's holding a clear orange acrylic shield to protect his eyes from the ultraviolet light.

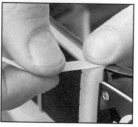

The light cures the fill in 20 seconds (I always give it 60). Erick uses files first, and then switches to strip-sanding with thin pieces of fine abrasive papers. After "running the grits" of these papers, he'll do the final buffing with cushioned Micro-Mesh finishing pads.

Fixing dents

The most common finish dents are small ones that are only in the finish. When only the finish is damaged, and is still adhering to the wood, my first approach is to heat the finish in the damaged area with a heat gun or hair dryer. As the finish warms, the dent will level itself into the undamaged surrounding finish to some extent. In many cases water-sanding and rubbing out won't even be necessary. Of course, don't over-heat the finish or it will bubble. This technique works best with lacquer, but it's okay for the poly finishes, too. Don't use this method on thin, vintage finishes—stick to the newer finishes with plenty of thickness.

Caution: Heating a finish can be dangerous. The finish—especially lacquer—can catch on fire! And the fumes of any finish when heated can be toxic. Work in a well-ventilated area, with a fire extinguisher at hand.

If the wood is undamaged, but the finish dent won't heat out with the above method, you can simply drop fill the finish as we did with chips. Look at these dents as smooth, clear-finished holes that need to be filled with finish—clear over clear. Lacquer finish dents will disappear using this method, due to lacquer's ability to melt in.

Steaming out damaged wood

Deep dents that have crushed the wood fibers can usually be swollen back out with steam. You'll lose the dented finish in the process, however, because the finish has to be removed in order to introduce water to the crushed wood fibers. After chipping out the bruised finish, dampen the wood with a rag dipped in warm water. Squeeze out the excess water from the rag and hold a damp edge against the dent. Carefully steam the rag with a hot soldering pencil or gun, but don't overcook it (I prefer my dents medium-

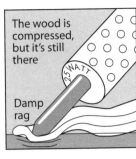

rare). The steam will generally raise the wood close to its original shape; remember that the wood is still there, but only crushed. Allow several hours for the wood to dry, and continue with a drop fill.

Syringe steaming Sometimes you'll find crushed wood and a solid finish on an instrument (especially a vintage one) that you simply don't want to mess with. Maybe it's in an area of color that you know is hard to match. Using an extremely fine syringe (such as an insulin syringe), inject water under the finish and heat both the wood and the finish simultaneously with a heat gun. Often the wood will swell back with the finish. This is more likely to work on softer woods like mahogany, and if it doesn't work, you can always chip away the finish, steam out the dent as we did earlier, and do a drop fill.

Rebonding a lifted finish Some dents don't damage the wood, but cause the finish to "lift" or lose its adhesion to the wood. This is most noticeable on dark woods or finishes. The finish gets a milky, whitish cast as if there were air or moisture underneath (which there is). Using a small syringe you can inject thinner or superglue under the finish and press it down gently to dry. Another approach is to slice the finish with a fresh #11 X-Acto knife and let the glue or thinner flow down through the cut to dissolve the finish. This works best on lacquer, of course.

Fixing scratches

With scratches, there isn't a clear-cut hole to deal with. Most scratches are irregular in shape and quite thin. On a lacquered guitar, brush a thin coat of lacquer thinner along the center of the scratch with a very thin, sharp-pointed artist's brush. This helps dissolve the line before the finish is applied. Apply the finish a dab at a time, once again using the brush tip to set lacquer into the scratch. Don't use a brush stroke; this can smear the work. Start at the farthest end and work your way towards yourself. If you have a good drop of lacquer on a brush tip, run a bead of it from your starting point for a good inch or so, until it runs dry, actually pulling the thick lacquer through the scratch. If a scratch is well filled and doesn't

need a second coat, let it dry many hours before leveling with well-soaked Finesse blocks or wet-or-dry sandpaper (1000-grit and up) that's been wrapped around a sanding block and dipped in water. Scratches in hard polyester finish should be filled with the super glue of your choice in much the same fashion, but use a toothpick dipped in glue instead of a brush. Never use a brush you care about with super glue, because that's the last time the brush will be used!

Redissolving a broken finish Sometimes what seems to be a scratch is actually cracked or broken finish. The finish isn't removed, as with a chip, but neither is it solid as with a smooth dent. On lacquer finishes, use the melt-in method of brushing on a solvent and following with finish. This type of repair is a situation where butyl-cellosolve works best.

If the finish doesn't choose to melt together well, you may be better off using an X-Acto knife to pry under the crushed finish and lever it out of the remaining solid finish. At this point you will have a jagged-edged hole with the bare wood showing, the same as a chip. Be careful not to pry into the wood itself. In the case of a lacquer finish, run a brush tip of thinner, Butyl Cellosolve or acetone (not too wet) into the dent to dissolve the hole's edges. Follow immediately with a drop of unthinned lacquer. Use the brush to set a thick drop of lacquer into the hole, but don't try to brush it on with a stroke. The lacquer will probably take all night to harden, and it may shrink a bit, requiring a second coat. Remember that a proper fill should slightly rise above the surrounding finish.

All of the touchups we've reviewed are to be leveled, wet-sanded and rubbed out. Remember that all of these touch-up methods are most easily performed on the instrument's edges, where it's easy to file, sand and polish. Once again, I caution you not to attempt repairs on the face or back of your guitar unless you have a lot of experience. Sanding and rubbing-out in these areas will contrast poorly with the surrounding finish. Repairs on the sides of guitars (especially solidbodies) are easier, since the curved shape usually offers an easier access for the leveling file and wet-sanding block. The narrow width is also easier to rub out. When working on a side touch-up, wet-sand and rub well away from the repaired area, blending it in with the surrounding finish.

Touching up color

All the techniques so far showed how to fix the clear topcoats. Most often you'll have to match some color, on the wood or in the finish, at the same time. To repair colored finishes, you must understand all the coloring information given in the basic finishing section at the start of this chapter. When touching up dings on colored finishes you'll be confronted with both transparent and opaque color situations.

Pay attention to what your eyes are telling you: just because you know a finish is supposed to be clear doesn't mean it really is. Most stains bleed out of the wood and into the clear finish to some degree, and a chip of vintage clear finish from an orange-stained Gretsch 6120 may be slightly orange even though it's supposed to be clear. Water stains don't bleed as much as oil or alcohol stains do. This means that a clear finish may have a weak, or strong, color in it (from bleeding) even if it wasn't sprayed as a shader to begin with. Clear finishes also yellow over the years.

✔ Touch up any scratches in the colored wood with waterbase stain—it's the safest and most forgiving (and it won't cut into the surrounding finish).

✔ If color has bled into the original finish, add alcohol or lacquer soluble stain to your clear finish for a matching drop fill. Do this if the finish has yellowed, too.

✔ Shaders (color in the clear finish) may have been applied over stains in the wood, and may be a uniform color (Gibson SG red) or a sunburst. Shaders are usually separated from the bare wood by a couple of coats of clear as a sealer, but not always. As mentioned above, sometimes color in the finish will migrate into wood (and the wood filler on open-grained woods) that wasn't stained originally.

✔ Add alcohol or lacquer soluble stain to your clear finish for a matching drop fill.

✔ If you're working on a non-lacquer finish (poly), you may not be able to find an appropriate clear color to shade superglue—in that case, use shaded lacquer for your drop fill.

✔ Dark shaders: some shader coats (especially the outer edge of a sunburst) are quite dark because many successive coats were sprayed. More often, a small amount of dark pigment (usually brown or black) was added to make the shader almost opaque. This is true of many Fender and Gibson sunbursts. You could lay on coats of shader all day, and not get dark enough to match without pigment. To darken a shader quickly, add liquid pigments or a bit of black lacquer.

✔ With stain, always go lighter than you expect is needed, working up carefully to the matching density without going too dark.

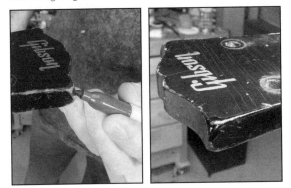

✔ A quickie solution for color finishes is to use artists' felt-tip markers. When the colored ink is dry, follow with the clear drop fill. The colors may change under lacquer or super glue, so experiment. Usually permanent markers do a better job than the inexpensive discount kind that are meant for kids' coloring books. I've worked wonders in a pinch with Magic Markers in yellows, reds, browns and especially black (great for black peghead-face touch-ups). With any colored pens or alcohol stains, always use less color than you think is needed, since these stains darken in time and look different under the clear drop fill that follows. (For a color test, practice on pieces of glass, ashtrays, mom's furniture or her jewelry.)

Solid color finish repairs

Solid-color drop fills are quite tricky to pull off. If the color isn't perfect it sticks out like a sore thumb. Professionals will often spray a large area to get a color match and not even try a drop fill. As mentioned, auto parts suppliers should have practically any color you'd need in acrylic lacquer, and Sherwin Williams can mix some colors of nitrocellulose lacquer.

The nitrocellulose lacquer used on guitars (also used for furniture and woodworking) differs from acrylic. In general, the two don't mix well, but small amounts can

be used for drop filling, as long as you give the finish plenty of time to dry. To be safe, you can follow an acrylic-lacquer color fill with a "sealer" coat of super glue before switching to nitrocellulose lacquer. Good color matches take lots of experience, so practice on yard sale special guitars until youre confident of your technique. No two finish repairs are the same. You need an arsenal of techniques and a broad knowledge base to pull them off successfully!

Cracked, flaking goldtop Another reader writes: *"The finish on my '55 Les Paul goldtop is flaking near the edges, and pieces are falling off! What can I do to stop this?"*

After more than three decades, the clear lacquer topcoats on goldtops can often "cold check" (usually across the grain), allowing the brittle lacquer to lift away from the dry bronze powder underneath. This flaking is most common near the edges that get the most wear, but you may also have problems near holes, such as at the tailpiece anchors. Try running super glue underneath the loose flakes and pressing the finish down with wax paper until it dries. Of course, this method is only effective around the edges—you can't glue down an entire loose finish, since you couldn't reach under it to the center of the instrument!

A warning: super glue dissolves many finishes, including nitrocellulose lacquer. It is this ability to melt the finish that makes super glue work so well for this job, but if you get any glue on top of the finish, forget it—you're in trouble. So be sparing with the amount that you use. If this is a fine old Les Paul, don't risk this; take it to a pro.

To get glue under the finish, use a piece of thin 2000-grit sandpaper or a feeler gauge to gently lift and probe under the flaking finish. Tilt the guitar body slightly in the direction you'd like the glue to run, and lay a drop of super glue onto the sandpaper probe. The glue will run along the paper and deeper under the finish. Be careful: This is extremely tricky business. An instant's hesitation, and the strip of paper will end up being permanently glued under the finish, so don't experiment on a '55 goldtop! Also, prying too hard can cause the brittle lacquer to pop off in large potato-chip size flakes, so be cool. When the flakes are glued tight, seal the peeling edges with a line of super glue to keep them from lifting up again.

Faking an aged finish

Sometimes you a finish repair needs to match a worn guitar finish with checking, crazing and the look of a guitar that's been around. In my shop, we use "relic" techniques to make repair work look original. This 1965 Fender Mustang is a good example. Someone did a hack job in trying to install a pickup; it looked like they'd taken wood out with their teeth! **Elliot John-Conry** patched in new wood, then did a beautiful fake on the finish, with the same sort of checking as the original surface.

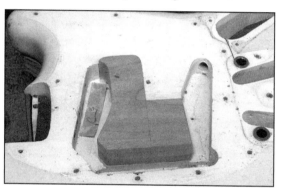

1 Elliot cleaned and squared up the damaged wood using a milling machine. He chose matching wood (alder) and carefully shaped the fill to line up with the original pickup cavity.

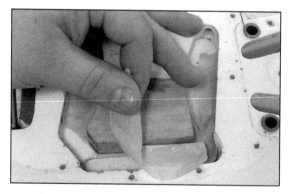

3 With masking tape protecting the surrounding original finish, he glued the plug in with slow-curing epoxy and left it clamped overnight. The glue squeeze-out comes off with the tape. Elliot will tape off the original finish when spraying the work.

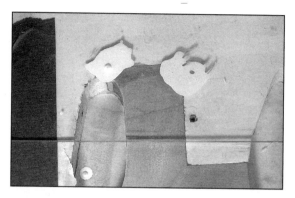

5 He tests his color match by putting the lacquer on a plate of glass over the guitar to give a good preview.

6 After drying, Elliot uses a #11 X-Acto blade to create checking to match the existing finish. There are all sorts of checking tricks, learned by studying many vintage finishes over a long period of time. We even keep photos of great vintage finishes and keep them on file; vintage Gibsons have check differently than Fenders, and a good finish-faker knows the diff!

Elliot's a young luthier doing work way beyond his years. Here's a picture of him when he was fifteen years old—getting his start in lutherie by doing neck jig work on his parents' kitchen table!

For more information on finishing, check out *Guitar Finishing Step-By-Step*, written by Don MacRostie and myself. Don and I also produced two finishing videos for StewMac: *Spray Finishing Basics* and *Sunburst Finishing*.

basic

How to pack a guitar 305
How to pack an amp 307

d.i.y.

deep

Chapter 17

Shipping a guitar or amp

basic

Packing a guitar for shipment

If you're buying/selling a guitar, or using an out-of-town repair shop, you need to get it safely from here to there. Guitars are shipped every day without a hitch. Manufacturers use heavy duty, brand new, properly sized cardboard boxes with cardboard inserts to stabilize the lower bout of the guitar case and the neck portion. Often no other packing is used or (apparently) needed. Save the good boxes if you get your hands on them; they're worth storing away for those unplanned occasions that you need to ship.

Good guitars should travel first class, in hardshell cases. If yours has a softshell case, buy a better one or keep the guitar at home. The same common sense cautions apply to shipping either acoustic or electric guitars. Start with the heaviest guitar shipping box you can find at your local music store. My favorites are the boxes from Martin, Gibson, Fender and Guild.

UPS, FedEx, DHL, and other shippers do a great job of handling all kinds of fragile and expensive stuff. When shipping exceptionally valuable guitars, talk with your shipper to make sure that the full amount you're thinking of is covered in case of a lost guitar. (It happens.)

How I box up a guitar

Remove any unnecessary items from the case's interior accessory box, and pack what you do leave in there well. Make sure that the lid can't open.

Tune down the strings until they're slack. During a fall, pressure from tuned-up strings can easily break a headstock on a Gibson. Fenders can handle almost any fall if packed well.

Slide something under the strings, protecting the nut and frets (cloth, paper towel, whatever). Protect an electric guitar's pickguard and pickups by sliding folded paper over them. With an archtop, pad all around the bridge with paper pushed under the strings and tail-piece, or remove the bridge entirely.

Be sure that the tuners are securely in the peghead and can't vibrate loose to rattle around inside the case.

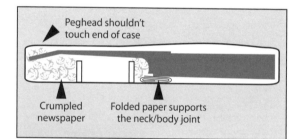

Peghead shouldn't touch end of case

Crumpled newspaper

Folded paper supports the neck/body joint

See that the neck rests in its support cradle. Don't depend on the cradle to keep the guitar in place. The headstock shouldn't be able to touch the case, and it should be supported all around with wadded balls of newspaper. For acoustics, fold some paper and support the back of the guitar under the neck block area if there's a gap between it and the case.

The guitar shouldn't move inside when you shake the case. If it does, pad the waist and bout areas with paper.

Drop a layer of crushed newspaper balls into the bottom of your shipping box, and lower the case into it. Center the case in the box (below) and fill the box snugly

Lots of crumpled newspaper

Fragile Please!

Fragile

on all sides with paper balls; use a stick to push them down where you can't reach.

If your box still has the original cardboard fillers inside, use them and/or the crushed newspaper. Stiff cardboard placed in the right areas can really firm up a box. Use gummed, fiber-reinforced tape to seal the box when it's full.

Clearly print the shipping address on the box. I always print "Fragile, Please" on all four sides (I think that adding the word "please" is important), and draw a picture of a broken long-stemmed wine glass—the international "fragile" symbol.

Insure the guitar for more than it's worth, pay the UPS person, say your prayers and you're done. You'll be in good shape.

Katie Erbise
9/07

Packing an amp for shipment

I worry more about shipping amps than guitars. Amps are bulky and heavy, and it's not always easy to find a proper shipping box—and it's imperative that an amp doesn't shift around in its box. (If I buy an amp over the phone, I quiz the seller to be sure they know how to package an amp and are willing to follow my guidelines.)

Recently I shipped this Fender Vintage Reissue '65 Deluxe Reverb using a computer box. It was sturdy cardboard, and big enough to allow for protective padding all around the amp.

Measure the amp, and don't stop box hunting until you find a high-quality, sturdy container. The box should be larger than the amp on all sides.

Coil the power cord and tie it with twist-ties so that you can lay it in the bottom of the amp cabinet. Be sure to unplug the speaker leads.

Remove the back panel and remove the tubes. Number each tube so that the recipient can install them in their proper sockets. Roll each tube in plastic bubble wrap, tape them, and put them into a container. I used a half-gallon plastic ice cream container with crushed newspaper for padding.

Place a layer of bubble wrap over the speaker and fill the cabinet with crushed newspaper. Pack the container holding the tubes into the newspaper. Reinstall the back panel.

Cut some styrofoam into snug-fitting pieces that fit the interior of the box exactly. I used 2" thick pieces for the front and back of the cabinet, and 1" thick pieces for the top, bottom and sides.

This amp's ready to go, protected inside and out. Tape the box with fiber-reinforced tape and call UPS.

basic

Basic tool list   309

d.i.y.

Do-it-yourselfer's tool list   310

deep

Professional's tool list   310
Sharpening chisels and scrapers   312

Chapter 18

Tools

basic

Basic tool list

Here's a player's tool kit, containing everything a well-adjusted guitarist needs to keep his or her guitar going. This list covers acoustics, electrics and basses.

Tuner A small electronic tuner, or an inexpensive A-440 pitch pipe or tuning fork.

String cutter Small end nippers or side cutters, perhaps as part of a needlenose pliers.

String winder Get one with a bridge pin puller if you play an acoustic.

Inspection mirror To check the insides acoustic guitar. A must if you're shopping for a flattop.

Screwdrivers Small Phillips and flat-blade screwdrivers for adjusting bridges and tightening parts.

Allen wrenches (hex drivers) for hardware adjustments on most electrics. The most common sizes for tremolos, locking nuts and bridge saddles:

.050", 1/16", 5/64", 3/32", 5/32", 7/64"
(1.5mm, 2.5mm, 3.5mm for imports)

Many domestic and imported guitars have truss rod adjusting nuts in the larger 3/16" to 7mm size, too. The Gui-tool combines Allen wrenches, screwdrivers and a string cutter all in one.

Socket-head nut driver for truss rod adjustments on many American guitars, notably Gibson (5/16") and Guild (1/4"). Sometimes they're too thick to get into the truss rod nut cavity; the long-shaft T-handle wrenches styled after those used by Gibson are my favorites.

Cleaner for dirty finishes and hardware. Naphtha (lighter fluid) is good for sticky or greasy spots. For light cleaning, use StewMac's Preservation Polish. For cleaning a really dirty guitar, use Meguiar's Mirror-Glaze #7.

6" stainless-steel ruler For setting string height. General makes a good one that you'll find in almost every hardware store.

Straightedge for neck adjustments. The two edges of a rafter square (hardware store item) work for guitar or

d.i.y.

bass. The more expensive precision straightedges are even better.

Radius gauge Stewart-MacDonald offers an inexpensive set of gauges, or make your own with the instructions on page 24.

Nail clippers (For your fingers, not your guitar.)

d.i.y.

Do-it-yourselfer's tool list

There's a big tool gap between a player's list and this list for the serious do-it-yourselfer. These are also the tools that a guitar technician carries on the road. I haven't repeated the player's tool list items mentioned above; the do-it-yourselfer owns all of those, as well.

Bar clamps Several 6" and 12" clamps for a general helping hand in repair work

Tin snips for cutting shielding foil and sheet materials

Needlenose pliers for electrical work (long and short handle versions)

Vise-Grips (locking pliers)

Multimeter for testing circuits, batteries, voltage, etc.

Soldering pencil or gun

Desoldering tool (solder-sucker)

Alligator clips, jumper cables (electrical connectors for testing)

Screwdrivers complete sets of small, large, Phillips, flat-blade and watchmaker's screwdrivers

Power screwdriver

Electric drill 3/8" (I like the cordless variety)

Drill bits fractional, by 64ths, from 1/16" to 1/2"

Dial caliper or micrometer

Dremel Moto-Tool w/bits, grindstones, etc.

Butane brazing torch (a luxury, not a necessity)

Electronic tuner (high quality)

Truss rod wrenches

Allen wrenches complete sets of metric and standard

Wire strippers

Tuner cleaner/degreaser

WD-40 spray lubricant

Fret-leveling file

Fret-rounding files

Nut-slotting files

Sandpapers

Steel wool

Safety glasses

Handsaws in several sizes

Circular saw hand-held electric (Skilsaw)

Jigsaw hand-held electric (sabre saw)

Precision straightedges for checking necks

Tape measure

Hammer

Crowbar and flat-bar

X-Acto knife with lots of #11 blades

Hacksaw and replacement blades

Vise for holding the work (a drill-press vise is handy)

 deep

Professional's tool list

This is a repair shop tool list—what it takes to operate a guitar repair shop. Repair shops are equipped similarly to shops that do only building, with most of the same tools, finishing equipment, etc. In other words, a repair shop is equipped to build almost anything, but not on a production basis.

Fret-bending pliers (both jaws ground to a basic fret shape for a good grip)

Small brass hammer for fretting

Flush-ground end nippers for removing frets and cutting them to size

Miniature flush ground nippers for fret removal

Dremel Moto-Tool, router base, and assorted bits

Radius gauges 7-1/4" to 20" for bridge and fret work

Taps and dies for re-tapping worn threads, tapping holes, all sorts of fabrication

Drill index set with fractional, letter and number bits

Hemostats straight and curved, for holding small parts during soldering

Feeler gauge set for measuring action, fret height, string height at nut, etc.

Thin palette knives and spatulas for mixing glues, separating wood joints, resetting necks, etc.

Straight and curved scrapers for flattening and smoothing wood

Vet's syringes and needles for glue injection

Infrared heat bulb to soften wood parts for removal (usually used with fingerboards)

Pressure cooker for steaming necks out

Hot plate for heating pressure cooker, boiling water, steaming, cooking lunch, etc.

Chisels full set

Diamond nut files full set

Precision nut files full set

Woodworking files nut files full set of rasps, etc.

Fret rounding files all you can find

Fret leveling file or 10" smooth mill file

Fret and fingerboard levelers (StewMac)

Three-in-One fret rounding file (Gurian file)

Diamond fret rounding files

6" triangle file for fret rounding

Spray guns and air compressor

Airbrush

Bridge plate removal tools

Bridge pin hole reamer

Buffer double-ended pedestal buffer

Buffing/polishing pads

Center punch

Jeweler's saw and extra blades for pearl cutting

Respirator

Fret-slotting saw

Fret tang nipper

FretBender

Fret radius blocks for sanding, dressing and prepping fingerboards

Neck heater for straightening necks

Tapered reamers (large 9/16" and small 3/8") for installing end pins and enlarging holes

Ball-bearing router bits for template routing

Routing templates for pickups, tremolos, etc.

Precision straightedges 6", 12",18", 24" and 30"

Razor saws for cutting nut slots, fret slots and all sorts of finely detailed work

File cleaner to clean wood and metal from file teeth

Bending iron for curving wood, patching sides, etc.

Scribe fine point awl tool

Inspection light to fit inside guitar bodies

Small brass spokeshaves (especially helpful for carving necks and bridges)

Vise with padded jaws large enough to clamp a neck from side to side

Glues (all types)

Finishing materials stains, fillers, sealers, topcoats

Workbenches the more the merrier

The following 13 varieties of clamps enable a shop to perform all sorts of repairs and building operations. They're used in neck resetting, as well as for gluing cracked sides, headstocks, bridges and braces.

Jorgensen pipe clamps (several for heavy gluing)

6" Jorgensen bar clamps (eight of these basic woodworking clamps for everything)

12" Jorgensen bar clamps (four of these)

4" C-clamps (eight)

2" C-clamps (twelve)

6" Ibex cast-aluminum bridge clamps (four)

7" Soundhole/bridge clamps (six)

9" Soundhole/bridge clamps (four)

5" Soundhole/bridge clamps (four)

7-1/2" cam clamps (four)

4-1/2" cam clamps (four)

Small spool clamps (eighteen)

Large spool clamps (eighteen)

Small spring clamps (eighteen)

deep

That's a good basic list of the tools a well-equipped shop should have. I'm sure I haven't listed everything—the most obvious omission being stationary power tools. Some shops have everything from thickness planers and sanders to vertical milling machines, and are equipped to manufacture almost anything. It isn't a must for a good repair shop to have that many power tools, but all of us dream of owning practically every tool there is. The three main stationary tools seen in most repair shops are a belt sander, a bandsaw and a drill press. With those power tools and access to a local cabinet or millwork shop for an occasional wood-dimensioning task, any instrument can be built or repaired.

Sharpening chisels and scrapers

Chisels and scrapers are the most important woodcutting tools you'll use, along with your X-Acto knife and plenty of #11 blades.

Chisels The Japanese are probably best at making and sharpening chisels. If you're buying your first good chisel, consider buying one of the Japanese versions; nothing sharpens quite as well. The English-made Marples are also a good choice. Woodcraft is a good source for these. Get yourself a "cheater" for sharpening: the roller honing guide allows you to set your chisel at the preferred angle and keep it there as you make smooth strokes lengthwise on the stone. Make your first chisel a 1/2" one, and get a

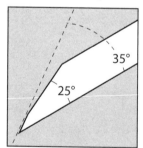

fine-grit synthetic/ceramic sharpening stone. These stones are easy to clean, don't wear out, and can be used without lubricant.

The most common angle for the bevel of a wood chisel is 35°. When

worn-out and blunted, chisel bevels are renewed by first being ground on a bench grinder to the proper angle, and then honed smooth on the stone. A good trick: If you first grind the initial bevel to a 25° angle, sharpening it to the required 35° bevel is quick and efficient.

Scrapers Sharpening a scraper is an art, and everyone has his own way of doing it. The idea is to clamp the scraper blade in a vise while you flatten and sharpen its thin edge, making it 90° to the sides. Do this with a smooth-mill metal file like the one used for fret leveling. Then hone the edge on your ceramic stone, holding it at 90° to the flat stone surface. Next lay the sharpened scraper on the edge of a firm surface and stroke the flat side of the scraper with a burnisher (a piece of steel that's harder than the scraper), holding it a few degrees off horizontal; this creates a burr on the thin edge. Now "turn" the burr by stroking the thin edge of the scraper with the burnisher, and you've got an edge that can cut shavings like a plane—a microplane. A scraper is usually held at an angle to the grain of the wood, and is often bent or curved slightly by flexing it with both hands. If you're lazy or in a hurry, you can use a scraper immediately after the filing stage, skipping the other steps. It won't work as well, and it's not proper, but I do it all the time with good results! Every third or fourth time, I do it right, following every step for a great edge.

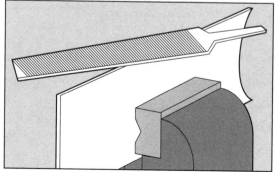

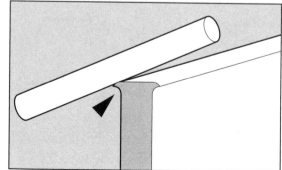

Chapter 19

Resources and schools

basic

d.i.y.

deep

Training for a career in lutherie   313
Schools   315
Suppliers   315
Books and DVDs   316
Lutherie organizations   316

⚒ deep

Getting started in lutherie as a career

I've been amazed by how many luthiers have told me they got started in the business with the help of this book and my DVDs. It's such a compliment that I don't know what to say. I'm glad to help, but I'd like to offer a piece of advice: if you're thinking seriously of becoming a luthier, consider getting some actual training from a school, or perhaps sign on as an assistant in a pro's shop. Years ago schools weren't an option, but today there are real opportunities to train in lutherie. I have visited several schools, including Red Wing Voc-Tech in Red Wing, Minnesota and Roberto-Venn in Phoenix, Arizona. They have exellent teachers and strong courses. A school that I know well is the Galloup School of Lutherie in Big Rapids, Michigan.

Bryan Galloup's facility is remarkable, always building and growing and better than ever. It has been the venue for the Great Northwoods Guitar Seminars hosted by Bryan and Susan Galloup and myself. These five-day seminars have seen a great bunch of luthiers teachnig and learning. In this one photo from the 1996 seminar,

the instructors include **Bryan Galloup**, **Lindy Fralin**, **Seymour Duncan**, yours truly, **Don MacRostie**, **Naoki Ogane**, **Frank Ford**, **Yasuhiko Iwanade** and **Roger Fritz**. Those guys represent a lot of years of experience!

Bryan's organized a great learning environment and a serious school with a structured programs, classroom space and everything needed to learn guitar building and repair. I asked Bryan to share his thoughts on the subject of lutherie schools. Here's Bryan:

"Becoming a luthier can be a tough gig if you have no training to get your your career started. The idea of guitarmaking schools is relatively new, especially for flattops and electric guitars. When I got into the business, reference materials were hard to come by. Just about every guitar repair meant making up my own techniques. I was lucky that my father was a master machinist and woodworker. He gave me a great foundation to build on. Then I met Dan and joined him in his shop in the early 1980s. That's how my lutherie training began.

"Back then, the market for used guitars hadn't yet skyrocketed. We felt pretty free to experiment, since the guitars didn't have the massive Vintage Value that they have today. Nowadays, a wrong repair can devalue and instrument worth tens of thousands of dollars. For new luthiers today, the pressure's on!

"In the 25 years since opening my school, I've had countless conversations with people thinking of becoming a luthier. I always emphasize that you want to be a well-rounded luthier, able to handle a wide variety of surprises that come through your door. That's what keeps your door open and pays the bills. Also, guitar building and repair skills go hand in hand; being good at both gives you an edge in today's market.

Apprenticeship "Apprenticeship is one option. After several years of doing music store guitar repairs, I start-

ed working with Dan. He taught me how to approach repairs and the history of lutherie and vintage guitars. I soaked up information like a sponge, so I know that apprenticeship is a great way to learn. But these opportunities are scarce; most established shops want trained apprentices.

Choosing a lutherie school A lutherie school, like any trade school, is a big investment, so be sure you're getting what you want and need out of it. You'll be learning to use woodworking machinery, so make sure the tools available are well maintained and safe. You'll be learning about finishing, so make sure you'll be using a professional spray setup. Choose a school that feels comfortable to you, with instructors that you feel you can work well with. And look over the course plan: is it clear what you'll be learning and what you'll be qualified for on completion? Don't settle for making it up as you go along.

Join the guitarmaking community In addition to your training, I recommend that you join the Association of Stringed Instrument Artisans and the Guild Of American Luthiers. These organizations are great sources information, and you'll be in touch with other luthiers of every experience level. They're good folks!

–Bryan Galloup

Schools

Galloup School of Lutherie

galloupguitars.com The Galloup School is a accomplished trade school with carefully designed programs built around the practical needs of someone wanting to earn a living in lutherie. Acoustics and electrics are the core of the school, but creating your business plan is included too. They even provide student housing for their Master Program.

Red Wing Area Vocational Technical Institute

southeastmn.edu Housed on the Red Wing Voc-Tech campus, the guitar building and repair school is roomy and modern. I taught a three-day workshop there once, and was impressed by the serious focus of the course. Across the hallway is the violin making/repair school. So you have serious learning on both sides of the hall.

Roberto-Venn School of Luthiery

roberto-venn.com The Roberto-Venn school is awesome. Year-round the weather is so perfect that they have a major woodshop outdoors with Mother Nature as a dust collector—the wind blows the sawdust out to the desert. I've been to Roberto-Venn once as an instructor with Frank Ford. It's a serious school, with students who are serious about learning.

Summit School of Guitar Repair

luthiers-international.com The Summit School is operated by Mike Jarvis, a veteran luthier well known in the music industry. Located in on Vancouver Island, it has to be a beautiful place (I haven't been there, but I'd like to). I say that Mike attends all the major music trade shows, and all the lutherie events that take place —usually with a half dozen students in tow. The Summit School is an authorized Buzz Feiten training center.

Timeless Instruments

timelessinstruments.com Not to be outdone for beautiful scenery or for quality teaching, David Freeman's Timeless Instrument school in Tugaske, Saskatchewan, Canada is primarily a building school — although a certain amount of repair work is addressed. David is a fine luthier who I've met at many lutherie events. I'll bet he's a great teacher.

Suppliers

Stewart-MacDonald

stewmac.com I often mention StewMac, where I'm on staff creating tools, instructions and the *Trade Secrets* e-mail newsletter. The reason I talk about StewMac isn't that I work there. Instead, it's the reason why I work there: it's the only place where so many skilled luthiers spend every day inventing new tools and supplying other luthiers. Go to their website for supplies and also for loads of free information.

Luthiers Mercantile International, Inc.

lmii.com LMI is another wonderful source for luthiers. These folks know the craft of lutherie, and they're a great source of tonewoods. My friend Frank Ford is a technical advisor to LMI, using his lutherie and machining skills to develop uniquely useful tools for them.

ALLPARTS

allparts.com Just what the name implies, ALLPARTS is parts galore. If we don't have it at StewMac, the next place I look is ALLPARTS.

Warmoth Guitar Products

warmoth.com Although Warmoth has a growing list of products and accessories, I'll always think of them as the very first "kit guitar" makers of bolt-on necks and bodies for electric guitar and bass.

Guitarmaker's Connection

martinguitar.com/1833 Martin Guitars' own shop for luthiers, where you can buy their guitar kits and related tools and supplies.

Woodcraft Supply

woodcraft.com The woodworker's store for me since 1969. The place to find tools that, while not lutherie-specific, are must-haves: chisels, sharpening stones, clamps, knives, burnishers, scrapers and a lot more.

USA Custom Guitars

usacustomguitars.com Makers of necks and bodies for electric guitars and basses, and specialists in knowing vintage instruments and specs.

Books

These books have all been invaluable to me at one time or another. You only need to find one piece of information that helps you look good in front of a customer or get the job done, and you've paid for the book several times over. If I could only buy one book from this list, it would be Don Teeter's *The Acoustic Guitar, Adjustment, Care, Maintenance and Repair.*

Donald Brosnac, *Guitar Electronics for Musicians*

Michael Dresdner, *The Woodfinishing Book*

A.R. Duchossoir, *The Fender Stratocaster 1954-1984*, and *The Fender Telecaster—The Detailed Story of America's Senior Solid Body Guitar, Guitar Identification* and *Gibson Electrics*

George Gruhn and Walter Carter, *Gruhn's Guide to Vintage Guitars*, GPI Books/Miller Freeman

Guild Of American Luthiers, *Lutherie Tools*

Hideo Kamimoto, *Complete Guitar Repair*

Adrian Legg, *Customizing Your Electric Guitar*

Tim Olsen and Cyndy Burton, *Lutherie Tools, Guild of American Luthiers*

Irving Sloane, *Guitar Repair, Classic Guitar Construction*, and *Steel-String Guitar Construction*

Don Teeter, *The Acoustic Guitar Vol. 1 and Vol. 2*

Tom Wheeler, *American Guitars: An Illustrated History*, and *The Guitar Book: A Handbook for Electric and Acoustic Guitarists*

Eldon Whitford, David Vinopal and Dan Erlewine, *Gibson's Fabulous Flattop Guitars*

DVDs

I've produced quite a few how-to DVDs on everything from fret dressing and nut making to installing tremolos, pearl inlaying, and spraying a finish. They're all offered at **stewmac.com**

Lutherie organizations

I belong to both of these organizations, and I wouldn't trade the times I've had at our conventions for anything. Both the GAL and ASIA are made up of people like us, so if you get seriously into guitar repair or building, join up!

Guild of American Luthiers (GAL)
luth.org The Guild is the oldest of these two organizations. They publish a quarterly journal, *American Lutherie*, and hold a biannual convention in Tacoma, Washington. Do yourself a favor and join the GAL. We all have a ball sharing and learning.

Association of Stringed Instrument Artisans
guitarmaker.org ASIA grew out of the GAL and became sort of an East coast version. (The two organizations are not connected, although they share many members). ASIA also produces a quarterly magazine, *Guitarmaker*.

With the ASIA and GAL, you don't have to choose one over the other: they're quite different from each other, and you should belong to both.

Index

A

ABR-1 bridge   *See:* bridge, Tune-O-Matic
   adjusting radius 92
acoustic body repairs 131–156
   clamps for acoustic repairs 132
   crack gluing 135, 137 *See also:* cracks
   glues for acoustic repairs 133
   gluing technique 134
   loose braces 143 *See also:* braces
   loose bridges 144 *See also:* bridge, acoustic, flattop
acoustic guitar amp 249
acoustic guitar amplification 240–249
acoustic pickups 240–249
   which to choose? 247–248
action   *See:* setup
Anke, Gerhard 216

B

Banks, Geoff 44
basic/d.i.y./deep 9
Beck, Jeff 44
bindings 225–227
   fixing loose binding 225–226
Bland, George 44
Boak, Dick 7
Bondo 151
bookmatched wood 145–146
Borisoff, David 119
Bosich, Dave 155
BPSSC System 239
braces
   gluing loose braces 143
Brawer, Gary 217
bridge
   acoustic, archtop 127–129
   fitting an archtop bridge 128
   acoustic, flattop 121–126 *See also:* bridge pins,
      bridge saddle, bridge plate
   fitting bridge pins 121
   loose bridges 144
   regluing the bridge 147–148
   removing the bridge 145–147
   bridge removal 145–147
   electric, non-tremolo 83–96

bridge *(cont.)*
   electric, tremolo 97–116
   fine-tuning a Strat tremolo 107–111
   Floyd Rose installation 97–100
   Floyd Rose setup 101–102
   Kahler installation and setup 103–105
   Kahler string hook replacement 106
   roller nuts 114–116
   Trem-Setter 111–114
   Tune-O-Matic 83–94
   adjusting 92
   repairs 93–94
bridge pad
   bridge pad damage 122
   bridge pad repair 149–152
bridge pins 121
   bridge pin holes 148, 151
bridge plate   *See:* bridge pad
bridge saddle, acoustic
   replacing a bridge saddle 124–126
bridge saddles, electric
   cleaning and de-rusting bridge saddles 94
   slotting Gibson saddles 91
BridgeSaver 149
Buzz Feiten Tuning System 66–68

C

Carlson, Brett 32
chips, fixing 279, 293, 295
clamping
   bar clamping, Martin style 133
   clamping cauls 133
   clamps for repair work 132
cleaners 1
cleaning
   fingerboard 4
   strings 4
Coleman, Erick 78, 277
Collins, Albert 50
compensation 63–65
cracks
   avoiding 6
   caused by shrinking pickguards 140
   clamping a long crack 142
   cracked end block 142
   crack gluing 135, 137, 142
   crack splinting 137
Craig, Larry 239
Cumpiano, William 14, 65

D

dents, fixing 279, 293, 301
Dubach, Michael 216

E

electronics 231   *See also:* pickups
    capacitors (caps) 235
    heat-shrink tubing 234
    potentiometers (pots) 235–236
    rewiring, modifications 260–273
    safety measures 250
    semi-hollowbody wiring 250
    shielding 238
    soldering technique 234
    supplies for electronics work 233–234
    switches 237–238
    tools for electronics work 231–232
    wiring diagrams 262–273
Elliott, Jeffrey 14, 39
endpin jack 245
Erlewine, Mark 291

F

Feiten, Buzz 66
finishing 279
    basic finishing schedule 279–286
    buffing 285
    candy apple red 290
    cherryburst, vintage 291
    clear topcoats 285
    color coats 284
    drop fills 295–300
    faking an aged finish 304
    finish repairs 292–302
    grain filling 283
    lake placid blue 289
    maple necks, vintage 288
    Pensa-Suhr finish 291
    safety measures 281
    sealer 284
    spraying 287
    stain 280, 289
    washcoat 283
    wet sanding, rubbing out 285
    wood preparation 279
Ford, Frank 21, 229, 246, 247, 248, 249

frets
    compression fretting 196–198
    Fender sideways fretting 209–212
    fret buzz 166
    fret dressing 177–184
    fret dressing tools 179
    fret files 171–173
    fret presses 205
    fret slots and tang size 213
    fretting bound fingerboards 207–209
    fretwire choices 190–193
    fretwork, what to expect from 169
    glue-in fretting 203–205
    hammer-in fretting 185, 194–196
    loose frets 170
    maple necks, fretting 212
    Martin bar-style fretting 199–201
    Martin T-fret technique 196
    neck jig for fretwork 214–216
    Plek machine 216
    refretting 184–189

G

Galloup, Bryan 68, 313
Garcia, Albert 29
Glaser, Joe 118, 216
Glaser Bender 118
glue
    crack gluing 135
    glues for repair 133
    gluing technique 134
    heat to loosen glue joints 146
    regluing a bridge 147–148
grain runout 145–146
Gruhn, George 77
Guy, Buddy 52

H

heat-shrink tubing 234   *See also:* electronics
Hedgecoth, John 77
Hipshot Bender 119
humidity 6
Humphrey, Thomas 39
hygrometer 6

I

iBeam pickup 248
Imbody, Gene 78
internal mics 248
intonation 65–66
    Buzz Feiten Tuning System 66–68

J

Jahnel, Franz 65
John-Conry, Elliot 278, 304

K

Kamimoto, Hideo 65
King, B.B. 57
Kirchen, Bill 165

L

lake placid blue 289
lemon oil 2
Lucille (B.B. King's guitar) 57–62
lutherie as a career 313
lutherie books 316
lutherie organizations 316
lutherie schools 315
lutherie suppliers 315

M

Malone, Bob 32
Martinez, Rene 44
McGannon, Mike 120
Michael, Brian 247, 248
Mooney, John 47
multimeter, using 235 *See also:* electronics

N

naphtha 1
Nashville bridge 84
Natelson, Jon 65
neck
    adjustment, typical 19
    bolt-on necks
    installation 161–164
    mounting screws 164
    shimming 163
    evaluation 15
    Fender bass neck shapes 159–161
    Fender guitar neck shapes 157–159
    relief 17
    relief, bass 19
    removal 153
    resetting 153–156
    sighting 15
    straightedges for 18
    truss rod adjustment 16
neck jig 214–216
nut replacement 219–224
    string spacing at the nut 223
    twelve steps for replacing a nut 220

O

Olander, Jimmy 118

P

Parsons/White Stringbender 117
Peat, Jim 288
peghead
    broken pegheads 166–168
Pettingill, Bob 84
pickguards
    acoustic, cracks caused by 140
    acoustic, curling 141
    regluing an acoustic pickguard 229–230
    shrinking Strat pickguards 227
pickup
    pickup height for Gibson 27–28
pickups 240 *See also:* acoustic pickups
    installing acoustic pickups 242–245
    pickup potting 276
    pickup remagnetizing 260
    pickup repair 256–259
    pickup replacement 251–255
    pickup wire color codes 253
    rewiring, modifications 260–273
    winding your own 274–278
piezo transducer pickups 240–244
Pigtail bridges, tailpieces 86
polish 2
potentiometers (pots) 235–236

R

radius 174
    bridge radius 24
    bridge radius, Fender 25
    compound radius fingerboards 174–176
    gauge 24
Ray, Will 119
roller nuts 114–116
Ross, Bruce 7
Rowen, Steve 86

S

Sadowski, Roger 32
sanding stick 173
Santana, Carlos 239
scalloped fingerboards 213
Schneider, Richard 14, 37
schools of lutherie 315
scratches, fixing 293, 301

setup
  10-step tremolo setup 29–31
  6-step bass setup 31–32
  8-step setup (guitar or bass) 28–29
  archtop acoustic setup 35
  basics of setup 24
  classical setup 36–40
  Fender setup 28–29
  Gibson setup (acoustic) 33
  Gibson setup (electric) 27
  low action and the blues 40–44
  Martin setup 34
  setups for pro players
    Albert Collins 50–52
    B.B. King 57–62
    Buddy Guy 52–57
    John Mooney's slide innovations 47–49
    Stevie Ray Vaughan and Jeff Beck 44–46
Shaw, Tim 235
shielding 238
shipping a guitar 305
shipping an amp 307
silicone 2
Smith, Ken 32
soldering
  string ends 11
soldering technique 234 See also: electronics
Stockwell, Randy 117
string benders 117–120
strings
  installing on acoustics 12
   avoiding bridge plate damage 122
  installing on classicals 11
  installing on electrics 9
string spacing 223
Suhr, John 239, 291
suppliers 315
swirl-mark remover 2

T

Taylor, Bob 7
Teeter, Don 65
Tobias, Michael 32
TonePros bridges, tailpieces 85–86
tools 309
  basic tool list 309
  do-it-yourselfer's tool list 310
  professional's tool list 310
  sharpening 312
Trance Amulet pickup 248
Trem-Setter 111–114
tremolo See: bridge, tremolo
truss rod
  adjustment 16
  adjustment, typical 19
  rescuing a broken truss rod 21
tuning machines 69–81
  installation 71–74
  making new tuners look old 78
  repair: damage from oiling 75
  repair: extracting broken screws 74
  repair: reconstructing knobs 80
  repair: replacing knobs 77
  Steinberger tuners 72

U

under-saddle pickups 240–244

V

Vaughan, Stevie Ray 44

W

wire, kinds of 233
wiring diagrams 262–273

DVD Included
What you'll learn in these fast-paced thirty minutes in Dan's shop

The once-over: electric

Body:	Inspecting for chips and cracks, loose binding, etc.
	Neck/body joint: checking for gaps, tightness
	Bridge problem due to factory error
Neck:	Inspect frets
	Look for evidence of a break at the peghead
	Check the tuners, replace if necessary
	Nut (example guitar has broken nut)
Truss rod:	Loosen, inspect and lubricate
	(Also applies to acoustics)
Wiring:	Checking and metering the pickup
	Controls: removing a knob, cleaning a dirty pot
Cleaning:	Removing stubborn dirt
	Don't use solvents or polish first
Dating:	Dating the guitar without a serial number

The once-over: acoustic

Body:	A separated glue seam
	Loose braces
	Check the bridge using a string package
Truss rod:	Same as electric
Inside:	Using an inspection mirror and light
	Brace troubles: using the inspection form provided on the DVD
	Bridge pad: ruined by badly installed strings
Neck:	Worn finish
	Inspect frets and nut

Guitar buyer's toolkit

Which tools to carry along when shopping

Intonation/compensation

Compensation explained

Intonation: you can do this yourself!

Tip: set a new bridge to play flat, then intonate

How to stop damaging your acoustic guitar when installing strings

Inside-the-body views of good/bad examples

Tip for installing at the bridge pin

Three ways to tie on to the tuner post:

> For heavy strings

> For most strings

> For repair work

Extras

Guitar inspection forms/drawings (PDF files to print from your computer)

Tool demo videos from stewmac.com